Imperial Glory

The Bulletins of Napoleon's
Grande Armée
1805–1814

With additional supporting documents

The first complete English translation

by

J David Markham

Greenhill Books, London,
Stackpole Books, Pennsylvania

Greenhill Books

Imperial Glory
first published 2003 by
Greenhill Books, Lionel Leventhal Limited, Park House
1 Russell Gardens, London NW11 9NN
www.greenhill books.com
and
Stackpole Books, 5067 Ritter Road, Mechanicsburg, PA 17055, USA

British Library Cataloguing in Publication data:
Napoleon I, Emperor of the French, 1769–1821
Imperial glory: the bulletins of Napoleon's Grande Armee
1. France. Armee – History – Napoleonic Wars, 1800–1815
2. Napoleonic Wars, 1800–1815 - Campaigns
I Title II. Markham, J. David
940.2'7344

ISBN 1-85367-542-3

Library of Congress Cataloging-in-Publication data available

Typeset by Palindrome
Printed and bound in Great Britain by
MPG Books Ltd, Victoria Square, Bodmin, Cornwall

CONTENTS

To the soldiers of the *Grande Armée*
and those who met them on the battlefield

PREFACE AND ACKNOWLEDGEMENTS

Napoleon's Bulletins are some of the most important documents of his military career, and rank high in military documents of history. Yet, until now, they have never been completely translated into English. The same can be said for most of the various reports and other documents that I have included in this book. It is my hope and belief that this book will fill an important historical role by providing English-speaking scholars whose French is less than fluent, or whose access to the often difficult to find documents is less than complete, with an opportunity to read this important historical material.

Translating 200-year-old French is a sometimes tricky business. The language is flowery and often obsolete, and the run-on (periodic) sentences would be the despair of modern French and English teachers everywhere. The early English partial translation suffers from the same problems.

Translation is as much an art as a science; word choice is not always obvious, and different translations of the same material often have subtle differences. I have provided a reasonably literal translation and have not attempted to be creative or to modernize Napoleon's words unduly. But I have felt free to modernize the sentence structure, verb forms or grammar when doing that would make the material more understandable, without losing any of the meaning or intended emphasis. I have also modernized the punctuation and, in a few cases, broken up some of those run-on sentences to make them comprehensible.

Another major problem with these documents is the spelling of names and places. The French often did not know how to spell the names of towns in such places as Poland, Latvia and Russia, and spelled them phonetically as best they could. They would also, for example, substitute the ending 'bourg' for the German 'burg'. To the extent possible, I have modernized the spelling of place names after researching through various atlases and other material. Where I was unable to do this, I used the spelling found in the Bulletins. The same is true for names of people. The Bulletins often misspelled names, including French names. Other names seem to have alternate spellings, even in French. Marshal Davout's name, for example, is often spelled Davoust. After researching numerous French and other sources, I made corrections when I could, and otherwise left them as they were.

During the campaign of 1805, France was using its own Revolutionary Calendar. I have included dates under that system in parenthesis to assist the reader in correlating the Bulletins with other material using that system.

As always, many people have been of great assistance. I can never say enough about the support and encouragement given me over the years by Don Horward and Ben Weider. The activities of the Consortium on Revolutionary Europe and the International Napoleonic Society, along with those of the Napoleonic Alliance, play a major role in my life.

Several good friends have been very helpful in the preparation of this book.

Jerry Gallaher, a Napoleonic scholar of the first rank, gave me many excellent suggestions and assisted with some of the translation. Doug La Follette reviewed much of the material and gave many helpful suggestions that have improved on what I have done. Bernadette Workman, a native French speaker, reviewed all of my translations and directly translated some of the documents for me. My wife Barbara worked with me on the translations and also provided some direct translations. She, Bernadette and Doug each reviewed the material with an eagle eye – that would be an Imperial Eagle, of course – and thus were enormous help in editing the final draft. Barbara's help and encouragement, and her toleration of my many hours in my library when we could be enjoying other activities, is what has made this entire project possible.

I greatly appreciate the effort made by Lionel Leventhal and Jonathan North of Greenhill in producing this work. They are a pleasure to work with, and it is an honour to be part of their team.

My thanks go to all of these people. They have combined to make this book an important work, and they share in the credit. Any errors or omissions are mine.

J DAVID MARKHAM
JANUARY 2003

MAPS

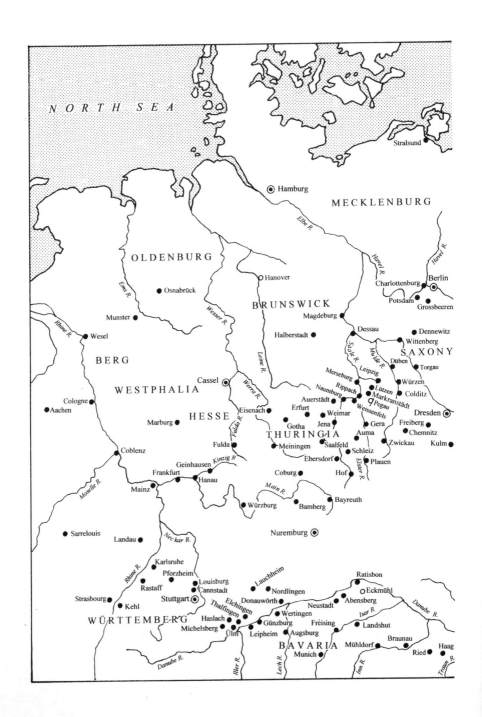

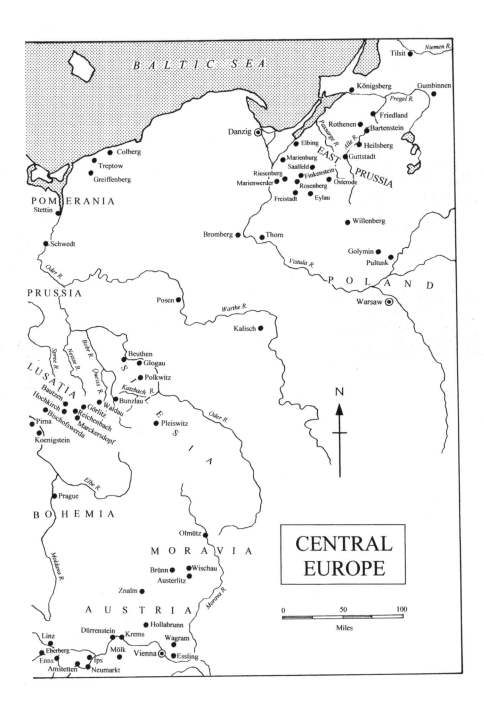

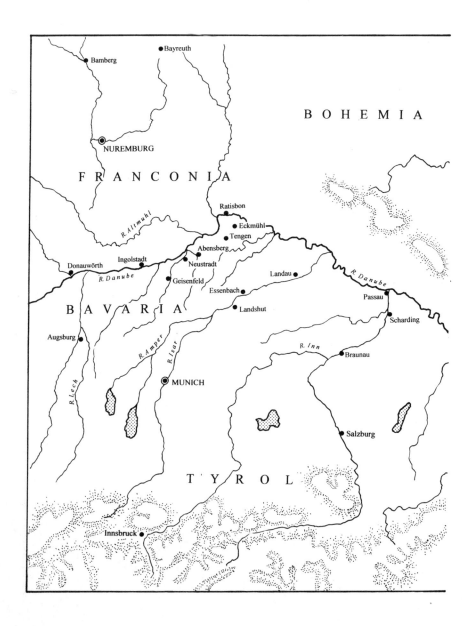

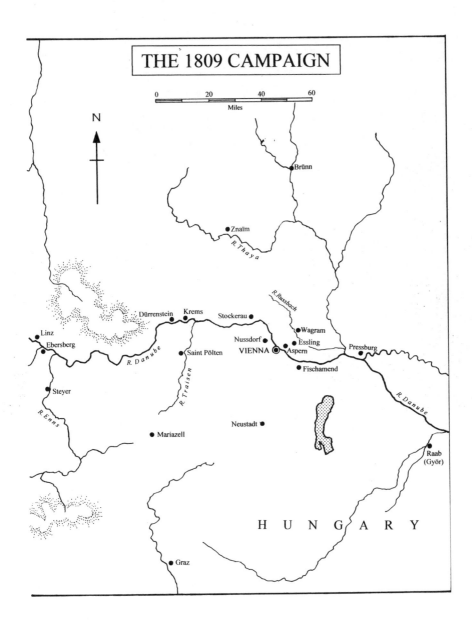

THE 1809 CAMPAIGN

ST PETERSBURG

THE RUSSIAN
CAMPAIGN
OF 1812

N

Pskov

Polotsk

Ula
Kamen   Vitebsk
Ostrovno
Beschenkovitschi
Tshashniki

Inkovo
Valutino

Liouvavitschi
Orsha
Dubrovna   Krasnoë
Smolensk
Kopiss

Bobr

Mohilev

R. Beresina

Semlevo   Viasma

Doroghoboui

Gjatsk
Borodino   Majaisk
Vereja
Borovsk
Medyn

MOSCOW

Voronovo
Vinkovo
Tarutino
Maloyaroslavetz

Kaluga

R. Oka

0   50   100   150

Miles

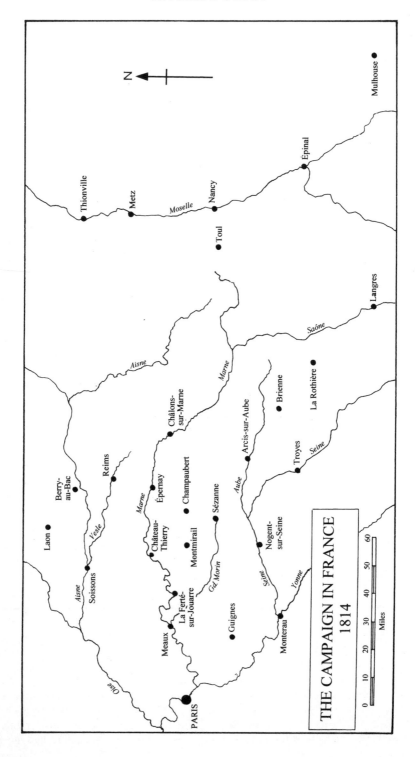

THE CAMPAIGN IN FRANCE
1814

A MODERN VIEW OF NAPOLEON'S BULLETINS

Since virtually the beginning of warfare, military leaders have kept diaries, issued bulletins and proclamations, and written memoirs of their campaigns. Alexander the Great had his own historian travel with him, and many of his generals wrote of their experiences. Accident, war and the burning of entire libraries by early Christian and Islamic fanatics have led to the sad fact that little remains of these documents.

Alexander had no previous examples to follow, but he did show his love of descriptions of war by carrying with him a copy of Homer's *Iliad*, which is one of the very first accounts of a battle. Of course the *Iliad* is probably more literature and mythology than history, but to him the two were inseparable.

Julius Caesar wrote his *Commentaries* while on campaign in Spain and Gaul. These positive and optimistic descriptions of his actions were meant for public consumption. He wrote them in the third person, as though someone else was observing the great Caesar in action, and they were distributed and posted in Rome. While part of their purpose was no doubt to give Romans an idea of what was happening in the furthest reaches of Rome's influence, the greater goal was to let Romans know how great a man Caesar was. They were the first and foremost examples of the use of military bulletins as propaganda, and they worked in a way that left the world in awe. They helped make Caesar wildly popular, and were a major contributary factor to his ultimate rise to power.

Caesar's *Commentaries* went far beyond that, however. They have been recognized as some of the greatest military literature ever written, and offer insight into the nature of Caesar and all that was a part of his campaigns. Great military leaders since then have studied them. Like Alexander with the *Iliad*, Napoleon carried Caesar's *Commentaries* with him on campaign.

Caesar was a great military leader who aspired to political leadership; his *Commentaries* were designed to help him achieve that goal. By 1805 Napoleon was already a very successful and powerful political leader; his campaigns, and their Bulletins, were designed to help him maintain his position and lend support for the reform programmes he hoped to achieve.

All governments and all leaders use a variety of methods to ensure that the public is aware of their political or military successes. Those exploits that are successful seldom need great embellishment, though they often get it. Those that are less than successful often are magically transformed into something more positive than reality would indicate. We call this effort to promote the activities of a government or of a leader 'propaganda'. That the term often has a negative connotation is more a reflection of its misuse than of anything inherently wrong with its use. The outright lies promulgated by some governments during wartime give propaganda a bad name! In the modern world, we often refer to any effort to put the best light on something, including political or military actions, as 'spin'.

Napoleon was a master at spin. As early as his 1796 campaign in Italy he was having prints produced showing heroic images that promoted his leadership. These prints were sold throughout France and contributed significantly to his growing popularity. His letters to the government were written with that in mind as well. He encouraged the production of commemorative medallions and other items to promote his image.

By 1805, Napoleon was Emperor and in control of the entire governmental spin apparatus.[1] He was able to have anything printed that he wanted and he made full use of that power. The official newspaper, *le Moniteur*, printed letters, proclamations, bulletins, reports, and anything else that would fulfill the joint role of educating and convincing the public.

That said, it must also be noted that much of what was published was reasonably accurate. The Bulletins are a good case in point. While they may not match the literary greatness of Caesar's *Commentaries*, they do offer a fascinating reflection of the mind of Napoleon; a reflection of the action on the battlefield, the political considerations, and the attitudes of the soldiers and officers of the *Grande Armée*.[2] While Napoleon could certainly be accused of adjusting the record from time to time, the Bulletins were generally reasonably accurate. His losses were sometimes described as 'considerable', and he would list specific officers that were lost, along with the numbers of men killed, wounded or taken prisoner. For example, on 16 September 1813, he describes an unfortunate turn of events by saying, 'The enemy has taken from us, in these different affairs, from 3,000 to 4000 prisoners, two eagles of two regiments and the cannon of the brigade.'

Even accuracy does not always reflect reality. In 1814, Napoleon was often successful in military operations where he was present, and the Bulletins are often upbeat in their description of those actions. Nonetheless, we read that suddenly the Allies are in Paris! Clearly it was more difficult to be honest about the situation when things were not going well.

If the numbers of enemy dead sometimes turn out to be inflated, and if French losses are sometimes understated, this would hardly make these Bulletins unique in the annals of history. A fair reading of them would give a pretty good idea when the *Grande Armée* was successful, and when it was not.

Nowhere is this clearer than in the Bulletins from the withdrawal from Moscow in 1812. For a time, the comments are straightforward and optimistic. Indeed, there is, in hindsight, sad irony when the 23rd Bulletin states, 'We have had for the last eight days a warmer sun than is experienced at Paris at this season. We do not perceive that we are in the north.'

Then the weather turns cold, and so do the Bulletins. No one can read them, especially the 28th and 29th, and not have compassion for what the troops were going through. The following passage from the 29th Bulletin of 3 December shows just how honest the Bulletins were prepared to be in telling the world of the horrors of that withdrawal:

> This army, so fine on the 6th, was very different on the 14th, almost without cavalry, without artillery and without transports. Without cavalry, we could not reconnoitre a quarter of a league's distance; without artillery, we could not risk a battle, and firmly await it: it was requisite to march, in order not to be constrained to a battle, which the want of ammunition prevented us from desiring; it was requisite to occupy a certain space, not

---

1 The best source on the subject of Napoleon and propaganda is Robert Holtman's *Napoleonic Propaganda* (London: Greenwood Press, 1969), first published by Louisiana State University Press in 1950. Sadly, Bob passed away in November 2001. He will be missed by all who knew him.
2 Literally the Great Army, Napoleon's army under his direct command from 1805 on was generally known by this term and we will use it throughout this book.

to be turned, and that too without cavalry, which could lead and connect the columns. This difficulty, along with a cold that suddenly came on, rendered our situation miserable. Those men whom nature had not sufficiently steeled to be above all the changes of fate and fortune lost their gaiety, their good humour, and dreamed but of misfortunes and catastrophes; those whom she has created superior to everything, preserved their gaiety, and their ordinary manners, and saw fresh glory in the different difficulties to be surmounted.

The Bulletins translated and presented here cover the period from 1805 to 1814. In 1813 and 1814, Napoleon discontinued the formal, numbered Bulletins, and instead used official reports sent to the Empress, and through her to the *Moniteur* and the public. This work refers to all these reports as Bulletins.

It is important to remember that the Bulletins, while appearing to be military publications, were really meant for general public consumption. They were Napoleon's ultimate propaganda opportunity while he was on campaign, and he made the most of it. It seems clear that Napoleon probably dictated most of the Bulletins himself or at the very least approved of them prior to their being sent to Paris. This, of course, is not true of the Bulletins of the Army of Italy in 1805, which were composed or approved by Marshal Masséna, or of Bulletins written by other commanders where Napoleon was not present.

The Bulletins were also meant for the consumption of the *Grande Armée*. Napoleon understood that his soldiers would be reading these Bulletins and it was important that in doing so they would read material that would increase their self-image. Thus the Bulletins and the various reports that were also widely published are careful to point out the valour and bravery of the soldiers, even in a losing cause. Individual units and officers are singled out for praise, and are often said to have 'covered themselves in glory', acted with 'unusual intrepidity', or attacked with 'impetuosity'. Napoleon wanted to make the soldiers proud and to give them credit for their performance. Often the Bulletins seem to be an endless list of soldiers and units worthy of praise. This is no accident, and in this goal it would appear the Bulletins enjoyed a great deal of success.

That said, Napoleon also used these Bulletins to criticize the performance of officers and soldiers. Thus in October of 1813, we read that, 'some battalions of marine artillerymen conducted themselves feebly.' In June 1813, Napoleon combines praise of one general with the recollection of the misdeeds of another:

> Hamburg had been lost during the last campaign by the pusillanimity of General St Cyr; it was to the vigour displayed by General Vandamme, on his arrival in the 32nd military division, that the preservation of Bremen was owing, and the present retaking of Hamburg.

On 21 February 1814, Napoleon is critical of one general's unwillingness to put up a proper defence:

> General of Brigade Montbrun, who had been charged with 18,000 men to defend Moret and the forest of Fontainebleau, abandoned them and retired on Essones. Yet the forest of Fontainebleau could be disputed foot by foot. The Major-General suspended General Montbrun, and sent him before a council of inquiry.

Given the importance of these Bulletins, it is not surprising that many scholars and general readers have sought access to them. Surprisingly, that access is not all that easy to obtain, even in French. The Bulletins were printed in the *Moniteur* and were also posted on town squares, in town halls and on church walls throughout France. Other newspapers would sometimes copy the *Moniteur's* version of the Bulletins or simply provide a summary. Large quantities of some of the Bulletins were printed for sale to the general public. Complete sets of the appropriate issues of the *Moniteur* or of the printed copies for posting or sale are, of course, quite rare.

In 1822, the first complete French language set of the Bulletins was published in *Bulletins Officiels de la Grande Armée, dictés par L'Empereur Napoleon; et Recueillis par Alexandre Goujon, Ancien Officier D'Artillerie Légère, Membre de la Légion d'Honneur*. (Paris: Alexandre Corréard, Libraire, 1822). This very rare two-volume set contains all of the Bulletins, as well as numerous other documents that appeared in the *Moniteur*, and is currently not readily available to scholars, let alone the general reader. Good fortune has placed a copy in my personal library and it is the primary document used as the French source for the translations presented here.

Another published French source for the Bulletins is the *Correspondance de Napoleon Ier; Publiée par ordre de l'empereur Napoleon III*. (Paris: Imprimerie Impériale, 1858–69). This 32-volume set is arguably the single most important reference on Napoleon. It contains more than 22,000 letters, proclamations, bulletins and other documents produced by Napoleon. The last three volumes contain material from Saint Helena. Surprisingly, it does not contain all of the Bulletins or any of the reports of the 1813 and 1814 campaigns, and does not contain any other important documents not written by Napoleon.

If the Bulletins are difficult to find in French, they are virtually impossible to find in English. Excerpts and the occasional complete Bulletin may appear in one publication or another, but, incredibly, until now a complete English translation has never been available.

When I began work on this project, I thought that there was one complete English set available, albeit in an extremely rare publication. Again, years of collecting a very extensive library led me to own a two-volume set entitled *Original Journals of the Eighteen Campaigns of Napoleon Bonaparte; Comprising All Those In Which He Personally Commanded In Chief; Translated From The French. To Which Are Added All The Bulletins Relating To Each Campaign, Now First Published Complete*. (London: J. Davis, no date). This publication contains a lengthy section entitled *Official Narratives of the Campaigns of Buonaparte, Since the Peace of Amiens Being A Complete Collection of The Whole of the Bulletins Published by Buonaparte to His Abdication* (London: J. Davis, 1817).

However, its title page notwithstanding, this publication is very incomplete and often quite inaccurate. In some cases a word or two is missing from a Bulletin. In other cases it is several paragraphs or pages that are missing, and a number of Bulletins are nowhere to be found. Many of these inaccuracies actually change the entire meaning of the Bulletin. For example, in one case the translation reads that a certain letter to the Emperor was 'vigorous and animated', while the French reads that the letter was 'pathetic'. Another example has the enemy being 'brave' while the French reads that the enemy was 'wretched'. These English translations, which one should note were done over 180 years ago, are often given to flowery language. A French phrase that reads in part 'He designated some places

4

for...' becomes 'He designed to point out the places for...' Thus, while this publication is a very interesting historical document, it is of modest value to one who would accurately read all the Bulletins, to say nothing of any of the other important and fascinating documents that we have included here.

There is an important lesson here: be skeptical of 19th-century translations of Napoleonic documents. This is not the first time that I have discovered these translations to be suspect.

What can we learn from the Bulletins and the other documents presented here? The Bulletins detail military movements and battles, single out individuals and military units for commendation, make sometimes biting political commentary and mourn the loss of great soldiers. They offer a window into the mind of Napoleon; what he was like on campaign, what he was thinking and what he took the time to do. Perhaps above all, they show how busy Napoleon could be and in how many directions his activities were often simultaneously directed. His reputation is of a man who was always busy and got little sleep, and the Bulletins certainly promote that image. He is often leaving a place at two in the morning, arriving at five and then immediately reviewing troops, perhaps for the greater part of a day. He is, not surprisingly, constantly on the move; the imperial headquarters rarely seems to be in the same place for more than a day.

Napoleon's primary consideration while on campaign is, naturally enough, the military matters with which he and his soldiers were dealing. There are, therefore, many pages detailing the movements of units under the command of one general or another and descriptions of the battles that followed. But Napoleon took time while on campaign to deal with other matters as well. For example, the Order of the Day on the Organization of Lithuania, issued 1 July 1812, provides incredible detail on the political and security organization of that state.

The status of Poland helped lead to the Russian campaign, and numerous references are made to that issue in the Bulletins and in other documents issued at the time. The issue of Poland had often been a difficult one for Napoleon, fraught as it was with great political risk. In the Bulletin of 1 December 1806, he seems desirous of referring the question to a higher power:

> Will the Polish throne be re-established, and will this great nation retake her existence and her independence? Shall she recall it to life from the grave? God alone, who holds in his hands all combinations of events, can resolve this great political question...

On 14 August 1813, in the middle of a serious campaign in Germany that was not going all that well, Napoleon took time out to address a legal matter in Brussels. He accused a jury of not following the law and issued instructions to suspend the findings and instigate a full investigation.

We see in these documents the humanity and compassion of Napoleon, especially towards his soldiers and their families. He is constantly rewarding soldiers with advancement or the Legion of Honour; this may be seen at least in part as simply a mechanism to inspire them to further effort. But we also read of a brave and wounded quartermaster who is to be given a suitable position at the palace of Versailles. After Austerlitz in 1805, we learn that the widows are to be given lifetime pensions. The surviving children are adopted by Napoleon, given the right to use the name 'Napoleon' and given education and a guaranteed position or, in the case of the girls, suitable marriage. This level of care for the families of fallen soldiers is perhaps unique. Throughout these Bulletins, we hear of other instances where Napoleon will take care of the families of fallen comrades.

We also see the sadness of war, and of Napoleon's grief at losing so many men and friends. For example, there is a lengthy description of his last moments with his friend and long-time military companion, Marshal Duroc. It is May of 1813, and Duroc, the Duke of Friuli and Grand Marshal of the Palace, has been mortally wounded by a cannonball. Napoleon visits him to pay his last respects to an old friend. It is a poignant scene, which cannot fail to touch the heart, and it is but one example of this aspect of Napoleon's humanity.

Some of the most interesting reading in the Bulletins and other documents is the political commentary. Napoleon understood the political importance of these Bulletins; they were an excellent way for him to reach not only his army and his people but also the people of his enemies. He knew full well, for example, that English newspapers were publishing translations of many of the Bulletins and that they would be read in the halls of power from London to Moscow. Most importantly, they were read in the halls of power in Paris. Thus, Napoleon used the Bulletins to promote his own interpretation of the political reasons for the various campaigns, reasons that were generally quite accurate.

England, of course, is his primary target for political commentary. Time after time Napoleon criticizes English policy and blames her for the wars. It was England, after all, who promoted and financed the various coalitions against Napoleon. It was also England who sheltered his enemies and trained and paid would-be assassins. Therefore, throughout these Bulletins we read of England's responsibility and of the actions of her 'hirelings'. Sometimes it is only in passing, as in this statement after victory at Ülm in 1805: 'We shall make the Russian army, which the gold of England has transported from the extremities of the universe, undergo the same fate.'

Later, in the 2nd Bulletin of 1805, he goes a bit further, even suggesting what should be the eventual political situation in England:

> There is not a man in all Germany who does not consider the English as the authors of the war, and the Emperors Francis and Alexander as the victims of their intrigues. There is no one who does not say that there will be no peace as long as England is governed by an oligarchy, and governed it will be in that way as long as George breathes. The accession of the Prince of Wales is therefore generally wished for on this account, that it will put an end to the power of the few, who in all countries are selfish and insensible to the misfortunes of the people.

On 8 July 1813, unhappy at the English treatment of the royal family of Sicily, Napoleon laments, 'so much ingratitude and treachery on the part of England towards princes who lost themselves for her, and who for 20 years gave her so much proof of their attachment and devotion, nauseates us with indignation!'

Now there's a phrase that leaves no room for interpretation!

England, of course, was not the only subject of Napoleon's negative political commentary. Next in line was probably Russia, whose European ambitions were often called into question. Interestingly, Napoleon often differentiates between the officers of the Russian army, whom he generally treats with respect, and the common soldiers. His greatest ire is directed at the Cossacks, whom he often calls barbarians or 'contemptible cavalry'. Napoleon would have us believe, perhaps with some justification, that when these barbarians were allowed to roam about the countryside, no one was safe. In February of 1814, Napoleon writes of the mistreatment of the French populace by the invading Russians and quotes the local citizens, 'You were right,' the inhabitants exclaimed while surrounding the Emperor, 'to tell us to rise in mass. Death is preferable to the vexations, the bad treatment, the cruelties which we have experienced for these 17 days.' That same month he relates, 'One cannot form an idea of the excesses committed by the Cossacks; there are no vexations, cruelties, crimes, which those hordes of barbarians have not committed.'

In the 15th Bulletin of 1805, we hear that the people of Austria and Bohemia are outraged at the Russians, 'who commit such pillage and violence in so frenzied a manner that they long for the arrival of the French to deliver them from these peculiar allies.'

Napoleon read the proclamations, bulletins and other documents of his opponents, and knew that they were also often published in France and elsewhere. These enemy documents were also often overt propaganda, or at least filled with material that questioned the successes of the *Grande Armée*. Napoleon's Bulletins were often used as damage control, to counter charges or rumours spread by the enemy. For example, in the 43rd Bulletin of 1807, he responds at length to published rumours of disease weakening his army. In other Bulletins, he counters reports that he has been defeated, or that his army of Italy is no more, or that some other disaster has occurred. This damage control aspect of the Bulletins should not be underestimated in its importance, and was meant both for the public and for the army.

War and government are a serious business, but these Bulletins occasionally show Napoleon's lighter side as well. While on campaign the *Grande Armée* would try to live off the land, and the Bulletins often report on the nature of the supplies found in captured enemy magazines, or storehouses. There are numerous references to the pleasure experienced when good supplies of wine were found. Better yet was the discovery of a cache of *eau-de-vie* (water of life), better known to the rest of us as brandy! In the 21st Bulletin of 1805, Napoleon notes:

> The vaults and cellars of the abbey were found full of excellent
> Hungarian wine, which was a great help to the army, which had needed it
> a long time. But we are now in wine country; there is a great deal of it in
> the vicinity of Vienna.

In the 44th Bulletin of 1806 he points out that he is providing for the needs of the soldiers, saying, 'We have taken measures for the delivery of a sufficient quantity of wine, in order to support the vigour of the troops.'

The Bulletins are laced with various examples of humour, sometimes subtle, sometimes ironic, other times rather blunt. Perhaps my favourite is found at the end of the 30th Bulletin in 1806. Napoleon is pointing out that according to enemy reports a number of his marshals and generals are falsely reported dead. He concludes by saying:

> All these people who make up news are really upset at our marshals and
> generals: they have killed Marshal Masséna at Naples; they killed in
> Germany both the Grand Duke of Berg and Marshal Soult. Fortunately
> this does not keep anyone from being in perfectly good health.

Another amusing example occurs in Napoleon's description of the battle of Golymin in 1807. Discussing the reports of the Russian army regarding the severity of their losses, he comments:

> Before this expedition, the Russian officers were saying that they had 150,000 men; today they pretend having had only half that number. Who to believe, Russian officers before the battle, or Russian officers after the battle?

As you can see, these Bulletins are not simply dry recitations of military action.

This book contains the first complete English translations of Napoleon's Bulletins from 1805 to 1814. It also includes numerous proclamations, letters, reports, treaties, and other documents that add to its value for historians and general readers alike. I have included a number of reports by marshals and generals on battles discussed in the Bulletins. This is especially true in 1812, a campaign of unusual interest and for which many such reports were available.

I have also added what I believe is a first-ever complete English translation of the Bulletins of the Army of Italy in 1805. Led by Marshal Masséna, that army played a key role in the campaign.

One thing that you will not find here is material from the campaign in Spain. Perhaps because that was such a long and drawn-out affair, neither of my two major sources have Bulletins from that campaign.

Napoleon's marshals, generals and other officials are usually referred to by their titles. To assist in their identification, I have included a list of titles and names. I have also added a brief list of major non-French people who are mentioned in the Bulletins, and have included a brief biographical sketch for these people. Finally, I include a short glossary of terms, some of which may be unfamiliar to most readers.

These Bulletins and other documents are a window into the campaigns and into the minds and hearts of those who fought in them. They tell us of the horror and hypocrisy of war, but also tell us of the compassion and glory. They are critical to a broad understanding of Napoleon's campaigns, and it is in that spirit that I present them to you.

CAMPAIGN IN GERMANY
1805

After the rupture of the Peace of Amiens between England and France, it was clear that Europe would soon be embroiled in another war. England was determined to crush Napoleon and was prepared to bankroll whatever coalitions against Napoleon she could form.

Napoleon, understanding this, had his *Grande Armée* across the English Channel at the port city of Boulogne. He wanted to invade England and put an end to the difficulties between them, but his lack of a proper navy ultimately doomed this idea.

Meanwhile, Russia and Austria, apprehensive of French ambitions and bitter over previous losses, had joined with England in a Third Coalition against the French. The Russians and Austrians began to move in central Europe, and the Austrians began actions in Italy. With Napoleon far to the west, they felt they had time to push the French back. They also felt that if Napoleon did counter their moves, he would first do so in Italy.

Napoleon had other ideas. The Austrians had moved against Bavaria, and the Austrian General Mack, occupying the town of Ülm, was far in advance of the Russian troops. Mack had expected the Russians to arrive much faster than they did. One reason why they did not was that while most of the world was using the Gregorian calendar adopted in the 16th century, the Russians were still using the Julian calendar established by Julius Caesar in 46 BCE, which was almost two weeks behind. In this and other campaigns, the Julian date will sometimes be given in parenthesis.

Napoleon took advantage of the situation. He moved his army with lightning speed and great secrecy across Europe, surrounded Ülm, shocking General Mack, and took the city without a fight. With a major portion of the Austrian army out of the fight, Napoleon then took Vienna without a fight, and moved north to face what was left of the Austrians, who were by then joined by the Russians. There, he manoeuvred the Coalition forces into doing just what he wanted them to do. The result was his greatest victory. It was truly the height of imperial glory.

While the military victory was complete, the political settlement left much to be desired. Napoleon was harsh toward Austria, and stripped her of several important territories. Prussia, too, was unhappy with the result, as she lost several territories to the new Confederation of the Rhine. Napoleon's allies, Württemberg and Bavaria, received territories at Prussia's expense. Only the Russians had little to complain about, as their army had been allowed to withdraw without much opposition.

The campaign of 1805, with its crowning victory at Austerlitz, was a great success, but it sowed the seeds for problems in the not too distant future.

Proclamation of the Emperor to the Army

29 September 1805 (7 Vendémiaire year 14)

Soldiers, the war of the Third Coalition has started. The Austrian army has crossed the Inn, violated the treaties, attacked and chased our ally from its capital… Even you had to rush in forced marches to the defence of our frontiers.

But already you have crossed the Rhine: we will not stop until we will have assured the independence of the Germanic corps, assisted our allies, and confounded the pride of the unjust aggressors.

We will never make peace without guarantee: our generosity will never again deceive our politics.

Soldiers, your Emperor is in your midst. You are only the advance guard of the great people; if it is necessary, all of it will rise up on hearing my voice to confound and dissolve this new league woven by the hatred and the gold of England.

But, soldiers, we have forced marches to do, some fatigues and privations of all kinds to endure; no matter what obstacles oppose us, we will vanquish them, and we will not rest until we have planted our eagles on the territory of the enemy.

NAPOLEON

By order of His Majesty: The Major-General of the Grande Armée,

MARSHAL BERTHIER

First Bulletin

Nördlingen, 7 October 1805 (20 Vendémiaire year 14)

The Emperor left Paris on 24 September and arrived at Strasburg on the 26th.

Marshal Bernadotte, who at the moment that the army had set out from Boulogne had advanced from Hanover towards Gottingen, started to march by Frankfort for Würzburg, where he arrived on 23 September.

General Marmont, who had arrived at Mentz, crossed the Rhine by the bridge of Cassel and advanced to Würzburg, where he joined with the Bavarian army and the corps under Marshal Bernadotte.

The corps under Marshal Davout crossed the Rhine on the 26th at Mannheim and marched by Heidelberg and Necker-Eltz, on the Necker.

The corps under Marshal Soult crossed the Rhine on the same day on the bridge that was thrown over it at Spire, and advanced towards Heilbronn.

Marshal Ney's corps crossed the same day by the bridge that had been thrown up opposite Durlach, and marched towards Stuttgart.

The corps under Marshal Lannes crossed the Rhine on the 25th at Kehl and advanced to Louisburg.

Prince Murat, with the cavalry of reserve, crossed the Rhine at the same place and on the same day, and remained for several days in position before the entrances of the Black Forest. His patrols, which often showed themselves to the enemy's patrols, induced them to believe it was our intention to penetrate by these entrances.

The great artillery park of the army crossed the Rhine at Kehl on 30 September and advanced to Heilbronn.

The Emperor crossed the Rhine on the 1st at Kehl, slept at Ettlingen the same evening, received there the Elector and Princes of Baden, and went to Louisburg, home of the Elector of Württemberg, in whose palace he took up his abode.

On the 2nd, the corps of Marshal Bernadotte, General Marmont, and the Bavarians who were at Würzburg joined and began their march for the Danube.

The corps of Marshal Davout marched from Necker-Eltz by the route of Meckmühl, Ingelfingen, Chreilshem, Dunkelsbuhl, Frembdingen, Oettingen, Haarburgh and Donauwörth.

The corps of Marshal Soult marched from Heilbronn and followed the route of Ochringen, Hall, Gaildorf, Abslgmund, Aalen and Nördlingen.

The corps of Marshal Ney marched from Stuttgart, following the route of Erslingen, Goppingen, Weissentein, Heidenheim, Neresheim and Nördlingen.

The corps of Marshal Lannes advanced from Louisburg, taking the road of Gross-Beutelsbach to Plüderhausen, Gmünd, Aalen and Nördlingen.

Here is the position of the army on the 6th:

The corps of Marshal Bernadotte and the Bavarians was at Weissenburg.

The corps of General Marmont was at Wassertrüdingen.

The corps of Davout was at Oettingen, straddling the Rednitz.

The corps of Marshal Soult at Donauwörth was in possession of the bridge of Munster, and repairing that of Donauwörth.

The corps of Marshal Ney was at Geislingen.

The corps of Marshal Lannes was at Neresheim.

Prince Murat, with his dragoons, stood on the banks of the Danube.

The men were in perfect health and burning with desire to engage the enemy. The enemy had approached the entrances into the Black Forest, where it seems it intended to make a stand and prevent our entering. It had fortified the Iller. Memmingen and Ülm were also fortifying in great haste.

Our patrols assert that the enemy has stopped its projects and appeared disconcerted at our new as well as unexpected movements.

The French and enemy patrols have frequently met: in those meetings we have taken 40 men of Latour's cavalry regiment prisoner.

This great and extensive movement has brought us, in the course of a few days, into Bavaria; it has enabled us to avoid the Black Mountains, the line of those parallel rivers which flow into the valley of the Danube; the difficulties of a state of operations which would always have been flanked by the entrances into the Tyrol, and finally it has placed us several marches behind the enemy, which has no time to lose to avoid its total destruction.

Proclamation of the Emperor of the French to the Bavarian Army

Bavarian soldiers, I have put myself at the head of my army to deliver your country from the most unjust of aggressors.

The House of Austria wants to destroy your independence and to include you in its vast states. You will be faithful to the memory of your ancestors who, sometimes oppressed, were never beaten down and always conserved this independence, this political existence, which are the first benefits of nations, like the faithfulness to the Palatine house is the first of your duties.

In good alliance with your sovereign, I have been struck by the signs of love that you have given him in this important circumstance. I know your bravery; I flatter myself that after the first battle I will be able to say to your prince and to my people that you were worthy of fighting in the ranks of the *Grande Armée*.

Second Bulletin

Donauwörth, 9 October 1805 (21 Vendémiaire year 14)

Events press upon each other with the greatest rapidity. The second division of the army corps of Marshal Soult, commanded by General Vandamme, by forced march halted but two hours at Nördlingen, arrived at Donauwörth at eight o'clock in the evening and seized the bridge that was defended by the regiment of Colloredo. Some men were slain and taken prisoner.

Prince Murat arrived at daybreak on the 7th with his dragoons. The bridge had just been repaired and the Prince proceeded to the Lech with the division of dragoons commanded by General Walther. He directed Colonel Watier, at the head of 200 dragoons of the 4th Regiment, to cross, and after a very brilliant charge Colonel Watier gained possession of the bridge and routed the enemy, which was double his force. The same day, Prince Murat slept at Rain.

On the 8th, Marshal Soult set out with the two divisions of Vandamme and Legrand to proceed on Augsburg, at the same time that General Saint–Hilaire advanced with his division along the left bank.

11

At daybreak on the 8th, Prince Murat, at the head of the divisions of dragoons of Generals Beaumont and Klein and of the division of carabiniers and cuirassiers commanded by General Nansouty, set out on his march to cut the route from Ülm to Augsburg. Arriving at Wertingen, he observed a considerable division of the enemy's infantry, supported by four squadrons of Albert's cuirassiers. He quickly surrounded the entire corps. Marshal Lannes, who was marching in the rear of these divisions of cavalry, arrived with the Oudinot division, and after an engagement of two hours all of the division of the enemy was captured: flags, cannon, baggage, officers and soldiers. It was composed of 12 battalions of grenadiers, which had arrived in a great hurry from the Tyrol to reinforce the army of Bavaria. Only tomorrow will the details of this truly brilliant action be made known.

Marshal Soult manoeuvred with his divisions all of the 7th and 8th on the left bank of the Danube for the purpose of cutting all the roads from Ülm and observing the corps of the army which appears to be still assembled in that city.

The corps of Marshal Davout arrived only on the 8th at Newburg.

The corps of General Marmont has also arrived there.

The corps of General Bernadotte and the Bavarians arrived at Eichstädt on the 2nd.

By the intelligence that has been obtained it appears that 12 Austrian regiments have left Italy to reinforce the army of Bavaria.

The official account of these movements and of these events will be interesting to the public, and will do the greatest honour to the army.

Third Bulletin

Zusmershausen, 10 October 1805 (18 Vendémiaire year 14)

Marshal Soult pursued the Austrian division which had taken refuge at Aicha, drove it from there, and at noon on the 9th entered Augsburg with the divisions of Vandamme, Saint-Hilaire and Legrand.

In the evening of the 9th, Marshal Davout, who crossed the Danube at Newburg, arrived at Aicha with his three divisions.

General Marmont, with the divisions of Boudet, Grouchy and the Batavian division of General Dumonceau, crossed the Danube and took a position between Aicha and Augsburg.

Finally, the army corps under Marshal Bernadotte with the Bavarian army commanded by Generals Deroy and Wrede took their position at Ingolstadt. The Imperial Guard, commanded by Marshal Bessières, proceeded to Augsburg, as did the division of cuirassiers under the orders of General Hautpoul.

Prince Murat, with the dragoon divisions of Klein and Beaumont and the division of carabiniers and cuirassiers under General Nansouty, hastened with all speed to the village of Zusmershausen, in order to intercept the road from Ülm to Augsburg.

Marshal Lannes, with the grenadier division of Oudinot and the division of Suchet, took a position the same day in the village of Zusmershausen.

The Emperor reviewed the dragoons at the village of Zusmershausen; he ordered a dragoon of the 4th Regiment named Marente to be presented to him, one of the bravest soldiers who in the crossing of the Lech had saved his captain, who but a few days before had cashiered him from his rank as an NCO [Non-Commissioned Officer]. His Majesty bestowed upon him the Eagle of the Legion of Honour. The brave soldier replied, 'I have only done my duty; my captain degraded me on account of some violation of discipline, but he knows that I have always been a good soldier.'

The Emperor next expressed his satisfaction to the dragoons of the conduct they displayed at the battle of Wertingen. He ordered each regiment to present a dragoon, on whom he also bestowed the Eagle of the Legion of Honour.

His Majesty expressed his satisfaction to the grenadiers of General Oudinot's division. It is impossible to imagine a finer corps, more animated with desire to take their measure against the enemy and more filled with honour and that military enthusiasm which presaged the greatest success.

Until we can give a detailed account of the battle of Wertingen, it may be appropriate to say a few words about it in this bulletin.

Colonel Arrighi, at the head of his regiment of dragoons, charged the regiment of cuirassiers of Duke Albert. The action was very hot. Colonel Arrighi had his horse killed under him, and his regiment burned with eagerness to rescue him. Colonel Beaumont of the 10th Hussars, fired with a true French spirit, had seized, in the middle of enemy ranks, a captain of cuirassiers whom he himself took prisoner after having cut down a cavalryman.

Colonel Maupetit, at the head of the 9th Dragoons, charged in the village of Wertingen; being mortally wounded, his last words were, 'Inform the Emperor that the 9th Dragoons have shown themselves worthy of their reputation, and that it charged and conquered with cries of 'Long live the Emperor!'"*

That column of grenadiers, the élite of the enemy's army, having formed in a square of four battalions was penetrated and cut down. The second battalion of dragoons charged in the wood.

Oudinot's division was impatient at the distance that still prevented them from attacking the enemy, but at the very sight of them the Austrians hastened their retreat; only one brigade was in time to charge.

All the cannon, flags, almost all the officers of the enemy's corps which fought at Wertingen were taken prisoner; a great number were killed: 2 lieutenant colonels, 6 majors, 60 officers, 4,000 soldiers, have fallen into our hands. The remainder was scattered, and what escaped owed their safety to a marsh that had stopped a column that was turning the enemy.

Squadron Chief Exelmans, aide-de-camp of Prince Murat, had two horses killed. It was he who carried the flags to the Emperor, who said to him, 'I know no man can be braver than you; I make you an Officer of the Legion of Honour.'

Marshal Ney, for his part, with the Malher, Dupont and Loison divisions, the division of foot dragoons of General Baraguey d'Hilliers and the division of Gazan, went back up the Danube and attacked the enemy in its position at Günzburg. It is now five o'clock and the cannon can be heard.

It rains heavily, but this does not slow down the forced marches of the *Grande Armée*. The Emperor sets the example on horseback day and night; he is continually in the midst of the troops and everywhere where his presence is necessary. Yesterday he rode 14 leagues. He slept in a small village, without servants, and without any kind of baggage. The Bishop of Augsburg had, however, illuminated his palace, and waited for His Majesty part of the night.

* *It has since become known that Colonel Maupetit is not dead of his wounds.*

Fourth Bulletin

Augsburg, 11 October 1805 (19 Vendémiaire year 14)

The battle of Wertingen was followed, 24 hours afterwards, by the action of

Günzburg. Marshal Ney marched with his corps, Loison's division against Langenau, and Malher's division against Günzburg. The enemy, who tried to oppose that march, was overthrown everywhere. In vain, Prince Ferdinand ran up in person to defend Günzburg. General Malher attacked it with the 59th Regiment. The action became dogged, hand to hand. Colonel Lacuée was killed at the head of his regiment, which despite the most vigorous resistance carried the bridge by force. The pieces of artillery that defended it were taken, and the fine position of Günzburg was now in our power. The three attacks of the enemy were useless; it retired with haste. Prince Murat's reserve arrived at Burgau and cut down the enemy in the night.

The detailed circumstances of the combat, which cannot be given for some days, will make known the officers who distinguished themselves.

The Emperor passed all the night of the 9th and part of the day of the 10th between the corps of Marshals Ney and Lannes.

The activity of the French army, the extent and complication of the combinations that entirely escaped the enemy, disconcerted it to the last degree.

The conscripts showed as much bravery and good will as the old soldiers. When they have been under fire one time they lose the name of conscripts, so all aspire to the honour of the title of soldiers.

The weather has continued to be very bad for several days; it is raining heavily again; the army, however, is in good health.

The enemy lost more than 2,500 men in the action of Günzburg. We took 1,200 prisoners and six pieces of artillery. We had 400 men killed or wounded. Major-General d'Aspre is among the prisoners.

The Emperor arrived at Augsburg on the 10th, at nine in the evening. The town has been occupied for two days.

The communication of the enemy's army is cut off at Augsburg and Landsberg, and is about to be cut off at Füssen. Prince Murat, with the corps of Marshals Ney and Lannes, is in pursuit. Ten regiments have been withdrawn from the Austrian army of Italy and are coming into position from the Tyrol. Several have already been taken. Some Russian corps, who also travel into position, are approaching the Inn, but the advantages of our position are such that we can make headway against everything.

The Emperor is lodged at Augsburg, at the Palace of the old Elector of Trèves, who has treated with great magnificence the suite of His Majesty during the time it took for his baggage to arrive.

Fifth Bulletin
Augsburg, 12 October 1805 (20 Vendémiaire year 14)

Marshal Soult marched with his army corps to Landsberg, and by this means has cut off one of the chief communications of the enemy. He arrived on the 11th, at four o'clock in the afternoon, and found there Prince Ferdinand's regiment of cuirassiers, who, with six pieces of artillery, moved by forced marches to Ülm. Marshal Soult charged with the 26th Regiment of Chasseurs. Prince Ferdinand's regiment was disconcerted, and the 26th Regiment was animated with such an ardour that Prince Ferdinand's regiment of cuirassiers took flight and left 120 soldiers prisoners, one lieutenant colonel, two captains, and two pieces of artillery. Marshal Soult, who had thought they would continue their route on Memmingen, had sent several regiments to cut them off, but they had retreated to the woods, where they rallied in order to take refuge in the Tyrol.

Twenty pieces of artillery and the pontoon equipment had crossed by Landsberg on the 10th. Marshal Soult sent General Sebastiani with a brigade of dragoons in pursuit of them. One hopes that he will catch them.

On the 12th, Marshal Soult directed his force to Memmingen, where he arrived at daybreak on the 13th.

Marshal Bernadotte marched all day on the 14th, and pushed his advanced guard to within two leagues of Munich. The baggage of several Austrian generals has fallen into the hands of the light troops. He took 100 prisoners from different regiments.

Marshal Davout advanced towards Dachau. His advanced guard has arrived at Maisach. The hussars of Blankenstein were put into disorder by his chasseurs, and in different actions he took 60 horsemen prisoner.

Prince Murat, with the reserve of the cavalry and the corps of Marshals Ney and Lannes, has placed himself directly opposite the enemy's army, the left of which is at Ülm and the right at Memmingen.

Marshal Ney is straddling the Danube, opposite Ülm.

Marshal Lannes is at Weissenhorn.

General Marmont is advancing by a forced march to take position on the height at d'Illertissen, and Marshal Soult outflanks from Memmingen the right of the enemy.

The Imperial Guard has left Augsburg for Burgau, where the Emperor will probably spend the night.

A decisive affair is about to take place. The Austrian army has almost all its communications cut off. It is nearly in the same situation as the army of Mélas was in at Marengo.

The Emperor was on the bridge of the Lech when the army corps of General Marmont marched. He caused each regiment to form a circle; he spoke to them of the situation of the enemy, of the imminence of a great battle and the confidence that he had in them. This speech took place in dreadful weather. The snow fell in abundance, and the troops were up to their knees in mud and felt a rather fierce cold; but the Emperor's words were like flames; listening to him, the soldier forgot his fatigues and his privations and was impatient for the hour of combat to arrive.

Marshal Bernadotte arrived at Munich on the 11th, at six o'clock in the morning: he took 800 prisoners and set out in pursuit of the enemy. Prince Ferdinand was at Munich. It appeared that this Prince had abandoned his army of the Iller.

Never will more events be decided in less time. Before the expiration of 15 days, the destinies of the campaign and the Austrian and Russian armies will be fixed.

Addendum to the Fifth Bulletin

[*Note: In the* Bulletins Officiels *and* Correspondance *this is listed as an addendum to the Fifth Bulletin, with the explanation that due to transportation difficulties it was often printed in Paris as Number Six, which is how it is listed in the 1817 English translation.*]

Elchingen, 16 October 1805 (23 Vendémiaire year 14)

Events of the greatest importance, the actions at Albeck, Elchingen and the taking of Ülm and Memmingen followed the actions at Wertingen and Günzburg.

Marshal Soult arrived on the 13th before Memmingen, immediately surrounded the town, and after some negotiation the commandant capitulated.

Nine battalions, two of which were grenadiers, are prisoner: a major-general, three colonels, many superior officers, ten pieces of artillery, a great deal of

15

baggage and ammunition of every kind were the result of this affair. All of the prisoners were immediately sent to headquarters.

At the same time Marshal Soult marched for Ochsenhausen for the purpose of reaching Biberach and cutting off the only retreat that lay open for the Archduke Ferdinand.

On the other hand, on the 12th, the enemy made a sortie from Ülm and attacked the division of Dupont, which occupied the position of Albeck. The battle was most relentless. Surrounded by 25,000 men, these 6,000 brave men opposed them on all sides and took 1,500 prisoners. These corps should not be astonished at anything; they were the 9th Light, the 32nd, 69th, and the 76th Line.

On the 13th, the Emperor went to the camp in front of Ülm and ordered the army of the enemy to be taken. The first operation was to take possession of the bridge and the position of Elchingen.

At daybreak on the 14th, Marshal Ney crossed this bridge at the head of Loison's division. The enemy opposed his taking possession of Elchingen with 16,000 men: the enemy was overthrown everywhere, lost 3,000 men who were made prisoners, one major-general, and was pursued to their entrenchments.

Marshal Lannes occupied the small heights that command the plain above the village of Pföl. The sharpshooters took the works that protected the bridge of Ülm; the confusion in the town was excessive. At this moment Prince Murat manoeuvred the divisions of Klein and Beaumont, which everywhere put the enemy's cavalry to flight.

On the 14th, General Marmont occupied the bridges at Unterkirch and Oberkirch and all the communications of the enemy, at the confluence of the Iller with the Danube.

On the 15th, at daybreak, the Emperor himself appeared before Ülm. The corps of Prince Murat and those of Marshals Lannes and Ney ranged themselves in battle formation to make an assault and force the entrenchments of the enemy.

General Marmont, with the division of dismounted dragoons of General Baraguey D'Hilliers, blockaded the town on the right bank of the Danube.

The day was dreadful: the troops were up to their knees in mud. The Emperor had not taken off his boots for eight days.

Prince Ferdinand had marched off in the night towards Biberach, leaving 12 battalions in the town and on the heights of Ülm, which were all taken, with a considerable quantity of cannon.

Marshal Soult occupied Biberach on the 15th, in the morning.

Prince Murat set out in pursuit of the enemy, which is in a dreadful condition.

Of an army of 80,000 men there are only 25,000 remaining, and one hopes that they will not escape us.

Immediately after his entrance into Munich, Marshal Bernadotte pursued the corps of General Kienmayer and took some wagons and prisoners from him.

General Kienmayer evacuated the area and re-crossed the Inn. In this way the promise of the Emperor was realized, and the enemy has been chased from all Bavaria.

Since the commencement of the campaign we have taken more than 20,000 prisoners, and taken from the enemy 30 pieces of artillery and 20 standards. On our side the loss has been but small. If we add to that the deaths and desertions, we may reckon the Austrian army is already reduced by one half.

So much devotion on the part of the soldiers, so many affecting proofs of love that they have given to the Emperor, and so many brilliant achievements would

16

require to be detailed more minutely. They shall be given as soon as these first operations of the campaign are terminated, and when it is positively ascertained how the wreck of the Austrian army will escape from Biberach and the position they will take.

At the battle of Elchingen, which was one of the most brilliant military achievements that can be cited, the 18th Regiment of Dragoons and their colonel Lefèvre, the colonel of the 10th Regiment of Chasseurs, Colbert, who had a horse killed under him, Colonel Lanjonquieres of the 76th, and a great number of other officers distinguished themselves.

The Emperor has his headquarters today at the abbey of Elchingen

Proclamation to the Army

Pfaffenhofen, 13 October 1805 (21 Vendémiaire year 14)
Soldiers, a month ago we were encamped on the shore of the ocean opposite to England, but an impious league compelled us to fly towards the Rhine.

It is but 15 days since we crossed that river, and the Württemberg Alps, the Necker, the Danube and the Lech. Those celebrated barriers of Germany have not slowed our march by a day, an hour or an instant. Indignation against a prince whom we have twice re-seated on his throne when it depended entirely on our pleasure to hurl him from it gave us wings. The enemy's army, deceived by our manoeuvres and the rapidity of our movements, is completely turned. It now fights only for its safety. It would gladly embrace an opportunity of escaping and returning home, but it is now too late. The fortifications that it erected at a great expense along the Iller, expecting that we would advance through the passes of the Black Forest, have become useless, since we have approached by the plains of Bavaria.

Without the army that is now in front of you, we should this day have been in London; we should have avenged ourselves for six centuries of insults, and restored the freedom of the seas.

But remember tomorrow that you are fighting against the allies of England; that you have to avenge yourselves from the affronts of a perjured prince, whose own letters breathed nothing but peace at the moment when he was marching his army against our ally; who thought us cowardly enough to suppose that we should tamely witness, without saying anything, his crossing of the Inn, his entrance into Munich and his aggression on the Elector of Bavaria. He believed us occupied elsewhere: let him for the third and the last time learn that we know how to be present in every place where the fatherland has enemies to combat.

Soldiers, tomorrow will be 100 times more celebrated than the day of Marengo; I have placed the enemy in the same position.

Remember that the most remote posterity will take note of that which each of you will do this memorable day.

Your progeny 500 years hence, who may place themselves under those eagles around which you rally, will know in detail everything that your respective corps shall achieve tomorrow, and the manner in which your courage shall confer on them eternal celebrity. This will constitute the perpetual subject of their conversation; and from age to age you will be held up to the admiration of future generations.

Soldiers, if I wished only to conquer the enemy, I should not have thought it necessary to make an appeal to your courage and your love for the country and for me; but merely to conquer him is doing nothing worthy either of you or your

17

Emperor. It is necessary that not a man of the enemy's army shall escape. That government, which has violated all its engagements, shall first learn its catastrophe by your arrival under the walls of Vienna; and, on receiving this fatal news, its conscience, if it listens to the voice of conscience, shall tell it that it has betrayed both its solemn promises of peace and the first of the duties bequeathed by its ancestors, the power of forming the rampart of Europe against the eruptions of the barbarians [Cossacks].

Soldiers who have been engaged in the combats of Wertingen and Günzburg, I am satisfied with your conduct; every corps in the army will emulate you. And I shall be able to say to my people: Your Emperor and your army have done their duty; perform yours; and the 200,000 conscripts whom I have summoned will hasten by forced marches to reinforce our second line.

NAPOLEON

Sixth Bulletin
Elchingen, 18 October 1805 (27 Vendémiaire year 14)

The day of Ülm was one of the greatest days of the history of France. The Emperor would have been able to take the city by assault, but 20,000 men defended by fortifications and motes filled with water would have resisted, and the strong desire of His Majesty was to prevent bloodshed. General Mack, the commander of the army, was in the city. It is the destiny of the generals opposing the Emperor to be taken prisoner in the towns. One remembers that after the fine manoeuvre of the Brenta, the old Field Marshal Würmser was taken prisoner in Mantua; Mélas was taken in Alessandria; Mack is a prisoner in Ülm.

The Austrian army was one of the finest Austria has ever had. It was composed of 14 regiments of infantry forming the army of Bavaria, 13 regiments of the Army of the Tyrol, and 5 regiments which had come into position from Italy, making a total of 32 regiments of infantry and 15 regiments of cavalry.

The Emperor had put the army of Prince Ferdinand in the same situation that he had placed Mélas. After having hesitated for a long time, Mélas made the noble decision to fight his way through the French army, which led to the battle of Marengo. Mack decided upon another solution. Ülm is the junction of many roads. He conceived of a plan for escape of his divisions by each of these roads and then to reunite them in the Tyrol and in Bohemia. The Hohenzollern and Werneck divisions departed by way of Heydenheim. A small division left by way of Memmingen. But the Emperor, since 12 October [20 Vendémiaire] rushed from Augsburg to Ülm, immediately disconcerting the enemy's projects, captured the bridge and the position at Elchingen, which took care of everything.

Marshal Soult, after taking Memmingen, took up the pursuit of other columns. Finally, Prince Ferdinand had only two courses of action: to remain encircled in Ülm or to try by some paths to rejoin the Hohenzollern division. That Prince chose the second, and set out to Aalen with four squadrons of cavalry.

However, Prince Murat was in pursuit of Prince Ferdinand. Werneck's division wanted to stop him at Langenau, but he took 3,000 prisoners, one of whom was a general, and captured two flags. At the same time Marshal Lannes manoeuvred his right by way of Aalen and Nördlingen to Heydenheim. The enemy's march was encumbered by 500 wagons and weakened by the combat of Langenau. In that combat Prince Murat was very satisfied with General Klein. The 20th Regiment of Dragoons, the 9th Regiment of Light Infantry, and the Chasseurs of the Imperial Guard particularly distinguished themselves. The aide-de-camp Brunet displayed great bravery.

This combat did not slow the march of Prince Murat. He marched rapidly on Neresheim, and at five o'clock on the afternoon of the 25th he arrived in front of Neresheim. In the combat that followed, General Klein's division of dragoons charged the enemy. Two flags, a general, and 1,000 men have been newly taken in the combat of Neresheim. Prince Ferdinand and seven of his generals only had time to mount their horses. Their dinner was found still on the table. For two days they were not able to rest. It seems that Prince Ferdinand will not able to escape from the French army except by disguising himself, or running away with a few squadrons by a different road through Germany.

The Emperor came upon a mass of enemy prisoners. Among them was an Austrian colonel who was astonished to see the Emperor of the French soaking wet, covered with mud and more fatigued than the least drummer boy of the army. One of the colonel's aides-de-camp told him what the Austrian prisoner had said, and the Emperor replied, 'Your master has wanted to make me remember that I was a soldier; I hope that he will realize that the throne and imperial crimson has not made me forget my first profession.'

The spectacle offered by the army on the 23rd was truly interesting. For two days there had been heavy rain and everyone was drenched. The soldiers had not received any rations, they were in mud up to their knees, but the sight of the Emperor made them happy, and the moment that he approached a column, in the same condition, the cry went up 'Long live the Emperor!'

It is also reported that the Emperor replied to the officers who surrounded him and who admired how, in the most painful moment, the soldiers forgot all their privations and expressed only pleasure at seeing him: 'They are right, because it is to spare their blood that I cause them such great fatigue.'

The Emperor, while the army occupied the heights that dominated Ülm, summoned the Prince of Lichtenstein, the major-general who was shut up in that place [Ülm], to make it known to him that he wished the city to surrender, saying that if it was taken by assault he would be obliged to do that which he had done at Jaffa, where the garrison was put to the sword. That was the sad right of war. But the Emperor wanted only to spare the garrison and the brave Austrian nation the necessity of an act so frightening; that Ülm was not tenable; that it should surrender. The Prince insisted that the officers and soldiers should be allowed to return to Austria. 'I will allow the officers but not the soldiers,' the Emperor replied, 'because who will guarantee me that they will not serve against me again!' Then, after a brief hesitation, he added: '*Eh bien*, I trust the word of Prince Ferdinand. If he is in Ülm, I want to give him proof of my esteem, and I grant him that which you request, hoping that the court in Vienna will not denounce the word of one of its princes.' Then being assured by the Prince of Lichtenstein that Prince Ferdinand was not in the city, 'Well then, I do not see,' said the Emperor, 'who can guarantee me that the soldiers will not serve again in the future.'

A brigade of 4,000 men occupies a gate of the city of Ülm.

In the night of the 24th/25th there had been a terrible rainstorm. The Danube flooded and broke most of its bridge, causing much trouble for our supplies.

During the 23rd Marshal Bernadotte pushed his advanced post to Wasserburg and Haag, on the road to Braunau. He captured 400 to 500 prisoners of war and 17 pieces of artillery of various calibres. Then, with his entry into Munich without the loss of a single man, Marshal Bernadotte took 1,500 prisoners, 19 cannon, 200 horses and a great amount of baggage.

The Emperor crossed the Rhine on 1 October, the Danube on the 6th at five o'clock in the morning, the Lech the same day at three in the afternoon. His troops entered Munich on the 12th. His advance guard arrived on the Inn the 15th. The same day he was master of Memmingen, and on the 16th Ülm.

He has taken from the enemy in combat at Wertingen, Günzburg, Elchingen, at Memmingen and Ülm, and at Albeck, Langenau and Neresheim, 4,000 men, as much infantry as cavalry, more than 40 flags, a very great number of pieces of artillery, baggage, vehicles, etc. And to achieve these great results, there had only been marches and manoeuvres.

In these combats the losses to the French army were less than 500 dead and 1,000 wounded. The soldiers frequently exclaimed, 'The Emperor has found a new method of making war; he makes use only of our legs and our bayonets.' Five-sixths of the army never fired a shot, which distressed them. But they had marched a great distance, and they redoubled their speed when they hoped to engage the enemy.

One is able to praise the army in two words: it is worthy of its commander.

One may consider the Austrian army as annihilated. The Austrians and the Russians will be obliged to make many appeals for recruits to resist the French army that has defeated an army 100,000 men strong while suffering almost no losses.

Seventh Bulletin

Elchingen, 19 October 1805 (26 Vendémiaire an 14)

On the 18th (26 Vendémiaire) at five o'clock in the morning, Prince Murat arrived at Nördlingen and succeeded in surrounding the Werneck division. That General had asked to surrender. The surrender that had been granted him will not take place until tomorrow. Lieutenant Generals Werneck, Baillet, Hohenzollern, Generals Vogel, Mackery, Hohenfeld, Weiber, and Dienesberg are prisoners on parole and on their word of honour allowed to return to their homes. The troops are prisoners of war and are sent to France. More than 2,000 cavalrymen were dismounted and a brigade of [French] foot dragons was mounted with its horses. We are assured that the Austrian army's reserve park, composed of 500 wagons, was also taken. It is presumed that the rest of the column of Prince Ferdinand must, at this time, be taken, Prince Murat having overthrown his right by Aalen and Marshal Lannes his left to Nördlingen. One awaits the result of these manoeuvres. Prince Ferdinand is left with very few troops.

Today, at two o'clock in the afternoon, the Emperor granted an audience to General Mack. At this audience Marshal Berthier signed with General Mack an addition to the capitulation which provided that the garrison of Ülm will evacuate the city tomorrow, the 20th. There are within Ülm 27,000 men, 3,000 horses, 18 generals and 60 to 80 field cannon.

Half of the Imperial Guard has already departed for Augsburg, but His Majesty has decided to remain until tomorrow to witness the surrender of the Austrian Army. With each passing day it becomes clearer that of this army of 100,000 men no more than 20,000 will have escaped; and this great accomplishment has been achieved without bloodshed.

The Emperor did not leave Elchingen today. He has endured fatigue and eight days of continuous rain and is need of a little rest. But rest is not compatible with the direction of this immense army. At all hours of the day and night officers arrive with reports, and the Emperor must give orders. He seems to be very satisfied with the activity and zeal of Marshal Berthier.

At three o'clock tomorrow afternoon, 27,000 Austrian soldiers, 60 pieces of artillery and 18 generals will march before the Emperor and lay down their arms. The Emperor has made a gift to the senate of the flags of Ülm. There will be twice as many as have been announced, that is to say, 80.

In these five days the Danube has overflowed with a violence that has not been seen for 100 years. The abbey of Elchingen, in which the Emperor has established his general headquarters, is situated on a hill from which one can see the country all around.

It is believed that the Emperor will leave for Munich tomorrow night. The Russian army has just arrived on the Inn.

Eighth Bulletin

Elchingen,20 October 1805 (28 Vendémiaire year 14)
The two surrenders announced in yesterday's bulletin have been received. Concluded by order of Prince Murat, one was signed by the chief of staff of Prince Murat, the other by General Fauconnet.

The Emperor spent today, from two in the afternoon to seven in the evening, on the heights near Ülm, where the Austrian army marched past him. Thirty thousand men, of whom 2,000 were of cavalry, 60 pieces of artillery and 40 flags have been given to the conquerors. The French Army occupied the heights. The Emperor, surrounded by his Guard, sent for the Austrian generals and kept them with him until their troops had filed off. He treated them with the utmost consideration. There were present, besides General-in-Chief Mack, eight generals and seven lieutenant generals. We will give in the following bulletin the names of the generals and the regiments.

The number of prisoners since the commencement of hostilities amounts to 60,000, and 80 flags have been taken, besides artillery, baggage, etc. Never were victories made more complete nor at less cost. It is believed that the Emperor, after dispatching his couriers, will set out during the night for Augsburg and Munich.

Ninth Bulletin

Elchingen, 21 October 1805
The Emperor has just issued the annexed proclamation with decrees.

At noon, His Majesty departed for Augsburg.

We are now in possession of an accurate number of the army that was shut up in Ülm. It consisted of 33,000 men, to which number the 3,000 wounded being added, makes the number of prisoners to 36,000. There were also found in the fortress 60 pieces of artillery with their supplies, and 50 flags.

There cannot be a more striking contrast than between the spirit of the French and that of the Austrian armies. In the French army heroism is carried to its extreme point. In the Austrian army discouragement is at its height. The soldier is paid with notes; he can send nothing home and is very ill-treated. The French think of nothing but glory. One could cite a thousand exploits like the following: Brard, a soldier of the 76th, was going to have his thigh amputated; death had laid hold of him. As the surgeon was preparing to perform the operation, he stopped him: 'I know that I shall not survive, but it doesn't matter. One man less will not prevent the 76th from marching against the enemy, in three ranks, with the bayonet in front.'

The Emperor has occasion to complain of nothing except the much too great impetuosity of the soldiers. The 17th Light Infantry, for example, which arrived before Ülm during the capitulation, rushed into the place; thus during the surrender the entire army wanted to mount an assault, and the Emperor was obliged to declare firmly that he did not want an assault.

The first column of the prisoners at Ülm has just begun its march for France.

Here is an account of the prisoners, at least those actually known, with the places where they are found: 10,000 at Augsburg, 33,000 at Ülm, 12,000 at Donauwörth and 12,000 already on their march for France. The Emperor said in his proclamation that we have taken 60,000 prisoner; it is probable that there will be more of them. He put the number of flags taken at 90; it is probable that we will also have more of them.

The Emperor addressed the Austrian generals, whom he sent for, as their army was filing past him, in the following terms, 'Gentlemen, your master carries on an unjust war. I tell you plainly, I don't know why I am fighting; I don't know what is wanted of me.

'It is not in this army alone that my resources consist; if it were so, my army and myself would make much headway. But I shall appeal to the testimony of your own prisoners of war, who will speedily pass through France; they will see what spirit animates my people and with what eagerness they flock to my flags. This is the advantage of my nation and my position. With a single word, 200,000 volunteers crowd to my flag and in six weeks become good soldiers; whereas your recruits only march from compulsion, and will become soldiers only after several years.

'I again give my brother the Emperor of Germany a piece of advice; let him hasten to make peace. It is the moment to recall that all empires have an end. The idea that the end of the dynasty of the House of Lorraine will have arrived must terrify him. I desire nothing on the Continent. I want ships, colonies, and commerce; and it is as much in your interest as ours.' General Mack replied that the Emperor of Germany had not wished for war, but was compelled to it by Russia. 'If that be the case,' said the Emperor, 'then you are no longer a power.'

Most of the generals have confessed how disagreeable this war was to them, and with what pain they saw a Russian army in their midst.

They blamed a blind system of politics that would bring into the centre of Europe a people accustomed to living in an uncultivated and rustic country, and who, like their ancestors, might take a fancy to settle in a milder climate.

The Emperor has welcomed with good grace Lieutenant General Klenau (whom he knew as the commander of the regiment of Würmser), as also the Lieutenant Generals Giulay, Gottershiem, Ries and the Prince of Lichtenstein, etc.

He consoles them in their misfortunes, and tells them that war has its fortunes, and that having been so often conquerors they could be sometimes conquered.

Proclamation of the Emperor Napoleon
to the soldiers of the *Grande Armée*

From Imperial Headquarters, Elchingen, 21 October 1805 (29 Vendémiaire year 14)

Soldiers of the *Grande Armée*, in 15 days we have made a campaign. What we proposed is accomplished. We have chased the troops of the House of Austria from Bavaria and re-established our ally in the sovereignty of his states. That army, which with equal ostentation and impudence came to place itself upon our frontiers, is annihilated. What signifies it to England? Her object is accomplished. We are no longer at Boulogne, and her subsidy will be neither more nor less.

Of 100,000 men who comprised that army, 60,000 are prisoners; they will go to replace our conscripts in the labours of our fields; 200 pieces of artillery, all the parks, 90 flags, all the generals, are in our power. Not 15,000 men of that army have escaped. Soldiers, I have announced to you a great battle; but thanks to the bad combinations of the enemy, I have been able to obtain the same success without running any risk; and, what is unprecedented in the history of nations, so great a result has not weakened us above 1,500 men out of combat.

Soldiers, this success is due to your boundless confidence in your Emperor, to your patience in enduring fatigues and privations of every kind and to your rare intrepidity.

But we shall not stop here: you are impatient to commence a second campaign. We shall make the Russian army, which the gold of England has transported from the extremities of the universe, undergo the same fate. To this combat is more especially attached the honour of the infantry; it is there that is to be decided, for the second time, that question which has already been decided in Switzerland and in Holland: if the French infantry is the second or the first in Europe. There are among them no generals against whom I can have any glory to acquire: all my care shall be to obtain victory with the least possible bloodshed: my soldiers are my children.

Decree

Elchingen, Imperial Camp, 21 October 1805
Napoleon, Emperor of the French and King of Italy
Considering that the *Grande Armée* has obtained, by its courage and its devotion, results that could not be hoped for but after a campaign,

And wishing to give it a proof of our imperial satisfaction, we have decreed, and decree as follows:

Article I The month Vendémiaire of the year 14 shall be reckoned as a campaign to all the individuals composing the *Grande Armée.*

This month shall be so charged to the state in the valuation of pensions and military services.

Article II Our ministers of war and of the public treasury are charged with the execution of this decree.

NAPOLEON

By the Emperor, THE MINISTER SECRETARY OF STATE, H B MARET

First Bulletin of the Army of Italy

18 October (26 Vendémiaire year 14)
At four o'clock in the morning, the General-in-Chief [Marshal André Masséna] had the bridge of the *Vieux-Château* of Verona attacked; the wall which blocked the middle of it was blown up with a petard; the two cuts made by the Austrians were made usable with large boards and planks, and 24 companies of voltigeurs flew to the other side of the river, followed by the first division.

The enemy strongly defended the passage; it was overthrown and routed from all his positions after a combat that lasted until six o'clock in the evening. It lost 7 pieces of artillery and 18 caissons.

We took 1,400 to 1,500 prisoners and almost as many killed or wounded; on our side we lost only a small number of combatants.

We have about 300 men only slightly wounded.

We immediately built a bridgehead at the bridge of the *Vieux-Château.*

The results of this great day will be made known later.

Tenth Bulletin

Augsburg, 22 October 1805 (30 Vendémiaire year 14)

Upon the capitulation of General Werneck near Nördlingen, Prince Ferdinand, with a corps of 1,000 horses and a portion of artillery park, had taken to flight. He threw himself into Prussian territory, and took the route by Gunzenhausen for Nuremberg. Prince Murat followed on his heels, and succeeded in overtaking him, which gave rise to a battle on the road between Fürth and Nuremberg in the night of the 21st. All the rest of the park of artillery and all the baggage, without exception, were taken. The Horse chasseurs of the Imperial Guard covered themselves with glory; they overthrew everything that opposed them and charged Mack's regiment of cuirassiers. The two regiments of carabiniers have sustained their reputation.

One is full of astonishment when considering the march of Prince Murat from Albeck to Nuremberg. Although always fighting, he marched faster than the enemy, which was two days' march before him. The result of this prodigious activity was the taking of 1,500 wagons, 50 pieces of artillery, 16,000 men, including the capitulation of General Werneck, and a great number of flags; 18 generals have laid down their arms, three have been killed.

Colonels Morland of the Chasseurs of the Imperial Guard, Cochois of the 1st Regiment of Carabiniers, Rouvillois of the 1st Regiment of the Hussars, and the aides-de-camp Flahaut and Lagrange were particularly distinguished. Colonel Cochois was wounded.

On evening of the 21st, Prince Murat slept at Nuremberg, where he rested the 22nd.

In the combat of Elchingen on the 15th, the 69th Regiment of Line was distinguished. After forcing the bridge in tight columns, they were deployed under fire of the Austrians with an order and sang-froid that filled the enemy with stupor and admiration.

A battalion of the Imperial Guard is entering Augsburg today. Eighty grenadiers each carried a flag. This spectacle produced in the inhabitants of Augsburg an amazement that the citizens of the entire region share.

The division of Württemberg has just arrived at Geislingen.

The battalions of chasseurs, which had followed the army since its passage through Stuttgart, have gone to conduct into France a column of 10,000 prisoners. The troops of Baden, 3,000 or 4,000 strong, are marching to Augsburg.

The Emperor has just made a gift to the Bavarians of 20,000 Austrian rifles for the army and the National Guard.

He has also just made a gift to the Elector of Württemberg of six pieces of Austrian artillery.

During the manoeuvre of Ülm, the Elector of Württemberg feared a moment for his wife and family, who then went to Heidelberg; and he disposed his troops to defend the heart of his states.

The Austrians are detested by all Germany, well convinced that, without France, Austria would treat them like its hereditary countries.

No idea can be formed of the misery of the Austrian army; they are paid in notes, by which they lose 40 per cent. Our soldiers with great pleasure call the Austrians soldiers of paper. They are without any credit. The House of Austria could not borrow 10,000 francs anywhere. The generals themselves have not seen a gold piece for many years. The English, the moment they heard of the invasion of Bavaria, made a little present to the Emperor of Austria, which has not made him richer; they have engaged to remit him the 48 millions which they had lent him during the last war. If this is an advantage to the House of Austria, it has already paid very dear for it.

Eleventh Bulletin
Munich, 26 October 1805 (4 Brumaire year 14)
The Emperor arrived at Munich on 24 October, at nine in the evening. The town was illuminated with a great deal of taste. A great number of people had decorated the front of their homes with emblems that expressed their sentiments.

At three in the morning, the great officers of the Elector, the chamberlains and gentlemen of the court, the ministers, the generals, the private counsellors, the diplomatic corps accredited by the Elector, the deputies of state of Bavaria, the magistrates of the city of Munich, all were presented to the Emperor, who carried on a long conversation on the economic affairs of their countries.

Prince Murat has arrived in Munich. He has exhibited in this expedition a prodigious activity. He never ceases to praise the gallant charge of the chasseurs of the Imperial Guard and of the carabiniers.

A treasure amounting to 200,000 florins fell into their hands, but they left it untouched and pushed on in pursuit of the enemy.

Prince Ferdinand escaped in the last action on the horse of a lieutenant of cavalry.

All the city of Nuremberg is impressed with the bravery of the French. A great number of Austrian deserters and runaways who have escaped into the province of Franconia have created great disorder there. All the enemy's baggage was taken.

This evening the Emperor attended the theatre, where he was greeted by demonstrations of very sincere joy and gratitude.

Today the Emperor, after seeing the departure of the troops of the corps of Marshal Soult, went to a hunt at Nymphenburg, vacation home of the Elector.

All are in movement; our armies have crossed the Isar, and are in full march for the Inn, where Marshal Bernadotte is on one side, General Marmont the other, and Marshal Davout will arrive this evening.

Twelfth Bulletin
Munich, 27 October 1805 (5 Brumaire year 14)
To the Fifth Bulletin of the Army should be annexed the capitulation of Memmingen, which was forgotten.

The works at the fortifications of Ingolstadt and Augsburg are, at the moment, carried on with the greatest activity.

Bridgeheads are constructed at all the bridges over the Lech, and magazines are established in their rear.

His Majesty has been highly satisfied with the zeal and activity of General of Brigade Bertrand, his aide-de-camp, whom he has frequently employed in reconnoitring.

His Majesty has given orders for the demolition of the fortifications of Ülm and Memmingen.

The Elector of Bavaria is expected here at any minute. The Emperor has sent his aide-de-camp, Colonel Lebrun, to receive him and to offer him escorts of honour on his route.

A *Te Deum* has been sung at Augsburg and at Munich. The attached proclamation has been posted in all the towns of Bavaria. The Bavarian people are full of good feelings; they are running to arms, and forming voluntary guards to defend their country against the incursions of the Cossacks.

Generals Deroy and Wrede manifest the utmost activity; the latter has taken many Austrian prisoners. He served in the Austrian Army during the last war, in which he was distinguished.

General Mack, having travelled quickly through Bavaria on his return to Vienna, met General Wrede at the advanced posts near the Inn. They had a long conversation on the manner in which the French treat the Bavarian army.

'We fare much better than with you,' said General Wrede, 'We are subjected neither to mortifications nor ill-treatment; and far from being the first to be exposed in combat, we are obliged to demand posts of danger, because the French prefer to reserve them for themselves. With you, on the contrary, we were sent to every quarter where there was a bad business to endure.'

A staff officer has just arrived from the army of Italy. The campaign began on the 18 October. That army will soon form the right of the *Grande Armée*.

The Emperor yesterday gave a concert to all the ladies of the court. He gave a particularly distinguished reception to Madame Montgelas, the wife of the Elector's prime minister and distinguished besides by her own merit.

He testified his satisfaction to Mr Winter, master of music to the Elector, on the excellent composition of his pieces, replete with spirit and talent.

Today, Sunday, 27 October, the Emperor attended mass in the chapel of the palace.

The following are the names of the Austrian generals taken prisoner. The number of officers is between 1,500 and 2,000. Each officer has given his word of honour not to serve; one hopes they will follow it exactly; if not, the laws of war will be enforced with the utmost rigour.

List of Austrian general officers taken prisoner in the actions of
Elchingen, Wertingen, Memmingen, Ülm, etc.

Baron Mack, Field-Marshal-Lieutenant, Quartermaster-General;
Prince Hesse-Homburg, Baron Stipsicz, Field-Marshal-Lieutenants;
Count Giulay, Baron Laudon, Count Klenau, Count Gottescheim, Count Riesch, Count Baillet, Count Werneck, Prince Hohenzollern, Field-Marshal-Lieutenants, Quarter-Master-Generals of the army of Prince Ferdinand;
Prince Lichtenstein, Baron Abel, Baron Ülm, Baron Weidenfeld, Count Auersperg, Count Ghenedegg, Count Fresnel, Count Sticker, Count Hermann, taken at Elchingen; Count Hermann, taken at Ülm; Count Richter, Count Dinnersberg, Count Mecséry, Count Vogel, Count Weber, Count Hohenfeld, Baron d'Aspre, Count Spangen, Major-Generals.

Thirteenth Bulletin

Haag, 28 October 1805 (6 Brumaire year 14)

The army corps under Marshal Bernadotte left Munich on the 26th; it arrived on the 27th at Wasserburg, on the Inn, and proceeded to Altenmarkt to sleep. Six arches of the bridge had been burned down. Count Minucci, Colonel of the Bavarian army, advanced from Rott to Rosenheim; he also found the bridge burned and the enemy on the other side. After a brisk cannonade, the enemy retired from the right bank; several Battalions of French and Bavarians crossed the Inn, and on the 28th at noon both the bridges were completely repaired. Colonels of the Engineers Morio and Somis were indefatigable in their exertions to re-establish the bridges. The enemy was hotly pursued as soon as the troops could cross; 50 of its rearguard were taken prisoner.

Marshal Davout, with his army corps, set out from Freising on the 26th and reached Mühldorf on the 27th. The enemy defended the right bank of the river, where they had some batteries very advantageously situated. The bridge had been so much destroyed that it was with difficulty repaired. At noon on the 28th, a considerable part of Marshal Davout's division had crossed over.

Prince Murat ordered a brigade of cavalry to cross the bridges of Mühldorf, had the bridges of Ötting and Marekhl repaired, and crossed them with a part of his reserve. The Emperor himself went to Haag.

The army corps of Marshal Soult bivouacked before Haag; the corps of Marshal Marmont sleeps this evening at Vilsbiburg; that of Marshal Ney at Landsberg; that of Marshal Lannes on the road from Landshut at Braunau. From all the information that has been received, it appears that the Russian army is retreating.

There has been a great deal of rain all day. All the country between the Isar and the Inn is nothing but a continuous forest of fir trees; the soil is excessively barren. The army has much reason to be satisfied with the zeal and attention of the inhabitants of Munich in supplying them with such provisions as they required.

Second Bulletin of the Army of Italy

29 October 1805 (7 Brumaire year 14)

The General-in-Chief had the enemy attacked this morning at five o'clock.

While on his left the division of General Séras crossed the Adige at Polo, and on his right that of General Verdier manoeuvred from Ronco to Albaro, the divisions of Generals Gardanne and Duhesme deploying before the bridge of the old castle of Verona, attacked the heights of Val-Pantena and turned the castle of Saint Felice; taking advantage of their position, the General-in-Chief forced the Austrians to evacuate Veronette. The palisades of the new bridge were immediately cut down; the division of mounted chasseurs under the orders of General Molitor crossed Veronette and marched on the road to Saint Michel, where the Austrians opposed us with infantry and cavalry protected by several cannon: several charges of cavalry were quickly executed, supported by the grenadiers of the Molitor division; in one of these charges the Guide squadron made 500 infantry put down their arms. The enemy was overthrown and chased from the village of Saint Michel to beyond Saint Martin. We have taken position at Vago.

The results of this day are 1,600 prisoners and two pieces of artillery. The Austrians left many men on the battlefield. Our loss is only a few men. We have about 100 wounded. The army is going to pursue its advantages.

The divisions and different corps have manoeuvred with precision, and the General-in-Chief praises the ardour and audacity of the troops during the attack; he has given testimony to His Majesty the Emperor and King of the burning desire they have of imitating the examples of the *Grande Armée* and that they deserve to have part of the noble rewards His Majesty confers upon them.

Fourteenth Bulletin

Braunau, 30 October 1805 (8 Brumaire year 14)

Marshal Bernadotte arrived at Salzburg at ten this morning. The elector had departed several days before. A corps of 6,000 men that was placed there had retreated hastily on the preceding evening.

The Imperial Headquarters were on the 28th at Haag, on the 29th at Mühldorf and on the 30th at Braunau.

Marshal Davout employed yesterday to repair the bridge of Mühldorf completely.

The 1st Regiment of Chasseurs made a fine charge against the enemy, killed 20 men and took several prisoner, among whom was a captain of Hussars.

During the day of the 29th, Marshal Lannes arrived with the light cavalry at the bridge of Braunau. He had set out from Landshut. The bridge was cut away. He immediately embarked 60 men in two boats. The enemy, which was pursued by the reserve under Prince Murat, has abandoned the city. The boldness of the Chasseurs of the 13th contributed to hasten the enemy's retreat.

The misunderstanding between the Russians and Austrians begins to show itself. The Russians plunder everywhere. The best-informed officers among them are perfectly aware that the war which they wage is impolitic, since they have nothing to gain against the French, whom nature has not placed in a situation to be their enemies.

Braunau, as we find, may be considered one of the finest and most useful acquisitions of the army. This fortress is surrounded with a wall fortified with bastions, drawbridges, a half-moon and ditches full of water. There are numerous magazines of artillery, and all are in good condition; but what will seem difficult to believe is that it is completely supplied with provisions. There we found 40,000 rations of bread ready to be distributed and more than 1,000 sacks of flour. The artillery of the fortress consists of 45 pieces of artillery, with double spare carriages, supplied mortars, and more than 40,000 cannonballs and howitzers. The Russians left behind about 100,000 powder charges, a great quantity of cartridges, lead, 1,000 muskets, and all the provisions necessary to support a long siege.

The Emperor has appointed General Lauriston, who arrived from Cadiz, governor of the place and he established the depot of the headquarters there.

Fifteenth Bulletin
Braunau, 31 October 1805 (9 Brumaire year 14)

Several Russian deserters have already arrived; among them is a sergeant-major native of Moscow, a man of some intelligence. One can easily imagine that he was questioned by everyone. He tells us that the Russian army is quite differently disposed now towards the French than it was in the last war; that the prisoners who had returned from France had spoken in high praise of it; that there were six in his company who, at the moment of departing from Poland, had been sent very far away; that if all the men who returned from France had been allowed to remain in the regiments, there can be no doubt but they would all have deserted; that the Russians were very sorry to fight for the Germans, whom they detest; and that they had a high opinion of French valour. He was asked if they loved the Emperor Alexander. He replied that they were too wretched to have any attachment for him; that the soldiers were fonder of the Emperor Paul, but that the nobility preferred the Emperor Alexander; that the Russians in general were very happy to leave their own country; that none of them wished to go back to Russia; and that they would rather establish themselves in other climates than return under the authority of so harsh a government; that they know the Austrians had lost every battle, and could only weep.

Prince Murat set out in pursuit of the enemy. He overtook the rearguard of the Austrians, 6,000 men strong, on the road from Mernbach. To see them and charge them was the same thing for the cavalry. This rearguard was dispersed on the heights of Ried. The enemy's cavalry then rallied to protect the passage of the infantry by a defile; but the first regiment of chasseurs and the division of dragoons under General Beaumont overwhelmed them and rushed into the defile along with the infantry of the enemy. The firing was rather sharp; but the darkness of the night saved this enemy division; part of them saved themselves in the woods; there were only 500 prisoners taken. The advanced guard of the division of Prince Murat took a position at Haag. Colonel Montbrun of the 1st Regiment of Chasseurs covered himself with glory.

The 8th Regiment of Dragoons maintains its old reputation. A quartermaster of this regiment having had his wrist shot off said, in the presence of the Prince as he was passing, 'I regret the loss of my hand, because it can no long serve our brave Emperor.' The Emperor, on learning of this event, said, 'There I recognize the spirit of the Eighth. Let an advantageous place, according to his rank, be given to this quartermaster in the Palace of Versailles.'

The inhabitants of Braunau, according to custom, carried to their houses a great part of the magazines of the fortress. A proclamation brought all back again. There are at present 1,000 sacks of flour, a great quantity of oats, magazines of artillery of every kind and 60,000 rations of bread, of which we are in great want; a part of it was distributed to the corps of Marshal Soult.

Marshal Bernadotte has arrived at Salzburg. The enemy retreated on the road of Carinthia and of Wels. A regiment of infantry wished to keep possession of the village of Hallein; it was obliged to retreat towards the village of Golling, where the Marshal hoped that General Kellermann would be able to cut off their retreat and capture them.

The inhabitants assure us that the Emperor of Germany, in his anxiety, came to Wels, where he learned of the disaster of his army. He also became acquainted there with the clamours of his Austrian and Bohemian subjects against the Russians, who commit such pillage and violence in so frenzied a manner that they long for the arrival of the French to deliver them from these peculiar allies.

Marshal Davout, with his army corps, took a position between Ried and Haag. All the other divisions of the army are advancing. But the weather is horrible; it has snowed half a foot deep, which has rendered the roads detestable.

Secretary of State Maret has joined the Emperor at Braunau.

The Elector of Bavaria has returned to Munich. The inhabitants of this capital received him with the greatest enthusiasm.

Several mails from Vienna have been intercepted. The most recent letters were dated 18 October; some included intelligence of the action at Wertingen; it created the greatest consternation there. Provisions were so expensive that few persons could afford to purchase them; famine threatened Vienna, and yet the harvest had been very productive; but the depreciation of the paper money, and of the *assignats* on which there was a loss of 40 per cent, had raised everything to a very high price. Everyone was persuaded that the Austrian paper money must be completely destroyed. The farmer would no longer exchange his produce for a paper currency of no value. There is not a man in all Germany who does not consider the English as the authors of the war, and the Emperors Francis and Alexander as the victims of their intrigues. There is no-one who does not say that there will be no peace as long as England is governed by an oligarchy, and governed it will be in that way as long as George breathes. The accession of the Prince of Wales is therefore generally wished for on this account, that it will put an end to the power of the few, who in all countries are selfish and insensible to the misfortunes of the people.

The Emperor Alexander was expected at Vienna, but he changed his mind. It is reported he has gone to Berlin.

3rd Bulletin of the Army of Italy

30 October 1805 (8 Brumaire year 14)

After the affair of the 29th (7th Brumaire) this army had taken position at Vago, two miles from Caldiero. At two in the afternoon on the 30th, the army attacked the enemy on the whole line. The Monitor division, forming the left, started the action; that of General Gardanne attacked the centre and that of General Duhesme attacked the right. These different attacks were superbly executed. The village of Caldiero was taken to the cries of 'Long Live the Emperor!' and the enemy was pursued as far as the heights.

At four-thirty, Prince Charles had his reserve advance; it has 24 grenadier battalions and several regiments. The battle then became livelier. His Majesty's troops displayed their normal intrepidity: the cavalry charged successfully several times; some grenadier battalions of reserve also were engaged, and the bayonet decided the fate of this day.

The enemy had used more than 30 pieces of artillery that was in its entrenchments. In spite of its tenacity in resisting, it was overthrown and pursued beyond Caldiero.

We have taken 3,500 prisoner; the battlefield is covered with Austrians; their dead and wounded equal in number that of their prisoners. Prince Charles has requested a truce in order that they might bury their dead.

Our loss is not very considerable compared to that of the enemy.

The Marshal General-in-Chief applauded the valour and devotion of the army; he will give an account of the fine actions which marked the day, and will show His Majesty the Emperor and King the names of the brave men to whom honour is due.

4th Bulletin of the Army of Italy

2 November 1805 (11 Brumaire year 14)

After the battle of the 30th (8 Brumaire), by the effect of the army's position before Caldiero and by the movements ordered to the Séras division on the 29th, an enemy column of 5,000 men commanded by a brigadier became separated from General Rosenberg's corps and found itself cut off and unable to return to the valleys or rejoin its army. The General-in-Chief, aware that it had gone on the 1st to the heights of Saint Leonard, sent one of his aides-de-camp to summon them to lay down their arms. The officer, General Hillinger, who commanded it, seeing he had no troops in front of him, manifested the intention to fight.

The 22nd Regiment of Light Infantry, at the head of which is Colonel Goguet, was ordered to advance before Veronette; the enemy made a movement towards him, and forced him to take position below the castle of Saint Felice. The General-in-Chief soon went there and sent four battalions of grenadiers to completely surround the enemy; General Charpentier, chief of staff in charge of these dispositions, executed them with precision, along with General Solignac.

A new summation was given to the enemy, who realized that it must resolve to lay down their arms. A capitulation was signed by the officer general commanding the enemy column and by General Solignac. We took 5,000 prisoner with arms and baggage, 70 officers, one brigadier, one major, one colonel, 80 horses, etc., etc.

Prince Charles, on his side, aware that one column of his army had been cut off and fearing he could be turned in his position, started to retreat. We learned that he had moved during the night; at daybreak we went to reconnoitre upon the line; the division of mounted chasseurs under the command of General Espagne and Gardanne's division of voltigeurs pursued the Austrians, who were harassed all day and from whom we took 600 prisoner.

Today we occupy Montebello; tomorrow the army will continue its march.

Sixteenth Bulletin

Ried, 2 November 1805 (11 Brumaire year 14)

Prince Murat has continued his march in pursuit of the enemy, sword in their back, and arrived on 31 October before Lambach. The Austrian generals, perceiving that their troops could not hold out, had eight battalions of Russians advance for the purpose of protecting their retreat. The 17th Regiment of Infantry of Line, the 1st Regiment of Chasseurs, and the 8th of Dragoons charged the Russians with impetuosity, and after a lively fusillade put them into disorder and drove them to Lambach. We took 500 prisoner, among whom were 100 Russians.

At ten in the morning, Prince Murat communicated that General Walther, with his division of cavalry, had taken possession of Wels. General Beaumont's division of dragoons and the 1st Division of the army corps of Marshal Davout, commanded by General Bisson, had taken a position at Lambach. The bridge over the Traun was cut; Marshal Davout substituted a bridge of boats. The enemy determined to defend the left bank of the river. Colonel Valterre of the 30th Regiment was one of the first to throw himself into a barge and crossed the river. General Bisson, while making his dispositions for crossing, received a musket ball in the arm.

Another division of the corps of Marshal Davout has advanced before Lambach, on the road from Steyer. The remainder of his army corps is on the heights of Lambach.

Marshal Soult will arrive this evening at Wels.

Marshal Lannes will arrive this evening at Linz.

Marshal Marmont is marching to turn the position on the banks of the Enns.

Prince Murat commends the conduct of Colonel Couroux, commander of the 17th Regiment of Infantry of Line. The troops could not possibly under any circumstances display more impetuosity and courage.

Immediately on his arrival at Salzburg, Marshal Bernadotte detached General Kellermann at the head of his advanced guard to pursue an enemy column, which was retreating by the road from Carinthia. It had taken shelter behind the fort of Lueg-Pass, in the gorge of Golling. Whatever the strength of its position, the carabiniers of the 27th Regiment of Light Infantry attacked it with impetuosity. General Werlé directed Captain Campocasso to turn the fort by almost impassable roads. Five hundred men, of whom three were officers, were made prisoner. The enemy column, 3,000 men strong, scattered to the winds. We found a great quantity of arms, and we hoped again to collect many prisoners. General Kellerman bestows praises on the conduct of Battalion Chief Dherbez-Latour. General Werlé has had his clothes pierced with bullets.

Our advanced posts announce from Wels that the Emperor of Germany had arrived there on 25 October; that he there learned the fate of his army at Ulm; and that he was convinced, with his own eyes, of the frightful ravages committed everywhere by the Russians and of the extreme discontent of his subjects. It is said that he has returned to Vienna without alighting from his carriage.

The ground is covered with snow; the rains have ceased; the cold has taken over; it is rather severe; it is by no means like the commencement of November, but the month of January. The drier weather has the advantage of being healthier and more favourable for marching.

Seventeenth Bulletin

Lambach, 3 November 1805 (12 Brumaire year 14)

Today, the 3rd, Marshal Davout has his advance posts near Steyer. General Milhaud, with the reserve of the cavalry under the orders of Prince Murat, entered Linz on 1 November; Marshal Lannes arrived there on the 3rd with his army corps. Considerable magazines were found at Linz, of which the inventories have not as yet been made; there are many sick in the hospitals, of whom about a hundred are Russians. We have taken some prisoners, of which 50 are Russian.

In the combat at Lambach, two pieces of Russian artillery were found among those taken; a Russian general and an Austrian colonel of hussars were killed.

The wound which General Bisson, commander of the first division of Marshal Davout's army corps, received in the arm is so serious as to prevent his serving the rest of the campaign. There is no danger, however. The Emperor has given General Caffarelli the command of that division.

Since the crossing of the Inn, we have taken from 1,500 to 1,800 prisoner, as many Austrians as Russians, without counting the sick.

The army corps of General Marmont left Lambach on 3 November at noon.

The Emperor has established his headquarters at Lambach, where it is believed he spent the night of the 12th.

The season continues severe. The ground is covered with snow; the weather is very cold.

We found at Lambach magazines of salt worth several millions. Several hundred thousand florins were found in the chest at Linz.

The Russians have completely devastated the area at Wels, Lambach and the surrounding villages. There are some villages where they have killed eight or ten peasants.

The agitation and disorder are extreme at Vienna. It is said that the Emperor of Austria has established himself in the Benedictine convent of Mölk. It would seem that in the rest of the month of November there will be major events of the greatest importance.

Mr Lezay, Minister of France at Salzburg, has had an audience with the Emperor at the moment when His Majesty set out from Braunau. Until then he had constantly resided at Salzburg.

We have no news from Mr de la Rochefoucauld; it is believed that he is still at Vienna. At the moment that the Austrian army crossed the Inn he asked for passports, which were refused him.

Several Russian deserters have arrived today.

5th Bulletin of the Army of Italy

5 November 1805 (14 Brumaire year 14)

After a few hours of rest at Montebello, the army pursued the enemy towards Vicence. The gates of the town had been walled; we summoned him to evacuate; the response was negative. A sentiment of humanity had dictated the summation of the General-in-Chief; we had no choice but to force the passage and directed cannon and howitzers against the gates, and unfortunately against the town itself. We entered it at daybreak. The enemy retreated with such precipitation that it abandoned 1,000 wounded and left some magazines in our hands. On that day, we took 800 prisoner.

The Austrians had retreated by the road to Bassano. The army followed them and continually encroached upon their rearguard. At the junction of the roads of Bassano and Treviso they headed towards the latter, burning behind them the bridges near the Palu. When we arrived at Saint Pierre we found this village occupied by a corps of troops, and we charged vigorously. The village was taken after a combat that gave us 600 prisoners and one piece of artillery.

We marched towards the Brenta. The advance guard arrived at the moment the enemy attempted to destroy the bridge. A strong cannonade was engaged from one bank to the other, which only night could stop.

The army bivouacked on the right bank. At four in the morning, several cavalry regiments with the voltigeurs in a group were able to ford the river while we repaired the bridge. The army set out again and we arrived at Cittadella in time to take out the last posts of the enemy. At five o'clock in the evening, we entered Castelfranco and our chasseurs already occupied Salratrunda and Albaredo. The General-in-Chief felt the necessity to give a few hours repose to the army.

In our march from Montebello we have taken more than 1,800 prisoner.

The division of the right marched towards Padua, where it should arrive today; that of the left marched by the 'sette communi' to Bassano, which it will occupy tomorrow.

The army is marching towards the Piave.

Eighteenth Bulletin

Linz, 5 November 1805 (14 Brumaire year 14)

Prince Murat does not lose sight of the enemy. It had left 300 or 400 men at Ebelsberg to retard the crossing of the Traun; but General Walther's dragoons threw themselves into boats, and under the protection of the artillery attacked the town with impetuosity. Lieutenant Billaudel, of the 13th Regiment of Dragoons, was the first to cross over in a small boat.

General Walther, after having crossed the bridge over the Traun, advanced on Enns. The brigade of General Milhaud met the enemy at the village of Asten, defeated them, pursued them to Enns and took 200 prisoner, 50 of whom were Russian hussars. Twenty Russian hussars were killed. The rearguard of the Austrians, supported by the Russian cavalry, was everywhere overthrown; neither one nor the other was able to stand a charge. The 22nd and 16th Regiments of Chasseurs and their Colonels Latour-Maubourg and Durosnel showed the greatest intrepidity. The aide-de-Camp to Prince Murat, Flahaut, has taken a ball in the arm.

During the day of the 4th, we have crossed the Enns, and today Prince Murat advanced in pursuit of the enemy. Marshal Davout arrived on the 3rd at Steyer; on the 4th during the day he took possession of the town and took 200 prisoner. The enemy made a show of defending it. General Beaumont's division of dragoons has maintained its reputation. The aide-de-camp of General Beaumont was killed. Both the bridges on the Enns are completely repaired.

At the battle of Lambach the Austrian Colonel Graff and the Russian Colonel Golofkin, were killed.

The Emperor of Austria, arriving at Linz, received complaints from the magistracy of the bad conduct of the Russians, who are not content to plunder but also have beaten the peasants, which has caused a number of villages to be deserted. The Emperor appeared extremely distressed at these excesses, and observed that he could not answer for the Russian troops as for his own and that they should endure in patience, which did not console the inhabitants.

A great many provisions were found at Linz, and a considerable quantity of cloth and clothes in the imperial factories. General Deroy, at the head of a corps of Bavarians, confronted at Lofer the advanced guard of a column of five Austrian regiments coming from Italy, completely defeated it and took 400 prisoner and three pieces of artillery. The Bavarians fought with the greatest persistence and extreme bravery. General Deroy himself was wounded by a pistol shot.

These minor actions gave rise to numerous instances of courage, on the part of the officers in particular.

The Major-General is occupied in drawing up a detailed account in which everyone will receive that share of glory that his courage has merited.

The Enns may be considered as the last line that defends the approaches to Vienna. It is said that the enemy intends to make a stand, and entrench itself behind the heights of Saint Pölten, within ten leagues of Vienna. Our advanced guard will be there tomorrow.

Nineteenth Bulletin
Linz, 6 November 1805 (15 Brumaire year 14)

The battle of Lofer has been very brilliant for the Bavarians. The Austrians occupied beyond Lovers an almost inaccessible defile, flanked on the right and left by peaked mountains. The summit was covered by Tyrolean chasseurs who knew every path. Three stone forts secure the mountains rendering access almost impossible. After a sharp resistance, the Bavarians overthrew everything, taking 600 prisoner, two pieces of artillery, and carrying all the forts. But at the last attack, Lieutenant General Deroy, commander-in-chief of the Bavarian Army, was wounded by a pistol shot. The Bavarians had 12 officers killed or wounded; 50 soldiers killed, and 250 wounded. The conduct of Lieutenant General Deroy merits the greatest praise; he is an old officer, full of honour and extremely attached to the Elector, of whom he is a friend.

All the time so far has been so busy that the Emperor has not yet been able to review the Bavarian army, nor to become acquainted with the brave men who compose it.

Prince Murat, after the capture of Enns, pursued the enemy anew. The Russian army had taken a position on the heights of Amstetten. Prince Murat attacked it with General Oudinot's grenadiers; the battle was rather relentless. The Russians were driven from all their positions, and left 400 dead on the battlefield and 1,500 prisoners. Prince Murat gives particular praise to General Oudinot; his aide-de-camp Lagrange was wounded.

Marshal Davout, on crossing the Enns at Steyer, particularly commends the conduct of General Heudelet, who commanded his advanced guard; he has continued his march and proceeded against Waidhofen.

All the intercepted letters state that all the furnishings of the Court are already embarked on the Danube, and that the French arrival at Vienna is awaited.

Twentieth Bulletin
Linz, 7 November 1805 (16 Brumaire year 14)

The combat of Amstetten has reflected great honour on the cavalry, and particularly on the 9th and 10th Regiments of Hussars and on the grenadiers of General Oudinot's division.

The Russians have since accelerated their retreat; in vain they cut the bridges over the Ips, which have been promptly re-established, and Prince Murat has reached the abbey of Mölk.

A reconnoitring party is moving on Bohemia. We have taken very considerable magazines, both at Freystadt and Mauthausen. Marshal Mortier, with an army corps, manoeuvred on the left bank of the Danube.

A deputation from the Senate has just arrived at Linz; the Elector of Bavaria is expected there in two hours.

Linz, November 1805 (17 Brumaire year 14)
The Elector of Bavaria and the Electoral Prince arrived at Linz yesterday evening. Lieutenant General Count Giulay, sent by the Emperor of Austria, arrived there in the night. He has had a very long conference with the Emperor. The object of his mission is not known.

In the combat of Amstetten we took 1,800 prisoner, 700 of whom were Russians.

Prince Murat has established his headquarters at the abbey of Mölk. His advanced posts are at Saint Pölten [Saint Hippolyte].

During the day of the 8th, General Marmont directed his march to Leoben. Arriving at Weyer, he encountered the regiment of Giulay, charged it, and took 400 prisoner, among whom were a colonel and several officers; he has pursued his route. All the columns of the army are in great manoeuvre.

Twenty-first Bulletin

Mölk, 10 November 1805 (19 Brumaire year 14)
On 7 November, the army corps of Marshal Davout advanced from Steyer towards Waidhofen, Mariazell and Lilienfeld. By this movement he entirely uncovered the left of the enemy, which was expected to make a stand on the heights of Saint Pölten, and from Lilienfeld he directed its march towards Vienna by a great carriage road that leads directly there.

On the 8th, the advanced guard of this marshal, while it was still many leagues from Mariazell, met the corps of General Merveldt, who was marching for Neustadt to cover Vienna on that side. General of Brigade Heudelet, commanding the advanced guard of Marshal Davout, attacked the enemy with the greatest vigour, routed them and pursued them the space of five leagues. The result of this battle of Mariazell was the capture of three flags, 16 pieces of artillery, and 4,000 prisoners, among whom are the colonels of the regiments of Joseph–Colloredo and Deutchmeister, and five majors.

The 13th Regiment of Light Infantry, and the 108th Line, conducted themselves perfectly.

On the 9th, in the morning, Prince Murat arrived at Saint Pölten. He directed General of Brigade of Dragoons Sebastiani to proceed towards Vienna. All of the court and the nobility had left that capital. It had been already announced at the advanced posts, that the [Austrian] Emperor was preparing to leave Vienna.

The Russian army effected its retreat to Krems by re-crossing the Danube, doubtless fearing to see its communications with Moravia cut off by the movement made by Marshal Mortier on the left bank of the Danube.

General Marmont must have passed Leoben.

The abbey of Mölk, in which the Emperor is lodged, is one of the finest in Europe. There is not, either in France or in Italy, any convent or abbey that can compare with it. It is in a strong position, and commands the Danube. It was one of the principal posts of the Romans, which was called the Iron House, built by the Emperor Commodus. The vaults and cellars of the abbey were found full of excellent Hungarian wine, which was a great help to the army, which had needed it a long time. But we are now in wine country; there is a great deal of it in the vicinity of Vienna.

The Emperor ordered that a particular safeguard should be put at the chateau of Lustschloss, a little country house of the Emperor of Austria, on the left bank of the Danube.

The avenues of Vienna on this side bear no resemblance to the ordinary avenues of the great capitals. From Linz to Vienna there is but one main road, a great number of rivers, such as the Ips, the Erlaf, the Mölk, the Trasen, etc., which have only bad wooden bridges. The country is covered with forests of fir. At every step there are impregnable positions in which the enemy endeavored in vain to make a stand. It had always to dread that it would be uncovered and turned by the columns that manoeuvred beyond their flanks.

From the Inn to here the Danube is superb, its points of view are picturesque, its navigation down the current is rapid and easy.

All the letters intercepted speak only of the frightful chaos that Vienna presents. The war has been undertaken by the Austrian cabinet against the advice of all the Princes of the Imperial Family. But Colloredo, led by his wife who, French, brought the bitterest hatred to her country; Cobentzl, accustomed to tremble at the very name of a Russian, persuaded that everything ought to give way before them, and in whom it is also possible that the agents of England may have found means to introduce themselves, and finally that wretch Mack, who had already played so great a role in the renewal of the second coalition: there are the influences that have been stronger than those of all prudent men and of all the members of the Imperial Family. There is not a man down to the meanest citizen or the lowest non-commissioned officer who does not feel that this war is advantageous only to the English; that they have fought only for them; that they are the authors of the misfortunes of Europe, in the same manner as by their monopoly they are the authors of the excessive high price of goods.

6th Bulletin of the Army of Italy
13 November 1805 (22 Brumaire year 14)
In its march on the Piave the army met only weak obstacles. From the Piave to the Tagliamento it saw fleeing in front of it a few corps of cavalry who seemed to observe it, but whose retreat was calculated in such a way as to avoid any engagement.

It is at the Tagliamento that the enemy appeared to want to wait for us. It had reunited on the left bank six regiments of cavalry and four of infantry, and its countenance led us to presume that it would strongly defend the passage. The General-in-Chief had decided only to have the position reconnoitered by some cavalry. General Espagne, commanding the division of mounted chasseurs, the dragoons under the orders of General Mermet and the cuirassiers under General Pully, had all gone to the river, while the Duhesme and Séras divisions marched on Saint Vilto, those of Generals Molitor and Gardanne headed toward Valvasone.

General Espagne had received orders to go on reconnaissance: on the 12th at six in the morning, a squadron that he had been able to cross was charged by a regiment of Austrian cavalry. He held up the attack with intrepidity and gave time to General Espagne to march and meet the enemy who soon was repulsed and put to route. Meanwhile, our artillery, having taken position, a cannonade started from one bank to the other; it was very lively and continued all day. The enemy had placed 30 cannon behind a trench; we only had 18, and our artillerymen kept their usual superiority. The divisions of infantry arrived that night. The General-in-Chief, satisfied with the advantages he had obtained, decided not to do the crossing immediately. He contented himself in making his dispositions for the next day, thinking he could then carry out much more decisive hits. The divisions were assembled at the indicated points at Saint Vilto and at Valvasone: it is on these points they were to cross the river, turn, and cut off the enemy.

Prince Charles, fearing the execution of this plan, did not want to wait until daylight in that position and at midnight he began his retreat on the road to Palma-Nova. The army crossed the Tagliamento with the regret of having no enemy left to fight; and it was then that they knew what the real results of the previous day were. The left bank of the river was still covered with men and horses that had perished as a result of our artillery. The army continued its march; the hope of meeting and fighting the enemy adds to its impatience and ardour.

They hear of all that the *Grande Armée* is doing, and the desire to back up its movements and to answer to the confidence the Emperor has placed in them causes them to be agitated and spurs them on.

The advance guard takes more prisoners each day, which will add to the numbers they already have. The weather is favourable; we are busy repairing the bridges of the Piave and the Tagliamento.

Twenty-second Bulletin

Saint Pölten, 13 November 1805 (22 Brumaire year 14)

Marshal Davout followed up his successes. All of Merveldt's corps is destroyed. That general saved himself with 100 Uhlans.

General Marmont is at Leoben. He took 100 cavalrymen prisoner. For three days Prince Murat has been within half a league of Vienna. All the Austrian troops had already evacuated the town. The National Guard did the duty there; it was animated with a very fine spirit.

Today, the 13th, the French troops have made their entry into this capital.

The Russians declined all the temptations that were held out to them to engage in battle on the heights of Saint Pölten (Saint Hippolyte). They crossed the Danube at Krems, and immediately after they had got over, they burned the bridge, which was very handsome.

At daybreak on the 11th, Marshal Mortier, at the head of six battalions, advanced towards Stein. He reckoned upon finding the rearguard there; but all of the Russian army was still there, their baggage not having passed by. Then they engaged in the battle of Dürrenstein, which will be forever celebrated in military annals. From six in the morning until four in the afternoon, these 4,000 brave fellows made headway against the Russian army and routed all those who opposed them.

Masters of the village of Leoben, they believed the labour of the day finished; but the enemy, irritated at having lost 10 flags, 6 pieces of artillery, 900 prisoners and 2,000 men killed, had marched in two columns, by difficult gorges, to turn the French. As soon as Marshal Mortier perceived this manoeuvre he marched straight against the troops who had turned him, and cut his way through the enemy's lines at the very moment that the 9th Regiment of Light Infantry and the 32nd Infantry of Line, having charged another Russian corps, had routed the corps after taking two flags and 4,000 prisoners.

This day was a day of massacre. Heaps of dead covered a circumscribed field of battle. More than 4,000 Russians were killed and wounded, and 1,300, among whom were two colonels, taken prisoner.

On our side the loss was considerable. The 4th and 9th Regiments of Light Infantry suffered most. The colonels of the 100th and 103rd were slightly wounded. Colonel Watier of the 4th Regiment of Dragoons was killed. His Majesty had chosen him to be one of his equerries; he was an officer of great worth; in spite of the difficulty of the terrain, he made a very brilliant charge on a Russian column; but he was struck by a ball and died in the mêlée.

It seems that the Russians are retreating by forced marches. The Emperor of Germany, the Empress, the minister and the court are at Brünn, in Moravia. All the persons of consequence have left Vienna. All the bourgeoisie have remained there. The Emperor Alexander is expected at Brünn, on his return from Berlin.

General Count Giulay has taken many journeys, carrying letters from the Emperors of France and Germany to each other. The Emperor of Germany will, no doubt, determine upon peace as soon as he obtains the assent of the Emperor of Russia.

In the meantime, the dissatisfaction of the people is at its extreme. They say at Vienna and in all the provinces of the Austrian monarchy that they are badly governed; that, for the sole interest of England, they have been drawn into this unjust and disastrous war; that Germany has been inundated by barbarians a thousand times more to be dreaded than all the scourges together; that the finances are in the greatest disorder; that the public fortune and the fortunes of individuals are ruined by the existence of a paper circulation which loses 50 per cent; they had enough misfortunes to fix, and that all the calamities of war should not have been added to them.

The Hungarians complain of the illiberality of the government, which does nothing for their industry, and which shows itself continually jealous of their privileges and uneasy at their national spirit.

In Hungary as well as in Austria, at Vienna as well as other towns, everyone is persuaded that the Emperor Napoleon wishes for peace and that he is the friend of all nations and of all great ideas.

The English are the perpetual objects of the curses of all the subjects of the Emperor of Germany, and of the most universal hatred. Is it not finally time that princes should listen to the voice of their people, and that they should keep themselves from the fatal influence of the English oligarchy?

Since the crossing of the Inn, the *Grande Armée* has taken, in the different affairs of advanced posts and different actions that have taken place, about 10,000 prisoner.

If the Russian army had wanted to wait for the French, it would have been lost; many divisions of the army are actively pursuing them.

Twenty-third Bulletin

Palace of Schönbrunn, 14 November 1805 (23 Brumaire year 14)

At the battle of Dürrenstein, 4,000 French, who were attacked on the 11th by 25,000 or 30,000 Russians, maintained their position, killed from 3,000 to 4,000 of the enemy, took some flags and took 1,300 prisoner. The 4th and 9th Regiments of Light Infantry and the 100th and 32nd Regiments of Infantry of line covered themselves with glory. General Gazan displayed a great share of bravery and conduct. The Russians, the day after the battle, evacuated Krems and left the Danube, leaving 1,500 prisoners in a state of the greatest want. We found in their field hospitals a great many who had been wounded and who had died in the night.

It appeared to have been the intention of the Russians to wait for reinforcements at Krems, and to maintain their position on the Danube. The battle of Dürrenstein disconcerted their plan. They have seen, from what 4,000 French had done, that which was coming to them from an equal force.

Marshal Mortier set out in pursuit of them, while other army corps crossed the Danube by the bridge of Vienna to outflank them on the right, and the corps of Marshal Bernadotte is marching to turn their left wing.

Yesterday, the 13th, at ten in the morning, Prince Murat passed through Vienna. At daybreak, a column of cavalry advanced to the bridge over the Danube, which it crossed after some conferences with the Austrian generals. The enemy's engineers, which were ordered to burn the bridge, attempted it several times but could not succeed in doing it.

Marshal Lannes and General Bertrand, aide-de-Camp to the Emperor, were the first who crossed over the bridge. The troops did not stop at Vienna, but pursued their march to follow their orders.

Prince Murat established his headquarters in the house of Duke Albert. Duke Albert has been a great benefactor to the city. In several quarters they lacked water; he had fresh water sent to them, and spent very large sums of his own money for that purpose.

The House of Austria has neither other foundry nor another arsenal than those at Vienna. The Austrians had no time to carry off above the fifth, or a fourth of their artillery, and of considerable material. We have ammunition enough to last for four campaigns, and to renew our trains of artillery four times over if we should lose them.We also have siege provisions enough to arm a great number of places.

The Emperor has taken up his residence in the palace of Schönbrunn. He went to Vienna today at two o'clock in the morning. He spent the rest of the night visiting the advanced posts on the left bank of the Danube, as well as the positions, and in satisfying himself personally that the duty was properly done. He returned to Schönbrunn at daybreak.

The weather has become very beautiful; the day, though cold, is one of the finest since the commencement of winter. Commerce and all transactions go on at Vienna as usual. The inhabitants are full of confidence and very tranquil in their homes. The population of the town amounts to 250,000 souls. It is not supposed that 10,000 people have left it on account of the absence of the court and the persons of distinction.

The Emperor received at noon Mr Wrbna, who is at the head of the administration of all Austria.

The army corps of Marshal Soult passed through Vienna at nine o'clock this morning; that of Marshal Davout is passing through it at this moment.

General Marmont has had at Leoben different small advantages from advanced posts.

The Bavarian army is growing greatly every day. The Emperor has just made new presents to the Elector. He has given him 15,000 muskets taken in the arsenal of Vienna, and has ordered all the artillery to be restored to him which Austria had taken in the Bavarian states on former occasions.

The town of Kufstein has surrendered into the hands of Colonel Pompei.

General Milhaud followed the enemy on the road to Brünn, as far as Wolkersdorf. Today at noon he took 600 prisoner and a park of 40 pieces of harnessed artillery.

Marshal Lannes arrived at Stockerau at two o'clock in the afternoon. There he found an immense store of clothing, 8,000 pairs of shoes and half boots, and cloth enough to make greatcoats for all the army.

Several boats freighted with artillery, leather, and articles of clothing that were going down the Danube have also been stopped.

Order of the Day

Chief of Staff, Imperial Headquarters at Vienna, 14 November 1805
The Emperor expresses his satisfaction to the 4th Regiment of Light Infantry, the 100th Line, the 9th Light Infantry, the 32nd Line, for the intrepidity that they displayed at the battle of Dürrenstein, where their firmness in holding the position that they occupied compelled the enemy to abandon its on the Danube.

His Majesty expresses his satisfaction to the 17th and 30th Regiments of the Line, which at the combat of Lambach made headway against the rearguard of the Russians, defeated them and took 400 prisoner.

His Majesty also expresses his satisfaction to Oudinot's grenadiers, who, at the battle of Amstetten drove the Austrians and Russians from their excellent and formidable positions and took 1,500 prisoner, of whom 600 were Russians.

His Majesty is satisfied with the 1st, 16th, and 22nd Regiments of Chasseurs, with the 9th and 10th Regiments of Hussars, for their good conduct in all the charges which have taken place from the Inn to the gates of Vienna, and for the 800 Russians taken prisoner at Stein.

Prince Murat, Marshal Lannes, the cavalry reserve, and their army corps entered Vienna on the 13th, took possession of the bridge over the Danube the same day, prevented it from being burned, crossed it immediately and set out in pursuit of the Russian army.

We found in Vienna more than 2,000 pieces of artillery, an arsenal containing 100,000 muskets, ammunition of all kinds; finally, everything to equip three or four armies for a campaign.

The people of Vienna appear to view the army with friendship.

The Emperor orders the greatest respect for estates, and that the greatest respect should be shown for the inhabitants of this capital, who view with pain the unjust war that has been made, and who show to us by their conduct as much friendship as they show hatred against the Russians, a people who by their barbarous habits and manners should inspire all civilized nations with the same sentiments.

THE MAJOR-GENERAL, MARSHAL BERTHIER

Twenty-fourth Bulletin

Palace of Schönbrunn, 15 November 1805 (24 Brumaire year 14)
At the battle of Dürrenstein, the Austrian Major-General Schmidt, who directed the movements of the Russians, was killed, as well as two Russian Generals. It appears that Colonel Watier is not dead, but that his horse was wounded in a charge and that he was taken prisoner. This news gave greatest satisfaction to the Emperor, who has a particular regard for this officer.

A column of 4,000 Austrian infantry and a regiment of cuirassiers traversed our posts, which allowed them to pass due to a false report of a suspension of arms that prevailed in the army. Here may be discovered the extreme facility of the French character, which, brave in the moment of battle is often of a most considerate generosity when not fighting.

General Milhaud, commanding the advanced guard of Marshal Davout's corps, took 191 pieces of artillery, with all the caissons of ammunition, and 400 men. Thus, almost all of the artillery of the Austrian monarchy is in our power.

The palace of Schönbrunn, in which the Emperor resides, was built by Maria Theresa, whose portrait is to be found in almost every apartment. In the office where the Emperor is working there is a marble statue of this sovereign. The Emperor, on seeing it, remarked that if that great queen were still living she would not allow herself to be influenced by the intrigues of a woman such as Madame Colloredo. Constantly surrounded as she always was with the chief persons of her kingdom, she would have known the inclination of her people; she would not have had her provinces ravaged by the Cossacks and Muscovites; she would not have consulted, in order to make up her mind to make war on France, a courtesan like Cobentzl, who, too well informed respecting court intrigues, dreads to disobey a foreign woman invested with a pernicious authority, which she abuses; a scribe like Collembach; and finally a man so universally detested as Lambertie. She would not have given the command of her army to such men as Mack, appointed, not by the choice of the Sovereign, not by the confidence of the nation, but by England and Russia. It is, in effect, a remarkable thing, this unanimity of opinion in a nation entirely adverse to the decision of the court; the citizens of every class, all the enlightened men, all the princes, are alike opposed to the war. It is said that Prince Charles, on his setting out for the army of Italy, wrote again to the Emperor to show him the imprudence of his determination and predicted to him the destruction of the monarchy; the Elector of Salzburg, the Archdukes, the principal persons, used the same language. The whole Continent should regret that the Emperor of Germany, who means well, who sees better than his ministers, and who, in many respects, might be a great Prince, is so diffident of himself and lives so constantly isolated. He would learn from the chief persons of the empire who esteem him to set a just value on himself; but not even one of them, who know and cherish the interests of the country, ever approach the interior of his palace. This isolation, which is imputed to the influence of the Empress, is the cause of the hatred that the nation has conceived against this princess. As long as this order of things shall exist, the Emperor will never learn the wishes of his people and will be always the puppet of the underlings whom England bribes and who surround him from fear that he might become enlightened. There is but one voice at Vienna, as well as at Paris; the misfortunes of the Continent are the fatal work of the English.

All the columns of the army are in full march, and are already in Moravia, several days' march beyond the Danube. A cavalry patrol has already come to the gates of Pressburg, the capital of Upper Hungary. It intercepted the courier from Venice at the very moment that he was seeking to enter that town. The dispatches of this courier have informed us that the army of Prince Charles was retiring in great haste in the hope of arriving in sufficient time to assist Vienna.

General Marmont writes that the corps that advanced to Ödenburg by the valley of Mur had evacuated that district after having destroyed all the bridges, a precaution that put them out of all danger of being hotly pursued.

The number of prisoners taken by the army increases at each instant.

His Majesty gave audience today to the Batavian Major-General Bruce, brother-in-law to the Grand Pensionary, who came to compliment the Emperor on the part of Their High Mightiness of the States of Holland.

The Emperor has not yet received any of the authorities of Vienna, but only a deputation of the city, which on the day of his arrival came to meet him at

Sieghartskirchen. It was composed of Prince Zinzendorf, Prelate Seidenstetten, Count Veterani, Baron Kess, the Burgomaster of the city, Mr Wohebben and General Burgeois of the corps of engineers.

His Majesty received them with much kindness and told them that they could assure the people of Vienna of his protection.

General of Division Clarke is appointed Governor of High and Low Austria. Councillor of State Daru is appointed *intendant général* [quartermaster].

Twenty-fifth Bulletin
Schönbrunn, 16 November 1805

Prince Murat and the corps of Marshal Lannes encountered the Russian army yesterday at Hollabrünn; a cavalry charge took place, but the enemy immediately abandoned the ground leaving 100 loaded carriages behind.

The enemy having been reinforced and his dispositions for attack made, an Austrian flag of truce advanced and asked permission for the Russian troops to separate from the Austrians. This request was granted.

Soon after, Baron Winzingerode, aide-de-camp-general to His Majesty the Emperor of Russia, presented himself to the advanced posts, and asked leave to capitulate for the Russian army. Prince Murat thought it his duty to assent to this measure; but the Emperor was not able to approve this capitulation. He immediately set out to the advanced posts.

The Emperor was not able give his approval because this capitulation is a kind of treaty, and because Winzingerode was not furnished with full powers on the part of the Emperor of Russia. But His Majesty, when ordering his army to march, declared, that if the Emperor Alexander, being in the neighbourhood, would ratify the convention, he was ready, on his part, to do the same.

General Vialannes, commanding the cavalry of Marshal Davout, has entered Pressburg. General Count Palffy has written a letter to which Marshal Davout replied. The two letters are attached.

A corps of 3,000 Austrians was entrenched near Waldmünchen, at the outlet of Bohemia. General Baraguey d'Hilliers, at the head of three battalions of grenadiers on foot, marched against this corps, which hastened to abandon its position. General Baraguey d'Hilliers was at Treinitz, in Bohemia, on the 9th. He hoped to cut into the corps.

Marshal Ney had orders to seize the Tyrol, and has acquitted himself with his usual intelligence and intrepidity. He has turned the forts of Scharnitz and of Luetasch, and seized them by force of arms. He has taken prisoner in this affair 1,800 men, a flag and 16 field pieces of artillery.

On 16 November, at five in the afternoon, he made his entry into Innsbruck; he found an arsenal with a considerable amount of artillery, 16,000 muskets and an immense quantity of powder. The same day he entered Hall, where he also found very great and very rich magazines, of which there is not yet an inventory.

The Archduke John, who commanded in the Tyrol, escaped by Luschthal. He had ordered a colonel to remit all the magazines to the French and to recommend to their generosity 1,200 sick at Innsbruck.

To all these glorious trophies may be added a scene that touched the soul of every soldier. In the last war, the 76th Regiment of Line lost two flags in the Grisons. This loss was, for a long time, the subject of deep affliction to all the corps. These brave fellows knew that Europe had not forgotten their disgrace, although their courage was uncensurable. The flags, subjects of so noble a regret, were found in the arsenal at Innsbruck; an officer recognized them. All the soldiers soon crowded around. When Marshal Ney had the colours restored to the 76th with great ceremony, tears fell from the eyes of all the old soldiers. The young conscripts felt themselves elated in the assistance they had given in the recovery of the honours snatched from their elders by the vicissitudes of war. The Emperor has ordered that the remembrance of this touching scene should be consecrated by a painting. The French soldier has a feeling for his colours that borders on tenderness. They are the object of his affections, like a present from the hands of a mistress.

General Klein has made an incursion into Bohemia with his division of dragoons. He has seen everywhere the Russians in horror; the devastations committed by them make one tremble. The irruptions of these barbarians, called in by the government itself, have almost extinguished every remnant of affection in the hearts of the Austrians for their Prince. 'We and the French,' say the Germans, 'are the sons of the Romans; the Russians are the children of the Tartars. We would rather a thousand times have the French armies against us than such as the Russians for our allies.' At Vienna the mere name of a Russian excites terror. These savage hordes are not contented with pillage for their subsistence; they carry off, they destroy, everything. A wretched peasant who possesses in his cottage only his clothes excites no pity in them. The rich man who occupies a palace can not hope to assuage them by his wealth; they would pillage him and leave him naked under the devastated ruins.

Doubtless this will be the last time that the European governments will call in such fatal help. If they were capable of wanting it again, they would have to pay these allies with an uprising of their own nation. A hundred years hence it will not be in the power of any Prince of Austria to introduce Russians into his states.

There are, notwithstanding, a great number of officers in this army, men of education, whose manners are polished and whose spirit enlightened; but that which is said of an army is always taken from the natural instinct of the mass that composes it.

Letter from General Count Palffy

General,

His Royal Highness the Archduke Palatine, in his role of supreme military and civil head of Hungary, has charged the undersigned to declare that His Highness has established along the western frontier of this kingdom a cordon of non-military guards, supported by very small detachments of cavalry, composed of invalids and recruits for the sole purpose of arresting the progress of the marauders in the Austrian army who may be present, and thus there is no question of any sort of hostility, these detachments being ordered to retire whenever the French troops shall approach the frontier.

Thus, in the circumstances in which these weak detachments are placed, they can only be looked on as outposts of observation, withdrawing at the approach of the French army. His Royal Highness has ordered the heads of the houses of invalids, seminary schools, officers on pension, individuals employed in the offices of accounting of the regiments and military hospitals, to remain at their posts, persuaded that the general or commandant of the French troops will not refuse them the necessary protections, and that he will want to give his orders that the columns of the French army that enters Hungary would commit no excesses, aware that no sort of opposition will be made to the French troops. In consequence of such a declaration, the undersigned may have to treat with the commandant of the French troops, relative to several very interesting subjects.

He also solicits a rendezvous on parole in a vessel in the middle of the Danube.

He accordingly awaits your response, and has the honour to be, his very humble servant,

LEOPOLD, COUNT PALFFY, MAJOR-GENERAL AND COMMANDANT AT PRESSBURG

The answer of Marshal Davout to General Count Palffy

General,

I have submitted to His Majesty the letter you sent to the commandant of my light cavalry. His Majesty has charged me to inform, through you, His Highness the Archduke Palatine, that he is ready to consider as neutral the Hungarian nation, to forbid the entry of his army into Hungary, if, on his part, the Archduke Palatine and the Hungarian nation would retire their troops, make no insurrection, continue to supply Vienna with provisions; and, finally, conclude between the Hungarian nation and His Highness the Archduke Palatine and the Emperor of the French a convention tending to maintain harmony between the two countries. I have been authorized to let any officer pass whom his Royal Highness the Archduke Palatine may choose to send to my sovereign, to treat with him on these preliminaries. I am happy in the opportunity of performing any good office agreeable to your compatriots, and to assure the well-being and the repose of a nation so estimable in many respects as the Hungarian nation.

I have the honour to be, General,

Your very humble servant,

THE MARSHAL OF THE EMPIRE, ONE OF THE COLONELS-GENERAL
OF THE GUARD OF HIS MAJESTY THE EMPEROR AND KING, LOUIS L DAVOUT

7th Bulletin of the Army of Italy

Headquarters of Gorizia, 17 November 1805 (26 Brumaire year 14)

The enemy, after abandoning to us the banks of the Tagliamento, had started to retreat on Balma-Nova. It did not attempt to defend that place, which it could have held, and we met its last posts only a few miles from there. A few skirmishes of no interest took place, however, and we took a few prisoners.

On the 16th, the army formed two columns and advanced on the Isonzo. The advance guard, under the orders of General Espagne, entered Gradisca before nightfall, where the Austrians gave only a weak resistance. The mounted chasseurs then went back up the right bank of the river to advance on Gorizia, and the Séras division established itself, at the same time, on the left bank at Sagrado.

The next day, the Molitor, Gardanne and Partouneaux divisions followed the right bank of the Isonzo with the intention of crossing it beyond Gorizia; but the bridge equipage had not yet arrived and the crossing could not take place on that point.

The Séras and Duhesme divisions were marching on Rubin and Savona. Their advance posts were on the heels of the enemy. There was an engagement after which the enemy dispersed in great disorder; their artillery escaped us only by the favor of nightfall; we repulsed them as far as the walls of Gorizia.

The General-in-Chief took his dispositions for a general attack on the morning of the 17th; the Austrians had not let themselves be exposed to it. They took advantage of the night to retreat in haste. General Espagne is pursuing them with the cavalry and light infantry. He has orders to chase them as far as Liebach.

The army has taken position before the Isonzo; 300 new prisoners are taken in his rear and we see more of them arriving constantly. The magazines established at Udine and Palma-Nova have fallen into our hands.

The General-in-Chief praises the sustained activity of the army; it surmounts with courage and gaiety the fatigues and privations inevitable in such a rapid march. He is pleased to give testimony of it to His Majesty the Emperor and King.

Twenty-sixth Bulletin

Znaïm, 18 November 1805 (27 Brumaire year 14)

Prince Murat, told that the Russian generals immediately after the signing of the convention were marching with a part of their army towards Znaïm, and that from all appearances the other part was about to follow them and escape, had them told that the Emperor had not ratified the convention, and that therefore he was going to attack. In fact, Prince Murat, having made his dispositions, advanced towards the enemy and attacked them on the 16th at four o'clock in the afternoon, which brought on the battle of Guntersdorf, in which a part of the Russian army, composing the rearguard, was routed, lost 12 pieces of artillery, 100 baggage wagons, 2,000 prisoners and 2,000 more remained on the field of battle. Marshal Lannes attacked the enemy in front, and while General Dupas's brigade of grenadiers turned their left Marshal Soult turned their right with General Levasseur's brigade of the Legrand division, consisting of the 3rd and 18th Regiments of Line. General of Division Walther charged the Russians with a brigade of dragoons and took 300 prisoner.

The brigade of grenadiers of General Laplanche-Mortières distinguished themselves. Were it not for the night, nothing could have escaped. There were bayonet attacks several times. Some battalions of Russian grenadiers showed intrepidity. General Oudinot was wounded; his two aides-de-camp squadron chiefs, Demangeot and Lamotte, were also wounded by his side. General Oudinot's wound will prevent him from serving for 15 days. In the meantime, the Emperor, wishing to give the grenadiers a mark of his esteem, has named General Duroc their commander.

The Emperor advanced his headquarters to Znaïm the 17th, at three o'clock in the afternoon. The Russian rearguard was obliged to leave their hospitals at Znaïm, where we found a considerable quantity of flour and oats. The Russians retired towards Brünn, and our advanced guard pursued them halfway, but the Emperor having learned that the Emperor of Austria was there, wished to give a proof of his respect for that Prince and halted the day of the 13th.

The fort of Kufstein was taken by the Bavarians.

General Baraguey d'Hilliers made an incursion as far as Pilsen, in Bohemia, and obliged the enemy to leave its position. He took some magazines and fulfilled the object of his mission. The dismounted dragoons travelled with rapidity over the mountains covered with ice and fir trees which separate Bohemia from Bavaria.

It is not possible to form an idea of the horror that the Russians have inspired in Moravia. In retreating, they set fire to the finest villages and they murder the peasantry. Thus, the inhabitants breathe easy in seeing them leave; they exclaim, 'Our enemies have left us.' In speaking of them, they characterize them as *barbarians* who have brought ruin upon them. This does not apply to the officers, who are in general quite different from the soldiers. Many of them are of distinguished merit; but the army has a savage instinct that is unknown in our European armies.

When we ask the inhabitants of Austria, of Moravia, and of Bohemia, if they love their Emperor, 'We did love him,' they answer, 'but how would we continue to love him? He has brought the Russians.'

It was reported at Vienna that the Russians had defeated the French army and that they were marching towards Vienna. A woman cried out in the streets, 'The French are beaten, and here come the Russians.' The alarm was general; fear and stupefaction prevailed in Vienna. Behold, however, the result of the fatal counsels of Cobentzl, Colloredo and Lambertie. Therefore, these men are detested by the nation, and the Emperor of Austria can never recover the confidence and love of his subjects, without sacrificing them to the public's hatred; and one day, sooner or later, this must happen.

Twenty-seventh Bulletin

Pohrlitz, 19 November 1805 (28 Brumaire year 14)

Since the combat of Guntersdorf the enemy has continued its retreat with the greatest haste. General Sebastiani followed it with his brigade of dragoons with their swords in its back. The immense plains of Moravia facilitated his pursuit. On the 18th, at the heights of Pohrlitz, he cut the retreat of several and during the day took 2,000 Russians prisoners of war.

Prince Murat entered Brünn, the capital of Moravia, on the 18th at three in the afternoon, always following the enemy.

The enemy has evacuated the town and the fortress, which is a well-built work capable of withstanding a regular siege.

The Emperor has established his headquarters in Pohrlitz.

Marshal Soult is stationed with his army corps at Niemtschitz.

Marshal Lannes is before Pohrlitz.

The Moravians have more hatred for the Russians, and friendship for us, than the inhabitants of Austria.

The country is superb and much more fertile than Austria.

The Moravians are stunned to see, in the middle of their immense plains, the people of the Ukraine, of Kamchatka, and the great Tartars, and the Normans, the Gascons, the Bretons and the Burgundians coming to blows and cutting each other's throat without, however, their country having anything in common or there being between them any political interest; and they have the rather good sense to say, in their bad Bohemian, that human blood has become merchandise in the hands of the English. A big Moravian farmer said not long ago to a French officer, in speaking of the Emperor Joseph II, that he was the emperor of the peasants and that if he had continued to live he would have exempted them from the feudal rights that they paid to the religious convents.

We have found at Brünn 60 pieces of artillery, 300,000 charges of powder, a great quantity of wheat and flour and very considerable stores of clothing.

The Emperor of Germany has retired to Olmütz.

Our posts are at one march from this place.

Twenty-eighth Bulletin

Brünn, 21 November 1805 (30 Brumaire year 14)

The Emperor entered Brünn on the 20th at ten o'clock in the morning.

A deputation of the Moravian States, with a bishop at its head, came to meet him. The Emperor reviewed the fortifications and ordered the arming of the citadel, in which he found more than 6,000 muskets, a great number of munitions of war of every kind, and, among other things, 400,000 charges of gunpowder.

The Russians had collected all their cavalry, which formed a corps of about 6,000 men, and wanted to defend the junction of the roads leading from Brünn and Olmütz. General Walther contained them the whole day, and by different charges forced them at last to abandon their ground. Prince Murat caused General Hautpoul's division of cuirassiers and four squadrons of the Imperial Guard to advance.

Though our horses were extremely fatigued, the enemy was charged and routed. It left more than 200 men, cuirassiers and élite dragoons, on the battlefield; 100 horses remained in our hands.

Marshal Bessières, commander of the Imperial Guard, has executed, at the head of four squadrons of the Guard, a brilliant charge that routed and cut down the enemy. There is no comparison between the silence of the Guard and the cuirassiers and the howling of the Russians. This Russian cavalry is well mounted, well equipped; they show intrepidity and resolution; but the men do not appear to know how to use their sabres, and in this regard our cavalry has a great advantage. We have several men dead and about 60 wounded, among whom are included Colonel Durosnel of the 16th Chasseurs and Colonel Bourdon of the 11th Dragoons.

The enemy has retired several leagues.

Twenty-ninth Bulletin

Brünn, 23 November 1805 (2 Frimaire year 14)

Marshal Ney has occupied Brixen, after having taken many enemy prisoner. He found in the hospitals a great number of sick and wounded Austrians. On 17 November he seized Klausen and Botzen.

General Jellacic, who defended Voralberg, is cut off.

Marshal Bernadotte has occupied Iglau. Some divisions of his corps have entered Bohemia.

General Wrede, commanding the Bavarians, has taken a company of Austrian artillery, 100 horses, 50 cuirassiers and several officers.

He has taken a considerable store of oats and other grains, and many harnessed wagons full of the baggage of several Austrian regiments and officers.

Adjutant commandant Maison has taken 200 dragoons of Latour and cuirassiers of Hohenlohe prisoner on the road of Iglau to Brünn. He charged another detachment of 200 men and took 150 prisoners.

We have reconnoitred as far as Olmütz.

The Court has evacuated that place and has retreated into Poland.

The winter begins to become very severe. The French army has taken position; its avant-guard is protected by the very strong fortress of Brünn, which they have already begun arming and putting in a better state of defence.

8th Bulletin of the Army of Italy

Headquarters of Gorizia, 23 November 1805 (2 Frimaire year 14)

The army keeps the position it has taken on the left bank of the Isonzo. The advance guard, under the orders of General Espagne, advanced on Vipacco, has pushed back the enemy as far as Gauz and in several vigorous charges has taken 100 prisoner. The whole enemy cavalry retreated by the road; a considerable part of their infantry took the road of the valley of Istria to reach that of Oberleybach. Five companies of voltigeurs pursue the enemy in that direction, while our advance posts have already gone on reconnaissance of the entrenchments of Prevald, and are taking the direction of Liebach.

The General-in Chief had the Séras division start to march on Trieste. The Austrians, seeing our approach, have evacuated the place and abandoned 300 wounded. A corps of troops followed them on the road of Liebach and took 50 men prisoner.

Two regiments of dragoons, supported by the infantry, advanced on our left, on the Chiusodi-Pletz which was defended by the two infantry regiments of Strasoldo and Deligné, with a few cavalry. All the posts were abandoned the very next day after the arrival of our troops. General of Brigade Lacour, who commands them, was ordered to enter Villach and to attempt to open communications with the *Grande Armée* whose movements, without a doubt, caused the retreat of the enemy who would have feared being surrounded. There has also been a detachment dispatched on Ponteba Veneta, where a strong enemy force had not dared to wait for us.

In all these movements, we have taken close to 400 prisoner.

The General-in-Chief left near Padua the corps of troops which had come from Naples. He joined one of the *Grande Armée's* divisions, the Corsican Legion, and the 2nd Italian Regiment. Lieutenant-General Gouvion Saint-Cyr, who commands these forces, observes Chiozza and Brondolo. He is ready to pounce on the Russians and the English should they disembark as they menace to do on the Italian coasts.

9th Bulletin of the Army of Italy
Headquarters of Gorizia, 26 November 1805 (5 Frimaire year 14)
The General-in-Chief had learned by several reports and also in a letter from General Vial, ambassador of His Majesty the Emperor and King at Berne, that a corps of the Austrian army, which had been cut off by the manoeuvres of the *Grande Armée*, would march down the mountains of the Tyrol. He calculated that this column, in that situation, would either try to cross the army's line to arrive at the lagoons of Venice and join the troops already there, or advance by Filtro and Belluno to join what was left of the army of Prince Charles, by Liebach. In the first hypothesis, the position of the right wing, which he had left to observe Venice under the command of Lieutenant-General Gouvion Saint-Cyr, told him that the enemy would not imprudently attempt to pass; in the second hypothesis, he had placed at Ponteba and at the Chiusa-di-Pletz, several regiments of cavalry and infantry under the command of Generals of Brigade Lacour and Lanchantin. No matter what direction the enemy column took, the situation of the army on the Isonzo would permit the detachment of sufficient forces in time to cut them off, while the advance guard would continue its march on Liebach.

The column, composed of 7,000 infantry and 1,200 horses, commanded by the Prince of Rohan, attacked Bassano on 23 November and and easily took out the weak detachment of 150 men who formed the garrison, and then advanced towards Castelfranco.

As soon as Lieutenant-General Saint-Cyr learned of this, he determined that the enemy's goal was, in fact, to cross our line, unaware of how strong it was, and prepared to receive him well.

The General-in-Chief who had thought of everything, but not wishing to leave anything to chance, took some measures to bring by forced marches on the Piave, General Partourneaux's division of grenadiers, two brigades of the Duhesme and

Séras divisions, the division of cuirassiers and a brigade of dragoons; the cuirassiers were to go back up the Piave by Il-Bosco-Del-Mantello and turn the position of Bassano. The Gardanne division, advancing at the same time on Venzone, was to reinforce the detachments sent to the two Ponteba, to cut off all of the enemy's retreat in the event it had already taken the road of Belluno and of the Pieva-Di-Cadore, to reach Villach and join Prince Charles at Liebach. The General-in chief had left the remaining troops on the Isonzo, under the command of General Duhesme, and was marching towards the Piave himself, to assist in the movements he had ordered.

Lieutenant-General Saint-Cyr was manoeuvring to recognize the enemy and stop him; he had formed a column taken from the Régnier, Lecchi and Verdier divisions: he was, himself, at Campo San-Pietro with the Polish regiment commanded by General Peyri. General Régnier, at Navale, had orders to march on 24 November, at daybreak, on Castelfranco. The enemy had arrived the day before and knowing they were in a difficult position, anticipated the attack; he fell violently upon the Régnier division, which met the attack with vigour and soon overthrew the enemy, who made several more charges and fell against the same welcome from our troops each time.

Meanwhile, Lieutenant-General Saint-Cyr had the Polish regiment make a movement and turned the enemy; it was then a complete rout as far as Castelfranco, where our troops arrived at the same time as the Austrians. All those that had not perished or been taken on the battlefield asked to capitulate. Six thousand infantrymen and 1,000 horses remained in our power; this is much more than the number of our combatants that opposed them; but they had perceived their defeat as inevitable, as they considered the effect of the dispositions which threatened them from all sides. General Prince Rohan, in command of the corps, several colonels and many officers are among the prisoners; six flags and one standard, 12 pieces of artillery, their caissons and large baggage are also the result of our victory. There were two standards lost in the mêlée. We have to regret only 100 men unable to fight. We found our men made prisoners at Bassano.

A corps of Croats, presumed to have been part of the column, is expected at the entrances of the mountains: it will be difficult for them to escape us; we have taken some measures such that they will share the same fate.

Lieutenant-General Gouvion Saint-Cyr showed great ability in the manoeuvres; he praises the bravery and talents of the Régnier division. He cites with honour the chiefs of the 10th and 56th Regiments of Line, Chief of Battalion Clavel who commands the Swill battalion, the chiefs of the Grabinski brigade and of the Bialowiski and Clopski battalions.

General of Brigade Lacour is at Villach; he pushes his advance posts on Klagenfurt and is close to being able to communicate with the *Grande Armée*.

The advance guard under the command of General Espagne takes prisoners constantly. The roads of Idria and of Liebach are covered with killed horses, broken caissons and thousands of abandoned musket balls.

Decree

Brünn, 28 November 1805 (7 Frimaire year 14)
Napoleon, Emperor of the French, King of Italy,
We have decreed and decree the following:
   Article I There will be a contribution of one hundred million francs (money of France) levied on Austria, Moravia and the other provinces of the

House of Austria occupied by the French army.

Article II This amount is given as gratification to the army according to the statement of distribution that we have decreed.

Article III The price of all the magazines of salt, tobacco, guns, powder and war munitions which are not necessary for arming our army and which our general of artillery will not have transported to France, and which will need to be sold, will be deposited in the coffers of our army to be distributed in the form of gratification.

Article IV From the first funds which will come into this distribution, as well as those coming from the contribution of the Souabe, there will be paid three months of pay in gratification to every general, officer and soldier who has been or will be wounded in the present war.

Article V Our minister of war is in charge of the execution of the present decree.

(Signed) NAPOLEON

By the Emperor, THE MINISTER SECRETARY OF STATE, H B MARET

To the Army

On bivouac, 1 December 1805 (10 Frimaire year 14)

Soldiers, the Russian army is before you to avenge the Austrian army at Ülm. They are the same battalions you beat at Hollabrünn, and which you have constantly pursued since then.

The positions we occupy are formidable; and when they march to turn my right, they shall present me their flank.

Soldiers, I shall myself direct all your battalions; I shall keep at a distance from the firing, if with your accustomed bravery you carry confusion and disorder into the enemy's ranks; but if victory be for a moment doubtful, you shall see your Emperor expose himself to the first blows; for victory cannot hesitate on this day above all, when the honour of the French infantry is at stake, which is so important to the honour of the whole nation.

Let not, under pretext of carrying off the wounded, the ranks be thinned, and let each be well imbued with this thought, that we must conquer these hirelings of England who are animated with so great a hatred against our nation.

This victory will finish our campaign, and we shall resume our winter quarters, where we shall be joined by the new armies forming in France; then the peace that I will make will be worthy of my people, of you and of me.

NAPOLEON

Thirtieth Bulletin

Austerlitz, 3 December 1805 (12 Frimaire year 14)

On 27 November, the Emperor, on receiving the communication of the full powers of Messrs Stadion and Giulay, offered beforehand an armistice in order to spare the effusion of blood, if the envoys had the power to arrange it and to come to a definitive accommodation. But it was easy for the Emperor to perceive that they had other designs; and as the hope of success could come to the enemy only from the side of the Russian army, he easily conjectured that the 2nd and 3rd armies had arrived, or were on the point of arriving, at Olmütz, and that the negotiations were only a ruse of war to lull his vigilance to sleep.

On the 28th, at nine in the morning, a horde of Cossacks supported by Russian cavalry made Prince Murat's advanced posts fall back, surrounded Wischau, and took 50 foot soldiers of the 6th Regiment of Dragoons. In the course of the day the Emperor of Russia returned to Wischau and the whole Russian army took a position behind that city.

The Emperor sent his aide-de-camp, General Savary, to compliment the Emperor of Russia as soon as he knew of the arrival of that Prince in the army. General Savary returned at the moment the Emperor was reconnoitring the fires of the enemy's outposts at Wischau. He greatly praised the good welcome, the graces and the good personal sentiments of the Emperor of Russia, and the same from the Grand Duke Constantine, who gave him every kind of care and attention; but it was easy to understand from the conversation he had for three days with some 30 fops who, under different titles, surround the Emperor of Russia, that presumption, inconsiderateness and imprudence reigned in the decisions of the military cabinet, as much as they had reigned in those of the political cabinet.

An army so conducted could not but commit faults. The Emperor's plan was from that moment to wait for them and to watch the moment for profiting by them. He immediately ordered his army to retreat in the night as if he had been defeated, took a good position three leagues in the rear, and laboured with much ostentation at fortifying it and establishing batteries.

He proposed an interview to the Emperor of Russia, who sent him his aide-de-camp, Prince Dolgorucki. That aide-de-camp could remark that everything breathed reserve and fear in the appearance of the French army. The placing of the strong guards, the fortifications made with such haste; everything showed to the Russian officer an army half beaten.

Contrary to the Emperor's custom, who never receives with so much circum-spection the *parlementaires* at his headquarters, he went himself to the advanced posts. After the initial compliments, the Russian officer wanted to discuss political questions. The Russian discussed everything with impertinence difficult to imagine. He was in the most absolute ignorance of the interests of Europe and the situation of the Continent. In a word, he was a young trumpeter for England. He spoke to the Emperor as he speaks to Russian officers, whom he has long disgusted by his haughtiness and improper conduct. The Emperor contained his indignation and the young man, who has a real influence over the Emperor Alexander, returned with a conviction that the French army was on the eve of its ruin. One may be convinced, above all, of what the Emperor must have suffered when it is known that towards the close of the conversation he proposed to him to cede Belgium and to place the Iron Crown upon the head of the most implacable of the enemies of France.

All these different steps had their due effect. The young heads that direct the Russian affairs have given themselves up, without measure, to their natural presumption. It was no longer a question of beating the French army, but of turning it and taking it: it had only done so much through the cowardice of the Austrians. We are assured that several old Austrian generals who had made campaigns against the Emperor warned the council that it was not with that confidence that one ought to march against an army that contained so many old soldiers and officers of the first merit. They said they had seen the Emperor, re-duced to a handful of men under the most difficult circumstances, regain victory by rapid and improvised operations and destroy the most numerous armies; that here, however, no advantage had been obtained; on the contrary, all the affairs with the rearguard of the first Russian army had been in favour of the French army. But this presumptuous youth countered that with the bravery of the 80,000 Russians, the enthusiasm inspired by the presence of their Emperor, the élite corps of the Imperial Guard of Russia and, what probably they dared not say, their talents, of which they were astonished the Austrians would want to underestimate their power.

On 1 December, the Emperor, from the heights of his camp, saw with indescribable joy the Russian army beginning, within twice the distance of cannon-shot from his advanced posts, a flank movement to turn his right. He perceived then to what a pitch presumption and ignorance of the art of war had misled the councils of that brave army. He said, several times, 'Before tomorrow night, that army is mine.' Yet the enemy's sentiment was far different. It appeared before our posts within pistol-shot; it defiled by flank march upon a line four leagues long, in passing the length of the French army, which seemed not to dare to leave its positions. It had but one fear, that the French army should escape. Everything was done to confirm the enemy in this idea. Prince Murat sent out a small corps on the plain; but all at once it seemed astonished at the immense force of the enemy, and returned in haste. Therefore everything tended to confirm the Russian general in the miscalculation that he had stopped the operation.

The Emperor put the annexed proclamation in the order of the day.

At night, he wished to visit all the posts on foot and incognito; but he had not gone many steps when he was recognized. It would be impossible to depict the enthusiasm of the soldiers upon seeing him. Lighted straw was placed in an instant upon the tops of thousands of poles, and 80,000 men appeared before the Emperor, saluting him with acclamations: some to celebrate the anniversary of his coronation, others saying that the army would tomorrow offer its bouquet to the Emperor. One of the oldest grenadiers went up to him and said, 'Sire, you need not expose yourself; I promise you, in the name of the grenadiers of the army, that you shall only have to fight with your eyes and that we will bring you tomorrow the colours and artillery of the Russian army to celebrate the anniversary of your coronation.' The Emperor said, upon his return to his guardhouse, which consisted of a miserable straw cabin without a roof that the grenadiers had made for him, 'This is the finest evening of my life; but I regret to think that I shall lose a good number of these brave fellows. I feel, by the pain it gives me, that they are indeed my children, and in truth I often reproach myself for this sentiment, for I fear it will terminate in rendering me unfit to carry on war.'

If the enemy had seen the sight, it would have terrified them; but the unthinking enemy continued its movements and hastened with quick steps to its ruin.

The Emperor made his dispositions for battle immediately. He sent off Marshal Davout in great haste to the convent of Raigern. He was, with one of his divisions and a division of dragoons, to keep the enemy's left wing in check in order that, upon a given signal, it might be completely surrounded. He gave the command of the left wing to Marshal Lannes; of the right to Marshal Soult; of the centre to Marshal Bernadotte, and all the cavalry, which was reunited at a single point, to Prince Murat. The left of Marshal Lannes leaned on Santon, a superb position that the Emperor had fortified and mounted with eighteen pieces of artillery. From the preceding evening he had entrusted the keeping of that firm position to the 17th Regiment of Light Infantry, and certainly it could not be guarded by better troops. The division of General Suchet formed the left of Marshal Lannes; that of General Caffarelli formed his right and was supported at the same time by the cavalry of Prince Murat; the latter had before it the hussars and chasseurs under the orders of General Kellermann and the divisions of dragoons of Walther and Beaumont, and, in reserve, the cuirassier divisions of Generals Nansouty and Hautpoul, with 24 pieces of light artillery.

Marshal Bernadotte, that is to say the centre, had on his left the division of General Rivaud, leaning on the right of Prince Murat and, on their right the division of General Drouet.

Marshal Soult, who commanded the right of the army, had on his left the division of General Vandamme, in his centre the division of General Saint-Hilaire, and on his right the division of General Legrand.

Marshal Davout was detached on the right of General Legrand, who guarded the road between the lakes and the outlets of the villages of Sokolnitz and Telnitz. He had with him the Friant division, and the dragoons of the division of General Bourcier. The division of General Gudin was directed to march at daybreak from Nicolsburg to stop the corps of the enemy that might have outflanked the right wing.

The Emperor, with his faithful companion in war Marshal Berthier, his first aide-de-camp Colonel Junot and his *état-major*, was in reserve with the ten battalions of his Guard and the ten battalions of General Oudinot's grenadiers, part of whom were commanded by General Duroc.

This reserve were ranged in two lines, in columns by battalion, at distance of deployment, having in the intervals 40 pieces of artillery served by the cannoneers of the Guard. It was with this reserve that the Emperor intended to push forward wherever it would have been necessary. One can say this reserve alone was worth an army.

At one in the morning, the Emperor mounted his horse to visit the posts, reconnoitre the fires of the camp of the enemy and get an account of what the guards had been able to learn of the movements of the Russians. He heard that they had passed the night in drunkenness and tumultuous cries, and that a corps of Russian infantry had appeared in the village of Sokolnitz, occupied by a regiment of the division under General Legrand, who had orders to reinforce it.

On the 2nd, day finally dawned. The sun rose bright; and this anniversary of the coronation of the Emperor, upon which one of the greatest feats in arms of the century was to be performed, was one of the finest days in autumn.

This battle, which the soldiers persist in calling the Day of the Three Emperors, which others call the Day of the Anniversary, and which the Emperor named the battle of Austerlitz, will be ever memorable in the annals of the great nation.

The Emperor, surrounded by all the marshals, waited only for the horizon to clear to issue his last orders. At the first rays of the sun, the orders were issued and each marshal rejoined his corps at full gallop. The Emperor said, in passing along the front of several regiments, 'Soldiers, we must finish this campaign by a thunderbolt that shall confound the pride of our enemies,' and instantly hats were placed at the point of bayonets, and cries of 'Long live the Emperor' were the true signal of battle. A moment afterwards, the cannonade began at the extremity of the right, which the enemy's advanced guard had already outflanked. But the unexpected meeting with Marshal Davout stopped the enemy short, and the battle was engaged.

Marshal Soult put himself in motion at the same moment, proceeded to the heights of the village of Pratzen with Generals Vandamme and Saint-Hilaire's division, and entirely cut off the enemy's right, whose movements became uncertain. Surprised by the flank march while it was fleeing, believing itself to be attacking and seeing itself attacked, it considered itself as half defeated.

Prince Murat was in motion with his cavalry. The left, commanded by Marshal Lannes, marched in echelons by regiments, as though in an exercise. A tremendous cannonade took place along the whole line. Two hundred pieces of artillery and nearly 200,000 men made a dreadful noise. It was really a combat of the giants. Not an hour had elapsed, and the enemy's whole left was cut off. Its right had already reached Austerlitz, the headquarters of the two emperors, who had to march immediately to the Emperor of Russia's Guard to try to re-establish communication of the centre with the left. A battalion of the 4th Line was charged by the Russian Imperial Guard cavalry and was pushed back; but the Emperor was not far away; he perceived this movement, ordered Marshal Bessières to go to the succour of his right with his invincibles, and the two Guards were soon engaged. Success could not be doubted; in a moment the Russian Guard was routed: colonel, artillery, flags, everything was taken. The regiment of the Grand Duke Constantine was annihilated; he owed his own safety only to the swiftness of his horse.

From the heights of Austerlitz the two emperors beheld the defeat of all the Russian Guard. At the same moment, the centre of the army, commanded by Marshal Bernadotte, advanced. Three of his regiments made a very fine cavalry charge. The left, commanded by Marshal Lannes, made three charges; all the charges were victorious. General Caffarelli's division was distinguished. The divisions of cuirassiers seized the batteries of the enemy.

At one in the afternoon the victory had been decided. It had not been uncertain for one moment. Not a man of the reserve was necessary and did not take any part.

The cannonade was sustained no more than on our right. The enemy's corps, which had been surrounded and driven from all the heights, was on a flat and near a lake. The Emperor went there with 20 pieces of artillery. This corps was driven from position to position, and we saw the horrid spectacle, such as was seen at Aboukir: 20,000 men threw themselves into the water and drowned in the lake.

Two columns, each of 4,000 Russians, laid down their arms and surrendered themselves prisoners. The enemy's entire artillery park is taken. The results of this day are 40 Russian flags, among which are the standards of the Imperial Guard, a considerable number of prisoners (the chief of staff does not yet know how many; we have already an account of 20,000), 12 or 15 generals, at least 15,000 Russians killed, left on the field of battle. Though we have not yet the report, we may, at the first glance, estimate our loss at 800 killed and 1,500 or 1,600 wounded. This will not surprise the military, who know that it is only in a rout that men are lost, and no other corps but the battalion of the 4th was penetrated. Among the wounded are General Saint-Hilaire, who, wounded at the beginning of the battle, remained the whole day on the field; he is covered with glory; Generals of Division Kellerman and Walther; Generals of Brigade Valhubert, Thiebault, Sebastiani, Compans and Rapp, the Emperor's aide-de-camp. It was the latter who, in charging at the head of the grenadiers of the Guard, captured Prince Repnine, Captain of the Chevaliers of the Imperial Guard of Russia.

With respect to the men who distinguished themselves, it was the whole army that covered itself with glory; it constantly charged to the cry of 'Long live the Emperor,' and the idea of celebrating so gloriously the coronation again animated the soldier.

The French army, though fine and numerous, was less numerous than the enemy's army, which was 105,000 men strong, having 80,000 Russians and 25,000

Austrians. Half of this army is destroyed; the rest has been completely routed, and the greater part threw away their arms.

This day will cost tears of blood at Saint Petersburg. May it cause the gold of England to be rejected with indignation, and may that young Prince, who has so many virtues to be called to be the father of his subjects, tear himself from the influence of those 30 fops whom England artfully pays and whose impertinence injures his intentions, makes him lose the love of his soldiers, and throws him into the most ill-judged operations. Nature, in endowing him with so many great qualities, had named him to be the consoler of Europe. Perfidious councils, by rendering him the auxiliary of England, will place him in history in the rank of men who perpetuating the war on the Continent will have consolidated the British tyranny upon the seas and produced the misery of our generation. If France can arrive at peace only by the conditions the aide-de-camp Dolgorucki proposed to the Emperor and which Mr Novosiltzof was ordered to bring, Russia should not obtain them were her army encamped upon the heights of Montmartre.

In a more detailed relation of this battle, the chief of staff will make known what each corps, each officer and each general has done to render the French name illustrious and to give proof of their love to their Emperor.

On the 3rd, at daybreak, Prince John of Lichtenstein, commanding the Austrian army, came to the Emperor's headquarters, established in a barn; he had a long audience.

Nevertheless, we pursue our successes. The enemy has retreated on the road from Austerlitz to Göding. In this retreat it presents its flank. The French army is already on its rear and follow it with swords at its back.

Never was there a more horrible field of battle. From the middle of the immense lakes we hear still the cries of thousands of men who could not be assisted. It will take three days before all the wounded enemy will be evacuated to Brünn; the heart bleeds. May so much bloodshed, may so many miseries fall at length on the perfidious islanders who are the cause of it! May the cowardly oligarchs of London bear the burden of so many evils!

Proclamation

Headquarters at Austerlitz, 3 December 1805

Soldiers! I am pleased with you. On the day of Austerlitz, you have justified what I expected from your intrepidity. You have decorated your eagles with an immortal glory. In less than four hours an army of 100,000 men, commanded by the Emperors of Russia and Austria, has been cut down or dispersed. Those who escaped your iron have drowned in the lakes. Forty flags, the standards of the Russian Imperial Guard, 120 pieces of artillery, 20 generals and more than 30,000 prisoners are the results of this day, to be celebrated forever. That infantry, so vaunted, and superior to you in numbers, could not resist your impact, and henceforth you have no rivals to fear. Thus, in two months the third coalition is conquered and dissolved. Peace can no longer be at a great distance; but, as I promised to my people before crossing the Rhine, I will only make a peace that gives you some guarantees and assures some recompenses to our allies. Soldiers! When the French people placed the Imperial Crown on my head, I entrusted you to keep it always in a high state of glory, which alone could give it value in my eyes; but at that moment our enemies thought to destroy and demean it; and that Iron Crown, which was gained by the blood of so many Frenchmen, they would have compelled me to place on the head of our cruellest enemies; an extravagant and foolish proposal, which you have ruined and confounded the very day of the anniversary of your Emperor's coronation. You have taught them that it is easier for them to defy us and to threaten us than to vanquish us. Soldiers! When everything necessary to the happiness and prosperity of our country has been achieved, I will lead you back to France. There you will be the objects of my most tender solicitudes. My people will see you again with joy, and it will be enough for you to say: 'I was at the battle of Austerlitz,' for them to reply, 'There is a brave man!'

NAPOLEON

Thirty-first Bulletin

Austerlitz, 5 December 1805 (14 Frimaire year 14)

The Emperor left Austerlitz yesterday, and is gone to the advanced post near Ziaroschitz. He is at the place of his bivouac. The Emperor of Germany arrived soon after. These two monarchs had an interview that lasted two hours. The Emperor of Germany did not conceal on his own part, or that of the Emperor of Russia, all the contempt that the conduct of England had inspired. 'They are the merchants,' he repeated, 'who put the Continent to fire to secure for themselves the commerce of the world.'

These two princes have agreed on an armistice and the principal conditions of peace, which will be negotiated and concluded in a few days. The Emperor of Germany also made known to the Emperor that the Emperor of Russia wished to make a separate peace; that he would entirely abandon the affairs of England and no longer maintain any interest in them. The Emperor of Germany several times repeated in the conversation, 'there was no doubt that in the quarrel with England, France was right.' He also requested a truce for the remains of the Russian army. The Emperor observed to him that the Russian army was surrounded, that not a man of them could escape, 'but,' he added, 'as I wish to do something agreeable to the Emperor Alexander, I will allow the Russian army to pass. I will halt the march of my columns; but Your Majesty must promise me that the Russian army shall return to Russia and evacuate Germany and Austrian and Prussian Poland.' 'That is the intention of the Emperor Alexander,' responded the Emperor of Germany, 'I can assure you of it: besides, in the course of the night your own officers may convince you of the fact.'

We are assured that the Emperor said to the Emperor of Germany, when he was introduced to the fires of his bivouac, 'I receive you in the only palace I have lived in for two months.' The Emperor of Germany replied with a smile, 'You have turned this habitation to such good account, that you have reason to be pleased with it.' This, at least, is what is believed to have been heard. The numerous attendants of the two monarchs were not too far away for them to have been able to hear many things.

The Emperor accompanied the Emperor of Germany to his carriage and presented the two Princes of Lichtenstein and General Prince Schwarzenberg to him. After this, he returned to sleep at Austerlitz.

The details are being collected for giving a fine description of the battle of Austerlitz; a great number of engineers are surveying the plan of the field of battle. The loss of Russians has been immense. Generals Kutusov and Buxhowden have been wounded. Ten or 12 generals have been killed. Several aides-de-camp of the Emperor of Russia and a great number of officers of distinction have been killed. It was not 120 pieces of artillery that were taken, but 150. The enemy columns that threw themselves into the lakes were favoured by the ice; but some cannon shot broke it, and some entire columns were drowned. The evening of that day, and during several hours of the night, the Emperor went through the battlefield and had the wounded removed; a horrible sight if ever there were one! The Emperor, who was mounted on a very fast horse, passed along with the rapidity of lightning, and nothing was more affecting than to see those brave men recognize him at once. Some of them forgot their sufferings, and exclaimed, 'Is the victory quite certain at least?' Others, 'I have suffered these eight hours, and since the commencement of the battle I have been deserted, but I have done my duty well.' Others said, 'You ought to be well satisfied with your soldiers today.' To every wounded soldier the Emperor left a guard to take him to the ambulances provided for the wounded. It is horrible to mention that 48 hours after the battle there were still a great number of wounded Russians that could not be dressed. All the French were dressed before night. Instead of 40 flags, at this hour 45 have been brought in, and the remains of many more have been found.

Nothing can equal the gaiety of the troops at their bivouacs. Whenever they see an officer belonging to the Emperor, they exclaim, 'Is the Emperor pleased with us?'

In passing before the 28th Line, which has a number of the conscripts of Calvados and the Lower Seine, the Emperor said to it, 'I hope that the Normans will distinguish themselves today!' They have kept their word; the Normans did distinguish themselves. The Emperor, who knows the composition of each regiment, said something applicable to each, and this expression came and spoke to the hearts of those to whom it was addressed; it became their rallying word in the midst of the fire. He said to the 57th, 'Remember that some years ago I gave you the title of The Terrible.' We should name all the regiments of the army; there was not one of them that did not perform prodigies of bravery and intrepidity. We might almost say that death became afraid, and fled before our ranks to fall upon the ranks of the enemy. Not a corps made a retrograde movement. The Emperor said, 'I have fought 30 battles like this, but I seen none where the victory was so decided and the fates so little balanced.'

The Guard on foot of the Emperor could not engage; they cried in rage. They absolutely insisted on doing something. 'Be satisfied to do nothing,' the Emperor said to them, 'you have to engage as the reserve; it will be so much the better if there be no need for you today.'

Three colonels of the Russian Imperial Guard are taken, with the general who commanded it. The hussars of this Guard made a charge on Caffarelli's division; in this one charge they lost 300 men, who remained upon the field of battle. The French cavalry proved their superiority and acted perfectly. At the end of the battle, the Emperor sent Colonel Dallemagne with two squadrons of his Guard as partisans to scour the neighborhood of the battlefield at his discretion and bring back the deserters. He took many flags, 15 pieces of artillery and 1,500 prisoners. The Guard regrets very much Colonel Morland of the Horse Chasseurs, who was killed by grapeshot as he was charging the artillery of the Russian Imperial Guard. This artillery was taken, but the brave colonel found death. We have had no general killed. Colonel Mazas of the 14th Line, a brave man, was killed. Many commanders of battalions were wounded. The light troops were rivals with the grenadiers. The 55th, 43rd, 14th, 36th, 40th, 17th... but we dare not name any corps, it would be an injustice to the others; they all did the impossible. There was not an officer, a general, not a soldier, who was not determined to conquer or perish.

We must not conceal an incident that does honour to the enemy. The commander of the artillery of the Russian Imperial Guard had just lost his cannon. He met the Emperor: 'Sire,' said he, 'have me shot, I have just lost my cannon.' 'Young man,' replied the Emperor to him, 'I appreciate your tears, but one may be beaten by my army and still be entitled to glory.'

Our advanced posts have arrived at Olmütz. The Empress and all the court fled in all haste.

Colonel Corbineau, Equerry to the Emperor, commanding the 5th Regiment of Chasseurs, had four horses killed under him. He was himself wounded on the fifth horse after having taken a flag. Prince Murat speaks in high terms of the brilliant manoeuvres of General Kellerman, of the fine charges by Generals Nansouty and Hautpoul, and, in fact, of all the generals, but he does not know who to name because he would have to name them all.

The soldiers of the train have merited the esteem of the army. The artillery did appalling mischief to the enemy. When a report of it was made to the Emperor, he said, 'These successes give me pleasure, for I do not forget that it was in this corps I began my military career!'

The aide-de-camp to the Emperor, General Savary, had accompanied the Emperor of Germany after the interview, to learn if the Emperor Alexander had adhered to the surrender. He found the remains of the Russian army without artillery or baggage, and in appalling disorder. It was midnight. General Merveldt had been driven from Göding by Marshal Davout. The Russian army was surrounded so that a single man could not escape. Prince Czartoryski introduced General Savary to the Emperor. 'Tell your master,' said this Prince, 'that I am leaving; that yesterday he has performed miracles and that this day has increased my admiration for him; that this is a predestination of Heaven; that it will require a century to make my army equal to his.But can I withdraw with safety?' 'Yes, Sire,' said General Savary to him, 'if Your Majesty ratifies that which the Emperors of France and Germany agreed upon during their interview.' 'And what is that?' 'That the army of Your Majesty shall retire to its home by the routes prescribed by the Emperor; and that it will evacuate Germany and Austrian Poland. Upon these conditions I have His Majesty's authority to move to our advanced posts, which have already turned you, and to give them orders to cover your retreat, the Emperor wanting to respect the friend of the First Consul.' 'But what guarantee would be necessary for that?' 'Sire, your word.' 'I give it to you.' This aide-de-camp left immediately at full gallop to Marshal Davout, to whom he communicated orders to halt all movements, and to remain quiet. May this generosity of the Emperor of the French be not so soon forgotten in Russia as that noble proceeding of the Emperor, who sent back 6,000 men to the Emperor Paul with so much respect and marks of esteem for him.

General Savary had conversed an hour with the Emperor of Russia and had found him to be a man of heart and of sense, notwithstanding the misfortunes which he had met. This monarch asked him the details of the day. 'You were inferior to me,' he said, 'and yet you were superior at all the points of attack.' 'Sire,' responded General Savary, 'it is the art of war and the fruit of 15 years of glory. It is the 40th battle fought by the Emperor.' 'That is true; that is a great man of war. For me, it is the first time that I have seen fire; I have never had the pretension to measure myself with him.' 'Sire, when you gain the experience, you will perhaps excel him.' 'I shall return to my capital; I came to assist the Emperor of Germany; he has informed me that he is satisfied; I am also.'

In his interview with the Emperor of Germany, the Emperor said to him: 'Mr and Madame Colloredo, Messrs Paget and Razoumofski, are one and the same with your minister Cobentzl; these are the true causes of the war, and if Your Majesty shall continue to give yourself up to those intriguers you will ruin all your affairs, and alienate the hearts of your subjects, you, who have so many qualities deserving to be loved and happy.'

An Austrian major presented himself at the advanced post, bearing dispatches from Mr Cobentzl for Mr Stadion at Vienna. The Emperor said, 'the advice of his sister and Madame Colloredo.'

The Emperor has paid very great attention to Prince John of Lichtenstein. He said several times, 'How, when there are men of such high distinction, can one allow his affairs to be conducted by fools and intriguers?' In fact the Prince of Lichtenstein is one of the most distinguished men, not only for his military talents but also for his character and knowledge.

It is known that the Emperor observed, after his conference with the Emperor of Germany, 'This man makes me commit an error, for I could have followed up my victory and taken the whole Russian and Austrian army, but at least several tears less will be shed.'

Thirty-second Bulletin

Austerlitz, 6 December 1805 (15 Frimaire year 14)

General Friant, at the battle of Austerlitz, has had four horses killed under him. Colonels Conroux and Demoustier acted remarkably. The examples of courage are so numerous, that as fast as they are reported to the Emperor he observes, 'It will take all my power to make proper recompense to all those brave people.'

The Russians, in combat, have a custom of taking off their haversacks. As the entire Russian army had been routed, our soldiers have taken all of the haversacks. We have also taken a great part of their baggage and the soldiers have found a great deal of money in it.

General Bertrand, who had been detached after the battle with a squadron of the Guard, has picked up a great number of prisoners, 19 pieces of artillery and many carriages filled with effects. The number of cannon taken up to this hour has climbed to 170 pieces. The Emperor expressed some dissatisfaction that plenipotentiaries were sent to him on the eve of the battle, and that the diplomatic character was thus prostituted. This is worthy of Mr Cobentzl, whom all the nation regards as one of the principal authors of all its unhappiness.

Prince John of Lichtenstein came to find the Emperor at the château of Austerlitz. The Emperor accorded him a conference of several hours. It is remarkable that the Emperor converses very freely with this general officer. This prince has concluded an Armistice of the following tenor with Marshal Berthier:

Mr Talleyrand is going to Nicolsburg, where the negotiations are to be opened.

Armistice concluded between Their Imperial Majesties of France and Austria

His Majesty the Emperor of the French, and His Majesty the Emperor of Germany, desiring to come to final negotiations to put an end to the war which desolates their two states, have previously agreed upon the commencement of an armistice, which will last until the conclusion of a definitive peace or the rupture of the negotiations; and in that case, the armistice shall not cease for 15 days after the rupture; and the cessation of the armistice shall be announced to the plenipotentiaries of both powers, at the headquarters of their respective armies.

The conditions of the armistice are:

Article 1 The line of the two armies shall be, in Moravia, the Circle of Iglau, the Circle of Znaïm, the Circle of Brünn, the part of the Circle of Olmütz on the right bank of the little river of Trezeboska, before Priesnitz, to the spot where that river empties into the Mark; and the right bank of the Mark to the junction of that bank with the Danube, Pressburg being included.

No French or Austrian troops shall on any occasion be stationed within five or six leagues of Halitch, on the right bank of the Mark.

The line of both armies shall include in the territory to be occupied by the French army, all Upper and Lower Austria, Tyrol, the State of Venice, Carinthia, Styria, Carniola, the country of Görlitz and Istria; finally, in Bohemia, the Circle of Montabaur, and the whole space to the east of the route from Tabor to Lima.

Article 2 The Russian army shall evacuate the states of Austria and Austrian Poland; that is to say, Moravia and Hungary, within the period of 15 days, and Galicia within a month. The routes shall be prescribed to the Russian army, that it may be always known where they are, as well as to prevent any misunderstanding.

Article 3 There shall be in Hungary no *levée en masse* or insurrection, and in Bohemia no extraordinary recruiting for troops, nor shall any foreign army be permitted to enter the territory of the House of Austria.

The negotiators for both powers shall meet at Nicolsburg, for proceeding directly to the opening of negotiations, in order to effect, without delay, the re-establishment of peace and good harmony between the two emperors.

The duplicates of this instrument are hereby signed by us, Marshal Berthier, Minister of War, Major-General of the *Grande Armée*, Plenipotentiary of His Majesty the Emperor of the French and King of Italy, and Prince John of Lichtenstein, Lieutenant-General and Plenipotentiary to His Majesty the Emperor of Austria, King of Hungary, etc.

At Austerlitz, 6 December 1805 (15 Frimaire year 14)

MARSHAL BERTHIER

JOHN, PRINCE OF LICHTENSTEIN, LIEUTENANT–GENERAL

Thirty-third Bulletin

Austerlitz, 7 December 1805 (16 Frimaire year 14)

General-in-Chief Buxhowden has been killed, with a great number of other Russian generals whose names are not yet known. Our soldiers have collected a great quantity of decorations. The Russian General Kutusov has been wounded, and his son-in-law, a young man of great merit, has been killed.

We have counted the dead; the result is 18,000 Russians killed, 600 Austrians, and 900 French. We have 7,000 wounded Russians. All together we have 3,000 wounded French. General Roger Valhubert is dead as a result of his wounds. He had written to the Emperor an hour before his death, 'I would have wanted to do more for you; I am dying within the hour. I do not regret my life, as I have shared in a victory that assures you a happy reign. When you sometimes remember the names of those brave men who were devoted to you, think of my memory. It will be enough to say to you that I have a family: I do not need to recommend them to you.'

Generals Kellermann, Sebastiani and Thiebault are out of danger. Generals [Van-] Marisy and Dumont are wounded, but much less gravely.

One will be doubtless pleased by the different decrees issued by the Emperor in favour of the army; they are attached.

The corps of General Buxhowden, which was on the left, had 27,000 men. Not one rejoined the Russian army. The corps had spent several hours under the fire of 40 pieces of artillery, one part of which was served up by the artillery of the Imperial Guard, and under the fusillade of the divisions of Generals Saint-Hilaire and Friant. The massacre has been horrible; the loss of the Russians can not be estimated at less than 45,000 men, the Emperor of Russia will not return to his home with more than 25,000 men.

Let this lesson profit the young prince and let him abandon the counsel that England has bought. Let him take back the true role that suits his country and his character and at last shake off the yoke of these vile oligarchs of London. Catherine the Great knew well the genius and resources of Russia when, in the first coalition, she did not send an army and contented herself with helping the members of the coalition by her counsels and by her wishes. But she had the experience of a long reign and of the character of her nation. She had reflected on the dangers of coalitions. This experience couldn't be acquired at 24 years of age.

When Paul, her son, marched the armies against France he well understood that the shortest errors are better, and after a campaign he pulled back his troops. If Voronzov, who is at London, was not more English than Russian one would have to have had very small idea of his talents to suppose that he had been able to think that 60,000, 80,000 or 100,000 Russians would have managed to dishonour France, to make her subject to the yoke of England, to make her abandon Belgium and to force the Emperor to deliver his Iron Crown to the degenerate race of the kings of Sardinia.

The Russian troops are brave, but much less brave than the French troops; their generals are of an experience and their soldiers of an ignorance and of an inertia that makes their armies, in truth, not very formidable. And besides, in supposing some victories to the Russians it would have been necessary to depopulate Russia to arrive at the insane goal that the oligarchs of London had prescribed for her.

The battle of Austerlitz was given on the tomb of the celebrated Kaunitz. This circumstance has made a very great impression on the minds of the Viennese. Having strong prudence and good conduct, and always maintaining good harmony with France, he had brought Austria to a high degree of prosperity.

Here are the names of the Russian generals taken prisoner; many others are dead on the battlefield. There are 400 or 500 officers prisoner, of which there are 20 majors and lieutenant colonels, and more than 100 captains. Prszybyzewski, Wimfen, Müller-Zakomelski, Müller, Berg, Selekov, Stryck, Szerliakof, Prince Repnine, Prince Sibirski, Adrian, Lagonof, Sulima, Mezenkof, Woicikof.

The Emperor has sent for Talleyrand, who is at Vienna, to come to Brünn. The negotiations are going to be opened at Nicolsburg.

Mr Maret has joined His Majesty at Austerlitz, where the Emperor has signed the papers of the ministers and the Council of State.

The Emperor has slept this evening at Brünn.

Proclamation

From our imperial camp of Austerlitz, 7 December 1805 (16 Frimaire year 14)
Napoleon, Emperor of the French, King of Italy, has decreed and decrees the following:

Article I The widows of the generals killed at the battle of Austerlitz will
   receive a pension of 6,000 francs for the rest of their lives; the widows of

colonels and majors, a pension of 24,000 francs; the widows of lieutenants and non-commissioned officers, a pension of 800 francs; the widows of soldiers, a pension of 200 francs.

Article II Our Minister of War is in charge of the execution of the present decree, which will be added to the Order of the Day of the army and included in the Bulletin of the laws.

(Signed) NAPOLEON

By the Emperor, THE MINISTER SECRETARY OF STATE, H B MARET

Decree

From our imperial camp at Austerlitz, 7 December 1805 (16 Frimaire year 14)

Napoleon, Emperor of the French, King of Italy, has decreed and decrees the following:

Article I We adopt all the children of French generals, officers and soldiers killed in the battle of Austerlitz.

Article II They will all be provided for and reared at our expense; the boys in our imperial palace of Rambouillet and the girls in our imperial palace of Saint Germain. The boys will later be placed and the girls married, by us.

Article III Independently from their baptism and family names, they will have the right to add that of Napoleon. Our Grand-Judge will help with filling out all the forms required by the Civil Code.

Article IV Our Grand-Marshal of the Palace and our Controller-General of the Crown are charged, each in his own concern, with the execution of the present decree, which will be added to the Order of the Day of the army and included in the Bulletin of the laws.

NAPOLEON

By the Emperor, THE MINISTER SECRETARY OF STATE, H B MARET

Thirty-fourth Bulletin

Brünn, 10 December 1805 (19 Frimaire year 14)

The Emperor today received Prince Repnine, who had become a prisoner at the battle of Austerlitz, at the head of the Horse Guard, of which he was the colonel. His Majesty said to him that the Emperor Alexander should not be deprived of such brave men, and that he would be able to join with all the prisoners of the Russian Imperial Guard, and return with them to Russia. His Majesty expressed regret that the Emperor of Russia had wanted to go to battle, and has said that this monarch if he had believed it the night before he would have spared the blood and the honour of his army.

Prince John of Lichtenstein arrived yesterday, with full powers. The conferences between him and Talleyrand are in full course.

The first aide-de-camp Junot, whom His Majesty had sent to the Emperors of Germany and Russia, has seen the Emperor of Germany at Holics, who received him with a great deal of grace and distinction. He has not been able to complete his mission, as the Emperor Alexander had already set out quickly for Saint Petersburg, as had General Kutusov.

His Majesty received at Brünn Mr Haugwitz and was extremely satisfied with all that this plenipotentiary said to him, and received him in the most distinguished manner, as he always defended from dependence on England, and that it is to his counsels that one ought to attribute the great consideration and prosperity that Prussia enjoys. One would not be able to say so much about another minister, who, born in Hanover, has not been inaccessible to the rain of gold. But all these intrigues have been and will be impotent against the good spirit and great wisdom of the King of Prussia. The French nation, besides, does not depend on anyone; and 150,000 more enemies would do nothing more than prolong the war. France and Prussia, in the present circumstances, have had to praise the Duke of Brunswick, Misters Mollendorf, Knobelsdorf, Lombard, and especially the King himself. The English intrigues have often appeared to gain some ground, but in the final analysis one could not arrive at any conclusion without first considering the question head on; all the intrigues have failed before the will of the King. In truth, those who conduct these intrigues surprisingly abuse his confidence. Prussia can not have a more solid and disinterested friend than France.

Russia is the sole power in Europe that can make a war of fantasy. After a battle lost or won the Russians can withdraw into their land. France, Austria and Prussia, on the contrary, have to think for a long time about the results of the war; one or two battles are insufficient to exhaust all possibilities.

The peasants of Moravia kill the Russians everywhere they come across them in isolation; they have already massacred 100 of them. The Emperor of the French has given orders for cavalry patrols to travel the countryside to prevent excesses. Since the enemy army retired, the Russians left after them were under the protection of the victor. It is true that they have committed so many disorders, so many brigandages, that one ought not be surprised by this vengeance. They maltreated the poor as well as the rich; 300 blows of the baton were given for light offences. There is no mischief that they did not commit. Pillage, burning the villages, massacre, such were their games; they even killed some priests at their altars. Misfortune to the sovereign who will ever draw such a scourge on his territory! The battle of Austerlitz was a European victory, since it has brought down the prestige that was connected to the name of these *barbarians*. This word can not apply, however, either to the court or to a very great number of officers, or to the inhabitants of the villages, who are, on the contrary, civilized in spite of the corruption.

Thirty-fifth Bulletin
Brünn, 11 December 1805 (20 Frimaire year 14)

The Russian army began its march to return to Russia on 8 December, in three columns; the first took the road of Kraków and Therespol; the second by Kaschau, Lemberg and Brodi; and the third by Trynau, Waitzen and Husiatyn. The Emperor of Russia left at the head of the first column, with his brother the Grande Duke Constantine.

Independent of the field artillery, the Russians lost a whole park of artillery of 100 cannon with their ammunition wagons.

The Emperor has gone to see this park. He has ordered that all these pieces should be sent to France. It is without example that in a single battle from 150 to 160 pieces of artillery should be taken, having been fired and served in the action.

Squadron Chief Challopin, aide-de-camp of Marshal Bernadotte, has been killed.

Colonels Lacour, of the 5th Regiment of Dragoons; Digeon of the 26th Chasseurs; Bessières of the 11th Chasseurs, brother of Marshal Bessières; Gérard, Colonel, aide-de-camp of Marshal Bernadotte; and Marès, Colonel, aide-de-camp to Marshal Davout, have been wounded.

Battalion Chiefs Perrier of the 36th Regiment of Infantry of Line; Guye, of the 4th Line; Schwiter of the 57th Line; the Squadron Chiefs Grumblot of the 2nd

Regiment of Carabiniers; Didelon of the 9th Dragoons; Boudinhon of the 4th Hussars; the battalion Chief of Engineers Abrissot; Rabier and Mobillard of the 55th Line; Proffil of the 43rd; and Squadron Chiefs Tréville of the 22nd Chasseurs and David of the 2nd Hussars, have been wounded.

Squadron Chiefs of Horse Chasseurs of the Imperial Guard Beurmann, Bohn and Thiry have been wounded.

Captain Thervay of the Horse Chasseurs of the Guard is dead as a result of his wounds.

Captain Geist, Lieutenants Bureau, Barbanègre, Guyot, Fournier, Addet, Bayeux and Renno of the horse chasseurs of the Guard, and Lieutenants Menager and Rollet of the horse grenadiers of the Guard have been wounded.

Thirty-sixth Bulletin

Schönbrunn, 14 December 1805 (23 Frimaire year 14)

We will recall with great interest the deeds of valour that have illustrated the *Grande Armée*.

A carabinier of the 10th Light Infantry had his left arm carried away by a cannonball: 'Help me,' he cried to his comrade, 'to take off my cartridge-box and hasten forward to avenge my loss. I want no other assistance.' The wounded man then put his sack on his right arm and marched alone to the ambulance.

General Thiebault was dangerously wounded and was carried off by four Russian prisoners. Six wounded Frenchmen saw them, chased the Russians, and seized the stretcher, saying, 'It is an honour belonging to us alone to carry a wounded French general.'

General Valhubert had his thigh carried away by a cannonball. Four soldiers approached to take him up; 'Remember the order of the day,' he said to them in a voice of thunder, 'and join your ranks. If you return victors, you may carry me off after the battle is ended; if you are beaten, I attach no more value to life.'

The loss of this general is the only one we have to lament; all the other wounded generals are in full recovery.

The battalions of skirmishers of the Po and the Corsican skirmishers comported themselves bravely in the defence of the village of Sokolnitz. Colonel Franceschi, with the 8th Hussars, was remarkable for his courage and good conduct.

We have drained the lake on which a great number of Russians tried to escape on the day of the battle of Austerlitz, and have pulled out 49 pieces of artillery and a great quantity of dead bodies.

The Emperor arrived here the day before yesterday, the 12th, at ten in the evening.

Yesterday the Emperor received the deputation from the Mayors of Paris, presented by Prince Murat.

Mr Dupont, Mayor of the 7th *arrondissement* made a speech.

The Emperor answered that he saw the deputation with pleasure, and that notwithstanding the fact that he received them in the palace of Maria Theresa, still the day when he should again find himself in the midst of his good citizens of Paris would be to him a feast day. He said they had been close enough to see the misfortunes of war, and that from the view which presented itself he was persuaded that all the French should consider the law of conscription as wholesome and sacred, if they did not want to see their homes devastated some day and the beautiful territory of France handed over, as Austria and Moravia, by the ravages of the barbarians; that in their relations with the middle class of Vienna they had been assured that they appreciate the justice of our cause and the fatal influence of England and of various corrupt men. He added that he wished for peace, but a peace as would secure the welfare of the French people, that the betterment of commerce and industry were always hindered by the insatiable greed of England.

His Majesty then informed the deputies of his intention to present to the cathedral of Paris the Russian flags taken in the battle on the anniversary of his coronation, and that he meant to entrust these trophies in their hands, in order that they might be delivered to the Cardinal Archbishop.

Letter of His Imperial Majesty Emperor and King to the Cardinal Archbishop of Paris

From our palace at Brünn, 11 December 1805

My Cousin, we have taken 45 flags from our enemy, the day of the anniversary of our coronation: that day when the Holy Father, his Cardinals and all the Clergy of France offered their prayers in the sanctuary of Notre Dame for the prosperity of our reign. We have resolved to deposit these flags in the church of Notre Dame, cathedral of our good city of Paris. We have ordered, in consequence, these flags to be presented to you, that they may be preserved in your metropolitan church. Our intention is that every year on this day a solemn mass may be celebrated in our staid cathedral in memory of the brave men dead for the fatherland that day, in commemoration of the valour exhibited on that day, which mass will be followed by the thanksgiving to the God of Armies for the victory which he has been pleased to give us. This letter has no other end, we pray God to take you, my cousin, into his holy and worthy keeping.

(Signed) NAPOLEON

By the Emperor, THE SECRETARY OF STATE, H B MARET

Order of the Day

From our imperial headquarters at Schönbrunn, 25 December 1805 (4 Nivôse year 14)

The Emperor spent Monday reviewing the divisions of carabiniers and cuirassiers of Generals Nansouty and Hautpoul.

His Majesty, after the review, experience veritable satisfaction at seeing in such great shape those brave regiments of cuirassiers which have given him so much proof of their courage in the current campaign, notably in the battle of Austerlitz.

Tuesday, His Majesty passed in review the Vandamme division. The Emperor charged Marshal Soult to inform the troops that he was satisfied with this division, and to see again, after the battle of Austerlitz, in such good shape and so numerous the battalions who have acquired so much glory and have contributed so much to the success of this day.

Arriving at the first battalion of the 4th Regiment of Line, which had been injured at the battle of Austerlitz and had lost its eagle there, the Emperor said to them: 'Soldiers, what have you done with the eagle I have given you? You had sworn that it would be used as your point of rally and that you would defend it with your life. Have you kept your promise?' The major responded that the flag-carrier had been killed in a charge at the moment of the greatest mêlée and that nobody had noticed it in the midst of all the smoke; that, however, the division had made a movement to the right; that the battalion had supported this movement and that it was not until much later that they had realized that they had lost their eagle; that the proof that he had been reunited and that he had not been broken is that a moment later they had overthrown two Russian battalions and taken two flags, which he offered to the Emperor, hoping it would offer them the merit of receiving another eagle from the Emperor. The Emperor was slightly uncertain, then he said, 'Officers and soldiers, do you swear that not one of you realized the eagle was lost; and that if you had you would have rushed to take it back or perished on the field of battle, because a soldier who has lost his flag has lost everything?' At that moment a thousand arms went up: 'We swear it, and we swear also that we will defend the eagle that you will give us with the same intrepidity we used to take the two flags we are presenting to you.' 'In this case,' said the Emperor, smiling, 'I will give you back your eagle.'

The Major-General reminds marshals and generals, chief commanders at the battle of Austerlitz, of the request made of them of an account, certified by the administrative councils, of the corps which served under their orders at that battle, verified by the inspectors of review and bearing their visa, stating the widows and children of French officers and soldiers killed on that memorable day, so that they can enjoy the benefits of the two decrees of the 16th Frimaire [7 December] included in the Order of the Day of the 17th [8 December]. The colonels must feel how important it is to accelerate the execution of these two decrees, which give fortune and assure the well-being of the widows and children of their comrades dead on the field of honour.

THE MAJOR-GENERAL, MARSHAL BERTHIER

Thirty-seventh Bulletin

Schönbrunn, 26 December 1805 (5 Nivôse year 14)

Here is the position of the army today:

Marshal Bernadotte occupies Bohemia.

Marshal Mortier, Moravia.

Marshal Davout occupies Pressburg, capital of Hungary.

Marshal Soult occupies Vienna.

Marshal Ney occupies Corinthia.

General Marmont, Styria.

Marshal Masséna, Carniola.

Marshal Augereau remains on reserve in Suabia.

Marshal Masséna is with the army of Italy, which has become the 8th Corps of the *Grand Armée*.

Prince Eugene is Commander-in-Chief of all the troops in the Venetian territories and the Kingdom of Italy.

General Saint-Cyr is advancing by great marches towards Naples to punish the treason of the Queen, and to remove from the throne this criminal woman who with so much impudence has violated all that is sacred among men.

One tried to intercede for her with the Emperor; he replied, 'Were hostilities to commence and the nation to support a war of 30 years, so atrocious an act of perfidy cannot be pardoned. The Queen of Naples has ceased to reign. This last crime has completed her destiny; let her flee to London, to increase the number of intriguers and form a sympathetic writing committee with Drake, Spencer Smith, Taylor, Wickham; she may also invite, if she please, Baron d'Armfelt, Messrs Fersen, d'Entraigues and the monk Morus.'

Mr Talleyrand is at Pressburg, where they are negotiating. The pleni-potentiaries of the Emperor of Austria are Prince John of Lichtenstein and

General Giulay.

Prince Charles has asked to see the Emperor. His Majesty will have an interview tomorrow with this Prince at the hunting lodge of Stamersdorf, three leagues from Vienna.

The Emperor is to review today the division of Legrand, near Laxenburg.

The Emperor takes no recreation at Vienna; he has given audience to very few.

For some days the weather has been rather cold. Today it is very fine. The Emperor has made a great many promotions in the army and in the Legion of Honour; but the commissions that he has at his disposal are scarcely sufficient to recompense so many brave men.

The Elector of Württemberg has sent to the Emperor the Ribbon of the Grand Order of Württemberg, with three others, which have been conferred on Senator Harville, First Equerry to the Empress, to Marshal Kellerman and General Marmont. The Emperor has presented the Grand Ribbon of the Legion of Honour to the Elector, the Electoral Prince and Prince Paul, his sons; and to his brothers, Prince Eugene-Frederic Henry and William-Frederick Philip; he became acquainted with the last two Princes as he passed through Louisburg, and has been happy to give them a proof of the opinion that he conceived of their merit.

The Electors of Bavaria and Württemberg are to assume the title of Kings, a reward that they have deserved by the attachment and friendship that they have shown His Majesty on all occasions.

The Emperor expressed his dissatisfaction that at Mayence a proclamation had been published, signed with his name, that was full of absurdity. It is dated from Olmütz, where the Emperor has never been, and what is more extraordinary, it was inserted in the Order of the Day of the army of Mayence. Whichever person was the author, he shall be punished according to the rigour of the laws. Can there be a greater crime in a civilized state that to misuse the name of a sovereign?

The Emperor of Austria is still at Holics.

A great number of the wounded have recovered. The army is in a better state than ever it was. Prince Murat reports that the number of his cavalry has almost doubled since the battle of Austerlitz. All the horses that, as a result of forced marches, remained on the road are refreshed and have joined their corps. More than 2,000 pieces of artillery have been sent from Vienna to France. The Emperor has given orders that there shall be a room prepared in the Napoleon Museum to receive all the curiosities collected at Vienna.

He has ordered restored to Bavaria all the cannon and flags taken in 1740. The Bavarians then made a common cause with France, but France was then governed by a pusillanimous priest.

The people of Italy have displayed great energy. The Emperor said many times, 'Why don't my people of Italy appear with glory on the world scene? They are full of spirit and passions: it will consequently be no difficult task to give them the proper military qualities.' The Italian cannoneers of the Royal Guard were covered with glory at the battle of Austerlitz, and merited the esteem of all the old French artillerymen. The Royal Guard always marched with the Imperial Guard, and everywhere showed themselves worthy to do so.

Venice is to be united to the Kingdom of Italy.

The cities of Bologna and Brescia are always the first to distinguish themselves by their energy; accordingly the Emperor, in receiving the address of these towns, observed, 'I know that the villages of Bologna and Brescia, *sono mie di cuore* [are mine from the heart].'

The Emperor has strongly approved of the dispositions made by Prince Louis for the defence of Holland, the excellent position he has taken at Nimègue and the measures he has proposed for protecting the northern frontier.

Treaty of Peace between the Emperor of Germany and Austria and the Emperor of the French

Done and signed at Pressburg, 26 December 1805

His Majesty the Emperor of Germany and Austria, and His Majesty the Emperor of the French, King of Italy, equally animated with a desire to put an end to the calamities of war, have resolved to proceed without delay to the conclusion of a definitive treaty of peace, and have in consequence named as plenipotentiaries, to wit: His Majesty the Emperor of Germany and of Austria, Prince John of Lichtenstein, Prince of the Holy Roman Empire, Grand Cross of the Military Order of Maria Theresa, Chamberlain, Lieutenant-General of the armies of his said Majesty the Emperor of Germany and of Austria and proprietor of a regiment of hussars; and Count Ignaz Giulay, Commander of the Military Order of Maria Theresa, Chamberlain of his said Majesty the Emperor of Germany and Austria, Lieutenant-General of his armies and proprietor of a regiment of infantry; and His Majesty the Emperor of the French, King of Italy, Charles Maurice Talleyrand Perigord, Grand Chamberlain, Minister of Foreign Relations of his said Majesty the Emperor of the French and King of Italy, Grand Cordon of the Legion of Honour and Knight of the Red and the Black Eagle of Prussia; who having exchanged their full powers have agreed as follows:

Article I There shall be from the date of this day peace and friendship between His Majesty the Emperor of Germany and Austria, and His Majesty the Emperor of the French, King of Italy, their heirs and successors, their states and subjects respectively, forever.

Article II France shall continue to possess in property and sovereignty the duchies, principalities, lordships, and territories beyond the Alps, which were before the present treaty united and incorporated with the French Empire or governed by the laws and government of France.

Article III His Majesty the Emperor of Germany and Austria, for himself, his heirs, and successors, recognizes the disposition made by His Majesty the Emperor of the French, King of Italy relative to the principalities of Lucca and Piombino.

Article IV His Majesty the Emperor of Germany and Austria renounces, as well for himself, as for his heirs and successors, that part of the states of the republic of Venice, ceded to him by the treaties of Campo Formio and Luneville, which shall be united in perpetuity to the Kingdom of Italy.

Article V His Majesty the Emperor of Germany and of Austria acknowledges His Majesty the Emperor of the French as King of Italy. But it is agreed that, in conformity with the declaration made by His Majesty the Emperor of the French at the moment when he took the crown of Italy, that as soon as the parties named in that declaration shall have fulfilled the conditions therein expressed, the crowns of France and Italy shall be separated forever and cannot in any case be united on the same head. His Majesty the Emperor of Germany binds himself to acknowledge, on the separation, the successor His Majesty the Emperor of the French shall appoint himself as King of Italy.

Article VI The present Treaty of Peace is declared to comprehend their most

Serene Highnesses the Electors of Bavaria, Württemberg, and Baden, and the Batavian Republic, allies of His Majesty the Emperor of the French in the present war.

Article VII The Electors of Bavaria and Württemberg having taken the title of King without ceasing nevertheless to belong to the Germanic confederation, His Majesty the Emperor of Germany and Austria acknowledge them in that character.

Article VIII His Majesty the Emperor of German and Austria, as well for himself, his heirs, and successors, as for the princes of his house, their heirs and successors respectively, renounces the principalities, lordships, domains and territories, hereinafter specified: cedes and abandons to His Majesty the King of Bavaria the Margravate of Burgau and its dependencies, the Principality of Eichstädt, the part of the territory of Passau belonging to the Elector of Salzburg and situated between Bohemia, Austria, the Danube and the Inn; the country of Tyrol, comprehending therein the principalities of Brixen and Botzen, the seven Lordships of the Voralberg, with their detached dependencies, the country of Hohenems, the county of Königsegg-Rothenfels, the Lordships of Tetnang and Argen, and the town and territory of Lindau.

To His Majesty the King of Württemberg, the five cities of the Danube, to wit, Ehingen, Munderkingen, Reidlingen, Mengen, and Sulgau, with their dependencies, the upper and lower County of Hogenberg, the Landgravate of Nellenburg and the Prefecture of Altorff, with their dependencies, the city of Constance excepted; that part of Brisgau which extends in the possessions of Württemberg, and situated to the east of the line, drawn from Schlegelberg to Molbach, and the towns and territories of Willingen and Brentingen.

To His Most Serene Highness the Elector of Baden the Brisgau (with the exception of the branch and separate portions above described), the Ortenau and their dependencies, the city of Constance and the commandery of Meinau.

The principalities, lordships, domains, and territories above mentioned, shall be possessed respectively by Their Majesties the Kings of Bavaria and Württemberg and by His Most Serene Highness the Elector of Baden, as well in paramount as in full property and sovereignty, in the same manner, by the same titles, and with the same rights and prerogatives, with which they were possessed by His Majesty the Emperor of Germany and Austria, or the princes of his house, and not otherwise.

Article IX His Majesty the Emperor of Germany and Austria acknowledges the debts contracted by the House of Austria for the benefit of private persons and public establishments of the country, making at present an integral part of the French Empire; and it is agreed that his said Majesty shall remain free from all obligation, with respect to any debts whatsoever which the House of Austria may have contracted, on the ground of the possession and of securities on the soil of the countries which it renounces by the present treaty.

Article X The country of Salzburg and of Berchtolsgaden belonging to his Royal and Elector Highness Prince Ferdinand shall be incorporated with the Empire of Austria; and His Majesty the Emperor of Germany and Austria shall possess them in full property and sovereignty, but by the title of a Duchy only.

Article XI His Majesty the Emperor of the French, King of Italy, engages himself to obtain, in favor of the Archduke Ferdinand, Elector of Salzburg, the cession by His Majesty the King of Bavaria of the Principality of Würzburg, such as it has been given to his said Majesty by the recess of the deputation of the Germanic Empire, of 25 February 1803.

The Electoral title of His Royal Highness shall possess in full property and sovereignty in the same manner and on the same conditions that he possessed the Electorate of Salzburg. And with respect to debts, it is agreed that the new possessor shall stand charged only with those debts resulting from loans formally agreed to by the states of the country, or the expenses incurred for the effective administration of the said country.

Article XII The dignity of Grand Master of the Teutonic Orders, its rights, domains, and revenues, which before the present war were dependencies of Mergentheim, the chief place of the order; the other rights, domains, and revenues which shall be found to belong to the Grand Mastership at the time of the exchanges of the ratifications of the present treaty; as well as the domains and revenues in possession of which the said order shall be, at the same epoch, shall become hereditary in the person and descendants in the direct make line, according to the order of primogeniture in which ever of the Princes of the Imperial House as shall be appointed by His Majesty the Emperor of Germany and Austria.

His Majesty the Emperor Napoleon promises his good offices to obtain, as soon as possible, for His Royal Highness the Archduke Ferdinand a full and entire indemnity in Germany.

Article XIII His Majesty the King of Bavaria shall occupy the city of Augsburg and its territory, and unite them to his states in full property and sovereignty. In the same manner the King of Württemberg may occupy, unite to his states and possess in full property and sovereignty the country of Bendorff, and His Majesty the Emperor of Germany and Austria engages himself to give no opposition.

Article XIV Their Majesties the Kings of Bavaria and Württemberg, and His Most Serene Highness the Elector of Baden shall enjoy over the territories ceded, as well as over their ancient estates, the plenitude of sovereignty and all the rights resulting from it, which have been guaranteed to them by His Majesty the Emperor of the French, King of Italy, in the same manner as His Majesty the Emperor of Germany and Austria, and His Majesty the King of Prussia, over their German States. His Majesty the Emperor of Germany and Austria, both as chief of the Empire and as co-estates, engages himself not to oppose any obstacle to the execution of the acts that they may have made or will make in consequence.

Article XV His Majesty the Emperor of Germany and Austria, as well for himself, his heirs, and successors, as for the princes of his house, their heirs and successors, renounces all the rights, as well of sovereignty, as of paramount right to all pretensions whatsoever, actual or eventual, on all the states, without exception, of Their Majesties, the Kings of Bavaria and Württemberg and of His Most Serene Highness the Elector of Baden, and generally on all the states, domains, and territories comprised in the circles of Bavaria, Franconia and Swabia, as well as to every title taken from the said domains and territories: and reciprocally, all pretension, actual or eventual, of the said states to the charge of the House of Austria or its princes are, and shall be, forever extinguished: nevertheless, the renunciations contained in the present article do not concern the properties, which are by the 11th article. Or which shall be, by virtue of the 12th article above, conceded to their royal Highnesses the Archdukes named in the said articles.

Article XVI The title of the domains and archives, the plans and maps of the different countries, towns, and fortresses ceded by the present treaty shall be given up in the space of three months from the date of the exchange of the ratifications to the persons that shall have acquired the property of them.

Article XVII His Majesty the Emperor Napoleon guarantees the integrity of the Empire of Austria in the state in which it shall be in consequence of the present treaty of peace; as well as the integrity of the possessions of the Princes of the House of Austria, pointed out in the 11th and 12th articles.

Article XVIII The high contracting parties acknowledge the independence of the Helvetia republic, as established by the act of mediation, as well as the independence of the Batavian Republic.

Article XIX The prisoners of war made by France and her allies from Austria, and by Austria from France and her allies, and who have not been yet restored, shall be restored within 40 days from the date of the exchange of the ratifications of the present treaty.

Article XX All commercial communications and relations are re-established in the two countries on the same footing as before the war.

Article XXI His Majesty the Emperor of Germany and Austria and His Majesty the Emperor of the French, King of Italy, shall maintain between them the same ceremonial as to rank and etiquette as was observed before the present war.

Article XXII Within five days from the exchange of the ratifications of the present treaty, the town of Pressburg and its environs to the extent of six leagues, shall be evacuated. Ten days after the said exchange, the French and the troops of the allies of France shall evacuate Moravia, Bohemia, the Viertel Unter Wiener Wald, the Viertel Unter Manhardtsberg, Hungary and all of Styria. In the ten following days they shall evacuate the Viertel Wiener Wald and the Viertel Ober Manhardtsberg; and finally, in the space of two months from the exchange of the ratifications, the French troops and the allies of France shall evacuate all of the hereditary states of His Majesty The Emperor of Germany and of Austria, with the exception of the fortress of Braunau, which shall remain for one month at the disposal of His Majesty the Emperor of the French, King of Italy, as a place of depot for the sick and for the artillery. No requisition, of whatever nature, shall be made of the inhabitants during that month. But it is agreed that at the expiration of the said month, no corps whatever of Austria troops can be stationed or introduced within a circuit of six leagues around the said fortress of Braunau. It is in like manner agreed that each of the places which are to be successively evacuated by the French troops within the times above mentioned shall not be taken possession of by the Austrian troops until 48 hours after the evacuation. It is also agreed that the magazines left by the French army in the places which they shall successively evacuate shall remain at its disposal; and that the high contracting parties shall make an arrangement relative to all contributions of war whatsoever imposed on the different hereditary states occupied by the French army, an arrangement in virtue of which the raising of the said contributions shall entirely cease from the day of the exchange of the ratifications. The French army shall draw its provisions and its sustenance from its own magazines, established on the routes by which it is to proceed.

Article XXIII Immediately after the exchange of the ratification of the present treaty, commissaries shall be named on both sides to give up and to receive in the names of their respective sovereigns all parts of the Venetian territory, and occupied by the troops of His Majesty the Emperor of the French and King of Italy. The city of Venice, the Lagoons and the possessions of the mainland shall be given up in the space of 15 days; Venetian Istria, and Dalmatia, the Mouths of the Cataro, the Venetian Isles in the Adriatic, and all the places and forts which they contain, in the space of six weeks from the exchange of the ratifications. The respective commissaries will take care that the separation of the artillery belonging to the republic of Venice from the Austrian artillery be exactly made, the former being to remain entirely to the Kingdom of Italy. They will determine by a mutual agreement the kind and nature of the objects, which being the property of the Emperor of Germany and of Austria, are consequently to remain as his disposal. They will agree either on the sale to the Kingdom of Italy of the objects mentioned above, or their exchange for an equivalent quantity of artillery, or other objects of the same or a different nature, which shall have been left by the French armies in the hereditary States. Every facility and every assistance shall be given to the Austrian troops, and to the civil military administrations, to return into the Austrian States by the most convenient and sure ways, as well as to the conveyance of the imperial artillery, the naval and military magazines and other objects which are not comprehended in the stipulations of sale or exchange which may be made.

Article XXIV The ratification of the present Treaty shall be exchanged within the space of eight days, or sooner if possible.

Done and signed at Pressburg 25 December 1805

(L..S.) CHARLES MAURICE TALLEYRAND
(L.S.) JOHN, PRINCE OF LICHTENSTEIN
(L.S.) IGNAZ, COUNT GIULAY

We have approved the above treaty, in all and each of its articles therein contained; we declare that it is accepted, ratified, and confirmed; and we promise that it shall be inviolable. In faith of which we have given these presents, signed with our hand, countersigned and sealed with our Imperial Seal at the Palace of Schönbrunn 27 December 1805.

By the Emperor Napoleon. THE MINISTER SECRETARY OF STATE, H B MARET
THE MINISTER OF FOREIGN RELATIONS, CHARLES MAURICE TALLEYRAND.

Proclamation of the Emperor Napoleon to the Army

Schönbrunn, 27 December 1805 (6 Nivôse year 14)

Soldiers, peace between me and the Emperor of Austria has been signed. You have in this late season made two campaigns; you have performed everything I expected

72

from you. I am setting out to return to my capital. I have accorded advancement and recompense to those who were the most distinguished. I will perform for you everything I have promised. You have seen that your Emperor has shared with you all dangers and fatigues; I wish also that you come to see him surrounded with all that grandeur and splendour which becomes the sovereign of the first nation in the universe. I will give a great festival at Paris in the first days of May; you shall all be there; and after we will go where we will call the happiness of our country and the interest of our glory.

Soldiers, during the three months which are necessary for your return to France, be the model of all armies: you have now to give examples, not of courage and intrepidity, but of strict discipline. May my allies have nothing to complain of in your passage, and on arriving on the sacred territory, conduct yourselves like children in the middle of their family; my people will conduct themselves towards you as they must do towards their heroes and their defenders.

Soldiers, the thought that I shall see you all, in less than half a year, assembled around my palace, is pleasing to my heart; and I feel beforehand the most tender emotions. We will celebrate the memory of those who, in these two campaigns, are dead in the field of honour, and the world shall see that we are ready to imitate their example; and, if necessary, to do still more than we have done against those who attack our happiness or allow themselves to be seduced by the corrupting gold of the eternal enemies of the Continent.

NAPOLEON

Proclamation to the inhabitants of Vienna

Schönbrunn, 27 December 1805

Inhabitants of Vienna! I have signed a peace with the Emperor of Austria. As I am about to return to my capital, I must express to you the esteem in which I hold you, and the satisfaction I have felt at your conduct during the time you were under my law. I have given you an example that so far has had no parallel in the history of nations; 10,000 men of your national guards have remained armed and have guarded your gates; your whole arsenal has continued in your power while I have followed the most hazardous fortunes of war. I have trusted in your sentiments of honour, good faith, of loyalty; you have justified my confidence.

Inhabitants of Vienna, I know that you have all criticized the war that the ministers sold to England have set off on the Continent. Your Sovereign is aware of the conduct of these corrupt ministers; he has, in consequence, acted entirely according to the great qualities that distinguish him, and henceforth I hope for happier days for you and for the Continent.

Inhabitants of Vienna, I have little shown myself among you, not from contempt or vain pride but I have not wanted to destroy in you any of the sentiments that you owe to the prince with whom I wanted to conclude a speedy peace. As I am now about to leave you, receive from me as a present that proves my esteem for you, your intact arsenal, which by the laws of war had become my property; use it always for the maintenance of order. All the evils you have suffered you must attribute to the misfortunes inseparable from war; and every kind of indulgence with which my armies have treated your countries is due to the esteem you have deserved.

(Signed) NAPOLEON

CAMPAIGN IN PRUSSIA
1806–7

The achievements of the campaign of 1805 were short-lived. By October 1806, a Fourth Coalition of England, Prussia and Russia had formed. As usual, England was the primary financial backer and the Continental armies were to bear the brunt of the action. In this case, England and Russia were delighted to send Prussia against Napoleon. King Frederick William, egged on by his wife, the aristocracy, and his Coalition partners, demanded that Napoleon dissolve the Confederation of the Rhine. Prussia began to mobilize, but Napoleon struck first.

The once-proud Prussian army was a shadow of its former self. At Jena and Auerstädt on 14 October 1806, Napoleon destroyed the Prussian army, finishing them as a fighting force. Only Marshal Bernadotte's failure to support adequately either Napoleon or Davout kept the victory from being a total rout.

Napoleon then moved on the Russians. On 7–8 February the two sides fought the bloody but indecisive battle of Eylau in Poland. After a break for winter in Warsaw, where he had a love affair with Countess Marie Walewska, Napoleon crushed the Russians on 14 June at the battle of Friedland. This finished the Fourth Coalition. Napoleon and Tsar Alexander met on a raft on the Niemen River and signed a treaty of alliance.

Proclamation of the Emperor Napoleon to his Army

Soldiers, the order for your return to France was given; you had already taken several marches toward home. Triumphal festivals awaited you, and every preparation was made in the capital for your reception.

But while we abandoned ourselves too much to confident security, new plots were being organized under the mask of friendship and alliance. The cry of war was resounded in Berlin; every day for two months we have received more provocation.

The same faction, the same spirit of giddiness, which 14 years ago brought the Prussians into the plains of Champagne, dominate in their advice. If it is no longer Paris that they want to burn and destroy from roof to foundation, today they want to plant their flags in the capital of our allies; it is Saxony that they have forced by a disgraceful transaction to renounce her independence, making her one of their many provinces; it is in short your laurels that they wish to tear away from your brows. They want us to evacuate Germany. The senseless beings! They should know it would be a thousand times easier to destroy the capital rather then tarnish the honour of the children of the great nation and of her allies. Their plans were then confounded: they found in the plains of Champaign their defeat, death and shame; but the lesson of experience disappears, and there are men in whom the sense of hatred and envy never dies.

Soldiers! There is not one of you who would return to France by any other road but the road of honour. We will not return except under an arch of triumph.

What! Have we braved the seasons, the seas and the deserts, vanquished Europe several times as it was allied against us, have we borne our glory of the Orient and the Occident, only to return today in our country like deserters, after abandoning our allies, and to hear that the French Eagle retreated frightened at the prospect of the Prussian army…? But they have already arrived at our advanced positions.

Let us march, since moderation has been unable to bring them out of their baffling intoxication. Let the Prussian army again have the fate it met 14 years ago. Let them learn that it is easy to increase territory and power with the friendship of a great people, its enmity, which, without renouncing every degree of wisdom and reason cannot be provoked, is more terrible than the tempests of the ocean.

Given at our imperial headquarters at Bamberg, 6 October 1806,

NAPOLEON

THE MAJOR-GENERAL PRINCE OF NEUFCHÂTEL AND VALENGIN,

MARSHAL BERTHIER

Letter of His Majesty Emperor and King

Senators,

We left our capital to join our army in Germany the moment we learned with certainty that it was threatened on its flanks by unexpected movements. Scarcely had we arrived at the frontiers of our states, when we recognized how much our presence was necessary there, and to applaud ourselves for the defensive measures we had taken previously to our departure from the centre of our Empire. Already the Prussian armies, in an attitude of war, were in motion everywhere. They had crossed their frontiers, Saxony was invaded, and the wise prince who rules that country was forced to act, against his will, against the interest of his people. The Prussian armies had arrived in front of the cantonments of our troops. Provocations of every kind, and even acts of violence, had signalled the spirit of hate which animated our enemies; and the moderation of our soldiers, who, tranquil while they beheld all these movements, astonished at receiving no order, rested in the double confidence that they get from courage and a sense of justice.

Our first duty was to cross the Rhine ourselves, to form our camps, and let the cry of war be heard. It resounded in the hearts of all our warriors. Marches, combined and rapid, carried them in an instant to the place we had indicated. All our camps are formed: we are about to march against the Prussian armies, and repel force them with force. However, we must say that our heart is sensibly affected by that continued preponderance which the genius of evil upholds in Europe, which is incessantly employed in counteracting the designs we are forming for the tranquillity of Europe, for the repose and happiness of the present generation; which attacks all cabinets, by all kinds of seduction, and misleads those it cannot corrupt, blinding them to their true interests, and throwing them into the midst of parties, without any other guide than the passions with which it inspired them.

The cabinet of Berlin itself has not chosen with deliberation the side it takes. It has been artfully induced to do so by malicious contrivance. The King finds himself suddenly 100 leagues from his capital, on the frontiers of the Con-federation of the Rhine, in the midst of his army, and in front of French troops, who were dispersed throughout their cantonments, and who thought they had a right to depend on the ties which united the two states, and on the protestations made on all occasions by the Court of Berlin.

In a war so just, in which we only take arms in our own defence, which we have not provoked by any act, by any pretension, and for which it would be impossible for us to assign the true cause, we reckon entirely on the support of the laws, and on that of our people, who are called on by the present circumstances to give new proofs of their love, their devotion and their courage. On our part, no personal sacrifice will be painful to us, no danger will stop us, whenever it will be necessary to maintain the rights, the honour and the prosperity of our people.

Given in our Imperial Headquarters of Bamberg, 7 October 1806

NAPOLEON

By the Emperor, THE MINISTER AND SECRETARY OF STATE, H B MARET.

First Bulletin

Bamberg, 8 October 1806

The peace with Russia, concluded and signed on 26 July, and negotiations with England, which were drawing towards a conclusion, brought alarm to Berlin. The vague rumours multiplied, and the consciousness of the wrongs of this cabinet towards other powers, and the successive betrayals, led it to believe the rumours that one of the secret articles in the treaty with Russia gave Poland to Prince Constantine with the title of King, that Silesia was to be given to Austria in exchange for the Austrian portion of Poland and that Hanover was to be given to England. Thus it was persuaded that these three powers were in accord with France, and that this accord resulted in an imminent danger to Prussia.

The betrayals of Prussia towards France went back to a very distant epoch. First, she had armed herself to profit by our internal disorders. She was seen ready to come forward at the moment of the invasion of Holland by the Duke of York; and during the events of the last war, although she had no cause of complaint against France, she took up arms again, and signed, 1 October 1805, the famous Treaty of Potsdam, which was in less than a month replaced by the Treaty of Vienna.

She had betrayed Russia, who cannot forget the unexecuted Treaty of Potsdam and the subsequent conclusion of the Treaty of Vienna.

Her betrayals towards the Emperor of Germany, and all Germans, more numerous and more ancient, were well known. She always acted in opposition to the Diet. When the Germans were at war, she was at peace with their enemies. Her treaties with Austria were never executed, and she uniformly studied to excite stronger powers to combat, in the view of gaining, at the moment of peace, the fruits of her cleverness and their success.

Those who suppose that so much versatility of conduct comes from a defect of morality on the part of the reigning prince would be making a great error. For 15 years, the Court of Berlin has been a kind of stage upon which different parties fought and triumphed in turn, the one for war, the other for peace. The least important political circumstance, the smallest incident, often gave the advantage to one or the other; and the King, in the midst of these opposing passions, in the middle of this maze of intrigues, floated uncertainly without ceasing to be an honourable man.

On 11 August, a messenger of the Marquis Lucchesini arrived at Berlin, and delivered, in the most positive terms, the assurance of those supposed dispositions by which France and Russia had agreed upon by the treaty of 20 July to restore the Kingdom of Poland, and remove Silesia from Prussia. The partisans of war were immediately enflamed, they did violence to the personal sentiments of the King; 40 couriers were dispatched from Berlin in one night, and an appeal to arms was instantly decided.

The news of this sudden explosion was received at Paris on the 20th of the same month. It was sad to see an ally so grossly deceived; full explanations, and precise assurances were immediately communicated; and as manifest error was the sole motive for these unexpected armaments, it was hoped that reflection would calm such turmoil which really lacked motive. However, the treaty signed at Paris was not ratified at Saint Petersburg; and communications and intelligence of various kinds were speedily forwarded to inform Prussia that the Marquis Lucchesini had received his knowledge from very suspect meetings in the capital with men of intrigue, with whom he habitually associated. As a result, he was recalled; it was announced that the Baron Knobelsdorf, a man of frank and open character, and of perfect morality, was appointed to succeed him.

This extraordinary envoy arrived shortly at Paris. He was the bearer of a letter from the King of Prussia, dated 13 August.

This letter, full of friendly terms and pacifying declarations, was answered by the Emperor in an unreserved and appropriate manner. The day following that of the departure of the courier with this answer, accounts were received that airs and songs of the most outrageous nature against France were sung in the theatre at Berlin; that immediately after the departure of Mr Knobelsdorf, the armaments had been redoubled, even though men with presence of mind would have blushed at these false reports, the war faction, blowing discord on all sides, had so exalted all the heads that the King himself could not resist the torrent.

We began to understand at that time at Paris that the party for peace had been alarmed by the lies and deceitful assurances, and had lost all its advantages, while the war faction, profiting from the error in which the adversaries had been thrown, had added provocation after provocation, and accumulated insult after insult; so that things had arrived to such a point that they could not come out of this situation except by war.

The Emperor saw then that such was the force of these circumstances that he could not avoid taking arms against his ally. He therefore ordered preparations.

Everything was happening in Berlin with great rapidity. The Prussian army entered Saxony. They arrived on the frontiers of the Confederation, and insulted the outposts.

On 24 September, the Imperial Guard left Paris for Bamberg, where it arrived on 6 October. Orders were issued for the army, and everything started to move.

The Emperor set out from Paris on 25 September; on the 28th he arrived at Mentz; on the 2nd of October, at Würzburg; and on the 6th, at Bamberg.

The same day, two shots were fired by the Prussian hussars at a French field officer, in view of the armies.

On the 7th, His Majesty the Emperor received a courier from Mentz, sent by the Prince of Bénévent with two important dispatches. One was a letter from the King of Prussia, containing 20 pages, which, in fact, was nothing but a paltry pamphlet against France, such as those produced by the writers of the English cabinet, at 500 pounds per annum! The Emperor did not finish reading it, turned to those around him and said, 'I pity my brother the King of Prussia; he does not hear the French. Surely, he cannot have read this rhapsody?' This letter was accompanied by the celebrated note of Mr Knobelsdorf. 'Marshal,' said the Emperor to Marshal Berthier, 'they give us a rendezvous of honour for the 8th. Never a Frenchman has missed it; but, as they say a beautiful Queen is there, who desires to see battle, let us be courteous, and march to Saxony without going to bed!' The Emperor was right to speak this way, for the Queen of Prussia is with the army, dressed like an Amazon, wearing the uniform of their regiment of dragoons, and writing 20 letters a day to excite incendiary feelings from all sides. He seems to see the confused Armide, setting fire to her own palace. Next to Her Majesty, Prince Louis of Prussia, a brave and courageous young man, incited by the war faction, vainly hopes to gain honour and renown in the vicissitudes of war.

Following the examples of those two great people, all the adherents of the court seem eager for war. But when war shall present itself in all its horrors, everyone will excuse themselves from having been culpable, and to have brought down the thunder of war upon the peaceable provinces of the north; then, by a natural consequence, we will see those who started the war not only find it nonsensical, but they will excuse themselves of having provoked it, saying they wanted it but in another time: but also to put the blame on the King, an honest man, who was merely the dupe of their own intrigues and artifices!

Here is the disposition of the French army:

The army must march from three positions. The right, consisting of the troops of Marshals Soult and Ney and a division of Bavarians, departed from Amberg and Nuremberg, united at Bayreuth, and then advanced on Hoff, where they arrived on the 9th.

The centre, composed of the reserve of the Grand Duke of Berg, the corps of the Marshal Prince of Ponte Corvo and Marshal Davout, and the Imperial Guard, advanced by Bamberg towards Kronach; it arrived on the 8th at Saalburg, and from there by Saalburg and Schleiz towards Gera.

The left, consisting of the corps of Marshals Lannes and Augereau, advanced from Schweinfurt towards Coburg, Grafenthal and Saalfeld.

Second Bulletin

Auma, 12 October 1806

The Emperor set out from Bamberg the 8th, at three o'clock in the morning, and arrived at Kronach at nine. His Majesty traversed the forest of Franconia at daybreak on the 9th, proceeded to Ebersdorf, and from there to Schleiz, where he was present at the first combat of the campaign. He returned to sleep at Ebersdorf; he proceeded on the 10th to Schleiz, and arrived the 11th at Auma, where he slept after passing the day at Gera. The headquarters leaves this instant to Gera.

All the orders of the Emperor have been most successfully executed.

On the 7th, Marshal Soult advanced to Bayreuth. On the 9th, he pushed on to Hoff, where he took possession of the enemy's magazines and took several prisoners. He advanced to Plauen on the 10th.

Marshal Ney followed his movement half a day behind him.

On the 8th, the Grand Duke of Berg advanced with the light cavalry from Kronach towards Saalburg; he was attended by the 25th Regiment of Light Infantry. A Prussian regiment appeared inclined to defend the crossing of the Saale; but after a cannonade of half an hour, apprehensive of being turned, it abandoned its position and the Saale. On the 9th, the Grand Duke of Berg advanced on Schleiz, where a Prussian general with 10,000 men was posted. The Emperor arrived at noon, and ordered the Prince of Ponte Corvo to attack and take possession of the village, wanting to have it before the end of the day. The Marshal did his planning and put himself at the head of his columns. The village was taken, and the enemy was pursued. Without the night, the biggest part of this division would have been taken. General Watier, with the 4th Regiment of Hussars and the 5th of Chasseurs, made a fine and spirited charge against three Prussian regiments. Four companies of the 27th Light Infantry, which were posted in a plain, were charged by the Prussian hussars, but these turned as the French infantry received the Prussian cavalry. Two hundred Prussian cavalrymen remained on the battlefield; General Maison commanded the French infantry. An enemy colonel was killed, two cannon taken, 300 men were taken prisoner and 400 men killed; our loss was just a few men. The Prussian infantry threw down their arms and fled, horrified, from the French bayonets! The Grand Duke of Berg led several of the charges, sword in hand.

On the 10th, the Prince of Ponte Corvo moved his headquarters to Auma. On the 11th, the Grand Duke of Berg arrived at Gera. General of Brigade Lasalle, of the cavalry of reserve, cut off an escort of the enemy's baggage; the French hussars captured 500 covered wagons and open carriages. Our light cavalry is covered with gold; the bridges' equipment and several important objects are part of the convoy.

The left wing has been equally successful. Marshal Lannes entered Coburg on the 8th, and went towards Grafenthal on the 9th. He attacked on the 10th at Saalfeld the advanced guard of Prince Hohenlohe, which was commanded by Prince Louis of Prussia, one of champions of the war. The cannonade only lasted two hours; it proceeded only with half of the division of General Suchet. The Prussian cavalry was overthrown by the 9th and 10th Regiments of Hussars. The Prussian infantry was unable to make an orderly retreat; part was overthrown in a marsh, the remainder was dispersed in the woods. We took 1,000 prisoners, 600 men remained on the battlefield, and we took 30 cannon. Upon seeing his people retreating, Prince Louis of Prussia, as a brave and loyal soldier, fought hand to hand with a sergeant of the 10th Regiment of Hussars. 'Surrender, Colonel,' said the hussar, 'or you are dead!' The Prince answered with a blow of his sabre. The sergeant responded by running him through the body, and the Prince fell dead. If the last instant of his life was that of a bad citizen, his death was glorious, and worthy of regret. He died as any good soldier desires to die. Two of his aides-de-camp were killed at his side. We found on him letters from Berlin, which showed that the project of the enemy was to attack immediately, and that the war faction, at the head of which were the Queen and the young Prince, had always feared the pacific intentions of the King, whose love for his subjects, they thought, would induce him to temporize, thereby foiling their cruel wishes. It may now be said the first blows of the war have killed one of its authors!

Neither Dresden nor Berlin is covered by an army. Turned on its left, caught red-handed at the moment when it committed itself to the most hazardous operations, the Prussian army, at the very outset, is placed in the most critical position. It occupies Eisenach, Gotha, Erfurt and Weimar. On the 12th, the French army occupied Saalfeld and Gera, and marches on Naumburg and Jena. Parties of light cavalry inundate the plains of Leipzig.

All the intercepted letters describe the councils of the King as distracted by conflicting opinions, always deliberating, never unanimous in decision. Uncertainty, alarm and terror seem already to succeed arrogance, inconsideration and folly!

Yesterday, the 11th, in passing through Gera in front of the 27th Regiment of Light Infantry, the Emperor charged the colonel to testify as to his satisfaction of the regiment regarding its good conduct.

In all these conflicts we have not to regret the loss of any officer of rank. The highest was Captain Campobasso, of the 27th Light Infantry, a brave and loyal officer. We have not had 40 killed and 60 wounded.

Third Bulletin

Gera, 13 October 1806

The battle of Schleiz, with which the campaign opened, and which has been very fatal to the Prussian army, and that of Saalfeld, which followed on the next day, have spread consternation among the enemy. All the intercepted letters say there was much alarm at Erfurt, where the King, the Queen, the Duke of Brunswick, etc., were consulting upon the measures that should be taken, without being able to agree. But while they are deliberating, the French army continues its march. To this spirit of effervescent and excessive boasting, critical observations begin to succeed upon the uselessness of the war; the injustice of taking it out on France; the impossibility of being assisted; the unwillingness of the soldiers, upon what they have not done; together with a thousand other observations, which are always in the mouths of the multitude, when princes are weak enough to consult them upon matters of great political interest which are above their reach.

However, on the evening of the 11th, the scouts of the French army were at the doors of Leipzig; the headquarters of the Grand Duke of Berg were between Zeitz and Leipzig; those of the Prince of Ponte Corvo at Zeitz; the imperial headquarters, with the Imperial Guard and the army corps of Marshal Soult at Gera, and the army corps of Marshal Ney at Neustadt. On the first line the army corps of Marshal Davout is at Naumburg; that of Marshal Lannes is at Jena; that of Marshal Augereau at Kala. Prince Jérôme, to whom the Emperor had confided the command of the allies, and of a corps of Bavarians, has arrived at Schleiz, after having blockaded the fort of Collembach with one of his regiments.

The enemy, cut off from Dresden, was still at Erfurt on the 11th, and endeavouring to collect his columns that he had sent towards Cassel and Würzburg, to take the offensive, wishing to open the campaign by an invasion in Germany.

The Weser, on which the enemy had raised batteries, the Saal, which it also pretended to defend, and the other rivers, are all turned much in the same manner as was practised on the Iller last year; so that the French army lines the banks of the Saal, with their rear towards the Elbe, and at the same time they are marching against the Prussian army, which has its rear towards the Rhine; a position so bizarre cannot fail to produce events of great importance.

The weather, since we commenced the present campaign, has been excellent, the country plentiful, and the soldiers full of vigour and health. We make marches of ten leagues without having a single straggler; and never was the army in a finer condition. However, the King of Prussia's intentions have been executed: he wished that the French army should evacuate the territory of the Confederation on 8 October, and they have evacuated it; but instead of re-crossing the Rhine, they have crossed the Saal.

Fourth Bulletin

Gera, 13 October 1806, ten in the morning

Events rapidly succeed each other. The Prussian army is taken by surprise, its magazines carried off, and it is turned. Marshal Davout arrived at Naumburg on the 12th at nine in the evening, where he seized the magazines of the enemy, some prisoners and got possession of a superb train of 18 copper pontoons, with their appendages. It appears that the Prussian army is marching to gain Magdeburg, but the French army has gained three marches on them.

The anniversary of the affair at Ülm will be celebrated in the history of France.

The annexed letter [not included here], which has been intercepted, will inform you of the real state of the public mind: but the battle, of which the Prussian officer speaks, will take place in the course of a few days, and the result of it will determine the fate of the war. The French should have no uneasiness respecting the result.

Fifth Bulletin

Jena, 15 October 1806

The battle of Jena has wiped away the disgrace of the battle of Rossbach, and in seven days concluded a campaign, which has wholly quieted all the dreadful preparations for war with which the Prussian heads were so much possessed.

The following was the position of the army on the 13th:

The Grand Duke of Berg and Marshal Davout were with their army corps at Naumburg, having parts at Leipzig and Halle.

The corps of Marshal Prince of Ponte Corvo was on the march to come up to Dörnberg.

The corps of Marshal Lannes advanced to Jena.

The corps of Marshal Augereau was in position at Kala.

The corps of Marshal Ney was at Rötha.

The headquarters were at Gera. The Emperor was on the march to proceed to Jena.

The corps of Marshal Soult was on the mach from Gera, to take a closer position on the intersection of the roads to Naumburg and Jena.

Here is the position of the enemy:

The King of Prussia wanted to start hostilities on 9 October by bearing down with his right wing on Frankfort, his centre on Würzburg, and his left on Bamberg. All the divisions of his army were disposed for the accomplishment of this plan; but the French army, turning on the extremity of its left wing, was found in a few days at Saalburg, at Lobenstein, at Schleiz, at Gera and at Naumburg. The Prussian army, seeing itself turned, occupied the days of the 9th, 10th, 11th and 12th in calling in its detachments; and, on the 13th, formed itself into order of battle between Kappelendorf and Auerstädt, being about 150,000 men strong.

On the 13th, at two o'clock in the afternoon, the Emperor came to Jena, and, on a small plateau that was occupied by our advanced guard, reconnoitred the positions of the enemy, which seemed to be manoeuvring to attack the next day, and to force the different passes on the Saal. The enemy made a vigorous opposition, and seemed by their dispositions, on an inaccessible position on the highway between Jena and Weimar, to think that the French could not debouch on the plain without previously forcing that passage. It did not appear possible, in fact, to bring the artillery to play on the plateau, which was so small that four battalions could scarcely open out their ranks on it. The men were set at work all night to make a road in the rock, and at length succeeded in bringing the artillery on the height.

Marshal Davout received orders to debouch by Naumburg and to defend the defiles of Kösen, if the enemy wanted to march on Naumburg, or to reach Apolda and fall on his rear, in case the enemy remained in the same situation it was.

The corps of Marshal Prince of Ponte Corvo was destined to debouch from Dörnberg, in order to fall on the rearguard of the enemy, whether it went in force towards Naumburg or whether it went towards Jena.

The heavy cavalry, which had not yet rejoined the army, could not be entirely brought on by midday. The cavalry of the Imperial Guard was at a distance of 36 hours march, no matter the heavy marches that it might have performed since it left Paris. But there are moments in war when no consideration should balance the advantage of being the first to attack the enemy. The Emperor placed on the plateau, which was occupied by the advance guard, which the enemy seemed to have neglected, and across from whom they were in position, all the corps of

Marshal Lannes. This corps was placed under the care of General Victor; each division formed a wing. Marshal Lefebvre ordered the Imperial Guard into a square battalion on the highest point. The Emperor camped in the midst of his brave men. The night presented a remarkable spectacle to observe: two armies light the air with their fires; one army is spread along a line of six leagues, while the fires of the other seemed to be brought into one small point; and in both armies there was a lot of activity and motion. The fires of the two armies were at half-cannon-shot distance from each other; the sentinels were almost touching, and there was not a single motion on either side that could not be heard from the other.

The corps of Marshals Ney and Soult spent the whole night marching. At daybreak all the army took arms. The Gazan division was in three lines on the left of the plateau. The Suchet division formed the right. The Imperial Guard occupied the summit of the plateau. Each of these corps had cannons between them. From the town and the neighbouring valleys we had made some openings that had allowed easier deployment for the troops which could not be positioned on the plateau; perhaps it was the first time that an army had to pass through such a small opening. A thick fog darkened the day. The Emperor passed in front of several lines. He advised the soldiers to stay ready against this Prussian cavalry that had been said to be so fearless. He told them to remember that it was only one year since they had taken Ülm, that the Prussian army, as the Austrian army, was today cornered, having lost its line of operation and its magazines; that it was no longer fighting at this moment for glory but for its retreat; that, looking to make a breakthrough at different points, the army corps that let it go by would lose its honour and reputation. Hearing this animated speech, the soldiers answered by shouting 'Let's march!' The skirmishers started the action. The fusillade became sharp. No matter how good the enemy position was, it lost it and the French army coming onto the plain started to organize itself for the battle. The biggest part of the enemy army, which would attack only once the fog had dissipated, took arms. A corps of 50,000 men on the left took position to cover the defiles of Naumburg and to take the openings of Kösen; but Marshal Davout had already anticipated this. The two other corps, a total of 80,000 men, brought themselves to the front of the French army that was coming from the plateau of Jena. The fog covered the two armies for two hours, but eventually dissipated and was replaced by a beautiful autumn sun. The two armies saw each other at a distance of a small cannon shot from each other. The left part of the French army was next to a village and some woods and was commanded by Marshal Augereau. The Imperial Guard separated it from the centre, which was occupied by the corps of Marshal Lannes. The right was formed by the corps of Marshal Soult: Marshal Ney had only a corps of 3,000 men which were the only troops of his army corps that had arrived. The enemy army was numerous and showed a large cavalry. Its manoeuvres were executed with precision and rapidity. The Emperor would have liked to have waited two more hours to start the battle, so that he could wait in the position that he had taken after the morning attack for the troops that were supposed to join him, most particularly his cavalry. But the French enthusiasm overtook him. Several battalions had already engaged at the village of Hollstedt. He saw the enemy start to move to repulse them. Marshal Lannes received orders right away to march at intervals to help the village. Marshal Soult had attacked some woods on the right. The enemy, having made a movement from its right on our left, Marshal Augereau then started to push them back. In less than an hour, the action became general: 300,000 men, with 700 or 800 cannon, were sowing death everywhere, and offered one of those very rare spectacles of history. From one part to another, they constantly manoeuvred as in a parade. Among our troops there was never any disorder. The victory was never uncertain for a moment. The Emperor always had near him, independent of the Imperial Guard, a good number of troops in reserve in order to take care of any unforeseen circumstance.

Marshal Soult having taken the woods that he had been attacking for two hours, made a move forward. At the same time, someone told the Emperor that the French reserve cavalry division was starting to move into position, and that two new divisions of the corps of Marshal Ney were being placed at the rear on the battlefield. All of the troops that were in reserve started to move to the front line, and, finding themselves supported in this position, overturned the enemy in the wink of an eye and sent it in full retreat. The retreat was orderly for the first hour. It became an awful disorder from the moment that our divisions of dragoons and cuirassiers, with the Grand Duke of Berg at their head, were able to take part in the whole affair. These brave cavalrymen, shaking from seeing the victory decided without them, threw themselves everywhere they encountered an enemy. The Prussian cavalry and infantry were unable to sustain the shock. In vain the enemy infantry formed into square battalions. Five of these battalions were destroyed. Artillery, cavalry, infantry: everything was overthrown and taken. The French arrived at Weimar at the same time as the enemy, which was pursued for six leagues.

On our right, the corps of Marshal Davout was really prodigious. Not only did he contain but also he beat for more than three leagues the biggest part of the enemy troops, which were supposed to come in on the side of Kösen. This marshal showed a distinguished bravery and strength of character that is the first quality of a man of war. He was seconded by Generals Gudin, Friant, Morand, Daultane, chief of staff, and by the rare intrepidity of his brave army corps.

The results of the battle are 30,000 to 40,000 prisoners; there are some coming in each moment; 25 to 30 flags, 300 cannon and some immense storehouses of sustenance. Among the prisoners there are more than 20 generals, some of them lieutenant generals, among them Lieutenant General Schmettau. The number of dead in the Prussian army is huge. We count that there are more than 20,000 killed or wounded; Field Marshal Mollendorf was wounded; The Duke of Brunswick was killed. General Rüchel was killed. Prince Henry of Prussia was mortally wounded. According to the deserters, the prisoners and the *parlementaires*, the confusion and consternation are extreme in what is left of the enemy army.

On our side we have only to regret among the generals the loss of General of Brigade Dehilly, an excellent soldier; among the wounded, General of Brigade Conroux; among the dead colonels, Colonel Vergès of the 12th Regiment of the Infantry of Line; Lamotte of the 36th; Barbanègre of the 9th of Hussars; Marigny of the 20th of the Chasseurs; Harispe of the 16th Light Infantry; Dulembourg of the 1st Dragoons; Nicolas of the 61st of the Line; Viala of the 81st; Higonet of the 108th.

The hussars and the chasseurs showed an audacity worthy of the biggest praises. The Prussian cavalry was unable to hold up in front of them, and all of the charges they did in front of the infantry were good ones.

We are not talking about the French infantry; it has been recognized for a long time that it is the best infantry in the world. The Emperor declared that the French cavalry, after the experience of the last two campaigns, and of this last battle, had no equal. The Prussian army has in this battle lost all retreat and all its lines of operations. Its left pursued by Davout, took its retreat on Weimar, at the same time that its right and its centre were leaving Weimar going towards Naumburg. The confusion was extreme. The King had to leave through the fields at the head of his cavalry regiment.

Our losses are evaluated at 1,000 or 1,100 killed and 3,000 wounded. The Grand Duke of Berg at this moment has moved to Erfurt where there is an enemy corps commanded by Marshal Mollendorf and the Prince of Orange.

The chief of staff is preparing an official account of the details of this battle and all the services rendered by the different army corps and regiments. If this can add a few things to the titles with which the army has the esteem and consideration of the nation, nothing could add to the tender sentiments that were felt by those who were witness to the enthusiasm and love that it gave to the Emperor at the heated part of the combat. If there had been one moment of hesitation, even the cry of 'Long live the Emperor!' would enliven the courage and determination of all the souls. At the highest point of the mêlée the Emperor, seeing that his flanks were menaced by the cavalry, galloped to order some manoeuvres to change the front into squares. He was interrupted often by cries of 'Long live the Emperor!' The Imperial Guard on foot could see with regret which was hard to hide that everyone was in the middle of the battle while it was totally inactive. Several voices cried 'Forward!' 'What is it?' said the Emperor, 'It could only be a young man who doesn't have a beard who would be so presumptuous as to think he knows what I should do. Let him wait. Let him have commanded 30 battles before giving me advice.' It was actually just some youth whose young courage was impatient to show itself.

In such a hot mêlée, while the enemy was losing all its generals, we must thank the providence that was helping our army. No high-ranking man was killed or wounded. Marshal Lannes had a sword that shaved his breast without wounding him. Marshal Davout had his hat taken off and a large number of shells in his clothes. The Emperor was always surrounded everywhere he went by the Prince of Neufchâtel, Marshal Bessières, the Grand Marshal of the Palace Duroc, the Grand Écuyer Caulaincourt, and of his aide-de-camp and *écuyers de service*. A part of the army still has not fought or is still without having fired their guns.

Sixth Bulletin

Weimar, 15 October 1806, evening

Six thousand Saxons, and more than 300 officers, have been taken prisoner. The Emperor assembled the officers and told them that he saw with pain that their army made war against him; that he had only taken up arms to assure the independence of the Saxon nation, and to prevent it from being incorporated with the Prussian monarchy; that his intention was to send them all home, if they would give him their word never to serve against France; that their sovereign, with whose good qualities he was well acquainted, had been extremely weak in thus ceding to the threats of the Prussians, and in letting them enter his territory; that all these doings must come to an end; that the Prussians must confine themselves to Prussia, and in no respect meddle with the affairs of Germany; that it behoved the Saxons to unite themselves with the Confederation of the Rhine, under the protection of France, a protection that was not new to them, seeing that for the space of two centuries, without France, they would have been invaded either by Austria or by Prussia; that the Emperor had taken up arms only when Prussia had invaded Saxony; that he needed to put an end to these aggressions; that the

Continent needed repose; and that, in spite of the intrigues and base passions that stirred several courts, it was necessary that repose exist, if necessary at the cost of the fall of some thrones.

Indeed, all the Saxon prisoners have all been sent home, with a proclamation from the Emperor to the Saxons, and with assurances that their nation was not considered as enemies. Attached is the declaration signed by the Saxon officers.

Declaration of the Saxon Officers

We, the undersigned general, colonels, lieutenant colonels, majors, captains and other Saxon officers, swear on our word of honour not to bear arms against His Majesty the Emperor of the French, King of Italy, and his allies, and we make the same oath and give the same pledges in the name of all the NCOs and soldiers who were taken prisoner with us, and mentioned in the attached list; even if we receive the formal order of our Sovereign the Elector of Saxony.

Jena, 15 October 1806
(The signatures follow)

Seventh Bulletin

Weimar, 16 October 1806

On the morning of the 15th, the Grand Duke of Berg surrounded Erfurt. On the 16th, the fortress capitulated. By this means, 14,000 men, of whom 8,000 were wounded and 6,000 able to bear arms, became prisoners of war, among whom are the Prince of Orange, Field-Marshal Mollendorf, Lieutenant General Larisch, Lieutenant General Graver, Major-Generals Lossow and Zweiszel. A park of 120 pieces of provisioned artillery has also fallen into our power.

Prisoners are being brought in daily.

The King of Prussia has sent an aide-de-camp to the Emperor, with an answer to the letter that the Emperor had written to him before the battle; but the King of Prussia answered only afterwards. The approach of the Emperor Napoleon was the same as that which he made to the Emperor of Russia before the battle of Austerlitz. He says to the King of Prussia 'The success of my arms is not uncertain. Your troops will be beaten, but it will cost me the blood of my children. If that can be spared by any arrangement compatible with the honour of my crown, there is nothing that I would not do to spare blood so precious. To my eyes, it is only honour which would be more precious than the blood of my soldiers.'

It appears that the remainder of the Prussian army has fallen back on Magdeburg. Of this immense and fine army, only the debris is gathered.

Eighth Bulletin

Weimar, 16 October 1806, evening

The different corps of the army that follow the enemy announce at each moment the taking of prisoners, baggage, artillery, magazines and munitions of every kind. Marshal Davout has just taken 30 cannon; Marshal Soult, a convoy of 3,000 tons of flour; Marshal Bernadotte, 1,500 prisoners. The enemy's army is so scattered and mixed with our troops that one of its battalions came into one of our camps, believing itself within its own.

The King of Prussia strives to reach Magdeburg. Marshal Mollendorf is very ill at Erfurt; the Grand Duke of Berg has sent him his physician.

The Queen of Prussia has been several times in view of our posts. She is in continual trances and alarms. The day before she had passed her regiment in review. She ceaselessly stirred up the King and the generals. She wanted blood: the most precious blood has been shed. The most outstanding generals are those who the first blows felled.

General of Brigade Durosnel, with the 7th and 20th of Chasseurs, has made a bold charge that has had the greatest effect. The Major of the 20th Regiment has distinguished himself in this. General of Brigade Colbert, at the head of the 4th Hussars and 12th Chasseurs, has made several charges on the enemy's infantry, which had the greatest success.

Ninth Bulletin

Weimar, 17 October 1806

The garrison of Erfurt has marched out, and many more people were found there than was at first thought. There is a great quantity of magazines in the fortress. The Emperor has named General Clarke Governor of the city and citadel of Erfurt, and the neighbouring country. The citadel of Erfurt is a fine octagon, bastioned with casements and well armed. This is a precious acquisition that will serve as a support point in the middle of our operations.

In the 5th Bulletin it was said that we had taken from 25 to 30 flags. There are already 45 at headquarters. It is probable that there will be more than 60. These are the flags given by Frederick the Great to his soldiers. Those of the regiment of the Guard, those of the regiment of the Queen, hand-embroidered by this princess, are found in this number. It appears that the enemy wishes to collect its force at Magdeburg, where we are now marching from all sides. The different corps of the army are in its pursuit by different routes. Couriers arrive every moment announcing that some entire battalions are cut off, some pieces of artillery taken, some baggage, etc.

The Emperor is lodged at the Palace of Weimar, where the Queen of Prussia lodged several days before. It appears that what is said of her is true. She is a woman with a very pretty figure but little spirit, incapable of seeing the consequences of what she does. It is necessary today, rather than accusing her, to feel sorry for her because she ought to have great remorse for the evils that she has done to her country and for the influence that she has exercised on her husband the King, whom one must present as a perfectly honest man who wishes for peace and the well-being of his people.

Tenth Bulletin

Naumburg, 18 October 1806

Among the 60 flags that had been taken at the battle of Jena are found several belonging to the King of Prussia's Guards, and one belonging to the bodyguards, upon which the caption is written in French.

The King of Prussia has request an armistice for six weeks. The Emperor answered that it was impossible, after a victory, to give the enemy time to rally.

The Prussians, however, have so industriously spread the report, that a great many of our generals having met them, believed that his armistice had been concluded.

Marshal Soult arrived at Greussen on the 16th, in pursuit of the column where the King was, which is estimated to be 10,000 or 12,000 men strong. General Kalkreuth, who commanded it, had Marshal Soult told that an armistice had been concluded. This Marshal replied that it was impossible that the Emperor had made that error; that he would believe in this armistice when it had been officially announced to him. General Kalkreuth expressed his desire to see Marshal Soult, who went to the advanced post. 'What do you want of us,' the Prussian general said to him, 'the Duke of Brunswick is dead; all our generals are killed, wounded, or taken; the greatest part of our army is in flight; your successes are rather great. The King has requested a suspension of arms, it is impossible that your Emperor should not grant it.' 'General,' answered Marshal Soult, 'for a long time we have been treated thus. People appeal to our generosity when they are vanquished, and forget, the moment after, the magnanimity that we have been accustomed to show. After the battle of Austerlitz, the Emperor granted an armistice to the Russian army; this armistice saved the army. Observe the unworthy manner in which the Russians act today. It is said that they wish to return: we burn with impatience to see them again. If there had been as much generosity among them as among us, they would have left us to remain at peace at last, after the moderation that we have shown in victory. We have in no way provoked the unjust war that you wage against us. You have declared it with gaiety of heart. The battle of Jena has decided the fate of the campaign. Our profession is to do you all the injury we can. Lay down your arms, I will await in that situation the orders of the Emperor.' The old General Kalkreuth saw that he had nothing to say in reply. The two Generals separated, and hostilities recommenced the moment after: the village of Greussen was taken, and the enemy routed and pursued with the sword at its back.

The Grand Duke of Berg, and Marshals Soult and Ney should, during the days of the 17th and 18th, reunite by combined movements, and crush the enemy. They will, without doubt, have rounded up a considerable number of deserters; the plains are covered with them, and the roads are encumbered with carriages and baggage of every sort.

Never was there a greater victory signalized by greater disasters. The reserve, commanded by Prince Eugene of Württemberg, has arrived at Halle. Thus we are only at the ninth day of the campaign, and already the enemy is obliged to put forward its last resource. The Emperor marches towards it: it will be attacked tomorrow if it remains in its position at Halle.

Marshal Davout has gone today to take possession of Leipzig, and throw a bridge over the Elbe. The Imperial Guard on horse has at last joined us.

Independently of considerable storehouses found at Naumburg, a great number have been found at Weissenfels.

General-in-Chief Rüchel has been found in a village, mortally wounded; Marshal Soult has sent him his surgeon. It appears as if it were a decree of Providence that all those who have pushed this war have been struck by the first blows.

Eleventh Bulletin

Merseburg, 19 October 1806

The number of prisoners that have been taken at Erfurt is more considerable than one would have believed. The passports given to officers who are to return home on parole, in virtue of one of the articles of capitulation, has mounted to 600.

The corps of Marshal Davout took possession of Leipzig on the 18th.

The Prince of Ponte Corvo, who was at Eisleben on the 17th to cut off some Prussian columns, having learned that the reserve of His Majesty the King of Prussia, commanded by Prince Eugene of Württemberg, had arrived at Halle, marched there. After having made his dispositions, the Prince of Ponte Corvo caused Halle to be attacked by General Dupont, and left the division Drouet in reserve on his left: the 32nd and 9th Regiments of Light Infantry crossed the three bridges at the charge, and entered the city, supported by the 96th. In less than an hour, the enemy was completely routed. The 2nd and 4th Regiments of Hussars, and the whole division of General Rivaud, traversed the city and chased the enemy from Dienitz, from Peissen and from Rabat. The Prussian cavalry endeavoured to charge the 8th and 96th Regiments of Infantry, but it was vigorously received and repulsed.

The reserve of the Prince of Württemberg was most completely routed and pursued for the space of four leagues.

The results of this combat, which merit a particular and careful detail, are 5,000 prisoners, of whom two are generals, and three colonels, four flags and 34 cannon.

General Dupont conducted himself with a great deal of distinction.

General of Division Rouyer has had a horse killed under him.

General of Division Drouet has taken the entire regiment of Treskow.

On our side the loss amounts only to 40 men killed and 200 wounded. The Colonel of the 9th Regiment of Light Infantry has been wounded.

General Léopold Berthier, major chief-of-staff to the Prince of Ponte Corvo, has comported himself with distinction.

As the result of the combat of Halle, there are no more of the enemy's troops that have not suffered.

The Prussian General Blücher, with 5,000 men, has passed through the divisions of dragoons of General Klein, which had cut him off. Having alleged to General Klein that an armistice had been concluded for six weeks, that General had the simplicity to believe him.

The ordinance officer near the Emperor, Montesquiou, who had been sent with as a parliamentary to the King of Prussia two days before the battle, has returned. He had been carried away for several days with the enemy deserters. He depicts the disorder of the Prussian army as inexpressible. Nevertheless, on the eve of the battle their boasting was unequalled. The question was about nothing less than to cut off the French army, and to take from it columns of 40,000 men. The Prussian generals aped, as much as they could, the manners of Frederick the Great.

Although we are in their country, the generals appeared to be in the most complete ignorance of our movements. They believed that on the little plateau of Jena there were no more than 4,000 men; however, the greatest part of the army had debouched on that plateau.

The enemy's army retreats in considerable force on Magdeburg. It is probable that several columns will be intercepted before it arrives here. No news has been received for several days from Marshal Soult, who has been detached with 40,000 men to pursue the enemy army.

The Emperor has crossed the field of the battle of Rossbach. He has ordered that the pillar that had been erected there should be transported to Paris. The headquarters of the Emperor were, on the 18th, at Merseburg. On the 19th, he will be at Halle. Very considerable magazines of every kind have been found in the latter city.

Twelfth Bulletin

Halle, 19 October 1806

Marshal Soult has pursued the enemy as far as the gates of Magdeburg. Several times the Prussians endeavoured to take a position, and were always routed.

Considerable stores have been found at Nordhausen, and even a wagon of the King of Prussia, filled with silver.

During the five days that Marshal Soult has been employed in the pursuit of the enemy, he has taken 1,200 prisoners, and taken 30 cannon, and from 200 to 300 wagons.

The first object of the campaign has been accomplished. Saxony, Westphalia and all the countries situated on the left bank of the Elbe are delivered from the presence of the Prussian army. That army, beaten and pursued with the sword at its back for more than 30 leagues, is today without artillery, without baggage, without officers, reduced below a third of that which it was eight days ago; and, what is still worse than that, it has lost its morale and all confidence in itself.

Two corps of the French army are on the Elbe, occupied in constructing bridges.

The headquarters are at Halle.

The following letter that has been intercepted contains a strong detailed picture of the situation of the Prussians after the battle of Jena.

Translation

My Very Dear Spouse,

I am still alive and feeling well after having assisted in the unhappy battle. But, alas, I can not stop myself from telling you that we have lost half our army as well as our better generals. My battalion conducted itself perfectly under fire; but it has lost its cannon in the retreat. My company alone has lost 40 men and Lieutenant Schweidnitz. If I wanted to give you a glimpse of all our misfortune, it would take me an infinite time. All the baggage of our army corps has been taken at Weimar; we have not even been able to save our domestics.

I arrived in the evening of the 16th at Nordhausen, horseless and deprived of everything. The army is in full retreat on Magdeburg. His Royal Majesty has received a strong contusion; however, he is bearing up well. You can tell Schuberten that her eldest son has been killed, and that no one knows what has become of the other, as well as Jarusch, Michalzeck and Joseph Tyralla. We are missing in addition five NCOs, four musicians, three artillerymen and two sappers, as well as all of the grenadiers. Jablonouski has lost all his people, Fontanius the same. They are all naked as worms. Only one major was able to keep a horse. Several generals are killed. We are missing Sanitz and Malchitz. The Duke of Brunswick has lost both eyes from a musket shot. Rüchel and Winning are dead. A lot of the regiments are without officers; others have officers and no soldiers. Our loss is immense. One no longer distinguishes the corps: everything is pell-mell. The battalions of Lostin, Borck and Grodana no longer exist. They made up part of the rearguard, which has been entirely hacked to pieces. One can not have any idea of the furious energy with which the French have pursued us. You can write to me at the army corps at Magdeburg.

Nordhausen, 17 October 1806

Thirteenth Bulletin

Halle, 20 October 1806

General Macon, commander at Leipzig, has given to the bankers, merchants and traders of that city the attached notification. Since the tyrants of the seas will not respect any flag, it is Emperor's intention to seize all their merchandise and to truly blockade them in their island.

There were found in the military magazines of Leipzig 15,000 quintals of flour and a great quantity of other types of provisions.

The Grand Duke of Berg arrived at Halberstadt on the 19th. On the 20th, he inundated the whole plain of Magdeburg with his cavalry, even to the mouth of the cannon. The enemy's troops, consisting of isolated detachments, the lost men, will be taken at the moment they will present themselves to enter the place.

A regiment of the enemy's hussars believed that Halberstadt was still occupied by the Prussians; it has been charged by the 2nd Hussars, and has sustained a loss of 300 men.

General Beaumont has taken 600 men of the King's Guard, and all the equipment of that corps. Two hours before, two companies of the Royal foot Guards had been taken by Marshal Soult.

Lieutenant General Count Schmettau, who had been taken prisoner, has just died at Weimar.

Thus of this fine and superb army, which a few days ago threatened to invade the Confederation of the Rhine, and which inspired its sovereign with such confidence that he dared to order the Emperor Napoleon to leave Germany before 8 October if he did not want to be constrained by force, of this fine and superb army, we say, there remains only debris and unformed chaos which merits more the name of a mob than that of an army. Of 160,000 men whom the King of Prussia had, it would be difficult to gather more than 50,000, and those without artillery and without baggage, partly armed, and partly disarmed. All these events justify what the Emperor said in his first proclamation, when he expressed himself thus: 'Let them learn that if it is easy to acquire an increase of lands and of power with the friendship of a great people, its enmity is more terrible than the tempests of the ocean.'

Nothing, indeed, resembles more the present state of the Prussian army than the debris of a shipwreck. It was a fine and numerous fleet, which pretended to nothing less than to sweep the seas; but the impetuous north winds have raised the ocean against it. There only returns to port a small part of the crews, who have only found salvation by saving themselves on some debris.

The attached letters truly depict the situation of affairs.

Another letter, also attached, shows in what respect the Prussian cabinet was duped by false appearances. It took the moderation of the Emperor Napoleon for weakness. Because that monarch did not wish for war, and did everything reasonable to avoid it, it was concluded that he was not prepared, and that he had need of 200,000 conscripts to recruit for his army.

The French army, however, was no longer cooped up in the camps of Boulogne; it was in Germany. Mr Charles-Louise Hesse and Mr Haugwitz would have been able to count it. Let us recognize then the will of that Providence that has not left to our enemies the eyes to see, the ears to hear, the judgement and the ability to reason.

It appears that Mr Charles-Louise Hesse coveted only Mayence. Why not Metz? Why not the other places west of France? Don't tell us any longer that the ambition of the French forced you to take up arms; confess that it is your own ill-judged ambition that has excited you to war. Because there was a French army in Naples, and another in Dalmatia, you planned to fall on the great people, but in seven days your plans have been confounded. You wished to attack France without running any risk, and already you have ceased to exist.

It is stated that the Emperor Napoleon, having, before he left Paris, assembled his ministers, said to them, 'I am innocent of this war; I have done nothing to provoke; it did not enter my calculations. Let me be defeated if it is of my making. One of the principal motives of the confidence which I have that my enemies will be destroyed is that I see in their conduct the finger of Providence, who, wishing that traitors may be punished, has so far set aside all wisdom in their councils, that when they think to attack me in moment of weakness, they chose the moment when I am the strongest.'

Fourteenth Bulletin

Dessau, 22 October 1806

Marshal Davout arrived on the 20th at Württemberg, and surprised the bridge on the Elbe at the moment when the enemy was setting fire to it.

Marshal Lannes is arrived at Dessau; the bridge was burnt; he immediately put men to work to repair it.

Marquis Lucchesini presented himself at the advanced posts with a letter from the King of Prussia. The Emperor sent the Grand Marshal of his Palace, Duroc, to confer with him.

Magdeburg is blockaded. General of Division Legrand, on his march against Magdeburg, captured some prisoners. Marshal Soult has his posts round the city. The Grand Duke of Berg sent there his Major Chief of Staff, General Belliard. This general saw the Prince of Hohenlohe there. The language of the Prussian officers was greatly changed. They loudly demanded peace. 'What does your Emperor want?' they say to us, 'Will he always pursue us with the sword in our backs? We have not a moment's rest since the battle.' These gentlemen were doubtless accustomed to the manoeuvres of the Seven Years War. They requested three days to bury their dead. 'Think of the living,' answered the Emperor, 'and leave to us the care of burying the dead, there is no need of a truce for that.'

Confusion is extreme in Berlin. All the good citizens who groaned at the false direction given to the policy of their country justly reproach the firebrands excited by England, with the sad effects of their leadership. There is only a cry against the Queen in all the country.

It appears that the enemy is seeking to rally behind the Oder.

The Sovereign of Saxony has thanked the Emperor for the generosity with which he has treated him, and which is going to wrest him from Prussian influence. However, a good number of his soldiers have perished in all this confrontation.

The headquarters on the 21st was at Dessau.

Fifteenth Bulletin

Wittenberg, 22 October 1806

Here is the information we have collected concerning the causes of this strange war.

General Schmettau, (dead, a prisoner at Weimar), drew up a memoir, written with much force, in which he established that the Prussian army ought to regard itself as dishonoured; that it was, however, in a state to beat the French; and that it was necessary to make war. General Rüchel (killed) and Blücher (who only saved himself by a subterfuge, and by abusing the French good faith) subscribed to this memoir, which was drawn up in the form of a petition to the King. Prince Louis Ferdinand of Prussia (killed) supported it by every type of sarcasm. The flame spread through every head. The Duke of Brunswick (wounded very grievously), a man known for being without discretion and without character, was enrolled in the war faction. At last, the memoir, thus supported, was presented to the King. The Queen undertook to position the spirit of this prince, and to make known to him what was thought of him. She reported to him that it was said that he was not brave, and that if he did not make war, it was because he was afraid of putting himself at the head of his army. The King, really as brave as any Prussian prince, gave way, without giving up his private opinion that he was making a big mistake.

We should single out the men who did not share illusions of the war partisans. These are the respectable Field Marshal Mollendorf and General Kalkreuth.

We are assured that after the fine charge of the 9th and 10th Regiments of Hussars at Saalfeld, the King said, 'You pretended that the French cavalry was worth nothing; see, nevertheless, what the light cavalry is doing; and judge what the cuirassiers will do. These troops have acquired their superiority by 15 years of combat. We would have to have as many to become their equal; but who among us could be so much the enemy of Prussia as to desire this terrible proof?'

The Emperor, already master of all the communications and stores of the enemy, wrote, on the 12th of this month the attached letter that he sent to the King of Prussia by the ordinance officer Montesquiou.

This officer arrived at four in the afternoon of the 13th at the quarters of General Hohenlohe, who kept him there and took the letter of which he was the bearer. The King of Prussia's camp was two leagues behind. That Prince should therefore have received a letter of the Emperor at no later than six in the evening. We are, however, assured, that he did not receive it until nine o'clock in the morning on the 14th; that is to say, when the battle was already begun.

It is also reported that the King of Prussia said then 'If this letter had arrived sooner, perhaps we might not have fought; but these young men have their heads so raised, that if it had been a question of peace yesterday, I should not have led back a third of my army to Berlin.' The King of Prussia had two horses killed under him, and he received a musket ball in his sleeve.

The Duke of Brunswick has had all the blame in this war. He has ill conceived and ill directed the movements of the army. He believed the Emperor was at Paris, when he found them on his flanks; he thought to have the lead in the movements, and he found himself already turned.

As for the rest, on the day before the battle, there was already consternation among the chiefs. They perceived that they were ill posted, and that they were going to play the last gamble of the monarchy. They all said, 'Well! We shall pay in person,' the common sentiments of men who preserve little hope.

The Queen was always to be found at the headquarters at Weimar. It was necessary at last to tell her that circumstances were serious, and that on the morrow great events for the Prussian monarchy could occur. She was desirous that the King should bid her to go away, and in effect she was reduced to the necessity of going away.

Lord Morpeth, sent by the court of London to haggle over the Prussian blood, (a mission really unworthy of a man like him) arrived on the 11th at Weimar, charged to make seducing offers and to propose considerable subsidies. The horizon was already very cloudy. The cabinet was not willing to see this envoy; it told him that there was little safety for his person, and it encouraged him to return to Hamburg, there to await events. What would the Duchess of Devonshire have said, had she seen her son-in-law charged with spreading the flame of war, and coming to offer poisoned gold, obliged to retrace his steps sadly in great haste? One can only be indignant to see England thus compromise some estimable agents, and play a role so odious.

We have as yet no news of a treaty between Prussia and Russia, and it is certain that up to now no Russian has appeared on Prussian territory. In other respects, the army strongly desires to see them: they will find Austerlitz in Prussia.

Prince Louis Ferdinand of Prussia and the other generals who have succumbed to the first French blows are today designated as the principle driving forces of this incredible frenzy. The King, who has taken all the chances in it and who supports all the misfortunes that have resulted from it, is, of all the men led by her, the one who remained the most uninvolved.

There is at Leipzig such a quantity of English goods that 60 millions have been already offered to redeem them.

One may ask what will England gain by all this? She might have recovered Hanover, kept the Cape of Good Hope, preserved Malta, made an honourable peace and restored tranquillity to the world. She was willing to excite Prussia against France, to push the Emperor and France to the end. Well! She has conducted Prussia to her ruin, procured the greatest glory for the Emperor, and the greatest power to France; and the time approaches when we may declare England in a state of Continental blockade. Is it then with blood that the English hoped to feed their commerce and revive their industry? Great mischief may come upon England. Europe will attribute to them the loss of that minister, an honest man, who wanted to govern by great and liberal ideas, and for whom the English will one day weep with tears of blood.

The French columns are already marching on Potsdam and Berlin. Deputies from Potsdam have arrived to request protection.

The Imperial Headquarters is today at Wittenberg.

Sixteenth Bulletin

Wittenberg, 23 October 1806

The Duke of Brunswick has sent his Marshal of the Palace to the Emperor. That officer was entrusted with a letter, in which the Duke recommended his states to the protection of His Majesty.

The Emperor said to him, 'If I were to demolish the city of Brunswick, and if I did not leave one stone upon another there, what would your Prince say? Does not the law of retaliation authorize me to do at Brunswick what he wanted to do in my capital? To announce a plan to demolish cities may be insane; but to attempt to deprive a whole army of brave men of their honour, to ask him to leave Germany by daylong marches only at the warning of the Prussian army, that would be something that posterity would find hard to believe. The Duke of Brunswick never should have permitted such an outrage. When one has grown grey under arms, one ought to respect the honour of military men; moreover, it was not in the plains of Champagne that this general had been able to acquire the right to treat the French flags with such contempt. Such a warning dishonours only the soldier who makes it. That dishonour does not belong to the King of Prussia; it attaches to the chief of his military council, to the general to whom, in these difficult circumstances, he had confided his affairs; in the end it is the Duke of Brunswick alone whom France and Prussia can accuse of the war. The frenzy with which that old general set the example encouraged a set of turbulent young men, and led the King contrary to his own thought and personal conviction. However, sir, tell the inhabitants of the country of Brunswick that they will find the French generous enemies; that I wish to soften the rigours of war with regard to them; and that the trouble that the passage of troops could occasion will be against my inclination. Tell General Brunswick that he shall be treated with all the attention due to a

Prussian officer, but that I cannot recognize a sovereign in a Prussian general. If it happens that the House of Brunswick loses the sovereignty of its ancestors, it can only be ascribed to the author of two wars, who in one war would have sapped the great capital to its foundation, and who in the other attempted to dishonour 200,000 brave men, who perhaps might be conquered, but who would never be surprised out of the path of honour and glory. Much blood has been shed in a few days; great disasters weigh upon the Prussian monarchy. How blameable is the man, who by a single word might have prevented them! If, like Nestor, bringing up a word in the midst of the councils, he had said, 'Be silent, ye inconsiderate youth; women, return to your spindles and to the management of your domestic concerns!' And you, Sire, believe the companion of the most illustrious of your predecessors; since the Emperor Napoleon does not wish for war, do not place him in the alternative of war or dishonour; do not engage yourselves in a dangerous contest with an army that boasts of 15 years spent in glorious labours, and that victory has accustomed to every sacrifice. Instead of holding this language, which agreed so well with the prudence of his years and with the experience of so long a career, he has been the first to rise the cry 'To arms!' he has even been faithless to the ties of blood, in arming a son against his father; he has threatened to place his flags on the palace of Stuttgart, and to accompany those proceeding with invectives against France: he was declared the author of that insane manifesto, which he has denied for these 14 years, although he could not deny that he had given it the sanction of his signature.'

It has been remarked that during this conversation the Emperor, with that warmth with which he is often animated, often repeated, 'To overturn and destroy the habitations of peaceable citizens is a crime which can be repaired by time and money; but to dishonour an army, to wish that it should fly from Germany before the Prussian eagle, is a baseness that none but the person who advised it could be capable of committing.'

Mr Lucchesini is always at the headquarters. The Emperor has refused to see him, but it is observed that he has frequent conferences with the Grand Marshal of the Palace, Duroc.

The Emperor has ordered to make a present from the great quantity of English cloth that has been found at Leipzig, of a complete set of clothes to each officer and of a greatcoat and a morning coat to each soldier.

The headquarters is at Kropstadt.

Seventeenth Bulletin

Potsdam, 25 October 1806

The corps of Marshal Lannes arrived at Potsdam on the 24th.

Marshal Davout's corps entered Berlin on the 25th, at ten in the morning.

The corps of Marshal Prince of Ponte Corvo is at Brandenburg. Marshal Augereau's corps will enter Berlin tomorrow, the 26th.

The Emperor arrived at Potsdam yesterday, and entered the palace. In the afternoon he went to inspect the new palace, Sans-Souci, and the positions around Potsdam. He found the location and the layout of the château of Sans-Souci very pleasant. He stayed some time in the chamber of Frederick the Great, the hangings and furniture of which are the same now as at the time of his death.

Prince Ferdinand, the brother of the great Frederick, remains at Berlin.

There are 500 pieces of artillery in the arsenal of Berlin, several thousand weight of powder, and a great quantity of arms.

General Hulin is named Governor of Berlin.

General Bertrand, aide-de-camp to the Emperor, has gone to Spandau; the fortress is defended; he has manned it with the dragoons of the Dupont division.

The Grand Duke of Berg has gone to Spandau to pursue a Prussian column that marches from Spandau to Stettin, and which we hope to cut off.

Marshal Lefebvre, commander of the Imperial Guard on foot, and Marshal Bessières, commander of the Imperial Guard on horse, have arrived at Potsdam on the 24th, at nine o'clock in the evening. The Imperial Guard on foot has made 14 leagues in one day.

The Emperor is staying all day the 25th at Potsdam.

Marshal Ney's corps is blockading Magdeburg.

Marshal Soult's corps crossed the Elbe a day's journey from Magdeburg, and followed the enemy to Stettin.

The weather continues to be superb; it is one of the most beautiful autumns that one has seen.

In route, the Emperor, having gone from Wittenberg to Potsdam on horseback, has been surprised by a storm and stopped at the house of the Grand *Veneur* of Saxony. His Majesty was very surprised to hear himself called by his name by a lovely woman; she was an Egyptian, the widow of a French officer of the army of Egypt, and who has been in Saxony for three months; she has been living at the home of the Grand *Veneur* of Saxony who had welcomed her and treated her honourably. The Emperor has given her a pension of 1,200 Francs and has taken it upon himself to find a position for her child. 'It's the first time,' said the Emperor, 'that I stopped for a storm; I had a premonition that a good action awaited me here.'

It is remarked as unusual that the Emperor Napoleon arrived at Potsdam and entered into the same apartment, the same day, and almost the same hour as the Emperor of Russia at the time of the voyage that this prince made last year, which has been so fatal to Prussia. It is from this moment that the Queen left the care of her interior affairs and the grave occupations of the dressing table to meddle in the affairs of state, to influence the King and to spark off everywhere the fire with which she had been possessed.

The sane part of the Prussian nation regards this trip as one of the greatest misfortunes that has befallen Prussia. One can have no idea of the activity of the Prussian faction to carry the King to war in spite of himself. The result of the celebrated oath, taken on the tomb of Frederick the Great on 4 November 1805, was the battle of Austerlitz and the evacuation of Germany by the Russian army by forced marches. Forty-eight hours after this event, a plate was engraved on this subject that one sees in every shop, and which makes even the peasants laugh. One sees on it the fine Emperor of Russia, near him the Queen, and on the other side the King, raising his hand over the tomb of the Great Frederick; the Queen herself, draped in a shawl, much in the same manner as the London engravers represent Lady Hamilton, rests her hand on her heart, looking at the Emperor of Russia. One cannot conceive how the police of Berlin could allow such a pitiful satire to be disseminated.

At any rate, the shade of the great Frederick could only have been indignant at this scandalous scene. His genius, his spirit and his wishes were with the nation that he so much esteemed, and of which he said 'If he was their King, a cannon-shot should not be fired in Europe without his permission.'

Eighteenth Bulletin

Potsdam, 26 October 1806

The Emperor reviewed the Foot Guard, composed of 10 battalions and 60 artillery pieces, served by the horse artillery. These troops, which have felt so many fatigues, had the same uniforms as on parade in Paris.

At the battle of Jena, General of Division Victor received a shell, which gave him a contusion. He has been obliged to keep to his bed for several days. General of Brigade Gardane, aide-de-camp of the Emperor, has had a horse killed and has been lightly wounded. Some superior officers have been wounded, others have had horses killed, and they rival each other in their courage and zeal.

The Emperor has been to see the tomb of Frederick the Great. The remains of this great man are enclosed in a wooden coffin, covered with copper. It is placed in a vault, without any ornaments, trophies or any distinctions to recall his great actions.

The Emperor has presented to the *Hôtel des Invalides* at Paris the sword of Frederick, the ribbon of his Order, the Black Eagle, his general's belt, and also the flags that his Guard carried in the Seven Years War. The old invalids of the army of Hanover will welcome, with a religious respect, all that belonged to one of the premier captains of whom history conserves the remembrance.

Lord Morpeth, the English envoy to the Prussian cabinet, found himself during the day of Jena only six leagues from the battlefield. He heard the cannon. A courier soon came to announce to him that the battle was lost, and in a moment he was surrounded by deserters who pushed him from all sides. He ran away, exclaiming, 'I must not be taken.' He offered 60 guineas for a horse; he obtained one, and saved himself.

The citadel of Spandau, three leagues from Berlin and four from Potsdam, strong because of its placement in the midst of water, having a garrison of 1,200 men, and a great quantity of ammunition and provisions, was surrounded in the night of the 24th. General Bertrand, the Emperor's aide-de-camp, had already reconnoitred the place. The cannon were placed to hurl shells and to intimidate the garrison. Marshal Lannes had the commandant sign the attached capitulation.

Large magazines of tents, clothing, etc., have been found at Berlin; we are employed in taking inventories.

Marshal Soult pursues a column commanded by the Duke of Weimar. It presented itself the 23rd before Magdeburg; our troops have been there since the 20th. It is probable that this column, 15,000 men strong, will be cut off and taken. Magdeburg is the first rendezvous point of the Prussian troops. Many of the corps are returning there. The French are blockading them.

A letter from Helmstedt, recently intercepted, contains curious details. It is attached.

The Princes of Hatzfeld, Busching (the superintendent of the police), the President of Kircheisen, Formey (a privy councillor), Mr Polzig (councillor of the municipality), Messrs Ruck, Sieger, and Hermensdorf (councillors sent as deputies from the city of Berlin) have this morning delivered the keys of the city of Berlin to the Emperor at Potsdam. They were accompanied by Mr Groote (privy councillor of finances) and the Barons Vichnitz and Eckarlstein. They have said that the noises that had been spread concerning the spirit of this city were false, that the middle class and the mass of people had seen the war with pain; that a handful of women and of young officers alone had made this racket. There was not a single sensible man who had not seen what one had to fear and who could divine what one had to hope. Like all the Prussians, they accuse the trip of the Emperor Alexander for the misfortunes of Prussia. The change that has been worked in the spirit of the Queen, who from a timid and modest woman occupied with her household, has become turbulent and war-like, has been a sudden revolution. She has suddenly wanted to have a regiment, to go to council, and she has led the monarchy so well that in a few days she has brought it to the brink of a precipice.

The headquarters is at Charlottenburg.

Nineteenth Bulletin

Charlottenburg, 27 October 1806

The Emperor, having left Potsdam today at noon, has been to visit the fortress of Spandau. He has given his orders to General of Division Chasseloup, commander of the engineers of the army, on the improvements to be made the fortifications of this fortress. It is a superb work; the magazines are magnificent. Wheat, grain and oats to feed the army for two months, and munitions to double the provision of the artillery were found at Spandau. This fortress, situated on the Sprée at two leagues from Berlin, is an invaluable acquisition. In our hands it will sustain two months of siege. If the Prussians have not defended it, it was because the commander had not received an order and that the French arrived there at the same time as the news of the lost battle. The batteries were not assembled and the fortress was disarmed.

To give an idea of the extreme confusion that prevails in this monarchy, it is sufficient to say that the Queen, upon her return from her ridiculous and sad trips to Erfurt and Weimar, spent the night at Berlin without seeing anyone; that the people have been for a long time without any news of the King; that no one has provided for the safety of the capital, and that the middle class have been obliged to meet to form a provisional government.

Indignation is at its height against the authors of the war. The manifesto, which the people of Berlin call a scandalous libel in which no grievance has been articulated, has whipped up the nation against the author, a miserable scribe named Gentz, one of those men without honour who sell themselves for money.

Everybody is witness that the Queen is the author of the difficulties that the Prussian nation suffers. Everywhere we hear it said, 'A year ago she was so good, so sweet; but since that fatal meeting with the Emperor Alexander how she has changed!'

There had been no order given in the palaces, so that the sword of the great Frederick, the belt that he wore during the Seven Years War and his ribbon of the Black Eagle, were found at Potsdam. The Emperor took these trophies with eagerness, saying, 'I would rather have these than 20 million.' Then thinking a moment of to whom he would entrust the precious deposit: 'I shall send these to my old soldiers war of Hanover, I will make a gift of them to the governor of the *Hôtel des Invalides*; they will remain there.'

There was found in the apartment that the Queen occupied at Potsdam the portrait of the Emperor of Russia, which that prince had presented to her. There was found at Charlottenburg her correspondence with the King covering the period of three years, together with some memoirs written by English authors to prove that nations were under no obligation to observe any treaty made with the Emperor Napoleon, but to turn itself completely on the side of Russia. These documents, above all, are historical documents; they demonstrate, if it needs demonstration, how unfortunate princes are when they allow women to have influence on political affairs. The notes, reports and state papers were scented with musk, and were found mixed with scarves and other objects on the dressing table of the Queen. This princess had turned the heads of all the women in Berlin; but today they have been very changed. The first deserters have been received badly; with irony one reminds them of the day they sharpened their sabres on the squares of Berlin wanting to kill everyone and to cut down everything.

General Savary, sent with a detachment of cavalry to seek the enemy, has informed us that Prince Hohenlohe, compelled to leave Magdeburg, was, on the 25th, between Rathenau and Ruppin, retreating to Stettin.

Marshal Lannes was already at Zehdenick; it is probable that the remains of the enemy will not escape without being attacked.

This morning a corps of Bavarians was to enter Dresden; but we have not yet received any news on the subject.

Prince Louis Ferdinand, who had been killed in the first affair of the campaign, was publicly nicknamed the Little Duke of Orleans at Berlin. This young man abused the King's goodness to the point of insulting him. It was he who, at the head of a troop of young officers, went to the house of Mr Haugwitz when that minister came back from Paris, and broke his windows. One does not know whether one ought to be more astonished by such audacity or by such weakness.

A great part of that which had been directed from Berlin to Magdeburg, and to the Oder, has been intercepted by the light cavalry. More than 60 boats loaded with clothing, meal and artillery have already been stopped. There are some regiments of hussars that have more than 500,000 Francs. There is an account that they have exchanged their gold for money at a loss of 50 per cent.

The palace of Charlottenburg, where the Emperor resides, is situated one league from Berlin, upon the Sprée.

Twentieth Bulletin

Charlottenburg, 27 October 1806

As the military movements are no longer uncertain, they are still more interesting, by the contrivances of marches and manoeuvres. The indefatigable Grand Duke of Berg was at Zehdenick on the 26th, at three o'clock in the afternoon, with a brigade of light cavalry under General Lasalle, while the division of dragoons, under the Generals Beaumont and Grouchy, were marching to the same point.

The brigade under General Lasalle contained the enemy, who opposed it with 6,000 cavalry. This was all of the cavalry of the Prussian army who, having abandoned Magdeburg, formed the advanced guard of Prince Hohenlohe's corps, directing their march towards Stettin. At four in the afternoon, when both divisions of the dragoons had arrived, the brigade of General Lasalle attacked the enemy with its usual intrepidity, which has always formed the character of the French hussars and jaegers in this campaign. The enemy's line, though formed three deep, was broken; it was pursued into the village of Zehdenick, and thrown into confusion in the defiles. The Queen's Regiment of Dragoons endeavoured to re-form, but the dragoons of Grouchy's division soon showed themselves, charged the enemy, and made a horrible carnage among them. A part of these 6,000 cavalry were driven into the marshes; 300 remained upon the field; 700 with their horses were taken prisoner; the colonel and a great number of officers of the Queen's Regiment are part of this number. The flag of the regiment was taken. Marshal Lanne's corps is in full march to support the cavalry. The cuirassiers are marching in columns on the right, and another army corps is advancing towards the Gransee. We will arrive at Stettin before this army, which, attacked in its march in the flank, is already overwhelmed by its head. Demoralized as it is, there is reason to hope that not nothing will escape, and that all of that part of the Prussian army, which lost two days without any advantage at Magdeburg, in order to collect themselves, will not be able to reach the Oder.

This combat of the cavalry of Zehdenick has its own interest as a martial achievement; neither party had any infantry; the events of this campaign have proved that it could not hold its own against forces less than half their number.

One of the adjuncts of the general staff, taken prisoner by the enemy in Thuringia as he was carrying orders to Marshal Mortier, was conveyed to Custrin, where he saw the King. He says that very few fleeing men had arrived on that side of the Oder, either there or at Stettin or at Custrin; he scarcely saw any infantry.

Twenty-first Bulletin

Berlin, 28 October 1806

Yesterday, the 27th, the Emperor made his solemn entry into Berlin. He was attended by the Prince of Neufchâtel, Marshals Davout and Augereau, his Grand Marshal of the Palace, his great Écuyer, and his aides-de-camp. Marshal Lefebvre opened the march at the head of the Imperial Guard on foot; the cuirassiers of Nansouty's division were drawn up in order of battle along the road. The Emperor marched between the grenadiers and chasseurs on horse of his Imperial Guard. At three in the afternoon he arrived at the palace, where he was received by Grand Marshal of the Palace Duroc. An immense crowd had assembled along the road. The avenue from Charlottenburg to Berlin is very good, and the entrance through the gate was superb. It was a most beautiful day. All of the civil administration, presented by General Hulin, Commandant of the fortress, came to offer the keys of the city to the Emperor. This body then went to His Majesty's residence. General Prince Hatzfeld was at their head.

The Emperor gave the order that the 2,000 richest middle class get together at the city hall to name 60 among them who would make up the municipal corps. The 20 cantons will furnish a guard of 60 men each, which will add up to 1,200 of the richest middle class to guard the city and police it. The Emperor said to the Prince of Hatzfeld, 'Do not present yourself before me, I am in no need of your services; go back to your own land.' He received the chancellors and the ministers of the Prussian King.

On the 28th, at nine in the morning, the ministers of Bavaria, of Spain, of Portugal and the Porte, who were in Berlin, were admitted to an audience of the Emperor. He told the minister of the Porte to send a courier to Constantinople to inform his court of what had taken place, and to declare that now the Russians would not enter Moldavia, nor undertake anything against the Ottoman Empire. Afterwards His Majesty received all of the Protestant and Calvinist clergy. There are more than 10,000 or 12,000 French refugees at Berlin, whose predecessors took refuge there in consequence of the Edict of Nantes. His Majesty told them that they had just rights to his protection, and that their privileges and their cult would be maintained. His Majesty advised them to concern themselves with their own affairs, to remain peaceable, and pay obedience and respect to Caesar.

The Courts of Justice were presented by the Chancellor. His Majesty conversed with the members of the Courts of Appeal, and informed himself as to the manner in which justice was being rendered.

The Count of Néale presented himself into the room of the Emperor. His Majesty told him, 'Well, Sir, your ladies wished for war, and here is the result: it becomes you to manage your household better.' Letters had been intercepted from the Count's daughter. 'Napoleon,' said these letters, 'does not want to go to war, let others carry on the war against him.' 'No,' said His Majesty to Count Néale, 'I do not want war. Not that I doubt my prowess, as you have suggested, but because the blood of my people is precious to me, and because my first duty is to not spill it except for their honour and safety. The people of Berlin are victim of the war, while those who have excited it have left them, and have become deserters. I shall reduce those noble courtiers to such extremities that they shall be compelled to beg for their bread.'

While trying to convey his intentions to the municipal corps, 'I hear,' said the Emperor, 'that we break the windows of no one. My brother the King of Prussia ceased to be a King since the day he did not have Prince Louis Ferdinand hanged, when he was daring enough to break the windows of his ministers.'

Today, the 28th, the Emperor mounted his horse to review Marshal Davout's corps. Tomorrow His Majesty will review Marshal Augereau's corps.

The Grand Duke of Berg and Marshals Lannes and the Prince of Ponte Corvo are in pursuit of the Prince of Hohenlohe. After the gallant affair with the cavalry at Zehdenick, the Grand Duke of Berg advanced to Templin, where he found a great quantity of provisions and the dinners prepared for the Prussian generals and their troops.

At Gransee, Prince Hohenlohe changed his route, and took the road to Fürstenberg. It is probable that, being cut off from the Oder, he will be surrounded and taken prisoner.

The Duke of Weimar is in a similar situation with respect to Marshal Soult. This Duke seems to wish to cross the Elbe at Tangermünde, in order to approach the Oder. On the 25th, Marshal Soult warned him. If he is caught, not a man will escape; if he succeeds in crossing the Oder, he will fall into the hands of the Grand Duke of Berg, Marshal Lannes and the Prince of Ponte Corvo. A part of our troops are on the Oder. The King of Prussia has crossed the Vistula.

Count Zastrow was presented to the Emperor on the 27th, at Charlottenburg, and delivered a letter from the King of Prussia.

At this same moment the Emperor receives an aide-de-camp from Prince Eugène who announces a victory over the Russians in Albania.

Here is the proclamation the Emperor made to his soldiers.

Proclamation to the Army
Imperial Camp at Potsdam, 26 October 1806
Soldiers! You have justified my expectations, and worthily answered the confidence of the French people.

You have supported privations and fatigues with as much courage as you have shown intrepidity and coolness in the mist of combat. You are the worthy defenders of the honour of my crown and of the glory of the great people. As long as you are animated with this spirit, nothing will be able to withstand you. The cavalry have vied with the infantry and artillery; I no longer know to which branch I ought to give preference; you are all good soldiers.

These are the results of our labours: one of the premier military powers of Europe, which so lately dared to propose to us a shameful capitulation, is annihilated. The forests and defiles of Franconia, the Saal and the Elbe, which our fathers would not have crossed in seven years, we have crossed in seven days, and fought in the interval four engagements and a great battle. We have preceded at Potsdam and Berlin the renown of our victories. We have taken 60,000 prisoners, taken 65 flags, among which are those of the King of Prussia's Guards, 600 cannon, 3 fortresses and more than 20 generals. However, almost half of you regret having not yet fired a musket shot. All the provinces of the Prussian monarchy as far as the Oder are in our power.

Soldiers, the Russians boast of coming to us. We will march to meet them, and thus spare them half the trip. They shall again find Austerlitz in the heart of Prussia. A nation which has so soon forgotten the generosity we showed it after that battle, in which its emperor, court and the wreck of its army owed their safety to the capitulation we accorded them, is a nation which does not know how to fight against us successfully.

Nevertheless, while we march to meet the Russians, new armies, formed in the interior of the Empire, come to take our place, in order to keep our conquests. All my entire people have risen, indignant at the shameful capitulation that the Prussian ministers, in their delirium, proposed to us.

Our roads and our frontier towns are full of conscripts who burn to march in our footsteps. Henceforth we will be no longer be the sport of a treacherous peace, and we will not lay down our arms until we have obliged the English, those eternal enemies of our nation, to renounce both the scheme of disturbing the Continent and the tyranny of the seas.

Soldiers, I can no better express to you the sentiments that I have, than to tell you that I carry in my heart for you the love you show me every day.

NAPOLEON

Twenty-second Bulletin

Berlin, 29 October 1806

Events succeed each other with rapidity. The Grand Duke of Berg arrived at Hasleben on the 27th with a division of Dragoons. He had sent General Milhaud to Boitzenburg, with the 13th Regiment of Chasseurs, and the brigade of light cavalry under Lasalle, to Prentzlow. Informed that the enemy was in force at Boitzenburg, he went off to Wichmansdorf. He had scarcely arrived there when he perceived that a brigade of the enemy's cavalry had gone to the left, with the intention of cutting off General Milhaud. To see them, charge them and throw the King's gendarmes into the lake was the affair of one moment. This regiment, believing itself lost, asked to capitulate. The Prince, at all times generous, granted their wish. Five hundred men alighted and delivered up their horses. The officers returned home on their parole. Four flags belonging to the Guard, all of gold, were the trophies of the small engagement of Wichmansdorf, which was only the prelude to the splendid one of Prentzlow.

These celebrated gendarmes, who experienced such great commiseration after their defeat, were the same who, for three months, excited riots in the city of Berlin by every sort of provocation. They went under the windows of Mr Laforest, the French minister, to sharpen their sabres; sensible people shrugged their shoulders; but the inexperienced youth and passionate women like the Queen saw in this ridiculous swaggering a sure prognostic of the great destinies which awaited the Prussian army.

Prince Hohenlohe, with the wrecks of the battle of Jena, attempted to reach Stettin. He had been obliged to change his route because the Grand Duke of Berg was at Templin before him. He wished to debouch from Boitzenburg on Hasleben. But he was deceived in his movement. The Grand Duke of Berg imagined that the enemy would endeavour to reach Prentzlow; the conjecture was well founded. The

Prince marched all night with the division of dragoons under Generals Beaumont and Grouchy, which was preceded by the light cavalry under the command of General Lasalle. The first posts of our hussars arrived at Prentzlow at the same time as the enemy, but they had to fall back on the 28th in the morning, upon facing the superior forces deployed by Prince Hohenlohe. At nine, the Grand Duke of Berg arrived at Prentzlow, and at ten saw the enemy's army in full march. Without losing time in vain motions, the Prince ordered General Lasalle to charge in the suburbs of Prentzlow, and sent to support him Generals Grouchy and Beaumont, with their six pieces of light artillery. He gave orders for three regiments of dragoons to cross over the small river of Golnitz, which leads to Prentzlow, to attack the enemy's flank, and gave directions to his other brigade of dragoons to turn the town. Our brave cannoneers on horseback placed their pieces so well, and fired with such assurance, that they rendered uncertain the enemy's motions. At this moment General Grouchy received orders to charge, and his brave dragoons did so with the greatest intrepidity. Cavalry, infantry, artillery, all were overthrown in the suburbs of Prentzlow. Our troops might have entered the town pell-mell with the enemy, but the Prince preferred sending him a summons by General Belliard. The gates of the town were already burst open. Deprived of all hope, Prince Hohenlohe, one of the principal firebrands of this impious war, capitulated, and passed before the French army with 16,000 infantrymen, almost all guards or grenadiers, six regiments of cavalry, 45 flags, and 64 pieces of harnessed artillery. All the King of Prussia's guards who had escaped from the battle of Jena have fallen into our power. We are in possession of all the flags of the King's horse and foot guards. Prince Hohenlohe, Commander-in-Chief after the wounding of the Duke of Brunswick, a Prince of Mecklenburg Schwerin, and several generals are our prisoners.

'But nothing is done, while there remains anything to be done,' wrote the Emperor to the Grand Duke of Berg. 'You have outstripped a column of 8,000 men commanded by General Blücher; let me soon learn that they have experienced the same lot.'

Another 10,000 men have crossed the Elbe, commanded by the Duke of Weimar. According to all appearances, both he and his whole column will be surrounded.

Prince Augustus Ferdinand, brother to Prince Louis, killed at Saalfeld, and son of Prince Ferdinand, brother of the Great Frederick, has been taken by our dragoons, sword in hand.

Thus this great and fine Prussian army has disappeared, like an autumnal fog at sunrise. Generals-in-chief, generals commanding the army corps, princes, infantry, cavalry, artillery: none remain. Our advance guard has entered Frankfurt on the Oder; the King of Prussia has gone further. He has not 15,000 men left; and for such a result, we have scarcely met with any loss.

General Clarke, Governor of Erfurt, has made a Saxon battalion capitulate, which was wandering without direction.

On the 28th, the Emperor reviewed the corps of Marshal Davout, under the walls of Berlin. He has filled all the vacancies and rewarded the brave. He then assembled the officers and petty officers in a circle, and addressed them: 'Officers and petty officers of the 3rd Corps of the army, you covered yourselves with glory at the battle of Jena: I shall preserve the eternal memory of it. The brave men who were killed died with glory. We ought to wish to die under such glorious circumstances.' In reviewing the 12th, 61st and 85th Regiments of Line, who felt the greatest loss in this battle, as it fell on them to make the greatest efforts, the Emperor was affected at seeing killed, or grievously wounded, many of his old soldiers whose devotion and bravery he was acquainted with for 14 years past. The 12th Regiment, above all, has shown intrepidity worthy of the highest praise.

Today, at twelve o'clock, the Emperor reviewed the 7th Corps, commanded by Marshal Augereau. This corps has suffered very little. One half of the soldiers have not had an occasion to fire a shot, but they all had the same intrepidity. The appearance of this corps was magnificent. 'Your corps alone,' said the Emperor, 'is stronger than all that remains to the King of Prussia, and you do not compose a tenth of my army!'

All the unmounted dragoons whom the Emperor has caused to come to the *Grande Armée* are now mounted, and there are at the grand depot at Spandau 4,000 horses saddled and bridled, which we do not know what to do with, because there are no horsemen in want of any. We wait with impatience for the arrival of the depots.

Prince Augustus was presented to the Emperor at the palace of Berlin, after the review of the 7th Corps of the army. The Prince was sent home to his father, Prince Ferdinand, to rest and get his wounds dressed.

Yesterday, before going to review the corps of Marshal Davout, the Emperor paid a visit to the widow Princess of Prince Henri, to Prince and Princess Ferdinand, who have always been noted for the distinguished manner in which they have received the French.

In the palace where the Emperor stays at Berlin is the sister of the King of Prussia, electorate Princess of Hesse-Cassel. This princess is pregnant. The Emperor gave orders to his Grand Marshal of the Palace to take care she be not disturbed with the noise and bustle of the headquarters.

The last Bulletin relates the manner in which the Emperor received the Prince of Hatzfeld at his audience. A few moments after, the Prince was arrested. He would have been sent before a military commission, and inevitably condemned to death. Some letters from this prince to Prince Hohenlohe, intercepted at the advanced posts, had given information that, although he said he was charged with the civil government of the town, he informed the enemy of the movements of the French. His wife, the daughter of minister Schulenburg, came to throw herself at the feet of the Emperor; she thought her husband was arrested on account of the hatred that the minister Schulenburg bore to France. The Emperor soon dissuaded her of this belief, and made known to her that papers had been intercepted that proved that her husband was acting a double part, and that the laws of war were strict on such a thing. The Princess was given to believe that her enemies had lied. 'You know the writing of your husband,' said the Emperor, 'I am letting you be the judge.' He had the intercepted letter brought to him and gave it to her. This woman, more than eight months pregnant, fainted with each word that showed her how much her husband was compromised and whose writing she recognized. The Emperor was touched by her pain, her confusion, and the anguish that tore her apart. 'Well!' he told her, 'You hold this letter, throw it in the fire; with this piece destroyed I will no longer be able to have your husband condemned.' (This touching scene was happening by the fireplace.) Madame Hatzfeld did not wait for him to tell her a second time. Immediately after, the Prince of Neufchâtel received orders to give her back her husband. The military commission was already formed. Only the letter of Mr Hatzfeld could condemn him: three hours later, and he would have been shot.

Twenty-third Bulletin

Berlin, 30 October 1806

The Duke of Weimar crossed the Elbe at Havelberg. Marshal Soult proceeded on the 29th to Rathnau, and on the 30th to Wüsterhausen.

On the 29th, the column of the Duke of Weimar was at Rheinsberg, and Marshal Prince of Ponte Corvo was at Fürstenberg. There is no doubt that these 14,000 men either have already fallen or are falling at this moment into the power of the French army. General Blücher also left Rheinsberg in the morning of the 29th with 7,000 men to proceed to Stettin, but Marshal Lannes and the Grand Duke of Berg had three days march in advance of him. This column has fallen into our power, or will fall into it in less than 48 hours.

In the last bulletin, we gave an account that in the matter of Prentzlow, the Grand Duke of Berg had made the Prince of Hohenlohe and his 17,000 men lay down their arms. On the 29th, an enemy column of 6,000 men likewise surrendered into the hands of General Milhaud at Pasewalk. This gives us 2,000 saddled and bridled horses along with some sabres. There are now more than 6,000 horses that the Emperor has at Spandau, after having mounted all his cavalry.

Marshal Soult, having arrived at Rathnau, came across five squadrons of Saxon cavalry that have asked to surrender. He made them sign the attached capitulation. This means 50 more horses for the army.

Marshal Davout has crossed the Oder at Frankfort. The Bavarian and Württemberg allies, under the orders of Prince Jérôme, are marching from Dresden to Frankfort.

The King of Prussia has left the Oder and has crossed the Vistula; he is at Graudenz. The places of Silesia are without garrisons and without provisions. It is probable that the fortress of Stettin will not be slow in falling into our power. The King of Prussia is without army, without artillery, without muskets. It is an exaggeration to evaluate at 12,000 or 15,000 men that he will have been able to gather on the Vistula. Nothing is as strange as his movements at this moment. It is a kind of hunt where the light cavalry, which lies in wait for the army corps, is constantly diverted by the enemy columns that are cut off.

We have taken, up to this hour, 150 flags, among which are some hand-embroidered by the beautiful queen, a beauty as fatal to the people of Prussia as Helen was to the Trojans.

The police of the [Prussian] Guard have crossed Berlin to be returned prisoners at Spandau. The people who have seen them so arrogant a few weeks ago have seen them completely humiliated.

The Emperor today ordered a great parade which lasted from eleven this morning to six this evening. He has seen in detail all his foot and horse Guard and the regiments of carabiniers and cuirassiers of the Nansouty division; he has made different promotions, taking everything into account in the greatest detail.

General Savary, with two regiments of cavalry, has already reached the corps of the Duke of Weimar and put in place communication to transmit information to the Grand Duke of Berg, to the Prince of Ponte Corvo and to Marshal Soult.

We have taken possession of the states of the Duke of Brunswick. It is believed that the Duke has taken refuge in England. All his troops have been disarmed. If this prince has justly merited the hatred of the French people, he has also incurred that of the Prussian people and army: of the people, who accuse him of being one of the authors of the war; of the army, which complains of his manoeuvres and of his military conduct. The errors in calculation of the young gendarmes are pardonable; but the conduct of this old Prince, 72 years old, is an excess of delirium and catastrophe to him would not excite any regrets. How respectable can age be if the boasting and inconsiderations of youth are joined to the frailties of age?

Twenty-fourth Bulletin

Berlin, 31 October 1806

Stettin is in our power. While the left wing of the Grand Duke of Berg's corps, commanded by General Milhaud, forced a Prussian column of 6,000 men to put down their arms at Pasewalk, the right wing commanded by General Lasalle, commanded the town of Stettin to surrender, and imposed on it the attached capitulation. Stettin is a town in a good state of defence, well armed and provided with palisades. One hundred sixty cannon, considerable magazines, a garrison consisting of 6,000 fine troops taken prisoner, many generals: such is the result of the capitulation of Stettin, which can only be explained by the extreme discouragement which the destruction of the great Prussian army has produced on the Oder, and over all the territory on the right bank of that river.

Of that whole fine army of 180,000 men, none of it crossed the Oder. All have been taken prisoner, killed, or still wander between the Elbe and the Oder, and will be taken before four days are up. The number of prisoners will climb to nearly 100,000 men. It is unnecessary to dwell on the importance of the taking of the town of Stettin, which is one of the most commercial towns in Prussia, and which secures to the army a fine bridge on the Oder and a fine line of operations.

As soon as the columns commanded by the Duke of Weimar and General Blücher, which are cut off on the right and left and pursued on the rear, shall surrender, the army will take a few days rest.

Nothing has yet been learned respecting the Russians. We long much to see 100,000 of them arrive, but the reports of their march we are afraid are mere noise; they dare not meet us. The battle of Austerlitz is still before their eyes. But what bothers the people of good sense is to hear the Emperor Alexander and his directing senate declare that it was the allies who were defeated. It is well known over all Europe that there is hardly a family in Russia that does not mourn, and it is not merely the loss of their allies they deplore. Besides, 195 pieces of Russian artillery that were taken and are now at Strasburg were not the cannon of their allies. The 50 Russian flags that are hung up on the church of Notre Dame at Paris are not the flags of their allies. The crowds of Russians who died in our hospitals or are imprisoned in our towns were not the soldiers of the allies.

The Emperor Alexander, who commanded so great an army at Austerlitz and Wischau, and who displayed so much ostentation, did not, it seems, command the allies. The Prince who capitulated and bound himself to evacuate Germany by forced marches, was doubtless no allied prince. We can only shrug our shoulders when we hear such things. Such, however, are the consequences of the weakness of princes, and the corruption of ministers. It would have been a more plain and a more honourable course for the Emperor Alexander, had he ratified the treaty of peace which his plenipotentiary signed, and thereby given repose to the Continent. The longer the war continues, the more the illusion of the power of Russia will vanish, and it will end by being annihilated: it was the wise policy of Catherine to produce a great impression by the display of her power, and she succeeded no less in that object than the present ministers, with their extravagant efforts and folly, succeed in rendering the influence of Russia ridiculed in Europe.

On the 21st, the King of Holland arrived with the advanced guard of the army of the north at Gottingen On the 26th, Marshal Mortier arrived at Fulda, with the two divisions of the 8th Corps of the *Grande Armée*, commanded by Generals Lagrange and Dupas.

At Munster, in the country of Main and in other Prussian states, the King of Holland found magazines and artillery. At Fulde and at Brunswick, the arms of the Prince of Orange and of the Duke have been removed. Neither of these princes will reign again. They were the principal instigators of this new coalition.

The English would make no peace; they will make it, but France will include more coasts and states in her federal system. Here is the report that the Prince of Hohenlohe addressed to the King of Prussia after the capitulation of his army corps, and which has been intercepted. [This report is not included.]

Twenty-fifth Bulletin

Berlin, 2 November 1806

Today General Beaumont presented to His Majesty the Emperor 50 new flags and standards recently taken from the enemy. He rode through the principal streets of the town with his dragoons whom he commands, bearing these trophies of victory. The number of flags taken since the battle of Jena amounts, at this moment, to 200.

Marshal Davout surrounded and summoned Custrin, and the fortress surrendered, and 4,000 prisoners have been taken there. The officers return home on their parole, but the soldiers are to be sent to France: 90 pieces of artillery were found on the ramparts. This fortress, which was in very good shape, is situated in the middle of the marsh, and possessed considerable magazines. It is one of the most important conquests of the army; it gives us the command of all the places on the Oder.

Marshal Ney is about to attack Magdeburg, and it is probable that that fortress will not make much resistance.

On the 31st, the Grand Duke of Berg had his headquarters at Friedland. It appears from his manoeuvres that he intends to attack the column commanded by the Prussian General Bilon. General Beker had an action with General Boussart's brigade of dragoons on a plain in the front of the little town of Anklam. The enemy, both cavalry and infantry, was thrown into complete confusion, and General Becker came into the town with the enemy, whom he forced to capitulate. The result of this capitulation has been 4,000 prisoners of war; the officers were dismissed on their parole, and the soldiers were forwarded to France. Among the prisoners we found the Regiment of the Hussars of the King's Guard, who, after the Seven Years War, were presented with tigerskin cloaks by the Empress Catherine as a mark of her approbation of the conduct of that corps.

The military chest belonging to General Bilon's corps, and a part of its baggage, had been removed over the Penne, and were on the territory of Swedish Pomerania. The Grand Duke of Berg demanded this property.

On 1 November, in the evening, the Grand Duke had his headquarters at Dimnin.

General Blücher and the Duke of Weimar, being cut off from Stettin, made a movement to the left as if to return on the Elbe, but Marshal Soult had anticipated this manoeuvre, and there is no doubt but that both corps will fall into our hands.

The Marshal has concentrated his army corps at Stettin, where more cannon and magazines are found every day.

Our scouts have already entered Poland.

Prince Jérôme, with an army formed of the Bavarian and Württemberg troops, proceeds to Silesia.

His Majesty has appointed General Clarke Governor-General of Berlin and of all Prussia, and has already laid down the principles according to which the internal government of the country is to be administered.

The King of Holland advances on Hanover, and Marshal Mortier on Cassel.

Twenty-sixth Bulletin

Berlin, 3 November 1806

We have not yet received the news of the taking of the columns of General Blücher and the Duke of Weimar. Here is the situation of these two enemy divisions and that of our troops. General Blücher, with his column, directed himself on Stettin. Having learned that we were already in that town and that we had gained two marches on him, he fell back from Gransee where we were arriving at the same time as he was, on Neustrelitz, where he arrived on 30 October without stopping there, and directing himself on Wharen, where we suppose he arrived the 31st, with the project of looking to pull back on the side of Rostock, to embark there.

On the 31st, six hours after his departure, General Savary, with a column of 600 horses, arrived at Strelitz where he has taken prisoner the Prussian Queen's brother, who is general at the service of the King.

On 1 November, the Grand Duke of Berg was at Demmin, where he was hurrying to arrive at Rostock and cut General Blücher off from the sea.

Marshal the Prince of Ponte Corvo had gone beyond General Blücher. This marshal, on the 31st, was with his army corps at Neubranderberg, and was starting to march on Wharen, which exposed him to General Blücher during the day of the 1st.

The column commanded by the Duke of Weimar had arrived on 29 October at Neustrelitz; but knowing that the road to Stettin was cut off and having met the French advanced guard, he withdrew on the 29th towards Wistock. On the 30th, Marshal Soult had learned this from the hussars and was starting to march on Wertenhausen. He could not help but to meet him on the 31st or the 1st. These two columns were taken yesterday or today at the latest.

Here are their forces. General Blücher has 30 cannon, 7 battalions of infantry and 1,500 cavalrymen. It is difficult to evaluate the force of this corps; its equipment, its wagons, its munitions were all taken. He is in a pitiful situation.

The Duke of Weimar has 12 battalions and 35 squadrons in good shape, but he does not have one piece of artillery.

Such are the feeble debris of all of the Prussian army. There will be nothing left of it. These two columns taken, the power of Prussia is annihilated, and it has almost no soldiers left. If we evaluated at 10,000 men the number that retired with the King on the Vistula, it would be greatly exaggerating.

Mr Schullermburg presented himself at Strelitz to ask for a passport to Berlin. He said to General Savary: 'It has been eight hours since I saw passing in front of me the debris of the Prussian monarchy; you will have them today or tomorrow. What inconceivable destiny this is! Lightning has struck us.' It is true that since the Emperor has entered the campaign he has not taken a moment to rest. He is always in forced marches, constantly guessing the movements of the enemy. The result is such that there is no example like it in history. Of more than 150,000 men who presented themselves at the battle of Jena, not one escaped to take the news beyond the Oder. Certainly, never was an aggression more unjust, never was war more untimely. May this example serve as a lesson to the feeble princes who instigate them; the cries and gold of England always excite nonsensical enterprises.

The Bavarian division commanded by General Wrede left from Dresden on 31 October. The one commanded by Deroy left on 1 November. The Württemberg column left on the 3rd. All these columns are headed towards the Oder; they form the army corps of Prince Jérôme.

General Durosnel was sent to Ödenburg with a unit of cavalry, immediately after we entered Berlin, to intercept all that would escape through the canal to the Oder. He has taken more than 80 boats full of munitions of all sorts that he sent to Spandau.

We found at Custrin some magazines of rations sufficient to feed the army for two months.

General of Brigade Macon, whom the Emperor had named commandant of Leipzig, died in this town of a putrid fever. He was a perfectly honest man. The Emperor was very distressed by his death.

Twenty-seventh Bulletin

Berlin, 6 November 1806

We found at Stettin a great quantity of English merchandise at the warehouse on the Oder; we found 500 cannon and some magazines with a considerable amount of rations.

On 1 November the Grand Duke of Berg was at Demmin and on the 2nd at Teterow, having his right on Rostock. General Savary was at Kratzeburg on the 1st, and at Warren and at Jabel very early on the 2nd. The Prince of Ponte Corvo attacked on the night of the 1st at Jabel, the enemy's rearguard. The combat was very sustained; the enemy's corps was often put into disorder; he would have been entirely taken if the lakes and the difficulty in passing the town of Mecklenburg had not saved it again that day. The Prince of Ponte Corvo, while charging with the cavalry, fell off his horse but did not get hurt. Marshal Soult arrived at Plau on the 2nd.

And so the enemy gave up on going to the Oder. Every day it changes its projects: seeing that the road to the Oder was closed to it, the enemy tried to retire on Swedish Pomerania; seeing this movement also intercepted, it wanted to return on the Elbe; but, Marshal Soult having anticipated it, it seems to take the direction toward the closed point of the coast. It must have been reaching the end by the 4th or 5th of November. Meanwhile, every day one or two battalions and even some squadrons of this column fall into our power. It no longer has any wagons or baggage.

Marshal Lannes is at Stettin.

Marshal Davout at Frankfort.

Prince Jérôme in Silesia.

The Duke of Weimar has left the command to return home, and left it to an unknown general.

Today the Emperor passed in review the division of dragoons of General Beaumont, on the square of the palace of Berlin; he has made several promotions.

All of the cavalrymen who were on foot went on to Potsdam, where we sent them some horses. General of Division Bourcier was charged with the direction of this large depot. Two thousand foot dragoons who were following the army are already mounted.

We work actively at arming the fortress of Spandau and to re-establish the fortifications of Wittenberg, of Erfurt, of Küstrin and of Stettin.

Marshal Mortier, who commands the 8th Corps of the *Grande Armée*, started his march on Cassel on 30 October. He arrived there on the 31st. Here is a note that the *chargé d'affaires* of France has presented to the Prince 24 hours ago. Here is also the proclamation that was made by Marshal Mortier. The Prince of Hesse Cassel, Marshal in the service of Prussia, and his son, a general in the same service, have withdrawn from it. The Prince, in answer to the note that was transmitted to him, requested permission to march at the head of his own troops, along with the French army, against our enemies. Marshal Mortier replied that he had no orders regarding such a proposition; but that the Prince having armed, after the declaration which had been made at Paris to Mr Malsbourg, his minister, the least further armament on his part would be considered as an act of hostility, as the Prussians had not violated his territories, but on the contrary were received with pomp by the Hereditary Prince; and that since they had evacuated Cassel following the military actions, it was only upon hearing the news of the battle of Jena that the armaments ceased at Cassel; and that truth be known, the Hereditary Prince was more desirous of marching at the head of Prussian troops, and to insult the French by all sorts of provocation.

He will pay for his frenzied conduct by the loss of his states. There is not a house in all Germany that has been so uniformly the enemy of France. For many years its sovereigns sold the blood of their subjects to England, in order to fight with it against France in the war of the two worlds. It is by the traffic of his troops the Prince has amassed great treasures, part of which, it is said, are locked up at Magdeburg, and part remitted to foreign countries. This sordid avarice has caused the catastrophe of his house, the existence of which on our frontiers is incompatible with the safety of France! It is finally time to extinguish that which may cause the unhappiness of 40 million people, and bring trouble and disorder to their very doors. The English may yet corrupt certain sovereigns by means of their gold, but the loss of the thrones of such sovereigns will be the inevitable consequence of such corruption. On the contrary, the allies of France will prosper and become larger. Their enemies will be dethroned.

The people of Hesse-Cassel will be happier. Discharged of these immense military chores, they will be able to cultivate their fields peacefully; freed from a great part of their taxes, they will be governed by generous and liberal principles, as are France and her allies. If the French had been conquered, their country would have been dismembered; it is just, therefore, that the serious consequences of war should attach to those who provided it, so that they may reflect more diligently in their advice before they start it. In this terrible game, the chances must be equal. The Emperor has ordered the fortresses of Hanau and Mauburg to be destroyed, all the magazines and arsenals to be removed to Mentz, all the troops disarmed, and the sovereign arms of Hesse-Cassel everywhere to be taken down.

What will follow will prove it is not an insatiable ambition or thirst for conquest which has caused the cabinet of the Tuileries to make this decision, but the necessity to put an end to this struggle and to cause a durable peace to succeed to this insensate war, instigated by the miserable and low manoeuvres of agents such as the Lords Paget and Morpeth.

Proclamation

Inhabitants of Hesse, I come to take possession of your country. It is the only way to spare you the horrors of war. You have been witness to the violation of your territory by Prussian troops. You have been scandalized by the welcome that your hereditary prince has given to them. Also, your sovereign and his son have ranks in the service of Prussia and they must obey the orders of the commandant in chief of the Prussian army. The quality of sovereign is incompatible with that of an officer in the service of a major power and with dependence on foreign tribunals.

Your religion, your laws, your customs, your privileges will be respected, discipline will be maintained; for yourself, do not be worried; have confidence in the great sovereign on whom your future depends; you will find in it only satisfaction.

EDOUARD MORTIER, MARSHAL OF THE EMPIRE

Twenty-eighth Bulletin

Berlin, 7 November 1806

Today His Majesty passed in review the dragoons of the division of General Klein, from eleven until three in the afternoon, on the square of the Palace of Berlin. He made several promotions. This division greatly distinguished itself at the battle of Jena, and broke several squares of the Prussian infantry. The Emperor then saw the defile of the great park of the army, the bridge equipment, and the park of the engineers: the big park is commanded by General of Artillery Saint-Laurent; the bridge equipment by Colonel Boucher, and the park of the engineers by General of Engineers Casals.

His Majesty conveyed to General Songis, Inspector General, his satisfaction of the approach that he was using to organize the different parts of the service of the artillery in this large army.

General Savary turned close to Wismar on the Baltic at the head of 500 horses of the 1st Regiment of Hussars and of the 7th Chasseurs; he too the Prussian General Husdunne prisoner with two brigades of hussars and two battalions of grenadiers. He has also taken several cannon. This column belongs to the corps that is being pursued by the Grand Duke of Berg, the Prince of Ponte Corvo and Marshal Soult, this corps, cut off in the area of the Oder and Pomerania, appears backed up near Lubeck.

Colonel Excelmans, commandant of the 1st Regiment of Chasseurs in the division of Marshal Davout, has arrived at Posen, the capital of greater Poland. He was received there with the most enthusiastic joy; the town was thronged with people and the windows were decorated as though it were a feast day; the cavalry could scarcely proceed along the streets.

General of Engineers Bertrand, aide-de-camp to the Emperor, has embarked on the lake of Stettin, to go on a reconnaissance of all the passes.

We formed at Dresden and at Wittenberg siege equipment for Magdeburg; the Elbe is covered. We hope that this fortress will not hold out long. Marshal Ney is appointed to direct the operations of the siege.

Twenty-ninth Bulletin

Berlin, 9 November 1806

The brigade of dragoons of General Beker appeared today at the parade.

His Majesty, wanting to give recompense for the good conduct of the regiments which composed the brigade of dragoons, has given several promotions.

A thousand dragoons, who had arrived at the army on foot and who were taken to the depot of Postdam, passed in review by Marshal Bessières yesterday; they were given a few pieces of equipment which they were missing, and they are leaving today to rejoin their respective corps, with some good saddles and mounted on good horses, which are the fruits of the victory.

His Majesty has ordered a contribution of 150 millions to be levied in the dominions of Prussia, and those of her allies.

After the capitulation of the Prince of Hohenlohe, General Blücher, who was following him, changed the direction of his progress and was able to join the column of the Duke of Weimar, which had previously joined that of Prince Frederick William Brunswick-Öls, son of the Duke of Brunswick. The three corps were then commanded by Blücher; some small corps joined them afterwards.

For many days these troops tried to penetrate through some roads that were left open by the French; but the combined movements of the Grand Duke of Berg, Marshal Soult and the Prince of Ponte Corvo had blocked all the passages.

At one time the enemy attempted to throw itself into Anklam, and afterwards into Rostock. Discovered in the execution of this project, it tried to return towards the Elbe; but in this it was also prevented. It then marched forward to reach Lubeck.

On 4 November, it took a position at Crevismulen; the Prince of Ponte Corvo cut off the rearguard, but could not make much impression on the main body, as he had no more than 600 cavalry, while the enemy was much stronger in that respect. General Watier, in this action, made some very fine charges, supported by Generals Pacthod and Maison, with the 27th Regiment of Light Infantry and the 8th Line.

It is worthy of remark, in this action, that a company of *éclaireurs* attached to the 94th Regiment commanded by Captain Razout, was surrounded by a few enemy squadrons, but the French light troops were not dismayed by the shock of the Prussian cuirassiers, they received it firmly, and kept up such a cool and well-directed fire on the assailants that the enemy retreated. We saw then the light cavalry on foot following the cavalry as fast as it could. The Prussians lost seven cannon and 1,000 men.

But on the evening of the 4th, the Grand Duke of Berg, who was advancing on the right, arrived with his cavalry against the enemy, whose ultimate object seemed, as yet, uncertain. Marshal Soult advanced by Ratzburg and the Prince of Ponte Corvo marched by Rena. He slept on the night of the 5th to the 6th at Schaumburg; he left from there at two in the morning. The Prince advanced to Schlukup on the Trave, and came up to a corps of 1,600 Swedes, who, at length, thought it proper to return from Lauenburg in order to embark on the Trave. A few discharges of cannon, however, disabled the vessels intended for their embarkation. The Swedes, after a show of resistance, laid down their arms.

A convoy of 300 wagons that General Savary had pursued from Wismar was surrounded by the column under the Prince of Ponte Corvo and captured.

In the meantime the enemy fortified itself in Lubeck. Marshal Soult advanced with such rapidity in his march from Matzeburg that he arrived at the gate of Mullen as soon as the Prince of Ponte Corvo was arriving at that of the Trave. The Grand Duke of Berg, with his cavalry, was between these two.

The enemy hastily endeavoured to strengthen the old walls of Lubeck, and place some batteries on the bastions, hoping, by these means, to gain at least a day on us, but it was mistaken, as the reconnoitring and the attack were almost immediate.

General Drouet, at the head of the 27th Light Infantry and the 94th and 95th Regiments of Line, carried the batteries with that coolness and intrepidity which peculiarly distinguishes the French troops! The gates were quickly forced, the bastions escalated, the enemy put to flight and the corps of the Prince of Ponte Corvo entered by the Trave.

The Corsican chasseurs, the skirmishers of the Po and the 26th Light Infantry composed the advanced guard of General Legrand; these had not, as yet, been engaged, and they were impatient to attack the enemy. They advanced with the speed of lightning: redoubts, bastions, ditches, all were cleared, and the corps of Marshal Soult entered the town at the gate of Mullen.

In vain the enemy attempted to defend itself in the streets, the squares, and was pursued everywhere. These places were covered with the dead. The two army corps arriving from two opposite sides joined in the middle of the town. Scarcely had the Grand Duke of Berg entered the place than he went in pursuit of those who were fleeing: 400 prisoners, 60 cannon, several generals and a great number of officers were killed or taken. Such were the results of this brilliant day.

Before daybreak on the 7th, the cavalry were mounted and the Grand Duke of Berg surrounded the enemy near Schwartau, with the brigade of Lasalle and the division of cuirassiers of Hautpoul. General Blücher, Prince Frederick William of Brunswick-Öls, and all the generals then came forward to the victors asking to sign a capitulation and defiled before the French army.

These two days' work destroyed the last corps that remained of the Prussian army, besides the remainder of the artillery, we have taken a number of flags, and 16,000 prisoners, of whom 4,000 are cavalry.

Thus the Prussian generals, who in the delirium of their vanity indulged in all sorts of sarcasms against the Austrian generals, have for the fourth time renewed a catastrophe similar to that of Ulm: 1st, in the capitulation of Erfurt; 2nd, by that of the Prince Hohenlohe; 3rd, in the rendering of Stettin; and 4th in the recent capitulation of Schwartau.

The city of Lubeck has suffered considerably: taken by assault, its streets, its squares, have been scenes of carnage. She attributes these calamities to those who drew the perils of war towards her walls.

Mecklenburg has been equally ravaged by the French and Prussian armies. A great number of troops crossing in difference directions and on forced marches in this territory were not able to find subsistence except at the expense of the country. This state is in intimately tied to Russia; its destiny will serve as an example to the German princes who look for distant relations with a power which is sheltered from the unhappiness that they bring upon them, and who does nothing to help those who are attached to them by ties of blood, or by the closest diplomatic relations. Dery, an aide-de-camp of the Grand Duke of Berg, caused a corps that escorted a considerable quantity of baggage that had pulled back behind the Peene to capitulate. The Swedes delivered the fleeing and the wagons. This capitulation produced 1,500 prisoners and a great quantity of baggage and carriages. Some regiments of cavalry have gained several hundred thousand *écus* [crowns].

Marshal Ney, who was charged with the siege of Magdeburg, bombarded that town. A number of houses were burned, the inhabitants have shown their discontent, and the commandant asked for a capitulation. A great number of cannon were found in the fortress; extensive magazines; 16,000 men drafted from more than 70 battalions, and military chests of several regiments.

During these important operations, several corps of our army arrived on the Vistula.

The Warsaw mail brought many letters from Russia, which of course were intercepted. From these we perceive that the fabrications of the English journals meet with much credit in Russia. For instance, that Marshal Masséna has been killed, that the city of Naples was taken and occupied by the Calabrians, that the King fled to Rome, and that the English, with 5,000 or 6,000 men, were masters of Italy; however, a little reflection will enable them to discover the fallacy of these reports. Does France no longer have an army of Italy? The King of Naples is in his capital; he has 80,000 French; he is master of the two Calabrias, while at Petersburg they imagine the Calabrians are at Rome. If a few galleys, armed and indoctrinated by this infamous Sidney Smith, the shame of the brave English military, killed unprotected individuals, and massacred wealthy, unoffending and peaceable proprietors, the gendarmerie and the scaffold have done them justice! The English navy will not disavow in the least the title of infamous given to Sidney Smith. Generals Stuart and Fox, and all the officers of the land, are indignant at seeing the English name associated with such brigands! The brave General Stuart has even publicly protested against these outrages, which seems to make the noble work of war an exchange of assassinations and brigandry; but when Sidney Smith was selected to execute the Queen's fury, we can only perceive in him one of those unprincipled instruments which governments do often employ, but whom they always abandon to that contempt, which they are the first to feel for them. The Neapolitans will one day be informed in detail of the letters circulated by Sidney Smith, the commissions he has authorized and the money he has expended for the executions of atrocities, in which he is himself the chief agent.

We also see, by the letters from Petersburg, and even in the official dispatches, that they imagine there are no French in Upper Italy: those persons, however, ought to be informed that independent of the army of Naples, there are more than 100,000 French troops in Italy, ready to punish those who should dare to attack it. They expect also every day at Petersburg to hear of the successes of the Division of Corfu; but they will shortly learn that this Division had scarcely landed at the mouths of the Cattaro when it was defeated by General Marmont, that a part of them had been captured and the remainder thrown back into its vessels: it is a very different thing to fight against French or the Turks, whom they hold in fear and partial oppression, by artfully fomenting discord and insurrections in the provinces!

Nevertheless, the Russians will not be embarrassed to shift the blame from themselves regarding these results.

A decree of the senate has declared that at Austerlitz it was not the Russians but their allies who had been beaten. If there should be another battle of Austerlitz on the Vistula, it will again be others than the Russians who will have been vanquished, although today, as it was then, their allies had no troops to join with theirs, and that their army could not be composed but of Russians.

The plan of the movements, and that of the marches of the Russian army, has fallen into the hands of the French chief of staff. From these, it is evident that there would be nothing more ridiculous than the plan of operations of the Russians, if their vain hopes of success had not been more ridiculous still.

General Lagrange has been declared Governor General of Cassel, and the territories of Hesse.

Marshal Mortier, with the troops under his command, is marching for Hanover and for Hamburg.

The King of Holland has blockaded Hameln.

It is necessary that the present war should be the last, and that its authors

113

should be severely punished, and that whoever in the future should want to take arms against the French people, should know, before engaging in such an enterprise, what can be the consequences of such action.

Thirtieth Bulletin

Berlin, 10 November 1806

The fortified town of Magdeburg surrendered on the 8th. On the 9th, the gates were occupied by French troops. Sixteen thousand men, nearly 80 pieces of artillery and magazines of every kind are in our hands.

Prince Jérôme has blockaded Glogau, the capital of Upper Silesia, by Brigadier-General Lefebvre, at the head of 2,000 Bavarian horses. The town was bombarded on the 8th by 10 howitzers, fired by the light artillerymen. The Prince commended the conduct of the Bavarian cavalry. General Deroy surrounded Glogau with his division on the 9th. A parley has been opened for its surrender.

Marshal Davout entered Posen with a corps of the army on the 10th. He is highly satisfied with the spirit that animates the Poles. The Prussian agents would have been massacred had not the French army taken them under its protection.

The heads of four Russian columns, each 15,000 men strong, had begun to enter the Prussian states by Georgemburg, Olita, Grodno and Jalowka: on 25 October, these advanced guards of columns had made two marches when they received news of the battle of the 14th, and of the consequent events; they withdrew immediately.

So many successes and events of such high importance should not slacken the military preparations in France. They should, on the contrary, be followed up with fresh energy, not to satisfy an insatiable ambition, but to fix bounds to the ambition of our enemies.

The French army will not leave either Poland or Berlin, until the Porte is re-established in all its independence, and until Wallachia and Moldavia have been declared to belong in complete sovereignty to the Porte.

The French army will not leave Berlin until the possessions of Spanish, Dutch and French colonies have been returned and a general peace made.

We have intercepted mail from Danzig in which we found many letters coming from Petersburg and Vienna. They use in Vienna a fairly simple ruse to spread false rumours. With each sample of the gazettes that are really toned down, they send in the same envelope a hand-written bulletin that contains the most absurd news possible. We read that France has no longer an army in Italy; that the whole country is on fire; that the state of Venice is in the greatest discontent and has taken up arms; that the Russians have attacked the French army in Dalmatia and have totally defeated it. As false and ridiculous as these claims may be, they arrive from so many places at the same time that they obscure the truth. We are authorized to say that the Emperor has 200,000 men in Italy, of which 80,000 are at Naples, and 25,000 in Dalmatia; that the Kingdom of Naples has not been troubled except by some brigands and assassins; that the King of Naples is master of all Calabria; that if the English want to arrive with regular troops they will find their match; that Marshal Masséna has had nothing but success and that the King is unworried in his capital, occupied by taking care of his army and the administration of his kingdom; that General Marmont, commanding the French army in Dalmatia, has completely beaten the Russians and the Montenegrins, between whom there is great division; that the Montenegrins accuse the Russians of having fought badly, and that the Russians reproach the Montenegrins with having fled; that, of all the troops of Europe the less proper to make war in Dalmatia are certainly the Russian troops; thus they represent themselves very badly.

However, the diplomatic corps, indoctrinated by the false directions given at Vienna, deceives the cabinets by these rhapsodies. False calculations are established upon that; and like all that is built on lies and on mistakes, it promptly falls in ruins, enterprises so badly calculated turn in ways that cause confusion to their authors. Certainly in the current war, the Emperor has not wanted to weaken his army of Italy; he has not taken out one man; he was content enough to bring eight squadrons of cuirassiers because the troops of this arm are not needed in Italy. These squadrons have not yet arrived in Innsbruck. Since the last campaign, the Emperor has, on the contrary, augmented his army of Italy by 15 regiments who were in the interior, and of 9 regiments of the corps of General Marmont. Forty thousand conscripts, almost all of the conscription of 1806, have started to march on Italy; and by the state of the situation of his army on 1 November, 25,000 had already arrived. As for the people of the Venetian states, the Emperor is very satisfied by the spirit that animates them. Thus His Majesty is busy taking care of the interests of the Venetians; he has ordered some work to prepare and better their port and to render the passage of Malmocco ready for vessels of all kinds.

All these people who make up news are really upset at our marshals and generals: they have killed Marshal Masséna at Naples; they killed in Germany both the Grand Duke of Berg and Marshal Soult. Fortunately this does not keep anyone from being in perfectly good health.

Thirty-first Bulletin

Berlin, 12 November 1806

On the 11th, at nine in the morning, the garrison of Magdeburg filed off, in presence of the division of the army under the command of Marshal Ney. We have 20 generals, 800 officers, and 22,000 prisoners, among whom are 2,000 artillerymen, with 54 flags, five standards, 800 pieces of artillery, 1,000,000 pounds of powder, a great assemblage of pontoons and an immense amount of artillery matériel.

Colonel Gérard and Adjutant Commandant Richard presented to the Emperor this morning, in the name of the 1st and 4th Corps, 60 flags taken from the Prussian corps under General Blücher at Lubeck. There were among them 22 standards. Four thousand horses, completely saddled, taken in that day are on their way to the depot at Potsdam.

In the 29th Bulletin it was stated that the corps under General Blücher put us in possession of 16,000 prisoners, including 4,000 cavalry. This was a mistake: there were 21,000 prisoners, including 5,000 mounted cavalry. Thus, in consequence of these two capitulations we have obtained 120 flags and standards and 43,000 prisoners. The number of prisoners taken since the commencement of the campaign exceeds 140,000, and that of the flags taken 250; the number of pieces of artillery taken from the enemy in the battlefield is in excess of 800; and that of the pieces taken at Berlin and the surrendered fortresses is in excess of 4,000.

Yesterday the Emperor reviewed his horse and foot Guard on the plain at the gates of Berlin. It was a great day.

General Savary has entered Rostock with his mobile column. He found there from 40 to 50 Swedish ships on their ballast, and he ordered them immediately sold.

Thirty-second Bulletin

Berlin, 16 November 1806

After the taking of Magdeburg and the battle of Lubeck, the campaign against Prussia is entirely finished.

The following was the situation of the Prussian army upon taking the field.

The corps of General Rüchel, said to be of Westphalia, consisted of 33 battalions of infantry, 4 companies of chasseurs, 45 squadrons of cavalry, one battalion of artillery and 7 batteries, independent from the units of the regiment.

The corps of Prince Hohenlohe consisted of 24 Prussian battalions and 25 Saxon battalions, 45 Prussian squadrons and 36 Saxon squadrons, two battalions of artillery, 8 Prussian and 8 Saxon batteries.

The army commanded by the King himself consisted of an advanced guard of 10 battalions and 15 squadrons commanded by the Duke of Weimar, and three divisions. The first, commanded by the Prince of Orange, consisted of 11 battalions and 20 squadrons. The second division, commanded by General Wartensleben, consisted of 11 battalions and 15 squadrons. The third division, commanded by General Schmettau, consisted of 10 battalions and 15 squadrons.

The corps of reserve of this army, which Kalkreuth commanded, consisted of two divisions, each of 10 battalions of the regiments of the guards or of the élite, and 20 squadrons.

The reserve, commanded by Prince Eugene of Württemberg, consisted of 18 battalions and 20 squadrons.

Thus the total of the Prussian army consisted of 160 battalions and 236 squadrons and 30 batteries, which made present under arms 115,000 infantry, 30,000 cavalry and 800 pieces of artillery, including the cannons of battalions.

All this army was at the battle of the 14th except the corps of the Duke of Weimar, which was still at Eisenach, and the reserve of the Prince of Württemberg; this totals the Prussian forces that were at the battle to 126,000 men.

Of these 126,000 men, not one has escaped. Of the corps of the Duke of Weimar, not a man has escaped. Of the corps of reserve of the Duke of Württemberg, which was beaten at Halle, not a man has escaped.

Thus these 145,000 men have all been taken, wounded or killed. All the flags and standards, all the cannons, all the baggage, all the generals have been taken, and nothing has crossed the Oder. The King, Queen, General Kalkreuth, and about 10 or 12 officers, are all that have fled. The King of Prussia has now remaining a regiment in the town of Gros-Glogau, which is besieged, one at Breslau, one at Brieg, two at Warsaw, and a few regiments at Königsberg, in all about 15,000 infantry and 3,000 to 4,000 cavalry. Part of these troops is shut up in strong places. The King cannot assemble at Königsberg, where he has at this moment fled, more than 3,000 men.

The Sovereign of Saxony has made a present of his portrait to General Lemarois, Governor of Württemberg, who being at Torgau, re-established order in a house of correction among 600 convicts who had armed themselves and threatened to plunder the town.

Yesterday, Lieutenant Lebrun presented to the Emperor four flags belonging to four Prussian squadrons commanded by General Pelet, and which General Drouet forced to capitulate near Lunenburg. They had escaped the corps of General

116

Blücher.

Major Ameil, at the head of a squadron of the 16th Chasseurs sent by Marshal Soult along the Elbe to pick up all that could possibly escape of the corps of General Blücher, has taken 1,000 prisoners, of which 500 are hussars, and has taken a great quantity of baggage.

Here is the position of the French army.

The division of cuirassiers of General Hautpoul, the divisions of dragoons of Generals Grouchy and Sahuc, the light cavalry of General Lasalle, being part of the reserve of cavalry that the Grand Duke of Berg had at Lubec, arrive at Berlin.

The head of the corps of Marshal Ney, who had forced the capitulation of Magdeburg, entered Berlin today.

The corps of the Princeof Ponte Corvo and Marshal Soult are on their way to Berlin.The corps of Marshal Soult will arrive there the 20th, that of the Prince of Ponte Corvo a few days after.

Marshal Mortier has arrived with the 8th Corps at Hamburg, to close the Elbe and the Weser.

General Savary has been charged to blockade Hameln with the Dutch division.

The corps of Marshal Lannes is at Thorn.

The corps of Marshal Augereau is at Bremberg and opposite Graudenz.

The corps of Marshal Davout is marching from Posen towards Warsaw, where the Grand Duke of Berg is headed with the other part of the reserve of cavalry, consisting of the division of dragoons of Generals Beaumont, Klein and Beker, the division of cuirassiers of General Nansouty and the light cavalry of General Milhaud.

Prince Jérôme, with the corps of the allies, is besieging Gros-Glogau; his siege equipment was formed at Custrin. One of his divisions is surrounding Breslau. He is taking possession of Silesia.

Our troops occupy the fort of Lenczyca, halfway between Posen and Warsaw. Magazines and artillery have been found there. The Poles show the best disposition; but this country is difficult as far as the Vistula; there is a lot of sand. It is the first time that the Vistula sees the Gallic Eagle.

The Emperor wants the King of Holland to return to his kingdom, to defend it himself.

The King of Holland has caused the corps of Marshal Mortier to take possession of Hanover. The Prussian Eagles and the Electoral arms were taken down together.

Thirty-third Bulletin

Berlin, 17 November 1806

The attached suspension of arms was signed yesterday at Charlottenburg. The season is rather advanced. This suspension of arms settles the quarters of the army. Part of Prussian Poland is thus occupied by the French army, and part of it is neutral.

His Majesty the Emperor of the French, King of Italy, and His Majesty the King of Prussia, in consequence of negotiations opened, since 23 October for the re-establishment of the peace so unhappily interrupted between them, have judged necessary to agree on a suspension of arms; and, for this purpose, they have appointed for their plenipotentiaries, to wit: His Majesty the Emperor of the French, King of Italy; General of Division Michel Duroc, Grand Insignia of the Legion of Honour, Knight of the Orders of the Black Eagle and Red Eagle of

Prussia, and of Fidelity of Baden, and Grand Marshal of the Imperial Palace; and His Majesty the King of Prussia, the Marquis of Lucchesini, his Minister of State, Chamberlain and Knight of the Orders of the Black Eagle and Red Eagle of Prussia, and General Frederick William of Zastrow, Chief of the Regiment, and Inspector General of Infantry and Knight of the Orders of the Red Eagle and of Merit; who after having exchanged their full powers, have agreed upon the following articles:

Article I The troops of His Majesty the King of Prussia, who are at present on the right bank of the Vistula, shall assemble at Königsberg and in royal Prussia from the right bank of the Vistula.

Article II The troops of His Majesty the Emperor of the French, King of Italy, shall occupy the part of Southern Prussia which is on the right bank of the Vistula as far as the mouth of the Bug, Thorn, the fortress and town of Graudenz, the town and citadel of Danzig, the towns of Colberg and Lenczyca, which shall be delivered to them for security; and in Silesia, the towns of Glogau and Breslau, with the portion of that province which is on the right bank of the Oder, and the part of that situated on the left bank of the same river, which will have for limit a line bordering upon that river, five leagues above Breslau, passing through Ohlau, Zobson, three leagues behind Schweidnitz, and without comprising it, and from there to Freiburg, Landshut, and joining Bohemia to Leiban.

Article III The other parts of Eastern Prussia or New Eastern Prussia, shall not be occupied by any of the armies, either French, Prussian or Russian, and if the Russian troops are there, His Majesty the King of Prussia engages to make them fall back to their own territory; as also not to receive any troops of that power into his states, during the time of the suspension of arms.

Article IV The fortresses of Hemeln and Nienberg, as well as those mentioned in Article II shall be delivered up to the French troops, with their arms and munitions, of which an inventory shall be made within eight days after the exchange of the ratifications of the present suspension of arms. The garrisons of these fortresses shall not be made prisoners of war, they shall be allowed to march to Königsberg, and they shall be allowed the necessary facilities for that purpose.

Article V The negotiations shall be continued at Charlottenburg, and if peace does not follow, the two high contracting parties engage not to resume hostilities until having after having given notice to each other ten days beforehand.

Article VI The present suspension of arms shall be ratified by the two high contracting powers, and the exchange of ratifications shall take place at Graudenz, at latest by the 21st of the present month.

In faith of which, the undersigned plenipotentiaries have signed the present, and have set to their respective seals.

Given at Charlottenburg, 16 November 1806

DUROC, LUCCHESINI, ZASTROW

Thirty-fourth Bulletin

Berlin, 23 November 1806

We have as yet no news that the suspension of arms concluded on the 17th has been ratified by the King of Prussia, or that any exchange of the ratification has yet taken place. Meanwhile, hostilities continue, nor will any suspension of them take place until the exchange of the ratification.

General Savary, to whom the Emperor had entrusted the command of Hameln, had arrived on the 19th at Ebersdorf in front of Hameln, and had a conference on the 20th with General Lecoq and the Prussian generals locked up in that place, and made them sign the capitulation: 9,000 prisoners, among whom are six generals, enough magazines to feed 10,000 men for six months, and munitions of all kinds, a company of horse artillery and 300 cavalry have fallen into our hands.

The only troops that General Savary had consisted of a regiment of light infantry and two Dutch regiments under General Dumonceau.

General Savary has this moment set off for Nienburg in order to force that fortress to capitulate, in which we believe there are 2,000 to 3000 men in its garrison.

A battalion of Prussians, 800 strong, who formed the garrison of Czentoskaw, on the frontiers of Prussian Poland, capitulated on the 13th to 150 chasseurs of the 2nd Regiment, united with 300 Poles who had taken up arms and advanced to that place. The garrison has been taken prisoner of war; there are a considerable amount of magazines.

The Emperor spent the day reviewing the infantry of the 4th Corps, commanded by Marshal Soult. He gave promotions and distributed rewards to each corps.

Thirty-fifth Bulletin

Posen, 28 November 1806

The Emperor left Berlin at two in the morning on the 25th and arrived at Custrin on the same evening about ten. On the 26th, he was at Mezerits, and on the 27th, at ten at night, he arrived at Posen. The next day His Majesty gave audience to the various orders of the Poles. Marshal Duroc continued his journey to Osterode, where he found the King of Prussia, who declared to him that a part of his states were in the possession of the Russians, that he was entirely dependent on them; consequently he could not ratify the armistice which had been concluded by his envoy, because it was not in his power to fulfil the stipulated conditions. His Majesty was headed to Königsberg.

The Grand Duke of Berg, with a part of the cavalry of the reserve and the corps under Marshals Davout, Lannes and Augereau, has entered Warsaw. The Russian General Bennigsen, who occupied the fortress before the French arrived, evacuated it on hearing that the French army was coming towards him and was going to engage him.

Prince Jérôme, with a corps of Bavarians, is at Kalitsch.

All the rest of the army has arrived at Posen or is in march by different directions to get there.

Marshal Mortier is marching on Anklam, Rostock and Swedish Pomerania, after having taken possession of the Hanseatic towns.

The surrender of Hameln was marked by some strange circumstances. Besides the garrison that was supposed to defend this place, a few Prussian battalions seem to have taken refuge there after the battle of the 14th. The officers were insubordinate against the generals, and the soldiers against the officers. Scarcely was the capitulation signed, when General Savary received the attached letter, number one, from the Commandant, General Von Schöler, which he answered by letter number two. In the meanwhile, the garrison was in a state of insurrection, and the first act of the mutineers was to break open the magazines where the brandy was deposited, and drink more than necessary. Soon, animated by the spirits, they began to fire upon each other in the streets, soldiers against soldiers, soldiers against officers, soldiers against citizens: the disorder was extreme. General Von Schöler sent courier after courier to General Savary, to request him to take possession of the place, even before the appointed time. To this the general consented, and advanced, and entered the place through a shower of bullets, he drove all the soldiers of the garrison through one of the gates into a neighbouring meadow. Then he assembled the officers, and told them that what had happened was due to their relaxed discipline, and had them sign their *cartel* and he re-established order in the town. We believe that in the tumult there have been several citizens killed.

Thirty-sixth Bulletin

Posen, 1 December 1806
The headquarters of the Grand Duke of Berg were, on 27 November, at Lowicz.

General Bennigsen, commander of the Russian army, hoping to keep the French from entering Warsaw, had sent an advanced guard to take positions along the river Drizura. On the 26th, the outposts of the respective armies joined each other, and the Russians were overthrown. General Beaumont crossed the Drizura at Lowicz, re-established the bridge, killed or wounded several Russian hussars, and took several Cossacks prisoner, and pursued the enemy as far as Blonic.

On the 27th some skirmishing took place between the advanced posts of cavalry of both armies; the Russians were pursued and some taken prisoner.

On the 28th, towards evening, the Grand Duke of Berg entered Warsaw with his cavalry. The corps of Marshal Davout entered there on the 29th. The Russians had re-crossed the Vistula, and burned the bridge.

It is difficult to describe the enthusiasm of the Poles. Our entrance into this great town was a triumph, and the sentiments that the Poles of all classes are showing since we arrived would be difficult to explain.

The love of their country and national sentiment is not only conserved whole in the heart of these people, but have grown stronger by misfortune: their first passion, their first desire, is to become a nation again. The powerful abandon their castles and come to implore with earnestness the restoration of their nation, and offer their children, their fortunes, and all their influence towards accomplishing that end. This spectacle is indeed moving. They have already everywhere resumed their ancient dress and their former customs.

Will the Polish throne be re-established, and will this great nation re-take her existence and her independence? Shall she recall it to life from the grave? God alone, who holds in his hands all combinations of events, can resolve this great political question; but certainly there have never been events more memorable, more worthy of interest, and, by a correspondence of sentiments which praises the French, stragglers who had committed excesses in other countries have been touched by the good reception from the people, and did not need any effort to comport themselves in a proper manner.

Our soldiers often observe that the solitary wildernesses of Poland are very different from the smiling fields of their own country; but they immediately add: 'They are good people, these Poles.' These people are really showing themselves in very interesting colours.

Proclamation

Imperial Headquarters, Posen, 2 December 1806

Soldiers!

A year ago, at this same hour, you were on the memorable field of Austerlitz. The horrified Russian battalions were fleeing, or, surrounded, were giving up their arms to the victors. The next day they expressed words of peace: but they were not true. As soon as they escaped the disasters of the third coalition by the effect of a generosity perhaps condemnable, they formed a fourth one. But the ally on whose military skill their principal hope rested is already no more. Its capitals, its fortresses, its magazines, its arsenals, 280 flags, 700 cannon and five great forts are in our power. Neither the Oder nor the Warta, the deserts of Poland, or the bad weather of the season, could stop us for a moment. You have braved all dangers, have surmounted them all, and every enemy has fled on your approach.

It is in vain that the Russians wanted to defend the capital of this ancient and illustrious Poland; the French Eagle hovers over the Vistula. The unfortunate but brave Poles, on contemplating you, France, they believe they are seeing again the legions of the great Sobieski returning from their memorable expedition.

Soldiers! We shall not lay down our arms until a general peace has confirmed and secured the power of our allies, until it has restituted to our commerce its liberty and its colonies. On the Elbe and on the Oder we have conquered Pondicherry, all our establishments in India, the Cape of Good Hope and the Spanish colonies. Who would give the right to the Russians to hope that they shall hold the balance of destiny in their hand? Who would give them the right to reverse such a just design? Them and us: are we not the soldiers of Austerlitz?

NAPOLEON

For the Emperor, The Prince of Neufchâtel, Minister of War, Major-General, Marshal Alexandre Berthier

Thirty-seventh Bulletin

Posen, 2 December 1806

Fort Czentoskoaw has capitulated: 600 men of the garrison, 30 pieces of artillery and some magazines have fallen into our hands. A treasure has been found, consisting of a number of valuables that had been dedicated by the Poles to the Holy Virgin, who is regarded as the patron of Poland. This treasure had been sequestered, but the Emperor ordered that it be given back.

The part of the army at Warsaw remains fully satisfied with the patriotism of the people of that city.

Today the city of Posen had a ball in honour of His Majesty, who was there for an hour.

A *Te Deum* was also performed today for the anniversary of His Majesty's coronation.

Thirty-eighth Bulletin

Posen, 5 December 1806

Prince Jérôme, who commands the army of the allies, after having closely blockaded Glogau and caused batteries to be constructed around that place, proceeded with the Bavarian divisions of Wrede and Deroy towards Kalitsch to meet the Russians, and left General Vandamme and the Württemberg corps to continue the siege of Glogau. The mortars and several pieces of artillery arrived on 29 November. They were immediately placed in battery. After a few hours' bombardment the place surrendered, and a capitulation was signed.

The allied Württemberg troops have displayed great gallantry. Two thousand five hundred men, considerable magazines of biscuit, wheat, powder, and nearly 200 cannon are the results of this important conquest, especially by the greatness of its fortifications and its situation. It is the capital of Lower Silesia.

The Russians have refused battle on this side of Warsaw, and have re-crossed the Vistula. The Grand Duke of Berg has crossed that river in pursuit of them, and has taken the suburb of Praga. He pursued them on the Bug. The Emperor has consequently given orders to Prince Jérôme to advance on his right, towards Breslau, and to surround that place, which will soon fall into our power. The seven fortresses of Silesia will be successively attacked and blockaded. Given the morale of the troops that are there, nothing would let us presume that they would resist for very long.

The little fort of Culmbach, called Plassenburg, had been blockaded by a battalion of Bavarians. Being furnished with provisions for several months, there was no reason to expect that it should have surrendered soon. The Emperor ordered artillery to be prepared at Kronach and Forcheim for battering this fort. On 24 November, 22 pieces of cannon were placed in battery, which caused the commander to surrender the fortress. Colonel Beker of the 6th Bavarian Regiment of Infantry of Line, who commanded the blockade, displayed much skill and activity in the situation in which he was placed.

The anniversary of the battle of Austerlitz and of the coronation of the Emperor was celebrated at Warsaw with very great enthusiasm.

Thirty-ninth Bulletin

Posen, 7 December 1806
General Savary, after having taken possession of Hameln, started towards Nienburg. The governor was causing difficulties regarding the capitulation. General Savary went into the place and after a few discussions he concluded a capitulation.

A courier has arrived with intelligence to the Emperor, that the Russians have declared war against the Porte; that Choczim and Bender are surrounded by their troops; that they have suddenly crossed the Dniester, and advanced as far as Jassy. It is General Michelson who commands the Russian army in Wallachia.

The Russian army commanded by General Bennigsen has evacuated the Vistula, and seems to have decided to bury itself in the interior.

Marshal Davout has crossed the Vistula, and has established his headquarters before Praga; his advanced posts are on the Bug. The Grand Duke of Berg remains at Warsaw.

The Emperor still has his headquarters at Posen.

Fortieth Bulletin

Posen, 9 December 1806
Marshal Ney has crossed the Vistula and entered Thorn on the 6th. He particularly commends Colonel Savary, who at the head of the 14th Regiment of Infantry and the grenadiers and voltigeurs of the 96th, and the 6th Light Infantry, was the first to cross that river. At Thorn he came to action with the Prussians, who, after a light combat, he compelled to evacuate the town. Some were killed, and 20 taken prisoner.

This affair offers a remarkable trait. The river, 400 *toises* wide, was carrying ice;

the boat occupied by our advanced guard was held back by the ice and could not be moved; from the other bank the Polish boatmen started across in the midst of a shower of bullets to help get the vessel afloat. The Prussian boatmen wanted to oppose this. A fist fight ensued between all of them. The Poles succeeded in throwing the Prussians into the water, and guided our boat to the right bank. The Emperor asked for the names of these brave fellows to reward them.

Today the Emperor received the deputation from Warsaw, consisting of Mr Gutakonski, Grand Chamberlain of Lithuania, Knight of the Orders of Poland; Gouzenski, Lieutenant General, Knight of the Orders of Poland; Lubenski, Knight of the same order; and Alexander Potocki and Rzetkowski, Knight of the Order of St Stanislas and Luszewski.

Forty-first Bulletin

Posen, 14 December 1806

General of Brigade Belair, of the corps of Marshal Ney, left Thorn on the 9th of this month and advanced on Galup. The 6th Battalion of Light Infantry, and Chief of Squadron Schoeny, with 60 men of the 3rd Regiment of Hussars, met a party of 400 enemy cavalry. The two advanced posts immediately came to an engagement. The Prussians lost an officer, five dragoons were taken prisoner and 30 men were killed, whose horses stayed in our power. Marshal Ney highly praises the conduct of Chief of Squadron Schoeny on this occasion. Our advanced posts arrived as far as Strasburg.

On the 11th, at six in the morning, a cannonade was heard on the side of the Bug river. Marshal Davout had ordered General of Brigade Gauthier to cross that river at the mouth of the Ukra, opposite the village of Okunin.

The 25th Line and the 89th, having crossed, were already covered by a bridgehead and had advanced half a league further, to the village of Pomiechowo, when a Russian division presented itself for the purpose of storming the village. Its efforts were useless, and it was repulsed with considerable loss. We had about 20 men killed or wounded.

The bridge of Thorn, which is constructed upon wooden piles, is re-established. They are re-establishing the fortifications of that town. The bridge from Warsaw to the suburb of Praga is completed; it is a bridge of boats. They are forming an entrenched camp at the suburb of Praga. General of Engineers Chasseloup is the chief director of these works.

On the 10th, Marshal Augereau crossed the Vistula between Zakroczin and Utrata. His detachments work on the right bank covering themselves by entrenchments. The Russians appear to have forces at Pultusk.

Marshal Bessières advances from Thorn with the 2nd Corps of reserve of the cavalry, composed of General Tilly's division of light cavalry, the dragoons of General Grouchy and Sahue and the cuirassiers of General Hautpoul.

Messrs Lucchesini and Zastrow, plenipotentiaries of the King of Prussia, passed through Thorn on the 10th, to join their master at Königsberg.

A Prussian battalion of the regiment of Klock has deserted the village of Brok. It directed itself on our posts by different roads. It is composed partly of Prussians and Poles. All are indignant at the treatment they receive from the Russians: 'Our Prince,' say they, 'has sold us to the Russians, we will not go with them.'

The enemy has burned the fine suburbs of Breslau: many women and children have perished in the flames. Prince Jérôme has given help to those unfortunate inhabitants. Humanity has won over the laws of war, which order to repulse in a place under siege the useless mouths that the enemy wants to send away. The bombardment has been commenced.

General Gouvion is named Governor of Warsaw.

Forty-second Bulletin

Posen, 15 December 1806

The bridge over the Narew, at its confluence with the Bug, is now finished. The bridgehead is finished, and armed with cannon.

The bridge over the Vistula, between Zakroczym and Utrata near the mouth of the Bug, is also finished. The bridgehead, armed with a great number of batteries, is a formidable work.

The Russian armies come in the direction of Grodno and Bielock, along the Narew and the Bug. The headquarters of their divisions were, on the 10th, at Pultusk, on the Narew.

General Dulauloy is named Governor of Thorn. The 8th Corps of the *Grande Armée*, commanded by Marshal Mortier, is advancing. Its right is at Stettin, its left at Rostock, and its headquarters at Anklam.

The grenadiers of the reserve of General Oudinot are arriving at Custrin.

The division of cuirassiers, lately formed under the command of General Espagne, is now at Berlin.

The Italian division of General Lechi is forming at Magdeburg.

The corps of the Grand Duke of Baden is at Stettin. In 15 days it will be able to enter the line. The hereditary Prince has constantly followed the headquarters, and was present at every affair.

The Polish division of Zayonchek, which was organized at Haguenau, is 6,000 men strong; it is now at Leipzig to get its clothing.

His Majesty has ordered a regiment to be raised in the Prussian states, on the other side of the Elbe, which is to assemble at Munster. Prince Hohenzollern Sigmaringen is named Colonel of that corps.

A division of the army of reserve of Marshal Kellermann has left from Mayence. The head of this division has already arrived at Magdeburg.

Peace with the Elector of Saxony and with the Duke of Saxe-Weimar has been signed at Posen.

All the Princes of Saxony have been admitted into the Confederation of the Rhine.

His Majesty has disapproved of the levy of contributions in the states of Saxe-Gotha and Saxe-Meiningen, so he has ordered the restitution of what has been raised. Those princes who have not been at war with France, and who have not furnished contingents to Prussia, were not subject to war contributions.

The army has taken possession of the town of Mecklenburg. This is a consequence of the treaty signed at Schwerin on 25 October 1805. By that treaty, the Prince of Mecklenburg granted a passage to the Russian troops commanded by General Tolstoï.

The season astonishes the inhabitants of Poland. It does not freeze. The sun appears every day, and it is quite autumnal weather.

The Emperor sets out tonight for Warsaw.

Forty-third Bulletin

Kutno, 17 December 1806

The Emperor has arrived at Kutno, at one o'clock in the afternoon, after having travelled all night in the *calèches du pays* [country carriage], as the thaw makes it impossible to travel in common carriages. The *calèches* in which Duroc, Grand Marshal of the Palace, travelled, was overturned. That officer has been severely hurt in the shoulder, but his hurt is not dangerous. This accident will oblige him to keep his bed for 8 or 10 days.

The bridgeheads of Praga, of Zakroczin, of Narew and of Thorn are acquiring a new degree of perfection every day.

The Emperor will be at Warsaw tomorrow.

The Vistula being extremely broad, all the bridges are 300 to 400 *toises*, which makes for a lot of work.

Forty-fourth Bulletin

Warsaw, 21 December 1806

Yesterday the Emperor inspected the works of Praga, where 8 fine redoubts, with palisades, bastions, etc., enclose a space of 1,500 *toises*, and 3 bastion fronts of 600 *toises* form an entrenched camp.

The Vistula is one of the largest rivers in the world. The Bug, though considerably smaller, is still larger than the Seine. The bridge over the Bug is completed. General Gauthier, with the 25th and 85th Regiments of Infantry, occupies the bridgehead, which General Chasseloup has fortified with great skill, so that this bridgehead, which only has 400 *toises* in extent, together with the marshes and the river, enclose an entrenched camp which is capable of protecting the whole army on the right bank from attack by the enemy. A brigade of the light cavalry of the reserve has skirmishes with the Russian cavalry every day.

On the 18th, Marshal Davout felt the necessity of strengthening and improving his camp upon the right bank of the river, and likewise occupying a small island at the mouth of the Ukra. The enemy perceived the importance of this post. A heavy fusillade of the advanced posts immediately commenced; but the victory and the island remained to the French. Our loss consisted of a few wounded. Captain of Engineers Clouet, a young man of great promise, received a ball in the chest. On the 19th, a regiment of Cossacks, assisted by the Russian hussars, endeavoured to surprise the advanced guard of light cavalry that was placed at the bridgehead of the Bug; but the advanced guard had taken such a position as to be secured from any surprise. The 1st of Hussars came on horseback. The colonel, at the head of a squadron, and the 13th came to assist it. The enemy was thrown back. In this small affair we had 3 or 4 men wounded, but the Colonel of the Cossacks was killed. Thirty men and 25 horses were left in our power. There is nothing so miserable and cowardly as the Cossacks; they are the shame of human nature. They cross the Bug and violate the Austrian neutrality every day, merely to plunder a house in Galicia or to compel the inhabitants to give them brandy, of which they are very fond; but our light cavalry is familiarized, since the last campaign, with the manner in which to combat these wretches, and notwithstanding their numbers and their hideous cry on these occasions, they await them without alarm, and it is well known that 2,000 of these wretches are not equal to the attack of the squadron of our cavalry.

Marshal Augereau crossed the Vistula at Utrata. General Lapisse entered Plonsk after drawing out the enemy.

Marshal Soult crossed the Vistula at Vizogrod.

Marshal Bessières was at Kikol on the 18th, with the 2nd Corps of the cavalry of reserve. His advanced guard arrived at Serpez. There have been several encounters between our cavalry and the Prussian hussars, of whom a great number have been taken prisoner. The right bank of the Vistula is totally cleared.

Marshal Ney, with his light corps, supports Marshal Bessières. He had arrived on the 18th at Rypin. He had his right supported by Marshal the Prince of Ponte Corvo.

Thus every corps is in motion, and if the enemy persists in staying in its position, a battle will take place in a few days. With God's help the issue cannot be uncertain. The Russian army is commanded by Marshal Kamenskoi, an old man about 75 years of age. Generals Buxhowden and Bennigsen command under him.

General Michelson has decidedly entered into Moldavia. There are accounts that he arrived at Jassy on the 29th of November. We are assured that his generals took Bender by storm and put everyone to the sword. So there is a war declared against the Porte without pretext or reason; but at Saint Petersburg it was thought that the moment had arrived when France and Prussia, the two powers who had the greatest interest in preserving the independence of Turkey, being at war, was the most favourable period for subjugating this power. Still, the events of one month have defeated that project, and the Porte will owe them its conservation.

The Grand Duke of Berg has a fever, but he is better.

The weather is a mild as at Paris in the month of October, but damp, which makes the roads difficult. We have taken measures for the delivery of a sufficient quantity of wine, in order to support the vigour of the troops.

The palace of the King of Poland is beautiful and well furnished. There are several noble palaces and private houses in Warsaw. Our hospitals are well established, which is no small advantage in this country. The enemy seems to have many sick; there are also many deserters. Of the Prussians we hear nothing; even whole corps have deserted to avoid that continual contempt which they might expect among the Russians.

Forty-fifth Bulletin

Paluki, 27 December 1806

Russian General Bennigsen had the command of an army that was estimated at 60,000 men. At first he intended to cover Warsaw; but he took a lesson from the renown of the past events which had taken place in Prussia, and decided to retreat towards the Russian frontiers. Without any engagement, the French armies entered Warsaw, crossed the Vistula, occupied Praga. In the meantime, Field Marshal Kamenskoi joined the Russian army just at the moment when General Bennigsen's corps formed a junction with that under Buxhowden. He was indignant at the retreat of the Russians; he believed that it compromised the honour of the arms of the nation, and he marched forward. Prussia time after time was complaining that it had been abandoned after it had been promised to be supported, saying that the road to Berlin was not by Grodno, Olita or Brezsc; that her subjects were feeling disaffection for their sovereign; and that the habit of beholding the throne of Berlin in the possession of the French was dangerous to him and favourable to the enemy. The Russians not only stopped their retreat, but they again began to advance. On 5 December, General Bennigsen re-established his headquarters at Pultusk. The orders issued were to prevent the French from crossing the Narew, to re-take Praga, and to occupy the banks of the Vistula until the moment when more important offensive operations could be adopted.

The reunion of Generals Kamenskoi, Buxhowden and Bennigsen was celebrated at the castle of Sierock with rejoicings and illuminations, which were seen from the towers of Warsaw.

Nevertheless, at the moment when the enemy was cheering itself with festivals, the Narew was crossed: 800 French threw themselves to the other side of this river at the mouth of the Ukra, entrenched themselves the same night, and when the enemy appeared next morning with the intention of forcing them back into the river, it was too late. The French were secure against every event.

Being informed of this change in the enemy's operations, the Emperor left Posen on the 16th; at the same moment he put his army in motion. Every report that was heard from the discourses of the Russians led us to believe that they wanted to take the offensive.

Marshal Ney had been master of Thorn for several days. He united the different corps of his army at Galup. Marshal Bessières, with the 2nd Corps of the cavalry of reserve, consisting of the divisions of dragoons of Sahuc and Grouchy and the division of Hautpoul's cuirassiers, marched from Thorn to proceed to Biezun. Marshal Prince of Ponte Corvo marched with his corps in support. Marshal Soult crossed the Vistula opposite Plock; and Marshal Augereau crossed opposite Zuckrocyn, where the utmost exertion was made to establish a bridge. The same activity was exerted in constructing that on the Narew.

On the 22nd, the bridge on the Narew was completed. All the reserve of cavalry instantly crossed the Vistula at Praga on their march to the Narew. Marshal Davout had collected all of his corps there. At one o'clock in the morning of the 23rd, the Emperor set out from Warsaw, and crossed the Narew at nine. On reconnoitring the Ukra and the considerable entrenchments thrown up by the enemy, he ordered a bridge to be thrown across at the confluence of the Narew and Ukra. By the zeal of the General of Artillery, the bridge was completed in two hours.

Night combat of Czarnowo

The Morand division crossed immediately to seize the entrenchments of the enemy near the village of Czarnowo. General of Brigade Marulaz supported the Morand division with his light cavalry. The division of dragoons of General Beaumont crossed immediately after. A cannonade was engaged at Czarnowo. Marshal Davout had General Petit with the 12th Line also cross so they could take out the redoubts of the bridge. Night came and all operations had to be concluded by moonlight; at two in the morning, the objective proposed by the Emperor was fulfilled. All the batteries of the village Czarnowo were taken out; those of the bridge were taken; 15,000 men who were defending these positions were routed in spite of their lively resistance.

A few prisoners and six cannon remained in our power. Several enemy generals were wounded. On our side, General of Brigade Boussart was slightly wounded. We have few dead but close to 200 wounded. At the same time, at the other end of the line of operations, Marshal Ney overthrew the rest of the Prussian army and pushed them into the woods of Lautenburg, causing them notable losses. Marshal Bessières had a brilliant cavalry charge and surrounded three squadrons of hussars, whom he took prisoner and took several pieces of artillery.

Combat of Nasielsk

On the 24th, the Reserve Cavalry and the corps of Marshal Davout started for Nasielsk. The Emperor gave command of the advance guard to General Rapp. At one league from Nasielsk, we met the advance guard of the enemy.

General Lemarois left with two regiments of dragoons to outflank a large wooded area and surround this advance guard. This movement was quickly executed. But the advance guard of the enemy, seeing the French army making no forward movement, suspected some scheme and did not hold. However, there were a few charges, in one of which Major Uvarov, aide-de-camp of the Emperor of Russia, was taken. Immediately after, a detachment arrived on the small town of Nasielsk. There was a lively cannonade. The enemy's position was good: it was backed up by marshes and some woods. Marshal Kaminskoi was in command. He believed that he could spend the night in that position while he awaited the arrival of other columns. This was in vain; he was chased from there and retreated several leagues. A few Russian generals were wounded, several colonels were taken prisoner, and several cannon were taken. Colonel Beker of the 8th Regiment of Dragoons, a brave officer, was mortally wounded.

Crossing of the Wrka

At the same moment, General Nansouty, with the Klein division and a light cavalry brigade, overthrew the Cossacks before Kursomz and the enemy cavalry who had crossed the Wrka at that point. The 7th Army Corps, commanded by Marshall Augereau, was carrying out the crossing of the Wrka at Kursomb and overthrew the 15,000 men who were defending it. The crossing of the bridge was brilliant, the 14th Line executed this in tight columns, while the 16th of Light Infantry set up a lively fusillade on the right bank. No sooner had the 14th left the bridge than it endured a cavalry charge which it resisted with intrepidity of the French infantry; but a wretched lancer penetrated as far as the head of the regiment and pierced the colonel who fell over dead. The colonel was a brave soldier and he was worthy of commanding such a brave corps. The point-blank firing executed by his regiment, which put the enemy's cavalry in such great disorder, was the first of the honours rendered in his memory.

On the 25th, the 3rd Corps, commanded by Marshal Davout, directed itself to Tykozyn, where the enemy had retreated. The 5th Corps, commanded by Marshal Lannes, took the direction of Pultusk, with the Beker division of dragoons.

The Emperor, with the biggest part of the cavalry of reserve, took the direction of Ciechanow.

Crossing of the Sonna

General Gardanne, who had been sent by the Emperor with 30 men of his Guard to observe the movements of the enemy, reported that it was crossing the Sonna River at Lopacksin and was headed towards Tycokzyn. The Grand Duke of Berg, who had remained sick at Warsaw, had not been able to resist his impatience to take part in the events which were about to take place. He left from Warsaw and rejoined the Emperor. He took two squadrons of Chasseurs of the Guard to observe the movements of the enemy's column. The brigades of the Light Cavalry of Reserve and the divisions of Klein and Nansouty hurried to join him. When he arrived at the bridge of Lopackzin, he found a regiment of Russian hussars who guarded it. This regiment was charged immediately by the Chasseurs of the Guard and overthrown into the river, with no other loss for the Chasseurs than a wounded cavalry sergeant.

Meanwhile, half this column had not yet crossed; it was crossing further up. The Grand Duke of Berg ordered it charged by Colonel Dalhmann, commanding the Chasseurs of the Guard, who took 3 pieces of artillery from the enemy and routed several of its squadrons.

While the column that the enemy had so imprudently sent on the right tried to reach the Narew to arrive at Tykoczyn, which was the meeting point, Tykoczyn was occupied by Marshal Davout, who took 2,000 of the enemy's baggage carts and a great number of stragglers who were picked up everywhere.

All of the Russian columns are cut off, wandering about in a disorder that it is difficult to imagine. The Russian general made the mistake of cantoning his army while the French army was on its flanks, even though separated by the Narew, but having a bridge on this river. If the season was good, we could predict that the Russian army would not retreat and would be lost without battle; but in a season when it is dark at four in the afternoon and where it is daylight at eight in the morning, the enemy we are pursuing has all the chances possible to escape, especially in difficult country, cut up by woods. In addition the roads are covered with four feet of mud, and the thaw continues. The artillery cannot make more than two leagues in one day. We anticipate that the enemy will withdraw from his unfortunate position: but it will lose all its artillery, all its wagons and all its baggage.

Here is what was the position of the French army on the 25th at night.

The left, composed of the corps of marshal the Prince of Ponte Corvo and of Marshals Ney and Bessières, marching from Biezun on the road to Grodno.

Marshal Soult was arriving at Chiechanow.

Marshal Augereau was marching on Golymin.

Marshal Davout enters Golymin and Pultusk.

Marshal Lannes is at Pultusk.

During these two days we have taken 15,000 to 16,000 prisoners, 25 to 30 cannon, 3 flags and one standard.

The weather here is extraordinary; it is warmer than it is in October in Paris; but it is raining, and in a country where there is no causeway, we are constantly in the mud.

Forty-sixth Bulletin

Golymin, 28 December 1806

Marshal Ney, charged with executing the manoeuvres by which he was to drive the Prussian Lieutenant General Lestocq from Ukra, to outflank and menace his communications, and by these means to cut off his communications with the Russians, has executed these movements with his accustomed ability and intrepidity. On the 23rd, General Marchand's division moved to Gurzno. On the 24th, the enemy was pursued to Kunzbrock. On the 25th, the rearguard of the enemy suffered some loss. On the 26th, the enemy having collected at Soldau and Miawa, Marshal Ney was determined to advance and attack. The Prussians were in possession of Soldau, with 6,000 infantry and about 1,000 cavalry, and, being defended by marshes and other obstacles about the place, they thought themselves secure against any attack. All these difficulties, however, were surmounted by the 69th and 76th Regiments. The enemy defended itself in all the streets of the place, and was everywhere driven with fixed bayonets. General Lestocq, observing the small number of troops that had attacked him, wished to re-take the place. In the course of the night he made four successive attacks, without effect. He afterwards retired to Neidenburg: 6 pieces of artillery, some flags and a great number of prisoners are the effects of this affair at Soldau. Marshal Ney praises General Vonderweidt, who was wounded. He also makes particular mention of Colonel Brünn, of the 69th, whose good behaviour was remarkable. On the same day the 59th marched to Lautenburg.

During the action at Soldau, General Marchand's division drove the enemy from Miawa, where a brilliant action also took place.

Marshal Bessières, with the 2nd Corps of the Reserve of Cavalry, had occupied Biezun as early as the 19th. The enemy, recognizing the importance of this post, and observing that the left wing of the French army wished to cut the Prussians off from the Russians, made an attempt to re-take the place; this gave rise to the battle at Biezun. On the 23rd, at eight o'clock, the enemy approached by various routes. Marshal Bessières had placed the only two companies of infantry he had near the bridge. When seeing the enemy approach in great numbers, he ordered General Grouchy to advance with his division to meet them. The enemy was already master of the village of Cormeden, into which it had already thrown a battalion of infantry.

Charged by General Grouchy's divisions, the enemy's line was soon broken. The Prussian infantry and cavalry, 6,000 strong, were thrown into confusion and driven into the marshes; 500 prisoners, 5 cannon and 2 flags are the fruits of this attack. Marshal Bessières bestows the highest praise on General Grouchy, General Roguet, and his Chief of Staff, General Roussel. Squadron Chief Renié, of the 6th Regiment of Dragoons, distinguished himself. Mr Launay, Captain of the élite company of the same regiment, was killed.

Mr Bourreau, aide-de-camp of Marshal Bessières, was wounded. Our loss is not very considerable. We had eight men killed and about 20 wounded. The two flags were taken by the dragoon Plet of the 6th Regiment of Dragoons and by the quartermaster Jeuffroy of the 3rd Regiment.

His Majesty, desiring that Prince Jérôme take the occasion to learn something, called him back from Silesia. This prince took part in all the battles that have taken place and often found himself at the advanced post.

His Majesty was satisfied with the conduct of the artillery, for the intelligence and intrepidity it showed in front of the enemy, be it in the construction of the bridges, or moving the artillery through the bad roads.

General Marulaz, commander of the Light Cavalry of the 3rd Corps, Colonel Excelmans of the 1st Chasseurs and General Petit showed proof of intelligence and bravery.

His Majesty recommended that in the official relations of different affairs we acknowledge a great number of individual actions which deserve to go into posterity; because it is for it and to live eternally in its memory that a French soldier affronts all dangers and all fatigues.

Forty-seventh Bulletin

Pultusk, 30 December 1806

The combat of Czarnowo, that of Nasielsk, that of Kursomb and the combat of cavalry at Luposzyn have been followed by that of Pultusk and Golymin; and by the complete and precipitate retreat of the Russian army, which has finished the present year's campaign.

Combat of Pultusk

Marshal Lannes could not arrive until the morning of the 26th, directly across from Pultusk, where, during the night, all of General Bennigsen's corps had assembled. The Russian divisions that had been defeated at Nasielsk, pursued by the 3rd division of the Corps of Marshal Davout, had arrived about two in the morning at Pultusk. At ten o'clock, Marshal Lannes began the attack, having his first line composed of the division of Suchet, the second line of Gazan's division and that of Gudin, of the 3rd Army Corps under the command of General Daultane, on his left wing. The engagement was very lively. After various engagements, the enemy was completely routed. The 17th Regiment of Light Infantry, and the 34th, covered themselves with glory. Generals Vedel and Claparède were wounded. General Trelliard, Commandant of the army corps, General Boussart, Commandant of a brigade of dragoons under General Beker, and also Colonel Barthelemy, of the 15th Dragoons, were wounded with grapeshot. Voisin, aide-de-camp to Marshal Lannes, and the aide-de-camp to General Suchet, Curial, were killed, and both have fallen with glory. Marshal Lannes was likewise grazed by a ball. The 5th Army Corps has shown in this circumstance what brave men can do, and the immense superiority of the French infantry over those of other nations. Marshal Lannes, though he had been sick for eight days, persisted in following the corps. The 85th Regiment sustained several charges of the enemy's cavalry with great coolness and success. During the night the enemy beat a retreat and reached Ostrolenka.

Battle of Golymin

While the corps of Bennigsen was at Pultusk and was being beaten there, the corps of Buxhowden was assembling at noon at Golymin. The Panin division of this corps, which had been attacked the day before by the Grand Duke of Berg, another division that had been beaten at Nasielsk, was arriving at the camp of Golymin by different roads.

Marshal Davout, pursuing the enemy from Nasielsk, caught up to it, charged it and took an area of woods from it near the camp of Golymin.

At the same time, Marshal Augereau, arriving from Golaczima, took the enemy in the flank. General of Brigade Lapisse, with the 16th of Light Infantry, carried away with bayonets a village that served as a point of support to the enemy. The Heudelet division was deploying and marching towards it. At three in the afternoon, the fire was getting hotter. The Grand Duke of Berg executed several marches with the greatest success in which the Klein division of dragoons distinguished itself. Meanwhile, the night arriving too soon, the battle continued until eleven at night. The enemy made its retreat in disorder, leaving its artillery, baggage, almost all of its bags and many dead. All of the enemy's columns retreated on Ostrolenka.

General Fenerolle, commanding a brigade of dragoons, was killed by a cannonball. The intrepid General Rapp, aide-de-camp to the Emperor, was wounded by a rifle shot at the head of his division of dragoons. Colonel Sémélé, of the brave 24th Line, was also wounded. Marshal Augereau had a horse killed under him.

In the meantime, Marshal Soult, with his army corps, had already arrived at Molati, two leagues from Makow, but the horrible mud, following rains and the thaw, stopped his march and saved the Russian army, of which not one man would have escaped without this incident.

The destinies of the armies of Bennigsen and Buxhowden were to end at the little river of Oreye; but all the movements were thwarted by the effect of the thaw, to such an extent that the artillery took two days to go three leagues. Nonetheless, the Russian army lost 80 cannon, all its wagons, more than 1,200 baggage carts and 12,000 men killed, wounded or taken prisoner. The movements of the French and Russian columns will be a subject of lively curiosity for military personnel, when they are traced on a map. They will see how very little there was that kept this whole army from being annihilated in few days, and this having as a cause only one mistake made by the Russian general.

We have lost 800 men killed and we have had 2,000 wounded.

Master of a large part of the enemy's artillery, of all the enemy's positions, having repulsed the enemy to more than 40 leagues, the Emperor put his army in winter quarters.

Before this expedition, the Russian officers were saying that they had 150,000 men; today they pretend having had only half that number. Who to believe, Russian officers before the battle, or Russian officers after the battle?

Persia and the Porte have declared war on Russia. Michelson attacks the Porte. These two great empires, neighbours of Russia, are tormented by the deceptive politics of the cabinet of Saint Petersburg, which has behaved for the last 10 years in their countries as it did for 50 years in Poland.

Mr Philippe Ségur, sergeant of the house of the Emperor, while going to Nasielsk, was ambushed by Cossacks who had placed themselves in a house in the woods behind Nasielsk. He killed two of them, but he was taken prisoner.

The Emperor asked for his release, but the Russian general had immediately sent him to Saint Petersburg.

Forty-eighth Bulletin

Warsaw, 3 January 1807

General Corbineau, aide-de-Camp to the Emperor, had set off from Poltusk with three regiments of light cavalry in pursuit of the enemy. After occupying Brok, he reached Ostrowiel on the 1st. On his march he picked up 400 Russian soldiers, several officers and a great quantity of baggage wagons.

Marshal Soult, with three brigades of light horse, part of LaSalle's division, has taken a position along the banks of the little river Orcye, in order to cover the cantonments of the army. Marshal Ney, the Prince of Ponte Corvo, and Marshal Bessières have cantoned their troops on the left bank. The light-armed corps, under Marshals Soult, Davout and Lannes, continues to occupy Poltusk and the banks of the Bug.

The enemy's army continues to retreat.

The Emperor arrived at Warsaw on 2 January.

We have had snow and frost for two day's continuance, but it has begun again to thaw, and the roads, which were becoming somewhat better, are now as bad as before.

Prince Borghèse has incessantly been at the head of the 1st Regiment of Carabiniers, which he commands. The brave carabiniers and cuirassiers testified the most anxious desire to meet the enemy; but the division of dragoons which came first into action, by carrying everything before them, left the former no opportunity of attacking the enemy.

His Majesty has appointed General La Riboisière a General of Division, and given him the command of the artillery of the Guard. He is an officer of the highest merit.

The troops of the Grand Duke of Würzburg compose the garrison of the city of Berlin. They consist of two regiments that make an excellent appearance.

The corps under Prince Jérôme continues to besiege Breslau. That beautiful city is in ashes. A disposition to wait the course of events, and the hope of being relieved by the Russians, have prevented the garrison from surrendering, but the siege makes progress. The Bavarian and Württemberg troops have merited the praise of Prince Jérôme and the esteem of the French army.

The Commandant of Silesia had collected the garrisons of the fortresses not yet blockaded, and formed out of them an army of 80,000 men, with which force he had commenced his march to interrupt the operations of the army besieging Breslau.

Against this force General Hedouville, the chief of Prince Jérôme's staff, detached General Montbrun, the commandant of the Württembergers, and General Minucci, commandant of the Bavarians. They came up with the Prussians at Strenien, put them to flight, and took 400 men, 600 horses and several convoys of provisions, which the enemy intended to send into the fortress. Major Hirscher, at the head of 150 Linange's light horse, attached two Prussian squadrons and completely routed them, taking 36 of them prisoners.

Forty-ninth Bulletin

Warsaw, 8 January 1807

Breslau has surrendered. The capitulation has not yet been received at the headquarters; neither has the inventory of the magazines of subsistence, or of the clothing and artillery, yet come to hand. They are, however, known to be very considerable. Prince Jérôme must have made his entry into the place. He is going to besiege Brieg, Schweidnitz and Kosel.

General Victor, commander of the 10th Army Corps, has marched to besiege Colberg and Danzig, and to take these places during the remainder of the winter.

Mr Zastrow, aide-de-camp to the King of Prussia, a wise and moderate man, who had signed the armistice that his master did not ratify, was, however, on his arrival at Königsberg, appointed Minister of Foreign Affairs.

Our cavalry is not far from Königsberg.

The Russian army is continuing its movement towards Grodno. We learn that in the last engagements it had a great number of generals killed and wounded. It evinces great discontents against the Emperor of Russia and the court. The soldiers say that if their army had been judged strong enough to fight with advantage against the French, the Emperor, his guards, the garrison of Saint Petersburg, and the generals of the court would have been conducted to the army by the same security which brought them to it last year; and that if, on the contrary, the events of Austerlitz and those of Jena made it be thought that the Russians could not obtain successes against the French army, they ought not to have been engaged in an unequal struggle. They say also, 'The Emperor Alexander has compromised our glory. We had always been vanquishers; we had established and shared the opinion that we were invincible. Things are greatly altered. For these two years past we have been led about from the frontiers of Poland to Austria, from the Dniester to the Vistula, and made to fall everywhere into the snares of the enemy. It is difficult not to perceive that all this is ill-managed.'

General Michelson is still in Moldavia. There is no news of his having marched against the Turkish army, which occupies Bucharest and Wallachia. The fears of that war are hitherto confined to the surrounding of Choczim and Bender. Great movements are taking place in all of Turkey to repulse such an unjust aggression.

General Baron Vincent is arrived from Vienna at Warsaw, carrying letters from the Emperor of Austria to the Emperor Napoleon.

There had been a great snowfall, and it had been freezing for three days. The use of sledges had given great speed to the communications, but the thaw has just begun again. The Poles assert that such a winter is without example in this country. The temperature is in reality milder than it generally is at Paris at this season.

Fiftieth Bulletin

Warsaw, 13 January 1807

At Ostrolenka, the French troops found several sick Russians whom the enemy had been unable to transport with it. Independent of the loss of the Russian army in killed and wounded, it has suffered still greater losses by the illnesses which increase in it from day to day.

The greatest disunion has occurred between Generals Kamenskoi, Bennigsen and Buxhowden.

All the territory of Prussian Poland has been evacuated by the enemy.

The King of Prussia has left Königsberg and is a refugee at Memel.

The Vistula, the Narew and the Bug had carried ice for several days; but the weather has improved and everything points to the winter being less harsh at Warsaw than it is in Paris this time of year.

On 8 January, the garrison of Breslau, consisting of 5,500 men, defiled before Prince Jérôme. The town has sustained considerable damage. From the first moment it was surrounded, the Prussian governor caused the three suburbs to be burned. The fortress was regularly besieged; we were already battering it in breach when it surrendered. The Bavarian and Württemberg troops distinguished themselves by their intelligence and bravery. Prince Jérôme is now surrounding and besieging, at the same time, all the other fortresses of Silesia; it is probable that they will not hold out long.

The corps of 10,000 men whom the Prince of Pless formed of the garrisons of the fortresses were cut to pieces in the engagements of 29 and 30 December.

General Montbrun, with the Württemberg cavalry, went to meet the Prince of Pless, near Ohlau, which he took possession of on the 28th, in the evening. On the following morning, at five o'clock, the Prince of Pless ordered him to be attacked. General Montbrun, taking advantage of the unfavourable position of the enemy's infantry, made a movement to the left, turned and killed a number of men, took 700 prisoners, took four cannon and as many horses.

The principal forces of the Prince of Pless, however, lay behind the Neisse, where he had assembled them after the engagement of Strehlen. He left Schurgalt and, marching day and night, advanced as far as the bivouac of the Württemberg brigade, which was drawn up in the rear of Hube, under Breslau. At eight in the morning, with 900 men he attacked the village of Grietern, occupied by two battalions of infantry, and by the Lilange light horses under the command of the adjutant-commandant Duveyrier; but he met with so vigorous a reception that he was forced to make a speedy retreat. Generals Montbrun and Minucci received orders immediately on their return from Ohlau to march on Schweidnitz to cut off the enemy's retreat. But the Prince of Pless made haste to disperse his troops, and made them return by detachments into the fortresses, abandoning in his flight a part of his artillery, a great deal of baggage and several horses. He had a number of men killed in this affair and left us 800 prisoners.

Letters received from Bucharest give some details concerning the preparations for war making by Bayracter and the Pacha of Widdin. On 20 December, the advanced guard of the Turkish army, consisting of 15,000 men, was on the frontiers of Wallachia and Moldavia. Prince Dolgorucky was also there with his troops. They were thus in the presence of each other. In passing Bucharest, the Turkish officers appeared to be very much animated; they said to a French officer who was in that town, 'the French shall see what we are capable of; we will form the right of the army of Poland; we shall show ourselves worthy to be praised by the Emperor Napoleon.'

Everything is in motion through this vast empire; the Sheiks and Ulemas give the impulsion, and every one flies to arms in order to repel the most unjust of aggressions.

Mr Italinski has so far only avoided being sent to the Seven Towers by promising that on the return of his messenger the Russians will have received orders to abandon Moldavia and restore Choczim and Bender.

The Serwiens, whom the Russians no longer disclaim as allies, seized an island of the Danube, which belongs to Austria, and from where they cannonade Belgrade. The Austrian government has ordered that it be re-taken.

Austria and France are also interested in not seeing Toldawia, Valashia, Lervia, Greece, Romania and Anatolia become the games of the ambition of the Muscovites.

The interest of England in this contest is at least as evident as that of France and Austria; but will she recognize it? Will she impose silence of the hatred that directs her cabinet? Will she listen to the lessons of politics and experience? If she shuts her eyes to the future, if she only lives from one day to the next, if she only listens to her jealousy against France, she might declare war against the Porte; she will make herself the ancillary of the insatiable ambition of the Russians; she will dig herself an abyss, of which she will only recognize the depth when she falls into it.

Fifty-first Bulletin

Warsaw, 14 January 1807

On 29 December, the annexed dispatch of General Bennigsen was received by the King of Prussia at Königsberg. It was immediately published and posted up throughout the town, where it excited the greatest transports of joy. The King was publicly complimented on the occasion, but on the 31st, in the evening, intelligence was given by some Prussian officers, corroborated by other advices from the country, of the real state of things. Sadness and consternation were now so much the greater, as every one had abandoned himself to joy. It was then resolved to evacuate Königsberg, and preparations were accordingly made for that purpose. The treasure and most valuable property were immediately sent to Memel. The Queen, who was quiet, embarked on 3 January for that town; the King set out from on the 6th to go there as well. The remains of General Lestocq's division also departed for the same, after leaving at Königsberg two battalions and a company of invalids.

The ministry of the King of Prussia is composed in the following manner:

General Zastrow is named Minister of Foreign Affairs.

General Rüchel, still ill of the wound he received at the battle of Jena, is appointed Minister of War.

President Sagebarthe is appointed Minister of the Interior.

The present forces of the Prussian Monarchy are as follows:

The King is attended by 1,500 troops, both foot and horse.

General Lestocq has scarcely 5,000 men, including the two battalions left at Königsberg with the company of invalids.

Lieutenant General Hamberger commands at Danzig, where he has a garrison of 6,000 men. The inhabitants have been disarmed, and it has been intimated to them that in case of alert the troops will fire on all those who shall leave their houses.

General Gutadon commands at Colberg, with 1,800 men.

Lieutenant General Courbière is at Graudenz, with 3,000 men.

French troops are in motion to surround and besiege these fortresses.

A certain number of recruits, whom the King of Prussia had caused to be assembled, and who were neither clothed nor armed, have been disbanded because there was no method of keeping them in order.

Two or three English officers were at Königsberg, and caused hopes to be entertained of the arrival of an English army.

The Prince of Pless has in Silesia, 12,000 or 15,000 men shut up in the fortresses of Breig, Neif, Schweidnitz and Kosel, which Prince Jérôme has caused to be surrounded.

We shall be silent concerning the ridiculous dispatch of General Bennigsen; we shall only remark that it contains something inconceivable. This General seems to accuse his colleague, General Buxhowden; he says that he was at Moscow. How could he be ignorant that Buxhowden had gone as far as Golymin, where he had been beaten? He pretended to have gained a victory, nevertheless he was in full retreat at ten at night, and this retreat was so hasty that he abandoned his wounded! Let him show us a single cannon, a single French standard, a single prisoner, but 12 or 15 men who might have been by the Cossacks in the rear of the army, while we can show him 6,000 prisoners, two flags, which he lost near Pultusk, and 3,000 wounded, whom he abandoned in his flight.

Should General Buxhowden have given, on his side, as true a relation of the engagement of Golymin, it will be evident that the French army was beaten, and that in consequence of its defeat it took possession of 100 pieces of ordnance, and 1,600 baggage wagons, all the hospitals of the Russian army, all its wounded, and the important positions of Sierock, Pultusk, Ostrolenka, and obliged the enemy to fall back 80 leagues.

With regard to the inference attempted to be drawn by General Bennigsen, from his not having been pursued, it is sufficient to observe that good care was taken not to pursue him because our troops outstretched him by two days' march, and that but for the bad roads that hindered Marshal Soult from following this movement, the Russian General would have found the French as Ostrolenka.

It remains for us only to seek what could be the intention of such a relation? It is the same, no doubt, that the Russians proposed to themselves at the battle of Austerlitz. It is the same, no doubt, as that of the Ukases, by which the Emperor Alexander declined accepting the grand insignia of the Order of St George, because, he said, he had not commanded at that battle, and accepted the small insignia for the success he had obtained in it, although under the command of the Emperor of Austria. He says furthermore he had the Grand Duke of Berg and Davout against him, while in fact he had only to cope with the division of Suchet and the corps of Marshal Lannes; the 17th Regiment of Light Infantry, and 34th Line, the 64th and 88th are the only regiments who fought against him. He must have reflected very little on the position of Poltusk, to suppose that the French would take possession of that town, commanded within pistol shot.

There is, however, one point of view under which the relation of General Bennigsen may be justified. No doubt they feared the effect which the truth might produce throughout Prussian and Russian Poland, which the enemy had to cross, had truth reached those countries previous to his being enabled to place hospitals and scattered detachments safe from all insult.

These relations, so evidently ridiculous, may still produce the advantages for the Russians of delaying for some days the ardour which faithful recitals will not fail to inspire the Turks with; and these are circumstances in which a few days form a delay of some importance. Experience, however, has proved that all wiles defeat their end, and that in all things simplicity and truth are the best means in politics.

Fifty-second Bulletin

Warsaw, 19 January 1807

The 8th Corps of the *Grande Armée*, commanded by Marshal Mortier, has detached a battalion of the 2nd Regiment of Light Infantry to Wollin; three companies of this battalion had scarcely arrived there, when before daybreak they were attacked by a detachment of 1,000 infantry and 150 horses, with four pieces of artillery, from Colberg. The French, not appalled by the enemy's great superiority of number, carried a bridge, took four pieces of artillery and 100 prisoners. The rest were put to flight, leaving behind a number of slain and wounded in the city of Wollin, the streets of which were covered with Prussian bodies.

The city of Brieg, in Silesia, has surrendered after a siege of five days. The garrison is composed of three generals and 1,400 men.

Poland, rich in grain and provisions, affords us a plentiful supply; Warsaw alone furnishes 100,000 rations per day.

No diseases prevail in the army, nor is it possible to take more care of the health of the soldiers than is done; although the winter season is already so far advanced, no severe frost has hitherto been experienced.

The Emperor is daily on the parade in front of the Palace of Warsaw, and reviews the different corps of the army, which, as well as the detachments of conscripts who arrive from France, are supplied with shoes and other necessaries out of the magazines of Warsaw.

Fifty-third Bulletin

Warsaw, 22 January 1807

Considerable magazines of provisions were found at Brieg.

Prince Jérôme continues his campaign of Silesia with activity. Lieutenant-General Deroy had already surrounded Kosel, and opened the trenches. The siege of Schweidnitz, and that of Neisse, are pursued at the same time.

General Victor, being on the way to Stettin in a carriage with his aide-de-camp and a servant, was taken prisoner by a party of 25 hussars, who were scouring the country.

The weather has grown cold: it is probable that in a few days the rivers will be frozen; the season, however, is not more severe than it usually is at Paris. The Emperor parades every day, and reviews several regiments.

All the magazines of the French army are in a train of organization; biscuit is made in all the bake-houses. The Emperor has given orders that large magazines be established, and that a great quantity of clothing should be made in Silesia.

The English, who can no longer gain credit for their reports that the Russians, the Tartars and the Calmucks are about to devour the French army, because it is well known, even in the coffee-houses of London, that their worthy allies cannot endure the sight of our bayonets, are now summoning dysentery, the plague and every kind of epidemic disease to their assistance. Were these calamities at the disposal of the Cabinet of London, not only our army but also our provinces and the whole class of manufacturers of the Continent, would, doubtless, become their prey. As this is not the case, the English content themselves with circulating, and causing their numerous emissaries to circulate, in every possible shape, the report that the French army is destroyed by disease. By their account, whole battalions are falling like those of the Greeks at the siege of Troy. This would be a very convenient way of getting rid of their enemies; but they must be made to renounce it. The army was never healthier; the wounded are recovering, and the number of dead is inconsiderable. There are not so many sick as in the last campaign; their number is even inferior to what it would have been in France in time of peace, according to the usual calculations.

Fifty-fourth Bulletin

Warsaw, 27 January 1807

Eighty-nine pieces of artillery, taken from the Russians, are ranged before the Palace of the Republic at Warsaw. They are those which were taken from Generals Kamenskoi, Bennigsen and Buxhowden in the battles of Czarnowo, Nasielsk, Pultusk and Golymin; and are the very same which the Russians drew along the streets of this city with so much ostentation, when not long ago they marched through them to meet the French. It is easy to conceive the effect that the sight of so grand a triumph must produce upon the people delighted with seeing the humiliation of enemies who have so long and so cruelly oppressed them.

There are several hospitals in the country which the army occupies, containing a great number of sick and wounded Russians. Five thousand prisoners have been evacuated to France, 2,000 escaped in the first moments of confusion, and 1,500 have entered among the Polish troops.

Thus, the battles engaged against the Russians have cost them a great part of their artillery, all their baggage and from 25,000 to 30,000 men, killed, wounded or prisoners.

General Kamenskoi, who had been represented as another Suvorov, has just been disgraced. It is reported that General Buxhowden is in the same situation; hence, it appears that General Bennigsen now commands the army.

Some battalions of light infantry belonging to Marshal Ney's corps had advanced 20 leagues from their cantonments; the Russian army took the alarm and made a movement on its right. These battalions have returned in the line of their cantonments, without sustaining any loss.

During this period, the Prince of Ponte Corvo took possession of Elbing and the country situated on the bank of the Baltic.

General of Division Drouet entered Christburg, where he took 300 prisoners from the regiment of Courbière, including a major and several officers.

Colonel Saint-Geniès, of the 19th Dragoons, charged another of the enemy's regiments and took 50 prisoners, among whom was the colonel commandant.

A Russian column had gone to Liebstadt, beyond the little river of Passarge, and had carried off half a company of voltigeurs of the 9th Regiment of the Line, who were at the advanced posts of the cantonment. The Prince of Ponte Corvo, informed of this movement, left Elbing, collected his troops, advanced with Rivaud's division towards the enemy, and met it near Mohrungen. On the 25th, at noon, the enemy's division appeared, 12,000 strong. We soon came to blows. The 8th Regiment of the Line fell upon the Russians with inexpressible bravery, to repair the loss which one of its posts had experienced. The enemy was completely routed, pursued four leagues, and compelled to re-cross the Passarge. Dupont's division arrived just as the engagement was concluded, and could take no part in it.

An old man, 117 years of age, has been presented to the Emperor, who has granted him a pension of 100 Napoleons, and has ordered him a 12 month's allowance in advance.

The weather is very fine. It is no colder than it should be for the health of the soldiers and the amendment of the roads, which are becoming passable.

On the right and centre of the army, the enemy is more than 30 leagues from our posts.

The Emperor went on horseback to make the tour of the cantonments. He will be absent from Warsaw eight or ten days.

Fifty-fifth Bulletin

Warsaw, 29 January 1807

Here are the details of the battle of Mohrungen:

The Marshal Prince of Ponte Corvo arrived at Mohrungen with the division of Drouet, on the 25th, at eleven in the morning, at the very moment when the General of Brigade Pacthod was attacked by the enemy.

The Marshal Prince of Ponte Corvo ordered an immediate attack of the village of Pfarresfeldeben, by a battalion of the 9th of Light Infantry. This village was defended by three Russian battalions, which were supported by three others. The Prince of Ponte Corvo ordered two other battalions to march, to support that of the 9th. The action was very sharp. The Eagle of the 9th Regiment of Light Infantry was taken by the enemy; but on the aspect of the affront with which this brave regiment was on the point of being covered forever, and that neither victory nor the glory acquired in 100 combats, would have purified the soldiers, animated with an inconceivable ardour, precipitated themselves on the enemy, which they routed, and recovered their eagle.

In the meanwhile, the French line, composed of the 8th Line, of the 27th of Light Infantry and of the 94th, was formed, and attacked the Russian line, which had taken its position on a rising ground. The fire of the musketry was very brisk, and at a point bank distance.

At this moment, General Dupont appeared on the road of Holland with the 32nd and 96th Regiments. He turned the right wing of the enemy. A battalion of the 32nd rushed upon the enemy with its usual impetuosity, put it to flight, killing many of them. The only prisoners they took were those who were in the houses. The Russians were pursued for two leagues, and were it not for the coming on of night, the pursuit would have been continued. Counts Pahlen and Gallitzin commanded the Russians. They left 1,200 dead on the battlefield, and lost 300 prisoners and several howitzers. We had 100 men killed and 400 wounded.

General of Brigade Laplanche distinguished himself. The 19th Dragoons made a fine charge against the Russian infantry. It is not only the good conduct of the soldiers and the talents of the generals that are most worthy to be remarked, but the rapidity with which the troops broke up from their cantonments and performed a march which would be reckoned extraordinary for any other troops, without a man being missing in the field of battle. It is this which eminently distinguishes soldiers who have no other impulse but that of honour.

A Tartar is just arrived from Constantinople, which place he left on the 1st of this month. He has been dispatched to London by the Porte. On 30 December, war with Russia had been solemnly proclaimed. The pelisse and the sword had been sent to the Grand Vizier: 28 regiments of Janissaries set out from Constantinople, and several others passed from Asia to Europe. The ambassador of

Russia, his whole suite, all the Russians in that city, and all the Greeks belonging to their party, to the amount of 700 or 800, left Constantinople on the 29th.

The English minister and two English vessels remained spectators in the affair and appeared to wait for orders from their government.

The Tartar passed through Widdin on 15 January. He found the roads covered with troops, who marched with cheerfulness against their eternal enemy; 60,000 men were already at Rodschuk, and 25,000, composing the advanced guard, were between that town and Bucharest. The Russians halted at Bucharest, which they occupied with an advance guard of 15,000 men.

Prince Suzzo was proclaimed Hospodar of Valachie. Prince Ypsilanti was proclaimed a traitor, and a price set upon his head.

The Tartar met the Persian Ambassador halfway from Constantinople at Widdin, and the Ambassador of the Porte, beyond that town.

The victories of Pultusk and Golymin were already well known in the Ottoman Empire. They heard this from the Turks before arriving at Widdin.

The temperature continues at two or three degrees below zero. It is the most favourable weather for the army.

Fifty-sixth Bulletin

Arensdorf, 5 February 1807

After the battle of Mohrungen, in which the Russian advance guard was defeated, the enemy retreated on Liebstadt, but on 27 January, several Russian divisions joined it and all were marching to the war theatre on the lower part of the Vistula.

The corps of General Essen, which was at first destined for Moldavia, and also a number of fresh regiments from different parts of the Russian empire, had rejoined the army corps.

The Emperor being informed of these events, ordered the Prince of Ponte Corvo to retreat, and also to favour the offensive operations of the enemy, in order to draw them towards the Lower Vistula. At the same time he ordered the whole army to break up from winter quarters.

The 5th Corps, commanded by General Savary because Marshal Lannes was ill, reunited at Brock on 31 January to keep at bay the corps of General Essen contained in the upper Bug.

The 3rd Corps was reunited at Mysiniez.

The 4th Corps at Willenberg.

The 6th Corps at Gilgenburg.

The 7th Corps at Niedenburg.

The Emperor left Warsaw and arrived on the evening of the 31st at Willenberg. The Grand Duke had been there for two days and had already collected all the cavalry.

The Prince of Ponte Corvo had successively evacuated Osterode, Tobau and fell upon Strasburg.

Marshal Lefebvre had gathered the 10th Corps at Thorn, for the defence of the left side of the Vistula and of this town.

On 1 February we began to advance. At Passenheim we fell in with the enemy, which constantly assumed the offensive; but here the Grand Duke fell upon it with several columns of cavalry, and entered the town sword in hand.

The corps of Marshal Davout have gone to Ortelsburg.

On the 2nd, the Grand Duke of Berg went to Allenstein with the corps of Marshal Soult.

Combat of Bergfried

The Emperor repaired to the village of Getkendorf, and put into battle the corps of Marshal Ney on the left, the corps of Marshal Augereau in the centre, and that of Marshal Soult on the right; the Imperial Guard was in reserve. He gave orders to Marshal Soult to repair to the road to Guttstadt and to take the bridge of Bergfried in order to debauch on the enemy's rearguard with all his army corps; a manoeuvre which gave this battle a decisive character. Vanquished, the enemy was lost with no recourse.

Marshal Soult sent General Guyot with his light cavalry to seize Guttstadt, where he took a great number of the enemy's baggage and 1,600 Russian prisoners. Guttstadt was his depot centre. But at the same time Marshal Soult repaired to the bridge of Bergfried with the Leval and Legrand divisions. The enemy, which felt the importance of this position to protect the retreat of its left flank, was defending this bridge with 12 of its best battalions. At three in the afternoon, the cannonade began. The 4th Regiment of Line and the 24th of Light Infantry had the glory of reaching the enemy first. They maintained their past reputation. These two regiments alone, and a battalion of the 28th in reserve, were enough to dislodge the enemy, cross the bridge, break through the 12 Russian battalions, take 4 cannon and cover the battlefield with dead and wounded. The 46th and the 55th who composed the second brigade were in the rear, impatient to begin their deployment; but already the enemy was in retreat, abandoning its good positions; this was a great omen for the next day!

At the same time, Marshal Ney was taking a wood where the enemy had backed up its right; the Saint-Hilaire division from the centre overtook the village; and the Grand Duke of Berg, with a division of dragoons placed by squadrons in the centre, passed the wood and swept the plain, to clear the front of our position. In these small partial attacks, the enemy was repulsed and lost 100 prisoners. Night, then, found these two armies facing each other.

The weather is superb for the season; there is three feet of snow; the thermometer is at 2 or 3 degrees.

At daybreak on the 4th, the General of Light Cavalry Lasalle scoured the plain with his hussars. A line of Cossacks and enemy cavalry rushed to place themselves in front of him. The Grand Duke of Berg formed his cavalry in line, and marched to reconnoitre the enemy. The cannonade started; but soon it became evident that the enemy had taken advantage of the night to beat a retreat and had left only a rearguard on the right, of the left and of the centre. We marched to the enemy and sent it in retreat for six leagues. The enemy's cavalry was overthrown several times; but the difficulty of the terrain opposed our cavalry's efforts. Before the end of the day, the French advance guard came to sleep at Deppen. The Emperor slept at Schlett.

At daybreak on the 5th, all of the French army was on the move.

At Deppen, the Emperor received a report that an enemy's column had not yet crossed the Alle, and was thus outflanked by our left, while the Russian army was still retreating on the roads of Arensdorf and Landsberg. His Majesty gave orders to the Grand Duke of Berg and Marshals Soult and Davout to pursue the enemy in that direction. He had Marshal Ney's corps cross the Alle with the division of light cavalry of General Lasalle and a division of dragoons, and gave him orders to attack the enemy's corps that was cut off.

Combat of Waterdorf

The Grand Duke of Berg, who had arrived at the height of Waterdorf, found himself in the presence of 8,000 to 9,000 cavalrymen. Several successive charges took place, and the enemy retreated.

Combat of Deppen

During this time, Marshal Ney was engaged and cannonading the enemy's corps, which was cut off. The enemy, for a moment, tried to force the passage, but found its death at the points of our bayonets. Overthrown as we charged, and sent into a complete rout, the enemy abandoned cannon, flags and other baggage. The other divisions of this corps seeing the condition of their advance guard, beat a retreat. By nightfall, we had already taken several thousands of prisoners, and taken 16 pieces of artillery.

Meanwhile, by these movements the largest part of the Russian army's communications were cut off. Their depots of Gustadt and Liebstadt, and a part of the magazines of the Alle, were taken by our light cavalry.

Our losses have been inconsiderable in all these small battles; we have 80 to 100 dead, 300 to 400 wounded. General Gardanne, aide-de-camp of the Emperor and governor of the pages, suffered a bad bruise to the chest. The colonel of the 4th Regiment of Dragoons was fatally wounded. General of Brigade Latour-Maubourg was wounded by a bullet in the arm. Adjutant Commander Lauberdiére, in charge of the detail of hussars, was wounded during a charge. The colonel of the 4th Regiment of Line was also wounded.

Fifty-seventh Bulletin

Prussian Eylau, 7 February 1807

On the 6th in the morning, the army started marching to follow the enemy: the Grand Duke of Berg, with Marshal Soult's corps, on Landsberg; the corps of Marshal Davout, on Heilsberg; and that of Marshal Ney, on Worenditt, to keep the corps which was cut off at Deppen from rising.

Combat of Hoff

Upon arriving at Glaudau, the Grand Duke of Berg met the enemy's rearguard and had it charged between Glandau and Hoff. The enemy deployed several lines of cavalry which appeared to support this rearguard, made up of 12 battalions, with the front on the heights of Landsberg. The Grand Duke of Berg made his dispositions. After different attacks on the right and the left of the enemy, which were backed up by a rise and a wood, the dragoons and cuirassiers of the division of General d'Hautpoult made a brilliant charge, overthrew and broke up two regiments of Russian infantry. The colonels, the flags, the cannon and most of the officers and soldiers were taken. The enemy army started marching to help support the rearguard. Marshal Soult had arrived; Marshal Augereau took position on the left, and the village of Hoff was occupied. The enemy sensed the importance of this position, and sent ten battalions marching to re-take it. The Grand Duke of Berg ordered a second charge to be made by the cuirassiers who took them in the flank and cut them to pieces. These manoeuvres are great exploits of arms and give the greatest honour to these intrepid cuirassiers. This day merits a particular relation. A part of the two armies passed the night of the 6th to the 7th across from each other. The enemy filed off during the night.

At daybreak, the French advance guard started marching and met the enemy's rearguard between the woods and the town of Eylau. Several regiments of enemy chasseurs on foot who defended it were charged and taken. Soon we arrived at Eylau and found that the enemy was in position behind that town.

Fifty-eighth Bulletin

Prussian Eylau, 9 February 1807

Combat of Eylau

A quarter of a league from the small town of Preussick-Eylau, there is a plateau which defends the debauch of the plain. Marshal Soult gave orders to the 46th and the 18th Regiments of Line to seize it. Three regiments which were defending it were overthrown; but at the same moment a column of Russian cavalry charged the extremity of the left of the 18th and caused disorder in one of its battalions. The dragoons of Klein's division noticed this in time; the troops became engaged in the town of Eylau. The enemy had placed several regiments in a church and a graveyard. There it gave a very obstinate resistance; and after a deadly battle for both sides, the position was seized at ten at night. The Legrand division took its bivouacs before the town, and the Saint-Hilaire division on the right of the town. The corps of Marshal Augereau took position on the left; the corps of Marshal Davout had, the day before, marched to overtake Eylau and fall on the left flank of the enemy if it did not change position. Marshal Ney was marching to overtake the enemy on its right flank. It is in this position that the night passed.

Battle of Eylau

On the following day, by the first dim ray of the morning, the Russians commenced the attack with a brisk cannonade. The Emperor took a position in the church which the Russians had defended with so much obstinacy on the day before. He made Marshal Augereau's corps advance, and the eminence upon which the church stood was cannonaded by 40 pieces of artillery belonging to his Guard. The armies were now within half a gunshot of each other. The thunder of the cannon was terrible. After the firing had continued for some time, the troops became impatient of suffering so much without anything decisive happening. Some manoeuvres then commenced on both sides, in order to obtain advantages over each other, and in the meantime a thick fall of snow came on, in consequence of which the troops could not discern one another at a distance of two paces. In this obscurity some of the corps lost their way, and the columns getting too much to the left wandered in uncertainty. This state lasted half an hour. When the weather cleared up, the Grand Duke at the head of the cavalry, supported by Marshal Bessières at the head of the Guard, and the division of Saint-Hilaire, advanced and attacked the enemy. This bold manoeuvre, which covered the cavalry with glory, had become necessary in consequence of the circumstances which our columns were placed. The enemy's cavalry, which endeavoured to oppose this manoeuvre, was completely routed. The slaughter was horrible. Two lines of Russian infantry were penetrated, and the third only maintained itself in consequence of having supported itself upon a wood. Some squadrons of the guards passed twice through all of the enemy's army.

This brilliant attack, had it not been for the wood, and some other difficulties of the ground, would have decided the victory. General Hautpoul was wounded. General Dahlmann perished gloriously in the attack. For the 100 dragoons or cuirassiers of the Guard which lay dead in the field, there were found beside them 1,000 of their enemies.

Marshal Davout, who had been detached to fall upon the rear of the enemy, but whose progress was much impeded by the weather, was at last enabled to execute his orders, and decided the victory. The enemy, after several vain endeavours to repulse that general, retreated, leaving its wounded and 16 pieces of artillery on the battlefield.

143

The number of killed and wounded in this action was on both sides very considerable, and it could not be otherwise when a constant fire was maintained from about 300 cannon for more than 12 hours, within a short distance of both armies.

Marshal Augereau was wounded in the battle. Generals Desjardin, Heudelet and Lochet are also wounded. General Corbineau is killed. Colonel Lacuée of the 63rd, and Colonel Lemarois of the 43rd were also killed. Colonel Bourvières of the 11th Regiment of Dragoons did not survive his wounds. They all died with glory. Our whole loss consists of exactly 1,900 killed, and 5,700 wounded, including 1,000 who are very badly wounded. But we have to set against this loss 7,000 Russians who have been counted dead on the battlefield.

The plan of the enemy, which had for its object to extend itself towards Thorn and to turn our left wing, has completely miscarried, and its attempt to carry it into execution has proved exceedingly fatal to them. It has cost it from 12- to 15,000 prisoners, as many in killed and missing, 45 pieces of artillery and 18 flags.

The Eagle of one of the battalions is lost, and has probably been taken by the enemy. The Emperor will give that battalion another standard after it has taken one from the enemy.

Having defeated this enterprise of the enemy, and driven it 100 miles from the Vistula, the army has returned to its cantonments and is going into winter quarters again.

Fifty-ninth Bulletin

Prussian Eylau, 14 February 1807

The enemy has taken a position behind the Pregel. Our patrols are before Königsberg, but the Emperor has thought proper to concentrate his army in winter quarters, in such manner that it may be in a condition to cover the line of the Vistula.

The number of cannon which have been taken since the battle of Bergfried is about 60. The 24 that the enemy had left at the battle of Eylau have been sent to Thorn.

The enemy has circulated the following notice. Everything in it is false. The enemy attacked the town and was constantly repulsed. It admits losing 20,000 men killed or wounded. Its loss is much greater. Its claim of taking 9 eagles is as false as that of taking the town.

The Grand Duke of Berg still has his headquarters at Württemberg, close upon the Pregel.

General Hautpoul has died of his wounds; his loss is generally deplored. Few soldiers have terminated their career so gloriously. His division of cuirassiers has distinguished itself in all the battles. The Emperor has given orders for removing his body to Paris.

General of Cavalry Bonardi Saint-Sulpice, wounded at the wrist, did not want to go to the hospital; instead he made a second charge. His Majesty was so pleased with his service that he named him general of the division.

On the 12th, Marshal Lefebvre advanced to Marienwerder, where he found 7 Prussian squadrons; he defeated them, and took 300 prisoners, among which were a colonel, a major and several officers, and 250 horses. Those who escaped fled towards Danzig.

(The notice announced in this Bulletin was never found attached to it.)

Proclamation to the Army

Prussian Eylau, 16 February 1807
Soldiers, we had begun to enjoy a little repose in our winter quarters, when the enemy attacked the first corps, and showed itself on the Lower Vistula. We broke up and marched against it. We have pursued it, sword in hand, 80 miles. It has fled to its strongholds, and retired beyond the Pregel. In the battles of Bergfried, Deppen, Hof and Eylau, we have taken from it 66 cannon, and 16 flags, besides its loss of more than 40,000 men killed, wounded or taken prisoner. The heroes who, on our side, remain in the field of honour, have died a glorious death. It is the death of a true soldier. Their relatives will always have a just claim to our care and beneficence.

Having thus defeated all the enterprises of the enemy, we shall return towards the Vistula, and resume our winter quarters. Those who shall dare to disturb these quarters shall have reason to repent; for, whether beyond the Vistula, or on the other side of the Danube; whether in the middle of winter, or in the beginning of autumn; we still will be found French soldiers, and the French soldiers of the *Grande Armée*.

Sixtieth Bulletin

Prussian Eylau, 17 February 1807
The conquest of Silesia is advanced. The fortress of Schweidnitz has surrendered. The Prussian Governor of Silesia is shut up in Glatz, after having been driven by General Lefebvre out of the positions of Frankenstein and Neurode. In these affairs the Württemberg troops behaved remarkably well. The enemy lost about 100 killed and 300 prisoners.

The siege of Kosel is conducted with vigour.

Since the battle of Eylau the enemy has reassembled behind the Pregel. We hoped to have driven it from that position, had the river remained frozen; but a thaw has commenced and this river is a boundary over which the French army has no interest to pursue it.

About 3,000 Russian prisoners who were at Willenberg have been set at liberty by a troop of Cossacks, consisting of 1,000 men.

The cold has entirely ceased; the snow is everywhere melted, and the season exhibits a singular phenomenon of the mild weather of the last days of April, in the middle of the month of February.

The army is entered into cantonments.

Sixty-first Bulletin

Landsberg, 18 February 1807
The battle of Eylau was at first considered as a victory by several of the enemy's officers. Such, indeed, was the belief at Königsberg, during the whole morning of the 9th; but the alarm was great when the Russian headquarters and the army arrived there. Soon after our cannon was heard, the French were seen in the possession of a height which dominated all of the Russian camp.

The Russian general declared that he would defend the town, which greatly increased the alarm of the inhabitants, who said, 'We shall share the fate of Lubeck.' It was fortunate, however, for this town, that it did not come within the plan of the French generals to drive the Russians from this position.

The number of dead in the Russian army, in generals and other officers, is very considerable.

In consequence of the battle of Eylau, more than 5,000 wounded Russians, found on the battlefield or in the neighbouring hospitals, have fallen into the hands of the victors. It is reckoned that the Russians had 15,000 wounded, besides the 5,000 which fell into the hands of the French.

The army has resumed its quarters. The districts of Elbing, Liebstadt and Osterode are the finest in the country, and the Emperor has chosen them for the cantonments of his left wing.

Marshal Mortier has gone back to Swedish Pomerania. Stralsund is blockaded; and it is to be regretted that the enemy has, without any reason, burned the fine suburb of Knipper. This fire presented a horrible spectacle. More than 2,000 persons are without homes or shelter.

Sixty-second Bulletin

Liebstadt, 21 February 1807

The right of the *Grande Armée* has been victorious, like the centre and the left. General Essen, at the head of 25,000 men, advanced to Ostrolenka on the 15th, along the two banks of the Narew; when he arrived at the village of Stanislawow, he met the advanced guard of General Savary, who commanded the 5th Corps.

On the 16th, at daybreak, General Gazan, with a part of his division, moved to the advanced guard. At nine in the morning, he met the enemy on the road to Novogorod, attacked, defeated and put it to the route. But, at the same moment, the enemy attacked Ostrolenka by the left bank. General Compana, with a brigade of the division of General Gazan, and General Ruffin, with a brigade of the division of General Oudinot, defended that small town. General Savary sent there the General of Division Reille, chief of the army. The Russian infantry, in several columns, endeavoured to carry the town. We let it advance half the length of the streets, when it was marched against and charged. It was three times cut down, and left the streets covered with the dead. The loss of the enemy was so great that it abandoned the town and took a position behind the sand hills that covered it.

The divisions of Generals Suchet and Oudinot advanced; at noon the heads of their columns arrived at Ostrolenka. General Savary drew up his little army in the following manner: General Oudinot commanded the left in two lines; General Suchet the centre; and General Reille, commanding a brigade of the division of Gazan, formed the right.He covered himself with all his artillery and marched against the enemy. The intrepid General Oudinot put himself at the head of the cavalry, made a successful charge, and cut in pieces the Cossacks of the rear guard of the enemy. The fire was very brisk; the enemy gave way on all sides, and was followed fighting for three leagues.

The next day the enemy was pursued several leagues, without realizing that its cavalry had been retreating the whole night. General Suvorov, and several other officers of the enemy are among the slain. The enemy has abandoned a great number of the wounded, 1,200 have been taken off the field, and more are being brought in every instant. Seven pieces of artillery and 2 flags are the trophies of this victory. The enemy has left 1,300 dead on the battlefield. On our side we have had 60 men killed, and from 400 to 500 wounded. But a loss more deeply felt is that of General of Brigade Campana, who was an officer of great merit and promise; he was born in the department of Marengo. The Emperor has been much grieved at his loss. The 103rd Regiment particularly distinguished itself in this affair. Among the wounded are Colonel Duhamel of the 21st Regiment of Light Infantry, and the Colonel of Artillery, Noury.

The Emperor has ordered the 5th Corps to go into winter quarters. The thaw is dreadful. The season will not permit anything great to be achieved; it is that of repose. The enemy first broke up from his quarters; it has repented it.

Sixty-third Bulletin

Osterode, 28 February 1807

Captain Auzouy, Captain of the Horse Grenadiers of the Imperial Guard, mortally wounded in the battle of Eylau, was lying on the battlefield. His comrades came to take him up and carry him to the hospital. He recovered his senses only to say to them, 'Let me alone, my friends; I die contented, since we have victory, and that I can die upon the field of honour, surrounded by the cannons taken from the enemy, and the wrecks of its defeat. Tell the Emperor that I have but one regret, which is that in a few moments I shall be no longer able to do any thing for his service, and the glory of our fine France... to her my last breath.' The effort he made to utter these words exhausted the little strength he had remaining.

All the reports we receive agree in stating that the enemy lost at the battle of Eylau 20 generals, 900 officers killed or wounded and upwards of 30,000 men disabled.

At the engagement of Ostrolenka, on the 16th, two Russian generals were killed, and three wounded.

His Majesty has sent the 16 stands of colours taken at the battle of Eylau to Paris. All the cannon are already sent off to Thorn. His Majesty has ordered that these cannon shall be melted down and made into a brazen statue of General Hautpoul, commander of the second division of cuirassiers, in his uniform of cuirassier.

The army is concentrated in its cantonments behind the Passarge, with its left supported by Marienwerder, at the island of Nogat, and at Elbing, countries which afford resources.

Being informed that a Russian division had marched towards Braunsberg, at the head of our cantonments, the Emperor ordered it to be attacked. The Prince of Ponte Corvo assigned this expedition to General Dupont, an officer of great merit. On the 26th, at two o'clock in the afternoon, General Dupont presented himself before Braunsberg, attacked the enemy's division, 10,000 strong, overthrew it with fixed bayonets, drove it from the town made it re-cross the Passarge; took from it 16 cannon, 2 stands of colours and took 2,000 prisoners. We had but very few men killed.

On the side of Guttstadt, General Leger-Belair repaired to the village of Peterswalde, at daybreak on the 26th, upon receiving advice that a Russian column had arrived during the night at that village, overthrew it, took General Baron Korff, who commanded it, his staff, several Lieutenant-Colonels and officers and 400 men. This brigade was composed of ten battalions, which had suffered so much that they formed only 1,600 men under arms.

The Emperor, in testimony of his satisfaction to General Savary for the engagement of Ostrolenka, has granted him the grand insignia of the Legion of Honour and called him about his person. His Majesty has given the command of the 5th Corps to Marshal Masséna, Marshal Lannes continuing to be sick.

At the battle of Eylau, Marshal Augereau, overrun with rheumatic pains, was sick and hardly in his senses; but the cannon awakes the brave; he flew in full gallop to the head of his corps, after getting himself tied upon his horse. He was constantly exposed to the greatest fire, and was even slightly wounded. The Emperor has just authorized him to return to France for the purpose of taking care of his health.

The garrison of Colberg and Danzig, availing themselves of the little attention paid them, had encouraged themselves by different excursions. An advanced post of the Italian division was attacked on the 16th at Stargard by a party of 800 men of the garrison of Colberg. General Bonfanti had with him only a few companies of the 1st Italian Regiment of Line, which took to their arms in time, marched with resolution against the enemy, and routed it. General Teulié, on his side, with the main body of the Italian division, the regiment of musketeers of the Guard, and the first company of Gendarmes on duty, repaired to surround Colberg. On arriving at Naugarten, he found the enemy entrenched, occupying a fort beset with cannon. Colonel Boyer, of the fusiliers of the Imperial Guard, gave an assault. Captain Montmorency, of the company of Gendarmes, made a successful charge. The fort was taken, 300 men taken prisoner, and six pieces of artillery carried off. The enemy left 100 men upon the battlefield.

General Dombrowski marched against the garrison of Danzig; he fell in with it at Dirschau, overthrew it, took 6,000 prisoners, took 7 pieces of artillery and pursued it for several leagues. He was wounded with a musket ball. Marshal Lefebvre arrived in the meantime at the head of the 10th Corps. He had been joined by the Saxons, and was marching to surround Danzig.

The weather is still changeable. It froze yesterday; it thaws today. The whole winter has passed in this manner. The thermometer has never been higher than five degrees.

Sixty-fourth Bulletin

Osterode, 2 March 1807

The town of Elbing furnishes great resources to the army: a great quantity of wine and brandy was found there. This country of the Lower Vistula is very fertile.

The ambassadors from Constantinople and Persia have entered Poland and are on their way to Warsaw.

After the battle of Eylau, the Emperor passed several hours each day upon the battlefield, a horrible spectacle, but which duty rendered necessary. It required great labour to bury all the dead. A great number of Russian officers slain were found with the insignia of their orders. It appears that among them was a Prince Repnine. Forty-eight hours after the battle, there were still upwards of 5,000 wounded Russians whom we had not been able to carry off. Brandy and bread were carried to them, and they were successively conveyed to the hospital. Let any one imagine to himself, upon the space of a square league, 9,000 or 10,000 dead bodies, 4,000 or 5,000 horses killed, whole lines of Russian knapsacks, broken pieces of muskets and sabres; the ground covered with cannonballs, howitzer shells and ammunition; 24 cannon, near which were lying the bodies of their drivers, killed at the moment when they were striving to carry them off. All this was the more conspicuous upon a ground covered with snow: this spectacle is calculated to inspire princes with the love of peace and an abhorrence of war.

The 5,000 wounded whom we had were all conveyed to Thorn, and to our hospitals on the left bank of the Vistula, in sledges. The surgeons observed with astonishment that the fatigue of this conveyance did no harm to the wounded.

Here are some details of the engagement of Braunsberg.

General Dupont marched against the enemy in two columns. General Bruyères, who commanded the right column, fell in with the enemy at Zagern and drove it towards the river which runs before this village. The left column drove the enemy towards Willenberg, and the entire division shortly after stretched out of the wood. The enemy, being driven from its first position, was obliged to fall back upon the river which covers the town of Braunsberg: it at first made a resolute stand, but General Dupont marched against it, overthrew it by a charge, and entered with the enemy into the town, the streets of which were choked up with the Russian slain.

The 9th of Light Infantry, the 32nd and the 96th Line, which compose this division, distinguished themselves. Generals Barrois and Lahoussaye, Colonel Sémélé, of the 24th Line, Colonel Meunier of the 9th Light Infantry, Battalion Chief Bouge of the 32nd Line, and Squadron Chief Hubinet of the 9th Hussars are deserving of particular praise.

Since the arrival of the French army on the Vistula, we have taken 89 pieces of artillery from the Russians in the engagements of Pultusk and Golymin; at the engagement of Bergfried, 4 pieces; at the engagement of Deppen, 16 pieces; at the retreat of Allenstein, 5 pieces; at the engagement of Hof, 12 pieces; the battle of Eylau, 24 pieces; at the engagement of Braunsberg, 16 pieces; and at the engagement of Ostrolenka, 9 pieces; total, 175 cannon.

It has been remarked upon this subject that the Emperor never lost any cannon in the armies that he has commanded, either in the first campaigns of Italy and Egypt, in that of the Army of Reserve, in that of Austria and Moravia, or in that of Prussia and Poland.

Sixty-fifth Bulletin

Osterode, 10 March 1807

The army has gone into cantonments behind the Passarge. The Prince of Ponte Corvo is at Holland and Braunsberg; Marshal Soult at Liebstadt and Mohrungen; Marshal Ney at Guttstadt; Marshal Davout at Allenstein, Hohenstein and Deppen; the headquarters are at Osterode; the Polish corps of observation, under General Zayonchek, is at Neidenburg; Marshal Lefebvre is before Danzig; the 5th Corps is upon the Omulew; a division of Bavarians, under the Crown Prince, is at Warsaw; the corps of Prince Jérôme in Silesia; the 8th Corps in observation in Swedish Pomerania.

The fortresses of Breslau, Schweidnitz and Brieg are being demolished.

General Rapp, aide-de-camp to the Emperor, is governor of Thorn.

Bridges are thrown over the Vistula at Marienburg and Dirschau.

On 1 March, the Emperor having been informed that the enemy, encouraged by the position of our army, had shown itself on the right bank of the Passarge, ordered Marshals Ney and Soult to advance, reconnoitre and drive the enemy back. Marshal Ney proceeded towards Guttstadt; Marshal Soult crossed the Passarge at Wormditt. The enemy's posts, which retreated with precipitation, were pursued to the distance of eight leagues. The enemy, observing that the French were not inclined to pursue it any further, and that our force was merely an advanced guard that had left their main body in the rear, brought forward two regiments of Russian grenadiers, and, in the course of the night, attacked our cantonments at Zechern. The 50th Regiment received them upon the point of the bayonet. The 27th and 39th Regiments also conducted themselves with great courage. In these small combats the Russians had nearly 1,000 of their men killed, wounded or taken prisoner.

After having thus disturbed the enemy, the army returned again to its cantonments.

The Grand Duke of Berg, being informed that a corps of cavalry had advanced to Willenberg, ordered the Prince of Borghèse to attack that place, who, at the head of his regiment, charged 8 Russian squadrons, overthrew, and put them to flight, taking 100 prisoner, including 3 captains and 8 officers.

Marshal Lefebvre has completely surrounded Danzig, and commenced the lines of circumvallation round that city.

Sixty-sixth Bulletin

Osterode, 14 March 1807

The *Grande Armée* remains in its cantonments, where it takes repose. Frequent skirmishes have taken place between the advanced posts of the two armies. Two regiments of Russian cavalry came on the 12th to harass the 69th Regiment of Infantry of Line in its cantonments, at Langenau, before Guttstadt. A battalion of this regiment flew to arms from an ambuscade and attacked and repulsed the enemy, which left 80 men on the field. General Guyot, who commanded the advanced posts of Marshal Soult, has, on his side, had several affairs of outposts with the enemy, in which he had the advantage.

After the little battle of Willenberg, the Grand Duke of Berg expelled the Cossacks from the whole of the right bank of the Alle in order to assure himself that the enemy was not hiding some movements. He went to Wartenburg, Seeburg, Mensgut and Bischofsburg. He had some engagements with the enemy's cavalry and took 100 Cossacks prisoner.

The Russian army appears to be concentrated on the side of Bartenstein on the Alle; the Prussian division on the side of Kreuzberg.

The enemy's army made a retrograde movement, and has approached nearer to Königsberg.

All of the French army is in cantonments: it is provisioned by the towns of Elbing, Braunsberg, and from the resources drawn from the island of Nogat, which is extremely fertile.

Two bridges have been erected over the Vistula, one at Marienwerder, the other at Marienburg. Marshal Lefebvre has completed the surrounding of Danzig. General Teulié has surrounded Colberg. Each of these garrisons have been driven into these towns after a slight engagement.

A division of 12,000 Bavarians commanded by the Prince Royal of Bavaria has crossed the Vistula at Warsaw, and is coming to join the army.

Sixty-seventh Bulletin

Osterode, 25 March 1807

On 14 March, at three in the afternoon, the garrison of Stralsund, taking advantage of a fog, made a sortie with 2,000 infantry, 2 squadrons of cavalry and 6 cannon, in order to carry a redoubt thrown up by General Dupas. This redoubt, which was open, without palisades and without cannon, was defended by a company of voltigeurs of the 58th Regiment of Line. The immense superiority of the enemy had no effect on these brave men; being reinforced by a company of voltigeurs of the 4th Line (Light Infantry) under Captain Barral, they resisted all the attempts of the Swedish brigade. Fifteen Swedish soldiers reached the parapet, but there found their death. All the enemy's attempts were equally fruitless. Sixty-two dead bodies of the Swedes were buried at the foot of the redoubt. It is supposed that 120 were wounded, and 50 were taken prisoner, though there were not more than 150 men in the redoubt. Several Swedish officers were found among the dead, distinguished by their military decorations. This instance of bravery has attracted the Emperor's attention. His Majesty his sent three orders of the Legion of Honour for the companies engaged. Captain Drivet, who commanded on this weak redoubt, highly distinguished himself.

On the 20th, Marshal Lefebvre ordered the brigade under General Schramm to cross over from the island of Nogat, in the Frisches-Haff, in order to cut off the communication between Danzig and the sea. The crossing was executed at three in the morning. The Prussians were routed, and 300 of them fell into our hands.

At six in the evening, the garrison sent out a detachment of 4,000 men to re-take the post; but they were repulsed, with the loss of some hundreds of prisoners and one piece of artillery.

General Schramm had under his command the 2nd Battalion of the 2nd Regiment of Light Infantry, and several Saxon battalions, who distinguished themselves. The Emperor has sent three orders of the Legion of Honour to be distributed among the Saxon officers; and three more for the privates, subalterns, and to the major who commanded them.

In Silesia the garrison of Neisse has made a sortie, but fell into an ambush. A regiment of Württemberg cavalry took these troops in flank, killed 50 and took 60 prisoner.

This winter in Poland seems to have resembled the winter at Paris, that is to say, variable. It freezes and thaws in alternate succession. However, we have the good fortune not to have any sick in the army. On the contrary, all accounts agree that the Russians have a great number of sick. The army remains tranquil in its cantonments.

The works that compose the bridgehead of Sierock, Modlin, Praga, Marienburg and Marienwerder are becoming more formidable every day; and the magazines are organized and are everywhere receiving provisions. Three hundred thousand bottles of Bordeaux wine were found at Elbing; and though each bottle cost four francs, the Emperor paid that price to the merchants and ordered the wine to be distributed among the army.

The Emperor has sent Prince Borghèse on a mission to Warsaw.

Sixty-eighth Bulletin

Osterode, 29 March 1807

On 17 March, at three o'clock in the morning, General of Brigade Lefebvre, aide-de-camp to Prince Jérôme, passed near Glatz, on this way to Wünschelburg, with three squadrons of light horse and a regiment of light infantry of Taxis, when 1,500 men, with two cannon, came out of the fortress. Lieutenant Colonel Gérard immediately attacked and drove them back into Glatz, after having taken 100 soldiers, several officers and two pieces of artillery.

Marshal Masséna is gone from Willenberg to Ortelsburg, and forced an entrance there for the division of Beker's dragoons, which he has reinforced with a detachment of Polish horse. There were some Cossacks at Ortelsburg, and several attacks were made, in which the enemy lost 20 men.

General Beker, as he was coming to resume his position at Willenberg, was attacked by 2,000 Cossacks. An ambush of infantry was formed, into which they fell and lost 200 men.

On the 26th, at five o'clock in the morning, the garrison of Danzig made a general sortie, which proved fatal. It was repulsed on all sides. A Colonel, named Kraków, who had a command of partisans, was taken with 400 men and two cannon, in an attack made by the 19th Regiment of Chasseurs. The Northern Polish Legion conducted itself in an excellent manner, and two Saxon battalions distinguished themselves.

As to the rest, there is nothing new. The lakes are still frozen, though there is some appearance of the approach of spring.

Sixty-ninth Bulletin

Finkenstein, 4 April 1807

The Gendarmes of the ordnance have arrived at Marienwerder, and Marshal Bessières has set out for that place, in order to review them. They have behaved remarkably well, and have displayed great courage in all the affairs in which they have been engaged.

General Teulié, who had conducted the blockade of Colberg, has, in that command, exhibited great activity and skill. The conducting of the siege is now entrusted to General Loison. On 19 March, the redoubts of Selnow were attacked and carried by the 1st Regiment of Italian Light Infantry. On this occasion the garrison made a sortie; but the company of carabiniers of the 1st Regiment of Light Infantry, and a company of dragoons, drove them back. The voltigeurs of the 19th Regiment of Line distinguished themselves greatly in the attack on the village of Allstadt. In that affair the enemy lost three cannon and 200 prisoners.

Marshal Lefebvre commands at the siege of Danzig, and General La Riboisière has the direction of the artillery. The latter corps shows itself in all circumstances worthy of the fame that it has so justly acquired. The French cannoneers will merit the name of élite troops. The manner in which the battalions of the train have performed their service has afforded perfect satisfaction.

The Emperor has given audience at Finkenstein to a deputation from the chamber of Marienwerder. It consisted of Count Von Gröben, Councillor Baron Von Schleinitz and Count Von Dohma, Director of the Chamber. The deputation represented to His Majesty the great hardships which the inhabitants had suffered from the war. The Emperor answered that he was affected by their sufferings, and that he would relieve Marienwerder, as well as Elbing, from the burden of any extraordinary contribution. He observed that there were evils belonging to the theatre of war which could not be avoided; that he participated in the regret which those evils occasioned, and would do everything in his power to mitigate them.

It is believed that His Majesty will this day set out on a short journey to Marienwerder and Elbing.

The 2nd Bavarian division has arrived at Warsaw.

The Crown Prince of Bavaria has gone to Pultusk to take the command of he first division.

The Hereditary Prince of Baden has marched at the head of his corps of troops to Danzig. The contingent of Saxe-Weimar has arrived upon the Warta.

There has not been a shot fired for a fortnight past at the advanced posts of the army.

The heat of the sun begins to be felt, but it is not yet sufficiently powerful to penetrate and thaw the earth. All is still bound in frost. Spring approaches slowly in this country.

A number of couriers arrive at the headquarters from Constantinople and Persia.

The health of the Emperor continues excellent; it is even remarked that it appears better than formerly. Some days His Majesty makes excursions to the distance of 40 leagues on horseback.

At Warsaw it was believed last week that the Emperor had arrived there about ten o'clock at night. The whole town was immediately and voluntarily illuminated.

The fortresses of Praga, Sierock, Modlin, Thorn and Marienburg begin to be put in a state of defence. The works of Marienwerder are planned. All these fortresses form bridgeheads on the Vistula.

The Emperor praises the activity of Marshal Kellermann in forming the provisional regiments, many of which have arrived in good condition and are incorporated in the army.

His Majesty also bestows great praise on General Clarke, Governor of Berlin, who displays equal activity and zeal in the important post confided to him.

Prince Jérôme, who commands the troops in Silesia, has also given proofs of great activity, and has exhibited a degree of skill and prudence that is, in general, only the fruit of long experience.

Seventieth Bulletin

Finkenstein, 9 April 1807

A corps of 400 Prussians, who embarked at Königsberg and landed on the peninsula opposite Pillau, advanced towards the village of Carlsberg. Mr Maingarnaud, aide-de-camp of Marshal Lefebvre, marched towards that point with a few men: he manoeuvred so dextrously that he took the 400 Prussians, among whom were 120 cavalry.

Several Russian regiments have entered Danzig by sea. The garrison has made several sorties.

The Polish legions of the north, and their commander Prince Michael Radziwill, have greatly distinguished themselves: they took about 40 Russians prisoner. The siege is carried on with activity. The siege artillery begins to arrive.

There is nothing new at the different posts of the army.

The Emperor has returned from Marienwerder and from a visit to the bridgehead on the Vistula. He reviewed the 12th Regiment of Light Infantry. The land and the lakes which are plentiful in this country are starting to thaw.

Seventy-first Bulletin

Finkenstein, 19 April 1807

The victory of Eylau, having frustrated all the plans that the enemy had formed against the Lower Vistula, has enabled us to surround Danzig and to commence the siege of that fortress. But it was necessary to draw the battering train from the fortresses of Silesia and along the Oder, so that it had to come 100 leagues in an area without roads. One hundred cannon are now on their way from Stettin, Custrin, Glogau and Breslau, and in a few days we shall be provided with everything necessary.

The Prussian General Kalkreuth has the command at Danzig. The garrison consists of 14,000 Prussians and 6,000 Russians. The inundations and marshes, several lines of fortifications, and the fort of Weichselmünde have rendered it difficult to surround the fortress.

Our works have come at 80 *toises* from Danzig; we have also several times affronted the covered roads.

Marshal Lefebvre tells us of the activity of a young man; as he was seconded by General Savary, this general became sick at the abbey of Oliva, which is a short distance away. His illness caused a great deal of worry for several days. General of

Brigade Schramm, General of Artillery La Riboisière and General of Engineering Kirgener, all have seconded Marshal Lefebvre in a great manner. General of Division of Engineers Chasseloup has just started for Danzig.

The Saxon, the Polish and the Baden troops, since the Hereditary Prince of Baden is at their head, are vying with each other in bravery.

The enemy has not tried any other means of coming to the assistance of Danzig than by sending a few battalions and some provisions to the fortress by sea.

In Silesia, Prince Jérôme continues the siege of Neisse vigorously.

Since the Prince of Pless has declined to act, Baron Kleist, aide-de-camp to the King of Prussia, is arrived at Glatz, by way of Vienna, with the title of Governor General of Silesia. He is accompanied by an English commissary, who must keep his eye upon the manner in which the 80,000 *livres* sterling are laid out which were given by England to the King of Prussia.

On the 13th of this month, that Prussian officer advanced from Glatz with a corps of 4,000 men and attacked General Lefebvre (who commands the corps of observation which covers the siege of Neisse) at Frankenstein. This operation has been ineffectual. Baron Kleist was repulsed with vigour.

On the 14th, Prince Jérôme fixed his headquarters at Münsterberg.

General Loison took command of the siege of Colberg. All necessary means are taken for the operation of this siege; there were delays caused by the reluctance to thwart the formation of the equipages of the siege of Danzig.

Marshal Mortier, who directs the siege of Colberg, went there, leaving General Grandjean to take position on the Peene with the observation corps.

The garrison of Stralsund, meanwhile, received several regiments of support, which came by sea, and having learned of the movement made by Marshal Mortier, debouched in force. General Grandjean, as instructed, crossed the Peene and took position at Anklam. The numerous Swedish flotillas gave them the advantage of landing on different points and to surprise a Dutch post of 30 men and an Italian post of 37 men. Marshal Mortier, having learned of these movements, advanced on the 13th on Stettin, and with all his forces manoeuvred to draw the Swedes, whose number is not quite 12,000 men.

For these two months past, the *Grande Armée* has been stationary in its positions. This time has been employed in renewing and replenishing the cavalry, and providing them with horses, repairing the arms, establishing large stores of biscuit and brandy and furnishing the soldiers with shoes. In addition to one pair in wear, each man has two more pairs in his knapsack.

Silesia and the Island of Nogat have furnished a number of good horses to the cuirassiers, to the dragoons and to the light cavalry.

In the first days of May, an army corps of observation, consisting of 50,000 French and Spanish troops, will be assembled on the Elbe: while Russia has assembled in Poland nearly all of her troops, there is only a part of the French military force in that country. This, however, is a consequence of the great difference which exists between the essential strength of the two countries. The 500,000 Russians, which the writers of newspapers made to march to the right and again to the left, only exist in their papers and in the imagination of some readers, who are the easier misled by being shown the immense extent of the Russian territory, without the least mention of its extensive deserts and uncultivated districts.

It is said that the Guards of the Emperor of Russia have reached the army. They will see on the first meeting, whether the Imperial Guard is annihilated, as the enemy's generals have asserted. That Imperial Guard is now more numerous than ever, and almost double the number it was at Austerlitz.

Exclusive of the bridge thrown across the Narew, another is forming on piles between Warsaw and Praga: the work is in a very forward state. The Emperor proposes to build three more on different points. The bridges on piles are stronger and more serviceable than those of boats. Although it is very laborious to construct such bridges across a river of 400 *toises* in breath, it is rendered easy through the skill and activity of the officers under whose direction it is performed, and from the abundance of timber.

The Prince of Bénévent is still at Warsaw, negotiating with the ambassadors of the Porte and of the Emperor of Persia. Independent of the services which he renders to the Emperor as a minister, some important operations are frequently entrusted to him relative to the needs of the army.

Finkenstein, where His Majesty has established his headquarters to be closer to his positions, is a very nice castle built by Mr Finkenstein, governor of Frederic II, and is now owned by a Mr Dohna, Grand-Marshal of the Prussian court.

The cold weather is again set in for these two days: the thaw is the only symptom we have of the spring; the earliest shrubs do not yet present the least sign of green.

Seventy-second Bulletin

Finkenstein, 23 April 1807

The operations of Marshal Mortier have had the desired effect. The Swedes had the imprudence to cross the river Peene, to advance upon Anklam and Demmin and to move towards Pasewalk. On the 16th, before daybreak, Marshal Mortier assembled his troops, advanced from Pasewalk on the road to Anklam, overthrew the posts at Belling and Ferdinandshof, took 400 prisoners and two cannon, entered Anklam at the same time with the enemy, and made himself master of the bridge on the Peene.

The column of the Swedish General Cardell was cut off. It remained at Uckermünde when we were already at Anklam. The Swedish General-in-Chief Armfelt has been wounded by grapeshot. All the enemy's magazines are taken.

The column of General Cardell, which has been cut off, was attacked on the 17th by General of Brigade Veaux, near Uckermünde, when the enemy lost 3 pieces of artillery and 500 men, which were taken. The rest escaped by getting on board the gunboats in the Pommersche-Haff; 2 more cannon and 100 men were taken near Demmin.

Baron Von Essen, who commands the Swedish army during the absence of General Armfeld, proposed an armistice to General Mortier, informing him that the King had granted him a special power to conclude the same. A peace, or even an armistice, granted to Sweden would accomplish the most sanguine wishes of the Emperor, who has always been very reluctant to carry on a war against a generous and brave nation, which, upon local and political grounds, is the friend of France. Must Swedish blood flow, either to protect or to subvert the Ottoman Empire? Is it to flow for maintaining the balance, or for supporting the slavery of the seas? What has Sweden to fear from France? Nothing. What has she to fear from Russia? Everything. These reasons are too evident not to prompt an enlightened cabinet, and a nation that possesses clearness of mind and independence of opinion, to put a speedy stop to the war. Immediately after the battle of Jena, the Emperor made known his desire to restore the ancient relations between Sweden and France. These first overtures were made to the Swedish minister at Hamburg, but rejected. The Emperor constantly directed his generals to treat the Swedes as friends with whom we are at variance, and with whom we shall soon be reconciled, from the nature of things. 'Behold the true interests of both nations. If they did us any harm, they would regret it; and we, on our part, should wish to repair the wrong that we may have done them. The interest of the state will at last rise superior to all differences and petty quarrels.' These were the Emperor's own words, in his orders. Animated by such sentiments, the Emperor ordered the military operations for the siege of Stralsund to be discontinued, and the mortars and cannon that were sent from Stettin for that purpose to be sent back. He wrote to General Mortier in the following words: 'I already regret what has been done. I am sorry that the fine suburb of Stralsund is burnt. Is it our business to hurt Sweden? This is a mere dream. It is our business to protect, not do her any injury. In the latter, let us be as moderate as possible. Propose to the Governor of Stralsund an armistice, or a cessation of hostilities, in order to ease the burden and lessen the calamities of war, which I consider as wicked because it is impolitic.'

On the 18th, the armistice was concluded between Marshal Mortier and Baron Von Essen.

The siege of Danzig continues.

On the 16th of April, at eight in the evening, a detachment of 2,000 men from the garrison of Glatz advanced with six cannon against the right wing of the post of Frankenstein. On the following day, the 17th, at daybreak, another column of 800 men marched from Silberberg. These troops, after their junction, advanced upon Frankenstein and commenced an attack at five in the morning, with an intent to attack General Lefebvre, who was posted there with a corps of observation. Prince Jérôme set off from Münsterberg when the first gun was fired, and arrived at Frankenstein at ten in the morning. The enemy was completely dispersed and pursued to the covered way of Glatz: 600 of them were taken, together with three pieces of artillery. One major and eight officers are among the prisoners: 300 men were left dead on the battlefield: 400 men that had escaped in the woods were attacked and taken at eleven in the morning. Colonel Beckers, commanding the 6th Bavarian Regiment of Line, and Colonel Scharfenstein of the Württemberg troops, have done wonders. The former would not leave the field of battle, although he was wounded in the shoulder; he showed himself everywhere at the head of his battalion, and everywhere performed wonders. The Emperor has granted to each of these officers the Eagle of the Legion of Honour. Captain Brockfeld, who provisionally commands the Württemberg horse chasseurs, has likewise distinguished himself; and it was he who took the several pieces of artillery.

The siege of Neisse is going on prosperously. One half of the town is already burnt, and the trenches are approaching very near the fortress.

Seventy-third Bulletin

Elbing, 8 May 1807

The Persian Ambassador has received his audience of leave. He brought some very fine presents to the Emperor from his master, and received in return the Emperor's portrait, enriched with very fine stones. He returns directly to Persia. He is a very considerable personage in his country, and a man of sense and great sagacity. His return to his country was necessary. It has been regulated that there shall henceforth be a numerous legation of Persians at Paris and of Frenchmen at Teheran.

The Emperor, at Elbing, reviewed from 18,000 to 20,000 cavalrymen cantoned near Nogat, which looks a lot like Holland. The Grand Duke of Berg commanded the manoeuvre. Never had the Emperor seen his cavalry in better shape.

The journal of the siege of Danzig will make known that our troops have lodged themselves in the covert way, that the fire of the town is extinguished, and will give the details of the fine operation which General Drouet directed, and which was executed by Colonel Aimé, the Battalion Chief, Arnaud, of the 2nd Light Infantry, and Captain Avy. This operation puts us in possession of an island, which was defended by 1,000 Russians and 5 redoubts mounted with artillery, and which is very important for the siege, since it is in the back position that our troops are attacking. The Russians were surprised in their guardhouse, 400 were slaughtered with the bayonet without having time to defend themselves, and 600 were taken prisoner. This expedition, which took place in the night of the 6th, was in a great measure performed by the troops of Paris, who covered themselves with glory.

The weather is growing milder; the roads are excellent; the buds appear on the trees; the fields begin to be covered with grass, but it will require a month before they afford fodder to the cavalry.

The Emperor has established at Magdeburg, under the orders of Marshal Brune, a corps of observation, which will consist of nearly 80,000 men, half Frenchmen and the other half Dutchmen and Confederates of the Rhine; the Dutch troops are to the number of 20,000 men.

The French divisions of Molitor and Boudet, which also form a part of this corps of observation, arrived on 15 May at Magdeburg. Thus we are able to receive the English expedition upon whatever point it may present itself. It is certain that it will disembark; it is not so certain that it will be able to re-embark.

Seventy-fourth Bulletin

Finkenstein, 16 May 1807

Prince Jérôme, having discovered that three advanced works of Neisse, alongside the Bielau, impeded the progress of the siege, ordered General Vandamme to occupy them. In the night from 30 April to 1 May, this General, at the head of the Württemberg troops, took the said works, put the enemy's troops by whom they were defended to the sword, took 120 prisoners and 9 cannon. Captains of Engineering Deponthon and Prost, the first officer of ordinance of the Emperor, marched at the head of the columns and showed great bravery. Lieutenants Hohenhorff, Bauer and Mühler were particularly distinguished.

On 2 May, Lieutenant General Camcer took command of the Württemberger division.

Since the arrival in the camp of the Emperor Alexander, it seems that a great council of war was held at Bartenstein, at which the King of Prussia and the Grand Duke Constantine assisted; that the dangerous situation of the city of Danzig was the subject of the deliberations of the said council, and that it was found Danzig could only be relieved in two ways: first, by attacking the French army, to cross the Passarge, and to take the change of a general engagement, the result of which (provided any advantage was obtained) would be to compel the French army to raise the siege of Danzig; the second, to throw succour into Danzig from the seaside. It seems that the first plan was deemed impracticable, unless the enemy would expose itself to be completely defeated and routed. It was therefore resolved to confine itself to the other plan of relieving Danzig by water.

In consequence thereof, Lieutenant General Kamenskoi, son of the Field

Marshal, embarked at Pillau with two Russian divisions formed of 12 regiments, and several Prussian regiments. On the 12th, the troops were landed from 66 transports, under convoy of three frigates, in the port of Danzig, under the protection of the fort of Weichselmünde.

The Emperor immediately ordered Marshal Lannes, who commands the reserve of the *Grande Armée*, to advance from Marienburg (where he has his headquarters), with the division of General Oudinot, to reinforce the army of Marshal Lefebvre. He arrived after an uninterrupted march, at the very moment when the enemy's troops were landing. On the 13th and 14th, the enemy made preparations for the attack. It was separated from the town by a distance of somewhat less than one league, but that part was occupied by French troops. On the 15th, the enemy advanced from the fort in three columns, with an intention to penetrate to the town along the right bank of the Vistula. General of Brigade Schramm (who was at the advanced posts with the 2nd Regiment of Light Infantry, and one battalion of Saxons and Poles) received the first fire, and resisted the enemy at the distance of a cannon shot from Weichselmünde. Marshal Lefebvre had repaired to the bridge, which is situated below on the Vistula, and ordered the 12th Regiment of Light Infantry, together with the Saxons, to cross over that way, to support General Schramm. General Gardanne, who was charged with the defence of the right bank of the Vistula, also pressed that way with the rest of his troops. The enemy was superior in numbers, and the contest was continued with equal obstinacy.

Marshal Lannes, with the reserve of Oudinot, was placed on the left bank of the Vistula, where it was expected the day before that the enemy would make its appearance; but when Marshal Lannes saw the movements of the enemy disclosed, he crossed the Vistula with four battalions of General Oudinot's reserve. All of the enemy's line and reserve were thrown into confusion, and pursued to the palisades, and at nine in the morning the enemy were shut up in the fort of Weichselmünde. The battlefield was strewn with dead bodies. Our loss consists of 25 killed, and 200 wounded. The enemy's loss is 900 killed, 1,500 wounded and 200 taken. The enemy, from the heights of its demolished and almost destroyed ramparts, was witness to all the action. It was dejected on seeing the hopes vanishing which it had formed of receiving succour. General Oudinot has killed three Russians with his own hand. Several of his officers were wounded. The 12th and 2nd Regiments of Light Infantry distinguished themselves.

The journal of the siege of Danzig will show that the works are carried on with equal activity, that the covered way is completed, and that we are occupied with preparations for crossing the ditch.

As soon as the enemy knew that its maritime expedition had arrived before Danzig, its light troops began to reconnoitre and alarm the whole line, from the position occupied by Marshal Soult on the Passarge, to that of General Morand on the Alle. They were received at the mouth of the musket by the voltigeurs, lost a considerable number of men and retired with more precipitation than they came.

The Russians also presented themselves at Malga, before General Zayonchek, the Commandant of the Polish corps of observation, and carried off one of his posts. General of Brigade Fischer pursued, routed them, and killed 60 men, one colonel, and two captains. They likewise presented themselves before the 5th Corps, and insulted General Gazan's advanced posts at Willenberg. This general pursued them several leagues. But they made a more serious attack on the bridge of Omulew at Drenzevo. General of Brigade Gérard marched against them with the 88th and drove them into the Narew. General Suchet arrived, pursued the Russians closely and defeated them at Ostrolenka, where he killed 60 men and took 50 horses.

On the same day, the 13th, the enemy attacked General Lemarois at the mouth of the Bug. This general had crossed that river on the 10th, with a Bavarian brigade and a Polish regiment, who, in the course of three days, had constructed several bridgeheads and had advanced to Winkovo with the intention of burning the rafts that the enemy had been at work upon during six weeks. His expedition completely succeeded, and the ridiculous work of six weeks was destroyed in a moment.

On the 13th, at nine o'clock in the morning, 6,000 Russians arrived from Nur and attacked General Lemarois in his entrenched camp. They were received by musketry and grape; 300 were killed. And when General Lemarois saw them on the borders of the ditch, he made a sally and pursued them with the sword in their loins. The Bavarian colonel of the 4th Regiment was killed. He is universally regretted. The Bavarians lost 20 men killed and about 60 wounded.

All the army is encamped in divisions of square battalions, in very sound positions.

These affairs of advanced posts have not occasioned any movements in the army. Everything is quiet at the headquarters. This general attack upon our advanced posts on the 13th seems to have had no other object than to occupy the French army, so as to prevent them from reinforcing the troops employed in the siege of Danzig. The hope of securing Danzig by means of a maritime expedition appears very extraordinary to self-informed military men, acquainted with the ground and the position occupied by the French army.

The leaves begin to appear; and the season resembles the month of April in France.

Seventy-fifth Bulletin

Finkenstein, 18 May 1807

Here are new details of the affair of the 15th. Marshal Lefebvre makes a very favourable report of General Schramm, to whom he, in a great measure, imputes the favourable issue of the affair at Weichselmünde.

On the morning of the 15th, at two o'clock, General Schramm had formed in order of battle, covered by two redoubts thrown up opposite the fort of Weichselmünde. He had the Poles on the left, the Saxons in the centre, the 2nd Regiment of Light Infantry on his right and the regiment of Paris in reserve. The Russian General Kamenskoi debouched from the fort at daybreak, and after two hours' hard fighting the 12th Regiment of Light Infantry, sent by Marshal Lefebvre from the left shore, and a battalion of Saxons, decided the victory. Scarcely a battalion belonging to Oudinot's corps had any occasion to take part in the action. Our loss is very trifling. Mr Paris, a Polish colonel, was killed. The loss of the enemy is greater than we supposed. We have buried 900 Russians. We cannot reckon its loss at less than 2,500 men. We observed no more movements on the part of the enemy, which seemed to confine itself very prudently within the circuit of the fortifications. The number of vessels sent off with the wounded was 14. The Emperor has issued a decree for making every person who distinguished himself on this occasion a member of the Legion of Honour; they are about 30 in number.

On the 14th, a division of 5,000 men, Prussians and Russians, but the majority Prussians, from Königsberg, debarked at Pillau, landed on the banks of the

Nehrung and advanced against our light cavalry as far as Kahlberg, who thought proper to fall back on Fürstenwerder. The enemy advanced to the extremity of the Frisch-Haff. We expected it would have penetrated from there to Danzig. A bridge thrown over the Vistula at Fürstenwerder made the crossing easy for our troops cantoned in the island of Nogat, so that the infantry might have attacked the enemy's rear; but the Prussians were too wary to proceed. The Emperor ordered General Beaumont, aide-de-camp to the Grand Duke of Berg, to attack them. On the morning of the 16th, at two o'clock, General of Brigade Albert advanced at the head of two battalions of grenadiers of the reserve, the 3rd and 11th Regiments of Chasseurs and a brigade of dragoons. He met the enemy about daybreak, between Passenwerder and Stegen, attacked it, routed, and closely pursued it 11 leagues, took 1,100 prisoner, killed and wounded a great number and took four pieces of artillery. General Albert was perfectly composed. Majors Chemineau and Salmon were distinguished. The 3rd and 11th Regiments of Chasseurs acted with great intrepidity. We have one captain of the 3rd Regiment of Chasseurs and 5 or 6 men killed, and 8 or 10 wounded.

Thus the enemy has suffered considerable losses, at various points, since the 12th.

On the 17th the Emperor caused the fusiliers of the Guard to manoeuvre: they are encamped near the castle of Finkenstein, in barracks equally as handsome as those at Boulogne.

On the 18th and 19th, the Imperial Guard will encamp upon the same spot.

Prince Jérôme is encamped in Silesia with a corps of observation, covering the siege of Neisse.

On the 12th, the Prince learned that a column of 3,000 men had left Glatz to surprise Breslau. He ordered General Lefebvre to advance with the 1st Bavarian Regiment and a detachment of 300 Saxons. In the morning of the 14th, the general came up with the enemy's rear near Canth, which he immediately attacked, made himself master of the village with the bayonet and took 150 prisoner: 100 of the Bavarian light cavalry fell upon those of the enemy, 500 in number, routed and dispersed them. The enemy again formed in order of battle, and offered resistance: 300 Saxons fled; this extraordinary conduct must have been the effects of dissatisfaction, as the Saxons have always behaved with valour ever since they joined the French. However, this unexpected event brought the 1st Bavarian Regiment into a very critical situation. They lost 150 men, who were taken prisoner, and they were compelled to beat a retreat, which they effected in good order. The enemy retook the village of Canth.

At eleven o'clock in the morning, General Dumuy, who had advanced from Breslau at the head of the 1,000 French dismounted dragoons, hussars and chasseurs, attacked the enemy in the rear: 150 of the hussars on foot re-took the village after a charge with the bayonet, took 100 prisoner, and liberated all the Bavarians made prisoners by the Prussians.

The enemy, in order to facilitate his retreat to Glatz, had separated in two columns. General Lefebvre, who left Schweidnitz on the 15th, fell in with two of these columns, killed 100, and took 400 prisoner, including 30 officers. A Polish regiment of lance bearers had arrived on the preceding evening at Frankenstein, and a detachment of these being sent to join General Lefebvre, by Prince Jérôme, distinguished themselves on this occasion.

The second column endeavoured to regain Glatz by crossing the Silberberg. Lieutenant Colonel Ducoudras, the Prince's aide-de-camp fell in with them and threw them in disorder. Thus a column of between 3,000 and 4,000 men that left Glatz was unable to return. They have been killed, taken prisoner or dispersed.

Seventy-sixth Bulletin

Finkenstein, 20 May 1807

A fine English corvette, copper-sheathed, with 24 cannons, having 120 English for her crew and laden with powder and ball, presented herself off Danzig, with an intention to enter that port. On approaching near our works, she was attacked from both the shores with a heavy shower of musketry and forced to surrender. A post of the regiment of Paris was the first to leap on board. An aide-de-camp of General Kalkreuth, who was on his return from the Russian headquarters, and several English officers, were taken on board the vessel. She is called the *Undaunted*, and had 60 Russians on board, besides the 120 English.

The enemy's loss in the affair of Weichselmünde, on the 15th, was greater than was at first supposed; a Russian column, which had held close to the sea, was put to the bayonet. There were 1,300 Russians buried.

On the 16th, a division of 7,000 Russians, commanded by General Tutshkov, advanced from the Brock to the Bug, and towards Pultusk, to oppose the execution of some new works for strengthening the bridgehead. These works were defended by six Bavarian battalions, under the command of the Crown Prince in person. The enemy advanced four times to the attack, and was four times repulsed by the Bavarians, and covered with grapeshot from the batteries of the different works. Marshal Masséna estimates the enemy's loss at 300 killed and twice as many wounded. The Bavarians were only 4,000 strong. The Crown Prince is particularly proud of Baron Wrede, Officer-General in the service of Bavaria, who distinguished himself. The loss for the Bavarians was 15 killed and 150 wounded.

The same mismanagement as in the attack of the 16th at Pultusk was displayed in the one the enemy made on the 13th against the works of General Lemarois; nor was its want of judgement less conspicuous in the preparation of a great number of rafts, which the enemy was preparing on the Bug for these six weeks past. The result was that these rafts, which took so long in preparation, were burnt in two hours' time; and that those repeated attacks upon works well-contrived, and defended by strong batteries, without a chance of success, have produced for it a considerable loss.

We are almost induced to think that the purpose of these attacks was to draw the attention of the French army to their right wing. But the position of the army was calculated, by anticipation, for every case and for all operations of attack and defence.

In the meantime, the important siege of Danzig is continued. The loss of that important fortress, and of the 20,000 men shut up within the same, will be severely felt by the enemy. A mine that was contrived near the outer bastion had the effect of blowing it up. A communication has been opened with the covered way by four entrances, and we are employed in filling up the ditch.

Today the Emperor reviewed the 5th Provisional Regiment. The first eight of those regiments have already been incorporated. The Genoese conscripts among those regiments are much extolled for their readiness and zeal.

Seventy-seventh Bulletin

Finkenstein, 29 May 1807

Danzig has capitulated. That fine city is our possession. Eight hundred pieces of artillery, magazines of every kind, more than 500,000 quintals of grain, well-stored cellars, immense collections of clothing and spices; great resources of every kind for the army; lastly, a fortress of the first order for strength on our left wing, as Thorn supports our centre, and Prague our right; these are the advantages obtained during winter, and which have signalized the leisure hours of the *Grande Armée*; this is, indeed, the first fruit of the victory of Eylau. The rigour of the season, the snow which has so often covered our trenches and the ice, which has added fresh difficulties, have not been obstacles to our operations. Marshal Lefebvre has braved all; he has animated with the same spirit the Saxons, the Poles, the troops of Baden, and has made them all march to his goal. The difficulties that the artillery had to conquer were considerable. One hundred pieces of artillery, 5,000 or 6,000 pounds weight of powder and an immense quantity of bullets have been drawn from Stettin, and the strong places in Silesia. It was necessary to surmount many difficulties in removing the artillery, but the Vistula afforded easy and expeditious means. The marines of the Guard have passed their boats under the fort of Graudenz with their accustomed skill and resolution. General Chasseloup, General Kirgener, Colonel Lacoste and in general all the officers of the engineers have served in the most distinguished manner. The sappers have shown an uncommon degree of intrepidity. The whole corps of artillery, under General La Riboisière, has sustained its reputation. The 2nd Regiment of Light Infantry, the 12th, and the troops of Paris, with Generals Schramm and Puthod, have distinguished themselves. A detailed journal of this siege will soon be drawn up with care. It will consecrate a great number of acts of bravery worth of being exhibited as examples, and such as must excite enthusiasm and admiration.

On the 17th, the mine blew up a lock-house, attached to the guard-house on the covered way. On the 19th, the descent and passage of the moat were executed at seven o'clock in the evening. On the 21st, Marshal Lefebvre having prepared everything for the assault, they were proceeding to the attack when Colonel Lacoste, who had been sent in the morning into the fortress on some business, signified that General Kalkreuth demanded to capitulate on the same conditions that he had formerly granted to the garrison of Mayence. This was agreed to. The Hagelsberg would have been stormed with very little loss, but the body of the place was yet entire. A large moat, full of running water, presented such difficulties that the besieged might have held out for 15 days longer. In this situation it appeared proper to grant them an honourable capitulation.

On the 27th, the garrison marched out with General Kalkreuth at its head. This strong garrison, which at first consisted of 16,000 men, was reduced to 9,000 men, of which number 4,000 have deserted. Among the deserters there are even officers. 'We will not,' they say, 'go to Siberia.' Many thousands of artillery horses have been given up to us, but they are in very bad condition. We are now drawing up the inventory of the magazines. General Rapp is named Governor of Danzig.

The Russian Lieutenant General Kamenskoi, after having been beaten on the 15th, retired under the fortifications of Weichselmünde. He remained there without venturing to undertake anything, and he has been a spectator of the surrender of the fortress. When he perceived that they were erecting batteries to burn his ships with red-hot balls, he embarked and retired. He has returned to Pillau.

The fort of Weichselmünde still held out. Marshal Lefebvre summoned it on the 26th, and while they were regulating the terms of capitulation, the garrison advanced from the fort and surrendered. The commandant, thus abandoned by the garrison, saved himself by sea, and thus we are in possession of the town and port of Danzig.

These events are a happy presage of the campaign. The Emperor of Russia and the King of Prussia were at Heiligenbeil. They might have conjectured the surrender of the fortress from the cessation of the fire. They might have heard the cannon from that distance.

The Emperor, to express his satisfaction to the besieging army, has granted a reward to each soldier.

The siege of Graudenz is now commencing under the command of General Victor. General Lazowski commands the engineers, and General d'Anthouard the artillery. Graudenz is strong from the number of its mines.

The cavalry of the army is in fine order. The Grand Duke of Berg has reviewed the division of light cavalry, two divisions of cuirassiers and one of dragoons, at Elbing on the 26th. The same day, His Majesty arrived at Bischofswerder and Strasburg, where he reviewed Hautpoul's division of cuirassiers and the division of dragoons of General Grouchy. He has been satisfied with their appearance and with the good condition of their horses.

The Ambassador of the Porte, Sid Mohammed Emen Vahid, had been presented on the 28th, at two o'clock, to the Emperor, by the Prince of Bénévent. He delivered his credentials to His Majesty, and remained an hour in this cabinet. He is lodged at the Castle, and occupies the apartments of the Grand Duke of Berg, who is absent on account of the review. It is confidently said that the Emperor told him that he and the Sultan Selim would be, forever after, inseparably connected, as the right hand and the left. All the good news respecting the success at Ismaîl and in Wallachia has just arrived. The Russians have been obliged to raise the siege of Ismaîl and evacuate Wallachia.

Seventy-eighth Bulletin

Heilsberg, 12 June 1807

Peace negotiations had taken place all winter long. A general congress had been proposed to France, at which all of the belligerent powers would be admitted except Turkey. The Emperor had been justly revolted by such a proposition. After several months of negotiations, it was agreed that all the belligerent powers, with no exception, would send plenipotentiaries to the congress, which would take place at Copenhagen. The Emperor let it be known that since Turkey was admitted and would join a common cause in the negotiations with France, there was no harm in England joining a common cause with Russia. The enemies then questioned on what basis the congress would have to negotiate. They had none to propose but waited for the Emperor to propose his basis of negotiations. The Emperor had no difficulty declaring that the basis for negotiations had to be equality and reciprocity between the two belligerent masses and that they would enter in a system of compensation.

The moderation, the clarity and the promptitude of this response left no doubt in the minds of the enemies of peace as to the pacific dispositions of the Emperor. They feared its effects and at the very moment they answered that there were no obstacles left to the opening of the congress, the Russian army came out of its cantonments and attacked the French army. Once again blood was spilt, but in this instance, France was innocent.

There is no pacific overture to which the Emperor would not have listened; there is no proposition to which he would not have responded; there is no trap laid by the makers of war that his will would not have set aside. Inconsiderately, they caused the Russian army to take up arms when they saw their measures frustrated, and these culpable enterprises were confounded. New failures fell upon the Russian armies; new trophies have crowned the armies of France. Nothing can more vividly prove that passion and interests foreign to those of Russia and Prussia direct the cabinet of these two powers, and drive their brave armies into new misfortune by forcing them into new battles: what circumstance is there for the Russian army to renew the hostilities? It is 15 days after the surrender of Danzig; it is when the reason no longer exists to lift the siege of this place, the importance of which would have justified all tentatives, and for the conservation of which no military could have been blamed for attempting three battles. These considerations are foreign to the passions that prepared the events of late. Preventing the opening of the negotiations, alienating two princes ready to get along, such is the aim that was proposed. What will the result be of such a proceeding? Where is the probability for success? All these questions are indifferent to those who want war. Where is their concern for the misfortunes of the Russian and Prussian armies? If they can prolong the calamities that weigh on Europe, their goal is fulfilled.

If the Emperor had seen no other interest but his glory, if he had made no other forecasts than those relative to his advantageous military operations, he would have opened the campaign immediately after taking Danzig; yet, though there was no truce, no armistice, he acted only for the hope of seeing the negotiations come to a fruitful end.

Battle of Spanden

On 5 June, the Russian army put itself in motion. Its divisions on the right attacked the bridgehead of Spanden, which General Frère defended with the 27th Regiment of Light Infantry. Twelve Russian and Prussian regiments made several ineffectual attempts. Seven times did they renew the attack, but were as often repulsed. The 17th Regiment of Dragoons charged the enemy immediately after the last assault, and forced it to abandon the battlefield and beat a retreat. Thus, during a whole day, two divisions attacked without success a single regiment, which, it must be admitted, was entrenched.

The Prince of Ponte Corvo, in visiting the entrenchments during the intervals of attack, received a slight wound, which will take him from his command 15 days. Our loss in this affair was trifling. The enemy lost 1,200 men and a number of wounded.

Battle of Lomitten

Two Russian divisions belonging to the centre attacked the bridgehead of Lomitten at the same time. General Ferey's brigade (part of Marshal Soult's corps) defended the bridgehead. The Russian general was killed, along with 1,100 men; 100 were taken, and a great many wounded. We had 120 men killed or wounded.

During this period, the Russian Commander in Chief, with the Grand Duke Constantine, the Imperial Guard and three divisions, attacked the positions of Marshal Ney at Altkirch, Amt, Guttstadt and Wolfsdorff. The enemy was repulsed everywhere: but when Marshal Ney perceived that the force opposed to him exceeded 40,000 men, he obeyed his orders and conducted his corps to Ankendorf.

Battle of Deppen

On the following day, the enemy attacked the 6th Corps in its positions at Deppen, on the Passarge. It was repulsed. The manoeuvres of Marshal Ney, his intrepidity, which he imparted to all this troops, the abilities displayed in this situation by General of Division Marchand and his officers, merit the highest praise. The enemy acknowledges having lost this day 2,000 killed and more than 3,000 wounded. Our loss was 160 killed, 200 wounded and 250 taken. The latter were for the most part taken by the Cossacks, who, on the morning of the attack, had got into the rear of the army.

The Emperor arrived at Marshal Ney's camp at Deppen on the 8th. He immediately gave the necessary orders. The 4th Corps marched to Wolfsdorff, where meeting the Russian division of Kamenskoi, which was on its way to rejoin the main body, the 4th Corps attacked it, deprived it of between 4- and 500 men, took 150 prisoner, and in the evening took its position at Altzirken.

Day of the 9th

On the 9th, the Emperor advanced to Guttstadt with the corps of Marshal Ney, Davout and Lannes, with his Guard and the cavalry of reserve. Part of the rearguard of the enemy, comprising 10,000 cavalry and 15,000 infantry, took a position at Glottau and attempted to dispute the way. The Grand Duke of Berg, after some very skilful manoeuvres, drove the enemy from all its positions. The light brigades of cavalry under Generals Pajol, Bruyères and Durosnel, and the division of the heavy cavalry under General Nansouty, triumphed over all the efforts of the enemy. In the evening at eight o'clock, we entered Guttstadt by main force: 1,000 prisoners, the taking of all the positions in advance of Guttstadt and the redoubts of the enemy infantry were the results of this day. The regiments of cavalry of the Russian Guard suffered more than any of the rest.

Day of the 10th

On the 10th, the army moved towards Heilsberg. It took several of the enemy's camps. About a quarter of a league beyond these camps the rearguard showed itself in position. It had between 15,000 and 18,000 cavalry and several lines of infantry. The cuirassiers of Espagne's division, the dragoon division of Latour-Maubourg and the brigade of light cavalry, made several charges and gained ground. At two o'clock, the corps under Marshal Soult was formed. Two divisions marched to the right, while the division of Legrand marched to the left, to seize on the extremity of a wood, the occupation of which was necessary in order to support the left of the cavalry and make various efforts to maintain themselves in the positions before Heilsberg. More than 60 cannon scattered death in supporting the enemy's columns, which our divisions nevertheless repulsed, with the most unprecedented intrepidity, and the characteristic impetuosity of the French. Several Russian divisions were routed, and at nine in the evening we found ourselves under the enemy's entrenchments. The fusiliers of the Guard, commanded by General Savary, were put in motion to sustain the division of Verdier; and some of the corps of infantry of the reserve, under Marshal Lannes, was engaged, it being already nightfall; they attached the enemy with the view of cutting off its communication with Landsberg, and succeeded completely. The ardour of the troops was such that several companies of the infantry of line insulted the entrenched works of the Russians. Some brave men met their death in the ditches of the redoubts at the foot of the palisades.

The Emperor passed the 11th on the battlefield. He there arranged the corps of the army and divisions, preparatory to a decisive action, such a one as should put an end to the war. All of the Russian army was collected. The Russian magazines were at Heilsberg. The Russians occupied a fine position, which nature had rendered very strong, and which they increased by the labour of four months.

165

At four in the afternoon, the Emperor ordered Marshal Davout to change his front, and push forward his left; this movement brought him upon the Lower Alle, and completely blocked up the road from Eylau. Every corps of the army had its post assigned to it; they were all re-assembled, the first corps excepted, which continued upon the Lower Passarge. Thus the Russians, who were the first to begin the battle, found themselves shut up in their entrenched camp, and were compelled to give battle in the position they had chosen themselves. It was for a long time believed they would make an attack on the 11th. At the moment when the French were making their dispositions, the Russians showed themselves, ranged in columns, in the midst of their entrenchments, fortified with numerous batteries.

But whether those entrenchments did not appear sufficiently formidable, after viewing the preparations which they saw before them, or whether the impetuosity which the French army had shown on the 10th had an effect upon them, they began to cross the Alle at ten o'clock at night, abandoning the whole country to the left, and leaving at the disposal of the conqueror their wounded, their magazines and their entrenchments, the result of long and painful labour.

On the 12th, at daybreak, all the corps of the army were in motion, and took different directions.

The houses of Heilsberg and its neighbourhood are filled with wounded Russians.

The result of the different affairs from the 5th to the 12th has deprived the Russian army of about 30,000 fighting men. They have left between 3,000 and 4,000 prisoners in our hands, 7 or 8 pairs of colours, and 9 pieces of artillery. According to the reports of the prisoners, several of the most eminent Russian generals have been killed or wounded.

Our loss amounted to 600 or 700 killed, 2,000 or 2,200 wounded and 300 prisoners. General of Division Espagne was wounded. General Roussel, chief of the staff of the Guard, had his head carried away by a cannonball. He was a distinguished officer.

The Grand Duke of Berg had two horses killed under him. Mr Segur, one of his aides-de-camp, lost an arm. Mr Lameth, Marshal Soult's aide-de-camp, was wounded. Mr Lagrange, Colonel of the 7th Regiment of horse Chasseurs, was killed. The detailed reports prepared by the Major-General will communicate particular acts of bravery and the names of those who were wounded in the memorable battle of 10 June.

Several thousand quintals of grain, and a great quantity of different kinds of provisions, have been found in the magazines of Heilsberg.

Seventy-ninth Bulletin

Wehlau, 18 June 1807

The combats of Spanden and Lomitten, the days of Guttstadt and Heilsberg, were only the prelude of still more important events.

On the 12th, at four in the morning, the French army entered Heilsberg. General Latour-Maubourg pursued the enemy with his division of dragoons, and Generals Durosnel's and Watiers' brigade of light cavalry to the right bank of the Alle, near Bartenstein. In the meantime, the light corps advanced in various directions, in order to pass the enemy to cut off his retreat to Königsberg, and get between the enemy and its magazines. Fortune favoured the execution of this plan.

On the 12th, at five o'clock in the afternoon, the Emperor took his Imperial

Headquarters to Eylau. Here, the fields were no longer covered with ice and snow; on the contrary, they presented one of the most beautiful scenes in nature. The country was adorned everywhere by beautiful woods, intersected by lakes and animated by handsome village.

On the 13th, the Grand Duke of Berg advanced towards Königsberg with his cavalry; Marshal Davout followed to support him. Marshal Soult advanced towards Kreuzberg; Marshal Lannes towards Domnau; Marshals Ney and Mortier towards Lampasch.

Meanwhile General Latour-Maubourg wrote that he had pursued the enemy's rearguard; that the Russians had abandoned a great number of wounded in their flight; that they had evacuated Bartenstein, and that they had directed their retreat on Schippeneil on the right bank of the Alle. The Emperor immediately proceeded towards Friedland. He ordered the Grand Duke of Berg, Marshals Soult and Davout, to manoeuvre against Königsberg, while he advanced with the corps of Ney, Lannes, Mortier, the Imperial Guard and the first corps, commanded by General Victor, on Friedland.

On the 13th, the 9th Regiment of Hussars entered Friedland, but was driven out of that place by 3,000 of the enemy's cavalry.

On the 14th, the enemy advanced on the bridge of Friedland, and at three in the morning a cannonade was heard. 'It is a fortunate day,' said the Emperor, 'It is the anniversary of the battle of Marengo.'

Marshals Lannes and Mortier were first engaged; they were supported by General Grouchy's dragoons, and by General Nansouty's cuirassiers. Several movements and actions took place. The enemy was stopped, and could not pass the village of Posthenem. Imagining that it had only a corps of 15,000 men opposed to it, the enemy followed the movements of our troops towards Königsberg; thus the French and Saxon dragoons and cuirassiers had the opportunity of making a brilliant attack, and of taking four cannon.

At five in the evening, the different army corps were at their appointed stations: on the right, Marshal Ney; in the centre, Marshal Lannes; on the left, Marshal Mortier; in reserve, the corps of General Victor and the Guard.

The cavalry, under the orders of General Grouchy, supported the left. The division of dragoons of General Latour-Maubourg was behind the right wing as a reserve; the division of dragoons under General Lahoussaye and the Saxon cuirassiers formed a reserve behind the centre.

Meanwhile, the enemy deployed all its army. It deployed its left to the town of Friedland, and its right wing a mile and a half in the other direction.

The Emperor, after reconnoitring the position, immediately decided to take the town of Friedland. Then suddenly changing his front and advancing his right, he commenced the attack with the first part of that wing.

At half past five, Marshal Ney began to move forward. Some shots from a battery of 20 cannons were the signal. At the same moment, the division of General Marchand advanced, sword in hand, upon the enemy and proceeded towards the tower of the town, being supported on the left by the division of General Bison. When the enemy perceived that Marshal Ney had left the wood in which his right wing had been posted, it endeavoured to surround him with some regiments of cavalry, and a multitude of Cossacks; but General Latour-Maubourg's division of dragoons rode up in full gallop to the right wing, and repelled the attack of the enemy. In the meantime, General Victor erected a battery of 30 cannon in the front of his centre. General Senarmont, who commanded this battery, pushed his works forward more than 400 paces and greatly annoyed the enemy. The several manoeuvres the Russians attempted in order to produce a diversion were all in vain. Marshal Ney was at the head of his troops, directing the smallest manoeuvres with that coolness and intrepidity peculiar to him, and maintained that example which has always distinguished his corps among the other corps of the *Grande Armée*. Several columns of the enemy that attacked his right wing were received with the bayonet and driven into the Alle. Thousands found their graves in that river, and some escaped by swimming; meanwhile, Marshal Ney's left wing reached the ravines, which encircle the town of Friedland. The enemy, which had posted the Imperial horse and foot Guards in ambush there, advanced with great intrepidity and attacked Marshal Ney's left, which for a moment was in confusion: but Dupont's division, which formed the right wing of the reserve, fell upon the Russian Imperial Guards, defeated them, and made a dreadful slaughter.

The enemy sent forward several other corps from his centre to defend Friedland. Vain efforts! Friedland was forced, and its streets bestrewed with dead bodies.

The centre, commanded by Marshal Lannes, was at the same time engaged. The attempts that the enemy had made upon the right wing of the French army being frustrated, it wished to try the effect of similar efforts upon our centre; it was, however, suitably received by the brave divisions of Oudinot and of Verdier, and the commanding Marshal.

The repeated attacks of the enemy's infantry and cavalry were incapable of obstructing the march of our columns. All the efforts of the brave Russians were exerted in vain. They were unable to start any action, and found their death on our bayonets!

Marshal Mortier, who during the whole day had given great proofs of coolness and intrepidity in supporting the left wing, now advanced and was in his turn supported by the fusiliers of the Guard under the command of General Savary. The cavalry, infantry and artillery: all were distinguished.

The Imperial Horse and Foot Guard, and two divisions of the first corps, were not in the action. The victory was never for a moment doubtful.

The battlefield is horrible to behold. It is not too much to estimate the number of the dead on the side of the Russians at from 15,000 to 18,000. The number of the dead on the French side was not 500, but we have 3,000 wounded. We have taken 80 cannons and a great number of caissons. A great number of flags have also fallen into our hands. The Russians had 25 of their generals killed, taken or wounded. Their cavalry has suffered an incalculable loss.

The carabiniers and the cuirassiers commanded by General Nansouty, and the different divisions of dragoons, performed remarkably. General Grouchy, who commanded the cavalry of the left wing, rendered important services.

General Drouet, Chief of Marshal Lannes' corps, General Coehorn, Colonel Reynaud of the 15th Line, Colonel Lajonquière of the 60th, Colonel Lamotte of the 4th Dragoons and Brigadier General Brun are wounded. General Latour-Maubourg is wounded in the hand. Colonel of the Artillery Destourneaux, Squadron Chief Hutin, first aide-de-camp of General Oudinot, are killed. Two of the Emperor's aides-de-camp, Mouton and Lacoste, are slightly wounded.

Night did not prevent us from pursuing the enemy; it was followed until eleven o'clock at night. During the remainder of the night, the cut-off columns tried to cross the Alle at several formidable places, and, the next day we saw caissons, cannon and harness everywhere in the river.

This battle of Friedland is worth to be numbered with those of Marengo, Austerlitz and Jena. The enemy was numerous, had fine cavalry, and fought with courage.

The next day, the 15th, the enemy endeavoured to assemble on the right bank of the Alle, and the French army had manoeuvres on the left bank to cut it off from Königsberg.

The heads of the columns arrived at the same time at Wehlau, a town situated at the confluence of the Alle and the Pregel.

The Emperor had his headquarters in the village of Peterswalde.

At daybreak on the 16th, the enemy, having destroyed all the bridges, took advantage of that obstacle to proceed on their retreat towards Russia.

At eight in the morning, the Emperor threw a bridge over the Pregel and took a position there with the army.

Almost all the magazines that the enemy had on the Alle have been thrown into the river or burnt. Some idea may be formed of the great extent of its loss by what remains to us. The Russians had storehouses in all the villages, which, in their passage, they everywhere burnt. We have, however, found more than 6,000 quintals of wheat in Wehlau.

Königsberg was abandoned on the arrival of the intelligence of the battle of Friedland. Marshal Soult has entered that place, where much wealth has been fund. We have taken there some 100,000 quintals of wheat, more than 20,000 wounded Russians and Prussians, all the ammunition that England has sent to the Russians, including 160,000 muskets that had not been landed. Thus has Providence punished those, who instead of negotiating with good faith to bring about a salutary peace, treated that object with derision, and regarded the repose taken by the conquerors as a proof of timidity and weakness.

The army now occupies the most beautiful country possible. The banks of the Pregel are rich. In a short time the magazines and cellars of Danzig and Königsberg will afford us new resources of superfluity and health.

The names of the brave men who have distinguished themselves cannot be contained within the limits of one bulletin. The staff is employed in collecting their deeds.

The Prince of Neufchâtel gave extraordinary proofs of his zeal and knowledge in the battle of Friedland. He was frequently in the hottest part of the action, and made arrangements that were of great advantage.

The enemy had renewed hostilities on the 5th. Their loss in the ten days that followed their first operations may be reckoned at 60,000 men, killed, wounded, taken, or otherwise put out of combat. A part of its artillery, the necessary supply of military stores, and all its magazines, on a line of more that 40 leagues, are lost to it. The French army has seldom obtained such great success with so little loss.

Eightieth Bulletin

Tilsit, 19 June 1807

During the time that the French armies distinguished themselves on the battlefield at Friedland, the Grand Duke of Berg arrived before Königsberg and took in flank the corps of the army commanded by General Lestocq.

On the 13th, Marshal Soult found the Prussian rearguard at Kreuzberg. The division of Milhaud's dragoons executed a fine charge, defeated the Prussian cavalry and took several pieces of artillery.

On the 14th, the enemy was compelled to shut itself up in Königsberg. About noon, two of the enemy's columns, which had been cut off before that place, attempted the bold effort of forcing their way, with a view of entering it. Six cannon, and from 3,000 to 4,000 men who composed this troop, were taken. All the suburbs of Königsberg were razed, and a considerable number of prisoners was taken.

The result of all these affairs is between 4,000 and 5,000 prisoners and 15 pieces of artillery.

On the 15th and 16th, Marshal Soult's corps was occupied before the entrenchments of Königsberg, but the advance of the main body towards Wehlau obliged the enemy to evacuate Königsberg, and this place fell into our hands.

The stores found at Königsberg are immense: 200 large vessels from Russia are still all loaded in the port. There was much more wine and brandy than we had any reason to expect.

A brigade of the division of Saint-Hilaire advanced before Pillau, to form the siege of that place; and General Rapp has sent off from Danzig a column ordered to go by the Nehrung, to raise before Pillau a battery that may shut the Haff. Vessels manned by marines of the Guard render us masters of this small sea.

On the 17th, the Emperor transferred his headquarters to the farm of Drucken, near Klein-Schirrau. On the 18th, he advanced them to Skaisgirren; and on the 19th, at two in the afternoon, he entered Tilsit.

The Grand Duke of Berg, at the head of the greater part of the light cavalry, some divisions of dragoons and cuirassiers, has followed the enemy in its retreat these last three days, and did much injury. The 5th Regiment of Hussars distinguished itself. The Cossacks were repeatedly routed, and suffered considerably in these different charges. We had a few killed or wounded: among the latter is the Squadron Chief Piéton, aide-de-camp to the Grand Duke of Berg.

After the crossing of the Pregel, opposite to Wehlau, a drummer was charged by a Cossack at full gallop; he took his lance to pierce the drummer, but the latter preserved his presence of mind, took his lance from him, disarmed the Cossack and pursued him.

A singular circumstance, which excited the laughter of the soldiers, occurred for the first time near Tilsit, where a cloud of Kalmouchs were seen fighting with arrows. We were sorry for those who gave the preference to the ancient arms over those of the modern; but nothing is more laughable than the effect of those arms against our muskets.

Marshal Davout, at the head of the 3rd Corps, defiled by Labiau, fell upon the enemy's rearguard and took 2,500 prisoner.

Marshal Ney arrived on the 17th at Insterburg, and there took 1,000 wounded and the enemy's magazines, which were considerable.

The woods, the villages, are full of straggling Russians, sick or wounded. The loss of the Russian army is enormous. It has not with it more than 60 cannon. The rapidity of our marches prevents us from being able as yet to ascertain how many pieces we have taken; but it is supposed that the number exceeds 120.

Near Tilsit, a communication was transmitted to the Grand Duke of Berg; and afterwards the Russian Prince, Lieutenant General Labanov, crossed the Niemen and had a conference for an hour with the Prince of Neufchâtel.

The enemy burned in great haste the bridge of Tilsit over the Niemen, and appeared to be continuing its retreat into Russia. We are on the confines of that empire. The Niemen, opposite Tilsit, is somewhat broader than the Seine. From the left bank we see a cloud of Cossacks, who form the rearguard of the enemy on the right bank.

Hostilities have already ceased.

What remained to the King of Prussia is conquered. That unfortunate prince has only in his power the country situate between the Niemen and Memel. The greater part of his army, or rather of the division of his troops, is deserting, being unwilling to go into Russia.

The Emperor of Russia remained three weeks at Tilsit with the King of Prussia. On receiving advice of the battle of Friedland, they both left the place with the utmost haste.

Eighty-first Bulletin

Tilsit, 21 June 1807

At the affair at Heilsberg, the Grand Duke of Berg passed along the line of the 3rd division of Cuirassiers, at the moment when the 6th Regiment had just made a charge. Colonel d'Avenay, commander of the regiment, his sabre dyed in blood, said, 'Prince, review my regiment, and you will find that there is not a soldier whose sword is not like mine.'

Colonels Colbert of the 7th Hussars and Léry of the 5th were remarkable for their brilliant intrepidity. Colonel Bordessoulle of the 22nd Chasseurs was wounded; Mr Gueheneuc, aide-de-camp to Marshal Lannes, was wounded in his arm.

The general aides-de-camp to the Emperor, Reille and Bertrand, rendered important services. The ordinance officers to the Emperor, Bongars, Montesquiou and Labiffe, deserve eulogies of merit for their conduct.

The aides-de-camp of Prince Neufchâtel, Captain Louis Périgord and Squadron Chief Piré, were remarkable.

Colonel Curial, commander of the fusiliers of the Guard, has been named General of Brigade.

General of Division Dupas, commander of a division under the orders of Marshal Mortier, rendered important services at the battle of Friedland.

The sons of Senators Pérignon, Clément Ris and Garran Coulon died with honour on the battlefield.

Marshal Ney proceeded to Gumbinnen, secured some of the enemy's artillery parks, many wounded Russians, and took a great number of prisoners.

Eighty-second Bulletin

Tilsit, 22 June 1807

An armistice has been concluded upon the proposition of the Russian general. The French army occupies all the Thalweg of the Niemen, so that there only remains to the King of Prussia the little town and territories of Memel.

Armistice between France & Russia

As His Majesty the Emperor of the French and His Majesty the Emperor of Russia are anxious to put an end to the war which has so long divided the two nations, they have in the meantime resolved to conclude an Armistice; their Majesties have named and empowered the following plenipotentiaries, viz., on the one part of the Prince of Neufchâtel, Major-General of the *Grande Armée*; and on the other part, Lieutenant General Prince Labanov von Rostov, Knight of the Order of St Anne, Grand Cross, etc., who have agreed upon the following preliminaries:

Article I An armistice shall take place between the French and the Russian armies, in order that, in the meantime, a peace may be negotiated, concluded and signed, to put an end to that bloodshed which is so contrary to humanity.

Article II If either of the two contracting parties shall incline to break this armistice, which God forbid!, the party so inclining shall be bound to signify this at the headquarters of the other army, and hostilities shall not again commence until one month after the above notification.

Article III The French and Prussian armies shall conclude a separate armistice, and officers shall be appointed for that purpose. During the four or five days requisite for the conclusion of this armistice, the French army shall undertake no hostilities against the Prussians.

Article IV The limits of the French and Russian armies, during the armistice, shall be from the Kurische-Haff, the Thalweg of the Niemen, and up the left bank of that river to the mouth of the Lorasna at Schaim, and pursuing the course of that river to the mouth of the Bobra, following this rivulet through Bojary, Lipsk, Sztabin, Dolistowo, Goniondz and Wizna, up to the mouth of the Bobra in the Narew, and from there ascending the left bank of the Narew by Tykoczyn, Suraz, Narew, to the frontiers of Prussia and Russia. On the Kurische-Nehrung the limits shall be at Nidden.

Article V His Majesty the Emperor of the French, and His Majesty the Emperor of Russia, shall name plenipotentiaries within the shortest time possible, who are to be provided with the necessary powers for negotiating, concluding and signing a definitive peace between these two great and powerful nations.

Article VI Commissaries shall be named on both sides in order to proceed immediately to the exchange of prisoners, which exchange shall take place by rank for rank, and man for man.

Article VII The exchange of the ratification's of the present armistice shall take place within 48 hours, or sooner, if possible, at the headquarters of the Russian army.

Done at Tilsit, 21 June 1807

MARSHAL, PRINCE OF NEUFCHÂTEL, ALEXANDER BERTHIER

PRINCE LABANOV VON ROSTOV

Approved Tilsit, 22 June 1807

NAPOLEON

By the Emperor, THE MINISTER AND SECRETARY OF STATE, H B MARET. I hereby ratify all the contents of the armistice concluded between the Marshal Prince of Neufchâtel, and Lieutenant General Prince Labanov von Rostov.

Proclamation of His Majesty and King to the Grande Armée

At the Imperial Camp at Tilsit, 22 June 1807

Soldiers, on 5 June we were attacked in our cantonments by the Russian army. The enemy mistook the causes of our inactivity. It found too late that our repose was that of the lion. It regrets having disturbed it.

In the days of Guttstadt, Heilsberg, in the ever memorable day of Friedland, in 10 days campaign, we took 120 cannon, 7 standards, killed or took 60,000 Russians, carried off all the enemy's magazines and hospitals and we remain masters of Königsberg, the 300 vessels that were there, laden with all sorts of ammunition, and 160,000 muskets that England sent to arm our enemies.

From the banks of the Vistula we have reached the banks of the Niemen with the rapidity of the eagle. You celebrated at Austerlitz the anniversary of the coronation, you celebrated this year, in an appropriate manner, the battle of Marengo, which put an end to the War of the Second Coalition.

Frenchmen, you have been worthy of yourselves and of me. You will return to France covered with laurels, after having obtained a glorious peace, which carries with it the guarantee of its duration. It is time that our country should live at rest, secure from the malignant influence of England. My benefits shall prove to you my gratitude, and the full extent of the love I bear you.

NAPOLEON

Eighty-third Bulletin

Tilsit, 23 June 1807
The fort of Neisse has capitulated. The garrison, 6,000 strong in infantry and 300 in cavalry, defiled on the 16th before Prince Jérôme. We found in the fortress 300,000 pounds of powder and 300 pieces of artillery.

Eighty-fourth Bulletin

Tilsit, 24 June 1807
The Marshal of the Palace, Duroc, went on the 23rd to the headquarters of the Russian army, on the other side of the Niemen, to exchange the ratifications of the Armistice, which had been ratified by the Emperor Alexander.

On the 24th, Prince Labanov, having requested an audience of the Emperor, was admitted on the same day at two in the afternoon; he remained a long time in the cabinet with His Majesty.

Marshal Kalkreuth is expected at the headquarters to sign the armistice with the King of Prussia.

On the 11th of June, at four o'clock in the morning, the Russians attacked Dronzewo in great force; General Claparède sustained the enemy's fire; Marshal Masséna rushed along the line, repulsed the enemy, and disconcerted its projects; the 17th Regiment of Light Infantry maintained its reputation; General Montbrun distinguished himself; a detachment of the 28th light infantry, and a piquet of the 25th dragoons, put the Cossacks to flight. All the enterprises of the enemy against our posts on the 11th and 12th turned to its own confusion.

It is already seen by the armistice that the left wing of the French army supports itself on the Kurische-Haff, at the mouth of the Niemen, from where our line extends itself towards Grodno; the right, commanded by Marshal Masséna, reaches to the confines of Russia, between the sources of the Narew and the Bug.

The headquarters are about to be removed to Königsberg, where every day new discoveries are made of provisions, ammunition and other effects belonging to the enemy.

A position so formidable is the result of successes the most brilliant; and while the enemy's army flees routed and destroyed, more than half the French army has not fired a musket.

Eighty-fifth Bulletin

Tilsit, 24 June 1807
Tomorrow, the two Emperors of France and Russia are to have an interview. For this purpose a pavilion has been erected in the middle of the Niemen, to which the

two monarchs will repair from each of its banks.

Few sights will be more interesting. The two sides of the river will be lined by the two armies, while their chiefs confer on the means of re-establishing order and giving repose to the existing generation.

The Grand Marshal of the Palace, Duroc, went yesterday, at three in the afternoon, to compliment the Emperor Alexander.

Marshal Count Kalkreuth was presented to the Emperor today: he remained an hour in His Majesty's cabinet.

The Emperor reviewed the corps of Marshal Lannes this morning. He made several promotions, gave rewards to those who distinguished themselves by their bravery, and expressed his satisfaction to the Saxon cuirassiers.

Eighty-sixth Bulletin

Tilsit, 25 June 1807

On 25 June, at one in the afternoon, the Emperor, accompanied by the Grand Duke of Berg, Prince Neufchâtel, Marshal Bessières, the Grand Marshal of the Palace Duroc and the Grand Equerry Caulaincourt, embarked on the banks of the Niemen in a boat prepared for the purpose. They proceeded to the middle of the river, where General La Riboisière, commander of the artillery of the Guard, had caused a raft to be placed, and a pavilion erected upon it. Close by it was another raft and pavilion for their Majesties' suite. At the same moment the Emperor Alexander set out from the right bank, accompanied by the Grand Duke Constantine, General Bennigsen, General Uvarov, Prince Labanov and his principal aide-de-camp, Count Lieven.

The two boats arrived at the same instant, and the two Emperors embraced each other as soon as they set foot on the raft. Together they entered the hall that was prepared for them, and remained there two hours. The conference having been concluded, the persons composing the suite of the two Emperors were introduced. The Emperor Alexander paid the handsomest compliments to the officers who accompanied the Emperor, who, on his part had a long conversation with the Grand Duke Constantine and General Bennigsen.

The conference finished, the two Emperors embarked, each in his boat. One conjectures that the conference has resulted in great satisfaction. Shortly after, Prince Labanov went to the French headquarters. An agreement has taken place that one half of the town of Tilsit is to be rendered neutral. The apartments appointed there for the residence of the Emperor of Russia and his court have been fixed upon. The Imperial Russian guard will cross the river, and be quartered in that part of the city destined to that purpose.

The great number of persons belonging to each army, who flocked to both banks of the river to view this scene, rendered it the more interesting, as the spectators were brave men, who came from the extremities of the world.

Eighty-seventh Bulletin

Königsberg, 12 July 1807

The Emperors of France and Russia, after 20 days' residence at Tilsit, where the Imperial Houses were in the same street and at no great distance, took leave of each other with the greatest cordiality, at three o'clock in the afternoon of the 9th.

The journal, which contains an account of what passed between them, will be very interesting to the two peoples.

At half past three, the Emperor Napoleon, having received a farewell visit from the King of Prussia, who returned to Memel, set out for Königsberg, where he arrived the 10th, at four in the morning.

Yesterday, the Emperor inspected the port of Königsberg in a boat manned by the marines of the Imperial Guard. Today, His Majesty will review Marshal Soult's corps, and at two o'clock in the morning tomorrow he will set out for Dresden.

The number of Russians killed in the battle of Friedland amounts to 17,500, the prisoners to 40,000, 18,000 of whom have already passed through Königsberg, 7,000 remain sick in the hospitals, and the rest have been conducted to Thorn and Warsaw. Orders have been issued to send them home to Russia without delay; 7,000 have already returned again to Königsberg. Those in France are to be formed into provisional regiments. The Emperor has ordered them to be clothed and armed.

The ratifications of the treaty of peace between France and Russia were exchanged at Tilsit, on the 9th. The ratification of the treaty of peace between France and Prussia, will be exchanged here today.

The plenipotentiaries charged with these negotiations were, on the part of France, the Prince of Bénévent; Princes Kourakin and Labanov, on the part of Russia; on the part of Prussia, Field Marshal Count Kalkreuth, and Count Goltz.

After such events as these, one cannot but smile when the great English expedition is mentioned, and at the new frenzy which animates the King of Sweden. Besides, we may remark that the army of observation between the Elbe and the Oder was 70,000 strong, exclusive of the *Grande Armée*, without including the Spanish divisions, which are now upon the Oder also. It would have been necessary for England to have brought her whole force together, her soldiers, her volunteers, fencibles, etc., in order to have made a diversion of any interest. But when we take into our account that England, under the present circumstances, has sent 6,000 men to Egypt, only to be slaughtered by the Arabs, and 7,000 men to the Spanish West Indies, we can alone feel sentiments of pity for the extravagant avarice with which that cabinet is tormented.

The peace of Tilsit put an end to the operations of the *Grande Armée*; but all the Prussian coasts and ports will remain closed to the English, and it is probable that the Continental blockade will not prove a vain word.

The Porte is included in the Treaty. The revolution that lately occurred at Constantinople was an anti-Christian revolution, which has nothing in common with the policy of Europe.

The Adjutant Commandant Guilleminot is gone to Bessarabia, where he will communicate to the Grand Vizier the intelligence of the peace, and the liberty given to the Porte to take part in it, as well as of the conditions of the treaty in which the Porte is interested.

Treaty between France and Russia

Treaty of Peace between His Majesty the Emperor of the French and King of Italy, and His Majesty the Emperor of all the Russias

Done at Tilsit, 7 July 1807

His Majesty, the Emperor of France, King of Italy, Protector of the Confederation of the Rhine, and His Majesty the Emperor of all the Russias, animated with the same interest in putting an end to the devastations of war, have, for this purpose, named and furnished with full power their plenipotentiaries: on the part of His Majesty the Emperor of the French and the King of Italy, Charles Maurice Talleyrand, Prince of Bénévent, his Great Chamberlain, and Minister of Foreign

Affairs, Grand Cross of the Legion of Honour, Knight of the Prussian Orders of the Black and Red Eagle and of the Order of St Hubert.

His Majesty, the Emperor of all the Russias, has, on his part, appointed Price Kourakin, his actual Private Advisor, Member of the Council of State, Senator and Chancellor of all the Orders in the Empire, Ambassador Extraordinary and Plenipotentiary of His Majesty of all the Russias to His Majesty the Emperor of Austria, Chevalier of the Russian Orders of St André, St Alexander, St Anne (first class), St Wolodomir (first class), and of the second class of the Prussian Orders of the Black and Red Eagle, of the Bavarian Order of St Hubert, of the Danish Order of St Daneborg, the Perfect Union of Danemare, Bailiff and Grand Cross of the Sovereign Order of St Jean of Jerusalem; and Prince Dimitry Labanov von Rostov, Lieutenant General of the Armies of His Majesty the Emperor of all the Russia, Chevalier of the Orders of St Anne (first class), of the Military Orders of St George, and of the of the Orders of Vladimir (third class).

The above-mentioned, after exchanging their full powers, have agreed upon the following Articles:

Article I From the day of exchanging the ratification's of the present treaties, there shall be perfect peace and amity between His Majesty the Emperor of the French and King of Italy, and His Majesty the Emperor of all the Russias.

Article II Hostilities shall immediately cease at all points by sea or land, wherever war is being fought, as soon as the intelligence of the present treaty shall be officially received. High-ranking parties shall dispatch couriers extraordinary, without delay, to their respective generals and commanders.

Article III All ships of war or their vessels belonging to the high contracting parties or its subjects which may be captured after the signing of this treaty, shall be returned or, if sold, the sale price shall be paid in full.

Article IV His Majesty the Emperor Napoleon, out of esteem for His Majesty the Emperor of all the Russias, and to afford to him a proof of his sincere desire to unite both nations in the bands of immutable confidence and friendship, wishes that all the countries, towns and territory, conquered from the King of Prussia, the ally of His Majesty the Emperor of all the Russias, should be restored; namely, that part of the Duchy of Magdeburg situated on the right bank of the Elbe River, Priegnitz; the Uckermark River; the Middle and New Mark of Brandenburg, with the exception of the Circle of Cotbus, in Lower Lusace, which shall belong to His Majesty, the King of Saxony; the Duchy of Pomerania; Upper, Lower, and New Silesia, and the County of Glatz; that part of the district of the Netze River which is situated to the northward of the road of Driesen and Schneidemühl, and to the northward of the line drawn from Schneidemühl through Waldau to the Vistula, and extending along the frontier of the Circle of Bromberg, and the navigation of the river Netze and of the canal of Bromberg, from Driesen to the Vistula and back, must remain open and free of all tolls, the Pomerie River; the island of Nogat, the country on the right bank of the Vistula and of the Nogat, to the west of Old Prussia, and to the northward of the Circle of Culm; the Ermeland River. Lastly, the Kingdom of Prussia, as it was on 1 January, 1772, together with the fortresses of Spandau, Stettin, Custrin, Glogau, Breslau, Schweidnitz, Neisse, Brieg, Kosel and Glatz, and in general all fortresses, citadels, castles and strongholds of the countries named above, in the same condition in which those fortresses, citadels, castles and strongholds may be at present; and also the city and citadel of Graudenz.

Article V Those provinces which, on 1 January, 1772, formed a part of the Kingdom of Poland, and have since, at different times, been subject to Prussia, with the exception of the countries named or alluded to in the preceding article, and of those which are described below in Article IX, shall become the possession of His Majesty the King of Saxony, with power of possession and sovereignty, under the title of the Duchy of Warsaw, and shall be governed according to a regulation, which will insure the liberties and privileges of the people of the said Duchy, and be consistent with the tranquillity and welfare of the neighbouring states.

Article VI The city of Danzig, with a territory of two leagues round the same, is restored to her former independence, under the protection of His Majesty the King of Prussia, and His Majesty the King of Saxony; to be governed according to the laws by which she was governed at the time when she ceased to govern herself.

Article VII For a communication between the Kingdom of Saxony and the Duchy of Warsaw, His Majesty the King of Saxony is to have the free use of a military road through the states of His Majesty the King of Prussia. This road, the number of troops that are allowed to pass at once, and the resting places, shall be fixed by a particular agreement between their Majesties, under the mediation of France.

Article VIII Neither His Majesty the King of Prussia, His Majesty the King of Saxony, nor the city of Danzig shall establish any rolls or taxes or any obstacles to the navigation of the Vistula river.

Article IX In order as far as possible to establish a natural boundary between Russia and the Duchy of Warsaw, the territory between the present confines of Russia, from the Bug to the mouth of the Lossona, shall extend in a line from the mouth of the Lossona along the towing path of the said river; and that of the Bobra, up to its mouth; that of the Narew from the mouth of that river as far as Suratz; from Lisa to its source near the village of Mien; from this village of Nurzuck, and from Nurzuck to the mouth of that river beyond Nurr; and finally, along the towing path of the Bug upwards, to extend as far as the present frontiers of Russia. This territory is forever united to the Empire of Russia.

Article X No person of any rank or station whatever, whose residence or property may be within the limits stated in the preceding article, shall be molested in his person, or effected in any way whatever regarding his rank, quality, estates, revenues, income or otherwise, or in consequence of any part, political or military, which he may have taken in the events of the present war terminated by this treaty. This provision shall apply specifically to the inhabitants of those provinces of the old Kingdom of Poland, which will be given to His Majesty the King of Prussia as the Duchy of Warsaw.

Article XI All contracts and engagements between His Majesty the King of Prussia, and the ancient possessors, relative to the public charges, the religious, military or civil benefits, of the creditors or pensioners of the old Prussian government, are to be settled between the Emperor of all the Russias, and His Majesty the King of Saxony; and to be regulated by their said Majesties, in proportion to their acquisitions, according to Article V and Article IX, and without any restrictions.

Article XII Their Royal Highnesses the Duke of Saxe-Coburg, Oldenburg, and Mecklenburg-Schwerin, shall each of them be restored to the complete and quiet possession of their estates; but the ports in the Duchies of Oldenburg and Mecklenburg shall remain in the possession of the French garrisons until the definitive treaty shall be signed between France and England.

Article XIII His Majesty the Emperor Napoleon accepts of the mediation of the Emperor of all the Russias, in order to negotiate and conclude a definitive treaty of peace between France and England; however, only upon condition that his mediation shall be accepted by England in one month after the exchange of the ratification of the present Treaty.

Article XIV His Majesty the Emperor of all the Russias, wanting on his part to show how ardently he desires to establish the most friendly and lasting relations between the two Empires, acknowledges His Majesty Joseph Napoleon, King of Naples, and His Majesty Louis Napoleon, King of Holland.

Article XV His Majesty the Emperor of all the Russias acknowledges the Confederation of the Rhine, the present state of the possessions of the princes belonging to it, and the titles of those which were conferred upon them by the act of confederation, or by the subsequent treaties of accession. His Said Majesty also promises, upon information being communicated to him by the Emperor Napoleon, to acknowledge those sovereigns who may hereafter become members of the Confederation, according to their rank specified in that act of confederation.

Article XVI His Majesty the Emperor of all the Russias cedes all his property in the right of sovereignty to His Majesty the King of Holland the manor of Jevor, in East Friesland.

Article XVII The present Treaty of Peace shall be mutually binding, and in force for His Majesty the King of Naples, Joseph Napoleon, His Majesty Napoleon, King of Holland, and the sovereigns of the Confederation of the Rhine, in alliance with the Emperor Napoleon.

Article XVIII His Majesty the Emperor of all the Russias also acknowledges His Imperial Highness Prince Jérôme Napoleon as King of Westphalia.

Article XIX The Kingdom of Westphalia shall consist of the provinces ceded by the King of Prussia on the left bank of the Elbe, and other states at present in the possession of His Majesty the Emperor Napoleon.

Article XX His Majesty the Emperor of all the Russias promises to recognize the limits which shall be determined by His Majesty the Emperor Napoleon, in pursuance of the foregoing Article XIX, and the cessions of His Majesty the King of Prussia, which shall be notified to His Majesty the Emperor of all the Russias, together with the resulting state of possession to the sovereigns for whose behalf they shall have been established.

Article XXI All hostilities shall immediately cease between the troops of His Majesty the Emperor of all the Russias and those of His Highness, at all points, wherever official intelligence shall arrive of the signing of the present treaty. The high contracting parties shall, without delay, dispatch couriers extraordinary to convey the intelligence, with the utmost possible expedition, to the respective generals and commanders.

Article XXII The Russian troops shall withdraw from the provinces of Valachie and Moldavia, but these provinces may not be occupied by His Highness' troops until after the exchange of the ratifications of the future definitive treaty of peace between Russia and the Ottoman Porte.

Article XXIII His Majesty the Emperor of all the Russias accepts the mediation of His Majesty the Emperor of the French and King of Italy, for the purpose of negotiating and concluding a peace advantageous and honourable to both Empires. Their respective plenipotentiaries shall repair to the place which shall be agreed upon by the two powers concerned, there to open and proceed with the negotiations.

Article XXIV The time periods within which the high contracting parties shall withdraw their troops from the fortresses that they are to evacuate, pursuant to the above stipulations, as also the manner in which the different stipulations contained in the present Treaty shall be executed, will be settled by a special agreement.

Article XXV His Majesty the Emperor of the French, King of Italy, and His Majesty the Emperor of all the Russias mutually ensure to each other the integrity of their possessions, and of those of the powers included in this present treaty, in the state in which they are now settled, or further to be settled, pursuant to the above stipulations.

Article XXVI Prisoners of war taken by the contracting parties, or included in the present treaty, shall be restored in a mass, and without any cartel of exchange on both sides.

Article XXVII The commercial relations between the French Empire, the Kingdom of Italy, the Kingdoms of Naples and Holland, and the Confederated States of the Rhine, on one side, and the Empire of Russia on the other, shall be replaced on the same footing as before the war.

Article XXVIII Protocol between the two Courts, the Tuileries and Saint Petersburg, with respect to each other, and also their respective ambassadors, ministers, and envoys, mutually accredited, shall be placed on the footing of complete equality and reciprocity.

Article XXIX The present Treaty shall be ratified by His Majesty the Emperor of the French, King of Italy, and His Majesty the Emperor of all the Russias. The ratifications shall be exchanged in this city within the space of four days.

Done at Tilsit, 7 July 1807 (25 June, Russian calendar)

[Signed]   CHARLES MAURICE TALLEYRAND, PRINCE OF BÉNÉVENT
PRINCE ALEXANDER KOURAKIN
PRINCE DIMITRY LABANOV VON ROSTOV

A true copy to the Minister of Foreign Affairs

[Signed]   C M TALLEYRAND, PRINCE OF BÉNÉVENT

Treaty between Prussia and France

Conditions of Peace between His Majesty the Emperor of the French and King of Italy, and His Majesty the King of Prussia. Done at Tilsit, July 9, 1807

His Majesty the Emperor of the French, King of Italy, and Protector of the Confederation of the Rhine, and His Majesty the King of Prussia, animated with the same desire of putting an end to the calamities of war, for that purpose appointed plenipotentiaries, namely: on the part of His Majesty the Emperor of France and King of Italy, Protector of the Confederation of the Rhine, Charles

Maurice Talleyrand, Prince of Bénévent, his High Chamberlain, and Minister for Foreign Affairs, Great Cross of the Legion of Honour, Chevalier of the Prussian Orders of the Black and Red Eagle and Order of St Hubert; and for His Majesty the King of Prussia, Marshal Count Kalkreuth, Knight of the Prussian Orders of the Black and Red Eagle, and Count Von Goltz, his Private Counsellor, Envoy Extraordinary, and Minister Plenipotentiary to His Majesty the Emperor of all the Russias, and Knight of the Prussian Order of the Black Eagle; who after the exchange of their several powers, have agreed on the following articles:

Article I From the day of the exchange of the ratifications of the present treaty, there shall be perfect peace and friendship between His Majesty the Emperor of the French, King of Italy, and His Majesty the King of Prussia.

Article II The part of the Duchy of Magdeburg which lies on the right bank of the Elbe; the Mark of Priegnitz, the Uckermark River, and the Middle and New Mark of Brandenburg, with the exception of the Circle of Cotbus, in Lower Lusach, which shall belong to His Majesty the King of Saxony; the Duchy of Pomerania; Upper, Lower and New Silesia, with the country of Glatz; the part of the district of the Netze River which lies north of the road from Driesen to Schneidemühl, and to the north of a line passing from Schneidemühl, and to the north of a line passing from Schneidemühl, by Waldau, to the Vistula river, and to the frontier of the Circle of Bromberg Pomerania; the Island of Nogat, and the country on the right bank of the Vistula and the Nogat, to the west of Old Prussia; and to the Circle Culm, the Ermeland River; and finally, the Kingdom of Prussia, as it was on 1 January, 1772, shall be restored to His Majesty the King of Prussia, with the fortresses of Spandau, Stettin, Custrin, Glogau, Breslau, Schweidnitz, Neisse, Brieg, Kosel, and Glatz; and, in general, all the places, citadels, castles, and forts of the above mentioned, shall be restored in the state in which they are now. The town and citadel of Grandenz, with the villages of Neudorf, Porschkou, and Swiekorzy, shall likewise be restored to His Majesty the King of Prussia.

Article III His Majesty the King of Prussia acknowledges His Majesty the King of Naples, Joseph Napoleon, and His Majesty the King of Holland, Louis Napoleon.

Article IV His Majesty the King of Prussia in like manner acknowledges the Confederation of the Rhine, and the present state of the possessions of the sovereigns of which it is composed, and the titles which have been bestowed on them, either by the act of confederation, or by the subsequent treaties. His Majesty likewise engages to acknowledge those sovereigns who, in future, shall become members of the said confederation, and the titles they may receive by their treaties of accession.

Article V The present Treaty of Peace and Amity shall be in common for His Majesty the King of Naples, Joseph Napoleon, for His Majesty the King of Holland, and for the Sovereigns of the Confederation of the Rhine, the allies of His Majesty the Emperor Napoleon.

Article VI His Majesty the King of Prussia, in like manner, acknowledges his Imperial Highness Prince Jérôme Napoleon as King of Westphalia.

Article VII His Majesty the King of Prussia cedes, in full right of property and sovereignty of the Kings, Grand Dukes and Dukes, and Princes, who shall be pointed out by His Majesty the Emperor of the French and King of Italy, all the Duchies, Marquisettes, Principalities, Counties, and Lordships, and in general all the territories and domains, and all territorial property of whatever kind, or by whatever title possess, by His Majesty the King of Prussia, between the Rhine and the Elbe, at the commencement of the present war.

Article VIII The Kingdom of Westphalia shall consist of the provinces ceded by His Majesty the King of Prussia, and of other states now in the possession of His Majesty the Emperor Napoleon.

Article IX His Majesty the King of Prussia shall recognize the arrangements made by His Majesty the Emperor Napoleon alluded to in the two preceding articles, and the occupation of the same by those sovereigns in whose favour he shall make such arrangements, as if they were contained and stipulated in the present treaty.

Article X His Majesty the King of Prussia renounces for himself, his heirs, and successors, all actual or future rights that he has or may claim,

　　1 on all territory without exception situated between the Elbe and the Rhine, other than those designated in Article VII.

　　2 on possessions of His Majesty the King of Saxony and of the House of Anhalt, situated on the right bank of the Elbe River. Likewise, all rights or claims of the states situate between the Rhine and the Elbe in the possession of His Majesty the King of Prussia, as they are defined by the present Treaty, shall be for ever extinguished and annulled.

Article XI All pacts, conventions, or treaties of alliance, that may have been publicly or privately concluded between Prussia and any countries on the left bank of the Elbe, and which have not been broken by the present war, shall remain without effect, and be considered as null and void.

Article XII His Majesty the King of Prussia cedes the Circle of Cotbus, in Lower Lusach, to His Majesty the King of Saxony, with full right of proprietorship and sovereignty.

Article XIII His Majesty the King of Prussia renounces forever possession to all the provinces which formerly constituted parts of the Kingdom of Poland, and after 1 January, 1772, having at different periods come under the dominion of Prussia, excepting Ermeland and the country to the west of Old Prussia, east of Pomerania, north of the Circle of Culm, and a line which passes from the Vistula by Waldau to Schneidemühl, and passes along the boundaries of Bromberg and the road from the Schneidemühl to Driesen, which provinces, with the town and citadel of Graudenz, and the villages of Neudorf, Parschken, and Schwierkorzy, shall in future be possess, with all rights of proprietorship and sovereignty, by His Majesty the King of Prussia.

Article XIV His Majesty the King of Prussia also renounces forever possession of the city of Danzig.

Article XV The provinces which His Majesty the King of Prussia renounces in Article XIII, with exception of the territories mentioned in the Article XVIII, shall be possessed with right of property and sovereignty by His Majesty the King of Saxony, under the title of a Duchy of Warsaw, and governed according to a constitution which shall secure the liberties and privileges of the people of that Duchy, and be conformable to the tranquillity of the neighbouring states.

Article XVI To secure a connection and communication between the

Kingdom of Saxony and the Duchy of Warsaw, the free use of a military road shall be granted to the King of Saxony through the states of His Majesty the King of Prussia. This road, the number of troops which shall pass through it at one time, and the places at which they may bivouac, shall be settled by a particular agreement between the two sovereigns, under the mediation of France.

Article XVII The navigation of the Netze River, and the canal of Bromberg, from Dresden to the Vistula and back, shall remain free from any toll.

Article XVIII In order to establish natural boundaries between Russia and the Duchy of Warsaw, the territory between the present boundaries of Russia, from the Bug to the mouth of the Lassosna, and a line which passes from the said mouth, and along the channel of that river, the channel of the Bobra to its mouth, the channel of the Narew from its mouth to Suratiz, the channel of the Lisa to its source near the village of Mien, and of the two neighbouring arms of the Nurzuck, rising near that village, and the channel of the Nurzuck itself to its mouth; and lastly, along the channel of the Bug, up the stream to the present boundaries of Russia, shall for ever be incorporated with the Russian Empire.

Article XIX The city of Danzig, with a territory of two miles circumference, shall be restored to its former independence, under the protection of His Majesty the King of Prussia and His Majesty the King of Saxony, and be governed by the rules by which it was governed when it ceased to govern itself.

Article XX Neither His Majesty the King of Prussia, nor His Majesty the King of Saxony, shall obstruct the navigation of the Vistula River, or establish any customs, duty or tolls of any kind.

Article XXI The city, port, and territory of Danzig, shall be closed for the duration of the present maritime war against the trade and navigation of Great Britain.

Article XXII No person of any rank or station whatever, whose residence or property may be within the limits stated in the preceding article, shall be molested in his person, or effected in any way whatever regarding his rank, quality, estates, revenues, income or otherwise, or in consequence of any part, political or military, which he may have taken in the events of the present war terminated by this treaty. This provision shall apply specifically to the inhabitants of those provinces of the old Kingdom of Poland, which will be given to His Majesty the King of Prussia as the Duchy of Warsaw.

Article XXIII In the same manner, no individual residing or possessing landed property in the countries which belonged to the King of Prussia, prior to 1 January, 1772, and which are restored to him by virtue of the preceding Article II; and, in particular, no individual of the Berlin police or civilian who have taken up arms in order to maintain tranquillity, shall be prosecuted in his person, his estates, rents, annuities or any income whatsoever, on account of any part which he may have taken in the events of the present war, or be subjected to any inquiry.

Article XXIV The arrangements, debts or obligations of any nature whatsoever, which His Majesty the King of Prussia may have contracted or concluded, prior to the present war, as possessor of the countries, domains, and revenues, which His Majesty cedes and renounces in the present treaty, shall be performed and satisfied by the new possessors, without any exception or reservations.

Article XXV The stocks and capital funds which belong to private persons, or public, religious, civil or military associations, in countries ceded by His Majesty the King of Prussia in this Treaty, or which he renounces by the private treaty, whether the said capitals be vested in the Bank of Berlin, the Maritime Society, or in any other manner, in the dominions of the King of Prussia, shall neither be confiscated nor seized. The owners of said funds shall be at liberty to dispose of the same, and they are to continue to enjoy the interest thereof, whether such interest be already due, or may yet become due at the periods stipulated in the conventions or bonds: the same shall, on the other side, be observed with regard to all funds and capitals which are vested by private individuals, or public institutions whatsoever, in such countries which are ceded or renounced by His Prussian Majesty by virtue of the present Treaty.

Article XXVI The archives which contain the titles of property, documents, and in general papers which relate to the countries, territories, dominions, as well as the maps and plans of the strongholds, citadels, castles and forts seated in the countries which His Majesty the King of Prussia cedes or renounces as a result of this Treaty, are to be delivered up by commissioners of His said Majesty, within three months after the exchange of the ratification of this Treaty, to commissioners of His Majesty the Emperor Napoleon, with regard to the countries seated on the left bank of the Rhine, and to commissioners of His Majesty the Emperor of all the Russias, and of the King of Saxony, and of the city of Danzig, with regard to all the countries which their said Majesties and the city of Danzig are in future to possess, by virtue of the present Treaty.

Article XXVII Until the day of the ratification of the future definitive treaty of peace between France and England, all the countries under the dominion of His Majesty the King of Prussia, without any exception whatsoever, shall be closed to the trade and navigation of the English. No shipment to be made from any Prussian port for the British Isles or British colonies, nor shall any ship which sailed from England, or her colonies, be admitted in any Prussian port.

Article XXVIII The necessary arrangements shall immediately be made to settle every point that relates to the manner and period of the surrender of the places that are to be restored to His Majesty the King of Prussia, and to the civil and military administration of the said countries.

Article XXIX The prisoners of war taken on both sides are to be returned without any exchange, and *en masse*, as soon as circumstances shall admit.

Article XXX The present Treaty is to be ratified by His Majesty the Emperor of the French, and by His Majesty the King of Prussia, and the ratifications shall be exchanged at Königsberg, by the undersigned, no later than six days after the signing of the treaty.

Done at Tilsit, 9 July 1807.

[Signed] CHARLES MAURICE TALLEYRAND, PRINCE OF BÉNÉVENT

MARSHAL COUNT KALKREUTH

AUGUSTE, COUNT GOLTZ

The ratifications of this Treaty were exchanged at Königsberg, on 12 July 1807.

CAMPAIGN IN AUSTRIA
1809

In April of 1809, Austria declared war against France. She had sensed that France was weakened by the campaign in Spain and sought to end French dominance of the Continent. As usual, England was willing to bankroll military activities against Napoleon, and the two formed the Fifth Coalition. In late April, Napoleon defeated the Austrians at the battles of Abensberg, Landshut, and Eckmühl, but the Austrian army retreated in good order.

In May, Napoleon took control of the Island of Lobau and crossed the Danube to face the Austrians at Aspern and Essling. High water and the destruction of his bridges cheated him of victory, but he retired in good order to the island.

Reinforced and reinvigorated, Napoleon moved against the Austrians and defeated them at the great victory of Wagram on 4–5 July 1809. Napoleon had won another campaign, but there were ominous signs. The Austrians had fought well, and the campaign had not been a textbook example of French superiority. Moreover, his Russian ally had done virtually nothing to help him; clearly Napoleon could no longer count on the Russians.

Still, in the campaign of 1809 Napoleon once again defeated his enemies and once again showed that the French army, with him at its head, was the best fighting force in Europe. The Treaty of Vienna left England isolated and, outside of Spain, brought peace to the Continent. That peace would last until 1812.

First Bulletin

Ratisbon, 24 April 1809

The Austrian army crossed the Inn on 9 April. That began the hostilities, and Austria declared an implacable war against France and her Allies, and the Confederation of the Rhine.

Here were the positions of the French Army and her Allies:

The corps of the Duke of Auerstädt at Ratisbon.

The corps of the Duke of Rivoli at Ülm.

The corps of General Oudinot at Augsburg.

The headquarters at Strasburg.

The three Bavarian divisions under the orders of the Duke of Danzig were placed as follows: the first division, commanded by the Prince Royal, at Munich; the second, commanded by General Deroy, at Landshut; and the third, commanded by General Wrede, at Straubing.

The Württemberg division at Heydenheim.

The Saxon troops encamped under the walls of Dresden.

The corps of the Duchy of Warsaw, commanded by Prince Poniatowski, in the environs of Warsaw.

On the 10th, the Austrian troops surrounded Passau, where they surrounded a battalion of Bavarians, and at the same time invested Kufstein, where there was another battalion of Bavarians. These movements took place without a shot being fired.

The Austrians published the attached proclamation in the Tyrol.

The Bavarian court left Munich for Dillingen

The Bavarian division that had been at Landshut went to Altdorf, on the left bank of the Isar.

The division under the command of General Wrede marched on Neustadt.

The Duke of Rivoli left Ülm for the environs of Augsburg.

From the 10th to the 16th, the enemy's army advanced from the Inn to the Isar; there were several skirmishes between parties of the cavalry in which the Bavarians were successful. On the 16th, at Pfaffenhofen, the 2nd and 3rd Regiments of Bavarian Light Horse completely routed the hussars of Stipschitz and the Rosenberg dragoons.

At the same time, the enemy appeared in large bodies for the purpose of debouching by Landshut. The bridge was broken down, and the Bavarian division commanded by General Deroy vigorously opposed this movement of the enemy; but being threatened by the columns that had crossed the Isar at Moorburg and Freising, this division retired in good order upon that of General Wrede, and the Bavarian army took a central position upon Neustadt.

Departure of the Emperor from Paris on the 13th

The Emperor learned by the telegraph in the evening of the 12th that the Austrian army had crossed the Inn, and he set out from Paris almost immediately. He arrived at Ludwigsburg at three o'clock on the morning of the 16th, and at Dillingen in the evening of the same day, where he saw the King of Bavaria, and passed half an hour with that Prince and promised to restore him to his capital in 15 days, to revenge the insults which had been offered to his house, and to make him greater than any of his ancestors had ever been. On the 17th, at two o'clock in the morning, His Majesty arrived at Donauwörth, where his headquarters was established, and immediately gave the necessary orders.

On the 18th the headquarters were moved to Ingolstadt.

Battle of Pfaffenhofen, on the 19th

On the 19th, General Oudinot left Augsburg and arrived by daybreak at Pfaffenhofen, where he met 3,000 or 4,000 Austrians, whom he attacked and dispersed, and took 300 prisoners.

The Duke of Rivoli arrived the next day at Pfaffenhofen with his army corps.

The same day, the Duke of Auerstädt left Ratisbon to advance to Neustadt and to draw near to Ingolstadt. It was then evident that the plan of the Emperor was to outmanoeuvre the enemy, who had formed near Landshut, and to attack them at the very moment when it, thinking it was commencing the attack, were marching to Ratisbon.

Battle of Thann, on the 19th

On the 19th, by daybreak, the Duke of Auerstädt began his march in two columns. The divisions of Morand and Gudin formed his right; the divisions of Saint-Hilaire and Friant formed his left. The Saint-Hilaire division arrived at the village of Pressing, and there met the enemy, superior in number but inferior in bravery, and there the campaign was opened by the battle that was most glorious to our arms. General Saint-Hilaire, supported by General Friant, overturned everything that was opposed to him, and took all the positions of the enemy, killed a great number, and took between 600 and 700 prisoners. The 72nd Regiment distinguished itself on that day; the 57th maintained its old reputation. Sixteen years ago this regiment obtained in Italy the name of the Terrible. In this action they maintained their claim to that title: they singly attacked six Austrian regiments in succession, and routed them.

On the left, at two o'clock in the afternoon, General Morand also fell in with an Austrian division, which he attacked in front, while the Duke of Danzig, with a corps of Bavarians that had marched from Abensberg, attacked them in the rear.

This division was soon driven from all its positions, and left several hundreds in killed and prisoners. The whole regiment of the dragoons of Leveneher was destroyed and its colonel killed by the Bavarian light horse.

At sunset the corps of the Duke of Danzig formed its junction with that of the Duke of Auerstädt.

In all these affairs Generals Saint-Hilaire and Friant were particularly distinguished.

Those unfortunate Austrian troops who had been led from Vienna with music and with songs, and under a persuasion that there was no longer any French army in Germany and that they would only have to deal with Württembergers and Bavarians, displayed in the strongest manner the resentment they felt against their chiefs for the error into which they had been led; and their terror was the greater when they saw those old bands which they had been accustomed to consider as their masters.

In all these battles our loss was inconsiderable compared with that of the enemy, which lost a number of generals and officers who were obliged to put themselves forward to give courage to their troops. The Prince of Lichtenstein, General Lusignan and others were wounded. The loss of the Austrians in colonels and officers of lower rank was extremely considerable

Battle of Abensberg, on the 20th

The Emperor resolved to beat and destroy the corps of the Archduke Louis and General Hiller, which amounted to 60,000 men. On the 20th, His Majesty took post at Abensberg: he gave orders to the Duke of Auerstädt to keep the corps of Hohenzollern, of Rosenberg and Lichtenstein, in check, while with the two divisions of Morand and Gudin, the Bavarians and the Württembergers, he attacked the army of the Archduke Louis and General Hiller in front, and caused the communications of the enemy to be cut off by the Duke of Rivoli, who passed by Freiburg, and from there proceeded to the rear of the Austrian army. The divisions of Morand and Gudin formed the left and manoeuvred under the orders of the Duke of Montebello. The Emperor determined to fight that day at the head of the Bavarians and Württembergers. He ordered the officers of these two armies to form a circle, and addressed them in a long speech. The Prince-Royal of Bavaria translated into German what he said in French.The Emperor made them aware of the confidence that he reposed in them. He told the Bavarian officers that the Austrians had always been their enemies; that they now wished to destroy their independence; that for more than 200 years the Bavarian standard had been displayed against the Austrians, but at this time he would render them so powerful that they alone should be able to resist the House of Austria.

He spoke to the Württembergers of the victories they had obtained over the House of Austria when they served in the Prussian army, and of the advantages that they had recently obtained from the campaign in Silesia. He told them all that the moment to conquer had come for carrying the war into the Austrian territory. This speech was repeated to the different companies by the captains, and the different dispositions made by the Emperor produced an effect that may easily be conceived.

The Emperor then gave the signal for battle, and planned manoeuvres to the particular character of these troops. General Wrede, a Bavarian officer of great merit, was stationed at the bridge of Siegenburg and attacked an Austrian division that was opposed to him. General Vandamme, who commanded the Württembergers, overtook the enemy's right flank. The Duke of Danzig, with the division of the Prince-Royal and that of General Deroy, marched toward the village of Neuhausen, in order to reach the great road from Abensberg to Landshut. The Duke of Montebello, with his two French divisions, forced the extremity of the enemy's left, and overthrew everything that was opposed to him and advanced to Rohr and Rosenberg. Our cannonade was successful on all points. The enemy, disconcerted by our movements, did not fight for more than an hour, and then beat a retreat. Eight standards, 12 pieces of artillery and 18,000 prisoners were the result of this affair, which cost us but few men.

Battle and taking of Landshut, on the 21st

The battle of Abensberg having laid open the flank of the Austrian army and all their magazines, by daybreak on the 21st the Emperor marched on Landshut. The Duke of Istria overthrew the enemy's cavalry in the plain before that city.

General of Division Mouton had the grenadiers of the 17th advance to the charge on the bridge, forming the head of the column. The bridge, which was of wood, was set on fire, but that was not an obstacle to our infantry, who forced it and penetrated into the city. The enemy, driven from its position, was then attacked by the Duke of Rivoli, who had advanced by the right bank. Landshut fell into our power, and with Landshut we took 30 pieces of artillery, 9,000 prisoners, 600 ammunition wagons, 3,000 baggage wagons, 3 superb bridge equipages and the hospitals and magazines that the Austrians had begun to form. Some couriers and aides-de-camp of the General-in-Chief Prince Charles, and some convoys of wounded men coming to Landshut and very surprised to find the enemy there, also fell into our hands.

Battle of Ekhmühl, on the 22nd

While the battle of Abensberg and that of Landshut produced such important consequences, the Archduke Charles had formed a junction with the Bohemian army under General Kolowrat and obtained some partial success at Ratisbon. One thousand of the 65th, who were left to guard the bridge of Ratisbon who had not received orders to retreat, having expended their cartridges and being surrounded by the Austrians, were obliged to surrender. This event made an impression upon the Emperor, and he swore that in 24 hours Austrian blood would flow in Ratisbon to avenge the insult that had been offered to his arms.

At the same time, the Dukes of Auerstädt and Danzig held in check the corps of Rosenberg, Hohenzollern and Lichtenstein. There was no time to be lost. The Emperor, on the 22nd in the morning, began his march from Landshut with the two divisions of the Duke of Montebello, the corps of the Duke of Rivoli, the cuirassiers of Nansouty and Saint-Sulpice and the Württemberg division. At two o'clock in the afternoon, he arrived opposite Ekhmühl, where the four corps of the Austrian army, consisting of 110,000 men, had taken a position under the command of the Archduke Charles. The Duke of Montebello attacked the enemy on the left, with the division of Gudin. On the first signal, the divisions of the Dukes of Auerstädt and Danzig, and the division of light cavalry of General Montbrun, debouched. One of the most beautiful sights which war can present then presented itself: 110,000 men attacked on all points, turned by their left, and successively driven from all their positions. The detail of the military events would be too long; it is sufficient to say that the enemy was completely routed; that it lost the greater part of its cannon and a great number of prisoners; that the 10th Light Infantry division Saint-Hilaire was covered in glory as it debouched on the enemy, and that the Austrians, driven from the woods which cover Ratisbon, were forced into the plain and cut off by cavalry. Senator General of Division Demont's horse was killed under him. The Austrian cavalry, strong and numerous, attempted to cover the retreat of their infantry, but they were attacked by the division of Saint-Sulpice on the right, and by the division of Nansouty on the left, and the enemy's line of hussars and cuirassiers routed; more than 300 Austrian cuirassiers were taken prisoner. As the night was falling, our cuirassiers continued their march to Ratisbon. The Nansouty division met with a column of the enemy that was escaping, attacked it, and compelled it to surrender; it consisted of three Hungarian battalions of 1,500 men.

The division of Saint-Sulpice charged another square of the enemy, where Prince Charles narrowly escaped being taken. He was indebted for his safety to the fleetness of his horse. This column was also broken and taken. Darkness at length compelled our troops to halt. In this battle of Ekhmühl, not above half of the French troops were engaged. The enemy, closely pressed, continued to defile all of the night in small divisions and in great confusion. All its wounded, the greater part of its artillery, 15 standards and 20,000 prisoners fell into our hands. The cuirassiers, as always, covered themselves with glory.

Battle and taking of Ratisbon, on the 23rd

On the 23rd, at daybreak, the army advanced upon Ratisbon; the advanced guard, formed by the division of Gudin and by the cuirassiers of Nansouty and Saint-Sulpice, very soon came in sight of the enemy's cavalry, which attempted to cover the city. Three successive charges took place, all of which were to our advantage. Eight thousand of their cavalry troops having been cut to pieces, the enemy precipitately re-crossed the Danube. During these proceedings, our light infantry tried to get possession of the city. By a most unaccountable disposition of his force, the Austrian general sacrificed six regiments there without any reason. The city is surrounded with a bad wall, a bad ditch and a bad counterscarp. The artillery having arrived, the city was battered with some 12-pounders. It was recollected that there was one part of the fortifications where, by means of a ladder, it was possible to descend into the ditch and to pass on the other side through a breach in the wall.

The Duke of Montebello caused a battalion to pass through this opening; they gained a position, and introduced themselves into the city. All those who made resistance were cut to pieces; the number of prisoners exceeded 8,000. In consequence of these unskilful dispositions, the enemy had no time to destroy the bridge, and the French crossed pell-mell with them to the left bank. This unfortunate city, which they were barbarous enough to defend, has suffered considerably. It was on fire during part of the night, but by the efforts of General Morand and his division, it was extinguished.

Thus, at the battle of Abensberg, the Emperor beat separately the two corps of the Archduke Louis and General Hiller. At the battle of Landshut, he took the centre of their communications and the general depot of their magazines and artillery. Finally, at the battle of Ekhmühl, the four corps of Hohenzollern, Rosenberg, Kolowrat and Lichtenstein were defeated. The corps of General Bellegarde arrived the day after the battle: they could only be witnesses of the taking of Ratisbon, and then fled into Bohemia.

In all these battles our loss amounted to 1,200 killed and 4,000 wounded. General of Division Cervoni, chief of staff to the Duke of Montebello, was hit by a cannonball, died, and is buried on the battlefield of Eckmühl; he was an officer of merit who served with distinction in our first campaigns.

In the combat of Peising, General Hervo, chief of staff of the Duke of

Auerstädt, was also killed. The Duke of Auerstädt regrets this officer whose bravery, intelligence and activity he admired. General of Brigade Clement, in command of a brigade of cuirassiers of the Saint-Sulpice division, had an arm taken off; he is an officer of courage and distinguished merit. General Schramm was wounded. The colonel of the 14th Chasseurs was killed in a charge. Altogether our loss in officers is not very considerable. The 1,000 men of the 65th who had been made prisoner have been for the most part re-taken. It is impossible to show more bravery and good will than that shown by the troops.

At the battle of Eckmühl, the corps of the Duke of Rivoli, having been unable to rejoin, this Marshal stayed constantly near the Emperor; it took orders and provided the execution of different manoeuvres.

During the assault of Ratisbon, the Duke of Montebello, who had designated the area of passage, had ladders carried by his aides-de-camp.

The Prince of Neufchâtel, in order to encourage the troops and at the same time give proof of confidence to the allies, marched several times at the advance guard with the Bavarian regiments.

The Duke of Auerstädt has given, in these different affairs, new proofs of his well-known intrepidity.

The Duke of Rovigo, with as much zeal as intrepidity, crossed several times the many legions, to appraise the different columns of the intention of the Emperor.

Of 222,000 men of which the Austrian army was composed, all have been engaged except 20,000 men, commanded by General Bellegarde. On the other hand, nearly one half of the French army has not fired a shot. The enemy, astonished by rapid movements, which were out of its calculation, was in a moment deprived of its foolish hopes and precipitated from a delirium of presumption to a despondency approaching despair.

Second Bulletin

Mühldorf, 27 April 1809

On the 22nd, the day after the battle of Landshut, the Emperor left that city for Ratisbon, and fought the battle of Ekhmühl. At the same time he sent the Duke of Istria with the Bavarian division under General Wrede, and Molitor's division, to proceed to the Inn and pursue the two corps of the Austrian army beaten at Abensberg and Landshut.

Marshal Duke of Istria arrived successively at Wilbisburg and Neumark, found there upwards of 400 carriages and equipages, and took from 15 to 1,800 prisoners in his march.

The Austrian corps found beyond Neumark a corps of reserve that had arrived upon the Inn. They rallied, and on the 25th gave battle at Neumark, where the Bavarians, notwithstanding their extreme inferiority, preserved their positions.

On the 24th, the Emperor had sent the corps of the Duke of Rivoli from Ratisbon to Straubing, and from there to Passau, where he arrived on the 26th. The Duke had the battalion of the Po cross the Inn. It took 300 prisoners, removed the blockade of the citadel and occupied Scharding.

On the 25th, Marshal Duke of Montebello had orders to march with his corps from Ratisbon to Mühldorf. On the 27th, he crossed the Inn and proceeded to the Salza.

Today, the 27th, the Emperor had his headquarters at Mühldorf.

The Austrian division commanded by General Jellacic that occupied Munich, is pursued by the corps of the Duke of Danzig.

The King of Bavaria has shown himself at Munich. He returned afterwards to

Augsburg, where he will remain a few days, intending not to fix his residence at Munich until Bavaria is entirely delivered from the enemy.

On the side of Ratisbon, the Duke of Auerstädt is gone in pursuit of Prince Charles, who, cut off from his communications with the Inn and Vienna, had no other resource than that of retiring into the mountains of Bohemia, by Waldmünchen and Cham.

With respect to the Emperor of Austria, he appears to have been before Passau, in order to besiege that place with three battalions of the *Landwehr* [militia].

All of Bavaria, the Palatinate, is delivered from the presence of the enemy's armies.

At Ratisbon, the Emperor passed several corps in review and caused the bravest soldiers to be presented to him, to whom he gave distinctions and pensions, and the bravest officers, to whom he gave baronies and lands. He has communicated his particular satisfaction to the divisions Saint-Hilaire and Friant.

Until this hour, the Emperor has carried on the war almost without equipage and guards; and one has remarked that in the absence of his guards he had always about him the allied Bavarian and Württemberg troops, wishing thereby to give them a particular proof of confidence. Yesterday, a part of the chasseurs and horse grenadiers of the Guard, the regiment of musketeers and a battalion of chasseurs on foot, arrived at Landshut.

From today to eight days from now, all the Guard will have arrived.

A report has been circulated that the Emperor has had his leg broken. The fact is that a spent ball grazed the heel of his boot, but did not touch the skin. Never was His Majesty in better health, though in the midst of the greatest fatigue.

It has been remarked as a singular fact, that one of the first Austrian officers made prisoners in this war was the aide-de-camp of Prince Charles, sent to Mr Otto with the famous letter purporting that the French army must retire.

The inhabitants of Ratisbon having behaved very well, and evinced that patriotic and confederated spirit which we have a right to expect from them, His Majesty has ordered that the damages done shall be repaired at his expense, and particularly the rebuilding of the houses burnt, the expense of which will be several millions.

All of the sovereigns and territories of the Confederacy evince the most patriotic spirit. When the Austrian minister at Dresden delivered the declaration of his court to the King of Saxony, this prince could not contain his indignation. 'You wish for war,' said the King, 'and against whom? You attack and you inveigh against a man, who three years ago, master of your destiny, restored your states to you. The proposals made to me afflict me; my engagements are known to all Europe; no Prince of the Confederacy will detach himself from them.'

The Grand Duke of Würzburg, the Emperor of Austria's brother, has shown the same sentiments, and has declared that if the Austrians advance to his territories, he should retire, if necessary, across the Rhine; so well are the insanity and the invectives of Vienna appreciated! The regiments of the petty princes, all the allied troops, are eager to march against the enemy.

A notable circumstance, which posterity will remark as a fresh proof of the signal bad faith of the house of Austria, is that on the day she wrote the annexed letter to the King of Bavaria, she published, in the Tyrol, the proclamation signed by General Jellacic. On the same day she proposed to the King to be neutral, and invited his subjects to rise. How can we reconcile this contradiction, or rather, how justify this infamy?

Proclamation

Donauwerth, 17 April 1809

Soldiers, The territory of the Confederation has been violated. The Austrian general wants us to flee at the sight of his arms, and that we should abandon our allies. I am arriving at lightning speed.

Soldiers, I was in your midst when the Austrian Sovereign came to my bivouac in Moravia; you heard him implore my clemency and swear to me of his eternal friendship. Victors in three wars, Austria owed everything to our generosity; three times she has perjured herself!!! Our past successes are our guarantee of the victory that awaits us.

Let us march, and upon sighting us, let the enemy recognize its vanquishers.

NAPOLEON

Order of the Day

Imperial Headquarters, Ratisbon, 24 April 1809

Soldiers, you have justified my expectations. You have supplemented your numbers by your bravery. You have gloriously marked the difference that exists between the soldiers of Caesar and the armed mobs of Xerxes.

In a few days we have triumphed in the three battles of Tann, Abensberg and Ekhmühl, and in the combats of Peising, Landshut and Ratisbon. One hundred pieces of artillery, 40 flags, 50,000 prisoners, three harnessed equipages, 3,000 wagons full of baggage, all the chests of the regiments, this is the result of the rapidity of your marches and your courage.

The enemy, intoxicated by a perjured cabinet, appeared no longer to preserve any recollection of you. Its awakening has been quick; you have appeared to it more terrible than ever. Lately it crossed the Inn and invaded territory of our allies; lately it presumed to carry the war into our country. Today, defeated and horrified, it flees in disorder. Already my advanced guard has crossed the Inn; before one month we shall be at Vienna.

NAPOLEON

By the Emperor, THE PRINCE OF NEUFCHÂTEL, MAJOR–GENERAL ALEXANDER

Third Bulletin

Burghausen, 30 April 1809

The Emperor arrived at Mühldorf at six in the evening of the 27th. His Majesty dispatched the division of General Wrede to Laufen on the Salza, in order to overtake the corps that the enemy had left in the Tyrol and which was retreating by forced marches. General Wrede overtook the enemy's rear on the 28th, near Laufen, took the baggage and took many prisoners; but the enemy had sufficient time to cross the river and burn the bridge.

On the 27th, the Duke of Danzig arrived in Wanesburg, and on the 28th, in Altenmarkt. On the 29th, General Wrede continued his march to Salzburg with his division: about three leagues from the town on the road to Laufen, he found the advanced posts of the enemy's army. The Bavarians pursued them closely and entered Salzburg with them. General Wrede assures us that the division of General Jellacic is completely dispersed. That general has thus been punished for the scandalous proclamation by which he put the dagger in the hands of the Tyrolese.

The Bavarians have taken 500 prisoners and found considerable stores in Salzburg.

On the 28th, at daybreak, the Duke of Istria arrived in Burghausen, and his advanced parties took post on the right bank of the Inn. The same day, the Duke of Montebello arrived in Burghausen, Count Bertrand exerted himself to the utmost to restore the bridge, which had been burnt by the enemy.

The rising of the river due to melting snow caused some delay in the work on the bridge. All the day of the 29th was used to continue the work. It was completed on the 30th, and all the army crossed the river.

On the 28th, a detachment of 50 horse chasseurs, commanded by Captain Margaron, arrived in Dittmoning, where he fell in with a battalion of the famous militia, styled *Landwehr*, which, on his approach, retreated to a neighbouring wood. Captain Margaron summoned them to surrender; after much deliberation, 1,000 men of that valiant militia, posted in a thick wood, altogether inaccessible to cavalry, surrendered to 50 chasseurs. The Emperor wished to see them; they really excited compassion; they are badly armed, worse accoutred, and commanded by retired officers of artillery.

The genuine arrogant and savage temper of the Austrians fully displayed itself in the moment of apparent success, when they occupied Munich. The High Bailiff of Mühldorf was arrested by them and shot. An inhabitant of Mühldorf, of the name of Stark, who had obtained a badge of distinction from the King of Bavaria for the services, which during the last war he rendered to the army, has been taken up and sent to Vienna to stand his trial. At Burghausen, the wife of the High Bailiff of Burghausen, Count Armansperg, came to implore the Emperor to help her get back her husband, who had also been sent to Linz and from there to Vienna, because in the year 1805 he did not comply with a requisition addressed to them on the part of the Austrians. This is the crime for which the Austrians have long resented him and for which he has suffered such an unjust vengeance.

The Bavarians will no doubt give a minute and faithful account of the acts of wanton cruelty committed by the Austrians in this country, that the memory thereof may be preserved by their most remote posterity, although it is extremely probable that this was the last insult that Austria will be able to offer to the allies of France. The Austrians have endeavoured, both in the Tyrol and Westphalia, to invite the inhabitants to rise in rebellion against their sovereigns.

Austria has raised numerous armies, divided into corps like the French army; her generals are publishing bulletins, proclamations, general orders – all in imitation of the French army. But the ass is not ennobled to a lion because he is covered with a lion's skin; the long ears betray the ignoble beast.

The Emperor of Austria has left Vienna, and on his departure published a proclamation, drawn up by Gentz, in the style and spirit of the most ridiculous performance of that kind. He is gone to Scharding, a position he has chosen precisely to be nowhere in particular, neither in his capital to govern his dominions, nor in the field, where he would have been no more than a useless encumbrance. It is difficult to see a prince weaker and more deceitful. When he was informed of the result of the battle of Ekhmühl, he left the banks of the Inn and retired into the interior of his dominions.

The town of Scharding, which had been occupied by the Duke of Rivoli, has suffered much. The Austrians on their retreat set fire to their magazines and burned half the town that belonged to them. They had no doubt some presentiment of their future fate and adopted the old adage, that what belonged to Austria shall no longer belong to her.

Fourth Bulletin

Braunau, 1 May 1809

On the crossing of the bridge at Landshut, Brigadier General Latour gave proofs of valour and coolness. Count Lauriston skilfully placed the artillery, and contributed much to the success of this brilliant affair.

The bishop and the principal authorities of Salzburg are gone to Burghausen to implore the clemency of the Emperor for the country. His Majesty gave them his assurance that they should never again come under the dominion of the House of Austria. They engaged to take measures for recalling the four battalions of the militia that the Circle had delivered, and of which part were dispersed and fled.

Today, 1 May, the headquarters are moved to Ried.

At Braunau, magazines were found with 200,000 rations of biscuit and 6,000 sacks of oats. We hope to find considerably more at Ried. The Circle of Ried has furnished three battalions for the militia, but the greater part of them have returned again to their habitations.

The Emperor of Austria was at Braunau three days. He was at Scharding when he heard of the defeat of his army. The inhabitants consider him as the principal cause of the war. The famous volunteers of Vienna passed through this place after their defeat at Landshut, throwing away their arms and in all haste carrying with them the alarm to Vienna.

On 21 April, an Imperial Decree was published in this capital, declaring the ports to be again opened to the English, the relations with this old ally renewed and hostilities against the common enemy begun.

General Oudinot has taken a battalion of 1,000 men prisoner between Altheim and Ried. This battalion was without cavalry and artillery. On the approach of our troops, they made it their duty to start firing, but being surrounded on all sides by the cavalry, laid down their arms.

His Majesty passed in review several brigades of light cavalry at Burghausen, among them the brigade of Hesse Darmstadt, to which he was pleased to express his satisfaction. General Marulaz, under whose command the troop stands, presented several of them. His Majesty was pleased to grant them decorations of the Legion of Honour.

General Wrede has intercepted a courier, on whom were found a number of letters, from which we may perceive the state of alarm that agitates the monarchy.

Fifth Bulletin

Enns, 4 May 1809

On 1 May, General Oudinot, after having taken 1,100 prisoners, penetrated beyond Ried, where he took 400 more, so that this day he took 1,500 men without firing a single shot.

The town of Braunau was a strong fortress of sufficient importance, since it commanded a bridge on the river that forms the frontier of Austria. In a spirit of inconsistency worthy of this weak cabinet, it destroyed a fortress situated on a frontier where it might be of great utility, in order to build one at Komorn, in the midst of Hungary. Posterity will with difficulty believe this excess of inconsistency and folly.

The Emperor arrived at Ried on 2 May, at one of the morning, and at Lambach at one of the afternoon of the same day.

At Ried were found a bakery with eight ovens, and magazines containing 20,000 quintals of flour.

The bridge of Lambach, on the Traun, had been cut by the enemy; it was re-established during the day.

On the same day, the Duke of Istria, commander of the cavalry, and the Duke of Montebello, with the corps of Oudinot, entered Wels. In this town were found a bakery, 12,000 or 15,000 quintals of flour and magazines of wine and brandy.

The Duke of Danzig, who arrived at Salzburg on 30 April, instantly caused one brigade to march towards Kufstein and another towards Rastatt, in the direction of the Italian roads. His advanced guard, pursuing General Jellacic, forced him from the strong post at Colling.

On 1 May, the headquarters of the Duke of Rivoli were at Scharding. Adjutant General Trinqualye, commanding the advanced guard of the division of Saint Cyr, met at Riedau, on the road to Neumarkt, with the advanced guard of the enemy. The Württemberg light horse, the Baden dragoons and three companies of voltigeurs of the 4th Regiment of the French line, as soon as they perceived the enemy, attacked and pursued it to Neumarkt. They killed 50 men and took 500 prisoners.

The Baden dragoons valiantly charged a half-battalion of the regiment of Jordis, and compelled them to lay down their arms. Lieutenant Colonel d'Emmerade, who commanded them, had his horse pierced with stabs from the bayonet. Major Saint-Croix took with his own hand a flag from the enemy. Our loss consists of 3 men killed and 50 wounded.

The Duke of Rivoli continued his march on the 2nd, and arrived at Linz on the 3rd. The Archduke Louis and General Hiller, with the remains of their corps, reinforced by a reserve of grenadiers and by all that the country could afford them, were before the Traun with 35,000 men; but menaced with being turned by the Duke of Montebello, they proceeded to Ebersberg, in order to cross the river.

On the 3rd, the Duke of Istria and General Oudinot marched towards Ebersberg and effected a junction with the Duke of Rivoli. They met the Austrian rearguard before Ebersberg. The intrepid battalions of the skirmishers of the Po, and the Corsican skirmishers, pursued the enemy, which was crossing the bridge, drove into the river the cannon, wagons and from 800 to 900 men, and took in the town from 3,000 to 4,000 men whom the enemy had left there for its defence. General Claparède, whose advanced guard was these battalions, pursued them. He halted at Ebersberg, and found 30,000 Austrians occupying a superb position. The Duke of Istria crossed the bridge with his cavalry in order to support the division, and the Duke of Rivoli ordered his advanced guard to be strengthened by the main body of the army. The remains of the corps of Prince Louis and General Hiller were lost without resource. In this extreme danger the enemy set fire to the town, which was built of wood. The fire spread in an instant in every direction. The bridge was soon enveloped, and the flames seized the joists, which it was necessary to cut. Neither cavalry nor infantry was able to act, and the division of Claparède alone, with only four cannon, fought for three hours against 30,000 men. This battle of Ebersberg is one of the finest military occurrences, the memory of which can be preserved by history.

The enemy seeing the division of Claparède cut off without any communication, advanced three times against it, and was always received and stopped by the bayonet. At length, after a labour of three hours, the flames were turned aside and a passage opened. General of Division Legrand, with the 26th Light Infantry and the 18th Line, marched towards the castle, which the enemy had occupied with 800 men. The sappers broke in the doors, and the flames having reached the castle, all who were within perished there. General Legrand afterwards marched to the assistance of Claparède's division. General Durosnel, who advanced by the right shore with 1,000 horse, joined him, and the enemy was obliged to retreat with great haste. On the first report of these events, the Emperor marched up by the right shore with the divisions of Nansouty and Molitor.

The enemy, who retreated with the greatest rapidity, arrived at night at Enns, burnt the bridge and continued his flight on the road to Vienna. His loss consists of 12,000 men, of which 7,500 are prisoners. We also possess four cannon and two flags.

The division of Claparède, which constitutes a part of the grenadiers of Oudinot, covered itself with glory. It has lost 300 men killed and 600 wounded. The impetuosity of the skirmishers of the Po and the Corsican skirmishers attracted the attention of our army. The bridge, the town and the position of Ebersberg will be lasting monuments of their courage. The traveller will stop and say, 'It is here, from these superb positions, from this long bridge, and this castle so strong from its situation, that an army of 35,000 Austrians were driven into flight by 7,000 Frenchmen.'

General of Brigade Coehorn, an officer of singular intrepidity, had his horse killed under him.

Second-Colonels Cardenau and Lendy were killed.

A company of the Corsican battalion pursued the enemy into the woods and alone took 700 prisoners.

During the affair of Ebersberg, the Duke of Montebello arrived at Steyer, where he rebuilt the bridge that the enemy had cut.

The Emperor sleeps today at Enns, in the castle of Prince Auersperg. Tomorrow will be spent in rebuilding the bridge.

The Deputies of the States of Upper Austria were presented to His Majesty at his bivouac at Ebersberg.

The citizens of all classes, and from all the provinces, allow that the Emperor Francis II is the aggressor; they expect great changes, and admit that the House of Austria has merited all its misfortunes. They accuse, even openly, the feeble, obstinate and perfidious character of their sovereign as the author of their afflictions; they manifest the deepest gratitude for the generosity that the Emperor Napoleon showed during the last war towards the capital and countries he had conquered. In common with all Europe, they are indignant at the resentment and hatred that the Emperor Francis II has not ceased to nourish against a nation that had been so noble and magnanimous towards him. Thus, in the opinion even of the subjects of our enemy, victory is on the side of the good cause.

Sixth Bulletin

Saint Pölten, 9 May 1809

Marshal the Prince of Ponte Corvo, who commands the 9th Corps, composed in a great measure of the Saxon army and which has marched near the Bohemian frontier, spreading disquietude everywhere, has caused the Saxon General Gutschmid to march to Egra. This general has been well received by the inhabitants, whom he has ordered to disarm the *Landwehr*. On the 6th, the headquarters of the Prince of Ponte Corvo were at Retz, between Bohemia and Ratisbon.

A man named Schill, a sort of brigand who was covered with crimes during the last campaign of Prussia, and who had obtained the rank of colonel, has deserted from Berlin with his whole regiment and repaired to Württemberg on the Saxon frontier. He has surrounded that town. General Lestocq has issued an order against him as a deserter. This ridiculous movement was concerted with the party that wished to send fire and blood through Germany.

His Majesty has ordered the formation of a corps of observation of the Elbe, which will be commanded by the Duke of Valmy and composed of 60,000 men. The advanced guard is already moving to proceed to Hanau.

Marshal Duke of Montebello crossed the Enns at Steyer on the 4th, and arrived on the 5th at Amstetten, where he met the enemy's advanced guard. General of Brigade Colbert caused the 20th Regiment of Chasseurs à Cheval to charge a regiment of Uhlans, of whom 500 were taken. The young Lauriston, 18 years of age, and who but six months ago was a page, after a singular combat vanquished the commander of the Uhlans and took him prisoner. His Majesty has granted him the decoration of the Legion of Honour.

On the 6th, the Duke of Montebello arrived at Mölk, the Duke of Rivoli at Amstetten, and the Duke of Auerstädt at Linz.

The remains of the corps of the Archduke Louis and General Hiller left Saint Pölten on the 7th. Two-thirds crossed the Danube at Krems; we pursued them to Mautern, where we found the bridge broken. The other third took the direction of Vienna.

On the 8th, the headquarters of the Emperor were at Saint Pölten.

The headquarters of the Duke of Montebello are today at Sieghartskirchen.

Marshal Duke of Danzig is marching from Saltzburg to Innsbruck, in order to attack in the rear the detachment which the enemy has still in the Tyrol, and which troubled the frontiers of Bavaria.

In the cellars of the abbey of Mölk, we found several thousand bottles of wine, which are very useful for the army. It is not until beyond Mölk that the wine country begins.

It follows from the accounts delivered, that the army has found, since the crossing of the Inn, in the different magazines of the enemy, 40,000 quintals of flour, 400,000 rations of biscuits, and some 100,000 rations of bread. Austria had formed these magazines in order to march forward. They have been of great use to us.

Seventh Bulletin

Vienna, 13 May 1809

On the 10th, at nine of the morning, the Emperor appeared before the gates of Vienna with the corps of Marshal Duke of Montebello. It was at the same hour, on the same day, and exactly one month after the Austria army had crossed the Inn, and the Emperor Francis II had rendered himself guilty of perjury, the signal of his ruin.

On 5 May, the Archduke Maximilian, brother of the Empress, a young prince 26 years of age, presumptuous and without experience, of an ardent character, assumed the government of Vienna, and issued two proclamations.

The talks were everywhere in the country that the entrenchments surrounding the capital were armed, that there had been redoubts built, that they were working on entrenched camps, and that the town was resolute to defend itself. The Emperor could scarcely believe that a capital so generously treated by the French army in 1805, and whose people are well-known for their good spirit and their wisdom, could have been fanaticized to the point of becoming engaged in an enterprise of such folly. Thus, he experienced sweet satisfaction when, approaching the large suburbs of Vienna, he saw a large population, women, children, old people, running towards the French army and welcoming our soldiers like friends.

General Conroux traversed the suburbs, and General Tharreau repaired to the esplanade that separates them from the city. At the instant he reached it, he was received by a discharge of musketry and cannon, and was slightly wounded.

Of 300,000 inhabitants who compose the population of Vienna, the city, properly so called, which is surrounded by a bastion and a counterscarp, scarcely contains 80,000 inhabitants and 1,300 houses. The eight *faubourgs* of the town, which have retained the name of suburbs and are separated from the city by a vast esplanade and covered on the side of the country by entrenchments, enclose more than 5,000 houses, and are inhabited by more than 220,000, who draw their subsistence from the city, where the markets and shops are.

The Archduke Maximilian had caused registers to be opened for collecting the names of the inhabitants who were willing to defend themselves. Only 30 individuals inscribed their names: all the others refused with indignation. Defeated in his hopes by the good sense of the people of Vienna, he collected ten battalions of the militia and ten battalions of the troops of line, composing a force of from 15,000 to 16,000 men, and threw himself within the fortifications.

The Duke of Montebello sent him an aide-de-camp with a summons; but some butchers, and a few hundred fellows, satellites of the of the Archduke Maximilian, rushed upon the *parlementaire*, and one of them wounded him. The Archduke ordered the wretch who had committed this infamous action to be led in triumph through the city, mounted on the horse of the French officer, and surrounded by the militia.

After this unheard of violation of the rights of people, the horrid spectacle was seen of one part of the city drawing upon the other part, and citizens directing their arms against their fellow citizens.

General Andréossy, appointed Governor of the city, organized in each suburb a municipality, a central committee of provisions, and a national guard, consisting of merchants, manufacturers and the good citizens of every class, armed to repress the proletariat and bad subjects.

The Governor-General caused a deputation of the eight suburbs to repair to Schönbrunn. The Emperor charged them to proceed to the city, in order to carry a letter written by Major-General Prince of Neufchâtel to the Archduke Maximilian. He recommended the Deputies to represent to the Archduke that if he continued to fire upon the suburbs, and if a single one of the inhabitants lost his life through his arms, this act of frenzy, this crime against the people, would forever break the bonds which attach subjects to their sovereigns.

The Deputation entered the city on the 11th, at ten in the morning, and their arrival was marked only by the redoubled fire from the ramparts. Fifteen inhabitants of the suburbs perished, and only two Frenchmen were killed.

The patience of the Emperor was wearied. He proceeded with the Duke of Rivoli to the arm of the Danube which separates the Prater (the fashionable promenade of Vienna) from the suburbs, and ordered two companies of voltigeurs to occupy a small pavilion on the left bank, in order to cover the raising of a bridge. The battalion of grenadiers that defended the passage was driven back by the voltigeurs, and by the grapeshot of 15 pieces of artillery. At eight of the evening, the pavilion was occupied and the materials of the bridge collected. Captain

Portales, aide-de-camp of the Prince of Neufchâtel, and Susaldi, aide-de-camp of General Boudet, were among the first to swim across the river, in order to seek the boats on the opposite shore.

At nine of the evening, a battery of 20 cannon, raised by Generals Bertrand and Navelet at 100 *toises* from the fortifications, began the bombardment: 1,800 shells were shot in less than four hours, and soon the whole town appeared to be in flames. One must have seen Vienna, its houses of eight or nine stories, its narrow streets, and numerous population within so narrow a compass, in order to form an idea of the tumult, disorder and disasters which such an operation could not but occasion.

The Archduke Maximilian had, at one in the morning, caused two battalions to march in close column, in order to attempt re-taking the pavilion, which covered the raising of the bridge. The two companies of voltigeurs who occupied this pavilion received them with a discharge of musketry, which with the 15 pieces of artillery from the right side, destroyed a part of the column, and forced them to flee in great disorder.

The Archduke lost all presence of mind in the midst of the bombardment, and especially at the moment when he heard that we had crossed an arm of the Danube and were on the march to cut off this retreat. As feeble and weak as he had been rash and arrogant, he was the first to flee and re-cross the bridge. The respectable General O'Reilly learned only by the flight of the Archduke that he was invested with the command.

At daybreak on the 12th, this general made an announcement to the advanced guard that the firing would cease, and that a deputation was about to be sent to the Emperor.

This deputation was presented to His Majesty in the park of Schönbrunn. It was composed of:

Colonel Dietrichstein, Provisional Marshal of States; the Prelate of Klosterneuburg; the Prelate of Scotland; Count Pergen; Count Veterani; Baron Bartenstein; Mr Mayenberg; Baron Hasen, *référendaire* of Lower Austria; all members of the State Council; the Archbishop of Vienna; Baron Lederen, Captain of the Town; Mr Wohlleben, Burgomaster; Mr Mäher, Vice-Burgomaster; Messrs Egger, Pinck and Heyss, councillors of the magistrate.

His Majesty assured the deputies of his protection. He expressed the pain which the inhuman conduct of their sovereign had given him, who had not feared to deliver up his capital to all the calamities of war, who, himself striking a blow at his rights, instead of being the King and father of his subjects, had evinced himself their enemy and tyrant. His Majesty assured them that Vienna should be treated with the same indulgence and favour that had been displayed in 1805. The deputation answered this assurance by expressions of the liveliest gratitude.

At nine of the morning, the Duke of Rivoli, with the Saint Cyr and Boudet divisions, took possession of the Leopoldstadt.

During this time, Lieutenant General O'Reilly sent Lieutenant General Veaux and Colonel Belloute to negotiate for the capitulation of the place. The annexed capitulation was signed in the evening, and on the 13th, at six of the morning, the grenadiers of Oudinot's corps took possession of the city.

Proclamation to the Army

Schönbrunn, 13 May 1809
Soldiers, a month after the enemy has crossed the Inn, on the same day, at the same hour, we entered Vienna.

Its *Landwehr*, its uprisings in mass, its ramparts created by the ineffectual rage of the princes of the House of Lorraine could not withstand the sight of you. The princes of this House have abandoned their capital, not like soldiers of honour who cede to the circumstances and the setbacks of the war, but like the perjured who are pursued by their own remorse. While fleeing Vienna, their farewell to the inhabitants was murder and fire; like Medea, they have, by their own hand, slaughtered their children.

Soldiers, the people of Vienna, according to the expression of the deputation of its suburbs, forsaken, abandoned, widowed, will be the objects of your consideration. I take the good inhabitants of Vienna under my special protection: as for the turbulent and the wretched, I will make of them an exemplary justice.

Soldiers! Let us be good to the poor peasants and to the good population who deserve our esteem: let us not keep any arrogance of our successes; let us see in it a proof of the divine justice who punishes the ungrateful and the perjured.

NAPOLEON

Eighth Bulletin

Vienna, 16 May 1809

The people of Vienna praise the Archduke Reinier. He was governor of Vienna, but when the revolutionary measures ordered by the Emperor Francis II came to his knowledge, he refused to retain the government. The Archduke Maximilian was therefore appointed in his stead. This young prince, who displayed all the thoughtlessness that could be supposed to belong to his age, declared that he would bury himself under the ruins of the capital. He collected altogether all the restless, the indolent and the worthless, of whom there is always a multitude in a great city, furnished them with pikes, and distributed all the arms which were in the arsenal. In vain did the inhabitants represent to him that a great city, raised by infinite labour and expense to so high a pitch of grandeur, ought not to be exposed to the horrors of devastation with which war is accompanied. Those representations, however, only excited his madness, and his fury rose to such a height that he gave no other answer but the order to fire bombs and howitzers on the suburbs, which could kill the inhabitants only. The French were protected by their fortifications, and could derive a further security from the practice of war. The people of Vienna experienced the most painful anxiety, and the town was believed to be lost, when the Emperor Napoleon, to save the capital from the disasters of a prolonged defence, by rendering all defence immediately useless, ordered the troops to cross the arm of the Danube and to take possession of the Prater.

At eight o'clock, an officer informed the Archduke that a bridge was established at that quarter, that a great number of the French had crossed by swimming and were already on the other side of the river. At this news, the hotheaded Prince grew pale and was filled with terror. He crossed the Prater in all haste, sent every battalion he met back beyond the bridges, and made his escape without having formed any arrangement for the defence of the town, and even without transferring to any person the command that he was abandoning. This however, was the very same man who but an hour before had boldly pretended that he would bury himself under the ruins of the capital. The fate of the House of Lorraine was foreseen by all intelligent persons, though in other respects of the most opposite opinions.

Manfredini obtained an audience of the [Austrian] Emperor, in which he represented to him that this war would long weigh heavy on his conscience, that it would bring about the downfall of his House, and that the French would soon be at Vienna, 'Bah! Bah!' replied the Emperor, 'they are all in Spain.'

Thugut, in pursuance of the confidence that the Emperor formerly placed in him, took the liberty of making repeated representations.

The Prince of Ligne said aloud, 'I thought I was old enough not to have outlived the Austrian monarch.' And when the old Count Wallis saw the Emperor set out to join the army, he said, 'There is Darius running to meet an Alexander: he will experience the same fate.'

Count Louis Cobentzl, the chief promoter of the war of 1805, was at this time lying on his deathbed; but 24 hours before he expired, he addressed a pathetic letter to the Emperor. 'Your Majesty,' he wrote, 'ought to consider yourself as fortunate with respect to the situation in which the Peace of Pressburg has placed you. You are in the second rank among the powers of Europe, which is the same that your ancestors occupied. Avoid a war for which no provocation is given, and which will produce the ruin of your house. Napoleon will conquer, and will then have the right to be inflexible,' etc.

This last act of Count Cobentzl rendered his departing moments truly interesting.

The Prince of Zinzendorf, Minister for Foreign Affairs, several statesmen, who, like him, remained free from the contagion and fatal blindness of the moment, several other persons of distinction, and all that were respectable among the burgers entertained the same sentiments, and spoke in the same manner. But the wounded pride of the Emperor Francis II, the hatred of the Archduke Charles against Russia, and the displeasure with which he viewed the close union between Russia and France, the gold of England, which had purchased the minister Stadion, the levity and, in consequence of some dozens of women, or effeminate men, the hypocrisy and false reports of Count Metternich, the intrigues of the Razoumofski, the Dalphozzos, the Schlegels, the Gentzes and other adventurers whom England maintains for the purpose of sowing discord on the Continent, have promoted this foolish, sacrilegious war.

Before the French were victorious in the battlefield, it was said that they were few in number; that there were no more of them in Germany; that the corps consisted entirely of conscripts; that the cavalry were without horses; that the Imperial Guard had revolted, and that the Parisians were in insurrection against the Emperor Napoleon. After we had conquered, however, the French army was innumerable; it had never been formed of more veteran or brave troops; the attachment of the soldiers to the Emperor Napoleon tripled and quadrupled their force; the cavalry was well mounted, numerous and formidable; the artillery was better served than that of any other nation, and moved with the rapidity of lightning, etc.

Weak princes! Corrupt cabinets! Ignorant, fickle, inconsequent men! Such are the snares that England has these 15 years constantly spread for you, and into which you still readily fall. But the catastrophe you prepared is accomplished, and the peace of the Continent is forever secured.

Yesterday the Emperor reviewed General Nansouty's division of heavy cavalry. He bestowed much praise on the appearance of this fine division, which, after so severe a campaign, exhibited 5,000 horses in order of battle. His Majesty filled up the vacancies by new appointments, and bestowed the title of Baron, with an estate, on the bravest officer; and the decoration of the Legion of Honour, with a pension of 1,200 Francs, on the bravest cuirassier of each regiment.

We found at Vienna 500 pieces of artillery, a vast number of gun carriages and muskets, a great quantity of powder, abundance of ready-made military accoutrements and a heap of bullets and cast iron. Only ten houses were destroyed during the bombardment. The people of Vienna remarked that this misfortune had justly fallen on those who were the most zealous promoters of the war, and they perceived then that General Andréossy directed the batteries.

The appointment of this general to the government of Vienna has proved highly satisfactory to all the inhabitants. He had left behind in the capital an honourable recollection, and enjoys the general respect of the people.

A few days rest have greatly benefited the army; and the weather is now so fine, we have scarce any sick. The wine distributed to the troops is in abundance, and of excellent quality.

The Austrian monarchy had made astonishing efforts for the support of this war. It is calculated that the preparations have cost above 300 millions in paper. The mass of bills in circulation exceeds in value 1,500 millions. The court of Vienna has carried off the plates of this sort of *assignat* [useless currency], for which a part of the mines of the monarch are mortgaged, that is to say, their security is a property almost chimerical, and over which the holders of the notes have no control. While these notes, that the public could not convert and which daily decreased in value, [were in circulation], the court, through the bankers of Vienna, bought up all the gold that could be procured, and sent it to a foreign country. A month has scarcely elapsed since chests full of gold ducats, sealed with the Imperial seal, were forwarded by the north of Germany to Holland.

Ninth Bulletin

Vienna, 19 May 1809

While the army was taking some repose at Vienna, while its corps were re-uniting and while the Emperor was reviewing the troops, in order to distribute rewards to the brave men who had distinguished themselves, and filling the vacancies that had occurred, every necessary preparation was made for the important operation of the crossing of the Danube.

After the battle of Eckmühl, Prince Charles, being driven to the other side of the Danube, had no other refuge than the mountains of Bohemia.

By pursuing the remains of Prince Charles' army into the interior of Bohemia, the Emperor might have taken from him his artillery and baggage, but this advantage was not sufficient to counterbalance the hardships to which the army would have been exposed during the march of 15 days, through a miserable, mountainous and devastated country.

The Emperor adopted no plan which might delay his entrance into Vienna even for a day, as he rightly conjectured that in the state of excitation which prevailed it would be attempted to present some obstacles by defending the town, which has a very good breastwork provided with bastions. Besides, his army of Italy demanded all this attention, and the idea that the Austrians were in possession of his fine province of Friuli and Piave never permitted him to repose.

Marshal Duke of Auerstädt remained in position before Ratisbon while Prince Charles retreated into Bohemia; and immediately after he proceeded by Passau and Linz to the left bank of the Danube, thus gaining four marches on that Prince. The corps of the Prince of Ponte Corvo acted upon a like system, and made a movement towards Egra, which obliged Prince Charles to direct the corps of General Bellegarde towards the same point; but the Prince of Ponte Corvo made a bold counter-march towards Linz, which he reached before General Bellegarde, who being aware of this counter-march also moved towards the Danube.

These manoeuvres, performed from day to day, according to circumstances, have delivered Italy; have thrown the barriers of the Inn, of the Salza, of the Traun, and all the enemy's magazines, out of defence; have reduced Vienna; have dissolved the militia and the *Landwehr*, have completed the overthrow of the corps of the Archduke Louis and General Hiller, and have still further withered the fame of the enemy's general. This commander, being aware of the march of the Emperor, was to make a movement towards Linz, to cross the bridge and unite with the corps of the Archduke Lewis and General Hiller. The French army, however, was there for some days before he could approach to form a junction. He had hoped perhaps that he could effect his junction at Krems, but that was a vain hope. He was again four days too late, and General Hiller, when re-crossing the Danube, was obliged to burn the great bridge of Krems. Finally, he hoped to be able to effect a junction at Vienna, but he was again several days behind.

The Emperor has caused a bridge to be thrown over the Danube, across from the village of Ebersdorf, two leagues below Vienna. The river is at this place divided into several branches, and is 400 *toises* broad. This work was only commenced yesterday the 13th, at four o'clock in the afternoon. Molitor's division was conveyed across to the left bank, and routed the weak detachments that disputed the ground with it, and attempted to cover the last branch of the river.

Generals Bertrand and Pernety are superintending the construction of two bridges, of which one is more then 240 and the other more than 130 *toises* long, communicating between each other by an island. It is hoped that the works will be finished tomorrow.

All the accounts we receive induce us to believe that the Emperor of Austria is at Znaim.

There is still no rising in Hungary. In want of arms, saddles and money, and not much attached to the house of Austria, this nation appears to have refused all kind of assistance.

General Lauriston, His Majesty's aide-de-camp, has marched at the head of the Baden infantry, and General Colbert's brigade of light cavalry, from Neustadt to Brucken on the Simeringberg, which is a high mountain dividing the waters that run into the Black Sea and the Mediterranean. In the course of this difficult march he took 100 prisoners.

General Duppelin has marched towards Mariazell. He has disarmed about 1,000 of the *Landwehr*, and taken several hundred prisoners.

Marshal Duke of Danzig has advanced to Innsbruck. He encountered, on the 14th at Wörgl, General Chasteler and his Tyrolese, overthrew him and took 700 prisoners and 11 pieces of artillery.

Kufstein was relieved on the 12th. His Majesty's chamberlain, Mr Germain, who was shut up in the fortress, conducted himself with propriety.

Here is position of the army today: the corps of Marshals the Dukes of Rivoli and Montebello, and the grenadier corps of General Oudinot, are at Vienna along with the Imperial Guard. The corps of Marshal Duke of Auerstädt has returned between Saint Pölten and Vienna. Marshal Prince of Ponte Corvo is at Linz with the Saxons and Württembergers, and has a corps of reserve at Passau. Marshal Duke of Danzig is with the Bavarians at Salzburg and Innsbruck.

Colonel Count Czernichev, aide-de-camp of the Emperor of Russia, who had been sent to Paris, arrived at the headquarters as the army was entering Vienna.

He has since served in the army, and attends on His Majesty. He has brought intelligence respecting the Russian army, which was unable to break up from its cantonments before the 10th or 12th of May.

Tenth Bulletin

Ebersdorf, 23 May 1809

Opposite Ebersdorf the Danube divides into three branches separated by two islands. The distance from the right bank to the first island is 140 *toises*: this island has a circumference of about 1,000 *toises*. From this island to the greater island is 120 *toises*, and here the stream runs with the greatest force. The larger of the two islands is called In-der-Lobau, with a circumference of 7,000 *toises*, and the water that separates it from the main land is 70 *toises* broad. The first villages that appear after crossing are Gross-Aspern, Essling and Enzersdorf. The crossing of such a river as the Danube, in the presence of an enemy well acquainted with all the local circumstances, and who has the inhabitants on his side, is one of the greatest military enterprises that can be imagined.

The bridge over the arm of the river which separates the right bank from the first island, and the bridge from this island to that of Lobau, were erected on the 19th. Molitor's division had been conveyed to the great island on the 18th by rowing boats.

On the 20th, the Emperor crossed this island and caused a bridge to be thrown over the last arm of the Danube, between Aspern and Essling. This arm being not quite 70 *toises* broad, only 15 pontoons were required for the operation, which were fixed within three hours by Colonel Aubry, of the artillery.

Colonel Saint-Croix, aide-de-camp of Marshal Duke of Rivoli arrived first on the left bank, in an open boat.

General Lasalle's division of the light cavalry, with Molitor and Boudet's divisions, crossed during the night.

On the 21st, the Emperor, accompanied by the Prince of Neufchâtel and the Dukes of Rivoli and Montebello, examined the position of the left bank and determined the field of battle, posting the right on the village of Essling and the left on the village of Gross-Aspern. Both villages were immediately occupied.

On the 21st, at four in the afternoon, the enemy's army showed itself and appeared to have for its object to defeat our advance guard and to drive it into the river. Vain enterprise! Marshal Duke of Rivoli was the first attacked at Aspern, by the corps of General Bellegarde. He manoeuvred with the divisions of Molitor and Legrand, and threw in total confusion all the attacks that the enemy made that evening. The Duke of Montebello defended the village of Essling, and Marshal Duke of Istria covered the plain with the light cavalry and Espagne's division of cuirassiers, protecting at the same time Enzersdorf; the contest was lively, the enemy having two cannon and 90,000 men collected from the remains of all the Austrian corps.

Espagne's division of cuirassiers, which made several fine charges, advanced in two squares and took 14 pieces of artillery, but a ball killed General Espagne while fighting gloriously at the head of this troops. He was a brave man, and in every respect eminent and praiseworthy. General of Brigade Fouler was likewise killed in a charge.

General Nansouty arrived in the evening on the battlefield, with the single brigade commanded by General Saint-Germain, and distinguished himself by several brilliant charges. At eight o'clock the action terminated, and we remained masters of the field.

During the night, General Oudinot's corps, Saint-Hilaire's division, two brigades of light cavalry and the train of artillery, crossed the three bridges.

On the 22nd the Duke of Rivoli was the first engaged at four in the morning. The enemy made several successive attacks, in order to re-take the village. At last the Duke of Rivoli, tired of acting on the defensive, attacked the enemy in his turn, and overthrew it. General Legrand distinguished himself by the coolness and intrepidity that characterize him.

General of Division Boudet was stationed at the village of Essling, and had orders to defend that important position.

Observing that the enemy occupied a very wide space between his right and left wing, it was resolved to penetrate by his centre. The Duke of Montebello led the attack. General Oudinot was on the left, Saint-Hilaire's division was on the centre, and Boudet's division was on the right wing. The enemy's centre would not withstand the sight of our troops. In a moment everything was borne down before them. The Duke of Istria made several brilliant and successful charges. Three columns of infantry were charged and cut down by the cuirassiers. The Austrian army was on the point of being destroyed, when at seven in the morning an aide-de-camp of the Emperor came to inform him that the sudden rise of the Danube had set afloat a great number of trees, which were cut down during the recent events at Vienna, and rafts which had been left on the bank; and that the bridges which formed the communication between the right bank and the little island, and between the little island and that of Lobau, had thereby been carried away. The rapid swell, which usually does not take place until the middle of June on the melting of the snow, has been accelerated by the premature heat that has for some days prevailed. All the reserve parks of artillery which were advancing, were by the loss of the bridges detained on the right bank, as was also a part of our heavy cavalry, and all of the Duke of Auerstädt's corps. This dreadful mishap induced the Emperor to put a stop to the movements forward. He ordered the Duke of Montebello to keep the battlefield that he had won, and then to take his position, with the left wing resting on a curtain-work, which covered the Duke of Rivoli, and his right wing at Essling. The artillery and infantry carriages that were in our reserve park could not now be brought across the river.

The enemy was in a most frightful state of rout at the moment when it learned that our bridges were broken down. The slackening of our fire, and the concentrating movement of our army, soon left it no doubt respecting this unforeseen events. All its cannon and artillery equipage, which were on the retreat, were again drawn out in line, and from nine in the morning to seven in the evening it made most astonishing exertions, supported by the fire of 200 pieces of artillery, to throw the French army into disorder; but all its efforts turned to his own disgrace. Three times it attacked the villages of Essling and Aspern, and three times it filled them with his dead. The fusiliers of the Guard, commanded by General Mouton, acquired great glory; they defeated the reserve, formed of all the grenadiers of the Austrian army, and the only fresh troops that remained to the enemy. General Gros put to the sword 700 Hungarians who had succeeded in entrenching themselves in the graveyard of Essling. The skirmishers under the command of General Curial performed their first service this day, and proved that they possessed courage. General Dorsenne, Colonel Commandant of the Old Guard, posted his troops in the third line, forming a brazen wall, which was alone capable of withstanding all the efforts of the Austrian army. The enemy discharged 40,000 cannon shot against us, while we, deprived of our reserve parks, were under the necessity of sparing our ammunition, lest some other unforeseen events should occur.

In the evening, the enemy returned to its old position, which it had left previous to the commencement of the attack, and we remained masters of the field. Its loss is very great; it is being estimated by the most experienced officers that it left 12,000 dead on the field. According to the reports of the prisoners, the enemy have had 23 generals and 60 superior officers killed or wounded. Lieutenant Field Marshal Weber and 1,500 men and four flags have fallen into our hands.

Our loss has also been considerable. We have 1,100 killed and 3,000 wounded. The Duke of Montebello was wounded by a cannonball in the thigh, at six o'clock in the evening of the 22nd; but an amputation has taken place and his life is out of danger. At first it was thought that he was killed, and being carried on a handbarrow to where the Emperor was, his adieu was most affecting. In the midst of all the anxieties of the day the Emperor gave himself up to the expression of that tender friendship which during so many years he has cherished for this brave companion in arms. Some tears rolled from his eyes, and turning to those who surrounded him, he said, 'It had to be, that this day my heart should be hit by such a pang as this, that I could abandon myself with any other care than that of my army.' The Duke of Montebello was unconscious, but recovered himself in the presence of the Emperor: he embraced him and said, 'Within an hour you will have lost him who dies with the glory and the conviction of having been and of being your best friend.'

General of Division Saint-Hilaire is also wounded; he is one of the finest generals of France.

General Durosnel, aide-de-camp to the Emperor, was also killed by a cannonball, while he was carrying an order.

The soldiers displayed all that coolness and intrepidity which is peculiar to only the French.

The water of the Danube still increasing, the bridges of the Danube could not be restored during the night; the Emperor, therefore, ordered the army, on the 23rd, to cross from the left bank across the little arm, and take a position in the island of Lobau, protecting the bridgeheads.

The work for replacing the bridges continues. Nothing will be undertaken until they are secure, not only against the accidents of the water, but also against anything that may be attempted against them. The rise of the river and the rapidity of the stream require much labour and great caution.

On the 23rd, in the morning, when the army was informed that the Emperor had ordered it to retreat to the great island, nothing could exceed the astonishment of the brave troops; victorious on both days, they had supposed that the remainder of the army had joined them; but when they were told that the high water had carried away the bridges, and that its continued increase rendered the renewal of their ammunition and provisions impossible, and that any movement in advance would be absurd, it was with great difficulty they could be persuaded of the truth of the statement.

That bridges constructed of the largest boats of the Danube, secured by double anchors and cables, should be carried away, was a great and entirely unforeseen disaster; but it was extremely fortunate that the Emperor was not two hours later of being informed of it. The army in pursuing the enemy would have exhausted its ammunition, which it would have been impossible to replace.

One the 23rd a great quantity of rations was sent to the camp at Lobau.

The battle of Essling, of which a circumstantial report shall be made, pointing out the brave men who distinguished themselves therein, will, in the eyes of posterity, be a new memorial of the glory and inflexible firmness of the French army.

Marshals the Dukes of Montebello and Rivoli on that day displayed all the powers of their military character.

The Emperor has given the command of the 2nd Corps to General Count Oudinot, a general tried in 100 battles, in which he has always evinced the possession of equal courage and skill.

Eleventh Bulletin

Ebersdorf, 24 May 1809

Marshal Duke of Danzig is master of the Tyrol, and entered Innsbruck on the 19th, the whole territory having submitted.

On the 11th, the Duke of Danzig had taken the strong position of the Strub Pass, with seven cannon and 600 men.

On the 13th, after defeating Chasteler in the position of Wörgl, putting him to flight and taking all this artillery, he pursued him past Rattenberg, where the wretched fugitive was indebted for his safety only to the speed of his horse.

At the same time, General Deroy raised the blockade of the fortress of Kufstein, forming his junction with the troops commanded in person by the Duke of Danzig. This marshal greatly praises the conduct of Major Palm, Battalion Chief of the Bavarian light infantry, of Lieutenant Colonel Hapermann, of Captain Haider, of Captain Bernard of the 3rd Regiment of the Bavarian Light Horse, of his aides-de-camp Montmarie, Maingarnaud and Montélegir, and of Squadron Chief Fontange, general staff officer.

Chasteler entered the Tyrol with a handful of wretched men, and preached insurrection, plunder and murder. He saw several thousand Bavarians and 100 French soldiers slaughtered before his eyes. He even encouraged the murderers by his own praises and stirred up all the cruelty of these mountain boors. Among the French who perished in this massacre were about 60 Belgians, all countrymen of Chasteler. That wretch, loaded with the favours of the Emperor, to whom he owed the restoration of his property, amounting to several millions, is insusceptible to the feeling of gratitude, as well as to the affection which even barbarians entertain for the people of the country of their birth.

The Tyrolese detest the men whose treacherous conduct instigated them to rebellion, and who thereby brought upon them all its consequent evils. The rage against Chasteler is so great, that when, after what happened at Wörgl, he took refuge at Hall, they attacked him with cudgels and gave him such a drubbing that he kept his bed for two days and did not venture to make his appearance, except to request a capitulation: he was told, however, that no capitulation would be granted to a highway robber, upon which he fled towards the mountains of Corinthia.

The valley of the Ziller was the first that submitted, laid down its arms and gave hostages. The remainder of the territory has followed this example. All the chiefs have ordered the boors to return to their homes, and they are leaving the mountains and returning to their villages. The town of Innsbruck and all the villages have sent deputies to the King of Bavaria to offer pledges of their fidelity, and to supplicate his mercy.

The Voralberg, who had been misled by the exasperating proclamations and artifices of the enemy, will follow the example of the Tyrol, and that part of Germany will then be completely freed from all the horrors and misfortunes of popular insurrection.

Battle of Urfahr

On the 17th, at two in the afternoon, three Austrian columns under the command of Generals Grainville, Bucalwitz and Somariva, and supported by a reserve under General Jellacic, attacked General Vandamme at the village of Urfahr, in the front of the bridgehead at Linz. At the same moment, Marshal the Prince of Ponte Corvo came to Linz with the cavalry and the first brigade of Saxon infantry, General Vandamme, at the head of the Württemberg troops, and four squadrons of Saxon hussars and dragoons, vigorously repulsed the two first columns of the enemy, drove it from its position, took from it six pieces of artillery, took 400 prisoners, and threw it into rout. The third column of the enemy appeared on the heights of Berslingberg at seven in the evening, and its infantry in a moment crowned the ridge of the neighbouring mountains. The Saxon infantry fell on the enemy with fury, drove it from his position, and took 300 prisoners and several ammunition wagons.

The enemy had retired in confusion to Freystadt and Haslac. The hussars sent out in pursuit brought in many prisoners, 500 horses, muskets, and a number of wagons and caissons that were found in the woods. The loss of the enemy amounts to 2,000 in killed and wounded, besides prisoners. Our whole loss in killed, wounded and prisoners is not 400.

Marshal the Prince of Ponte Corvo gave a lot of praise to General Vandamme. He also praised the conduct of Saxon General-in-Chief Leschwitz, who while 65 years of age acted with the ardour of a young man, of General of Artillery Mossel, of General Gérard and of Lieutenant Colonel aide-de-camp Hamelinaie.

Army of Italy

The Viceroy Commander-in-Chief informs the Minister of War of the continuation of the operations of the army of Italy.

According to the reports by prisoners, the loss of the enemy at the battle of the Piave is as high as 10,000 men. Field Marshal Lieutenant Wauzall is among the dead: one of the two Generals named Giulay has been mortally wounded.

After the battle of the Piave, the enemy, vigorously pursued, was reached at Sacile at the moment he attempted to establish some redoubts to gain some time; he was attacked and put to rout, and we have taken several hundred prisoner.

The next day, the 10th, the pursuit continued and the advance guard brought back a great number of prisoners: two battalions of the 23rd of Light Infantry, which had been heading for Brugnera, reached the rear of an enemy column and took 500 men and one cannon from it.

On the 11th, all the army crossed the Tagliamento: it joined the Austrian army at three in the afternoon at Saint Daniel. General Giulay occupied the heights with several regiments of infantry, several squadrons of cavalry and five pieces of artillery. The Archduke John was there in person and had ordered to hold until the last extremity, to give time to the remainder of the army to defile in the long valley of the Fella. The position was attacked immediately: the enemy was chased out of all the heights and put into a great disorder, and at midnight our advance guard took position on the Ledra. In the combat of Saint Daniel the enemy lost two cannon, 600 men killed or wounded; the flag and 1,500 men of the regiment of Rieski were taken. We have had 200 men killed or wounded.

On the 12th, General Grouchy chased the enemy as far as beyond the Isonzo, took 800 prisoners, and at Udine took all the magazines, pontoons and many equipment wagons.

On the same day, Colonel Gifflenga, at the head of a squadron of the 6th Hussars and one squadron of the Queen's Dragoons, joined a column that was retreating to Genova. He at once charged and overthrew the enemy, took 800 men, eight of them officers, and a flag of the regiment of François Jellacic.

The pursuit continues with the same activity.

Twelfth Bulletin

Ebersdorf, 26 May 1809
We worked all day on the 23rd, all that night, and all day the 24th to restore the bridges.

At daybreak on the 25th, they were ready. The wounded, the empty caissons and all objects necessary for success were moved to the right bank of the Danube.

The Danube being likely to rise until 15 June, it is intended that in order to be able to depend on the bridges we plant in the front some poles driven into the ground, to which is to be fastened the large iron chain which the Turks had destined for the same purpose, but which was taken from them by the Austrians, and was [then] found in the arsenal of Vienna. This measure, and the fortifications which are constructed on the left bank of the Danube, will enable us to manoeuvre on both sides of that river.

Our light cavalry is posted opposite Pressburg, on the lake of Neusiedler.

General Lauriston is in Styria, on the Simeringberg and Bruck.

Marshal Duke of Danzig is on great marches, at the head of the Bavarian troops, hastening to join the army near Vienna.

The Chasseurs à Cheval of the Imperial Guard arrived here yesterday; the dragoons will arrive today; and within a few days the horse grenadiers and 60 pieces of artillery attached to the Guard will arrive.

By the capitulation of Vienna, 7 field marshal-lieutenants, 9 major-generals, 10 colonels, 20 majors and lieutenant colonels, 100 captains, 150 lieutenants, 200 second lieutenants and 3,000 non-commissioned officers and soldiers were made prisoners of war, exclusive of those who were in the hospital and whose number amounts to thousands.

Thirteenth Bulletin

Ebersdorf, 28 May 1809
During the night of the 26th and 27th, our bridges on the Danube were carried away by the waters and the mills which have been set free. We had not time to finish the piles and fix the great iron chain. Today one of the bridges has been re-established, and we expect the other will be completed tomorrow.

The Emperor spent yesterday on the left bank surveying the fortifications which are raising on the island of Lobau, and in order to inspect some regiments of the Duke of Rivoli's corps, stationed at this sort of bridgehead.

At noon on the 27th, Captain Bataille, aide-de-camp of the Viceroy, brought the agreeable tidings of the arrival of the army of Italy at Bruck. General Lauriston had been sent in advance, and the junction took place on the Semmeringberg. A chasseur of the 9th, who was proceeding as scout to a detachment of the army of Italy, met a chasseur of a platoon of the 20th, sent by General Lauriston. After having observed each other for some time, they discovered that they were

Frenchmen, and embraced. The chasseurs of the 20th proceeded to Bruck to the Viceroy, and the chasseur of the 9th repaired to General Lauriston to inform him of the approach of the army of Italy. For 12 days the two armies had received no intelligence of each other. On the evening of the 26th, General Lauriston was at Bruck, at the headquarters of the Viceroy.

The Viceroy has displayed during all the campaign a calmness and an extent of observation that are the presages of a great general.

In the relation of facts that have graced the Army of Italy during these last 20 days, His Majesty has marked with pleasure the destruction of the corps of Jellacic. It was this general whose insolent proclamation enkindled the fury and sharpened the daggers of the Tyrolese. Pursued by the Duke of Danzig, in danger of being flanked by the brigade of General Duppelin, whom the Duke of Auerstädt had dispatched by way of Mariazell, he ran as into a snare upon the front of the army of Italy.

The Archduke John, who, so short a time since in the excess of his presumption, degraded himself by his letter to the Duke of Ragusa, evacuated Graz yesterday, the 27th, taking with him hardly 20,000 or 25,000 men of the fine army with which he entered Italy. Arrogance, insults, excitements to revolt, all his actions, which bear the stamp of rage, have turned to his shame.

The people of Italy have conducted themselves as the people of Alsace, Normandy or Dauphine would have done. On the retreat of our soldiers, they accompanied them with their vows and their tears. They led back individuals who had lost their way, by back roads, five days' march to the army. When any prisoners or wounded French or Italians were brought by the enemy into their towns or villages, the inhabitants brought them assistance and during the night endeavoured to disguise them and assist them in their flight.

The proclamations and the discourses of the Archduke John inspired only contempt and scorn: and it would be difficult to describe the joy of the people of the Piave, the Tagliamento and of the Friuli when they saw the army of the enemy fleeing in disorder, and the army of the sovereign and of the country returning in triumph.

When the papers were examined which belonged to the Intendent of the Austrian army, who was at the head both of the government and the police, and who was taken at Padua, with four carriages, the proof of the love which the people of Italy bear to the Emperor was then discovered. Everybody refused the places offered them; no one was willing to serve Austria, and among seven million men who compose the population of the kingdom, the enemy could not find more than three wretches who did not repel seduction.

The regiments of Italy, who had distinguished themselves in Poland, and who had emulated in the campaign in Catalonia the most ancient French campaigns, covered themselves with glory in every engagement. The people of Italy are marching with rapid strides to the last period of a happy change. That beautiful part of the Continent to which are attached so many great and illustrious recollections, which the Court of Rome, that swarm of monks, and its own divisions, had ruined, is appearing with honour again on the theatre of Europe.

All the details which arrive from the Austrian Army show that on the 21st and 22nd its loss was enormous. The élite troops of the army have perished. The good folks of Vienna say that the manoeuvres of General Danube saved the Austrian army.

The Tyrol and the Voralberg are completely subjected. Carniola, Styria,

Carinthia, the territory of Salzburg, Upper and Lower Austria, are pacified and disarmed.

Trieste, that city where the French and Italians suffered so many insults, has been occupied. The colonial English merchandise has been confiscated. One circumstance in the capture of Trieste has been most agreeable to the Emperor: the delivery of the Russian squadron. It had received orders to fit out for Ancona, but, detained by contrary winds, it had remained in the power of the Austrians.

The junction of the army of Dalmatia will soon take place. The Duke of Ragusa began his march as soon as he heard that the army of Italy was on the Isonzo. It is hoped that he will arrive at Laybach before the 5th of June.

The robber Schill, who assumed, and with reason, the title of general in the service of England, after having prostituted the name of the King of Prussia, as the satellites of England prostitute that of Ferdinand of Seville, has been pursued and chased into an island of the Elbe. The King of Westphalia, independently of 15,000 men of his own troops, had a Dutch division and a French division; and the Duke of Valmy has already united at Hanau two divisions of the corps of observation, commanded by Generals Rivaud and Despeaux, and composed of the brigades Lameth, Clément, Taupin and Vaufreland.

The pacification of the Souabe has made available the corps of observation of General Beaumont, who is at Augsburg, and where there are more than 5,000 dragoons.

The rage of the princes of the House of Lorraine against Vienna may be painted with one stroke. The capital is fed by 40 mills raised on the left bank of the river. They have removed and destroyed them.

Army of Italy

The Viceroy Commander-in-Chief informs the Minister of War of the continuation of the operation of the army of Italy.

After the crossing of the Tagliamento, and the advantages gained at the combat of Saint Daniel, the rearguard of the enemy, which was still being pursued with the sword at its back, was reached at Venzonne by our advance guard under the command of General Dessaix. It attempted to hold its ground but was soon overthrown, and we took 450 prisoners, among whom were several officers of the staff. General Colloredo, who was in command, was wounded by a fireball in the thigh. Our loss is 2 killed and 54 wounded.

The enemy had burned all the bridges of the Fella, but these obstacles have been overcome. The enemy had fortified itself in the Malborghetto fort and on Mount Predel. These positions have been turned; the first, under fire from the fort and without losing any men; the second by the valleys of Raccanala and of Dogna. The troops in charge of these movements met the enemy near Tarvisio, and took this town at a charge.

The fort of Malborghetto has been cannonaded on the 17th from five in the morning until nine-thirty. The assault was then ordered. In the space of half an hour, all the blockhouses and palisades were assaulted and crossed, and the enemy pursued and forced with great carnage as far as its entrenchments. It left 300 men on the place; we took 350 prisoners, 2 howitzers, 5 3-pounder cannon, 1 6-pounder and 2 12-pounders, and considerable magazines. Taking this fort, which was called the *Osopo de la Carinthia*, cost us only 80 men unable to fight. We owe the small number of our wounded to the rapidity with which our troops rushed the enemy. The Prince Viceroy praises General Grenier, who directed the action under his orders; General Durutte; General Pacthod, who was the first to enter the entrenchments of the enemy; the Battalion Chief Amoretti, who was wounded; Battalion Chief Colas of the 102nd, and Captain Gérin of the artillery. The grenadiers and voltigeurs of the 1st Line, of the 52nd, of the 62nd and of the 102nd particularly distinguished themselves.

On the same day and immediately after taking the fort of Malborghetto, the Prince Viceroy proceeded towards Tarvisio, where another victory crowned this day. The enemy was established on the other side of the small valley, narrow and deep, where the Schlittza flows, occupying with five regiments of line and several battalions of Croats, a double line of redoubts elevated one on top of the other and stocked with 25 pieces of artillery. One could see on its rear a large number of cavalry. These corps were commanded by Generals Giulay and Frimont.

Our advance guard, supported by the Abbé and Valentin brigades, attacked the front, and the Fontanelli division attacked the left of the enemy. This division, which still did not have its artillery, was not stopped by the fire of the enemy batteries, which it answered by charging and overthrowing at bayonet point all that was in front of it. The enemy left in great disorder, and the advance guard finished the job of sending its in a complete rout. It left on the battlefield a great number of dead men, 3,000 prisoners and 17 pieces of artillery. We have not had 200 men unable to fight. Generals Fontanelli and Bonfanti, Colonel Zucchi of the Italian 1st Line, and Major Grenier of the 60th Line, have distinguished themselves.

The army artillery, as well as the Séras division, was stopped by the fort of Predel. The Viceroy ordered Major Grenier to proceed with three battalions and two pieces of artillery in the valley of Raïbell to attack the fort from the rear, while General Séras, who was aware of this movement, would attack from the front. In the space of one quarter of an hour the fort was taken and everything that was in the palisades hit by the sword. The garrison was 400 men strong: only two escaped. We found eight pieces of artillery in the fort.

On the 19th, 20th and 21st, the army arrived from Tarvisio to Villach, Klagenfurt and Saint Weit.

On the 22nd, 23rd and 24th, the army entered Freisach, Unzmarkt and Knittelfeld.

The right wing of the army, under the command of General Macdonald, and composed of the Broussier and Lamarque divisions, and the Pully division of dragoons, had been directed towards Görlitz. They crossed the Isonzo on the 14th, and on the 15th took position beyond Görlitz, in spite of the efforts of the enemy. We took at Görlitz 11 cannon, two mortars and many artillery supplies.

On the 17th, the Broussier division broke through the enemy before Prevald and obliged him to retreat quickly on Laybach. The Lamarque division, which marched by the roads of Podvel and of Poderay, routed the enemy everywhere in the passes, took 400 prisoners, one of them a colonel, and 15 officers, and also took one cannon.

On the 18th, General Schilt entered Trieste and in his march took 400 to 500 prisoners.

On the 20th, General Broussier forced the capitulation of the forts of Prevald: 2,000 men put down their arms. We took 15 cannon and a considerable quantity of war munitions and rations.

On the 21st, the forts of Laybach were reconnoitred and closely surrounded. On the 22nd, Marshal Macdonald ordered General Lamarque to attack on the left, General Broussier was to attack on the right, and the cavalry was placed so that they could cut off the enemy's retreat. On the same day, in the evening, these forts, which had cost Austria an enormous amount of money and were defended by 4,500 men, asked to capitulate. Generals Giulay and Zach, upon seeing the dispositions for attack, had fled with a few hundred men. One Lieutenant-General, 1 colonel, 3 majors, 131 officers and 4,000 men put down their arms. We found in the forts and entrenched camp 65 guns, 4 flags, 8,000 rifles and considerable magazines.

The Prince Viceroy makes praises of General Macdonald, who directed all the operations of the right wing of the army. Generals of Division Lamarque and Broussier distinguished themselves.

At the time the army of Italy arrived at Knittelfeld, the Prince Viceroy was informed that the remains of General Jellacic's corps, who had escaped the army from Germany, had been joined at Rotenmann by several battalions arriving from the interior, and formed a corps of 700 to 800 men taking the direction of Leoben. The Séras division received orders to start a forced march in order to arrive at the fork of the roads before the enemy. On the 25th, at nine in the morning, his advance guard met the enemy, which was debouching by the road of Mautern. The enemy formed itself on the advantageous position of Saint Michel, its right leaning on some scarped mountains, its left at the Muer, and its centre occupied a plateau, the access to which was difficult. General Séras was in charge of attacking in front with a brigade of his division and one of the Durutte division commanded by General Valentin. He had, behind his line the 9th and 6th of mounted Chasseurs, commanded by Colonels Triaire and Delacroix, aides-de-camp of the Prince. General Durutte was in reserve with the rest of his division. Around two o'clock, the attack started on the whole line; everywhere the enemy was overthrown; the plateau was taken and the cavalry finished off the rout. Eight hundred Austrians were left on the battlefield, 1,200 were wounded, 4,200, of whom 70 are officers, were taken prisoner. We took two cannon and one flag. General Jellacic, with two other generals and 60 dragoons, fled as fast as they could. General Séras entered Leoben at six o'clock in the evening, where he took 600 more men. A similar number fled into the mountains after having thrown down their arms.

And so, all that remained of the corps of General Jellacic has been destroyed during that day. We have 500 men unable to fight. The Prince Viceroy gives praises in particular of General of Division Séras, of Generals Roussel and Valentin, of Colonels Delacroix and Triaire, of Adjutant Commander Forestier, of Captain Aimee of the 9th Chasseurs, who has taken one flag, of Lieutenant Bourgeois of the 102nd who, with four mounted chasseurs and eight infantrymen, took 600 prisoner, and of Sergeant Rivoine of the 6th of Chasseurs, who took one cannon after having killed the cannoneers who attended it.

The next day, the 26th, at noon, the army of Italy arrived at Bruck where it joined General Lauriston and the army of Germany.

Proclamation

Soldiers of the army of Italy, you have gloriously attained the goal that I had given you; the Somering witnessed your junction with the *Grande Armée*.

Welcome! I am pleased with you!

Surprised by a treacherous enemy before your columns were united, you had to retreat as far as the Adige. But there you received the order to march forward, you were on the memorable field of Arcole, and there you swore on the Manes [spirits] of our heroes that you would triumph. You have kept your word at the battle of the Piave, at the combats of Saint Daniel, of Tarvis, of Görlitz; you assaulted and took the forts of Malborghetto, of Pradel, and caused the capitulation of the enemy's division entrenched in Prevald and Laybach. You had not yet crossed the Drave, and already 25,000 prisoners, 60 battle pieces, 10 flags, had shown your valour. Since then, the Drave, the Save, the Muer, have not delayed your march. The Austrian column of Jellacic, which was the first to enter Munich, which gave the signal for the massacres in the Tyrol, surrounded at Saint Michel, fell on your bayonets. You gave prompt justice to these wretches who stole away from the wrath of the *Grande Armée*.

Soldiers! This Austrian army of Italy, which one moment soiled my provinces by their presence, who had the pretension to break my Iron Crown, beaten, dispersed, annihilated, thanks to you, will be an example of this motto: *Dio la mi diede, guai a chi la tocca* [God gave it to me, beware he who touches it].

NAPOLEON

By the Emperor, THE PRINCE OF NEUFCHÂTEL, MAJOR-GENERAL OF THE
ARMY
ALEXANDER [BERTHIER]

Fourteenth Bulletin

Ebersdorf, 1 June 1809

The bridges upon the Danube are completely re-established; to these have been added a flying bridge, and all the necessary materials are preparing for another bridge of rafts. Seven pile-drivers are employed to strike the piles, but the Danube being in many places 24 and 26 feet in depth, much time is spent in order to fix the anchors, when the pile-drivers are moved. However, our works are advancing and will be finished in a short time.

General of Brigade of Engineers Lazowski is supervising works on the left bank on a bridgehead of 1,500 *toises* in extent, and which will be surrounded by a trench full of running water.

The 44th crew of the flotilla of Boulogne, commanded by Captain of Ships Baste, has arrived. A great number of boats, cruising around the islands, protect the bridge and render great service. The battalion of marine workmen labour in the construction of little armed barges, which will serve to completely command the river.

After the defeat of the corps of General Jellacic, Mr Mathieu, Captain Adjutant of the staff of the army of Italy, was sent with an orderly dragoon on the road to Salzburg, who have successively met with a column of 650 troops of line and a column of 2,000 militia, both of whom were cut off and had lost their way; they, on being summoned to surrender, laid down their arms.

General of Division Lauriston has arrived at Ödenburg, the first country town of Hungary, with a strong advanced guard. There appears to be some ferment in Hungary, where men's minds are divided, the greater part of them not seeming favourable to Austria.

General of Division Lasalle has his headquarters opposite of Pressburg, and pushes his posts to Altenburg and Raab [Györ].

Three divisions of the army of Italy are arrived at Neustadt. The Viceroy has been at the headquarters of the Emperor for the last two days.

General Macdonald, who commands one of the corps of the army of Italy, has entered Graz. There have been found in this capital of Styria immense stores of provisions, clothing and equipments of every kind.

The Duke of Danzig is at Linz. The Prince of Ponte Corvo is marching on Vienna. General of Division Vandamme, with the Württembergers, is at Pölten, Mautern and Krems.

Tranquility reigns in the Tyrol; cut off by the movements of the Duke of Danzig and of the army of Italy, all the Austrians who had imprudently engaged in that point have been destroyed; some by the Duke of Danzig, others, such as the corps of Jellacic, by the army of Italy. Those who were in Swabia had no other resource than to endeavour to cross Germany as partisans, directing their march by the Upper Palatinate. They formed a small column of infantry and cavalry, which, after escaping from Lindau, was met by Colonel Reiset, of General Beaumont's corps of observation. It was cut off at Neumark, and the entire column, officers and soldiers, laid down their arms.

Vienna is tranquil; bread and wine are in abundance; but meat, which this capital used to draw from the bottom of Hungary, begins to be scarce. Contrary to all reasons of policy and motives humanity, the enemy does all in its power to starve their fellow-citizens and this city, although it contains their wives and children. How different is this from the conduct of our Henry IV, who supplied a city then hostile to us, and besieged by him, with provisions!

The Duke of Montebello died yesterday at five in the morning. Shortly before, the Emperor passed an hour with him. His Majesty sent his aide-de-camp for Dr Franc, one of the most celebrated physicians in Europe. The wounds were in good condition, but a dangerous fever had made the most fatal progress in the course of a few hours. All the assistance of the art was useless. His Majesty ordered that the body of the Duke of Montebello should be embalmed and conveyed to France, there to receive the honours that are due to his elevated rank and eminent services. Thus dies one of the most distinguished soldiers that France ever produced. In the many battles in which he was engaged, he had received 13 wounds. The Emperor was deeply afflicted by this loss, which will be felt by all of France.

Fifteenth Bulletin

Ebersdorf, 2 June 1809

The army of Dalmatia has obtained the greatest successes. It has defeated all that it has opposed in the battles of Mount Kitta, Gradchatz, Liéca and Ottechatz. General in Chief Sloissevitch has been taken.

The Duke of Ragusa arrived on 28 May at Fiume, and thus the army of Italy has formed a junction with the *Grande Armée*, of which the army of Dalmatia forms the right. The reports of the Duke of Ragusa respecting these different events shall be published.

On the 28th, an English squadron, consisting of four ships of the line, two frigates and a sloop, appeared before Trieste, with an intention of taking the Russian squadron. General Count Caffarelli had just arrived at that port. As the town was disarmed, the Russians landed 40 pieces of artillery, 24 of which were 36-pounders and 16 were 24-pounders.They have placed their cannon in a battery, and the Russian squadron came up broadside on. Everything was ready to receive the enemy, who seeing that it had failed in his design, went off.

One thousand Austrians, having crossed from Krems to the right bank of the Danube, have been overthrown by the Württemberg troops, which took 60 of them prisoner.

Sixteenth Bulletin

Ebersdorf, 4 June 1809

The enemy had thrown upon the right bank of the Danube, opposite to Pressburg, a division of 9,000 men, who entrenched themselves in the village of Engerau. The Duke of Auerstädt attacked them yesterday with the sharpshooters of Hesse Darmstadt, supported by the 12th Regiment of Infantry of Line. The village was speedily carried. A major and eight officers of Beaulieu's regiment (one of them the grandson of Field Marshal Beaulieu) and 400 privates were taken prisoner. The rest of this regiment were killed, wounded or driven into the water. The remains of the enemy's division found in an island the necessary protection for their re-crossing the river. The sharpshooters of Hesse Darmstadt acquitted themselves extremely well.

The Viceroy of Italy today has his headquarters at Ödenburg.

All the valuable effects belonging to the Court have been conveyed from Bude to Peterwardein, where the Empress has retired.

The Duke of Ragusa has arrived at Laybach.

General Macdonald is master of Graz. He surrounded the citadel, which seemed disposed to make some resistance.

In the battle of Essling, on the 21st and 22nd of last month, Brigadier General Fouler was wounded in making a charge, and thrown from his horse. A similar accident befell General of Division Durosnel, aide-de-camp to the Emperor, as he was carrying orders to a division of cuirassiers who were charging the enemy. We have had the satisfaction of learning that these two generals, and 150 soldiers whom we believed to be lost, were only wounded, and that they were left lying among the wheat, where they were taken prisoner at the moment when the Emperor, on learning that the bridges had been broken down, ordered the troops to concentrate themselves between Essling and Gross-Aspern.

The Danube falls, but from the continuance of the warm weather we fear that it will rise again.

Seventeenth Bulletin

Vienna, 8 June 1809

Colonel Gorgoli, aide-de-camp of the Emperor of Russia, has arrived at the imperial headquarters with a letter from that sovereign for His Majesty. He has announced that the Russian army, which is marching upon Olmütz, had crossed the frontiers on 24 May.

The Emperor, the day before yesterday, reviewed his Guard, infantry, cavalry and artillery. The inhabitants of Vienna admired the number, fine appearance and excellent condition of these troops.

The Viceroy has gone with the army of Italy to Ödenburg in Hungary. It appears that the Archduke John intends to rally his army on the Raab.

The Duke of Ragusa arrived with the army of Dalmatia, on the 3rd of this month, at Laybach.

The heat is very great, and persons acquainted with the Danube assure us that in a few days it will overflow. We shall employ this time to finish driving the piles, independent of the bridges of boats and rafts.

All the accounts that we receive from the enemy state that the towns of Pressburg, Brünn and Znaim are full of wounded. The Austrians themselves estimate their loss at 18,000 men.

Prince Poniatowski, with the army of the Duchy of Warsaw, is pursuing the advantages he has gained. After the taking of Sandomir, he took the fortress of Zamosé, where the enemy suffered a loss of 3,000 men and 30 pieces of artillery. All the Poles who are in the Austrian army desert. The enemy, after having failed before Thorn, has been vigorously pursued by General Dombrowski. Archduke Ferdinand will derive nothing from his expedition but disgrace. He must have arrived in Austrian Silesia with his force reduced to one-third.

Senator Wybicki had distinguished himself by his patriotic sentiments and his activity.

Count Metternich has arrived at Vienna; he is to be exchanged at the advanced posts for the French legation, to whom the Austrians, contrary to the law of nations, had refused passports and had taken to Pest.

Eighteenth Bulletin

Vienna, 13 June 13 1809
The division of General Chasteler, which had raised the Tyrol, proceeded on the 4th of this month to the environs of Klagenfurt, in order to throw itself into Hungary. General Rusca marched against it, and a severe engagement took place where the enemy was beaten, when 900 prisoners were taken.

Prince Eugene with a large corps manoeuvres in the centre of Hungary.

For some days past the Danube has risen a foot.

General Gratien, with a Dutch division, having marched to Stralsund, where Schill had entrenched himself, carried the entrenchments by assault. Schill gave orders to burn the town to secure his retreat, but had not the time. Schill himself was killed in the great square, near the *Corps de Garde*, at the moment when he fled and was endeavouring to reach the port in order to embark.

The Archduke Ferdinand evacuated Warsaw precipitately on 2 June, so that all of the Grand Duchy is abandoned by the enemy's army, while the troops under the command of Prince Poniatowski occupy three-fourths of Galicia.

Affairs of Poland

The enemy continues its retreat with the same precipitancy. On 28 May, 12 Polish lancers, who were on a reconnaissance, met 110 Austrian dragoons at Skirniewice, who were withdrawing on Rawa; they routed them and took 11 prisoners. In the morning of the 30th, General Kosinski, commanding the advance guard, after entering Lowicz proceeded to Sochaczew where he did not find any enemy, who appears to be retreating on the Pilica. A few reports, however, seem to announce that the largest part of the Austrian troops is proceeding towards High Silesia. They commit excesses everywhere; they steal supplies, cattle and horses. The new levies of all the departments are taking place with the greatest rapidity and the greatest success.

The Archduke Ferdinand, despite the agreement he had with Prince Poniatowski, and the promise he had made not to demand any contributions, has imposed one of 400,000 florins on the city of Warsaw. He furthermore demanded that there should be brought to him the proceeds of the territorial taxes, of the estates rents and the remaining amount of a forced loan which had been established in 1808 and the payment of which was not due until 1810. Following the example of the chief, the colonels, the officers and the soldiers were trying to ruin the country by every means possible. These measures foretold of the evacuation of Warsaw, and it happened soon after.

Prince Poniatowski wrote to the Prince of Neufchâtel, from the headquarters at

Jrzeni, on 25 May, that General of Brigade Roznicki had taken Jaroslaw on the 24th, where he took prisoner a Colonel, 25 officers and 900 men.

The occupation of this town entirely intercepts communications between Kraków and Leopold, and assures the army of the possession of three-quarters of Galicia. The advance posts were one day's march from Kraków.

The last reports received at the Grand Duchy regarding the army of Prince Poniatowski state that he has taken Brody, the last town of Galicia, near the border, and that he found there considerable magazines and an abundant amount of supplies.

Here is the proclamation published by Prince Serge Gallitzin upon the arrival of the Russian army in Galicia.

Proclamation

The war that broke out between France and Austria could not have been viewed with indifference by Russia.

All sorts of efforts and care were taken on our side to suppress this fire before it became a blaze. It was declared to the Austrian court, from the beginning, that by virtue of the treaties and the narrowest agreements that subsist between the two Emperors of Russia and of the French, Russia would act conjointly with France.

Austria did not choose to consider these representations, which should have carried a lot of weight for her; but she masked her war preparations under the pretext of her defence, until, at last, by aggressive measures she exposed the arrogant schemes of her ambition and lit the torch of war.

Consequently, Russia could not exempt herself from taking part in this war, her role having been established by solemn treaties. As soon as the news reached Russia, she broke all ties that existed between her and Austria, and ordered her army to advance to the borders of Galicia.

Upon entering in that country to take action against Austria and repulse by force her deployed forces, the Commander-in-Chief of the army, according to His Majesty the Emperor's orders, has to declare to the tranquil inhabitants of Galicia in a most solemn manner that Russia has no enmity against any of them, and that the army, no matter where it might be in its movements, will respect the personal safety of everyone, secure properties, and will not disturb the interior peace or general tranquility.

The Commander-in-Chief will prove by the facts, how sacred these principles are to him.

Done at the headquarters, 19 May 1809

PRINCE GALLITZIN, COMMANDER-IN-CHIEF, INFANTRY GENERAL AND
KNIGHT OF THE ORDERS

Nineteenth Bulletin

Vienna, 16 June 1809

The anniversary of the battle of Marengo has been celebrated by the victory of the Raab, which the right wing of the army, under the command of the Prince Viceroy, has obtained over the united corps of the Archduke John and the Archduke Palatine.

Since the battle of the Piave, the Viceroy has pursued the Archduke John at the point of the bayonet. The Austrian army hoped to canton itself at the source of the Raab, between Saint Gotthard and Körmond.

On 5 June, the Viceroy advanced from Neustadt, and established his headquarters at Oedenburg, in Hungary.

On the 7th he followed up his movements, and arrived at Güns. General Lauriston, with his corps of observation, formed a junction on his left.

On the 8th, General Montbrun, with his division of light cavalry, forced the crossing of the Rabnitz, near Sovenyhaga, routed 300 cavalry of the Hungarian insurrection, and drove them towards Raab.

On the 9th, the Viceroy proceeded towards Sarvar. The cavalry of General Grouchy fell in with the enemy's rearguard at Vasvár and took some prisoners.

On the 10th, General Macdonald arrived from Graz at Körmond.

On the 11th, General Grenier came up at Karako with a column of the enemy's flank corps which defended the bridge. He, however, crossed the river in force. General Debroc made a brilliant charge with the 9th Hussars upon a battalion of 400 men, 300 of whom were taken prisoner.

On the 12th, the army crossed by the bridge of Merse near Pápa. The Viceroy, from a height, observed the whole hostile army in battle array. General Montbrun, General of Cavalry and officer of great expectation, debouched in the plain and charged the enemy's cavalry, which he completely overthrew, after having made many skilful and vigorous manoeuvres. The enemy had already begun to retreat; the Viceroy passed the night at Pápa.

On the 13th, at five in the morning, the army marched towards Raab. Our cavalry and the Austrian's cavalry showed themselves near the village of Szanach. The enemy was defeated, and we took 400 prisoner.

The Archduke John, having united with the Archduke Palatine near Raab, took a fine position on some heights; the right wing rested upon Raab, a fortified town, and the left covering the road of Komorn, another strong fortress in Hungary.

On the 14th, at eleven in the evening, the Viceroy drew up his army in order of battle, and with 35,000 men attacked 50,000 of the enemy. The zeal of our troops is still animated by the recollection of the memorable victory that has sanctified this day. All the soldiers shouted with joy when they saw the enemy, which was placed in three lines consisting of from 20,000 to 25,000 men of the remains of the fine army of Italy, which had already imagined itself master of Italy; of 10,000 men under General Haddick and formed with the reserve of Hungary's strong places; of 5,000 to 6,000 men of the remains of Jellacic's corps, and the other corps of the Tyrol which had joined the army through the passes of Carinthia; and of 10,000 or 12,000 of the Hungarian insurrection, cavalry and infantry.

The Viceroy placed his army, General Montbrun's cavalry, the brigade of General Colbert and the cavalry of General Grouchy on his right wing; the corps of General Grenier formed two platoons, whereof General Séras' division was the right one; in the front an Italian division commanded by General Baraguey d'Hilliers formed a third platoon. The reserve of General Puthod formed the reserve; General Lauriston, with this corps of observation, supported by General Sahuc, formed the extremity of the left wing, and watched Raab.

At two in the afternoon the cannonade began. At three, the 1st, 2nd and 3rd platoons were engaged in hand combat. The fire from the musketry was lively; the first line of the enemy was overthrown; but the second withstood for a moment the impetuosity of our first echelon, which being speedily reinforced, also overthrew the line of the enemy. The enemy's reserve then appeared. The Viceroy, who followed all the movements of the enemy, marched, on his side, with his reserve. The fine position of the Austrians was taken, and at four the victory was decided.

The enemy, which was in complete rout, could not easily unite if a defile had not opposed the movement of our cavalry. Three thousand prisoners and six cannon, are the memorials of this achievement. The enemy left 3,000 dead on the battlefield, among whom is a major-general. Our loss amounts to about 900 killed or wounded. Among the first is Colonel Thierry of the 23rd Regiment of Light Cavalry, and among the latter, Brigadier General Valentine and Colonel Espert.

The Viceroy makes particular mention of Generals Grenier, Montbrun, Séras and Douthomars. The Italian Severoli division has shown a lot of precision and composure. Several generals had their horses killed; four aides-de-camp to the Viceroy were slightly wounded. This prince was constantly in the middle of the biggest mêlée. The artillery under the command of General Lorbier maintained its reputation.

The battlefield at Raab had long been pitched upon by the enemy, which had announced far in advance that it would make a stand in that fine position. On the 15th it was closely pursued on the road of Komorn and Pest.

The inhabitants of the country remain tranquil and take no part in the war. The Emperor's Proclamation has set men's minds reflecting. It is known that the Hungarian nation always desired its independence. The part of the Insurrection that is now with the army was raided by the last Diet; it is in arms, and does duty.

Twentieth Bulletin

Vienna, 20 June 1809

When the news of the victory of Raab arrived at Buda, the Empress, as well as everything which was a part of the government, immediately left it.

The enemy's army was pursued during the 15th and 16th. It crossed the Danube over the bridge of Komorn.

The town of Raab has been surrounded; we hope to be masters of this important place in a few days. We found considerable magazines in the suburbs.

We have taken the superb entrenched camp of Raab, which could contain 100,000 men; the column destined to defend it was cut off and could not reach it. A courier coming from Bude was intercepted. The dispatches he carried, written in Latin, advise of the effect produced by the battle of Raab. The enemy inundates the country with false reports; this is part of the system adopted for stirring up the lower classes.

Count Metternich left Vienna on the 18th. He will be exchanged, between Komorn and Buda, with Mr Dodun and the other persons of the French Legation. Mr d'Epinay, ordnance officer of His Majesty, arrived from Petersburg. He passed at the headquarters of the Russian army.

Prince Serge Gallitzin entered Galicia on the 3rd, in three columns; that of General Levis by Drohicyn; that of Prince Gortchakov by Therespol, and that of Prince Suvorov by Wlodzimirz.

Twenty-first Bulletin

Vienna, 22 June 1809

An aide-de-camp of Prince Joseph Poniatowski is arrived from the headquarters of the army of the Grand Duchy. On the 10th of this month, Prince Serge Gallatin was to be at Lublin, and his advance guard at Sandomir.

The enemy pleases itself in spreading ephemeral Bulletins, in which it reports a victory every day. According to its account, it took 20,000 muskets and 2,000 cuirasses in the battle of Essling. It says that on the 21st and 22nd it was master of the battlefield; it has had printed and circulated an engraving of that battle, in which we see the enemy striding over both shores, and its batteries traversing the islands and the battlefield in every direction. The enemy also imagines a battle, which it calls the battle of Kittsee, in which a number of French have been killed or taken. These childish reports hawked about by small columns, like that of Schill, are tactics employed to disquiet and rouse the country.

General Marziani, who was taken prisoner in the battle of Raab, has arrived at the headquarters. He says that since the battle of the Piave, the Archduke John has lost two-thirds of his army: that he afterwards received recruits which scarcely filled the vacancies, and who do not understand the use of arms. He reckons the loss of the Archduke John and Archduke Palatine in the battle of the Raab at 12,000 men. According to the report of the Hungarian prisoners, the Palatine was on that day the first to take flight.

A few people had wished to put in opposition the force of the Austrian army at Essling, estimated at 90,000 men, with the 80,000 men that have been taken prisoner since the opening of the campaign! They have shown very little reflection. The Austrian army entered upon the campaign with nine corps of 40,000 men each; and they had in the interior corps of recruits and *Landwehr*, so that Austria really had more than 400,000 men under arms. From the battle of Abensberg to the taking of Vienna, they reckon that including Italy and Poland we have taken 100,000 prisoners from the enemy, and he has lost 100,000 men in killed, deserted and dispersed. There still remain to it, therefore, 200,000 men, distributed as follows: the Archduke John had, in the battle of Raab, 50,000 men; the principal Austrian army was, previous to the battle of Essling, 90,000 men; there remained 25,000 men with the Archduke Ferdinand at Warsaw, and 25,000 men were dispersed in the Tyrol and Croatia and spread in bands on the confines of Bohemia.

The Austrian army at Essling, was composed of the 1st Corps, commanded by General Bellegarde, the only one which had not been engaged and which was still entire, and the wrecks of the 2nd, 3rd, 4th, 5th and 6th Corps, which had been crushed in the preceding battles. If these corps had suffered no loss, and had united such as they were at the commencement of the campaign, they would have formed 240,000 men. The enemy had no more than 90,000; thus we see how enormous the losses are which it has suffered.

When the Archduke John entered in the campaign, his army was composed of the 8th and 9th Corps amounting to 80,000 men. At Raab he had only 50,000. But in these 50,000 were included 15,000 Hungarians of the insurrection. His loss was therefore really 45,000 men.

The Archduke Ferdinand entered Warsaw with the 7th Corps, consisting of 40,000 men. He is reduced to 25,000. His loss is therefore 15,000 men.

We see how these different calculations are made and verified.

The Viceroy has, with 30,000 French, beaten 50,000 men at Raab.

At Essling, 90,000 men have been beaten and retained by 30,000 French, who would have completely routed and destroyed them if the carrying away of the bridges had not caused a want of ammunition.

The great efforts of Austria have been the result of paper money and the resolution of the Austrian government to risk all. In the danger of bankruptcy, which would have brought about a revolution, she has preferred to add 500 millions to the mass of her paper money, and try a last effort to have it circulated through Germany, Italy and Poland. It is very probable that this consideration has influenced, more than any other, her determinations.

Not a single regiment has been drawn from Spain except the Imperial Guard.

General Count Lauriston continues the siege of Raab with the greatest activity: the town has been on fire for 24 hours and this army – which at Essling has gained so great a victory that she took 20,000 muskets and 2,000 cuirassiers; which at Kittsee killed so many and took so many prisoners; which, according to its apocryphal bulletins has gained such great advantages at the battle of Raab – tranquilly sees its principal places besieged and burnt, Hungary inundated by parties, and to save its Empress, its *dicastères*, all the precious effects of government, has removed them to the frontiers of Turkey and to the utmost extremity of Europe.

An Austrian major had the temerity to cross the Danube at the mouth of the March, in two boats. General Gilly-Vieux met him with some companies, drove him into the water and took 40 prisoners.

Twenty-second Bulletin

Vienna, 24 June 1809

Raab has capitulated. This city forms an excellent position in the centre of Hungary; it is defended by bastions, its moats are full of water, and a flood covers a part of it. It is situated at the confluence of three rivers: it resembles, on a small scale, the reduction of the great entrenched camp, where the enemy hoped to assemble and exercise the Hungarian insurrection, and where it had constructed immense works. The garrison, 1,800 strong, was insufficient. The enemy intended to have left 5,000 men, but by the battle of Raab its army was separated from that place. The city has suffered considerably from a bombardment of eight days, which has destroyed its finest edifices; all that could be said as to the inutility of a defence was ineffectual: it was misled by the hope of being relieved.

Count Metternich, after having remained three days at the advanced posts, has returned to Vienna. The secretary of embassy, Dodun, and the persons attached to the allied legations, who had not withdrawn previous to the capture of Vienna, were evacuated on the confines of Hungary, when intelligence of the loss of the battle of Raab reached Buda.

Two battalions of *Landwehr*, two squadrons of Uhlans and one battalion of troops of line, forming together 2,500 men, have entered Bayreuth. They have, as usual, distributed proclamations and endeavoured to excite insurrections. At the same time, General Am-Ende entered Dresden with three battalions of line, three battalions of *Landwehr* and some squadrons of cavalry drawn from different corps, forming in all from 7,000 to 8,000 men.

The King of Westphalia has joined the 10th Corps, and is on his march. The Duke of Valmy has put in motion, from Hanau, the advanced guard of the army of reserve that he commands.

Twenty-third Bulletin

Vienna, 28 June 1809

On the 25th of this month, His Majesty reviewed a great number of troops on the heights of Schönbrunn. We observed a fine line of 8,000 cavalry, of which the Guard formed a part, in which there was not one regiment of cuirassiers. There was also a line of 200 pieces of artillery. The appearance and martial air of the troops excited the admiration of the spectators.

On Saturday the 24th, at four o'clock in the afternoon, our troops entered Raab; on the 25th, the garrison, prisoners of war, set out. According to an estimate made, it is found to amount to 2,500 men.

His Majesty has given to General of Division Narbonne the command of this place, and of all the administrative subdivisions of Hungary surrendered to the French arms.

The Duke of Auerstädt is before Pressburg. The enemy works at the fortification; it is intimated to it to cease these works, unless it wished to draw upon the peaceable inhabitants the greatest misfortunes; the enemy took no notice of it; 4,000 bombs and shells have compelled it to renounce its project, but fire broke out in this unfortunate city and several quarters have been burnt.

The Duke of Ragusa, with the army of Dalmatia, crossed the Drau on the 22nd, and marched to Graz.

On the 24th, General Vandamme embarked 300 Württembergers, commanded by Major Kechler, at Mölk, in order to throw them upon the opposite shore and gain intelligence. The debarkation has been effected. These troops routed two companies of the enemy, and took two officers and eighty men of the regiment of Mittrovski prisoners.

The Prince of Ponte Corvo and the Saxon army are at Saint Pölten.

The Duke of Danzig, who is at Linz, ordered General Wrede to reconnoitre on the left bank. All the enemy's posts were repulsed. Several officers and 20 men were taken. The object of this reconnoitring was also to procure intelligence.

The city of Vienna is plentifully furnished with meat; the supply of bread is more difficult, on account of the impediments in grinding. In respect to the subsistence of the army, it is secured for more than six months; it has rations, wine and vegetables in abundance. The wines of the cellars of the convents have been placed in a magazine, to furnish distributions to the army. Several million bottles have been collected.

On 10 April, at the very time when the Austrian general prostituted his character and spread a snare for the King of Bavaria, by writing the letter which has appeared in all the public papers, General Chasteler excited the Tyrol to insurrection, and surprised 700 French conscripts who were going to Augsburg, where their regiments were, and who were marching in the confidence of peace. Obliged to surrender and taken prisoner, they were massacred. Among them were 80 Belgians, born in the same town as Chasteler. Eighteen hundred Bavarians taken prisoner at the same time were also massacred. Chasteler, who commanded, was witness to these horrors. He not only made no opposition to them, but he is accused of having smiled at the massacre, hoping that the Tyrolians, having to dread the vengeance due to a crime which they could not hope would be pardoned, would thus be more firmly engaged in their rebellion.

When His Majesty was made aware of these atrocities, he found himself in a difficult situation. If he had chosen to have recourse to reprisals, 20 generals, 1,000 officers and 80,000 men, taken prisoner during the month of April, might have satisfied the Manes [spirits] of the unfortunate French, so cowardly slaughtered. But prisoners do not appertain to the power for which they have fought; they are under the safeguard of the honour and generosity of the nation that has disarmed them. His Majesty considered Chasteler as acting without recognition; for, notwithstanding the furious proclamations and violent language of the princes of the House of Lorraine, it was impossible to believe they could approve such crimes; His Majesty, in consequence, published the following:

Order of the Day

Imperial headquarters, Enns, 5 May 1809

By order of the Emperor, the person named Chasteler, would-be general in the service of Austria, the mover of the insurrection in the Tyrol, charged with being the author of the massacres committed on the Bavarian and French prisoners by the insurgents, shall, upon being taken prisoner, be carried immediately before the military commission, and if need be, shall be shot within 24 hours.

THE PRINCE OF NEUFCHÂTEL, VICE CONSTABLE, MAJOR-GENERAL OF THE ARMY

ALEXANDER

At the battle of Essling, General Durosnel, carrying an order to an advanced squadron, was taken prisoner by 25 Uhlans. The Emperor of Austria, proud of so easy a triumph, caused to be published an Order of the Day, conceived in the following terms:

Copy of a letter from His Majesty the Emperor of Austria, to Prince Charles Wolkersdorf, 25 May 1809

My dear brother, I have learned that the Emperor Napoleon has declared the Marquis of Chasteler out of the protection of the law of nations. This unjust conduct, contrary to the usages of nations, and of which there is no example in the latter periods of history, obliges me to have recourse to reprisals. In consequence, I order that French Generals Durosnel and Fouler shall be kept as hostages, to undergo the same fate and same treatment as the Emperor Napoleon shall make General Chasteler suffer. It is repugnant to my feelings to give such an order, but I owe it to my brave warriors, and to my brave people, who may be exposed to a similar fate while fulfilling their duties with ardent devotion I charge you to make known this letter to the army, and to send it by a parliamentary to the Major-General of the Emperor Napoleon.

FRANCIS

As soon as this order of the day came to the knowledge of His Majesty, he ordered the arrest of the Prince Colloredo, Prince Metternich, Count Pergen and Count Hardegg, and that they should be conveyed to France to answer for the lives of Generals Durosnel and Fouler. The Major-General wrote to the chief of staff of the Austrian army the following letter:

To the Major-General of the Austrian Army.

Schönbrunn, 6 June 1809

Sir,

His Majesty the Emperor has learned of an order given by the Emperor Francis, which declares that the French Generals Durosnel and Fouler, whom the circumstances of war have placed in his power, shall answer for the punishment which the laws of justice may inflict on Monsieur Chasteler, who has put himself at the head of the insurgents of the Tyrol, and who has permitted the slaughter of 700 French prisoners and between 18,000 and 1,900 Bavarians, a crime unheard of in the history of nations, and which might have caused a terrible reprisal on 40 field marshal lieutenants, 36 major-generals, more than 300 colonels or majors, 1,200 officers and 80,000 soldiers, if His Majesty did not consider prisoners as placed under his faith and honour, and had not besides proof that the Austrian officers in the Tyrol have been as indignant at the action as ourselves.

His Majesty, however, has ordered that Prince Colloredo, Prince Metternich, Count Frederic and Count Pergen shall be arrested and conveyed to France, to answer for the safety of Generals Durosnel and Fouler, threatened by the order of the day of your sovereign. These officers may die, sir, but they shall not die without being revenged: this vengeance shall not fall on any prisoners, but on the relatives of those who shall order their death.

As to Mr Chasteler, he is not yet in the power of the army; but if he should be taken, you may be assured that he will be delivered to a military commission, and that his trial will take place. I request your Excellency to believe the sentiments of my high consideration.

THE MAJOR–GENERAL, ALEXANDER

The city of Vienna and the corps of the states of Lower Austria solicited the clemency of His Majesty, and requested to send a deputation to the Emperor Francis, to convince him of the impropriety of the proceeding with respect to the Generals Durosnel and Fouler, to represent that Chasteler was not condemned, that he was not arrested, but only accused before the tribunals; that the fathers, wives, children and property of the Austrian generals were in the hands of the French, and that the French army was determined, if a single prisoner was put to death, to make an example of which posterity should long preserve the remembrance.

The esteem that His Majesty entertains for the good inhabitants of Vienna and the states determined him to accede to this request. He granted permission to Messrs Colloredo, Metternich, Pergen and Hardegg to remain at Vienna, and to the deputation to set out for the headquarters of the Emperor of Austria.

This deputation has returned. The Emperor Francis has replied to these representations that he was ignorant of the massacre of the French prisoners in the Tyrol; that he pitied the miseries of the capital and the provinces; that his ministers had deceived him, etc. The deputies reminded him that all prudent men see with pain the existence of a handful of intriguers, who, by the measures they advise, by the proclamations, orders of the day, etc., which they cause to be adopted, endeavour only to foment passions and hatred, and to exasperate an enemy who is master of Croatia, Carniola, Carinthia, Styria, Upper and Lower Austria, the capital of the Empire and a great part of Hungary, that the sentiments of the Emperor for his subjects ought to incline him to calm rather than irritate the conqueror, and to give to war the character natural to it among civilized nations, since it is in the power of the conqueror to render more heavy the evils which press on the half of the monarchy.

It is said the Emperor Francis answered that the greater part of the writings mentioned by the deputies were fictitious, and that those, the existence of which was not denied, were more moderate; that the editors were besides French clerks, and that even when these papers did contain some inconvenient things, they were not perceived until the mischief was done. If this answer, which is publicly reported, is authentic, we have no observation to make. It is impossible not to perceive the influence of England, for this small number of men, traitors to their country, is certainly in the pay of that power.

When the deputies went to Buda, they saw the Empress. It was a few days before she had been obliged to leave this city. They found her changed, depressed and in consternation at the evils which threatened her house. The opinion of the monarchy is extremely unfavourable to the family of this princess. It is that family which excited the war. The Archdukes Palatine and Reinier are the only Austrian princes who defended the maintenance of the peace. The Empress was far from foreseeing the events that have taken place. She has shed many tears; she has shown great alarm at the thick cloud that covers the future. She spoke of peace; she requested peace; she conjured the deputies to speak to the Emperor Francis in favour of peace. They reported that the conduct of the Archduke Maximilian had been disowned, and that the Emperor of Austria had sent him into the interior of Hungary.

Twenty-fourth Bulletin

Vienna, 3 July 1809

General Broussier had left two battalions of the 84th Regiment of Line in the town of Graz, and proceeded to Wildon to join the army of Dalmatia.

On 26 June, General Giulay appeared before Graz with 10,000 men, composed, it is true, of Croats and frontier regiments. The 84th, which was cantoned in one of the suburbs of the town, repelled all attacks of the enemy, routed it everywhere, took 500 men prisoner, and two flags, and maintained himself in his position 14 hours, giving time to General Broussier to come to his assistance. This combat, of one against ten, covered the 84th and its Colonel Gambin with glory. The flags were presented to His Majesty at the parade. We have to regret that 20 of these brave fellows were killed and 92 wounded.

On the 30th, the Duke of Auerstädt attacked one of the islands of the Danube, at a small distance from the right bank, opposite Pressburg, where the enemy had some troops. General Gudin directed this operation with skill; it was executed by Colonel Decouz and the 31st Regiment of Infantry of Line, which this officer commands. At two o'clock of the morning, this regiment, partly in small boats and partly swimming, crossed a very narrow arm of the Danube, seized the island, routed the 15,000 men who were upon it, and took 250 prisoner, among whom were the colonel and several officers of the regiment of Saint Julian, and took three pieces of artillery, which the enemy had landed for the defence of the island.

At length there exists no longer any Danube, as far as concerns the French army. General Count Bertrand has raised works that excite astonishment and inspire admiration.

Over the breadth of 400 *toises*, and over a very rapid river, he has in a fortnight raised a bridge formed of 60 arches, on which three carriages can pass abreast. He has built a second bridge upon piles eight feet broad; but this is for infantry only. Next to these two bridges is a bridge of boats; we can, therefore, cross the Danube in three columns. These three bridges are secured against all assaults, even against the effects of fire ships and incendiary machines, by barricades raised on piles between the island, in different directions, the furthest of which are at 250 *toises* from the bridges. When these immense works are contemplated, they might be thought to be the labour of many years; they were, however, the works of 15 to 20 days. These works are defended by bridgeheads, each 1,600 *toises* of development, formed of redoubts surrounded by ditches full of water.

The Island of Lobau is a strong place: there are stores of rations, 100 pieces of large calibre and 20 mortars or howitzers of siege in battery; opposite Essling, on the last arm of the Danube, there is a bridge which was raised yesterday by the Duke of Rivoli. It is covered by a bridgehead built at the time of the first crossing.

General Legrand, with his division, occupies the woods before the bridgehead.

The hostile army is in order of battle, covered by redoubts; the left is at Enzersdorf, the right at Aspern; a few discharges of musketry from the advance posts have taken place.

Now that the crossing of the Danube is secured, and our bridges are sheltered from every attempt, the fate of the Austrian monarchy will be decided in a single battle.

The waters of the Danube were, on 1 July, four feet above the lowest, and thirteen feet below the highest point. The rapidity of the river at this part is, when the waters are high, from seven to twelve feet; when the water is at moderate level, four feet six inches each second, and stronger than at any other point. In Hungary it diminishes a great deal; and at the place where Trajan raised a bridge, it is almost unnoticeable. There, the Danube is 450 *toises* broad; here it is only 400. The bridge of Trajan was a stone bridge, the work of several years. Caesar's bridge over the Rhine was raised, it is true, in eight days, but no loaded carriage could pass over it.

The works on the Danube are the most beautiful military works ever formed.

Prince Gagarin, aide-de-camp general of the Emperor of Russia, arrived at Schönbrunn at four of the morning the day before yesterday, at the moment the Emperor was mounting on horseback. He had set out from Petersburg on 8 June. He has brought intelligence of the march of the Russian army in Galicia.

His Majesty has left Schönbrunn; he has been encamped two days. His tents are very beautiful, and made in the style of the Egyptian tents.

Excerpt of a letter of Prince Poniatowski to His Most Serene Highness the Prince of Neufchâtel

At the headquarters of Pniow, 10 June 1809

The Archduke Ferdinand, disquieted on his rear by the march of General Zayonchek, who had already crossed the Pilica at the height of Pulawy, had gathered all his forces in the environs of Sandomir and appeared to be looking for a way to penetrate on that side. On the 5th of this month, a corps of about 8- to 10,000 men under the orders of General Schauruth having attempted to approach the place, was repulsed with considerable losses in killed and wounded. The enemy also lost 300 men who were taken prisoner.

On the 7th, Archduke Ferdinand marched in person against the place. He was immediately attacked, and this second attempt had no better success than the first. He appeared then to abandon that enterprise, and to divide the attention of Prince Poniatowski's troops, he debouched with part of his forces by the High Vistula; consequently, General Schauruth crossed the river at Polanice and advanced to the Vistula, a river that is fordable on all points.

Prince Poniatowski, awaiting the approaching Russian army, a division of which is to join his troops on the 12th to support his operations, reinforced the garrisons of the fortresses of Sandomir and of Zamosé, forming the two extremities of line, folded back at the mouth of the San the bridge he had on the Vistula, concentrated his forces and took position on the San, at the height of Pniow and of Czekay.

The new levies are continuing in Galicia with the greatest activity: four regiments of infantry and four regiments of cavalry, levied at the expense of the inhabitants, are already assembled, clothed and equipped.

Proclamation of the King of Saxony to the Polish People

Frédéric Auguste, by the grace of God, King of Saxony, Duke of Warsaw, etc.

Poles! Already the army that had invaded our Duchy of Warsaw has been forced by the victories of your great regenerator and by the valor of our troops to abandon the capital and return home.

After having thanked Divine Providence for the protection she accorded us, we make it our duty to utilize the first moments of the re-establishment of our government to express to you the sentiments excited in us by the patriotism and the attachment the nation has developed in such a sparkling manner, in this moment of distress.

The enemy had entered in the country with a numerous army; it did not seem possible to resist him: but he soon learned to recognize the power of valour, conducted by a chief as brave and as clever as our War Minister, Prince Poniatowski.

Poles! Your battalions, created by the great hero, and to which he inspired that courageous spirit you demonstrated with great proof under his eyes, have shown that they were worthy of their creator. Inferior in numbers, not only they have resisted the enemy, but they have attacked him with success. They carried the victory in the provinces dominated by the enemy, and covered themselves with glory.

On her side, all of the nation has shown that the spirit of valour and patriotism of the ancient Poles was still hers. The aggression by a numerous enemy, far from intimidating her, only served to incite her to make voluntary and extraordinary offers, to sacrifice individual fortunes: she gave everything for the defence of the fatherland. The departments tried to outdo each other: wanting to see who could increase the army of line with more people, who would furnish the necessary supplies, who would bring the biggest levy to oppose the enemy. They proved that the love of the fatherland is a distinctive quality of the nation, and made themselves worthy of serving as a model. And so, Providence has thus also crowned with success her generous efforts.

Our Council of State, by its loyalty, its zeal, its wise measures, and also by continuing its activity, using its different moves, seconded by all the other constitutional authorities animated with the same sentiments, succeeded in keeping the government working as well as circumstances permitted.

Poles! The fatherland owes her salvation to you, she owes you the approval of your great regenerator, to the eyes of whom the courageous conduct of the army and the ardent zeal of the nation have not escaped. She owes you the increase of her consideration for your neighbours: she owes you the glory of the Sovereign to reign on such a nation.

Even from a distance, our heart has always been near you: your situation has always been present in our minds. Your patriotism, your loyalty and your attachment to our person have increased, if that is possible, ours for you; and we could not bring you the help that our heart had wished, it is with pain that we saw ourselves prevented from it by the circumstances.

Polish nation! Tranquillity is returned to you, and with it the constitutional government. Our most precious care will be to heal the scars of the country caused by the war, to discover and recompense those who have merited it, and to re-establish the order necessary to your future happiness. As for you, you will contribute to it by a perfect confidence in this government, which will be directed only by our paternal intentions.

Given at Frankfurt-on-the-Main, 24 June 1809

FRÉDÉRIC-AUGUST

By the King, THE MINISTER SECRETARY OF STATE, STANISLAS BREZA

Proclamation of the King of Saxony to His Subjects

We, Frédéric-August, by the Grace of God, King of Saxony, Duke of Warsaw, etc., etc.

Divine Providence has until now shown itself so much in favour of our Reign that we found ourselves in the pleasant obligation to offer it this tribute of our ardent recognition, and we fulfilled this obligation with so much the more zeal that our heart knows no bigger pay than to know that those who have been placed in our care are happy.

We particularly had, in the last few years, many reasons to bless God's goodness, when we recovered from the hands of the generous victor our States already lost, and this happiness became even more precious when being personally acquainted with this great man, we joined to the sentiments of gratitude those of the most sincere admiration for his qualities, which we could not appreciate enough, and has motivated, without reserve, this true esteem upon which our alliance rests as solidly as our treaties; which makes it doubly inviolable.

Even at the present time, so teaming with disquiet, it has not been for us a feeble consolation to see our kingdom in such a state of almost perfect tranquillity, while war having relit the torch, renewed its devastations in other countries. The truth be known, the circumstances led us to believe that it was necessary to abandon for a time our good city of Dresden and to establish our residence in the town of Leipzig, which is its neighbour. We had hoped, however, to remain there without trouble for our loyal subjects, since, according to the course of the war, an enemy invasion in our States did not appear anything but less than likely.

It has been all the more painful for us to see this hope deceived, and to be obliged to leave and go beyond Leipzig, until we passed the line of troops coming out of Bohemia to enter Saxony and Franconia, could surround our person and our royal family and we found ourselves sheltered from danger.

Today our trust in the divine Providence lets us live in the hope that it will bless our efforts to free the fatherland from the presence of the enemy, and that, supported by the forces of His Majesty the King of Westphalia, our loyal neighbour and ally, we will soon be able to return.

We believe it our duty, dear and loyal Saxons, to let you share this hope from afar, for your tranquillity. Meanwhile, we publicly thank you, in the interim, to endure your situation with calm and dignity; do not lend an ear to what the enemy has to say, and we thank you for having given new proof of your love and your affections towards us, which makes our felicity that our heart gives so well in return.

It is with all the more confidence that we invite you to attach yourselves more and more to our principles, which until now, under the divine protection, have always caused the country's happiness, to imbue yourselves with it, and to shelter yourselves from the prejudices that the ill-meaning people might try by propagating erroneous opinions. It has not been unknown to us that there are, in our States, a few people, some feeble and lost, the others guided by perverse intentions, who not only profess a way of thinking which is contrary to our system, to the principles of our government, to the sentiments which have inspired us by just reflections on our position, but who still have the audacity to oppose by their remarks, and even by their actions.

It is therefore directed in the most express manner, to the diverse authorities of our kingdom, to redouble their attention on those whose opinions such as these render suspect, but particularly on those who could become culpable, either by the very inconvenient expression of these opinions, or even by actions which would disturb order, as well as the propagation of news, by which the worries of our well-intentioned citizens could be awakened, and who could betray in part the efforts of our zeal for the repose of our subjects, and, in general, not to neglect anything so that our subjects conduct themselves according to the sentiments we have just stated, and that our beneficent intentions be exactly fulfilled; and for greater notoriety, we have signed the presents by our hand, and affixed to it our royal seal. Given at Frankfurt-on-the-Main, 18 June 1809

FRÉDÉRIC-AUGUST

(L.S.) GEORGE-GUILLAUME, COUNT OF HOPFGARTEN

Twenty-fifth Bulletin

Wolkersdorf, 8 July 1809
The works raised by General Count Bertrand, and the corps he commands, had, since the beginning of the month, entirely subdued the Danube. His Majesty instantly resolved to collect his forces in the island of Lobau, quickly march upon the Austrian army, and bring on a general engagement. It was not that the position of the French army was not a very fine one at Vienna; master of the whole right bank of the Danube, having in his power Austria and a considerable portion of Hungary, he enjoyed the greatest plenty. If some difficulties had been experienced in providing sustenance for the people of Vienna, this was due to an ill-organized administration, from embarrassments, which were every day diminishing, and from difficulties that were naturally produced by the situation in which the country was placed, in a land in which the trade in grain is an exclusive privilege of the government. But how could the troops continue to be separated from the hostile army, by a canal of 300 or 400 *toises* in breadth, when the means of crossing over had been prepared and secured? This would have given credibility to the impostures which the enemy had scattered with so great profusion throughout its own and neighbouring countries: this would have cast a doubt over the occurrences at Essling, and would finally have authorized the supposition of there being, in fact, a substantial equality between armies so different, of which one was animated and in some measure reinforced by the multiplicity of its successes and victories, while the other was dispirited by the most striking reverses.

All the intelligence concerning the Austrian army showed that it was considerable; that it had been recruited by numerous bodies of reserve, by the levies from Moravia and Hungary, and by all the *Landwehr* of the provinces; that its cavalry had been re-mounted by requisitions in all the circles, and its draughts of artillery tripled by immense levies of horses and carriages in Moravia, Hungary and Bohemia. To add new chances in their favour, the Austrian generals had raised military works, of which the right was protected by Gross-Aspern and the left by Enzersdorf, and the intervals between them were covered by redoubts, surrounded by palisades and defended by more than 150 pieces of battering artillery taken from the fortresses of Bohemia and Moravia. It was inconceivable how the Emperor, with his experience in war, could think of attacking works so powerfully defended, backed by an army estimated at 200,000 men, made up as much by troops of line as militia and troops from the insurrection, and who were supported by 800 or 900 pieces of field artillery. It appeared simpler to throw some fresh bridges over the Danube, a few leagues lower down, and thus render useless the battlefield prepared by the enemy. But in this latter case it was not thought practicable to avert the inconveniences which had already nearly proved fatal to the army, and succeed, in the course of two or three days, in protecting these new bridges from the machines of the enemy.

On the other side, the Emperor was tranquil. Works were raised upon works in the island of Lobau; and several bridges on piles, and several rows of breakwaters, were fixed at the same place.

This situation of the French army placed between these two great difficulties had not escaped the enemy. It was aware that its army, too numerous and unwieldy, would be exposed to certain destruction if it acted on the offensive; but at the same time, it believed it was impossible to dislodge it from the central position, in which it covered Bohemia, Moravia and a part of Hungary. It is true that this position did not cover Vienna, and that the French were in possession of this capital. But this possession was, to a certain degree, disputed, since the Austrians remained masters of one bank of the Danube, and prevented the arrival of the articles most indispensable to the subsistence of so great a city. These were the reasons of hope and fear, and the subject of conversation in the two armies.

On 1 July, at four o'clock in the morning, the Emperor moved his headquarters to the island of Lobau, which had been named by the engineers the island Napoleon; a small island, to which had been given the name of the Duke of Montebello, and which bore upon Enzersdorf, had been armed with 10 mortars and 20 18-pounders. Another island, called Espagne, had been armed with six pieces of battering artillery, 12-pounders and four mortars. Between these two islands a battery had been raised, equal in force to that of the island Montebello, and in like manner bearing upon Enzersdorf. These 62 pieces of battering artillery had the same object, and were, in two hours, to destroy the little town of Enzersdorf, drive away the enemy, and demolish the works. On the right, the island Alexander, with four mortars, two 10-pounders and 12 6-pounders, battering cannon, were to bear upon the plain and protect the operations of the bridges.

On the 2nd, Pelet, squadron chief and aide-de-camp of the Duke of Rivoli, crossed over to the Mill Island with 500 voltigeurs, and took possession of it. This island was also furnished with cannon. It was joined to the Continent, on the left bank, by a small bridge. In the front, a little fleche was raised, and this redoubt was called Petit. In the evening the redoubts of Essling appeared to be jealous of these works; not doubting that they were a first battery, formed to act against themselves, they fired upon them with great activity. This was precisely the intention in having seized this island. The attention of the enemy was to be drawn to this point, in order to conceal from it the real objective of the operation.

Passage across the arm of the Danube to the Island Lobau

On the 4th, at ten in the evening, General Oudinot caused 1,500 voltigeurs to be embarked on the great arm of the Danube, commanded by General Conroux. Colonel Baste, with 10 gunboats, conveyed them, and disembarked them beyond the little arm of this island Lobau, in the Danube. The batteries of the enemy were soon crushed, and it was driven from the woods to the village of Mühlleuten.

At eleven in the evening, the batteries raised against Enzersdorf received orders to begin their firing. The howitzers set this unfortunate little town on fire, and in less than half an hour the enemy's batteries had ceased to operate.

Battalion Chief Dessalles, director of the equipment of bridges, and the engineer of the marine —, had prepared in the arm of the island Alexander, a bridge of 80 *toises*, of a single piece, and five great ferryboats.

Colonel Saint-Croix, aide-de-camp of the Duke of Rivoli, embarked in barges with 2,500 men, and landed on the left bank.

The bridge of a single piece, the first of the kind that has hitherto been made, was fixed in less than five minutes, and the infantry crossed over it with great rapidity.

Captain Bazelles fixed a bridge of boats in an hour and an half.

Captain Peyerimoff formed a bridge of rafts in two hours.

Thus, at two o'clock in his morning, the army had four bridges, and had debouched on the left 1,500 *toises* below Enzersdorf, protected by the batteries, and the right upon Wittau. The corps of the Duke of Rivoli formed the left; that of Count Oudinot, the centre; and that of the Duke of Auerstädt, the right; the corps of the Prince of Ponte Corvo, the Viceroy and the Duke of Ragusa, the Guard and the cuirassiers formed the second line and the bodies of reserve. Utter darkness, a violent thunderstorm and rain, which fell in torrents, rendered this night as frightful as it was propitious to the French army, and was about to be glorious to it.

On the 5th, with the first rays of the sun, everyone perceived what had been the project of the Emperor, who was then with his whole army, arranged in order of battle at the extremity of the enemy's left, having turned all its entrenched camps, having rendered its works useless, and thus obliging the Austrians to abandon their positions, and come and offer it battle on the spot that was convenient to him. The great problem was thus resolved, and without crossing the Danube on other points, without receiving any protection from the works he had raised, he forced the enemy to fight three quarters of a league from its redoubts. From that moment the greatest and happiest results were presaged.

At eight in the morning, the batteries, which had played upon Enzersdorf, had produced such an effect that the enemy was obliged to let that town be occupied by no more than four battalions. The Duke of Rivoli dispatched his first aide-de-camp, Saint-Croix, against it, who did not meet with a great resistance, and took prisoner all who remained in it.

Count Oudinot surrounded the castle of Sachsengang, which the enemy had fortified, forced 900 men who defended it to capitulate, and took 12 pieces of artillery.

The Emperor then had all the army deploy itself along the immense plain of Enzersdorf.

Battle of Enzersdorf

In the meanwhile, the enemy, confounded in all its projects, gradually recovered from its astonishment and endeavoured to regain some advantages in this new field of battle. For this purpose it detached several columns of infantry, a considerable number of pieces of artillery, and all its cavalry, as well of the line as the new levies, in order to attempt to outflank the right of the French army. As a result it came to occupy the village of Rutzendorf. The Emperor ordered general Oudinot to carry this village, to the right of which he sent the Duke of Auerstädt, in order to proceed to the headquarters of Prince Charles, going always from the right to the left.

From noon until nine in the evening the French armies manoeuvred on this immense plain. All the villages were occupied, and when the French had reached the heights of the entrenched camps of the enemy, they fell of their own accord, as if by enchantment. The Duke of Rivoli caused them to be occupied without resistance. It was thus that we seized the works of Essling and Gross-Aspern, and the labour of 40 days was of no use to the enemy. It made some resistance in the village of Raschdorf, which the Prince of Ponte Corvo caused to be attacked and carried by the Saxons. The enemy was overwhelmed everywhere and crushed by the superiority of our fire. This immense battlefield was covered with its remains.

Battle of Wagram

Quickly alarmed by the progress of the French army, and the great successes which it obtained, with scarcely any effort, the enemy put all its troops in motion, and at six in the evening it occupied the following position: its right from Stadelau to Gerasdorf, its centre from Gerasdorf to Wagram, and its left from Wagram to Neusfedel. The French army had its left at Gross-Aspern, its centre at Raschdorf and its right at Glinzindorf. In this position the day seemed almost at a close, and we had expected a great battle the next day; but this was avoided, and the position of the enemy was intersected so as to prevent it from forming any plan, by taking possession in the night of the village of Wagram. Then its line, already of an immense length, taken suddenly by the chances of combat, the remaining bodies of his army dispersed without order or direction, and we would succeed easily and without any serious engagement. The attack on Wagram took place, and our troops took possession of this village; but a column of Saxons and a column of French in the dark mistook each other for enemies, and this operation failed.

We then prepared for the battle of Wagram. It appears that the dispositions of the French general and the Austrian general were inverted. The Emperor passed the night reassembling his forces towards his centre, where he was in person, within cannon-shot of Wagram. To that end, the Duke of Rivoli moved on the left of Aderklaa, leaving at Aspern a single division, with orders to fall back, in case of necessity, upon the island of Lobau. The Duke of Auerstädt received the order to go beyond the village of Grosshofen that he might approach the centre. The Austrian general, on the contrary, weakened his centre, to secure and augment his extremities, which he still farther extended.

On the 6th at daybreak, the Prince of Ponte Corvo occupied the left, having the Duke of Rivoli in a second line. The Viceroy connected him with the centre, where the corps of Count Oudinot, that of the Duke of Ragusa, those of the Imperial Guard, and the divisions of cuirassiers, formed seven or eight lines.

The Duke of Auerstädt marched from the right to reach the centre. The enemy, on the contrary, put Bellegarde's corps in motion for Stadelau. The corps of Kolowrat, Lichtenstein, and Hiller, connected this right with the position of Wagram, where Prince Hohenzollern was, and with the extremity of the left at Neusiedel, where the corps of Rosenberg debouched in order also to outflank that of the Duke of Auerstädt. The corps of Rosenberg, and that of the Duke of Auerstädt, moving in the opposite direction, encountered each other with the first rays of the sun and gave the signal of battle. The Emperor instantly repaired to this point, ordered the Duke of Auerstädt to be reinforced by the division of the Duke of Padua's cuirassiers, and the corps of Rosenberg to be attacked in flank by a battery of 12 guns, of the division of Count Nansouty. In less than three-quarters of an hour, the fine corps of the Duke of Auerstädt overcame of the corps of Rosenberg, defeated it and drove it beyond Neusiedl with considerable loss.

In the meantime, a cannonade commenced along all of the line, and the enemy's dispositions were engaged moment by moment. All of his left was secured with artillery. One might have said that the Austrian general was not fighting for victory but was looking only for the means of gaining by it. This disposition of the enemy seemed so absurd that some snare was apprehended, and the Emperor delayed some time before he ordered these easy dispositions which he had to make to annul those of the enemy, and render them fatal to it. He ordered the Duke of Rivoli to make an attack on the village occupied by the enemy, and which somewhat strained the extremity of the centre of the army. He ordered the Duke of Auerstädt to turn the position of Neusiedl, and there to push on upon Wagram; and he formed the Duke of Ragusa's troops, and those of General Macdonald, in column, to carry Wagram at the moment the Duke of Auerstädt should debauch.

While these proceedings were taking place, information was received that the enemy was making a furious attack upon the village carried by the Duke of Rivoli; that our left was outflanked by 3,000 *toises*, that a brisk cannonade was already heard at Aspern, and that the space between Aspern and Wagram seemed to be covered with an immense line of artillery. There was no longer any room for doubt. The enemy had committed an enormous fault, and we had only to profit by it. The Emperor ordered General Macdonald to form the divisions of Broussier and Lamarque in column of attack. He ordered the division of Nansouty to support them with the Guard on horse and a battery of 60 guns belonging to the Guard and 40 of different other corps. General Count Lauriston, at the head of this battery of 100 pieces of artillery, marched at a trot against the enemy, advanced without firing to within half gun-shot distance, and there opened a prodigious fire, which silenced that of the enemy and spread death among its ranks. General Macdonald then advanced at the quick charge. General of Division Reille, with the brigade of fusiliers and sharpshooters of the Guard, supported General Macdonald. The Guard had made a change of front, in order to render this attack infallible. In the wink of an eye, the enemy's centre lost a league of ground; its right became alarmed, and perceiving the dangerous position in which it was placed, rapidly fell back. The Duke of Rivoli, at that moment, attacked it in front. While the rout of the centre struck consternation and forced the movement of the right of the enemy, the left was attacked and outflanked by the Duke of Auerstädt, who had carried Neusiedl, and who, having gained the elevated plain, was marching upon Wagram. The divisions of Broussier and Gudin covered themselves with glory.

It was only then ten o'clock in the morning; and even the least discerning men saw that the fate of the day was decided and the victory was ours.

At noon, Count Oudinot marched upon Wagram to assist the attack of the Duke of Auerstädt. He was successful, and carried that important position. As early as ten o'clock, the enemy fought only to effect its retreat; at noon this was manifest; it was conducted in disorder; and long before dark the enemy was out of sight. Our left was posted at Iedlersee and Oberstdorff; our centre upon Ebersdorf, and the cavalry of our right extended their posts as far as Shönkirchen.

At daybreak on the 7th, the army was in motion, marching on Korneuburg and Wolkersdorf, and had some posts near Nicolsburg. The enemy, cut off from Hungary and Moravia, had been forced to fall back on Bohemia.

Such is the narrative of the battle of Wagram, a battle decisive and ever memorable, in which from 300,000 to 400,000 men, and from 1,200 to 1,500 pieces of artillery, contended for great interests, upon a battlefield, studied, planned and fortified by the enemy for several months. Ten pairs of colours, 40 cannon, 20,000 prisoners, including between 300 and 400 officers, and a considerable number of generals, colonels and majors are the trophies of this victory. The battlefields are covered with the slain, among whom are the bodies of several generals, and, among others, one called Norman, a Frenchman, traitor to his country, who prostituted his talents against her.

All the enemy's wounded have fallen into our hands. Those whom it had evacuated at the commencement of the action were found in the adjacent villages. It may be calculated that the result of this battle will be that of reducing the Austrian army to less than 60,000 men.

Our loss has been considerable; it is estimated at 1,500 killed and from 3- to 4,000 wounded. The Duke of Istria, at the moment when he was preparing for an attack with the cavalry, had his horse shot dead by a cannonball, which fell upon his saddle, and slightly grazed his thigh. General of Division Lasalle was killed by a musket ball. He was an officer of the greatest merit, and one of our best light cavalry generals. The Bavarian General Wrede, and Generals Séras, Grenier, Vignolle, Sahuc, Frère and Defrance, were wounded. Colonel Prince Aldobrandini was wounded in the arm by a musket ball; the majors of the Guard, Daumesnil, Corbineau and Colonel Saint-Croix were also wounded; the adjutant commandant, Duprat, was killed; the colonel of the 9th Infantry of Line fell on the field of battle. That regiment has covered itself with glory.

The officers of the staff are preparing a list of our losses.

A particular circumstance of this great battle is that the columns nearest Vienna were only about 1,200 *toises* from it. The numerous population of the capital covered the turrets, the steeples, the roofs of the houses and every elevated situation to witness this great spectacle.

The Emperor of Austria had left Wolkersdorf on the 6th, at five in the morning, and ascended a tower, from which he had a view of the battlefield, and where he remained until noon. He then set off in all haste.

The French headquarters arrived at Wolkersdorf on the morning of the 7th.

Twenty-sixth Bulletin

Wolkersdorf, 9 July 1809

The enemy retreated in the utmost disorder. We have collected a part of its equipment. Its wounded has fallen into our hands; we have already counted more than 12,000; all the villages are filled with them. In five of its hospitals alone we have found more than 6,000.

The Duke of Rivoli, pursuing the enemy by Stockerau, has already arrived at Hollabrünn.

The Duke of Ragusa had at first followed him on the road to Brünn, which he left at Wolkersdorf, in order to take that of Znaim. At nine o'clock this morning, he met a rearguard at Laa, which he routed: he took 900 of them prisoner. Tomorrow he will be at Znaim.

The Duke of Auerstädt has arrived today at Nicolsburg.

The Emperor of Austria and Prince Anthony, with a suite of about 200 chariots, coaches and other carriages, slept on the 6th at Erensbrünn, on the 7th at Hollabrünn, on the 8th at Znaim, from where they set out on the 9th in the morning. According to the relation of the country people who conducted them, their dejection was extreme.

One of the princes of Rohan was found wounded on the battlefield. Lieutenant Field Marshal Wussakowicz is among the prisoners.

The artillery of the Guard covered itself with glory. Major Aboville, who commanded, was wounded. The Emperor has made him General of Brigade. The chief of a squadron of artillery, Grenner, has lost an arm. These intrepid artillerymen displayed all the power of this terrible weapon.

The Chasseurs à Cheval of the Guard charged and drove back on the day of the battle of Wagram three squares of infantry. They took four pieces of artillery. The Polish light horse of the Guard charged a regiment of lancers. They took the Prince of Auersperg prisoner, and captured two pieces of artillery.

The Saxon hussars of Albert charged the cuirassiers of Albert, and took their flags. It was a very singular thing to see two regiments belonging to the same colonel fighting against each other.

It appears that the enemy is abandoning Moravia and Hungary, and is retiring into Bohemia.

The roads are covered with the men belonging to the *Landwehr*, and the mass uprising, who are returning to their houses.

The losses, which desertion is adding to those the enemy has sustained in killed, wounded and prisoners, are concurring to annihilate its army.

The numerous letters that have been intercepted are a striking picture of the discontent of the hostile army, and the disorder that reigns in it.

Now that the Austrian monarchy is without hope, it would evince being ill acquainted with the character of those who govern it not to expect that they will humiliate themselves as they did after the battle of Austerlitz. At that epoch, they were, as now, without hope, and they exhausted all protestations and oaths.

During the day of the 6th, the enemy sent a few hundred men to the right of the Danube to make observations. They re-embarked after having lost a few men killed or taken prisoner.

The heat was excessive on these days. The thermometer was almost constantly at 26 degrees.

Wine is in great abundance. In one village 3,000,000 pints were found. Happily, it is not of bad quality.

Twenty of the most considerable villages in the beautiful plain of Vienna, such as are seen in the neighbourhood of a great capital, have been burnt during the battle. The just hatred of the nation is loud against the criminal men who have drawn upon it all these calamities.

General of Brigade Laroche entered Nuremberg on 28 June with a corps of cavalry, and proceeded towards Bayreuth. He met the enemy at Besentheim, charged it with the first provisional regiment of dragoons, sabred all who opposed him, and took two pieces of artillery.

Twenty-seventh Bulletin

Znaim, 12 July 1809

On the 10th the Duke of Rivoli beat the enemy's rearguard before Hollabrünn.

At noon on the same day, the Duke of Ragusa, who had arrived on the heights of Znaim, saw the enemy's baggage and artillery filing off toward Bohemia. General Bellegarde wrote to him that Prince John of Lichtenstein would repair to the Emperor with a mission from his master, for the purpose of treating for peace; and in consequence desired a suspension of arms. The Duke of Ragusa replied that it was not in his power to accede to such a proposition; but that he would acquaint the Emperor with it. Meanwhile he attacked the enemy, took from it an excellent position, took some prisoners, and took two flags.

On the morning of the same day, the Duke of Auerstädt had crossed the Taya opposite Nicolsburg, and General Grouchy had beaten Prince Rosenberg's rearguard, taking 450 men of Prince Charles's regiment.

At noon on the 11th, the Emperor arrived opposite Znaim. The battle had begun. The Duke of Ragusa had outflanked the town, and the Duke of Rivoli had taken the bridge and had occupied the tobacco factory. In the different engagements this day, we had taken 3,000 men, two flags and three pieces of artillery. General of Brigade Bruyères, an officer of very great promise, has been wounded. General of Brigade Guiton made a fine charge with the 10th cuirassiers.

The Emperor, informed that Prince John of Lichtenstein, who had been sent to him, had arrived within our posts, ordered the fire to cease. The annexed

Armistice was signed at midnight, at the Prince of Neufchâtel's. The Prince of Lichtenstein was presented to the Emperor in his tent, at two o'clock in the morning.

Suspension of Arms between His Majesty the Emperor of the French and King of Italy, and His Majesty the Emperor of Austria

Article I There shall be a suspension of Arms between the armies of His Majesty the Emperor of the French, King of Italy, and of His Majesty the Emperor of Austria.

Article II The line of demarcation shall be, on the side of Upper Austria, the frontier which separates Austria from Bohemia, the Circle of Znaim, that of Brünn, and a line drawn from the frontier of Moravia upon Raab, which shall be at the point where the frontier of the Circle of Brünn touches the March, and descending the March to the conflux of the Taya; from there to Saint John and the road to Pressburg and a league round the town; the great Danube to the mouth of the Raab; the Raab to the frontiers of Styria; Styria, Carniola, Istria and Fiume.

Article III The citadels of Brünn and Graz shall be evacuated immediately on the signature of the present Armistice.

Article IV The detachments of Austrian troops that are in the Tyrol and the Voralberg shall evacuate those two countries, and the fort of Sachsenburg shall be given up to the French troops.

Article V The magazines of provisions and clothes, which shall be found in the countries to be evacuated by the Austrian army, and which belong to it, may be evacuated.

Article VI In relation to Poland, the two armies shall take the line that they at present occupy.

Article VII The present suspension of arms shall continue for a month, and 15 days' notice shall be given before hostilities recommence.

Article VIII Commissaries on either side shall be named for the execution of the present articles.

Article IX From tomorrow, the 13th, the Austrian troops shall begin their evacuation of the countries designated in this suspension of arms; and shall retire by daily marches. The fort of Brünn shall be given up to the French army on 14 July, and that of Graz, on the 16th.

Made and concluded between us the undersigned, charged with full powers from our respective sovereigns, the present Armistice, the Prince of Neufchâtel, Major-General of the French army, and Baron Wimpffen, Major-General and Chief of Staff of the Austrian army.

At the camp before Znaim, 12 July 1809

ALEXANDER

WIMPFFEN

Twenty-eighth Bulletin

Vienna, 14 July 1809

The Danube has risen six feet. The bridges of boats that had been constructed before Vienna, since the battle of Wagram, have been broken by the effects of this rise, but the bridges at Ebersdorf are solid and permanent; none of them has suffered. Those bridges, and the works of the island of Lobau, are the admiration of the military persons of Austria. They avow that such works during war are without example since the time of the Romans.

The Archduke Charles having sent Major-General Weissenwolf to compliment the Emperor, and since Baron Wimpffen and Prince John of Lichtenstein having come upon the same courteous errand in his name, His Majesty has thought proper to send to the Archduke, the Duke of Friuli, Grand Marshal of the Palace, who found him at Budweis and spent part of yesterday at his headquarters.

The Emperor left his camp at Znaim yesterday at nine o'clock in the morning, and arrived at the palace of Schönbrunn at three in the afternoon.

His Majesty has visited the environs of the village of Spitz, which forms the bridgehead of Vienna. General Bertrand has been charged with the execution of different works, which must be marked out and begun this day.

The bridge of piles at Vienna will be re-established with the least delay possible.

His Majesty has named as Marshals of the Empire General Oudinot, the Duke of Ragusa, and General Macdonald. The number of marshals was 11; this nomination will make it 14. There still remain two vacancies. The places of Colonel General of the Swiss and Colonel General of the Chasseurs are also vacant.

The Colonel General of the Chasseurs is, according to our constitution, a Grand Officer of the Empire.

His Majesty has testified his satisfaction with the manner in which the surgery has been served, and particularly with the services of the principal surgeon, Heurteloup.

His Majesty, passing through the field of battle on the 7th, caused a great number of wounded to be taken off, and left there the Duke of Friuli, Grand Marshal of the Palace, who remained there all day.

The number of wounded Austrians in our power amounts to 12,000 or 13,000. The Austrians have had 19 generals killed or wounded. It has been remarked as a singular fact, that most of the French officers, whether of old France or of the new provinces, who were in the Austrian service, have perished.

Several couriers have been intercepted, and among their letters has been found a regular correspondence of Gentz with Count Stadion. The influence of this wretch in the leading determination of the Austrian cabinet is hereby materially proved. Such are the instruments that England employs, like a new Pandora's box, to raise storms and spread poisons on the Continent.

The Duke of Rivoli's corps encamps in the circle of Znaim; that of the Duke of Auerstädt in the circle of Brünn; that of the Duke of Ragusa in the circle of Korneuburg; that of Marshal Oudinot before Vienna at Spitz; that of the Viceroy on Pressburg and Graz. The Imperial Guard returns to the environs of Schönbrunn.

The harvest is very fine and abundant everywhere. The army is cantoned in a beautiful country, and rich in provisions of all kinds, wine particularly.

Treaty of Peace between France and Austria, 15 October 1809

Napoleon, by the Grace of God, and the Constitution of the Empire, Emperor of the French, King of Italy, Protector of the Confederation of the Rhine, etc., having seen and considered the Treaty concluded, determined and signed at Vienna on the 14th of this month, by Nompère de Champagny, our Minister for Foreign Affairs, in virtue of the full powers to that end given him by us, and Prince John of Lichtenstein, Marshal of the Armies of His Majesty the Emperor of Austria, equally provided with full powers, which Treaty is the following:

His Majesty the Emperor of the French, King of Italy, Protector of the

Confederation of the Rhine, Mediator of the League of Switzerland; and His Majesty the Emperor of Austria, King of Hungary and Bohemia, being equally animated with the desire of putting an end to the war which has arisen between them, have resolved to negotiate without delay a definitive Treaty of Peace, and for that purpose have appointed as their plenipotentiaries, namely:

His Majesty the Emperor of the French, King of Italy, Protector of the League of the Rhine, Jean Baptiste Nompère, Count of Champagny, Duke of Cadore, Grand Eagle of the Legion of Honour, Commander of the Order of the Iron Crown, Knight of the Order of St André of Russia, Grand Dignitary of that of Order of the Two Sicilies, Grand Cross of the Orders of the Black and Red Eagle of Prussia, of the Orders of St Joseph Würzburg, of the Order of Fidelity of Baden, of the Order of Hesse-Darmstadt, His Majesty's Minister for Foreign Affairs; and His Majesty the Emperor of Austria, King of Hungary and Bohemia, Prince Jean of Lichtenstein, Knight of the Order of the Golden Fleece, Grand Cross of the Order of Maria Theresa, Chamberlain, Marshal of the Armies of His Said Majesty the Emperor of Austria, and Proprietary Commander of a Regiment of Horse in his service.

Who having previously exchanged their full powers, have agreed upon the following Articles:

Article I There shall be, from the day of the exchange of the ratifications of the present Treaty, peace and friendship between His Majesty the Emperor of the French, King of Italy, Protector of the Confederation of the Rhine, and His Majesty the Emperor of Austria, King of Hungary and Bohemia, their heirs and successors, their States and subjects respectively, forever.

Article II The present peace is also declared to be common with His Majesty the King of Spain, His Majesty the King of Holland, His Majesty the King of Bavaria, His Majesty the King of Saxony and His Majesty the King of Westphalia, His Most Eminent Highness the Prince Primate to Their Royal Highnesses the Grand Duke of Baden, the Grand Duke of Berg, the Grand Duke of Hesse-Darmstadt, the Grand Duke of Würzburg, and all the Princes and Members of the Confederation of the Rhine, the Allies of His Majesty the Emperor of the French, King of Italy, Protector of the League of the Rhine in the present war.

Article III His Majesty the Emperor of Austria, King of Hungary and Bohemia, cedes, for himself, his heirs and successors, Princes of his House, and their respective successors, the principalities, seigniorial domains, and territories hereinafter mentioned, and also all titles which may accrue from the possession their properties, whether manorial or held by them under an church title, that these lands include.

He cedes and transfers to His Majesty the Emperor of the French, to form part of the Confederation of the Rhine, and to be placed at his disposition for the interest of the Sovereigns of the League:

The lands of Salzburg and Berchtolsgaden; that part of Upper Austria, located on the further side of a line running from the Danube near the village of Strass, including Weissenkirch, Wildersdorff, Michelbach, Gruit Mukenhoffen, Helst and Jedina; there in the direction of Schwanstadt, the town of Schwanstadt on the Alle, and there ascending along the bank of that river, and the lake of the same name to the point where the lake touches upon the territory of Salzburg.

His Majesty the Emperor of Austria shall only retain in property the woods belonging to the Salzkammergut, which are part of the territory of Mondace, with liberty to cut and carry there the brushwood, but without enjoying any right of sovereignty upon that territory.

He also cedes to His Majesty the Emperor of the French, King of Italy, the Country of Gorizia, the Manor of Montefalcone, the government and city of Trieste, Carniola with its dependencies on the on the Gulf of Trieste, the Circle of Villach, in Corinthia, and all the territories lying on the right bank of the Save, from the point where that river leaves Carniola, along its course to where it touches the frontiers of Bosnia: namely a part of provincial Croatia, six districts of military Croatia, Fiume, and the Hungarian coastline, Austrian Istria, or the district of Castua, the islands depending on the ceded territories, and all other territories however named, upon the right bank of the Save; the middle stream of the said river serving as the boundary between the two States.

Lastly, the Manorial Domain of Rhazums lying in the land of Grisons.

He cedes and makes over to His Majesty the King of Saxony, the territory of Bohemia depending upon and included in the territory of the Kingdom of Saxony, namely the parishes and villages of Guntersdorf, Taubentranke, Gerlachsheim, Lenkersdorf, Schirgiswalde, Winkel, etc.

He cedes and abandons to His Majesty the King of Saxony, to be united to the Duchy of Warsaw, all of western or New Galicia, a district round Kraków, on the right bank of the Vistula, to be hereafter ascertained, and the Circle of Zamosé in Eastern Galicia. The district around Kraków, upon the right bank of the Vistula, shall in the direction of Podgorze, have for its circumference the distance from Podgorze to Wieliczka. The line of demarcation shall pass through Wieliczka, and to the westward touch upon Scavina, and to the eastward upon the Beek, which falls into the Vistula at Brzdegy.

Wieliczka and all of the territory of the salt mines shall belong in common to the Emperor of Austria, and the King of Saxony. Justice shall be administered therein in the name of the Municipal Power; there shall be quartered there only the troops necessary for the support of the Police, and they shall consist of equal numbers of those of both nations. The Austrian salt from Wieliczka, in its conveyance over the Vistula, and through the Duchy of Warsaw, shall not be subject to any toll-duties. Wheat of all kinds, raised in Austrian Galicia, may also be freely exported across the Vistula.

His Majesty the Emperor of Austria, and His Majesty the King of Saxony, may form such an arrangement with regard to these boundaries, as that the Sacu, from the point where it touches upon the Circle of Zamosé, to its confluence with the Vistula, shall serve as the line of demarcation between both states.

He cedes and makes over to His Majesty the Emperor of Russia in the easternmost part of Galicia, a tract of territory containing a population of 400,000 souls, the city of Brody not, however, being included. This territory shall be settled amiably by Commissioners on the part of both Empires.

Article IV The Teutonic Order having been abolished in the States of the Confederation of the Rhine, His Majesty the Emperor of Austria, in the name of his Imperial Highness the Archduke Anthony, abdicates the Grand Mastership of that Order in his States, and recognizes the dispositions taken with regard to the property of the Order, located out of Austrian territory. Pensions shall be assigned to those who have been on the civil establishment of the Order.

Article V The debts funded upon the territory of the ceded provinces and allowed by the states of the said provinces, or accruing from expenses incurred for their administration, shall follow only the fate of those provinces.

Article VI The provinces which are to be restored to His Majesty the Emperor of Austria, shall be administered at his expense by the Austrian authorities, from the day of exchanging the Ratification of the present Treaty; and the Imperial Domains, wherever situated, from 1 November. It is nevertheless understood that the French army in this country shall take for their use whatever articles cannot be supplied by their magazines for the subsistence of the troops and wants of the hospitals, and also whatever shall be necessary for the conveyance of their sick and the evacuation of magazines. An arrangement shall be made between the High Contracting Parties respecting all war contributions, of whatever denomination, previously imposed on the Austrian provinces occupied by the French and allied troops. In consequence of this arrangement the levying of the said contributions shall cease from the day of the exchange of the Ratifications.

Article VII His Majesty the Emperor of the French, King of Italy, pledges to give no obstruction to the importation of merchandise into and from Austria by way of the port of Fiume; this, however, shall not include English goods or merchandise coming from English trade. The transit duties on the goods thus imported or exported shall be lower than upon those of all other nations except for the Kingdom of Italy.

An inquiry shall be instituted to ascertain whether any advantages can be allowed to the Austrian trade in the other ports ceded by this Treaty.

Article VIII The titles of domains, archives, plans and maps of the counties, towns and fortresses that have been ceded shall be given up within two months after the exchange of the Ratification.

Article IX His Majesty the Emperor of Austria, King of Hungary and Bohemia, agrees to surrender the yearly and back interest of the capital invested in securities of the Government, States, Bank, lottery or other public establishment, by subjects, companies or corporate bodies in France, the Kingdom of Italy, and the Grand Duchy of Berg.

Measures shall also be taken to completely liquidate the sum due to Mont St Thérèsa, now Mont Napoleon, at Milan.

Article X His Majesty the Emperor of the French agrees to grant a full and complete pardon to the inhabitants of the Tyrol and Voralberg who have taken a part in the insurrection, so that they shall not be prosecuted either in person or property.

His Majesty the Emperor of Austria equally agrees to grant a full and complete pardon to those inhabitants of the territories he retains in Galicia, whether civil or military, public officers, or private individuals, who have taken part in the levying of troops or the formation of judicial or municipal administrations; or in any other proceeding whatsoever during the war, which inhabitants shall not be prosecuted in their persons or property.

They shall have permission, during a period of six years, to dispose of their properties, of whatever description they may be; to sell their estates, even those that have been considered inalienable, such as trusts and entailed estates; to leave the country, and to carry with them the produce of these sales, in cash, or effects of any other description, without paying any duty for the same, or experiencing any difficulty or obstruction.

The same permission, and for the same period, shall be reciprocally allowed to the inhabitants and landholders in the territories ceded by the present Treaty.

The inhabitants of the Duchy of Warsaw possessing landed estates in Austrian Galicia, whether public officers or private individuals, shall enjoy the revenues thereof, without paying any duty thereon or experiencing any obstruction.

Article XI Within six weeks from the exchange of the present Treaty, posts shall be erected to mark the boundaries of Kraków, upon the right bank of the Vistula. For this purpose there shall be nominated Austrian, French and Saxon Commissioners.

The same measures shall be adopted within the same period upon the frontiers of Upper Austria, Salzburg, Villach and Carniola, as far as the Save. The Thalweg (mid-channel) of the Save shall determine what islands of that river shall belong to each power. For this purpose, French and Austrian Commissioners shall be nominated.

Article XII A military convention shall be forthwith entered into, to regulate the respective periods within which the various provinces restored to His Majesty the Emperor of Austria shall be evacuated. The said Convention shall be adjusted on the basis that Moravia shall be evacuated in 15 days; that part of Galicia which remains in possession of Austria, the city and district of Vienna, in one month; Lower Austria in two months, and the remaining districts and territories not ceded by this treaty shall be evacuated by the French troops and those of their allies in two and a half months, or earlier if possible, from the exchange of the Ratifications.

This same convention shall regulate all that relates to the evacuation of the hospitals and magazines of the French army, and the entrance of the Austrian troops into the territories evacuated by the French or their allies, and also the evacuation of that part of Croatia ceded by the present Treaty to His Majesty the Emperor of the French.

Article XIII The prisoners of war taken by France and her allies from Austria, and by Austria from France and her allies that have not yet been released shall be given up within 50 days after the exchange of the Ratifications of the present Treaty.

Article XIV His Majesty the Emperor of the French, King of Italy, Protector of the Confederation of the Rhine, guarantees the inviolability of the possessions of His Majesty the Emperor of Austria, King of Hungary and Bohemia, in the state in which they exist in consequence of the present Treaty.

Article XV His Majesty the Emperor of Austria recognizes all the alterations that have taken place, or may subsequently take place, in Spain, Portugal and Italy.

Article XVI His Majesty the Emperor of Austria, desirous to co-operate in the restoration of a maritime peace, accedes to the prohibitory system with respect to England adopted by France and Russia during the present maritime war. His Imperial Majesty shall break off all intercourse with Great Britain, and, with respect to the English government, place himself in the situation he held previous to the present war.

Article XVII His Majesty the Emperor of the French, King of Italy, and His Majesty the Emperor of Austria, King of Hungary and Bohemia, shall observe, with respect to each other, the same protocol in regard to rank and other points of etiquette as before the present war.

Article XVIII The Ratifications of the present Treaty shall be exchanged within six days, or sooner, if possible.

Done and signed at Vienna, 14 October 1809

J B NOMPÈRE DE CHAMPAGNY

JOHN, PRINCE OF LICHTENSTEIN

We have ratified, and hereby ratify the above Treaty, in all and every of the articles therein contained; declare the same to be adopted, confirmed, and established; and engage that the same shall be maintained inviolable.

In confirmation whereof we have hereto affixed our signature with our own hand, being countersigned and sealed with our Imperial Seal.

Given at our Imperial Camp at Schönbrunn, 15 October 1809

NAPOLEON

By the Emperor, CHAMPAGNY, MINISTER FOR FOREIGN AFFAIRS

H B MARET, SECRETARY OF STATE.

Certified by us, the Arch-Chancellor of State EUGÈNE NAPOLEON.

Twenty-ninth Bulletin

Vienna, 22 July 1809

Generals Durosnel and Fouler have arrived at the headquarters.

The conjectures we had formed regarding General Durosnel were found to be false. He was not wounded, his horse was not killed under him; but upon returning from taking the order to the Duke of Montebello on 22 May to concentrate his movement because of the breakup of the bridges, he crossed a ravine where he found 25 hussars whom he thought formed one of our posts. He did not realize they were the enemy until they assaulted him. Having heard nothing from him for a long time and taking into account other indications, we believed him to be dead.

General of Division Reynier has taken the command of the Saxons and occupied Pressburg.

Marshal Macdonald started marching to take possession of the citadel of Graz where he is expected to enter today.

Marshal Duke of Ragusa has encamped his troops on the heights of Krems.

His Majesty assists every morning at the parades of the Guard, which are very fine. The *vélites* and foot grenadiers of the Italian Guard are noticed for their excellent appearance.

Prince John of Lichtenstein, returning from Buda, was presented to His Majesty on the 18th; he was bringing a letter from the Emperor of Austria,

Count Bubna [-Littitz], Major-General aide-de-camp of the Emperor of Austria, had dinner several times with Count Champagny.

On the banks of the Danube, we have collected and repaired the commercial boats that had been dispersed by the events of the war, and they are being loaded with wood, vegetables, wheat and flour. We see them arriving every day.

The whole army is encamped.

Thirtieth Bulletin

Vienna, 30 July 1809

The 9th Corps, commanded by the Prince of Ponte Corvo, has been dissolved on the 8th. The Saxons who were a part of it are now under the command of General Reynier. The Prince of Ponte Corvo has gone to sea. In the battle of Wagram, the village was taken on the 6th between ten and eleven in the morning, and the glory belongs solely to Marshal Oudinot and his corps.

According to the intelligence taken, the house of Austria had been preparing for war for almost four years, that is to say, since the peace at Pressburg. Her military state during three years has cost her 300 million francs each year. And so, her paper money which was only worth one million francs at the time of the Peace of Pressburg, is now worth two millions.

The house of Austria entered the campaign with 62 regiments of line, 18 regiments of frontiers, 4 corps of legions, giving a total of 300,000 men under arms; 150 battalions of *Landwehr* under the command of retired officers and trained during ten months, forming 150,000 men, 40,000 men of the Hungarian insurrection, and 60,000 cavalry, artillery and sappers, which made the real number of forces from 500,000 to 600,000 men. Thus, the house of Austria believed herself sure of victory. She hoped to balance the destiny of France, at a time when our forces would have been united, she had no doubt about advancing on the Rhine, knowing that the majority of our forces and our finest regiments were in Spain. However, her armies are today reduced to less than a quarter of what they were, while the French army is twice what it was at Ratisbon.

These efforts, the House of Austria could only make once. It is a miracle attached to paper money. The legal tender value is so rare we do not believe that in the states of this monarchy there could be 60 million francs in cash. This is what supports the paper money, since nearly 2 millions, which, once reduced to one third, are only worth 600 to 700 millions, are the only thing necessary for circulation.

We found 22 pieces of artillery in the citadel of Graz.

The fortress of Saschenburg, situated on the debouch of Tyrol, was handed over to General Rusca.

The Duke of Danzig entered Tyrol with 25,000 men. He occupied Lovers on the 28th and has disarmed the inhabitants. He should be, at this time, at Innsbruck.

General Thielmann has entered Dresden.

The Duke of Abrantès is at Bayreuth. He has established his posts on the frontier of Bohemia.

CAMPAIGN IN RUSSIA
1812

The campaign in Russia is often seen as the source of Napoleon's downfall. It should be seen as the perhaps inevitable result of Napoleon's effort to isolate England economically through the Continental System and, perhaps, his weakened condition owing to the Peninsular campaign in Spain.

Tsar Alexander did not really want to go to war with Napoleon. His mother, however, was not happy with the alliance between Russia and France, and his nobles were very unhappy with the Continental System. They wanted English business, and soon the economic blockade had sprung some serious leaks.

Alexander had another problem with Napoleon: Poland. Napoleon had promised the Poles he would create an independent Polish state. As an interim measure, he had created the Duchy of Warsaw. These actions guaranteed Polish loyalty to his cause, but they enraged Alexander and his nobles. Alexander demanded that Napoleon abandon the Duchy. Napoleon refused, partly because he had given his word to the Poles and partly because he wanted a buffer between his empire and the Russians.

Alexander was the first to prepare for war. He convinced Sweden, largely run by its Crown Prince Jean-Baptiste Bernadotte, the former French Marshal turned traitor, to join an alliance with Russia against Napoleon, and then signed a peace treaty with Turkey. By April, he was ready for war, and delivered an ultimatum to Napoleon that demanded he abandon the Duchy of Warsaw.

This gave Napoleon little choice. He could not give in to the ultimatum, and he could not just sit and wait for Alexander to attack his territory. He would take the fight to Alexander, defeat him in a large pitched battle, and then dictate peace terms that would return the two great countries to their previous alliance.

That, at least, was the plan.

Napoleon assembled what at the time was the largest army in history. There were over 600,000 soldiers, about half of whom were French and about half of whom were from 20 other nations. No Russian force could hope to defeat this army.

That, as it happens, was the problem. Rather than fight such a formidable force, the Russians withdrew deep into their own country. The French had several opportunities to defeat major Russian forces, but delays and incompetence on the part of Napoleon's commanders deprived him of the one big battle he had wanted. Only at Borodino, with his forces greatly diminished, was Napoleon able to get his pitched battle. He won that battle, referred to as the Moskova in the Bulletins, and marched on to Moscow, but the victory was anything but complete, and the Russian army withdrew in good order.

After several weeks in Moscow, Napoleon finally decided to leave Russia. The story of this disastrous withdrawal is well known, and the later bulletins of this campaign give poignant testimony of the suffering endured by the soldiers.

First Bulletin

Gumbinnen, 20 June 1812
Towards the end of 1810, Russia altered her political system; the English spirit regained its influence, the Ukase respecting commerce was its first act.

In February 1811, five divisions of the Russian army left the Danube by forced marches and proceeded to Poland. By this movement Russia sacrificed Wallachia and Moldavia.

When the Russian armies were united and formed, a protest against France

244

appeared, which was transmitted to every cabinet. Russia that way announced that she felt no wish even to save appearances.

All means of conciliation were employed on the part of France: all were ineffectual.

Towards the close of 1811, six months afterwards, it was clear in France that all this could end only in war; preparations were made.

The garrison of Danzig was increased to 20,000 men. Stores of every description, cannons, muskets, powder, ammunition and pontoons, were conveyed to that place; considerable sums of money were placed at the disposal of the department of engineers for the augmentation of its fortifications. The army was placed on war readiness. The cavalry, artillery train and military baggage train were completed.

In March 1812, a treaty of alliance was concluded with Austria; the preceding month a treaty had been concluded with Prussia.

In April the 1st Corps of the *Grande Armée* marched for the Oder, the 2nd Corps to the Elbe, the 3rd Corps to the Lower Oder; the 4th Corps set out from Verona, crossed the Tyrol and proceeded to Silesia.

The Guard left Paris.

On 22 April, the Emperor of Russia took the command of his army, left Saint Petersburg and moved his headquarters to Vilna.

At the beginning of May, the 1st Corps arrived on the Vistula at Elbing and Marienburg, the 2nd Corps at Marienwerder, the 3rd Corps at Thorn, the 4th and 6th Corps at Plock, the 5th Corps assembled at Warsaw, the 8th Corps on the right of Warsaw and the 7th Corps at Pulawy.

The Emperor set out from Saint Cloud on 9 May; crossed the Rhine on the 13th, the Elbe on the 29th and the Vistula on 6 June.

Second Bulletin

Wilkowiszki, 22 June 1812

All means of effecting an understanding between the two empires became impossible. The spirit that controlled the Russian Cabinet hurried it on to war.

General Narbonne, aide-de-camp to the Emperor, was dispatched to Vilna and could remain there only a few days. By that was gained the proof that the demand, equally arrogant and extraordinary, which had been made by Prince Kurakin, and in which he declared that he would not enter into any explanation before France had evacuated the territory of her own allies in order to leave them at the mercy of Russia, was the *sine qua non* of that Cabinet, and he made that a matter of boast to foreign powers.

The 1st Corps advanced to the Pregel. The Prince of Eckmühl had his headquarters, on 11 June, at Königsberg.

Marshal Duke of Reggio, commanding the 2nd Corps, has his headquarters at Wehlau; Marshal Duke of Elchingen, commanding the 3rd Corps, at Soldapp; the Prince Viceroy at Rastenburg [Ketrzyn]; the King of Westphalia at Warsaw; Prince Poniatowski at Pultusk. The Emperor moved his headquarters on the 12th to Königsberg, on the Pregel: on the 17th to Insterburg, on the 19th to Gumbinnen.

A slight hope of accommodation still remained. The Emperor had given orders to Count Lauriston to go and see the Emperor Alexander, or his Minister for Foreign Affairs, and to ascertain whether there might not yet be some means of obtaining a reconsideration of the demand of Prince Kurakin and of reconciling the honour of France and the interest of her allies with the opening of a negotiation.

The same spirit that had previously swayed the Russian Cabinet, under various pretexts, prevented Count Lauriston from accomplishing his mission, and it appeared for the first time that an Ambassador under circumstances of so much importance was unable to obtain an interview, either with the Sovereign or his Minister. The Secretary of Legation, Prévost, brought this intelligence to Gumbinnen, and the Emperor issued orders to march for the purpose of crossing the Niemen. 'The conquered,' said he, 'assume the tone of conquerors: fate draws them on; let their destinies be fulfilled.' His Majesty submitted the following Proclamation to the Orders of the Army:

'Soldiers! The second war of Poland has commenced. The first was brought to a close at Friedland and Tilsit. At Tilsit, Russia swore eternal alliance with France, and war with England. She now violates her oaths. She refuses to give any explanation of her strange conduct, until the Eagles of France shall have re-crossed the Rhine, leaving our allies at her mercy. Russia is swept away by her fate; her destinies must be accomplished. Does she believe us degenerate? Are we no longer the soldiers of Austerlitz? She places us between dishonour and war: the choice cannot be in doubt. Let us, then, march forward! Let us cross the Niemen! Let us carry the war into her territory. The second war of Poland will be as glorious to the French arms as the first; but the peace that we shall conclude will carry its own guarantee and will put an end to that proud and haughty influence which Russia has for 50 years exercised in the affairs of Europe.

At our headquarters at Wilkowiszki, 22 June 1812

Third Bulletin

Kovno, 26 June 1812
On 23 June, the King of Naples, who commands the cavalry, transferred his headquarters to within two leagues of the Niemen, on its left bank. This Prince has under his immediate orders the corps of cavalry commanded by Generals Counts Nansouty and Montbrun; the one composed of the divisions under the command of Generals Counts Bruyères, Saint-Germain and Valence; the other consisting of the divisions under the orders of General Baron Watier and Generals Counts Sebastiani and Defrance.

Marshal the Prince of Eckmühl, commanding the first Corps, moved his headquarters to the skirts of the great forest of Pilwisky.

The 2nd Corps and the Guard followed the movement of the 1st Corps.

The 3rd Corps took the direction of Marienpol; the Viceroy, with the 4th and 6th Corps, which remained in the rear, marched upon Kalwary.

The King of Westphalia marched to Novogrudok, with the 5th, 7th and 8th Corps.

The 1st Austrian Corps, commanded by Prince Schwarzenberg, left Lemberg [Lwów] on the —, made a movement on its left, and drew near to Lublin.

The pontoon train, under the orders of General Eblé, arrived on the 23rd within two leagues of the Niemen.

On the 23rd, at two in the morning, the Emperor arrived at the advanced posts near Kovno, took a Polish cloak and cap from one of the light cavalry, and inspected the banks of the Niemen, accompanied only by General Haxo of the engineers.

At eight in the evening, the army was again in motion. At ten, General of Division Count Morand had three companies of voltigeurs cross, and at the same time three bridges were thrown across the Niemen. At eleven, three columns marched quickly over the three bridges. At a quarter past one, day began to appear. At noon, General Baron Pajol drove before him a cloud of Cossacks and took possession of Kovno with a single battalion.

On the 24th, the Emperor proceeded to Kovno.

Marshal the Prince of Eckmühl pushed forward his headquarters to Roumchicki and the King of Naples to Eketanoni.

During all of the 24th and 25th, the army was defiling on the three bridges. In the evening of the 24th, the Emperor ordered a new bridge to be thrown over the Vilia opposite Kovno and directed Marshal Duke of Reggio to cross it with the second Corps. The Polish light horse of the Guard crossed the river by swimming. Two men were drowning when they were saved by two swimmers of the 26th Light Infantry. Colonel Guéhéneuc, having imprudently exposed himself to afford them assistance, was himself in peril; a swimmer of his regiment saved him.

On the 25th, the Duke of Elchingen pushed on to Kormelou; the King of Naples advanced to Jigmoroni. The enemy's light troops were driven and pursued on every side.

On the 26th, Marshal Duke of Reggio arrived at Janów; Marshal Duke of Elchingen arrived at Skorouli. The light divisions of cavalry covered the whole plain to within ten leagues of Vilna.

Marshal Duke of Tarentum, who commands the 10th Corps, composed in part of the Prussians, crossed the Niemen on the 24th at Tilsit, and marched on Rosiena in order to clear the right bank of that river and to protect the navigation.

Marshal Duke of Belluno, commanding the 9th Corps and having under his orders the divisions Heudelet, Lagrange, Durutte and Partouneaux, occupies the country between the Elbe and the Oder.

General of Division Count Rapp, Governor of Danzig, has under his orders the Daendels division.

General of Division Count Hogendorp is Governor of Königsberg.

The Emperor of Russia is at Vilna with his Guards and one part of his army occupying Ronkonkoma and Kovtroki.

The Russian General Bagavout, commanding the 2nd Corps and a part of the Russian army, having been cut off from Vilna had no other means of safety than by proceeding towards the Dvina.

The Niemen is navigable for vessels of 200 or 300 tons as far as Kovno. The communications by water are also secured as far as Danzig, and with the Vistula, the Oder and the Elbe. An immense supply of brandy, flour, and biscuit is hastily taken from Danzig and Königsberg towards Kovno. The Vilia, which flows by Vilna, is navigable for smaller boats from Kovno to Vilna. Vilna, the capital of Lithuania, is also the chief town of all Polish Russia. For several months the Emperor of Russia has been in this city with a part of his Court. The occupation of this place will be the first fruit of victory. Several Cossack officers, and officers charged with dispatches, have been captured by the light cavalry.

Fourth Bulletin

Vilna, 30 June 1812

On the 27th, the Emperor arrived at the advanced posts at two in the afternoon, and put the army in motion for the purpose of approaching Vilna, and attacking the Russian army at daybreak of the 28th, should it wish to defend Vilna or retard its capture, in order to save the immense magazines which it had there. One Russian division occupied Troki and another division was on the heights of Waka.

At daybreak of the 28th, the King of Naples put himself in motion with the advanced guard and the light cavalry of General Count Bruyères. Marshal the Prince of Eckmühl supported him with his corps. The Russians everywhere retired. After exchanging some cannon-shot, they re-crossed the Vilia in all haste, burned the wooden bridge of Vilna and set fire to immense magazines, valued at many millions of roubles: more than 150,000 quintals of flour, an immense supply of forage and of oats and a great mass of clothing were burned. A great quantity of arms, in which Russia is in general deficient, and of warlike stores was destroyed and thrown into the Vilia.

At noon, the Emperor entered Vilna. At three o'clock the bridge over the Vilia was re-established. All the carpenters of the city repaired to it with zeal, and constructed a bridge, while the pontoon engineers at the same time constructed another.

The Bruyères division followed the enemy on the left bank. In a slight affair with their rearguard, about 50 carriages were taken from the Russians. There were some men killed and wounded; among the last was the Captain of Hussars, Ségur. The Polish light horse of the Guard made a charge on the right bank of the Vilia, put to rout, pursued and made prisoner a considerable number of Cossacks.

On the 25th, the Duke of Reggio had crossed the Vilia by a bridge thrown over near Kovno. On the 26th he marched on Javou, and on the 27th, on Chatoui. This movement obliged the Prince of Wittgenstein, Commandant of the 1st Corps of the Russian army, to evacuate all the Samogitia and the country lying between Kovno and the sea, and to retire upon Wilkomir after obtaining a reinforcement of two regiments of the Guards. On the 28th, a re-encounter took place. Marshal the Duke of Reggio found the enemy drawn up opposite Develtovo. A cannonade commenced; the enemy was driven from one position to another, and re-crossed the bridge with so much precipitation that it could not set fire to it. It lost 300 prisoners, among whom were several officers, and about 100 killed or wounded. Our loss amounts to about 50 men.

The Duke of Reggio praises the brigade of light cavalry commanded by General Baron Castex, and the 11th Regiment of Light Infantry, composed entirely of Frenchmen from the departments beyond the Alps. The young Roman conscripts have shown a great deal of intrepidity.

The enemy set fire to its large magazine at Wilkomir. Up to the last moments the inhabitants were pillaging some barrels of flour; we succeeded in recovering a part of it.

On the 29th, the Duke of Elchingen threw a bridge over the Vilia opposite Souderva. Some columns received a direction to march by the roads of Grodno and Volhynia, for the purpose of coming up with various Russian corps that were cut off and scattered.

Vilna is a city containing from 25,000 to 30,000 souls, with a great number of convents, fine public buildings and inhabitants full of patriotism. Four or five hundred young men of the University, over 18 and belonging to the best families, have requested to form a regiment.

The enemy is retiring upon the Dvina. A great number of staff officers and couriers are falling into our hands daily. We are obtaining proofs of the exaggeration of all that Russia has published with regard to the immensity of her means. Only two battalions to each regiment are with the army: the third battalions, the statements of the situation of which have been found in the intercepted correspondence of the officers of the regiment depots, do not in general amount to more than 120 or 200 men.

The Court set off from Vilna 24 hours after being apprised of our passage at Kovno. Samogitia [Zemaitija] and Lithuania are almost entirely liberated. The centralization of Bagration towards the north has very much weakened the troops that were to defend Volhynia.

The King of Westphalia, with the corps of Prince Poniatowski and the 7th and 8th Corps, must have entered Grodno on the 29th.

Different columns have set out to fall upon the flanks of the corps of Bagration, which, on the 20th, received orders to proceed by forced marches from Proujanoni towards Vilna, and the head of which had already arrived within four days march of the latter city; but events have forced it to retreat and it is now pursued.

Hitherto the campaign has not been bloody; there have been only manoeuvres: we have taken in all 1,000 prisoners. But the enemy has already lost the capital and the greater part of the Polish provinces, which were in a state of insurrection. All the magazines of the first, second, and third lines, the result of two years' care and valued at more than 20 million roubles, are consumed by flames or have fallen into our power. Finally, the headquarters of the French army is in the place where the Court was for six weeks.

Among the great number of intercepted letters, the following two are remarkable: the one from the quartermaster of the Russian army, who communicates that Russia, having already lost all her magazines of the first, second and third lines, is reduced to the situation of forming new ones in all haste; the other, from Duke Alexander of Württemberg, which shows that after a campaign of a few days the provinces of the centre are already declared in a state of war.

In the present situation of things, had the Russian army believed that they had any chance of victory, the defence of Vilna would have been equivalent to a battle; and in all countries, but particularly in that where we now are, the preservation of a triple line of magazines should have determined a general to risk the chances of it.

Manoeuvres alone have placed in the power of the French army a considerable portion of the Polish provinces, the capital and three lines of magazines. The magazines of Vilna were set on fire with so much precipitation that we have been able to save a great many things.

Order of the Day on the organization of Lithuania

At the Imperial Headquarters of Vilna, 1 July 1812

There will be a temporary government of Lithuania made up of seven members and one secretary-general. The commission of the temporary government of Lithuania will be entrusted with the administration of finances, of the subsistence, of the organization of the troops of the country, the formation of the national guards and the police. There will be in the service of the temporary commission of the government of Lithuania an imperial commissioner.

Each of the governments of Vilna, Grodno, Minsk and Byalistock will be administered by a commission of three members, presided over by an Intendant. These administrative commissioners will be under the orders of the temporary commission of the government of Lithuania.

The administration of each district will be given to a vice-prefect.

There will be for the town of Vilna a mayor, four deputies and one municipal council composed of 12 members. This administration will be in charge of the management of the city's estate, the surveillance of the relief establishments and the municipal police.

There will be formed at Vilna a national guard composed of two battalions. The force of the two battalions will be of 450 men.

There will be in each of the governments of Vilna, Grodno, Minsk and Byalistock a police force commanded by a colonel having under his orders two squadron chiefs for the governments of Vilna and of Minsk and one squadron chief for the governments of Grodno and of Byalistock. There will be one company of police in each district. Each company will be composed of 107 men.

The colonel of the police will reside at the chief town [*chef-lieu*] of the government. The residence of the officers and the placement of the brigades will be determined by the temporary commission of the government of Lithuania.

The officers, non-commissioned officers and volunteer policemen will be chosen from among the gentlemen proprietors of the district: no one can be exempt. They will be named this way: the officers, by the temporary commission of the government of Lithuania; the non-commissioned officers and volunteer police, by the administrative committee of the governments of Vilna, Grodno, Minsk and Byalistock.

The uniform will be the Polish uniform.

The gendarmerie will perform the service of police; it will provide assistance to the public authority; it will arrest the stragglers, looters and deserters, no matter which army they belong to. Our order of the day dated the — of last June will be published in each government, and in consequence there will be a military commission established.

The Major-General will appoint an officer-general or superior, French or Polish, of the troops of line, to command each government. The national guards, the gendarmerie and the troops will be under its orders.

NAPOLEON

Fifth Bulletin

Vilna, 6 July 1812

The Russian army was posted and organized in the following manner, at the commencement of hostilities:

The 1st Corps, commanded by Prince Wittgenstein, consisting of the 5th and 14th divisions of infantry and one division of cavalry, amounting in all to 18,000 men, including artillery and sappers, had been a considerable time at Chawli. It had since occupied Rosiena; and was, on 24 June, at Keydanoui.

The 2nd Corps, commanded by General Bagavout, consisting of the 4th and 17th divisions of infantry and one division of cavalry, constituting the same force, occupied Kovno.

The 3rd Corps, commanded by General Schomoalov, composed of the 1st division of grenadiers, one division of infantry, and a division of cavalry, amounting to 24,000 men, occupied Novo-Troki.

The 4th Corps, commanded by General Tutshkov, composed of the 11th and 23rd divisions of infantry and one of cavalry, in total 18,000 men, was stationed on the line from Novo-Troki to Lida.

The [Russian] Imperial Guard was at Vilna.

The 6th Corps, commanded by General Docturov, consisting of two divisions of infantry, and one of cavalry, amounting to 18,000 men, had formed a part of the army of Prince Bagration. In the middle of June, this corps arrived at Lida from

Volhynia, in order to reinforce the first army.It lay, at the end of June, between Lida and Grodno.

The 5th Corps, composed of the 2nd division of grenadiers, of the 12th, 18th and 26th divisions of infantry, and two divisions of cavalry, was, on the 30th, at Wolkowysk.Prince Bagration commanded this corps, which could probably amount to 40,000 men.

Lastly, the 9th and 15th divisions of infantry and a division of cavalry, commanded by General Markov, were at the extremity of Volhynia.

The crossing of the Vilia, which took place on 25 June, and the movement of the Duke of Reggio on Janów and towards Chatoui, obliged the corps of Wittgenstein to proceed towards Wilkomir and on its left; and this corps of Bagavout to make for Dvinsk by Mouchnicki and Gedroitse. These two corps were thus cut off from Vilna.

The 3rd and 4th Corps and Russian Imperial Guards retired from Vilna upon Niemenczin, Swentsiany and Widzeme. The King of Naples pressed them vigorously along the two banks of the Vilia. The 10th Regiment of Polish Hussars, which was at the head of the column of the division of Count Sebastiani, came up near Lébowo, with a regiment of Cossacks of the Guard which covered retreat of the rearguard, and charged at full gallop, killed nine and took about a dozen prisoners. The Polish troops, which up to this moment have engaged in a charge, have shown rare resolution. They are animated by enthusiasm and passion.

On 3 July, the King of Naples marched upon Swentsiany, and there he reached Baron de Tolly's rearguard. He gave orders to General Montbrun to charge; but the Russians did not wait for the attack, and retired with such precipitation that a squadron of Uhlans, which was returning from a reconnaissance on the side of Mikaïlitki, fell in with our outposts. It was charged by the 12th Chasseurs, and all were either taken or slain. Sixty men were taken with their horses. The Poles who are among these prisoners have applied to serve, and have joined rank, fully mounted, into the Polish troops.

At daybreak on the 4th, the King of Naples entered Swentsiany, the Marshal Duke of Elchingen entered Maliatoui and Marshal Duke of Reggio, at Avanta.

On 30 June, Marshal Duke of Tarentum arrived at Rosiena; he proceeded beyond that to Ponevieji, Chawli, and Tesch.

The immense magazines that the Russians had in Samogitia have been burned by themselves, which has occasioned an enormous loss not only to their finances but still more to the subsistence of the people.

The corps of Docturov, in other words the 6th Corps, was, however, without any orders until 27 June and had made no movement. On the 28th it assembled, and put itself in motion in order to proceed to the Dvina by marching on its flank. On the 30th, its advanced guard entered Soleinicki. It was charged by the light cavalry of General Baron Bordesoulle, and driven out of the village. Docturov, perceiving that he was anticipated, turned to the right and made for Oschmiana. General Baron Pajol arrived at that place with his light cavalry at the moment when Docturov's vanguard entered it. General Pajol charged. The enemy was sabred and overthrown in the town; it lost 60 men killed and 18 prisoners. General Pajol had 5 men killed, and a few wounded. This charge was made by the 9th Regiment of Polish Lancers.

General Docturov, seeing his route intercepted, fell back on Oschmiana. Marshal the Prince of Eckmühl, with a division of infantry, the cuirassiers of the division of Count Valence and the 2nd Regiment of Light Cavalry of the Guard, moved upon Oschmiana, in order to support General Pajol.

The corps of Docturov, thus cut off and driven towards the south, continued to prosecute the movement on the right by forced marches, with the sacrifice of its baggage, on Smorgoni, Donowcheff and Kobouïluicki, from where he made for the Dvina. This movement had been foreseen. General Nansouty, with a division of cuirassiers, the division of light cavalry of Count Bruyères and Count Morand's division of infantry, advanced to Mikaïlitchki with a view to cut off this corps. He arrived on the 3rd at Swir, at the time when it passed that place, and pushed it briskly. He took a large number of stragglers and obliged the enemy to abandon some hundreds of baggage carts.

The uncertainty, the anxiety, the marches and counter-marches that these troops had endured, the fatigues that they had undergone, must have made them suffer severely.

Torrents of rain fell for 36 hours without interruption.

The weather has suddenly changed from extreme heat to very severe cold. Several thousands of horses have perished by the effects of this sudden transition. Convoys of artillery have been stopped by the mud.

This terrible storm, which has fatigued both men and beasts, has unavoidably retarded our march; and the corps of Docturov, which successively fell in with the columns of General Bordessoulle, General Pajol and General Nansouty, has narrowly escaped destruction.

Prince Bagration, with the 5th Corps stationed further in the rear, marches towards the Dvina. He set out, on 30 June, from Wolkowysk to Minsk.

The King of Westphalia entered Grodno the same day. The Dombrowski division entered it first. The Hetman Platov was still at Grodno with his Cossacks. When charged by the light cavalry of Prince Poniatowski, the Cossacks were dispersed in every direction. Twenty were killed and 60 made prisoner. A bakery capable of baking 100,000 rations of bread, and some remains of the magazine were found at Grodno.

It has been foreseen that Bagration would fall back upon the Dvina by drawing as near as possible to Dvinsk; and General of Division Count Grouchy has been sent to Bogdanov. He was at Traboni on the 3rd. Marshal the Prince of Eckmühl, reinforced by two divisions, was at Wichnew on the 4th. If Prince Poniatowski has vigorously pressed the rearguard of the corps of Bagration, that corps will be compromised.

All the enemy's corps are in a state of the greatest uncertainty. The Hetman Platov was still ignorant on 30 June that Vilna had been two days in the possession of the French. He took a direction towards that city, as far Lida, where he changed his route and moved towards the South.

The sun, during all of the 4th, re-established the roads. Everything is now organizing at Vilna. The suburbs have suffered by the vast crowds of people that rushed into them during the duration of the tempest. There was a Russian army store there for 60,000 rations. Another has been established for an equal number of rations. Magazines are forming. The head of the convoys arrives at Kovno by the Niemen. Twenty thousand quintals of flour and a million rations of biscuit have just arrived here from Danzig.

Sixth Bulletin

Vilna, 11 July 1812

The King of Naples continued to follow the enemy's rearguard. On the 5th, he met the enemy's cavalry in a position upon the Dvina. He caused it to be charged by the brigade of light cavalry commanded by General Baron Subervie. The Prussian regiments, the Württembergers and Poles that form a part of this brigade charged with the greatest intrepidity. They overturned a line of Russian dragoons and hussars, and took 200 prisoner, with their horses. When they arrived beyond the Dvina, they broke down the bridges and showed a disposition to defend the crossing of the river. General Count Montbrun then brought up his five batteries of light artillery, which for several hours carried destruction into the ranks of the enemy. The loss of the Russians has been considerable.

General Count Sebastiani arrived on the same day at Vidzoni, whence the Emperor of Russia had departed on the preceding evening.

Our advanced guard is upon the Dvina.

General Count Nansouty was at Postavoui on 5 July. In order to cross the Dvina, he proceeded six miles farther on the right of the King of Naples. General of Brigade Roussel, with the 9th Regiment of Polish Light Cavalry and the 2nd Regiment of Prussian Hussars, crossed the river, overthrew six Russian squadrons, sabred a great number, and took 45 prisoner, with several officers. General Nansouty praises the conduct of General Roussel, and mentions with commendation Lieutenant Borke of the 2nd Regiment of Prussian Hussars, the NCO Kranse and the hussar Lutze. His Majesty has granted the insignia of the Legion of Honour to General Roussel and to the officers and NCOs named above.

General Nansouty took 130 Russian mounted hussars and dragoons prisoner.

On 3 July, communication was opened between Grodno and Vilna, by Lida. The Hetman Platov, with 6,000 Cossacks, when driven out of Grodno, moved towards Lida, and found there the French advanced posts. He descended to Ivié on the 5th.

General Count Grouchy occupied Witchnew, Traboui and Soubotnicki. General Baron Pajol was at Perchaï; General Baron Bordesoulle was at Blakechtoni; Marshal the Prince of Eckmühl was in advance of Bobrowitski, pushing heads of columns in every direction.

Platov retreated precipitately, on the 6th, to Nicolaew.

Prince Bagration, having set out in the beginning of July from Wolkowysk on his route for Vilna, was intercepted in his march. He returned back with a view to reach Minsk: anticipated there by the Prince of Eckmühl, he altered his direction, gave up his intention of proceeding towards the Dvina and moved towards the Borysthenes, by Bobrwitski, across the marshes of the Beresina.

Marshal the Prince of Eckmühl entered Minsk on the 8th. He found there considerable magazines of flour, hay, clothing, etc. Bagration had already arrived at Novi-Sworgiew; perceiving that he was anticipated, he sent orders to burn the magazines, but the Prince of Eckmühl did not give time for effecting these orders.

The King of Westphalia was on the 9th at Novogrudok; General Reynier at Slonim: stores, baggage-wagons, quantities of medicines and straggling parties fall into our hands every instant. The Russian divisions are straying in these countries without any previously arranged route, pursued on every side, losing their baggage, burning their magazines, destroying their artillery and leaving their places without defence.

General Baron Colbert took at Vileika a store of 3,000 quintals of flour, 100,000 rations of biscuit, etc. He found also at Vileika a chest containing 20,000 francs in copper money.

All these advantages have scarcely cost the French army a man. Since the opening of the campaign, there have been but about 30 killed in all the corps, about 100 wounded and 10 prisoners, while we have already taken from 2,000 to 2,500 Russians prisoner.

Prince Schwarzenberg crossed the Bug at Droghitschin, pursued the enemy in its different directions, and took many baggage-carts. Prince Schwarzenberg praises the reception he has met with from the inhabitants and the spirit of patriotism that animates these countries.

Thus, ten days after the opening of the campaign, our advanced posts are on the Dvina. Almost all of Lithuania, containing four million inhabitants, is conquered. The movements of war commenced at the crossing of the Vistula. The projects of the Emperor were from that time plainly unfolded, and he had no time to lose in carrying them into execution. Thus, the army has been making vigorous marches from the period of crossing that river, in order to advance by means of manoeuvres on the Dvina; for the distance between the Vistula and the Dvina is greater than that between the Dvina and Moscow or Petersburg.

The Russians appear to be concentrating themselves upon Dvinsk; they give out that it is their intention to wait for us and to give us battle before we enter their ancient provinces, after having abandoned Poland without a contest, as if they were constrained by justice and wished to restore a country badly acquired, inasmuch as it was not gained by treaties or by the right of conquest.

The heat continues to be very violent.

The people of Poland are excited on all sides. The White Eagle is hoisted everywhere. Priests, nobles, peasants, women; all call for the independence of their nation. The peasants are extremely jealous of the happiness of the peasants of the Grand Duchy, who are free; for whatever may be said to the contrary, liberty is considered by the Lithuanians as the greatest blessing. The peasants express themselves with a vivacity of elocution, which would not seem to belong to the climates of the north; and all embrace with transport the hope that the result of the struggle will be the re-establishment of their liberty: the peasants of the Grand Duchy gained by having liberty, not that they are richer, but that the proprietors are obliged to be moderate, just, and humane; because otherwise the peasants would leave their lands in order to seek better proprietors. Thus the noble loses nothing; he is only obliged to be just, and the peasant gains much. It must have been an agreeable gratification for the heart of the Emperor to witness, in crossing the Grand Duchy, the transports of joy and gratitude which the blessing of liberty granted to four million men, has excited.

Six regiments of infantry are just ordered to be raised by a new levy in Lithuania; and four regiments of cavalry have been offered by the nobility.

Seventh Bulletin

Vilna, 16 July 1812

His Majesty has had an entrenched camp erected on the right bank of the Vilia, surrounded by redoubts, and had a citadel constructed on the mountain on which was the ancient palace of the Jagellons. Thus, two bridges on piles are being constructed. Three bridges on rafts are already established on this river.

On the 8th, His Majesty reviewed a part of his Guard, composed of Laborde's and Roguet's divisions commanded by Marshal Duke of Treviso, and the Old

Guard under the orders of Marshal Duke of Danzig, in front of the entrenched camp. The fine appearance of these troops excited general admiration.

On the 4th, Marshal Duke of Tarentum set out from his headquarters in Rosiena, the capital of Samogitia, one of the finest and most fertile provinces in Poland; General of Brigade Baron Ricard, with a part of the 7th division, set out to march on Poniewiez; the Prussian General Kleist with a Prussian brigade had been sent upon Chawli; and the Prussian Brigadier Jeannerel, with another Prussian brigade, upon Telch. These three commanders have arrived at their destinations. General Kleist was only able to reach a single Russian hussar, the enemy having hastily evacuated Chawli after setting the magazines on fire.

General Ricard arrived at Poniewiez early on the morning of the 6th. He had the good fortune to save the magazines which were in it and which contained 30,000 quintals of flour. He took 160 prisoners, among whom were four officers. This small expedition does the greatest honour to the detachment of Prussian Hussars of Death who were charged with its execution. His Majesty has bestowed the Legion of Honour on the its Commandant, on Lieutenant Raven, NCOs Werner and Pormmereit, and Brigadier Grabowski, who distinguished themselves in this affair.

The inhabitants of the province of Samogitia are distinguished for their patriotism; they were free, their country was rich, but their destinies changed with the fall of Poland. The better and finest parts of the country were given by Catherine to Soubow:the peasants, free as they were, were compelled to become slaves. The flank movement made by the army upon Vilna having turned this fine province, which remained intact and will be of the utmost utility to the army. Two thousand horses are on their march to repair the losses of the artillery. Considerable magazines have been preserved. The march of the army from Kovno upon Vilna, and from Vilna upon Dvinsk and Minsk, had obliged the enemy to abandon the banks of the Niemen and rendered that river free, by which numerous convoys arrive at Kovno. We have at this moment more than 150,000 quintals of meal, 2,000,000 rations of biscuit, 6000 quintals of rice, a great quantity of brandy, 6000,000 bushels of oars, etc. The convoys succeed each other with rapidity; the Niemen is covered with boats.

The crossing of the Niemen took place on the 24th, and the Emperor entered Vilna on the 28th. The 1st Army of the West, commanded by the Emperor Alexander, is composed of nine divisions of infantry, and four of cavalry: driven from post to post, it now occupies the entrenched camp at Drissa, which holds the King of Naples, with the corps of Marshals the Dukes of Elchingen and Reggio, several divisions of the 1st Corps and cavalry of the Counts Nansouty and Montbrun. The 2nd Army, commanded by Prince Bagration, was on 1 July at Kobrin, where it had collected. The 9th and 15th divisions, under General Tormasov, were still farther off. On the first intelligence of the crossing of the Niemen, Bagration put himself in motion to march upon Vilna; he effected his junction with Platov's Cossacks, who were opposite Grodno. Arrived on the Ivié, he learned that the road to Vilna was shut against him. He discovered that the execution of the orders he had received would be rash, and cause his ruin, Soubotnioki, Troboui, Witchnew, Volojiuk, being occupied by General Grouchy, General Baron Pajol and the Prince of Eckmühl's corps; he therefore withdrew and took the direction of Minsk: but arriving midway towards that town, he learned that the Prince of Eckmühl had entered it. He again withdrew. From Newji he marched upon Slousk, and from there upon Bobruisk, from where he will have no other resource than that of passing the Borysthenes. Thus the two armies are completely cut off and separated, there being between them the distance of 100 leagues.

The Prince of Eckmühl has seized upon the strong fortress of Borisov, upon the Beresina. Sixty thousand pounds of powder, 16 pieces of siege artillery and some hospitals have fallen into his power. Considerable magazines were set on fire; a part was, however, saved.

On the 10th, General Latour-Maubourg sent the division of light cavalry commanded by Roznicki in advance towards Mir. It met the enemy's rearguard at a short distance from the town. A very brisk engagement took place. Notwithstanding the inferiority of the Polish division in number, it remained master of the field. General of Cossacks Grigoriev was killed, and 1,500 Russians were killed or wounded. Our loss, at the most, was not more than 500. The Polish light cavalry fought with the greatest intrepidity, and its courage supplied the want of number. The same day we entered Mir.

On the 13th the King of Westphalia had his headquarters at Nesvy.

The Viceroy has arrived at Dockchitsoui.

The Bavarians, commanded by General Count Gouvion Saint-Cyr, were reviewed by the Emperor on the 14th, at Vilna. Deroy's and Wrede's divisions were very fine. These troops have started their march on Sloubokö.

The Diet at Warsaw, being constituted into a general Confederation of Poland, has named Prince Adam Czartoryski its President. This Prince, aged 80 years, was 50 years ago Marshal of the Diet of Poland. The first act of the Diet was to declare the Kingdom of Poland re-established.

A deputation from the Confederation was presented to His Majesty at Vilna, and submitted to his approbation and protection the Act of Confederation.

Eighth Bulletin

Glubokoïë, 22 July 1812

The corps of the Prince Bagration is composed of four divisions of infantry, from 22,000 to 24,000 men, of Platov's Cossacks, forming 6,000 horse, and 4,000 or 5,000 cavalry. Two divisions of his corps (the 9th and 15th) wished to rejoin him by Pinsk; they were intercepted, and obliged to return in Volhynia.

On the 14th, General Latour-Maubourg, who followed the rearguard of Bagration, was at Romanov. On the 16th, Prince Poniatowski had his headquarters there.

In the affair of the 10th, which took place at Romanov, General Roznicki, commanding the light cavalry of the 4th Cavalry Corps, lost 600 men, killed, wounded or prisoners. We have no superior officers to regret. General Roznicki states that the bodies of Count Pahlen, General of Division, and of the Russian Colonels Adronov and Jesowayski, have been recognized on the battlefield.

Prince Schwarzenberg had his headquarters at Prazana on the 13th. On the 11th and 12th he occupied the important position of Pinsk, with a detachment, which took some men and considerable magazines. Twelve Austrian Uhlans charged 46 Cossacks, pursued them for several leagues and took six of them. Prince Schwarzenberg marches on Minsk.

General Reynier returned, on the 19th, to Slonim, to guarantee the Duchy of Warsaw from an incursion and to observe the two divisions of the enemy that had re-entered Volhynia.

On the 12th, General Baron Pajol, who was at Jghoumen, sent Captain Vandois with 50 cavalry to Khaloui. This detachment took there a park of 200 carriages belonging to Bagration's corps, and made prisoner 6 officers, 200 gunners, 300 men attached to the train and 800 fine artillery horses. Captain Vandois, finding himself 15 leagues distant from the army, did not think it practicable to carry off this convoy, and burnt it. He has brought with him the horses and the prisoners.

On the 15th, the Prince of Eckmühl was at Jghoumen. General Pajol was at Jachitsié, having posts on Swisloch. On learning this, Bagration renounced the idea of marching to Bobruisk, and proceeded 15 leagues lower down, on the side of Mozier.

On the 17th, the Prince of Eckmühl was at Golognino.

On the 15th, General Grouchy was at Borisov. A party that he sent on Star Lepel took considerable magazines and two companies of miners of eight officers and 200 men.

On the 18th, this general was at Kokanoff. On the same day, at two in the morning, General Baron Colbert entered Orcha, where he too possession of immense stores of flour, oats and clothing. He afterwards passed the Borysthenes, and proceeded in pursuit of a convoy of artillery.

Smolensk is in alarm. Everything is being evacuated to Moscow. An officer sent by the Emperor Alexander to cause the evacuation of the magazines at Orcha was quite astonished to find the place in the possession of the French. This officer was taken with his dispatches.

While Bagration was briskly pursued in his retreat, anticipated, separated, and removed from the main army, that army, commanded by the Emperor Alexander, retreated on the Dvina. On the 14th, General Sebastiani, following the enemy's rearguard, cut down 500 Cossacks and arrived at Drounïa.

On the 13th, the Duke of Reggio advanced upon Dvinsk, burnt the fine barracks which the enemy had constructed there, took a plan of the works, burnt some magazines and took 150 prisoners. After this diversion on the right, he moved on Drounïa.

On the 15th, the enemy, which was reunited from its entrenched camp of Drissa, to the number of from 100,000 to 120,000 men, being informed that our light cavalry did not keep a strict watch, threw over a bridge, sent across 5,000 infantry and 5,000 cavalry, attacked General Sebastiani unexpectedly, drove him back one league, and caused him a loss of 100 killed, wounded and prisoners, among whom were a captain and a sublieutenant of the 11th Chasseurs. General of Brigade Saint-Genies, who was mortally wounded, remained in the power of the enemy.

On the 16th, Marshal Duke of Treviso, with a part of the Foot Guard, and the Horse Guard, and the Bavarian light cavalry, arrived at Glubokoïë. The Viceroy arrived at Dockchistioui on the 17th.

On the 18th, the Emperor removed his headquarters to Glubokoïë.

On the 20th, the Marshals Dukes of Istria and Treviso were at Ouchatch, the Viceroy at Kamen, and the King of Naples at Disna.

On the 18th, the Russian army evacuated their entrenched camp of Drissa, defended by twelve palisaded redoubts united by a covered way and extending 3,000 *toises* on the river. These works cost a year of labour; we have levelled them.

The immense magazines they contained were either burnt or thrown into the water.

On the 19th, the Emperor Alexander was at Vitebsk [Vitsyebsk].

On the same day, General Count Nansouty was opposite Polotsk.

On the 20th, the King of Naples crossed the Dvina, and covered the right bank of the river with his cavalry. All the preparations the enemy had made to defend the passage of the Dvina have been useless. The magazines it had been forming at a great expense for these three years past have been entirely destroyed; the same has happened to its works, which, according to the reports of the people of the country, have cost the Russians in one year not less than 6,000 men. One can hardly guess on what ground they flattered themselves that they would be attacked in the encampments that they had entrenched.

General Count Grouchy has reconnoitred Babinowiczii and Sienno. On all sides we are marching on the Oula; this river is joined by a canal to the Beresina, which runs into the Borysthenes. Thus we are masters of the communication from the Baltic to the Black Sea.

In its movements the enemy has been obliged to destroy its baggage and to throw its artillery and arms into the rivers. All the Poles of his army avail themselves of his precipitate retreat to desert and await in the woods the arrival of the French. The number of Poles who have deserted the Russian army may be calculated to amount to at least 20,000 men.

Marshal Duke of Belluno, with the 9th Corps, is advancing upon the Vistula.

Marshal Duke of Castiglione has set out for Berlin to take the command of the 11th Corps.

The country between the Oula and the Dvina is very beautiful and in the highest state of cultivation. We often meet with beautiful *châteaux* and large convents. In the town of Glubokoië alone there are two convents, each of which may contain 1,200 sick.

Report of Marshal Duke of Tarentum to the Prince Major-General [Alexander Berthier]

Jacobstadt. 22 July 1812
My Lord,
I received at this instant (five in the evening) the report of General Grawert regarding the engagement that took place on the 19th at Ekau.

As soon as he arrived at Bauska, he replaced General Ricard, and while his infantry crossed the Aa he detached Colonel Roeder, aide-de-camp of the King and his chief of staff, with a detachment of 60 horses to reconnoitre the terrain. He met the enemy posts at about three leagues from Bauska, pushed them back easily, but soon perceived by their countenance that they had forces behind them. He sent word of this to General Grawert and at the same time requested two squadrons and half a battery of mounted artillery; but before they arrived, the enemy, which from a height had become convinced of the weakness of the detachment of Colonel Roeder, fell upon him. He valiantly defended himself so as not to lose the advantageous position he occupied. This inequitable combat kept becoming more brisk and very critical, when Major Stiern of the 1st Regiment of Dragoons arrived. This brave officer charged the enemy's cavalry with vigour, overthrew it completely, and pursued it into the wood, where he was stopped by the infantry fire.

The enemy lost in this charge a lot of men who can no longer fight, one officer and 20 men prisoners. The Prussian cavalry had one man killed and 20 wounded, among them three officers, particularly Captain Count Brandenburg, who received a lance in his chest, and two officers of the 1st Regiment of Dragoons, who, after getting their wounds bandaged, returned to the regiment and were fighting in the action of the evening. We hope that Count Brandenburg's wound is not dangerous (he is the natural brother of the King). According to the report of Colonel Roeder, Major Stiern and Count Brandenburg distinguished themselves.

The prisoners taken in this collision of cavalry have unanimously declared that, the day before, considerable reinforcements had arrived at Ekau, on which the enemy was advancing with one detachment of four battalions, a few squadrons of Uhlans, a *poulk* of Cossacks and several guns to retake Bauska, and also there was a concentration of very superior forces at Ekau, with 10 guns in battery.

Colonel Roeder remained on the terrain from which he had chased the enemy, and the latter placed himself at 2,000 steps opposite.

General Grawert having learned of this, took the resolution to send an order to General Kleist, whom in a first disposition I had sent to Kanken and to Drakin, on the great road of Herbergen to Riga, to proceed by the right bank of the Ekau to take the enemy in flank and in the back, while he prepared to attack it in front.

General Grawert marched on Ekau, and had repulsed by the cavalry and skirmishers on the right banks of this river what was still on the left, and waited in an advantageous position the arrival of General Kleist; as soon as he became aware of this by the first cannon shots, he approached the enemy, crossed the defile with the cavalry, artillery and the skirmishers, and sustained this attack by part of his infantry, while the other part advanced to guard the defile.

General Kleist was vigorously attacking on his side, leaning his left at the Ekau. The combat was lengthy and deadly, the Russians were defending their positions foot by foot; even a detachment which was entirely cut off fought until the last moment.

However, the bravery of the Prussian troops, even though their numbers were inferior, and the good conduct of the chiefs and the officers, triumphed over the Russians; they were forced on all points at eight thirty in the evening, and put to flight.

The result of the day is one flag taken, several hundred prisoners, among them some superior officers and others. The enemy has lost a considerable number of killed and wounded. The loss of the Prussians is important; among the killed are two very brave officers: Captain Esbeck of the 1st Dragoons, who had already distinguished himself that morning in the combat of cavalry under Colonel Roeder, and who charged with the greatest vigour the infantry on the night he was killed; Lieutenant Wallis of the 2nd Battalion of Fusiliers, who commanded the skirmishers and took them with impetuosity to the enemy. He fell dead on the field of glory.

General Grawert had not yet received the particular reports at the time his report left. He proposes to write one in more detail that will reveal the actions and the losses. The charges of the Prussian cavalry on the Russian infantry contributed much to the losses of this latter. None missed.

A long march and one combat in one day had exhausted this cavalry, and it was able to follow its advantages for only one mile.

General Grawert supposes that the enemy will once again take position between Edau and Riga, from where he plans on chasing him easier, because the action of the 19th has discouraged the Russians very much, while our troops are full of assurance. However, if it is true, as he has heard from several places, that the enemy is still waiting for some reinforcements, part of which arrived during the combat, he cannot be entirely sure to gain some ground, but he will do what he can.

It is General Lewis who is at the command of the Russian corps.

General Grawert tells me that it will be difficult for him to name the officers who distinguished themselves, because all, with out exception, were animated with the same bravery and desire to reach the enemy. As soon as he will have a moment, he will send me a more circumstantial report. He restrains himself to naming only General Kleist, who has so perfectly manoeuvred and charged the enemy with such vigour that he avows owing him the success of this day.

I still do not know if the detachment that proceeded to Mittau has arrived there.

General Grawert adds that if the day of the 19th has been so happy for the Emperor and the Prussian armies, it is to the activity and good dispositions of Colonel Roeder, his chief of staff, that he owes part of it. It is with as much circumspection as intrepidity that he directed the charges on the enemy, and animated the troops by his example.

I pray Your Highness to inform His Majesty the Emperor of the excellent qualities of this distinguished officer, on all counts, and to recommend him to His Grace. He is an officer full of merit.

General Grawert has the modesty to not name himself, nor to cite his officer or staff, although they all have distinguished themselves.

This glorious action, in this first start, promises some new advantages. I pray Your Highness to ask His Majesty for rewards, and that he give his approbation to the conduct of the Prussian corps.

Accept, My Lord, etc.

MARSHAL THE DUKE OF TARENTUM

Ninth Bulletin

Beschenkowitschi, 25 July 1812

The Emperor, taking the road of Ouchatch, established his headquarters at Kamen on the 23rd.

The Viceroy occupied, on the 22nd, with his advanced guard, the bridge of Botscheikovo. A reconnaissance of 260 horses, detached on Beschenkowitschi, came upon two squadrons of Russian hussars and two of Cossacks, charged them, and took or killed a dozen men, of whom one was an officer. Squadron Chief Lorenzi who was in command praises the conduct of Captains Rossi and Ferreri.

On the 23rd, at six o'clock in the morning, the Viceroy arrived at Beschenkowitschi. At ten he crossed the river and threw a bridge over the Dvina. The enemy was inclined to dispute the crossing, but its artillery was dismounted. Colonel Lacroix, aide-de-camp of the Viceroy, had his thigh broken by a ball.

The Emperor arrived at Beschenkowitschi on the 24th, at two o'clock in the afternoon. The division of cavalry of General Count Bruyères and the division of General Count Saint-Germain were sent on the route to Vitebsk. They rested when they had performed half their march.

On the 20th, the Prince of Eckmühl advanced upon Mohilev. The garrison of this town, which consisted of 2,000 men, had the temerity to wish to defend it; but they were sabred by the light cavalry. On the 21st, 3,000 Cossacks assailed the advanced posts of the prince of Eckmühl; they were the advanced guard of Prince Bagration, arrived from Bobruisk. A battalion of the 85th arrested this cloud of light cavalry and drove it back to a considerable distance. Bagration appears to have availed himself of the little activity with which he was pursued to advance on Bobruisk; and there he returned against Mohilev.

We occupy Mohilev, Orsha, Disna and Polotsk. We are marching on Vitebsk, where it appears the Russian army is concentrated.

Tenth Bulletin

Vitebsk, 31 July 1812

The Emperor of Russia and the Grand Duke Constantine have left the army and repaired to the capital. On the 17th, the Russian army left the entrenched camp of Drissa and marched towards Polotsk and Vitebsk. The Russian army that was at Drissa consisted of five army corps, each of two divisions, and of four divisions of cavalry. One army corps, that of Prince Wittgenstein, remained for the purpose of covering Saint Petersburg; the four other corps, having arrived on the 24th at Vitebsk, crossed to the left bank of the Dvina. The corps of Ostermann, with a part of the cavalry of the Guard, put itself in motion at daybreak on the 25th and marched on Ostrovno.

Battle of Ostrovno

On 25 July, General Nansouty, with the Bruyères and Saint-Germain divisions and the 8th Regiment of Light Infantry, encountered the enemy two leagues in advance of Ostrovno. The combat was engaged. Several charges of cavalry took place; all of them were in favour of the French. The light cavalry covered itself with glory. The King of Naples mentions the Piré brigade, composed of the 8th Hussars, and 16th Chasseurs, as having distinguished itself. The Russian cavalry, of which a part belonged to the Guard, was overthrown. The batteries that the enemy opened upon our cavalry were carried. The Russian infantry, who advanced to support their artillery, were broken and sabred by our light cavalry.

On the 26th, the Viceroy was marching with the Delzons division at the head of the columns; an obstinate action of the advanced guard, of from 15- to 20,000 men, took place a league beyond Ostrovno. The Russians were driven from their positions one after another. The woods were carried by the bayonet.

The King of Naples and the Viceroy mention with praise Generals Baron Delzons, Huard and Roussel. The 8th Light Infantry, the 84th and 92nd Regiments of Line, and the 1st Regiment of Croats, were distinguished.

General Roussel, a brave soldier, after being the whole day at the head of the battalions, was visiting the advanced posts at ten at night when a sentinel took him for an enemy, fired upon him, and the ball shattered his skull. He ought to have died three hours sooner, on the battlefield, by the hands of the enemy.

At daybreak on the 27th, the Viceroy made the Broussier division file off in advance. The 18th Regiment of Light Infantry, and the brigade of light cavalry of the Baron Piré, wheeled to the right. The Broussier division marched by the great road and repaired a small bridge that the enemy had destroyed. At daybreak, the enemy's rearguard, consisting of 10,000 cavalry was perceived drawn up in echelon on the plain, its right resting on the Dvina, and its left on a wood lined with infantry and artillery. General Count Broussier took position on an eminence with the 53rd Regiment, waiting until all of his division had passed the defile. Two companies of voltigeurs had marched in advance, alone; they skirted the bank of the river, advancing towards that enormous mass of cavalry, which made a forward movement and surrounded these 200 men, who were thought to be lost, and who ought to have been so. It happened otherwise. They concentrated themselves with the greatest coolness, and remained hemmed in on all sides for the whole hour; having brought down more than 300 horsemen of the enemy, these two companies gave the French cavalry time to arrive.

The Delzons division defiled on the right. The King of Naples directed the wood and the enemy's batteries to be attacked. In less than an hour all the positions of the enemy were carried, and it was driven across the plain beyond a

261

small river that enters the Dvina below Vitebsk. The army took a position on the banks of this river, at the distance of a league from the town.

The enemy displayed 15,000 cavalry and 60,000 infantry in the plain. A battle was expected next day. The Russians boasted that they wished to give battle. The Emperor spent the remainder of the day in reconnoitring the field and in making his dispositions for the next day; but at daybreak the Russian army was retreating in all directions towards Smolensk.

The Emperor was on a height very near the 200 voltigeurs who alone on the plain had attacked the right of the enemy's cavalry. Struck by their fine conduct, he sent to inquire what corps they belonged to. They answered, 'To the 9th; and three-fourths of us are lads of Paris.' 'Tell them,' said the Emperor, 'that they are brave fellows: they all deserve the cross!'

The results of the three actions of Ostrovno are 10 pieces of artillery of Russian manufacture taken, the cannoneers sabred; 20 caissons of ammunition; 1,500 prisoners; 5,000 or 6,000 Russians killed or wounded. Our loss amounted to 200 killed, 900 wounded and about 50 prisoners.

The King of Naples bestows particular praise on Generals Bruyères, Piré and Ornano, and on Colonel Radziwill, commandant of the 9th Polish Lancers, an officer of singular intrepidity.

The Red Hussars of the Russian Guard have been crushed. They lost 400 men, many of whom are prisoners. The Russians had three generals killed or wounded. A considerable number of colonels and superior officers of their army remained on the field of battle.

On the 28th at daybreak, we entered Vitebsk, a town of 30,000 inhabitants. It has 20 convents. We have found in it some magazines, particularly one of salt, valued at 15,000,000.

While the army was marching on Vitebsk, the Prince of Eckmühl was attacked at Mohilow.

Bagration crossed the Beresina at Bobruisk and marched upon Novoi Bickow. At daybreak on the 23rd, 3,000 Cossacks attacked the 3rd Regiment of Chasseurs and took 100 of them, among whom were the colonel and four officers, all wounded. The general beat [on the drums]; an action commenced. The Russian General Sicverse, with two élite divisions, began the attack. From eight in the morning until five in the afternoon, the firing was kept up on the edge of the wood, and at a bridge that the Russians wished to force. At five, the Prince of Eckmühl caused three élite battalions to advance, put himself at their head, overthrew the Russians, carried their positions and pursued them for a league. The loss of the Russians is estimated at 3,000 killed or wounded and 1,100 prisoners. We lost 700 killed and wounded. Bagration, repulsed, retired on Bickow, where he crossed the Borysthenes to advance towards Smolensk.

The battles of Mohilev and Ostrovno have been brilliant, and honourable to our army. We never have had engaged more than the half of the force which the enemy presented, the ground not being suitable for greater developments.

—◠—

Report of the Viceroy on the combats of 25, 26 and 27 July

I have the honour to address to Your Majesty the reports of the combats which took place on 25, 26 and 27 July, and to which the 4th Corps under my command took part.

Your Majesty had given the order to the King of Naples, who commands the army cavalry, to leave from Bechen-Kovisch and to proceed on the road of

Vitebsk. I received the order to put at his disposition the 8th Regiment of Light Infantry.

The King of Naples met the enemy before Ostrovno and engaged different charges of cavalry that obtained fine results. About 600 prisoners and 8 cannon were the trophies of that day. General of Division Delzons gives the account that the 8th had several engagements that he sustained with valour.

On the 26th, the King of Naples received the order to continue his movement on Vitebsk, and I received the order to march with a division to support the movement of the cavalry. I went before daylight to see the King of Naples and together we agreed on the time when the movement would start.

I gave the order to the 13th Division to follow the cavalry, to the 14th and the Guard to march behind the 13th Division, but by echelon, and at one hour of distance. The road traversed a wooded area and the 8th soon became engaged to open the road that the enemy disputed with some infantry. About ten o'clock in the morning, the 8th Regiment, after having chased all the sharpshooters of the enemy from the woods, met it formed and holding an advantageous position on a plateau of fine elevation, protected by numerous artillery, with a deep ravine in front and its left leaning on a forest so thick that it was impossible for a mass to penetrate it without breaking it up. It was the corps of General Ostermann, two infantry divisions strong, which occupied that position. Then I ordered General Delzons, who commanded the 15th Division, to form for the attack, with the Croat regiment and the 84th on the left of the road, the first deployed, the second in columns by division. A battalion of light infantry and the 92nd Regiment were placed in echelon by battalions on the right. The attack started; it was brisk and the enemy was approached with intrepidity. The Croats and the 84th folded up the battalions that were opposed to them. General Huard, who was in command of this attack, deployed in it as much valour as capacity. On the right, the light infantry and the 92nd experienced a much greater resistance; they had to penetrate the forest, debouch and form under fire from the enemy, who had placed its principal forces on his left. It was not without many efforts that General Roussel was able to take position at the entrance of the wood and chase the enemy from that position. The valour of the troops and obstinacy of the general in command were needed to succeed in an attack as difficult as this one.

Meanwhile, the centre and the left, who could not see the slow progress of the right, disputed in the forest, continued their successes. The enemy, who could see its left maintaining his position, sent its reserve on his right where it felt much more pressed. The Croats and the 84th were repulsed and outflanked.

The King of Naples, with his brilliant valour and the promptitude of lightning, made a vigorous charge of cavalry that stopped the enemy. Battalion Chief Ricard, with a company of carabiniers of the 8th, hastened to the head of the pieces: Battalion Chief Dumay and Captain Bonardelle, with a rare intrepidity, maintained great order in the artillery column; during this time, General Roussel debouched from the forest, charged the enemy with the 92nd in column, and made himself master of the position. The Croats and the 84th, supported by two battalions of the 106th Regiment held in reserve until that moment, recaptured their advantages. That is when all was re-established and we remained masters of the ground that the enemy had strongly disputed.

After a few moments of repose to rally the troops and re-form the columns, the enemy was once again pursued and promptly forced in all the positions it still wanted to defend. It was, in this manner, brought back to within two leagues of

Vitebsk, where the 13th Division took position around nine o'clock at night. The 14th was placed on the road, in second line, with the order to illuminate with some posts the banks of the Dvina. The Guard was also placed in the rear, on the right of the 13th division.

On the 27th, Your Majesty ordered the cavalry and the 4th Corps to continue the movement on Vitebsk. On that day, the 14th Division took the lead. General of Brigade Bertrand Sivray was detailed with the 18th of Light Infantry and three companies of voltigeurs. He seized a village occupied by the enemy on the right and followed the ridge of the heights of which he made himself the master. The rest of the division advanced, formed itself on the left of the road in presence of the enemy, established its artillery, silenced the one that opposed it, and forced the Russians to move their line back from the edges of the ravines they occupied, behind a burnt bridge.

General Broussier, making use of the retrograde movement of the enemy, crossed the river with his division, formed his regiments in a double square by echelon, under the protection of a lively fire from his artillery. The square of the 53rd was the closest. The enemy's cavalry tried several times to charge the squares, but the fire and the countenance of this regiment kept it back.

The first two companies of voltigeurs of the 9th Line who had crossed in the lead on the bridge, under the fire of the enemy, were directed with intelligence and bravery by Captains Guyard and Savary on the right flank of the enemy, and inflicted great losses upon it.

General Broussier praises all the regiments of his division. He particularly distinguishes the Battalion Chief Villemain, the 53rd, Captain Guyard of the 9th Line, and Lieutenant of Light Artillery Laguerinais, who received three hits with a lance while he defended the pieces that were under his command.

General Delzons cites as having particularly distinguished himself Colonel Serrant of the 8th Light, who was wounded; Battalion Chief of artillery Demay; Battalion Chief Richard of the 8th Light; Battalion Chief Livingston of the 92nd; Battalion Chief Chotard of the 84th; Captain Desjardins of the 8th Light; and Artillery Captain Bonardelle.

I present to Your Majesty the statement of the losses suffered by the 13th and 14th Divisions in these different engagements. One loss, which is badly felt, is that of General Roussel, who was killed at eleven o'clock at night, just as Your Majesty had visited the advanced posts. He was mistaken for the enemy.

I request from Your Majesty the blessings in favour of the officers and soldiers who behaved in the best way, and also the favour of the widow and children of General Roussel.

I am with the most profound respect, Sire, of Your Majesty,

The very devoted, the most tender and loyal subject,

EUGÈNE NAPOLEON

Report of Marshal Duke of Reggio to the Prince Major-General
Biada, 31 July 1812 at eleven o'clock at night
My Lord,

I have the honour to inform Your Most Serene Highness that on the 28th of this month I sent the troops of the army corps marching on Sebeji. The 5th Brigade of light cavalry and one battalion took position the same day at the ford of Sivochino, where I had a bridge established. The 1st and 2nd Divisions of infantry camped between Biala and Sipochina; the 3rd Division of infantry left from Disna and took position at Lozowka. The 6th Brigade of light cavalry, which was charged with covering the march of this division, was attacked towards evening by 14- to 1,500 horses, hussars of Grodno or Cossacks, who had crossed the Drissa at the ford of Valentsoui. The 8th Regiment of light cavalry, who took this attack almost alone, suffered a loss of nearly 80 horses, although they fought with a lot of courage. This brigade, harassed in its march, did not arrive at its position until eleven o'clock at night; on the other side, on the road of Sebeji, the 5th Brigade of light cavalry met two squadrons of the dragoons of Riga, which General Castex ordered to charge and from which we took a few prisoners.

It was learned from the reports and reconnaissance which took place on all the debouches during the day of the 29th that General Koulnieff occupied Valentsoui with 4,000 infantrymen, the regiment of hussars of Grodno, two regiments of Cossacks of 500 horse each, 6 pieces of artillery on horses and twelve pieces of artillery on foot, and that Prince Wittgenstein, with whom Prince Repnine had just joined, occupied Kokonow and Osveia.

On the 30th in the morning, I started for Kliatsoui with the 5th Brigade of light cavalry and the 1st Division of infantry. The 2nd Division and the cuirassiers followed this movement and took position at Glovitchsoui and Sakotliso. I left the 3rd Division of infantry to guard the ford of Sivochina and gave it the 6th Division of light cavalry to observe the fords of Zarnowisé and of Valentsoui.

When I arrived at Kliatsitsoui, about eleven in the morning, I at once pushed a few light troops on Jakoubovo, where the road to Osveia and Koslonovo passes; these troops met an enemy patrol, which they repulsed. General Legrand took position at Jakoubovo with the 25th Light, 56th Line and the 24th of Chasseurs à Cheval. I gave him orders to send his reconnaissance on the Sevoiana. During this time, the 23rd Chasseurs à Cheval, which I had sent on the road of Sebeji, brought me a young Russian officer who had come from Serej to Kliatsitsoui, where General Wittgenstein had met him. Soon after, the grand guard of this regiment took an aide-de-camp of this general, who also came from Sebeji, and who carried a few insignificant papers and the state of the artillery situation only. Around four o'clock in the afternoon, I was informed that my reconnaissance had returned, and that the enemy was advancing in force on Jakoubovo. It debouched and the combat was engaged with the 26th Light who made the finest defence and whom the Russians were unable to remove from the village. The enemy tried particularly to threaten the flank of the line, making itself master of a great wood which stands on the left of the basin where the village of Jakoubovo is situated. General Legrand threw there the 56th Line, against which the Russians sent great forces without unsettling it. General Maison's brigade came to the post itself, in echelons, to support the first line. I could not put in battery more than twelve pieces of artillery, being in a position squeezed on one side by a thick wood, and the other by houses. The basin, on the contrary, opening up on the side of the enemy, he used more than three times the artillery and deployed considerable forces. However, the combat was sustained without the least disadvantage until ten o'clock at night. I asked to bring the division of General Verdier and had it placed in reserve; as for the cuirassiers, I kept them in the rear, as it was impossible to use them on the terrain.

I think that the object of the enemy being to proceed on Sebeji to cover the road to Petersburg, it would not be so obstinate as to debouch by Kliatsitsoui; but this morning, at barely daylight, it renewed its attack. After a prodigious artillery fire, it attacked the castle of Jakoubovo; it was already in the yard when the 26th Light came at it at a charge, killed 300 men with the bayonet, took 500 prisoners and pursued the enemy as far as the woods. After this affair was done, it appeared to me that the enemy was in such a good position that I could not attack it with great hope for success; in fact, I had a defile behind me and I resolved to manoeuvre to lure it towards me.

I am being told at this moment that the enemy is making efforts in an attempt to make itself the master of the ford of the Drissa. I am giving orders to Generals Albert and Castex, in charge of guarding it, not to defend it; if the enemy crosses it, it will be doing what I want.

I have the honour, etc.

MARSHAL DUKE OF REGGIO

Report of [Russian] Lieutenant-General Count Wittgenstein to His Majesty the Emperor [Tsar Alexander]

Oswec, 31 July (11 August) 1812

I have been informed by my advance posts that the enemy was making, from Polotsk, every effort to take them out, and by the deserters and the prisoners that the French *Grande Armée* was increasing with the Bavarian and Württemberger troops. At the same time, I received from the war minister the notice of the junction of the two armies and the order to take offensive action, attacking the enemy in flank as soon as possible. Consequently I detached four squadrons under the orders of Major Bedragui, who has been charged with observing all the movements of the army of Macdonald and to inform me of it. I proceeded at once on the corps of Oudinot, whom I met on the evening of the 29th at four versts from Kochanova. Having taken immediately all the necessary dispositions, I vigorously attacked him yesterday with God's help. After eight consecutive hours of combat, the enemy was routed and pursued until night by the brave troops of His Imperial Majesty.

We have taken prisoner three officers and 250 soldiers. The loss of the enemy has been considerable as much in killed as in wounded. Its cuirassiers have particularly suffered, having made all the efforts possible to become the masters of our battery. I had them pursued by the Grodno hussars, who particularly distinguished themselves in this occasion. We have lost 400 men, as many killed as wounded. We especially deplore the loss of the brave Colonel Denissen, Chief of the 25th Regiment of Chasseurs, who was killed by a cannonball.

I propose to pursue the enemy as far as the Dvina.

Biada, 1 August 1812 at ten o'clock at night

My Lord,

Last night at 11 o'clock, the enemy made an attack on the troops in charge of guarding the ford of Sivoehina. They pulled back as they had been ordered to do. The enemy spent the rest of the night debouching, since at daylight it was ready to attack us. We were expecting this. The fire was engaged by a swarm of skirmishers, followed by columns that were advancing at a charge and uttering great cries; but the fire from our artillery, which was perfectly placed and was well delivered, at first moderated their ardour and soon caused them to deploy. Meanwhile, we were forming our columns and the three divisions were placed in such a way that they could successively replace each other in each position: when everything was ready, I ordered a charge. At first, the Russians made a brisk resistance, but to no avail. They were routed in the wink of an eye and thrown in the Drissa, leaving in our hands 14 cannon, 13 caissons and more than 2,000 prisoners. We had them beat a retreat three-quarters of a league to the river; that ground is covered with their dead. I have seldom seen a battlefield offering the sight of such carnage.

The division of General Legrand had the greatest part in this action. I later ordered General Verdier to pursue the enemy, and he pushed him back three leagues from the battlefield, on the road of Sebej, and caused him an enormous loss.

The enemy, since the 30th, has lost 3,000 to 4,000 prisoners, there are at least 4,000 killed or wounded, and it has not taken from us any prisoners. The generals, the officers, the troops, all have shown very rare valour. The light cavalry under the orders of General Castex made several very well-timed and successful charges.

I will inform later on Your Highness of the generals, officers and others who particularly distinguished themselves and for whom I will solicit the kindness of the Emperor.

I have the honour to be, etc.

MARSHAL DUKE OF REGGIO

First report of the King of Naples to the Emperor

Mattuzzevo, 1 August 1812

I arrived from Polostk to Beschenkowitschi at night on the 24th, and I marched according to the instructions that were given to me on the night of the 25th to rejoin the 1st Corps of cavalry and push with it on Vitebsk: the Viceroy was to support me. General Count Nansouty departed from his headquarters at Boudiloua and I rejoined him as he was already engaged with the enemy on the height of Ostrovno and master of its first position and of eight pieces of artillery that had been taken from it by the advance guard of the Bruyères division. This success was the result of a cavalry charge executed by General Piré, with as much bravery as intelligence. Meanwhile, General Ostermann, who had arrived in the morning from Vitebsk with all his corps, had taken position at some 100 *toises* in the rear, and opposed some infantry. I had the Saint-Germain division rapidly advance; I had it form its lines by brigades and all its artillery was placed into position. Then I saw debouching from a wood, at 50 *toises*, a Russian regiment of dragoons, who came to form on the right flank of the foreign brigade with which I was at the time. Making a change of front on the right, charging him, overthrowing him and destroying him almost entirely was the affair of an instant. A second charge of the Piré brigade, headed by General Count Ornano, was taking place on the embankment; it was stopped by the fusillade of the infantry.

Informed by some prisoners that I was facing all of the corps of Ostermann, I ordered the Delzons and Broussier divisions to proceed on the line. I had the two battalions of the 8th Regiment of Light Infantry advance, which His Majesty had put at my disposition that morning, and placed them along a small wood that was on my left, to support my first brigade of cavalry, which the fire from the infantry would necessarily force to retreat. Seeing this movement, about three Russian battalions passed from their left on the front of my cavalry to go meet these two battalions. I had them charged; they were forced to withdraw with considerable losses. I wanted to maintain my position until the Delzons division arrived, but the enemy had put in motion by a wood that was on my right 10 or 12 battalions, and seemed to want to outflank my right, a manoeuvre that would force me to abandon my position. Two other battalions emerged by my left on a regiment of cuirassiers and on the 9th of Lancers. At almost the same time, these four battalions were charged and destroyed, those on my left by the 9th Lancers and those on my right by the foreign brigade. I have seldom seen cavalry charging infantry with more courage and success.

Meanwhile, the Delzons division arrived and I had it march along the Dvina in order to take a position that threatened the Russians. This one movement stopped that of the enemy on my right, which hastily recalled its battalions to the centre in order to protect its retreat, which it executed immediately.

The two battalions of the 8th Regiment of Light Infantry repulsed two or three charges of the enemy's infantry, and constantly covered the front of my line; the artillery did a lot of harm to the enemy; it fired 1,500 cannonballs at close range.

Here is, Sire, the exact account of the combat of Ostrovno, the results of which have been 8 pieces of artillery taken, 700 to 800 prisoners and at least 5,000 to 6,000 Russians as many killed as wounded. Your Majesty has had the opportunity to judge the enemy's losses when passing on the battlefield.

I made it known to your Majesty, in my letter written on the field, the brilliant conduct of the generals who directed these different charges. Your Majesty will find in more detail, in the attached reports, the names of the braves who have more particularly distinguished themselves. May Your Majesty permit me to solicit for them the rewards they so justly merit. I owe particular praises to General Count Belliard, who was present in all the charges and who was most helpful to me in the execution of the different movements for which I had to give orders. I must also name to Your Majesty all the individuals of my staff, and ask for them your kindness.

I have the honour to ask from Your Majesty a rank of lieutenant for Mr Berthier, NCO at the 16th Regiment of Mounted Chasseurs, who was in the charge made by General Ornano, and who was one of the first to arrive on the pieces. The superior officers have shown great esteem for him.

I am of Your Majesty, Sire, the very affectionate brother,

JOACHIM NAPOLEON

Second report from the King of Naples to the Emperor

Mattuzzevo, 2 August 1812 at five in the morning
Sire,
I received, in the night of 25 to 26 July, a dispatch from Your Majesty, according to which I was to make a strong reconnaissance on the enemy, with a lot of artillery and the Delzons division to support it. I put in movement all of the 1st Corps of cavalry reserve and the two battalions of the 8th Light Infantry; the Delzons division followed the movement. My advance guard met the enemy's rearguard at about two leagues from Ostrovno. It was in an advantageous post, behind an extremely cut up ravine; it had some infantry and artillery and was covered on its front and on its flanks by some very bushy woods. We exchanged a few cannon shots. The two battalions were sent to stop the infantry, which was already making the head cavalry retreat. Meanwhile, the Delzons division arrived. Here the role of the cavalry had to end. The Viceroy made his dispositions. We marched to the enemy; we passed the ravine. The brigade of foreign cavalry has crossed the Dvina, was protecting our left flank and debouched on the plain: the rest of the light division was marching on the embankment as quickly as the Viceroy was pushing back the enemy's infantry. The cuirassiers were kept in reserve behind the ravine, and their cannon were put in battery. My right was guaranteed by some

immense woods and reconnoitred by numerous detachments. The enemy was vigorously driven to its second position, in the rear of the ravine where its reserve was. It then drove us back on the ravine; it was pushed back a second time. For the second time it vigorously drove us back. I perceived some confusion. I ordered a cavalry charge against a column of infantry that was audaciously marching in the plain. The brave Poles thrust themselves on the Russian battalions; not one man escaped, not one was made prisoner; the last men were killed as far as the woods. Immediately a charge started in all the square battalions of the infantry of Your Majesty, and General Girardin, who headed the battalions of the left, received an order to make a charge to the right and to proceed on the large embankment on the rear of the enemy. All the battalions that were on his right executed the same manoeuvre, and General Piré, with the 8th Regiment of Hussars on the right, vigorously charged all of the enemy's left, whose salvation it found in the woods and ravines that slowed our march. All the division followed the movement on the embankment: the cavalry debouched on the heights, facing five or six regiments of cavalry, which I ordered to start a cannonade. It was in that position that Your Majesty found me, and from where he had me pursue the enemy, which was hustled along as far as a ravine about one-and-a-half leagues from Vitebsk.

Here is, Sire, the account of the affair of the 26th, in which, according to the report of all the prisoners and deserters, the enemy suffered even more losses than the day before. We can evaluate the number of dead at 2,500 to 3,000; he had a great quantity of wounded; Your Majesty lost almost nobody.

I must again cite to Your Majesty General Count Belliard, who on this day gave new proofs of devotion and courage. It is to him that we owe the conservation of a part of the artillery of the Delzons division.

Captain Ferrari of the 8th Regiment of Hussars had his leg taken off by a cannonball. I have the honour to cite to Your Majesty for their good conduct, General Ornano, of whom I spoke in my first report of the 25th for his brilliant conduct and who showed the same bravery on the 26th; General Girardin, Colonel Flahaut and Captain Lecouteux, all three aides-de-camp of the Prince of Neufchâtel, and the Adjutant-Commandant Borelli. I must also cite Battalion Chief — who commands the 8th Regiment of Light Infantry, who has earned in these two days merit for the kindness of Your Majesty.

All of my aides-de-camp conducted themselves with the accustomed bravery. My equerries Garaffa and Campomel did not leave my side for an instant during these two days. I will not speak to Your Majesty of the day of the 27th, as everything happened before his eyes; I did nothing but execute his orders.

I am of Your Majesty, Sire, the very affectionate brother,

JOACHIM NAPOLEON

Eleventh Bulletin

Vitebsk, 4 August 1812

Intercepted letters from the camp of Bagration speak of the losses sustained by the corps in the battle of Mohilev and of the number of desertions from which it has suffered on the route. Every Pole has remained in his own country, so that this corps, which, including the Cossacks of Platov, amounted to 50,000 men, is now reduced to less than 30,000. It will meet the *Grande Armée* on 7 or 8 August, at Smolensk.

The following is the position occupied by the army on 4 August:

The headquarters is at Vitebsk, with four bridges on the Dvina.

The 4th Corps at Souraj, occupying Velij, Porietchè and Ousviaht.

The King of Naples at Roudina, with the three first corps of cavalry.

The 1st Corps, commanded by Marshal the Prince of Eckmühl, is at the mouth of the Beresina, on the Borysthenes, with two bridges over this last-mentioned river, and one bridge on the Beresina, with double bridgeheads.

The 3rd Corps, commanded by Marshal Duke of Elchingen, is at Liozna.

The 8th Corps, commanded by the Duke of Abrantès, is at Orcha, with two bridges and bridgeheads on the Borysthenes.

The 5th Corps, commanded by Prince Poniatowski, is at Mohilev, with two bridges and bridgeheads on the Borysthenes.

The 2nd Corps, commanded by Marshal Duke of Reggio, is on the Drissa, advanced before Polotsk, on the road to Sebej.

The Prince of Schwarzenberg is with his corps at Slonim.

The 7th Corps is upon Rozana.

The 4th Corps of cavalry, with a division of infantry, commanded by General Count Maubourg, is before Bobruisk and Mozyr.

The 10th Corps, commanded by the Duke of Tarentum, is before Dvinsk and Riga.

The 9th Corps, commanded by the Duke of Belluno, is assembled at Tilsit.

The 11th Corps, commanded by the Duke of Castiglione, is at Stettin.

His Majesty has sent the army into quarters of refreshment. The heat is excessive, greater than what it was in Italy. The thermometer is at 26 and 27 degrees. Even the nights are warm.

General Kamenskii, with two divisions of the corps of Bagration, having been cut off from that corps, and not being able to rejoin it, returned to Volhynia, effected a junction with the division of recruits commanded by General Tormasov, and marched on the 7th Corps. He surprised and cut off the Saxon Brigadier General Keugler, who had under his command an advanced guard of two battalions, and two squadrons of Prince Clément's regiment.

After six hours' resistance, the greater part of this advanced guard was killed or taken. General Count Reynier could not come up to their assistance sooner than two hours after the affair was over. Prince Schwarzenberg marched on 30 July to join General Reynier and push the war with great spirit against the enemy's divisions.

On the 19th, the Prussian General Grawert attacked the Russians at Eckau, in Courland, overthrew them, took 200 prisoner and killed a considerable number. General Grawert much commends Major Stiern, who, at the head of the 1st Regiment of Prussian Dragoons took a prominent part in the affair. When Grawert had effected a junction with General Kleist, he drove the enemy before him on the road to Riga, and surrounded the bridgehead.

On the 30th, the Viceroy sent a brigade of Italian light cavalry to Velij. Two hundred men charged four battalions of the depot, who were en route to Twer, broke them, and took 400 prisoners and 100 wagons loaded with military stores.

On the 31st, the aide-de-camp Triaire, who had been sent forward with the Queen's Regiment of Dragoons of the Royal Italian Guard, arrived at Ousviath, took a captain and 40 men prisoner, and took possession 200 carriages loaded with flour.

On the 30th, Marshal Duke of Reggio marched from Polotsk on Sebej. He met General Wittgenstein, whose corps had been reinforced by that of Prince Repnine. An engagement took place near the castle of Jakoubovo. The 16th Regiment of

270

Light Infantry obtained much glory. The Legrand division gloriously bore up against the fire of the entirety of the enemy's corps.

On the 31st, the enemy marched upon the Drissa in order to attack the Duke of Reggio upon his flank as he marched. The Marshal took up a position behind the Drissa.

On 1 August, the enemy was foolish enough to cross the Drissa, and to present itself in battle array in front of the 2nd Corps. The Duke of Reggio allowed half the corps to cross, and as soon as he perceived about 15,000 men and 14 pieces of artillery beyond the river, he unmasked a battery of 40 cannon, which played upon them with grapeshot for half an hour. At the same time the Legrand and Verdier divisions made a running charge with the bayonet and drove the 15,000 Russians into the river. All the artillery and military chests taken, 3,000 prisoners, among whom were several officers, and one of General Wittgenstein's Staff, together with 3,500 men killed or wounded, are the result of this affair.

The combat of Drissa, of Ostrovno and Mohilev might have been, in other wars, called three battles. The Duke of Reggio praises much General Count Legrand, who is remarkably cool in the field. He also applauds the conduct of the 26th Light Infantry, and the 56th Line.

The Emperor of Russia has ordered levies of men in the two governments of Vitebsk and Mohilow; but before his agents could reach those provinces, we were masters of them. These measures consequently have produced nothing.

We have found at Vitebsk proclamations issued by Prince Alexander of Württemberg; and we have learned that the people of Russia are amusing themselves with singing *Te Deum* on account of the victories obtained by the Russians!

Twelfth Bulletin

Vitebsk, 7 August 1812

At the battle of Drissa, the Russian General Koulnieff, a distinguished officer of the light troops, was killed; ten other generals were wounded; four colonels were killed.

General Ricard, with his brigade, entered Dvinsk [Dünaburg] on 1 August. He found eight cannon; all the remainder had been taken away. The Duke of Tarentum arrived there on the 2nd. Thus Dvinsk, which the enemy has been fortifying for five years, where it has expended several millions, which cost it more than 20,000 men during the labour, has been abandoned without firing a musket, and is in our power, like the other works of the enemy, and like the entrenched camp which it had on the Drissa.

In consequence of the taking of Dvinsk, His Majesty has ordered that a park of 100 pieces of artillery which he had formed at Magdeburg and which had advanced upon the Niemen, should retire to Danzig, and be put in depot in that place. At the commencement of the campaign, two besieging parks of artillery had been prepared: one against Dvinsk, the other against Riga.

The magazines of Vitebsk are provisioned and the hospitals organized. These ten days of repose are extremely useful to the army. The heat is, besides, excessive; we have it warmer here than in Italy. The harvest is superb; it appears that this extends to all Russia; last year it was bad everywhere. The crops will not begin to be cut before eight or ten days.

His Majesty has formed a large square before the palace that he occupies at Vitebsk. This palace is situated upon the left bank of the Dvina. Every morning at six there is a grand parade at which all the officers of the Guard appear. One of the brigades of the Guard, in full dress, takes turns to march.

Report of the Prince of Eckmühl to the Prince Major-General
Doubrowna, 7 August 1812
My Lord,

I have the honour to put under the eyes of Your Highness the report of the affair that took place on 23 July before Mohilow, between part of the troops of the 1st Corps and the Russian corps of Prince Bagration.

I entered Mohilow on the 20th. On the 21st, the 3rd Regiment of Chasseurs was attacked by the advance guard of Prince Bagration, who wanted to occupy that important town. That regiment lost 100 men and was brought back.

On the 22nd, I placed in position the 85th Regiment of Infantry of Line, under the orders of General Frédéricks.

General Bagration had arrived at Novoï-Brickow. He wanted to give battle to enter Mohilow. He had 4 infantry divisions, 5,000 Cossacks and 8,000 cavalrymen, a total of 35,000 men.

At Mohilow I only had the 57th, 61st and 111th Regiments of the Compans division (the 25th had been left with the Pajol brigade and the 1st Chasseurs on the Beresina, to cover Minsk), the 85th and 108th of the Dessaix division, the divisions of cuirassiers of General Valence, and the 3rd of Chasseurs à Cheval. The position of Salta-Naecka, of which I send a drawing to Your Highness, appeared proper for receiving the enemy well.

In the night of the 22nd, I had the bridge that is on the great road barricaded, and crenellated the inn, which is on the opposite side. The bridge of the mill on the right was cut by a company of sappers, and the houses of the area crenellated. The 85th was in charge of defending these posts, and to hold in the case of an attack, to give time to the other troops in echelons between this position and Mohilow, to arrive. Having taken these dispositions, I retired to Mohilow, to hasten the arrival of the Claparède division and of the detached troops of General Pajol.

On the 23rd, at seven in the morning, I received the report that the advance guard was being attacked; at eight o'clock, I found the 85th very briskly attacked. General Frédéricks, who commanded it, had taken some good dispositions, and during the whole day had displayed calm and a lot of intrepidity. The light artillery of the division and that of the 85th had been placed the night before. Their fire was very deadly, and after one hour of combat there were already more than 500 dead Russians. Twelve to 15 Russian pieces debouched from the wood and placed themselves in battle on the plateau of the mill, the bridge of which had been destroyed. Some regiments of Russian infantry began to form. A battalion of the 108th was sent to support the companies of the 85th, which were on the bridge; a few artillery pieces were opposed to those of the Russians. On that side the combat became very lively. The enemy forces were increasing constantly. The battalion of the 108th, which had repulsed the Russians, was obliged to cede to its numbers. General Guardet, with two battalions of the 61st, stopped the enemy's pursuit and made the Russians re-cross the ravine that they had passed while they pursued the 108th battalion.

While all this was taking place on the right, I ordered General Frédéricks, who was defending the debouches of the great road with great vigour, to have the defile crossed by a battalion of the 108th and a few companies of the 85th, and to charge the pieces of the enemy. This movement, which was executed with great decision and directed by Colonel Achard of the 108th Regiment, had a big influence on the movements of the left of the enemy, which was forced into a retrograde movement. The battalion commanded by Colonel Achard had taken prisoner an enemy battalion, which was later freed. The Colonel was wounded by a ball in the arm, and was unable to sustain himself on the heights he had occupied.

The enemy had advanced a considerable mass of infantry, formed in a tight column, to try to force, once again, the defile of the bridge. This column was advancing in the direction of Squadron Chief Pulimey, who stopped them with a very lively fire and caused them great losses. The number of enemy dead, which was already very considerable, has now doubled.

The action was still sustained very heated on one side and the other, and with a great inferiority on our side.

The other troops were in reserve on our right, where we presumed the enemy would take its forces, especially its numerous cavalry. About six in the evening, all my reconnaissance on the right having seen no enemies, the troops that had been in reserve, particularly the 111th, were directed on the great road. General Frédéricks received the order to renew his attack. A battalion of the 85th, which had been placed on the extreme right the night before, and one of the 61st, attacked the left of the enemy. The two attacks were successful; the enemy retired its artillery and its troops followed this movement on all points.

The 111th regiment and the 61st of the 5th Division, commanded by General Compans, were charged with pursuing the enemy as far as Novosieleki. Night stopped the pursuit at this place.

I owe the biggest praise to the conduct of these troops, in particular to that of the 85th Regiment. Not one soldier left his post to move the wounded, and the young and the old soldiers showed great valour. The old soldiers gave the honourable testimony to the young ones that there were no conscripts left in their regiments.

The enemy's loss was great. It left more than 1,200 dead on the battlefield and more than 4,000 wounded, of which 700 to 800 were left in our hands. Our loss amounts to 900 men killed or taken prisoner.

I reiterate the praises that I owe to General Frédéricks for his conduct, to all the officers of the staff who paid of their persons. One of them, aide-de-camp of General Haxo, was killed.

I make use of this occasion to pray Your Highness to ask His Majesty for rewards for several of them. I attach their case to that of the officers, NCOs and soldiers of the 4th and 5th Divisions who merit to be cited with distinction. I pray Your Highness to put these cases under the eyes of His Majesty and solicit for them his favours.

I am, etc., etc.,

MARSHAL THE PRINCE OF ECKMÜHL

Report of Marshal Duke of Elchingen to the Major-General
Bivouac of Vanosava, 7 Leagues from Smolensk, 14 August 1812, 11 P.M.

Monsignor,

I have the honour to report to Your Most Serene Highness that the troops of the 3rd Army Corps debauched this morning from Viwiaimin by the bridge of Chevalets on the Dnieper, near Khomino, to advance towards Krasnöe.

The Emperor having given me orders to quickly repair to that town where, according to a report given to His Majesty, the enemy had a regiment of infantry, my column's front arrived there at three o'clock in the afternoon. The 24th Regiment of Light infantry, supported by the remainder of the 10th Division, attacked the enemy with admirable audacity, and Krasnöe was overthrown in an assault without any hesitation.

The enemy, with 6,000 infantrymen, 1,200 horses and 10 cannon had established its echelons and showed good continence behind the town; but the infantry attacked it so boldly that it was forced to retreat, which it did in good order under the protection of its artillery, which served it well.

A half a league from Krasnöe, the cavalry under the command of the King of Naples also attacked and pursued the enemy. The Russian infantry, which had been abandoned by their cavalry, formed two tight columns at first, and then a large square that, although surrounded, continued a prompt retreat while still fighting.

Our light cavalry made more than 40 charges on that infantry. Several squadrons penetrated the enemy's square and cut off some battalions, but it was saved from a total loss by the inertia created by the mass that opposed us rather than the effect of its fire, which made more noise than mischief. The Russians were pursued until nightfall and as far as the defile of Kanosava. We took 8 cannon, 800 men prisoner and killed at least 1,000. Therefore, this division, which is the 27th, composed of four regiments of musketeers and two of chasseurs under the orders of General Niewierowski, must have lost, in killed, wounded and prisoners, half of its men.

According to most of the reports, there are not very many people at Smolensk, and it would appear that the enemy is marching on Porietche, to proceed to the Dvina.

The loss of the army corps is about 200 killed or wounded. I will ask the Emperor for favours to be awarded to those officers, NCOs and soldiers who particularly distinguished themselves.

I have the honour to be, etc.

MARSHAL THE DUKE OF ELCHINGEN

Report of Prince Schwarzenberg to the Prince Major-General
At Kobryn, 14 August 1812
My Lord,

I pray Your Most Serene Highness to bring to the attention of His Majesty the Emperor that the army of Tormasov, which had taken a position behind Horodezna and Podubne, was attacked on the 12th by that which I have the honour of commanding, beaten and pursued the next day, the 13th, to beyond Kobryn.

The enemy lost 3,000 men, as many killed as wounded. We took more than 500 prisoner. It has retired, during the night of the 12th to the 13th, all of its artillery beyond the Muchavetz, and we only took a few caissons from it. We arrived on the 13th, about one in the afternoon, with the heads of columns at Kobryn; the enemy troops crowned the heights on the left bank. Upon the arrival of the infantry, I had the bridge re-established and occupied a part of the place situated beyond that; but the enemy was showing a lot of infantry, and my troops were so fatigued I could only push on to one-and-a-half leagues on the road from Kobryn to Divin, which the enemy took with all its army.

Today I sent General Bianchi with two brigades, two batteries and 1,200 horses on the road to Divin. Two detachments are advancing on Antopol, and I have invited General Reynier to push some strong detachments towards Brzesc. These detachments left yesterday and I await their report.

The enemy has a very numerous artillery that is well attended.

I learned at Kobryn that General Gaplitz, with a corps of 7,000 men with which I had already dealt at Seniewitezc, arrived with 24 pieces of artillery that night after the battle. This was advantageous for me, as the enemy's cavalry that is part of the army of Tormasov is much more numerous than the one I have available to oppose him.

The greatest praises are due to General Count Reynier and to the Saxon troops which fought under his orders. It is to this General that I must principally assign the glory of the day of the 12th. The task of turning the left of the enemy fell partly upon him and he found, with the greatest activity, the means to attain this goal and he executed the attack with calm and vigour that we expect from an army chief so distinguished.

The Austrian troops who took part in this combat showed great ardour and fought with perseverance and admirable bravery. The brave Jérôme Colloredo regiment, although battered with grapeshot from a battery established on the height, and despite the loss of 18 officers and 300 men, passed in front a marsh we believed impassable to charge the flank of the enemy, which by strong attacks had forced the Saxon brigade of General Sahr[er] to fall back momentarily. This regiment drove down with the bayonet all that came before him and cleared this way the left flank of that brigade, which took advantage of it to re-establish the line.

The enemy having pushed a detachment of 1,000 men, 800 horses and a few cannons by Lohiezin on Iwantzewiezy, on the Czara, to worry the communications on Slonim, I ordered General Mohr to march and reach this detachment and deliver it as much mischief as possible.

I attach here, My Lord, the continuation of the journal and the copy of an order of battle found at the quarters of General Tormasov at Kobryn.

Accept, My Lord, etc.

SCHWARZENBERG

Report of the Duke of Elchingen to the Major-General

At the bivouac before Smolensk, near Dienowo, Golomisk, 16 August 1812

Monsignor,

I have the honour to report to Your Highness that the troops of the 3rd Army Corps started marching this morning from their position at Loubna and vicinity in order to advance on Smolensk.

The enemy defended the outskirts of the town with some dragoons and a great number of Cossacks; we were obliged to use the infantry to turn them out; this was executed in spite of a very lively fire from the artillery of the place.

A battalion of the 46th showed such ardour that I threw it at a charge against the right bastion of the enemy, thus I was able to ascertain if the enemy was in force. All the Russian infantry that defended the covered road was forced to enter into the town very quickly and in disorder.

I ordered a second battalion to march, not so much to support the first, but to protect its retreat. The enemy made a terrible fire of artillery and infantry on this battalion, which pulled back only when the masses of infantry came out of the place to rush it. The retrograde movement was done in great order and without the enemy daring to reach the trench to follow it. This victorious attack by one battalion against more than 4,000 infantrymen supported by 60 guns is the most courageous act of war that I have seen since I started in the war. It will give the enemy a fine idea of the courage of our troops.

I am with a profound respect, Monsignor, of Your Highness,

The very humble and very obedient servant,

MARSHAL DUKE OF ELCHINGEN

Report of Marshal Duke of Elchingen to the Major-General

At the bivouac before Smolensk, 17 August 1812, eleven p.m.

Monsignor,

I have the honour to report to Your Highness that the enemy has not ceased to bring out troops continuously from Smolensk to attack our posts, from five o'clock this morning until three o'clock this afternoon.

Per the order I received to assist the attack made on the right of the town by our troops of the 1st Corps, and to attack the bastion which had been attacked by the 46th yesterday, I had this same regiment march and it forced the enemy to evacuate its position. The 25th Division has also not ceased to fight all day.

We observed that shortly after the attacks began against the place, the enemy columns that had disappeared this morning came back and are once again deployed on the heights on the right of the Dnieper, so that the position of the enemy, tonight, appears to be the same as it was last night.

I am with profound respect, Monsignor, of Your Highness,

The very humble and very obedient servant,

MARSHAL THE DUKE OF ELCHINGEN

Thirteenth Bulletin

Smolensk, 21 August 1812

It appears that in the battle of Mohilev, won by the Prince of Eckmühl over Prince Bagration on 23 July, the loss of the enemy was considerable

The Duke of Tarentum found 20 cannon in Dvinsk, instead of eight as had been announced. He had several vessels pulled from the water that were laden with more than 40,000 bombs, and other projectiles. An immense quantity of ammunition was destroyed by the enemy. The ignorance of the Russians in constructing fortifications is apparent in the works of Dvinsk and Drissa.

His Majesty gave the command of his right to Prince Schwarzenberg by placing under his orders the 7th Corps. This Prince marched against General Tormasov, met and defeated him on the 12th; he pays the highest compliments to the Saxon and Austrian troops; Prince Schwarzenberg showed in these circumstances as much activity as talent. The Emperor has requested promotions and rewards for the officers of his army corps who have distinguished themselves.

On the 8th, the *Grand Armée* was placed in the following manner:

The Prince Viceroy was at Souraj, with the 4th Corps, his advanced guard occupying Vilij, Ousviath and Porietch.

The King of Naples was at Nikoulino; his cavalry occupied Inkovo.

Marshal the Duke of Elchingen, commanding the 3rd Corps, was at Liozna.

Marshal the Prince of Eckmühl, commanding the 1st Corps, was at Doubrowna. The 5th Corps, commanded by Prince Poniatowski, was at Mohilev.

The headquarters was at Vitebsk.

The 2nd Corps, commanded by the Duke of Reggio, was upon the Drissa.

The 10th Corps, commanded by the Duke of Tarentum, was upon Dvinsk and Riga.

On the 8th, 12,000 of the enemy's cavalry marched upon Inkovo, and attacked General Count Sebastiani's division, which for half a league was obliged to fight, retreating all the way, suffering and causing equal loss to the enemy. A company of voltigeurs, of the 24th Regiment of Light Infantry, forming part of a battalion of that regiment, which had been confided to the cavalry to maintain a position in a wood, was taken. We had about 200 killed or wounded; the enemy may have lost the same number of men.

On the 12th, the enemy's army having united at Smolensk, marched by different points, with as much slowness as hesitation, on Porietch and Nadra.

On the 10th, the Emperor resolved to march to the enemy and to take possession of Smolensk by proceeding by the other bank of the Borysthenes. The King of Naples and Marshal Duke of Elchingen set out from Liozna and marched on the Borysthenes, near to the mouth of the Beresina, opposite Khomino, where, on the night between the 13th and 14th, they threw two bridges over the Borysthenes.

The Viceroy set out from Souraj, and marched by Janoviczi and Liouvavitschi to Rasana, where he arrived on the 14th.

General Count Grouchy collected the 3rd Corps of cavalry at Rasana, on the 12th.

The Prince of Eckmühl collected all his corps at Doubrowna on the 13th.

General Count Eblé threw three bridges at Rasana on the 13th.

The Headquarters set out from Vitebsk, and arrived at Rasana on the 13th.

Prince Poniatowski set out from Mohilev, and on the 13th arrived at Romanoff.

On the 14th, at daybreak, General Grouchy marched on Liady, chased two regiments of Cossacks from it, and there found the corps of cavalry of General Count Nansouty.

The same day the King of Naples, supported by the Duke of Elchingen, arrived at Krasnöe. The enemy's 27th Division, consisting of 5,000 infantry supported by 2,000 cavalry, and 12 pieces of artillery, was in a position before that town: it was attacked and forced in an instant, by Marshal Duke of Elchingen. The 24th Regiment of Light Infantry attacked the small town of Krasnöe with the bayonet, with great intrepidity: the cavalry executed some admirable charges. General of Brigade Baron Bordesoulle and the 3rd Regiment of Chasseurs distinguished themselves. The taking of 8 pieces artillery, 14 caissons, 1,500 prisoners, with a battlefield covered with more than 1,000 Russian corpses, were the advantages of the battle of Krasnöe, in which the Russian division, consisting of 3,000 men, suffered a loss of half its number.

His Majesty, on the 15th, had his headquarters at Kovonitnia.

On the morning of the 16th, the heights of Smolensk were surrounded. The town presented to our view an enclosure of 4,000 *toises* around, 10 feet thick and 25 feet high, intersected with towers, several of which were armed with cannon of heavy calibre.

On the right of the Borysthenes we perceived and knew that the enemy faced about, and hastily retraced its steps to defend Smolensk. We knew that the enemy's generals had orders from their master to do battle and save Smolensk. The Emperor reconnoitred the town and placed his army in its position on the 16th. Marshal Duke of Elchingen had the left leaning on the Borysthenes, the Prince of Eckmühl the centre, Prince Poniatowski the right; the Guards were placed in reserve in the center, the Viceroy in reserve on the right, and the cavalry under the orders of the King of Naples at the extremity of the right; the Duke of Abrantès, with the 8th Corps, lost his way and had made a false movement.

The 16th and half of the 17th, we stayed in observation. A fire of musketry was kept up along the line. The enemy occupied Smolensk with 30,000 men, and the remainder of its army was forming upon the fine positions on the right bank of the river, opposite to the town, and communicating by three bridges. Smolensk is considered a strong town by the Russians, and the bulwark of Moscow.

On the 17th, at two in the afternoon, seeing that the enemy had not debouched, that it was fortifying itself in Smolensk, and that it refused battle, notwithstanding the orders it had received and the fine position it might have occupied, its right upon Smolensk and its left upon the banks of the Borysthenes, the enemy's general lacking resolution, the Emperor marched upon the right and ordered Prince Poniatowski to change his front, the right in advance, and to place his right to the Borysthenes, occupying one of the suburbs by posts and batteries, to destroy the bridge and intercept the communication of the town with the right bank. During this time, the Prince of Eckmühl received orders to attack two of the suburbs which the enemy had entrenched, 2000 *toises* distant from the town; and which were each defended by 7,000 or 8,000 infantry, and heavy cannon. General Count Friant had orders to complete the surrounding, by leaning his right towards Prince Poniatowski's corps, and his left to the right of the attack made by the Prince of Eckmühl.

At two in the afternoon, Count Bruyère's division of cavalry, having driven away the Cossacks and enemy's cavalry, occupied the plateau that is the closest to the bridge highest up the river. A battery of 10 pieces of artillery was established on this plateau, opened a fire of grapeshot upon that part of the enemy's army which was still on the right bank of the river, and quickly obliged the Russian masses of infantry to evacuate that position.

The enemy then placed two batteries of 20 cannon in a convent, to annoy the battery that played upon it and the bridge. The Prince of Eckmühl entrusted the attack of the suburbs on the right to Count Morand, and that of those on the left to General Count Gudin. At three, the cannonade commenced. At half-past four a very brisk fire of musketry began; and at five, the divisions of Morand and Gudin carried the enemy's entrenched suburbs, with a cool and rare intrepidity, and pursued it to the covered way, which was covered with Russian dead.

On our left, the Duke of Elchingen attacked the position which the enemy had outside the town, seized upon it, and pursued the enemy to the slope.

At five o'clock the communication of the town with the right bank became difficult, and could only be accomplished by isolated men.

Three batteries of breaching 12-pounders were placed against the walls at six in the evening; one by Friant's division, and the two others by Morand's and Gudin's divisions. We drove the enemy from all the towers by howitzers, which rained fire on them. General of Artillery Count Sorbier rendered the occupation of the covered way by the enemy impossible, by the enfilading [sweeping] battcries.

Nevertheless the enemy general, who from two in the afternoon perceived we had serious intentions against the town, sent two divisions, and two regiments of infantry of the Guard to reinforce the four divisions that were in the town. Those united forces composed half of the Russian army. The battle continued all night; three breaching batteries played with the utmost activity. Two companies of miners were attached to the ramparts.

The town was now on fire. In the middle of a fine August night, Smolensk offered the French a spectacle similar to that which an eruption of Vesuvius presents to the inhabitants of Naples.

An hour after midnight, the enemy abandoned the town, and retired across the river. At two o'clock, the grenadiers who first led to the attack no longer found resistance, the place was evacuated; 200 pieces of artillery and one of the first fine towns in Russia was in our power, and that too in sight of the whole Russian army.

The combat of Smolensk, which we might justly term a battle, 100,000 men having been engaged on the different sides, caused the Russians a loss of 4,700 men, left dead on the field; of 2,000 prisoners, the greater part of whom are wounded; and of 7,000 to 8,000 wounded. Among the dead were found five Russian generals. Our loss amounts to 700 killed and 3,100 or 3,200 wounded. General of Brigade Grabowski was killed, and Generals of Brigade Grandeau and Dalton wounded. All the troops have rivalled each other in intrepidity. The field of battle has offered to the view of 200,000 persons, who can attest it, the sight of one French corpse lying upon the bodies of seven or eight Russians: meanwhile, the Russians were protected by a part of the musketry fire from their trenches during a part of the days of the 16th and 17th.

On the 18th, we re-established the bridges over the Borysthenes that the enemy had burnt, but did not succeed in quenching the fire that consumed the town until the 18th, the French sappers having worked with great activity. The houses in the city were filled with dead and dying Russians.

Of 12 divisions, which composed the great Russian army, two divisions have been broken and defeated in the combats of Ostrovno, two met with the same fate in the battle of Mohilev, and six in the battle of Smolensk. It has only two divisions of the Guards that remain entire.

The deeds of bravery which rebound to the honour of the army, and which distinguished such numbers of soldiers in the battle of Smolensk, shall be the subject of a particular report. Never has the French army shown greater intrepidity than in this campaign.

Fourteenth Bulletin

Smolensk, 23 August 1812

Smolensk may be considered as one of the finest cities in Russia. Had it not been for the circumstances of war, which set it on fire and consumed immense magazines of colonial merchandise and goods of all kinds, this city would have been a great resource for the army. Even in its present state, it may be of the greatest utility in a military point of view. There are still large houses remaining that offer fine places for the establishment of hospitals; the province of Smolensk is very fine and fertile, and will furnish great resources for subsistence and forage. The Russians intended, since the events of the war, to raise a militia of peasant slaves, whom they had armed with bad pikes. They had already collected about 5,000 of them at this place; it was an object of raillery and derision even to the Russian army itself. They had already stated as the Order of the Day that Smolensk was to be the grave of the French; and that, although it had been deemed convenient to evacuate Poland, yet it was necessary to give battle at Smolensk, to prevent this barrier of Russia from falling into our hands.

The cathedral of Smolensk is one of the most celebrated Grecian churches in all Russia; the Episcopal palace forms a kind of town by itself.

The heat is excessive, the thermometer having risen to 26 degrees: the weather is much hotter here than in Italy.

Battle of Polotsk

After the battle of Drissa, the Duke of Reggio, knowing that the enemy's General, Wittgenstein, had been reinforced by the 12th and 3rd Battalions from the garrison of Dvinsk, and willing to draw him to an engagement near the defile below Polotsk, caused the 2nd and 6th Corps to be ranged in order of battle below Polotsk. General Wittgenstein followed him, attacked him on the 16th and 17th, and was vigorously repulsed. The Bavarian division of Wrede of the 6th Corps has distinguished itself. At the moment when the Duke of Reggio was making his dispositions to profit by the victory and to close the enemy in the defile, he was struck on the shoulder by a *biscaïen*. His wound, which is of a serious nature, obliged him to be transported to Vilna; but it does not appear that it should cause any worries later on.

General Count Gouvion Saint–Cyr has taken the command of the 2nd and 6th Corps. On the 17th, in the evening, the army retired beyond the defiles. General Verdier was wounded. General Maison has been recognized as General of Division, and has succeeded him in the command of his division. Our loss is estimated at 1,000 men killed or wounded. The loss of the Russians is triple to ours; we have taken 500 prisoners from them.

On the 18th, at four o'clock in the afternoon, General Gouvion Saint-Cyr, commanding the 2nd and 6th Corps, opened on the enemy by causing its right wing to be attacked by the Bavarian division of the Count Wrede. The battle extended the whole length of the line, and the enemy was thrown into a complete rout and pursued for two leagues, as long as daylight permitted; 20 pieces of artillery and 1,000 prisoners, have remained in the power of the French army. The Bavarian General Deroy was wounded.

Battle of Valutino

At daybreak on the 19th, the bridge being finished, Marshal Duke of Elchingen crossed over to the right bank of the Borysthenes and pursued the enemy. At one league from the town he encountered the last column of the enemy's rearguard. It was a division of 5,000 or 6,000 men stationed on fine heights. He caused them to be attacked with the bayonet by the 4th Regiment of Line Infantry and by the 72nd Line. The position was carried, and our bayonets covered the field of battle with dead: 3,000 or 4,000 prisoners fell into our hands. The fleeing enemy retired on the second column, which was posted on the heights of Valutino. The first position was carried by the 18th line, and towards four o'clock in the afternoon the musketry fire was kept up against all of the enemy's rearguard, which presented about 15,000 men. The Duke of Abrantès had crossed the Borysthenes at two leagues the right of Smolensk, and he found himself close upon the rear of the enemy; he might, therefore, by marching with determination, have intercepted the great road to Moscow and rendered the retreat of the rearguard difficult; but meantime the other columns of the enemy's army which were within range, being informed of the success and of the rapidity of the first attack, returned back the way they came. Four divisions then advanced to support their rearguard, and among others, the divisions of grenadiers, which until now had not come forward; 5,000 or 6,000 cavalry formed their right, while their left was covered by woods filled with skirmishers. It was of the greatest consequence to the enemy to keep this position as long as possible, it being a very fine one, and apparently unassailable; on our part we attached no less importance to taking it, in order to accelerate his retreat and cause to fall in our hands all the carriages filled with wounded and other articles whose evacuation was protected by the rearguard. This was what gave rise to the battle of Valutino, one of the finest feats of arms in our military history.

At six o'clock in the evening, the division of Gudin, which had been sent forward to support the 3rd Corps from the moment when we perceived the great succour that the enemy had sent to its re+rearguard, pushed forward a column on the centre of the enemy's position, was supported by the division of General Ledru, and after an hour's combat, forced the position.

General Count Gudin arriving with his division, was, at the commencement of the action, struck by a bullet that carried off his thigh; he died gloriously. This loss was deeply felt. General Gudin was one of the most distinguished officers in the army: he was estimable for his moral qualities, as much as for his bravery and intrepidity. General Gérard has taken the command of the division. We reckon that the enemy has had eight generals killed or wounded; one of its generals is taken prisoner.

On the following day, at three in the morning, the Emperor distributed rewards on the field of battle, to all the regiments which had distinguished themselves; and as the 127th, which is a new regiment, had behaved itself well, His Majesty granted this regiment the right of carrying an Eagle, a privilege it had not before enjoyed, never having until this time been present in any battle. These recompenses, given on the battlefield in the midst of the dead, the dying, the wounded, and the trophies of victory, offered a spectacle truly military and imposing. After this battle, the enemy precipitated its retreat in such a manner that on the day of the 20th our troops marched eight leagues without being able to find the Cossacks, and everywhere picking up the wounded and stragglers.

Our loss in the battle of Valutino has been 600 killed and 2,600 wounded. That of the enemy, as the battlefield shows, is triple; we have taken 1,000 prisoners, mostly wounded.

Thus the only two divisions that had not suffered by the preceding combats of Mohilev, of Ostrovno, of Krasnöe and of Smolensk, have now suffered at the battle of Valutino.

All the intelligence received confirms the account of the enemy running at full speed for Moscow; that its army has suffered much in the preceding engagements; and besides this, experiences a great desertion. The Poles say to them, when deserting, 'You have abandoned us without fighting; what right, then, can you have to exact from us to remain under your colours?' The Russian soldiers of the provinces of Mohilev and Smolensk likewise take advantage of the proximity of their villages to desert, and return to repose themselves in their own countries.

The division of Gudin attacked with so much intrepidity that the enemy was persuaded it was the Imperial Guard. This is, in one word, to pronounce the finest eulogy on the 7th Regiment of Light Infantry, and on the 12th, 21st and 127th Line who composed this division. The combat of Valutino may likewise be called a battle, as more than 80,000 men were engaged. It was, at least, an affair of vanguard of the first rank.

General Grouchy, who was sent with his corps on the route to Doubovichina, found all the villages filled with dead and wounded, and has taken three ambulances containing 900 wounded.

The Cossacks have surprised at Liozna a hospital of 200 sick Württemberg troops, which through negligence had not been forwarded to Vitebsk.

For the rest, in the midst of all these disasters, the Russians never cease to chant the *Te Deum*; they convert everything into a victory, but, in spite of the ignorance and brutality of these people, this begins to appear ridiculous to them, and even too gross.

Report to the Major-General

My Lord,

I suppose that the Duke of Reggio will have rendered Your Highness an account of the action of the 17th, or at least up to the moment when his wounds forced him to quit the field of battle. During the remainder of that day, the troops continued their successes, and at nine in the evening the Russians were repulsed at every point, after having suffered the most considerable losses, having attempted, in the course of the day, six or seven attacks that were repulsed with a bravery superior to the infatuation which brought them there. This affair reflects the highest honour on the division of Legrand, which was placed at the branching of the roads to Sebeji and to Nevel; and on the Bavarian corps placed on the left bank of the Polota, in the rear of the village of Spas, which the enemy was determined to retake, notwithstanding its having been driven out of it five or six times; and the 20th Division, as also General Wrede, who commanded it, have covered themselves with glory. The Bavarian General Vincenti, who is entitled to praise for the manner in which he conducted himself, was there wounded.

In the evening of that day I felt the necessity of attacking the enemy.

I took my measures for making the attack on the 18th, at four o'clock in the afternoon; I have performed impossibilities to deceive the enemy concerning my intentions. Towards one o'clock, I caused the equipage of the army that was in the rear of Polotsk to file off on the left bank of the Dvina, on the road to Oula. I made an appearance as if I would cause this movement to be covered and protected by the troops, which Marshal Duke of Reggio had caused to re-cross to the left bank. In the night between the 16th and 17th, they re-united behind Polotsk, at the tail of the equipages; the division of cuirassiers arrived there from Semenets, and the brigade of light cavalry of General Castex from Rondina.

At three in the afternoon, the column of baggage had defiled in sight of the enemy, and the above-mentioned troops re-crossed the Dvina, with the greatest part of the French artillery, and entered Polotsk. About five o'clock all the troops and artillery were in a position to debouche upon the enemy, without its even having observed our preparations. At five precisely, all the artillery opened its fire and our columns of infantry debouched under its protection to attack the enemy's left and centre. Wrede's division debouched to the right of the village of Spas and attacked the enemy's left with great bravery and skill. General Deroy's division marched from that village, the Legrand division on the left of the village, connecting itself by its left with Verdier's division, a brigade of which observed the enemy's right and was placed on the road of Gehinzeliva. Merle's division covered the front of Polotsk and part of its rear.

The enemy, though completely surprised, quite confident in its superior force and immense artillery, composed of 108 pieces, at first received our attacks with infinite calmness and composure; but in the end, before night, its left was completely forced, and its centre totally routed, after having defended its position with much bravery and great tenacity. We could have taken a very great number of prisoners if the woods had not been so near their position. The enemy abandoned to us the battlefield covered with an immense number of its killed, 20 pieces of artillery and 1,000 prisoners. On our side, we have had some killed and wounded; among the latter are Generals Deroy and Raglovich and Colonel Cologne, commanding the Bavarian artillery.

I cannot sufficiently eulogize Legrand, Wrede, Deroy, Raglovich and General of Artillery Aubry, who directed the artillery of the 2nd Corps with great distinction. General Merle, with only a part of his division, repulsed with great skill an attack that the enemy made on our left to protect its retreat to the wood. The Croats distinguished themselves in his charge, supported by a part of General Castex's cavalry. In general, I request the consideration of His Majesty; the troops have merited encouragement and rewards. His Majesty will give me great pleasure by dispensing his favour on Mr Mailly, my aide-de-camp, the bearer of this letter, whose zeal I have every reason for praising. I have also nothing but praise to bestow upon the Chief of the 2nd and the 6th Corps.

I have the honour to be Your Highness's most obedient humble servant,

COUNT GOUVION SAINT-CYR

Report of Marshal Duke of Elchingen to the Major-General

19 August 1812

My Lord,

The 3rd Corps has crossed on the right of the Dnieper this morning at four o'clock, reaching the heights where the Russian army had taken position yesterday. The small posts the enemy had near the convent have been forced to pull back; a few cannon shots have also taken out their light infantry, which occupied the plateau. As the regiments were forming, I directed the columns on the road to Moscow. When I arrived near Valutino, on the Stabna road, I found the enemy's rearguard in position; it was the army corps of Bagavout; the action was engaged with extreme rapidity and the combat lasted about two hours; at last, after a few very deadly charges, we took the position. The enemy retreated in great disorder and showed us nothing but Cossacks.

The Emperor then arrived on the battlefield and gave orders to march forward in the direction of Moscow.

At one-and-a-half leagues from Smolensk I met the rearguard of the army of General Barclay de Tolly; the 11th Division who opened the march overthrew the enemy without any hesitation, as far as the position of —, where I found a large portion of the Russian army in combat. I then had this division take position and wait for the 10th and the 25th to join it. Meanwhile the enemy, seeing itself as no longer pursued, decided to take the offensive and made great efforts to chase me from my position; but it was constantly repulsed and there are no words that can describe the devotion shown by the troops under my orders in this circumstance.

About five o'clock in the afternoon, General Gudin's division arrived behind me. I immediately took the necessary dispositions to take out the enemy's position. The division of General Gudin and that of General Razout were in charge of the attack; those of Generals Leduc and Marchand stayed in reserve. This attack and the defence of the enemy were terrible. We made ourselves masters of the plateau and of the enemy's position.

This affair may be considered one of the most intense that can be fought. It was very glorious for the arms of His Majesty, as General Barclay de Tolly, who was in command, had half of his army in action, while in the liveliest part of the combat only two French divisions were engaged.

I could not, Monsignor, make too big a praise of the courage of the troops and the great devotion of the officers. I will have many favours to request, and I will hasten the information to Your Highness as soon as I receive the detailed

statements from the generals of division and the chiefs of the corps.
I am with profound respect of Your Highness,
The very humble and obedient servant,

MARSHAL DUKE OF ELCHINGEN

Fifteenth Bulletin

Slavkowo, 27 August 1812

General of Division Zayonchek, who commanded a Polish division at the battle of Smolensk, was wounded. The behaviour of the Polish corps at Smolensk astonished the Russians, who used to despise them. They were struck with their steadiness, and the superiority that they displayed under these circumstances.

At the battles of Smolensk and Valutino the enemy lost 20 generals killed, wounded or taken, and a very great number of officers. The number of men killed, taken or wounded on these occasions may amount to from 25 to 30,000 men.

On the day after the battle of Valutino, His Majesty gave the 12th and 21st Regiments of Infantry of Line and the 7th Regiment of Light Infantry, a number of decorations of the Legion of Honour, to be bestowed on the captains, lieutenants, NCOs, and soldiers. The selections were made immediately, in a circle before the Emperor, and were confirmed with acclamations by the troops.

The following are the names of those who obtained this honourable distinction:

12th Regiment of Line Messrs Bretz, captain of the Grenadiers; Dehir, Petitjean, Micnelet, Carré, Lecu, Rumigni, captains; Beaulieu, first captain; Humbert, captain; Etienne, Rota, Lecler, Villemain, Rouby, Boyer, Berlan, Barzun, lieutenants; Vingard, tambour-major; Vaceron, sergeant; Gilbert, Frédéric, Ganavial, Marchudie, Georget (Louis), Gaudier, Becker, Varenne, Hugot, Pitois, Lefèvre, soldats; Houllier, cannonier.

21st Regiment of Line Messrs Rossi, Baron Victor, Caudron, Caillebot, Leroux, Cocriamont, captains; Deloux, Ourblain, Arnaud, Boisson, Fumé, Varguet, Viard, Lachenal, lieutenants; Caudron, Blanc, Carré, Roman, Chubuissot, Milard, sergeants; Basset, Ragot, adjutants; Pierron, Paccaud, Lagurande, sergeants.

7th Regiment of Light Infantry Messrs Roman, Seguinot, Cossot, Marchand, Moncey, captains; Butard, adjutant-major; Tournier, Delplace, Guiabert, Chasse, Masson, Boiste, Cosset, Delignon, Baby, Dufour, Painbot, Barezout, lieutenants; Salmeton, sapper; Guérin, sergeant-major; Redarez, adjutant NCO; Dandal, Soustel, Ledran, Saunier, Picard, sergeants; Bataille, trumpeter; Didier, Calvet, Prevot, Brillant, Vaines, soldiers.

Number of decorations granted	
To the 12th regiment	30
To the 21st regiment	25
To the 7th light	32
Total	87 decorations

In retiring, the enemy's army burns the bridges and destroys the roads in order to retard the march of the French army as much as possible. On the 21st, it had re-crossed the Borysthenes at Slob-Pniwa, still closely followed by our advance guard.

The commercial establishments at Smolensk were quite untouched on the Borysthenes, in a fine suburb to which the Russians set fire for the sole purpose of retarding our march a single hour. Never was war conducted with so much inhumanity:the Russians treat their own country as they would that of any enemy. The country is fine, and abundantly supplied with everything. The roads are superb.

Marshal Duke of Tarentum continues to destroy Dvinsk. The wooden materials, palisades, and the debris of the blockhouses, which were immense, served to make a bonfire in honour of 15 August [Napoleon's birthday].

Prince Schwarzenberg writes from Ossiati, on the 17th, that his advanced guard has pursued the enemy on the road to Divin, that he has taken some hundreds of prisoners, and obliged the enemy to burn his baggage. General Bianchi, however, who commands the advanced guard, has succeeded in seizing 800 baggage-wagons that the enemy could neither carry off nor burn. The Russian army under Tormasov has lost almost all its baggage.

The equipage for the siege of Riga has begun to move from Tilsit for the Dvina.

General Saint-Cyr has taken a position on the Drissa. The rout of the enemy at the battle of Polotsk on the 18th was complete. The brave Bavarian General Deroy was wounded on the field of honour, at the age of 72, after nearly 60 years' service. His Majesty has named him a Count of the Empire, with a revenue of 30,000 francs. The Bavarian corps behaved with much bravery. His Majesty has granted it rewards and honours.

The enemy indicated that it would make a stand at Doroghoboui. It had, according to custom, thrown up earth and constructed batteries. The army having shown itself in order of battle, the Emperor moved forward; but the enemy's general thought better of it, beat a retreat, and abandoned Doroghoboui, a city containing 10,000 souls and eight steeples. Headquarters were there on the 26th, and on the 27th at Slavkowo. The advanced guard is close to Viasma.

The Viceroy manoeuvres on the left, at two leagues from the great road; the Prince of Eckmühl on the great road; and Prince Poniatowski on the left bank of the Osma.

The capture of Smolensk appears to have had a sad effect on the spirits of the Russians. It was called Smolensk the sacred; Smolensk the strong; the key of Moscow; besides a thousand other common sayings. 'Whoever has Smolensk has Moscow', say the peasants.

The heat is excessive; it has not rained for a month.

The Duke of Belluno, with the 9th Corps, 30,000 strong, has set out from Tilsit for Vilna. This corps is to form the reserve.

Report of Marshal the Prince of Eckmühl to the Major-General
30 August 1812

My Lord,

In accordance with the orders of His Majesty, the 1st Corps of the *Grande Armée* has taken position before Smolensk on the 16th of this month in the following order:

The 3rd Division advanced to 600 *toises* from the place, leaning its left on the road of Krasnöe, where it joined the 3rd Corps. Its right stretched as far as the windmill that is on the road to Mohilow.

The 1st Division cut off the windmill by the left and joined by its right the 3rd Corps.

The three other divisions have been placed in the rear, a short distance away, as nightfall did not permit them to advance on the different points which had been assigned to them.

The 17th, the 3rd and the 1st Divisions stayed in the same position, while the 2nd advanced to the left of the 1st; the 4th remained at the ravine at the rear of this division, and the 5th has occupied the plateau of —.

On the 17th, His Majesty ordered that the enemy be ousted from its positions and pushed back into the place; the 1st, 2nd and 3rd Divisions that were on the first line were ordered to attack at the same time. The attack took place about noon. After having shaken the enemy with artillery fire, to which it responded from the fortress and from his redoubts, our troops marched forward and attacked on all points the enemy troops that opposed them.

The attack was very lively and the defence determined; however, everything gave way to the bravery of His Majesty's troops. The redoubts were taken; the battlemented houses were forced. The enemy was pursued and thrown back into the fortress, where it took refuge after great losses.

I cannot give too much praise of the conduct of our troops in this circumstance. Generals, officers and soldiers of all the arms, all competed with zeal, bravery and devotion for the service of His Majesty.

The 127th Regiment of Line, which was under fire for the first time, showed the most brilliant manner. I pray His Majesty to bestow his eagle upon this regiment, which is truly worthy of it.

I must especially cite with praise the 13th Light Regiment that, in spite of the assault from musketry fire and a hail of bullets, went up to the plateau he was to charge with the greatest bravery. General Dalton who headed this attack showed proof of the greatest bravery. We have to regret that he was put out of combat by a musket that hit him towards the end of the affair. General Friant was hit by a dead ball. Our loss has been very little in comparison with that of the enemy.

Generals of Division Morand, Friant, and Gudin gave in this affair more proof of their talents and valour.

I have the honour to address their particular reports to you, as well as the state of the soldiers who distinguished themselves and for whom I solicit the favours of the Emperor.

I pray Your Highness to bring these to the attention of His Majesty.

I also send request in favour of several officers of my general staff who showed much bravery and devotion and who serve with the greatest zeal.

I am with a profound respect, My Lord, the very Humble and Obedient Servant,

MARSHAL DUKE OF AUERSTÄDT, PRINCE OF ECKMÜHL

Sixteenth Bulletin

Viasma, 31 August 1812

The headquarters of the Emperor was, on the 27th, at Slavkowo, on the 28th, near Semlevo; on the 29th, in a castle one league in the rear of Viasma, and on the 30th, at Viasma; the army marched in three columns: the left formed by the Viceroy, proceeding by Kanouchkino, Znamenkoi, Kosterechkovo and Novoé; the centre, formed by the King of Naples, the corps of the Prince of Eckmühl, the Duke of Elchingen and the Guard, marching on the main road; and the right by Prince Poniatowski, marching on the left bank of the Osma by Volosk, Louchki Pokroskoé, and Slouckino.

On the 27th, the enemy, wishing to rest on the Osma opposite the village of Riebké, took a position with its rearguard. The King of Naples directed his cavalry on the left of the enemy, showing him 7,000 to 8,000 cavalry. A battalion of the enemy was penetrated by the 4th Regiment of Lancers. A hundred prisoners were the result of this small affair. The positions of the enemy were carried and it was obliged to quicken his retreat.

On the 28th, the enemy was pursued. The advanced guards of the three French columns came up with the rearguard of the enemy; they exchanged several cannon-shot. The enemy was driven everywhere.

General Count Caulaincourt entered Viasma on the 29th, at daybreak.

The enemy had burned the bridges, and set fire to several quarters of the city. Viasma is a town of 15,000 inhabitants: there are 4,000 burghers, merchants, and artisans; there are 32 churches. We found considerable resources in flour, soap, drugs, etc., and large stores of *eau-de-vie* [brandy].

The Russians burnt the stores, and the finest houses in the town were on fire at our arrival. Two battalions of the 25th were employed with much activity in extinguishing them. We got it under control, and saved three-quarters of the town. The Cossacks, before they left it, committed the most dreadful pillage, which has made the inhabitants say that the Russians think Viasma will be no longer under their dominion, since they treat it in so barbarous a manner. All the population of the towns retires upon Moscow. It is said there are now one million and a half souls in that great city. They fear the result of these crowds. The inhabitants say that General Kutusov has been appointed Commander-in-Chief of the Russian army and that he took the command on the 28th.

The Grand Duke Constantine, who had returned to the army, having fallen ill, has retired.

A little rain has fallen, which has laid the dust that incommoded the army. The weather today is very fine; it will last, as they believe, to 10 October, which gives us still 40 days' campaign.

Seventeenth Bulletin

Ghjat, 3 September 1812

The headquarters were, on 31 August, at Velitchéro; on 1 and 2 September, at Ghjat.

The King of Naples, with the advanced guard, had his headquarters on the 1st ten *versts* in advance of Ghjat; the Viceroy had his two leagues in advance on the left; and Prince Poniatowski had pushed forward two leagues on the right. Some discharges of artillery and attacks with the sabre were exchanged in each direction, and a few hundreds of prisoners were taken.

The Ghjat River empties into the Volga. Thus we are in possession of the course of those waters that flow into the Caspian Sea. The Ghjat is navigable to the Volga.

The city of Ghjat contains a population of 8,000 or 10,000 souls. Many of the houses are built of stone and brick; there are many parish churches and several manufactories of linen cloth. It is perfectly clear that agriculture has made great progress in this country within the last 40 years. It no longer bears any resemblance to the descriptions that are given of it. Potatoes, pulses and cabbages grow there in abundance: the granaries are full. At present it is the harvest season; and we enjoy now the same weather here as we have in France at the start of October.

The deserters, the prisoners and the inhabitants all agree that the greatest confusion prevails at Moscow and in the Russian army, which is distracted with a diversity of opinions and has suffered enormous losses in the different actions. Some of the generals have been changed. It appears that the opinion of the army is not favourable to the plans of General Barclay de Tolly; he is accused of having made his divisions fight in detail.

Prince Schwarzenberg is in Volhynia: the Russians flee before him.

Some sharp affairs have taken place before Riga; the Prussians have always had the advantage.

We have found in this place two Russian bulletins that give an account of the actions before Smolensk and of the battle of the Drissa. They have appeared sufficiently curious to be annexed to this Bulletin. When we shall receive the sequel of these Bulletins, they shall be sent to the *Moniteur*. It appears by their contents that the editor had profited by the instructions he received from Moscow, 'That the truth is not to be told to the Russian people, but that they are to be deceived with lies.' Smolensk was set on fire by the Russians. They set fire to the suburbs on the day after the battle, when they saw our bridge established over the Borysthenes. They also set fire to Doroghobouï, to Viasma and to Ghjat; but the French came up in time to extinguish it. This may be easily conceived. The French have no interest in burning those towns that belong to them and in depriving themselves of the resources that they afford. The cellars have been everywhere filled with brandy, leather and every type of article that is useful to an army.

If the country be wasted, if the inhabitants suffer more than a state of war warrants, the fault is with the Russians.

The army rested on the 2nd and 3rd in the vicinity of Ghjat.

It is positively asserted that the enemy is employed in forming an entrenched camp in front of Majaisk, and has established lines before Moscow.

At the battle of Krasnöe, Colonel Marbeuf of the 6th Light Cavalry was wounded with a bayonet at the head of his regiment, in the midst of a square of Russian infantry that he had penetrated with the greatest intrepidity.

We have thrown six bridges over the Ghjat.

Report of General Prince Poniatowski to the Major-General.

At the battlefield, 7 September 1812 at ten o'clock at night
My Lord,
I have the honour to apprise Your Most Serene Highness of today's activities.

At five in the morning, the 5th Corps started its movement going around the woods. We arrived on the old road from Smolensk to Moscow. We followed this road and at the debouch of the woods, in the plain, we saw a strong column of infantry near the village of Passarevo. I had re-established a battery of 6- and 12-pounders on a knoll on the left of the road; and after striking upon the column for some time, I had my infantry quickly advance and with brisk force seized the village of Passarevo, and in a second attack the small wood that is before the village.

The countryside is full of woods and thickets, from the small wood to the top of the knoll which dominates the whole plain and which was strongly occupied by the enemy. I set forth three battalions in extended order into the brushes that were full of a great number of Russian chasseurs on foot. A lively fusillade was at once engaged as well as a very strong cannonade, which lasted until noon. I gave orders to also take the knoll in an assault. The first battalions, with great efforts, were able to surround it; but even though they were supported by other battalions, it became impossible for them to sustain their efforts against a force infinitely superior. We were repulsed from the knoll, but we managed to maintain position in the underwood according to the order given by His Majesty, and I had my batteries continue to strike the summit of the knoll where the enemy had 12 large-calibre pieces.

We remained in that position until two o'clock in the afternoon when, noticing we were making considerable progress on the centre, I ordered another attack to be done on the knoll, seconded by the cavalry which arrived by the back of the knoll at almost the same time as the infantry, and we were able to establish ourselves there. The enemy made some efforts to recapture it; not only was it brusquely repulsed but I vigorously pursued it with some infantry, cavalry and mounted artillery as far as one league or more. The cavalry made several charges on the infantry, which suffered great losses. We took very few prisoner because the cavalry sabred everything that came its way after it had received several rounds. We only took one caisson containing munitions for 12-pounders, and a number of charged howitzers. The prisoners we took will be sent to the headquarters tomorrow morning. Meanwhile, I have the honour to send to Your Most Serene Highness an officer who has just abandoned the Russian flags, desiring, as a Pole, to serve his country. He is in a good position to give us some very good information. According to what he has told me, it would appear that today the 5th Corps saw in front of it the army corps of Tutshkov, composed of the grenadier division of Stroganov, named the second guard, and the division of Kanowitzin, more than two battalions of grenadiers in reserve, two regiments of militia, one regiment of Uhlans and one of hussars.

I cannot but applaud the happy result that I owe to the bravery and the zeal of the generals, officers and the troops. Before I can inform Your Most Serene Highness of the names of those who distinguished themselves, I would like to recommend to Your Most Serene Highness General Sebastiani, whose great advice helped me as much in the dispositions as did his vigorous action in the execution.

Tomorrow I will have the honour to transmit to Your Most Serene Highness the roll call with the exact loss suffered by the 5th Corps. The loss of the enemy has been extremely considerable, as witnessed by the battlefield and the declaration of the officer previously mentioned.

I await the orders of Your Most Serene Highness, and have the honour to be, etc.

The general commanding the 5th Corps
[Signed] JOSEPH, PRINCE PONIATOWSKI

Report from the King of Naples to the Major-General

Majaisk, 9 September 1812

On the 4th and 5th, the advance guard of His Majesty's army vigorously drove the rearguard of the enemy and chased it out of all his positions. The enemy showed much resistance on the 5th. Everyone did their duty on the 4th, and Count Perigord, Colonel of the 8th Mounted Chasseurs, distinguished himself in successfully pushing back several charges of a cavalry much stronger than his.

That night, His Majesty gave the order to attack the redoubt with the cavalry of the Compans division at the Polish corps.

General Compans prepared his attack columns and marched on the village of — situated at the foot of the redoubt and of the woods on the right. The cavalry supported it; master of the village and the woods, General Compans ordered a march to the redoubt, which was taken by the 61st Regiment at the end of the bayonet. Meanwhile, several charges of cavalry had taken place and the Russian cuirassiers were overwhelmed by the fire from our infantry and artillery, and by our cavalry.

The enemy returned at a charge with two columns of infantry to retake the redoubt, but it was vigorously received by the Compans division and obliged to retreat after a long fusillade. During this time, Prince Poniatowski repulsed on my right the enemy in front of him and overtook a mountainous position. The combat lasted until ten o'clock at night, and we took position.

The result of this day gives His Majesty a few prisoners, seven pieces of artillery and the position he had wanted to occupy.

Everyone did their duty; General Caland and Marquis Gulano, my aides-de-camp, were wounded.

I will address to the chief of staff the state of the officers, NCOs and soldiers who distinguished themselves the most, and solicit for them the advancement and rewards they deserve.

JOACHIM NAPOLEON

Reports on the battle of the Moskova
Report from the King of Naples to the Major-General
Majaisk, 9 September 1812

During the night of the 6th to the 7th, I received some general dispositions for the battle; I ordered the execution of these dispositions, and at 5 o'clock in the morning the 1st, 2nd and 4th Corps of Cavalry Reserve were in columns of each brigade, and at the foot of the redoubt.

The 1st Corps of Reserve was to support the attack of the 1st Army Corps, the 2nd that of the 3rd Army Corps. The 4th marched in reserve at the centre, and was to support either of those corps according to the need. His Majesty had placed the 3rd Corps of Reserve at the disposition of the Viceroy. Once the attack signal was given, everything was put in movement in that order.

The Emperor, upon receiving word that the Prince of Eckmühl had just been wounded, gave me orders to go to him and take command of the 1st Army Corps if the Prince was not in condition to resume his command. I returned to inform His Majesty that the Prince had told me his wound was only a contusion and that he was able to continue to command. A moment later, His Majesty told me to advance and see what was happening at the redoubts; I went there at a full gallop. As I arrived, our light troops entered the second redoubt from which they were repulsed. Some Russian cuirassiers were charging our light infantry, but they were received with a brisk fusillade from our infantry and pushed back quickly by the 1st Brigade of the Bruyères division.

A charge of the Württemberger regiment of the Beurmann brigade was made at the same time with great success upon the Russian infantry that was marching at the first redoubt, and was entirely sabred. Then, I ordered a charge at the second redoubt, which was definitely taken.

The whole 1st Corps of Cavalry received the order to take position behind these redoubts, and the 4th Corps also received orders to advance, cross the ravine and charge the cannon of the infantry which were at the village, a very important position for the enemy. General Latour-Maubourg, at the head of the Saxon cuirassiers, debauched on the enemy in spite of their infantry and artillery fire, charged it, sabred a large number and maintained his position. During this time,

General Nansouty, at the head of the 1st Division of cuirassiers under the orders of General Saint-Germain, charged vigorously all that was on the right of the two redoubts and swept the plain as far as the ravine of the village. At that moment, His Majesty dispatched Friant's division to me. General Dufour crossed the ravine at the head of the 15th Light Infantry regiment, routed the enemy and arrived on the major heights of the position that was behind the village. General Friant supported this movement with all the rest of his division placed in reserve by brigade. Then, I had General Caulaincourt, at the head of the 2nd Corps of Reserve, cross also; as soon as he arrived on the other side of the ravine I gave him orders to charge on his left all that was there of the enemy, and attempt to reach the big redoubt, which, taking us in the flank, caused us a lot of mischief each time it found a favourable occasion. That order was executed with as much rapidity as bravery. General Caulaincourt, at the head of the 2nd Division of cuirassiers under the command of General Watier, overthrew everything he met in front of him, and finding he had gone past the large redoubt on the left, came back and fell upon it and with the 5th of Cuirassiers took it from the enemy. This brave general died gloriously in that redoubt, which was held until the troops of the Gérard division arrived. However, the Russians formed several masses of infantry composed of the Russian Guard and of their reserve. Supported by a great number of cavalry, the enemy was marching to re-take the village. I had ordered the successive arrival of all the artillery of the cavalry and that of the Friant division. About 80 pieces of artillery were put in battery within grapeshot of the enemy masses. I ordered a rolling fire, which stopped the movements of the Russians. The Emperor was able to convince himself of the hardship inflicted by our artillery on the enemy when he surveyed the field of battle yesterday.

The Russian cuirassiers supported the movement of their infantry and charged several times the artillery, the cavalry and the French infantry. They were constantly repulsed with great losses, and the field of battle is covered with their dead. They lost a great number of horses in these different charges. The brigade of carabiniers under the orders of Generals Paultre and Chouard and the 11th and 12th Regiments of Chasseurs headed by General Pajol, as well as the Saint-Germain and Bruyères divisions, all have particularly distinguished themselves as they were in front.

The time had come to extinguish all the enemy's artillery fire and to seize its last position, which was forward of the left of the 3rd Corps. I ordered the Friant division to march; meanwhile, I ordered a vigorous charge to be made on the whole front. The enemy was overthrown, threw itself into the woods and retired its artillery; all the plain was cleared and the last position taken out: that is where I had the good fortune to meet His Majesty.

Here is the history of what the troops accomplished under my orders at the battle of the 7th. The corps of all the arms rivaled with zeal, courage and devotion for the service of the Emperor. As soon as the state of generals, officers, non-commissioned officers and soldiers who distinguished themselves reaches me, I will hastily release their names. However, I must particularly cite Generals Montbrun and Caulaincourt who died with glory on the battlefield. General Belliard had a horse killed under him and two wounded.

Generals Nansouty, Grouchy, Friant, Bordessoulle, Mourier, Queunot, Roussel, Chouard and Bessières distinguished themselves. Generals Latour-Maubourg, Pajol, Bruyères, Lahoussaye, Piré, Jacquinot and Dufour, as well as Generals Dery and Dumont, who marched at the head of different charges, all had horses killed or wounded.

I must also cite Generals Pignatelli, Rossetti; Colonels Romeuf, Gobert, Picerno and Berthemy (the latter was wounded); Squadron Chief Bonnafoux, also wounded; Prince Curiati and Lieutenants Beaufremont, Petitin and Pérignon. The latter, consumed by a fever, whom I wanted to send back, answered me this way, 'Sire, I ask Your Majesty to permit me to stay by your side; one is never sick on the day of a battle.'

I will cite Colonel Borelli and the officers of my staff whose case I have the honour to send to you and for whom I request the advancement from Your Majesty.

JOACHIM NAPOLEON

Report of Marshal Duke of Elchingen to the Major-General

Before Borodino, route of Majaisk, 9 September 1812

My Lord,

According to the orders of Your Most Serene Highness, the troops of the 3rd Corps took position on the 5th before the abbey of Kolinsky, on the left of the Kologha, and stayed at the ready to support the 1st Corps, a part of which had just attacked and taken the redoubt near the village of —.

On the 6th, the 3rd and 8th Corps formed on the height behind this redoubt; the day was spent in reconnoitring, and, the enemy holding its position behind Borodino, the battle was set for the 7th.

The instructions Your Highness addressed to me on the morning of the 7th expressed that with the 3rd and the 8th Corps, which the Emperor had put under my orders, I would hold the centre of the battle, leaning my right on the 1st Corps and my left on the 4th. I also had at my disposition the 3rd Corps of the cavalry reserves.

The Emperor ordered that the 1st Corps should start its attack along the wood, protected by batteries of 12-pounders, which had been constructed during the night; His Majesty gave me orders to attack at about 7 o'clock in the morning. I gathered the generals at once to review verbally the written instructions they had already received; the head of the troops read His Majesty's proclamation; it was welcomed by the soldiers with enthusiasm and to the cries of 'Long live the Emperor!' At once we started to march towards the enemy.

The divisions of the 3rd Corps advanced in the following order: the 10th, the 25th and the 11th; the first in column of attack, with its last regiments in column of battalions deployed at a distance of division, ready to form square and to serve as reserve. The 8th Corps was deployed on two lines.

The 10th division, after having repulsed all the sharpshooters and posts, approached the redoubt on the left of the enemy with the greatest valour, this redoubt was attacked at the same time by the troops of the 1st Corps, so that the 24th of Light Infantry and the 37th Line entered it pell-mell. The enemy, recovering from its first shock, turned around and went back to re-take the redoubt; but the 25th Division marched at that same moment to support the 10th and the enemy was repulsed. A charge I had executed by the 14th Brigade of Light Cavalry seconded the efforts and was successful.

While the 10th and 25th Divisions were engaged this way, the 11th marched on the redoubt of the centre and seized it. The enemy's renewed efforts, although making successively several charges of infantry and cavalry, were in vain; it retreated in great disorder and renounced re-taking its positions.

The 8th Corps then arrived on the heights; I directed it to the right to attack, along with the Poles, the left of the enemy, which they accomplished with a lot of vigour.

As soon as I perceived that the redoubt of the right had been taken by the troops of the 1st and 4th Corps, I directed myself on the enemy, outflanking its left until it retreated.

I could not give too much praise in the great devotion of the troops under my orders, and it is nice to think that the zeal that animates them will be appreciated by the Emperor, as His Majesty himself witnessed it.

The loss of the 3rd Corps has been 2,500 killed or wounded. The battlefield attests to the immense losses suffered by the enemy.

MARSHAL DUKE OF ELCHINGEN

Report of the Viceroy to the Major-General

Rouza, 10 September 1812

In accordance with the orders of His Majesty, the 4th Army Corps left on 5 September at six o'clock in the morning from its camp, forward of Lousos. After an hour's march, a brisk cannonade on my right alerted me that the enemy was resisting the troops that were advancing on the road to Moscow. His Majesty's instructions were to turn the redoubt of the enemy's army. I would then seize a village built on a height, which the Russians had neglected to occupy. As soon as they saw us the masters of this place, they started a retrograde movement. This movement could only take place under firing from our cannon charged with grapeshot, which took all the corps in flank or in the rear that passed within our reach. The enemy gathered with fresh troops arrived in its position at Borodino; some campaign works added a lot to the natural strength of the site. In the afternoon, the 4th Corps delivered a sustained artillery fire to support the attack His Majesty had ordered on the redoubt, against which the enemy army was leaning its left.

On the 6th, the day was spent in preparations and reconnaissance. His Majesty put the Morand and Gérard divisions at my disposition, as well as the corps of cavalry of General Grouchy, to which I joined the next day the brigade of light cavalry of General Guyon. In the evening the troops were disposed as follows:

The division of General Morand on the right, that of General Gérard behind it, farther to the right and in the rear the cavalry of General Grouchy, in charge of gaining the area which would allow the best use of his arm, as quickly as the circumstances would permit. At the centre and in echelon of the Gérard division was placed the Broussier division, with the Royal Guard on foot and on horse behind it in reserve. The Delzons division formed the extreme left. It was supported by the light cavalry division under the orders of General Ornano. During the night, General of Engineers Poitevin threw four bridges over the little river of Kologha, the banks of which were scraped and cut by a great many ravines and separated us from the enemy.

The order of His Majesty was to seize the village of Borodino as soon as I heard the cannonade well under way on my right, and advance as we made progress in that part. Thus, the next day, the 7th, at five thirty in the morning, General Delzons had the 106th attack the village of Borodino. At the moment when this brave regiment formed in a column entered the village, General Plauzonne, who guided it, fell mortally wounded from a gunshot. The 106th, carried away by its bravery, rapidly crossed the three bridges the enemy had established on the

Kologha behind the village and advanced towards the enemy lines. The Russians, persuaded that our intention was to debouch from that point to separate their wing from the centre, settled their attention on that point for several hours. The Adjutant-Commandant Boisserolle, whom I praise much, had replaced General Plauzonne; he took some excellent dispositions for the conservation of the village of Borodino, which according to the general instructions of the battle, was not to be passed.

While this was happening on my left, I had sent forward the division of General Morand, in charge of attacking the redoubt which covered the center of the enemy's army; it was formed, the first line deployed, the second by columns of battalions. In spite of 80 pieces of artillery and violent musketry fire, that brave division came out of the ravines and advanced very calmly on the plateau. The 30th Line crossed the bayonet and penetrated the redoubt; but they could not maintain their position. General Bonnamy, who marched at the head of the regiment, was wounded and taken in the redoubt. For the moment, our efforts had to concentrate on the conservation of the plateau: five lines of Russian infantry were advancing to reclaim it and were approaching the right of General Morand. Immediately I had the Gérard division start to form a little beyond and to the right of the first; the 7th Light was placed on the left, and I arranged the division of General Broussier to support them. The combat became engaged again along this whole line with extreme vigour. The enemy renewed its efforts to take away the plateau; but it was in vain. His Majesty's troops remained unshakable in their position.

In the hope of creating a useful diversion to disengage his centre, the enemy decided to make a big movement of cavalry by his right, while turning our left. Eight regiments and several thousand Cossacks totally overflowed this wing and the Russian artillery was doubled to cannonade the village. The brave Colonel of Artillery Demay was killed on the plateau. The light cavalry division of General Ornano, too weak to offer resistance to such considerable forces, retreated in order. The 2nd Line of General Delzons, which had been constantly supporting the troops that defended the village of Borodino, was rapidly formed into squares. This formation was not yet accomplished when the Croats received a charge that they repulsed with their fire. The enemy cavalry, reinforced by new squadrons, came to charge the 84th, which received it in the same manner. The forces of this cavalry were increasing each moment, it renewed successively its charges on the square of the Light 8th and the Croats, of the 84th and the 92nd; but everywhere it is received and sent back with the same vigour. The Hussars of the Russian Imperial Guard were particularly mistreated; the enemy gave up the idea of breaking down our infantry.

In the centre and to the right of the troops under my orders, the combat had continued with the same ardour. Upon returning from the left where my presence had been necessary, I made new dispositions for the attack of the great redoubt. Five battalions of the Gérard division, which had not been engaged, were placed on the right, the Broussier division in front and to the left. All this infantry rose at a charge and without firing; at the same time the cuirassiers that were on its right made a very brilliant charge and entered the redoubt. The 21st, 17th, 9th and 25th Line attacked the redoubt in front and in the flank, and seized it; there were still 21 pieces of artillery there. The enemy had formed in the rear on several lines and was covered by a ravine; I had it attacked; my troops crossed the ravine, overthrew the enemy and established themselves on the opposite plateau: the Russians, crushed, retreated. In spite of the obstacles of the terrain, General Grouchy executed a great charge with the division of cavalry of General Chastel who, at that moment supported the left of the infantry. General Grouchy was slightly wounded by a splinter of a shell.

I should cite all the regiments who were engaged; but the 106th, 9th, 30th and 21st Line have been remarkable by their calm and their intrepidity. My staff has particularly distinguished itself; it joined in several charges of infantry and cavalry. Almost all of the officers who are a part of it have been wounded or dismounted. I must especially mention to Your Highness the essential services given on that memorable day by Generals Morand, Guilleminot, Gérard, Almeras and Colonel Bertrand of the 106th.

My aide-de-camp Seve and the young Fontanes of Saint-Marcellin deserve to be cited in this report.

EUGÈNE NAPOLEON

Eighteenth Bulletin

Majaisk, 10 September 1812

On the 4th, the Emperor set out from Ghjat, and encamped near the post of Gritneva.

On the 5th, at six o'clock in the morning, the army put itself in motion. At two in the afternoon we perceived the Russians formed, with their right upon the Moskova, the left upon the heights on the left bank of the Kologha. At 1200 *toises* in advance of the left, the enemy had begun to fortify a fine height between two woods where it had placed 9,000 or 10,000 men. The Emperor, having reconnoitred it, resolved not to lose a moment and to carry this position. Orders were given to the King of Naples to cross the Kologha with the Compans division and the cavalry. Prince Poniatowski, who had marched on the right, was in a condition to turn the position. At four o'clock the attack commenced. In one hour the enemy's redoubt was carried, with the cannon; the enemy's corps driven from the wood and put to flight, leaving the third part in the field of battle. At seven in the evening the firing ceased.

On the 6th, at two o'clock in the morning, the Emperor surveyed the enemy's advanced posts: the day was passed in reconnoitring. The enemy was in a much-contracted position. Its left was weakened by the loss of the position on the day before: backed by a large wood, supported by a fine height, crowned by a redoubt, planted with 25 pieces of artillery. Two other heights, crowned with redoubts at 100 paces from each other, protected their line as far as a large village that the enemy had destroyed to cover the ridge with artillery and infantry and to support the centre. Its right extended behind the Kologha, in the rear of the village of Borodino; and was supported by two fine heights, crowned with redoubts and fortified with batteries. This position appeared strong and favourable. It was easy to manoeuvre and to oblige the enemy to evacuate it; but that would have been renouncing our object, and the position was not judged sufficiently strong to render it necessary to avoid fighting. It was easy to perceive that the redoubts were but half-formed, the moat shallow and with no palisades or pointed stakes. We reckoned the enemy's force at about 120,000 or 130,000 men. Our forces were equal, but the superiority of our troops was not doubtful.

On the 7th, at two in the morning, the Emperor was surrounded by the Marshals in the position taken two evenings before. At half past five o'clock, the sun rose without clouds: it had rained the preceding evening. 'This is the sun of

Austerlitz,' said the Emperor. Throughout the month of September it was as cold as a December in Moravia. The army accepted the omen. The drums beat, and the following order of the day was read:

Soldiers, behold the field of battle you have so much desired! Henceforth victory depends on you: it is necessary to us; it will give us abundance, good quarters for the winter, and a speedy return to your country. Behave yourselves as you did at Austerlitz, at Friedland, Vitebsk, at Smolensk, that the latest posterity may speak of your conduct this day with pride, that it may say of each of you, 'He was at that great battle under the walls of Moscow.'

At the Imperial camp on the heights of Borodino, 7 September, two o'clock in the morning.

The army answered with reiterated acclamations. The ground on which the army stood was spread with the dead bodies of the Russians killed two days before.

Prince Poniatowski, who was on the right, put himself in motion to turn the forest on which the enemy rested its left. The Prince of Eckmühl marched on the skirt of the forest, the Compans division at the head. Two batteries of 60 cannon each, commanding the enemy's position, had been constructed in the night.

At six o'clock, General Count Sorbier, who had armed the battery on the right with the artillery of the reserve of the Guard, commenced fire. General Pernety, with 30 cannon, put himself at the head of the Compans division, (4th of the 1st Corps,) who skirted the wood, turning the head of the enemy's position. At half-past six, General Compans was wounded; at seven, the Prince of Eckmühl had his horse killed. The attack advanced, the musketry was engaged. The Viceroy, who formed our left, attacks and carries the village of Borodino, which the enemy could not defend, that village being on the left bank of the Kologha. At seven, Marshal Duke of Elchingen put himself in motion, and under the protection of 60 cannon which General Foucher had placed the evening before against the enemy's centre bore upon the centre. A thousand pieces of artillery spread death on all sides.

At eight o'clock, the positions of the enemy were carried, its redoubts taken and our artillery crowned its heights. The advantage of position that the enemy's batteries had enjoyed for two hours now belonged to us. The parapets, which had been occupied against us during the attack, were now to our advantage. The enemy saw the battle lost, which it thought had only commenced. A part of its artillery was taken; the rest was withdrawn to its lines in the rear. In this extremity it attempted to restore the combat, and to attack with all its masses those strong positions that it was unable to protect. Three hundred pieces of French artillery placed on these heights thundered upon the enemy's masses, and its soldiers died at the foot of those parapets which it had raised a few days past with so much labour and as a protecting shelter.

The King of Naples made various charges with the cavalry. The Duke of Elchingen covered himself with glory and displayed as much intrepidity as coolness. The Emperor ordered a change of front, the right in advance; this movement made us masters of three parts of the field of battle. Prince Poniatowski fought in the wood with various successes.

There still remained to the enemy the redoubts to the right. General Count Morand marched there and captured them; but at nine in the morning, attacked on all sides, he could not maintain his position. The enemy, encouraged by this advantage, made its reserve and his last troops advance to try his fortune again. The [Russian] Imperial Guard formed a part of them. It attacked our centre, on which our right had pivoted. For a moment it was feared that the enemy might carry the village which was burnt; the Friant division advanced: 80 pieces of French cannon immediately arrest and then annihilate the enemy's columns, which stood for two hours in close order under the chain-shot, not daring to advance, unwilling to retire, renouncing the hope of victory. The King of Naples decided their uncertainty. He caused the 4th Cavalry Corps to make a charge; they penetrated the breaches that our cannon-shot had made in the condensed masses of the Russians and the squadrons of their cuirassiers; they dispersed on all sides. General of Division Count Caulaincourt, Governor of the Emperor's Pages, advanced at the head of the 5th Regiment of Cuirassiers, overthrew everything, and entered the redoubt on the left by its gorge. From this moment there was no longer any uncertainty. The battle was gained. He turned upon the enemy the 21 cannon that were found in the redoubt. Count Caulaincourt, who had distinguished himself in this fine charge, has terminated his destiny. He fell dead, struck by a bullet; a glorious death, and worthy of envy.

It was now two in the afternoon: the enemy had lost all hope; the battle was ended; the cannonade still continued; the enemy fought for retreat and safety, but no longer for victory.

The loss of the enemy is enormous; from 12,000 to 13,000 men, and from 8,000 to 9,000 Russian horses, have been counted on the field of battle: 60 pieces of artillery and 5,000 prisoners have remained in our power.

We have had 2,500 killed and thrice that number wounded. Our total loss may be estimated at 10,000 men, that of the enemy at from 40,000 to 50,000. Never was there seen such a field of battle. Out of six dead bodies, there were five Russians for one Frenchman. Forty Russian generals were killed, wounded or taken. General Bagration was wounded.

We have lost General of Division Montbrun, killed by a cannonball; General Count Caulaincourt, who was sent to occupy his place, was killed by a shot of the same kind an hour afterwards.

Generals of Brigade Compere, Plauzonne, Marion and Huard were killed; seven or eight generals were wounded, the majority of them slightly. The Prince of Eckmühl has received no injury. The French troops covered themselves with glory and displayed their great superiority over the Russian troops.

Such, in a few words, is a sketch of the battle of the Moskova, fought a few leagues in the rear of Majaisk, and 25 leagues from Moscow, near the little river of the Moskova. We fired 60,000 cannon-shot, which are already replaced by the arrival of 800 artillery carts, which passed Smolensk previous to the battle. All the woods and villages from the field of battle to this place are covered with dead and wounded. We have found here 2,000 killed or amputated Russians. A number of generals and colonels are prisoners.

The Emperor was never exposed; neither the Imperial Guard of foot or horse was engaged or lost a single man. The victory was never uncertain. Had the enemy, when driven from its entrenchments, not endeavoured to re-take them, our loss would have been greater than its; but it destroyed its army by keeping it, from eight o'clock until two, under the fire of our batteries and in obstinately attempting to regain that which it had lost. This was the cause of its immense loss.

Everyone was distinguished. The King of Naples and the Duke of Elchingen were particularly conspicuous.

The artillery, and particularly that of the Guard, surpassed itself. The actions that have rendered this day illustrious shall be made known in detailed reports.

Monsieur Bishop of —

The crossing of the Niemen, of the Dvina, the Borysthenes, the combats of Mohilow, of the Drissa, of Polotsk, or Ostrovno, of Smolensk, and the battle of Moskova, furnish many respective reasons for addressing thanks to the God of Armies; our will therefore is that on receiving this present letter you concert together with those whom it may concern. Assemble my people in the churches to chant prayers, conformably to the usage of the Church in similar circumstances.

This letter having no other object, I pray God to have you in his holy keeping. From our Imperial Quarters at Majaisk, 10 September 1812

NAPOLEON

By the Emperor, COUNT DARU, MINISTER SECRETARY OF STATE

Nineteenth Bulletin

Moscow, 16 September 1812

After the battle of the Moskova, the French army pursued the enemy toward Moscow by the three routes of Majaisk, Svenigorod and Kaluga.

The King of Naples was on the 9th at Koubinskoié, the Viceroy at Rouza and Prince Poniatowski at Fominskoië. The headquarters were transferred on the 12th from Majaisk to Peselina; on the 13th they were at the castle of Berwska; on the 14th, at midday, we entered Moscow. The enemy had raised some redoubts on Sparrow Mountain, two *versts* from the city, which it abandoned.

The city of Moscow is as large as Paris; it is an extremely rich city, full of palaces of all the nobles of the empire. The Russian governor [Count Fëdor] Rostopchin wished to ruin this fine city when he saw it abandoned by the Russian army. He had armed 3,000 malefactors, whom he had taken from the dungeons; he also summoned together 6,000 satellites and distributed arms among them from the arsenal.

Our advanced guard, arrived in the centre of the city, was received by a fusillade of musket fire from the Kremlin. The King of Naples ordered a battery of a few pieces of artillery to be engaged, dispersed this rabble, and took possession of the Kremlin.

We have found in the arsenal 60,000 new muskets and 120 cannon on their carriages. The most complete anarchy reigned in the city; some drunken madmen ran through its different quarters, and everywhere set fire to them. Governor Rostopchin had caused all the merchants and shopkeepers to be carried off through whose instrumentality order might have been re-established. More than 400 French and Germans were arrested by his orders; finally, he had taken the precaution of carrying off the firemen, with the fire engines, so that the most complete anarchy has desolated this great and fine city, and the flames are devouring it. We had found in it considerable resources of every kind.

The Emperor is lodged in the Kremlin, which is in the centre of the city like a kind of citadel, surrounded by high walls. Thirty thousand wounded or sick Russians are abandoned in the hospitals, without succour and without nourishment. The Russians acknowledge that they lost 50,000 men in the battle of the Moskova. Prince Bagration was mortally wounded. A list has been made of the Russian Generals wounded or killed in the battle; it amounts to between 45 and 50.

Twentieth Bulletin

Moscow, 17 September 1812

The Russians have sung the *Te Deum* for the battle of Polotsk. The *Te Deum* has been sung for the battles of Riga, for the battle of Ostrovno, and for that of Smolensk. According to the Russian accounts they were everywhere conquerors, and they had driven the French to a great distance from the field of battle. It was then amid the strains of the Russian *Te Deum* that the army arrived at Moscow. There they thought themselves conquerors; at least the populace thought so, for well-informed persons knew what was happening.

Moscow is the warehouse of Asia and Europe. Its storehouses were immense; every house was provided for eight months with necessities of every description. It was only the evening before, and the day of our entrance, that the danger became known. We found in the house of the miserable Rostopchin some papers and a letter half-written; he fled without finishing it.

Moscow, one of the finest and richest cities in the world, is no more.

On the 14th, the Russians set fire to the money market, the bazaar and the hospital. On the 16th, a violent wind started blowing; 300 to 400 brigands set fire in the city in 500 places at once, by orders of Governor Rostopchin. The majority of the houses are made of wood; the fire spread with prodigious rapidity, it was an ocean of flames. Churches, there were 1,600 of them; palaces, more than 1,000; immense magazines; almost everything has been consumed. The Kremlin was preserved.

This loss for Russia is incalculable, as well as for its commerce and its nobility who had left everything there. It is not evaluating too high the cost at several billion.

About 100 of these incendiaries have been apprehended and shot; all of them declared that they acted under the orders of Rostopchin and the director of the police.

Thirty thousand sick and wounded Russians have been burnt. The richest commercial houses in Russia are ruined. The shock must be considerable. The clothing, the magazines and the equipment of the Russian army have been consumed. They have thus lost everything: they would remove nothing, because they always thought it impossible for us to reach Moscow, and because they were willing to deceive the people. When they saw all in the hands of the French, they conceived the horrible project of destroying by fire this first capital, this holy city, the centre of the empire; and they have reduced to beggary 200,000 respectable inhabitants. This is the crime of Rostopchin, executed by felons liberated from the prisons.

The resources which the army had found are consequently much diminished: however, we have collected, and are still collecting, a number of necessaries. All the cellars are untouched by the fire; and the inhabitants, during the last 24 hours had saved many articles. They endeavoured to stop the progress of the flames, but the Governor had taken the horrid precaution of carrying off or destroying all the pumps.

The army is recovering from its fatigues: it has abundance of bread, potatoes, cabbages and other vegetables, meat, salted provisions, wine, brandy, sugar, coffee and, in short, provisions of all sorts.

The advanced guard is 20 *versts* on the road to Kazan, by which the enemy is retreating. Another French advanced guard is on the road to Saint Petersburg, where the enemy has not a single soldier.

The temperature is still that of autumn. The soldiers have found, and continue to find, a number of fur-trimmed coats and furs for the winter. Moscow was the depot of those articles.

299

Twenty-first Bulletin

Moscow, 20 September 1812

Three hundred incendiaries have been arrested and shot. They were armed with fuses six inches long, which they had between two pieces of wood. They had also explosives, which they threw upon the roofs of the houses. The miserable Rostopchin had these prepared on the pretext that he wished to send a balloon, full of combustible matter, into the French army. He thus got together the explosives and other materials, necessary for the execution of his project.

The fires subsided on the 19th and 20th. Three-quarters of the city is burned; among other palaces that beautiful one of Catherine, which had been newly furnished. Not more than a quarter of the houses remain.

While Rostopchin was taking away the pumps of the city, he left behind him 60,000 muskets, 150 cannon, more than 100,000 balls and shells, 1,500,000 cartridges, 400,000 pounds of gunpowder, 400,000 pounds of saltpetre and sulphur. It was not until the 19th that the powder, saltpetre and sulphur were discovered at a fine establishment half a league from the city. This is a matter of importance: we are now supplied with ammunition for two campaigns.

Every day we discover cellars full of wine and brandy.

Manufactures were beginning to flourish at Moscow; they are destroyed. The conflagration of this capital will throw Russia back 100 years.

The weather is becoming rainy. The greatest part of the army is in barracks in Moscow.

Twenty-second Bulletin

Moscow, 27 September 1812

Consul General Lesseps has been appointed Intendant of the Province of Moscow. He has organized a municipality and several commissions, all composed of the inhabitants of the country.

The fires have entirely ceased. We discover every day magazines of sugar, furs, clothes, etc.

The enemy's army appears to retire to Kaluga and Tula. Tula contains the greatest manufactory of arms in all Russia. Our advanced guard is on the Pakra.

The Emperor is lodged in the Imperial Palace of the Kremlin. We have found in the Kremlin several of the ornaments used at the coronation of the Emperors, and all the flags taken from the Turks for the last 100 years.

The weather is nearly the same as at the end of October at Paris. It rains a little, and we have had some white frosts. We are assured that the Moskova and the rivers of the country are not frozen over before the middle of November.

The greater part of the army is cantoned in Moscow, where it recovers from its fatigues.

Twenty-third Bulletin

Moscow, 9 October 1812

The advanced guard, commanded by the King of Naples, is upon the Nara, 20 leagues from Moscow. The enemy's army is at Kaluga. Some skirmishes have taken place for the last three days. The King of Naples has had all the advantages, and always drives the enemy from its positions.

The Cossacks hover upon our flanks. A patrol of 150 dragoons of the Guard, commanded by Major Marthod, has fallen into an ambush of the Cossacks between the road of Moscow and Kaluga. The dragoons sabred 300 of them, and opened themselves a passage; but they left 20 men upon the battlefield, who were taken; among them is the Major, mortally wounded.

The Duke of Elchingen is at Boghorodock. The advanced guard of the Viceroy is at Troitsksa, upon the road to Dmitrow.

The flags taken by the Russians from the Turks in different wars, and several curious things found in the Kremlin, have been sent off for Paris. We found in the principal church a Madonna enriched with diamonds and pearls, with the following attached inscription in the Russian language:

> The French and Poles having been conquered by the Russians, and the town of Danzig having been taken in 1733, the Empress Anne Iwanowa enriched, in 1740, with pearls and diamonds this image of the virgin, as actions of thanks for this event.

We have sent it to Paris.

It appears that Rostopchin has emigrated. At Voronovo he set fire to his castle, and left the following writing attached to a post:

> I have for eight years embellished this country-house, and I have lived happy in it in the bosom of my family. The inhabitants of this estate, to the number of 1720, leave it at your approach;[1] and I set fire to my house, that it may not be polluted by your presence. Frenchmen, I have abandoned to you my two Moscow houses, with furniture worth half a million roubles; here you will only find ashes.[2]
>
> [Signed] COUNT FËDOR ROSTOPCHIN

1 They have returned.

2 In truth he set fire himself to his country house, but his example has but few imitators. All the houses in the neighbourhood of Moscow are untouched.

The palace of Prince Kourakin is one of those that have been saved from the fire. General Count Nansouty is lodged there. We succeeded with great difficulty in withdrawing from the hospitals and houses on fire a part of the Russian sick. There remain about 4,000 of these wretched men. The number of those who perished in the fire is extremely great.

We have had for the last eight days a warmer sun than is experienced at Paris at this season. We do not perceive that we are in the north.

The Duke of Reggio, who is at Vilna, has entirely recovered. The enemy's General-in-Chief, Bagration, is dead of the wounds which he received in the battle of the Moskova.

The Russian army disavows the fire of Moscow; the authors of this attempt are held in horror among the Russians, they consider Rostopchin as a sort of Marat; he has been able to console himself in the society of the English Commissioner Wilson.

The Staff Major will cause the details of the battles of Smolensk and the Moskova to be printed, and point out those who distinguished themselves.

We have just armed the Kremlin with 30 cannon, and constructed *fleches* [arrow-shaped fortifications] at all the entrances of it. It forms a fortress; bakeries and magazines are established in it.

Twenty-fourth Bulletin

Moscow, 14 October 1812

General Baron Delzons has marched on Dmitrov. The King of Naples is with the advanced guard on the Nara, in presence of the enemy, which is occupied in recruiting their army by completing it from the militia.

The weather is very fine. The first snow fell yesterday. In 20 days, it will be necessary to be in winter quarters.

The troops that Russia had in Moldavia have joined General Tormasov. Those from Finland have been disembarked at Riga. They marched out and attacked the 10th Corps; they have been beaten: 3,000 men were made prisoner. We have not yet the official account of this brilliant affair, which does so much honour to General Yorck.

All our wounded have been removed to Smolensk, Minsk and Mohilev. A great number have been restored to health and have rejoined their corps.

A great many private letters between Saint Petersburg and Moscow make us well acquainted with the situation of this empire. The project of burning Moscow having been kept secret, the greater part of the nobles and private individuals had removed nothing.

The engineers have taken a plan of the city, and houses are marked which were saved from the flames. It shows that we did not succeed in saving more than 10 per cent part of the town; the other nine-tenths no longer exist.

Report of Marshal Gouvion Saint-Cyr to His Highness the Prince Major-General

20 October 1812

In my last communication of the 17th of the current month, I informed Your Highness that the next day I would probably have all the forces assembled under the orders of Count Wittgenstein on the 2nd Corps. I spoke to you of the reinforcements he had received from Petersburg, and amounting to 17,000 men, including 6,000 to 8,000 militiamen, picked up in Petersburg and in the environs. He also received the 21st Division, arriving from Finland: a part of this division had only engaged, passing near Riga, in an affair against the Prussians. It joined with the troops of Wittgenstein at Disna, on the 16th, at the time when he turned out the post I had placed there.

On the 18th, at six o'clock in the morning, Mr Wittgenstein emerged in the front of Polotsk with four columns, deploying his troops around my position and taking advantage of the enormous superiority he had, to take in the rear and, without any danger, the position I occupied on the left bank of the Polota, opposite the one he previously occupied on the Drissa.

His first serious attack was carried against a barbette battery that I had established in an advantageous position, and which we had to occupy at all cost so as not to give to the enemy the weakest part of my position, that is to say, the front of the town where the only obstacle was a timber stockade, the front of which I had covered but was not yet finished and was open everywhere, notably at the two little bastions that were to support it but were barely traced. However, I had a few pieces put there which served us well.

The battery of the Tuileries was taken and retaken three or four times: it was defended by the troops of the 8th Division under the command of General of Division Maison. The defence of this front of attack gave him much honour, as well as to the corps in charge of its defence, that is to say, the 2nd, 37th Regiments of Infantry of Line and the 11th of Light Infantry, and two squadrons of the 16th Regiment of Cuirassiers under the command of Remberg; two squadrons of light troops of the 8th Lancers and 20th Chasseurs under the command of Squadron Chief Curel, who supported the right of the 8th Division and whose conduct deserves the greatest praises in all the charges they received or made against forces so disproportionate to theirs.

The enemy deployed another of its columns before the front of the 6th Division under the command of General Legrand. The enemy directed its attack principally on a battery that was not finished, on the left bank of the Polota and which was becoming the centre of Legrand's division. Three or four times the enemy tried to take it and was always repulsed with the kind of losses one suffers when enterprises of this sort do not succeed. Until the afternoon, the enemy had not dared attack the front of the right bank of the Polta, where several points were well entrenched and finished; around four o'clock they emerged from the road of Seibet and of Riga and proceeded as a mob full of fury on the left flank of the town, supported by the column which was emerging from the road of the Nevel. I wanted to let them use all this ardour on two redoubts built and occupied by the Bavarian artillery and the soldiers necessary to its defence and under the orders of General Vicente; but the Swiss of the 2nd Division, under the command of General Merle, and the 3rd Regiment of Croats, against the agreed upon dispositions, advanced in a hurry to meet the Russians and fought that fury with bravery, order and sang-froid which was remarkable. We finally brought the attacking Russians under the walls of the town, where the carnage that had been taking place since the morning on all the points of the army ended with nightfall. The Russians, in spite of their superiority, left the ground covered with their dead and succeeded in none of their attacks.

Notwithstanding the successes obtained during that day, I was concerned during the evening as to what my cavalry could have met on the left bank of the Dvina. I had deprived myself of the biggest part of my cavalry during this day to be undisturbed on my rear. In the evening, General Corbineau, whose brigade's horses are extremely tired, had not penetrated beyond the Duschatz, and, according to his report, had met only some cavalry and infantry. As he was quite capable, having at his disposition three small battalions of Bavarian infantry, I awaited the next day with a lot of tranquillity.

On the 19th, at daybreak, we saw the enemy moving on the line, busy rectifying their position by forming a half circle around ours. Around ten in the morning the aide-de-camp of General Corbineau arrived, informing me that he had in front of his brigade 5,000 men and 12 squadrons of cavalry. I did not waste a moment, taking one regiment in each of the three divisions of the 2nd Corps, preferably taking what we could most easily take away from in front of the enemy who would not have missed renewing its attacks and waited only for the appearance of this corps whose arrival it anticipated with impatience.

About noon, these troops defiling on the height behind Polotsk, the enemy saw what had decided this movement, but believed it was some kind of a reserve behind Polotsk. I assembled these troops under the command of General Amey; I joined to it the 7th Regiment of Cuirassiers of the Doumerc division, who had not yet met the enemy on its way coming up the Dvina. At the same time I ordered that as soon as the dusk appeared the entire army re-cross on the left bank of the Dvina.

When night fell at the moment when we started to pull our the artillery from advanced works, some imprudent soldiers set fire on the barracks of General Legrand, and it moved in a moment on the entire line, giving the enemy the certitude that we were retreating. Then, it started all the batteries firing and threw on the town a quantity of howitzer shells and other incendiary projectiles to start fires, which only partially succeeded, hoping to prevent our movements of artillery and to blow up our caissons.

This cannonade and bombardment were sustained by a general attack. We could see as if in daylight because of the fires in the town, and this attack ceased only after the last man had reached the left bank of the Dvina; but in the midst of all these attacks and the tumult caused by the conflagration, the troops conducted themselves with extraordinary bravery, and the retreat was made in the best order. At midnight all the artillery was retired and the whole troop had re-crossed at two-thirty in the morning. At once I reinforced, with two regiments that had had crossed first, the troops that I had placed during the day under the command of General Amey and which had contained the enemy that night in the defiles near Smolensk, but were not yet in sight of the army of Mr Wittgenstein. He had with his troops a Bavarian column of 6,000 to 7,000 men strong. I assembled all of them under the command of Mr Merle, to whom I gave orders to march immediately to meet the corps of General Steingel, repulse them with vigour in order to throw them back beyond the Oschatz; having then the possibility of support from another part of the army, if it became necessary. At the moment when these troops started moving, we met those of the enemy.

Steingel's corps was overthrown and, after a big loss in killed, thrown to the other side of Bolonia, and leaving in our hands 1,200 to 1,500 prisoners, among whom were 18 officers of different ranks, one of them a captain of an English vessel employed on the staff of Steingel and saying he had been in the service of Russia for three weeks. This affair brings a lot of honour to Count Wrede, who directed it, and to General Amey, who seconded him.

I owe the greatest praise to the troops for their good conduct, the zeal and intelligence of the officers of all ranks and all arms, who supported me well, and amongst whom I will cite Generals Legrand, Merle, Baron Laurencez, my chief of staff Aubry, commanding the artillery of the 2nd Corps; Dode, commander of the engineers, and Adjutant Commander Dalbignac, who have acquired on that day new rights from the benevolence of His Majesty. In a few days I will have the honour to address to Your Highness the statement of the officers who merit advancement for their good conduct.

Our loss is not very considerable in comparison with that of the enemy, which is enormous. General Legrand had a horse killed under him and has two contusions; Colonel Gueheneuc, aide-de-camp of His Majesty, is among the wounded. I have the honour to inform Your Highness that a ball I received in my left foot keeps me from walking or riding on horseback, and will force me to leave the active command of the army corps for 10 to 12 days. I gave the command to Count Legrand. I plan to stay at a distance of one march from the army corps in order to be able to resume my functions, hoping I can be of help with my council to the army corps, if General Legrand approves of them. But I await, in a few days, Marshal Duke of Reggio and the 9th Corps of the Duke of Belluno that is marching. When we have joined, we will briskly push the Russian army.

MARSHAL GOUVION SAINT-CYR

Twenty-fifth Bulletin

Noilskoe, 20 October 1812

All the sick who were in the hospitals of Moscow have been evacuated on the 15th, 16th, 17th and 18th for Majaisk and Smolensk. The artillery caissons, the ammunition taken, a great quantity of curious things and two trophies were packed up and sent off on the 15th. The army received orders to make biscuit for 20 days and hold itself in readiness to march: effectively, the Emperor left Moscow on the 19th. The headquarters were the same day at Desna.

On the one hand, the Kremlin has been armed and fortified, and at the same time it has been mined, in order to blow it up.

Some think the Emperor wants to march upon Tula and Kaluga, to pass the winter in these provinces, and occupy Moscow by a garrison in the Kremlin.

Others suppose the Emperor will blow up the Kremlin, and burn the public establishments which remain, and that he will approach within 100 leagues of Poland, to establish his winter quarters in a friendly country, and near enough to receive everything which exists in the magazines of Danzig, Kovno, Vilna and Minsk, and recover from the fatigues of war.

The latter observe that Moscow is 180 leagues of bad road from Saint Petersburg, while Vitebsk is only 130 from Petersburg: that from Moscow to Kiow is 218 leagues, while from Smolensk to Kiow is but 112 leagues; from this they conclude that Moscow is not a military position. Or that Moscow no longer possesses political importance, since that town is burned and ruined for 100 years.

The enemy showed many Cossacks who annoyed our cavalry; the advanced guard of cavalry placed in advance of Vinkovo was surprised by a horde of these Cossacks, who were in the camp before we could mount on horseback. They took General Sebastiani's park of artillery, 100 baggage wagons and about 100 prisoners.

The King of Naples mounted on horseback with the cuirassiers and carabiniers, and, perceiving a column of light infantry of four battalions that the enemy sent to support the Cossacks, he charged it, broke it, and cut it in pieces. General Dezi, aide-de-camp to the King, a brave officer, was killed in this charge, which honours the carabiniers.

The Viceroy has arrived at Fominskoië. All the army is in march.

Marshal Duke of Treviso has remained at Moscow with a garrison.

The weather is very fine, like that in France during October, perhaps a little warmer; but on the first days of November we may expect cold.

Everything indicates that we must think of winter quarters. Our cavalry particularly require it. The infantry refreshed themselves at Moscow, and are very well.

Report of Lieutenant General Count Wrede

Vynovoska, near Babinetscky, 23 October 1812

Ignorant if Marshal Count Gouvion Saint-Cyr was able to give, for the last two days, any news to Your Excellency of the position I occupy with the 6th Bavarian Corps, the 1st Brigade of the French Light Cavalry and General L'Héritier's brigade of cuirassiers, I make it my duty to give information to Your Excellency of the movements I made since the day before yesterday.

Perhaps you have learned, Duke, that on the 19th the enemy who, on the 18th had been so bravely and completely beaten before Polotsk, has gained by its superior forces a lot of ground on General Corbineau, who was to block the crossing of the Oschatz by the enemy and to arrive by the rear on Polotsk.

As the enemy was about to emerge from the town of Polotsk, Marshal Count Gouvion Saint-Cyr sent for me, to compel me to take command of the troops he had assembled on the left bank to prevent the enemy from emerging. I took command as its skirmishers were about to come out of the wood. It is to a battalion of the brave 19th Regiment of French Infantry Line, which was the closest and to which I gave orders to cross the bayonet and charge, that I owe to have thrown the enemy back half a league in the defile, before nightfall.

After this expedition was done, Marshal Gouvion Saint-Cyr placed under my orders the 19th, 37th and 124th Regiments of Infantry; the 2nd Swiss Regiment, the 7th of Cuirassiers, and the brigade of General Corbineau to try, taking with me a Bavarian brigade not very strong in numbers, to repulse on the morning of the 22nd the enemy to the other side of the Oschatz.

I divided this corps in three columns, personally heading the centre column; that of the left under the command of General Baron Amey, and that of the right commanded by the Bavarian General Baron Strath; at four thirty in the morning the enemy attacked me in the defile at the moment when I was preparing my attack. As I had given orders not to shoot and use only the bayonet to pay the enemy for its insolence, in one and a half hours of time it was chased from the defile, which is three leagues in length. The brave 19th and 37th Line, under the command of the dignified General of Brigade Grundler, covered themselves with glory. Two colonels, one major, a great number of officers, and 1,800 men were taken prisoner. After having debouched from the wood, I attacked the main corps of General Steingel, which was placed on the left bank of the Oschatz, with numerous cavalry and some artillery. After a half hour of time, the Bavarian artillery which I had with me silenced that of the enemy and I crossed the Oschatz. If at that time General Baron Amey, who had orders to come down from Rudonia on the left of the Oschatz to take the enemy by the right flank, had arrived, it is believed that all the enemy corps would have been annihilated. I pursued the enemy on the road of Disna, when I received orders from Marshal Count Gouvion Saint-Cyr to return on Polotsk, His Excellency having resolved to wait for the arrival of the 9th Corps, commanded by Marshal Duke of Belluno.

DE WREDE

Twenty-sixth Bulletin

Borowsk, 23 October 1812

After the battle of the Moskova, General Kutusov took a position a league in advance of Moscow; he established several redoubts to defend the town; he remained there until the last moment. On 14 September, seeing the French army march towards him, he evacuated the position and passed through Moscow. He crossed that city with his headquarters at nine in the morning. Our advanced guard passed through it an hour after noon.

The commandant of the Russian rearguard requested to be allowed to defile in the city, without firing; he was allowed; but in the Kremlin, the villains, armed by the Governor, made some resistance, and was immediately dispersed. Ten thousand Russian soldiers were collected in the city the next and following days, into which they had dispersed by their thirst for plunder; they were old and good soldiers; they added to the number of prisoners.

On 15, 16 and 17 September, the Russian general commanding the rearguard said that they should fire no more, that they ought to fight no more, and talked much about peace. He marched on the road of Kolomna, and our advanced guard placed itself five leagues from Moscow, on the bridge of the Moskova. During this time, the Russian army left the Kolomna road and took that of Kaluga by crossroads. It thus made the half-tour of the city at six leagues distance. The wind carried clouds of flame and smoke. This march, according to the statements of the

Russian officers, was sombre and religious. Consternation filled their souls; they assert that officers and soldiers were so penetrated, that the most profound silence reigned throughout all the army, as during prayers.

We quickly perceived the enemy's march.

The Duke of Istria marched to Desna, with a corps of observation.

The King of Naples at first followed the enemy upon Podol, and afterwards marched on their rear, threatening to cut it off from the Kaluga road. Although the King had only with him the advanced guard, the enemy only allowed itself time to evacuate the entrenchments it had constructed, and marched six leagues backwards, after a glorious battle for the advanced guard. Prince Poniatowski took a position behind the Nara, at the confluence of the Istia.

General Lauriston having, on 5 October, gone to the Russian headquarters, the communications were re-established between our advanced posts and those of the enemy, who between themselves agreed not to attack each other without giving three hours' notice. But on the 18th, at seven in the morning, 4,000 Cossacks came out from a wood, situated within half a cannon-shot of General Sebastiani, forming the extreme left of the advanced guard, who had neither been occupied nor inspected that day. They made an attack upon this light cavalry at a time when they were on foot, at the distribution of flour. This light cavalry could not form but at a quarter of a league further. While the enemy penetrated by this opening, a park of 12 pieces of artillery and 20 caissons of General Sebastiani were taken in a ravine, with baggage wagons 10 in number, in all 65 wagons instead of 100 as stated in the last Bulletin.

At the same time, the enemy's regular cavalry and two columns of infantry penetrated by the opening. They hoped to gain the wood and the defile of Voronzov before us; but the King of Naples was there; he was on horseback; he marched and penetrated the Russian line of cavalry in 10 or 12 different charges. He perceived the division of six enemy battalions commanded by Lieutenant General Muller, charged, and penetrated it. This division was massacred. Lieutenant General Muller was killed.

While this was passing, Prince Poniatowski successfully repulsed a Russian division. The Polish General Fischer was killed by a ball.

The enemy not only suffered a loss superior to ours but had the blame of having violated the truce concluded between the advanced guard, a thing hardly ever done. Our loss amounts to 800 men, in killed, wounded and taken; that of the enemy is double. Several Russian officers were taken; two of their generals were killed; and this day the King of Naples has proved what presence of mind, valour and a knowledge of war can effect. In general, throughout all this campaign the Prince has shown himself worthy of the supreme rank in which he is placed.

However, the Emperor wished to oblige the enemy to evacuate his entrenched camp and drive them several marches back, in order to be able to proceed tranquilly to the countries chosen for his winter quarters, and actually necessary to occupy for the execution of his ulterior projects, on the 17th had ordered by General Lauriston to his advanced guard to place themselves behind the defile of Winkovo, in order that their movements might not be perceived. After Moscow had ceased to exist, the Emperor had determined either to abandon this heap of ruins or only occupy the Kremlin with 3,000 men; but the Kremlin, after 15 days' labour, was not judged sufficiently strong to be abandoned for 20 or 30 days to its own forces. It would have weakened and incommoded the army in its movements, without giving a great advantage. If we wished to protect Moscow from beggars and plunderers, 20,000 men would have been necessary. Moscow is, at present, a truly unhealthy and impure sink. A population of 200,000, wandering in the neighbouring woods, dying with hunger, comes there to seek what remains, and vegetables in the gardens, to support life. It appears useless to compromise anything whatever for an object which was of no military importance and which has now become of no political importance.

All the magazines which were in the city having been carefully examined, and the others emptied, the Emperor caused the Kremlin to be mined. The Duke of Treviso caused it to be blown up at two o'clock a.m. on the 23rd; the arsenal, magazines, all were destroyed. This ancient citadel, which dates back to the foundation of the monarchy, this first palace of the Czars, has been destroyed! The Duke of Treviso has started to march for Vereja. The Emperor of Russia's aide-de-camp, Baron Winzingerode, having on the 22nd attempted to penetrate at the head of 500 Cossacks, was repulsed and taken prisoner with a young Russian officer named Narishkin.

On the 19th, the headquarters were in the castle of Troitskoe; they remained there on the 20th. On the 21st they were at Ignatiew; the 22nd at Pominskoi, all the army having made two flank-marches; and the 23rd at Borowsk.

The Emperor reckons upon marching on the 24th to gain the Dvina, and taking a position that will bring him within 80 leagues of Petersburg and Vilna; a double advantage; that is to say, 20 marches nearer his means and his object.

Of 4,000 stone houses that were in Moscow, not more than 200 remain. It has been said a fourth part remained, because in that calculation 800 churches were included, a part of which are even damaged. Of 8,000 houses of wood, nearly 500 remain. It was proposed to the Emperor to burn what remained of the city, to treat the Russians in their own way, and to extend this measure round Moscow. There are 2,000 villages, and as many country houses and *chateaux*. It was proposed to form four columns of 2,000 men each and charge them with burning everything for 20 leagues round Moscow. That will teach the Russians, said they, to make war according to rule, and not like Tartars. If they burn a village or a house, we must answer them by burning 100.

The Emperor refused to allow these measures, which would have aggravated the misfortunes of this population. Of 9,000 proprietors whose castles would have been burned, 100 perhaps would have been supporters of Marat of Russia, but 8,900 are brave people, already too much the victims of the intrigue of some wretches. To punish 100 guilty persons, 8,900 would have been ruined. We must add that it would absolutely have left without resources 200,000 poor serfs, innocent of everything. The Emperor therefore contented himself with ordering the destruction of the citadel and military establishments, according to the usages of war, without doing any thing to ruin individuals already too unhappy by the consequences of the war.

The inhabitants of Russia do not recollect such a season as we have had for the last 20 days. It is the sun and fine days of a journey from Fontainebleau. The army is in an extremely rich country; it may be compared to the best in France of Germany.

Twenty-seventh Bulletin

Vereia, 27 October 1812

On the 22nd, Prince Poniatowski marched on Vereia. On the 23rd, the army was about to follow this movement; but, in the afternoon, we learned that the enemy had left its entrenched camp and was on the march to the little town of Malo-yaroslavetz. It was found necessary to march after it and obstruct its intentions.

The Viceroy received orders to march there. Delzons' division arrived on the left bank at six in the evening on the 23rd, took possession of the bridge and re-established it.

In the night between the 23rd and 24th, two Russian divisions arrived in the village and took possession of the heights on the right bank, which are extremely advantageous.

At daybreak on the 24th, the battle commenced. During this time, the enemy's army appeared quite whole, and took a position behind the town. The Delzons, Broussier and Pino divisions, and the Italian Guard, were successively engaged. This engagement does the greatest honour to the Viceroy and the 4th Corps of the army. Two-thirds of the enemy's army was engaged to maintain its position; but this was in vain, for the town was taken, as well as the heights. The enemy retreated so precipitately that it was obliged to throw 20 cannon into the river.

Towards night, Marshal the Prince of Eckmühl debouched with his corps, and all the army was in order of battle, with its artillery, on the 25th, in the position that the enemy occupied the night before.

The Emperor moved his headquarters on the 24th to the village of Ghorodnia. At seven in the morning, 6,000 Cossacks who had slipped into the wood made a general huzza in the rear of his position, and took six pieces of artillery, which were parked. The Duke of Istria set off at a gallop with all the Horse Guard. This horde was sabred; the artillery it had taken was recovered, and several of his wagons were captured; 600 of these Cossacks were killed, wounded or taken; 30 men of the guards were wounded and 3 killed. General of Division Count Rapp had a horse killed under him. The intrepidity of which this general has given so much evidence is shown on every occasion. At the commencement of the charge, the Cossack officers called the Guards, which they remembered, *muscardins de Paris* [Parisian dormice]. Major of Dragoons Letort acted with distinction. At eight o'clock, order was re-established.

The Emperor marched to Maloyaroslavetz, reconnoitred the position of the enemy, and ordered an attack for the next morning; but in the night the enemy retreated. The Prince of Eckmühl followed it for six leagues. The Emperor then let it go, and directed the movement upon Vereja.

On the 26th, the headquarters was at Borowsk, and on the 27th, at Vereia. Tonight the Prince of Eckmühl is at Borowsk, the Duke of Elchingen at Majaisk. The weather is beautiful, the roads are excellent; it is the end of autumn: this weather will last eight days longer, and by then we shall have arrived in our new position.

In the battle of Maloyaroslavetz, the Italian guard distinguished itself. It took the position and maintained it. General Baron Delzons, a distinguished officer, was killed with three balls. Our loss was 1,500 men killed or wounded; that of the enemy is 6,000 or 7,000. We found on the battlefield 1,700 Russians, among whom were 1,100 recruits dressed in grey jackets, having hardly served two months.

The old Russian infantry is destroyed. The Russian army would have no consistence but for the numerous reinforcements of Cossacks recently arrived from the Don. Well-informed persons assure us that in the Russian infantry only the first rank is composed of soldiers, and that the second and third ranks are recruits and militia, and who, notwithstanding the promises made them, have been incorporated. The Russians had three generals killed, and General Count Pino was slightly wounded.

Twenty-eighth Bulletin

Smolensk, 11 November 1812

The Imperial headquarters were, on 1 November, at Viasma, and on the 9th at Smolensk. The weather was very fine up to the 6th, but on the 7th winter began; the ground is covered with snow. The roads have become very slippery, and very difficult for carriage horses. We have lost many men by cold and fatigue; night bivouacking is very injurious to them.

Since the battle of Maloyaroslavetz, the advanced guard has seen no other enemy than the Cossacks, who like the Arabs, prowl upon the flanks and fly about to annoy.

On the 2nd, at two in the afternoon, 12,000 Russian infantry, covered by a cloud of Cossacks, intercepted the route, a league's distance from Viasma, between the Prince of Eckmühl and the Viceroy. The Prince of Eckmühl and the Viceroy marched upon this column, drove it from the road and overthrew it in the wood; took a major-general with a good number of prisoners, and carried off six pieces of artillery; since that time we have not seen the Russian infantry again, but only Cossacks.

Since the bad weather of the 6th, we have lost more than 3,000 carriage horses and nearly 100 of our caissons have been destroyed.

General Wittgenstein, having been reinforced by the Russian division from Finland and by a great number of troops from the militia, attacked Marshal Gouvion Saint-Cyr on 18 October; he was repulsed by that Marshal and General Wrede, who took more than 3,000 prisoner and covered the battlefield with his dead.

On the 20th, Marshal Gouvion Saint-Cyr, having been informed that Marshal Duke of Belluno was advancing with the 9th Corps to reinforce him, re-crossed the Dvina and marched to meet him, so that upon having effected a junction with him they could fight Wittgenstein and oblige him to re-cross the Dvina.

Marshal Gouvion Saint-Cyr bestows the highest eulogies upon his troops. The Swiss division distinguished itself by its sang-froid and bravery. Colonel Guéheneuc of the 26th Regiment of Light Infantry was wounded. Marshal Saint-Cyr received a ball in the foot. Marshal Duke of Reggio has arrived to replace him, and he has retaken the command of the 2nd Corps.

The health of the Emperor has never been better.

Twenty-ninth Bulletin

Molodetchna, 3 December 1812

Until 6 November the weather was fine, and the movement of the army executed with the greatest success. The cold weather began on the 7th; from that moment, every night we lost several hundred horses, which died at the bivouac. Arriving at Smolensk, we had already lost many cavalry and artillery horses.

The Russian army from Volhynia was opposed to our right: our right left the Minsk line of operations, and took for the pivot of its operations the Warsaw line. On the 9th, the Emperor was informed at Smolensk of this change in the line of operations, and presumed what the enemy would do. However hard it appeared to him to put himself in movement during so cruel a season, the new state of things demanded it. He expected to arrive at Minsk, or at least upon the Beresina, before the enemy; on the 13th, he left Smolensk; on the 16th he slept at Krasnöe. The cold, which began on the 7th, suddenly increased, and on the 14th, 15th and 16th the thermometer was 16 and 18 degrees below the freezing point. The roads were covered with ice; the cavalry, artillery and baggage horses perished every night, not only by hundreds, but by thousands, particularly the German and French horses. In a few days, more than 30,000 horses perished; our cavalry were on foot; our artillery and our baggage were without conveyance. It was necessary to abandon and destroy a good part of our cannon, ammunition and provisions.

This army, so fine on the 6th, was very different on the 14th, almost without cavalry, without artillery and without transports. Without cavalry, we could not reconnoitre a quarter of a league's distance; without artillery, we could not risk a battle and firmly await it: it was requisite to march in order not to be constrained to a battle, which the want of ammunition prevented us from desiring; it was requisite to occupy a certain space, not to be turned, and that too without cavalry, which could lead and connect the columns. This difficulty, along with a cold that suddenly came on, rendered our situation miserable. Those men whom nature had not sufficiently steeled to be above all the changes of fate and fortune, lost their gaiety, their good humour, and dreamed but of misfortunes and catastrophes; those whom she has created superior to everything, preserved their gaiety, and their ordinary manners, and saw fresh glory in the different difficulties to be surmounted.

The enemy, who saw upon the roads traces of that frightful calamity which had overtaken the French army, endeavoured to take advantage of it. It surrounded all the columns with his Cossacks, who carried off, like the Arabs in the desert, the trains and carriages that separated. This contemptible cavalry, which only makes noise and is not capable of penetrating through a company of voltigeurs, rendered itself formidable by favour of circumstances. Nevertheless, the enemy had to repent of all the serious attempts that it wished to undertake: they were overthrown by the Viceroy, before whom they were placed, and lost many men.

The Duke of Elchingen, who with 3,000 men made up the rearguard, had blown up the ramparts of Smolensk: he was surrounded, and found himself in a critical position, but he extricated himself from it with that intrepidity by which he is distinguished. After having kept the enemy at a distance from him during all of the 18th, and constantly repulsing it at night, he made a movement on the right, crossed the Borysthenes, and deceived all the calculations of the enemy. On the 19th, the army crossed the Borysthenes at Orsha; and the Russian army being fatigued, and having lost a great number of men, ceased from its attempts.

The army of Volhynia had moved on the 16th to Minsk, and marched on Borisov. General Dombrowski defended the bridgehead of Borisov with 3,000 men. On the 23rd, he was forced, and obliged to evacuate this position. The enemy then crossed the Beresina, marching on Bobr; the Lambert division formed the advanced guard. The 2nd Corps, which was at Tschereia commanded by the Duke of Reggio, had received orders to march on Borisov to secure for the army the crossing of the Beresina. On the 24th, the Duke of Reggio met the Lambert division four leagues from Borisov, attacked, defeated, took 2,000 prisoners, 6 cannon, 500 baggage wagons of the army of Volhynia, and threw the enemy on the right bank of the Beresina. General Berckheim, with the 4th Cuirassiers, distinguished himself by a fine charge. The enemy could only secure its safety by burning the bridge, which is more than 300 *toises* in length.

Nevertheless, the enemy occupied all the passages of the Beresina: this river is forty toises wide, and had much floating ice on it, but its banks are covered with marshes 300 *toises* long, which present great obstacles in clearing it.

The enemy's general had placed his four divisions at different debouches, where he presumed the French army would cross.

On the 26th, at daybreak, the Emperor, after having deceived the enemy by different movements made during the day of the 25th, marched on the village of Studianka, and caused, in spite of the enemy's division, and in its presence, two bridges to be thrown over the river. The Duke of Reggio crossed, attacked the enemy, and led him, fighting two hours. The enemy retired on the bridgehead of Borisov. General Legrand, an officer of the first rate merit, was badly, but not dangerously, wounded. During all of the 26th and 27th, the army crossed.

The Duke of Belluno, commanding the 9th Corps, had received orders to follow the movement of the Duke of Reggio, to form the rearguard and keep the Russian army from the Dvina that followed him in check. Partouneaux's division formed the rearguard of this corps. On the 27th, at noon, the Duke of Belluno arrived with two divisions at the bridge of Studianka.

Partouneaux's division set out at night from Borisov. A brigade of this division, which formed the rearguard and which was charged with burning the bridge, marched at seven in the evening, and arrived between ten and eleven o'clock; it sought its first brigade and its General who had departed two hours before, and which it had not met with in its route. Its searches were in vain. Some uneasiness was then conceived. All we have since been able to learn is that the first brigade set out at five o'clock, missed its way at six, went to the right in place of proceeding to the left, and marched two or three leagues in this direction; that, during the night, and benumbed with cold, it rallied at seeing the enemies' fires, which it mistook for those of the French army. Thus surrounded, it was taken. This cruel mistake must have caused us a loss of 2,000 infantry, 300 cavalry, and 3 pieces of artillery. Reports state that the General of Division was not with his column, and had marched alone.

All the army having crossed on the morning of the 28th, the Duke of Belluno guarded the bridgehead on the left bank; the Duke of Reggio, and behind him all the army, was on the right bank.

Borisov having been evacuated, the armies of the Dvina and Volhynia communicated; they planned an attack. On the 28th, at daybreak, the Duke of Reggio caused the Emperor to be informed that he was attacked. Half an hour afterwards, the Duke of Belluno also was attacked on the left bank. The army took to arms. The Duke of Elchingen immediately followed the Duke of Reggio, and the Duke of Treviso behind the Duke of Elchingen. The battle heated up. The enemy wishing to turn our right, General Doumerc, commanding the 5th Division of Cuirassiers that made part of the 2nd Corps that remained on the Dvina, ordered a charge of cavalry by the 4th and 5th Regiments of Cuirassiers, at the moment when the legion of the Vistula was engaged in the woods, to pierce the centre of the enemy. The enemy was defeated and put to rout. These brave cuirassiers successively pushed in four squares of infantry, and put to rout the enemy's cavalry, which came to the assistance of his infantry. Six thousand prisoners, two standards, and six pieces of cannon fell into our hands.

On his side, the Duke of Belluno vigorously charged the enemy, defeated him, took from 500 to 600 prisoners, and kept him from advancing within reach of the cannon of the bridge. General Fournier made a fine charge of cavalry.

In the battle of the Beresina, the army of Volhynia suffered much. The Duke of Reggio was wounded, but his wound is not dangerous. He received a ball in his side.

The next day (the 29th) we remained on the battlefield. We had to make our choice between two routes: that to Minsk, and that to Vilna. The road to Minsk led through the middle of a forest, and of uncultivated marshes, where it would be impossible for the army to subsist. On the other hand the road to Vilna led through a very fine country. The army being without cavalry, deficient in ammunition, and horribly fatigued by 50 days' march, carrying in its train all the sick and wounded of so many battles, stood greatly in need of getting to its magazines. On the 30th, the headquarters were at Plechnitsie [Plaszczenitzy]; on 1 December at Slaiki; on the 3rd at Molodetchna, where the army received the first convoys from Vilna.

All the wounded officers and soldiers, and whatever else that could be of encumbrance, with the baggage, etc., were sent off to Vilna.

To say that the army needs to re-establish its discipline, to refresh itself, to remount its cavalry, complete its artillery and its materiel – this is the result of the *exposé* that has just been made. Rest is its first requirement. The matériel and the horses are coming in; General Bourcier has already more than 20,000 horses for remounting in different depots. The artillery has already repaired its losses. The generals, officers and soldiers have suffered greatly from want. Numbers have lost their baggage by the loss of their horses, and several by the effect of the Cossacks' ambushes. The Cossacks have taken numbers of isolated persons, geographical engineers who were taking positions, and wounded officers who were marching without precaution, preferring running rather than marching slowly and going with the convoys.

The reports of the general officers commanding the different corps will make known what officers and soldiers have chiefly distinguished themselves, and the details of all these memorable events.

In all these movements the Emperor has continually marched in the middle of his Guard, the cavalry commanded by the Duke of Istria and the infantry commanded by the Duke of Danzig. His Majesty has been well pleased with the fine spirit shown by his Guard. They have always been ready to show themselves wherever their presence was needful, but circumstances have always been such that their appearance alone was sufficient, and that they never were in a situation that required them to charge.

The Prince of Neuchâtel, the Grand Marshal, the Grand Equerry, and all the aides-de-camp and military officers of the house of the Emperor have always accompanied His Majesty.

Our cavalry was dismounted to such a degree that it was necessary to collect the officers who had still a horse remaining, in order to form four companies of 150 men each.

The generals there performed the functions of captains, and the colonels of subalterns. This sacred squadron, commanded by General Grouchy, and under the orders of the King of Naples, did not lose sight of the Emperor in all these movements.

The health of His Majesty was never better.

Paris, 18 December 1812
On 5 December, the Emperor, having called together at his headquarters at Smorgoni, the Viceroy, the Prince of Neuchâtel and the Marshals Dukes of Elchingen, Danzig, Treviso, the Prince of Eckmühl, the Duke of Istria, told them that he had named the King of Naples his Lieutenant General to command the army during the severe season.

His Majesty, in passing through Vilna, was employed several hours with the

Duke of Bassano. His Majesty travelled incognito, in a single sledge, with and under the name of the Duke of Vicence. He examined the fortifications of Prague, surveyed Warsaw, and remained there for several hours unknown.

Two hours before his departure he sent for Count Potocki and the Minister of finance of the Grand Duchy, with whom he had a long conference.

His Majesty arrived at one o'clock in the morning on the 14th at Dresden, and stayed at the home of Count Serra, his minister. He spoke at length with the King of Saxony, and departed immediately by the route of Leipzig and Mayence.

CAMPAIGN IN SAXONY
1813

When Napoleon left Russia in 1812, he may well have expected Tsar Alexander to stay in Russia. Instead, Alexander began to see himself a liberator of central Europe and maybe even more. He pursued the French into the Duchy of Warsaw, and quickly formed an alliance with Prussia and England. The Prussians had been allied with France, but in December the Prussian General Yorck agreed to the Convention of Tauroggen, whereby his soldiers became neutral. Reacting to the diminished power of France, and to increased nationalism at home, King Frederick William III eventually agreed to the Convention of Kalisch on 28 February and joined the coalition against France. At that point it is unlikely that they sought the removal of Napoleon from the throne of France, but they did seek the elimination of the Duchy of Warsaw and the dismemberment of the Confederation of the Rhine.

Napoleon still had Austria as an ally, and was tied to that monarchy through his marriage to the Austrian princess Marie Louise. But the alliance with Austria was shaky at best. Austrian troops overtaken by the Russians as they left Russia were allowed to withdraw, and Austria failed to provide any direct assistance to Napoleon. Austria acted more like a neutral than an ally, and Prince Metternich was already planning to switch sides.

Still, Napoleon felt he could defeat the Russians and Prussians alone, as long as no one else joined on their side. He defeated the coalition at the battle of Lützen on 2 May, but his lack of horses, due to the great losses of them in Russia, prevented what could have been a decisive pursuit. Even so, he routed the allies at Bautzen on 20–21 May, though once again the lack of horses lessened the totality of his victory.

Napoleon's twin victories stunned the coalition forces, and on 4 June both sides agreed to an armistice. Austria offered to negotiate a settlement, but the proposals made by Austrian foreign minister Metternich were absurd on their face, as it demanded that Napoleon give up all gains since becoming First Consul.

The allies were not negotiating in good faith. Indeed, they used the break in the action to bring Sweden and Austria into the coalition, and on 13 August, Prussian General Blücher violated the armistice by advancing on Napoleon. Napoleon responded by crushing the allies at Dresden on 26–27 August, but was in turn defeated at Leipzig on 16–19 October. During the battle, the Saxon troops changed sides and fought against Napoleon. The battle might not have been a disaster, but but became one when the bridge over which Napoleon's forces were retiring in good order was prematurely blown up, costing Napoleon 20,000 men and the life of Prince Poniatowski. Bavarian General Wrede, following the Convention of Roed signed a few days earlier, then turned on Napoleon and vainly attempted to stop the French withdrawal to the Rhine. As the year ended, the allies were threatening France.

Moniteur, 4 April 1813
To Her Majesty the Empress-Queen and Regent
Situation of the French armies in the North, at 30 March
The garrison of Danzig had routed the enemy from all the heights of Oliva during the first days of March.

The Thorn and the Modlin garrisons were in very good shape. The corps that blocked Zamosé had moved away from there.

On the Oder, the fortresses of Stettin, Custrin and Glogau were not under siege. The enemy stood fast out of reach of the cannon from these fortresses. The garrison of Stettin had burned all the suburbs and prepared the terrain around the place.

The garrison of Spandau had also burnt all that could impede the defence of the place.

On the Elbe, on the 17th, we had blown up an arch of the bridge of Dresden, and General Durutte had taken position on the left bank. The Saxons had proceeded towards Torgau.

The Viceroy had left Leipzig and had taken his headquarters to Magdeburg on the 21st.

General La Poype was in command of the bridge and the square of Wittenberg, which were armed and well supplied for several months. We had worked to put it in good condition.

After he arrived at Magdeburg, the Viceroy sent General Lauriston on the right bank of the Elbe on the 22nd. General Maison had proceeded to Mockern and had pushed some posts on Burg and on Ziczar; he found only a few light troops, which he overthrew and from which he took or killed about 60 men.

On the 12th, General Carra Saint-Cyr, commanding the 32nd Military Division, had judged it suitable to re-cross on the left bank of the Elbe, and to leave Hamburg under the watch of the authorities and of the National Guard. From the 15th to the 20th, different insurrections took place in the departments of the Bouches-de-Elbe and of the Ems.

General Morand, who occupied Swedish Pomerania, having learned of the evacuation of Berlin, was retreating on Hamburg. He crossed the Elbe at Zollenpischer, and on the 17th joined General Carra Saint-Cyr. Two hundred men of the enemy's light troops having reached his rearguard, he had them charged and killed a few of their men. General Morand took position on the left bank and General Saint-Cyr proceeded towards Bremen.

On the 24th, General Saint-Cyr sent two mobile columns to advance on the batteries of Calsburg and Blexen, which had been taken by smugglers with the help of some peasants and a few English disembarkments. These columns put these insurgents in disorder and took possession of the batteries. The chiefs were taken and shot. The disembarked English were only 100 in number; we only took 40 of them prisoner.

The Viceroy had re-united his army, 100,000 men and 300 pieces of artillery strong, around Magdeburg, making manoeuvres on both banks.

General of Brigade Montbrun, who with a brigade of cavalry occupied Stendhal, having learned that the enemy has crossed the lower Elbe in some boats near Werden, proceeded there on the 28th, chased the enemy's light troops and entered Werden at a gallop. The 4th Lancers made a full charge in which they killed about 50 Cossacks and took 12 of them prisoner. The enemy returned in great haste to the right bank of the Elbe. Three large boats were sunk and a few small crafts capsized; they may have carried 60 horses and men. We saved 17 riders, among them two officers, one an aide-de-camp of General Dörnberg, who was in command of this column.

It appears that a corps of light troops, consisting of 1,000 horses, 2,000 infantrymen and six pieces of artillery, has been able to proceed towards Brunswick to excite Hanover and the Kingdom of Westphalia to revolt. The King of Westphalia went in the pursuit of this corps, and some other columns sent by the Viceroy are arriving on its rears.

Fifteen hundred men of the enemy's light troops crossed the Elbe near Dresden on the 27th, on little boats. General Durutte is marching towards them. The

Saxons had left that bridge unmanned when regrouping around Torgau.

The Prince of the Moskova arrived at Würzburg on the 26th, with his headquarters and army corps; his advance guard debouched from the mountains of the Turinge.

The Duke of Ragusa took his headquarters to Hanau on 22 March; his divisions were gathering there.

On 30 March, the advance guard of the observation corps of Italy had arrived at Augsburg. The whole corps was traversing the Tyrol.

On the 27th, General Vandamme arrived at Bremen. The Dumonceau and Dufour divisions had already passed Wesel.

Independently of the Viceroy's army, of the armies of the Main and of the King of Westphalia's corps, there will be, in the first two weeks of April, nearly 50,000 men in the 32nd Military Division, so that we can make a severe example of the insurrections that have troubled this division. The Count of Bentink, mayor of Vareil, had the infamy of placing himself at the head of the rebels. His estates will be confiscated, and he will have, by his treason, caused the ruin of his family forever.

During the whole month of March, there have been no actions. In all of these skirmishes, on of which being that of the 28th (at Werden) and by far the most considerable, the French army has always come out on top.

--

Moniteur, 15 April 1813
His Majesty the Emperor left today at one o'clock in the morning for Mayence.

To Her Majesty the Empress-Queen and Regent
Situation of the French Armies in the North, at 5 April.
The news from Danzig was satisfactory. The large garrison has formed camps outside of the town. The enemy held fast at a distance from the fortress and did not appear in a position to attempt any action. Two English frigates had been seen before the place.

At Thorn, there was nothing new. Time had been used to improve the fortifications.

The enemy had only a few forces in front of Modlin: General Daendels took advantage of the opportunity to make a sally; he repulsed the enemy's corps and seized a large convoy where, among other things, there were 500 steers.

The garrison of Zamosé is mistress of the country six leagues around, the enemy using only a few light cavalrymen to observe this place.

General Frimont and Prince Poniatowski were still in the same position on the Pilica.

Stettin, Glogau and Custrin were in the same shape. The enemy seemed to have projects on Glogau, the blockade of which had tightened.

The enemy corps that had crossed the Elbe at Werden on 27 March, and whose rearguard has been defeated on the 28th by General Montbrun and thrown into the river, had proceeded on Lüneburg.

On the 26th, General Morand left Bremen and advanced on Lüneburg, where he arrived on 1 April. The inhabitants, supported by a few light troops of the enemy, tried to show some resistance; the doors were broken down by cannon shots, about 30 of these rebels were put to the sword, and the town was subdued.

On the 2nd, the enemy corps, estimated at 3,000 to 4,000 men of cavalry, infantry and artillery appeared before Lüneburg. General Morand marched to meet it with his column composed of 800 Saxons and 200 French, with 30 horsemen and 4 cannon. A cannonade was engaged. The enemy had been forced out of several positions when General Morand was killed by a ball. The command was passed to a Saxon colonel. The troops, startled by the loss of their chief, fell back in the town, and, after defending themselves there for half a day, they capitulated in the evening. The enemy took prisoner 700 Saxons and 200 French. A part of them has been recovered.

The next day, General Montbrun, in command of the advance guard of the Prince of Eckmühl's corps, arrived at Lüneburg. The enemy, informed of their approach, had hastily evacuated the town and re-crossed the Elbe. The Prince of Eckmühl, who arrived there on the 4th, forced the enemy to withdraw all his troops from the left bank of the Elbe and ordered the occupation of Stade.

On the 5th, General Vandamme had reunited the Saint-Cyr and Dufour divisions at Bremen. General Dumonceau, with his division, was at Minden.

On 2 April, the Viceroy met a Prussian division in the front of Magdeburg, on the right bank of the Elbe, overthrew it, pursued it for several leagues, and took several hundred prisoners.

The Bavarian brigade, which is part of General Durutte's division, had an action on 29 March at Colditz with the enemy cavalry. This infantry has repulsed all the charges the enemy attempted on it, and killed more than 100 men; among them we recognized on colonel and several officers. The Bavarian loss was only 16 wounded men. Since then, General Durutte has continued his movement without trouble, to proceed on the Saale at Bernburg.

An enemy detachment of cavalry had entered Leipzig on the 3rd.

The Duke of Belluno was in observation at Calbe and Bernburg on the Saale.

—〜—

Moniteur, 16 April 1813

To Her Majesty the Empress-Queen and Regent
Situation of the French armies in the North, at 10 April

On the 5th, the 35th division, under the command of General Grenier, had an affair of advance posts on the right bank of the Elbe, four leagues from Magdeburg. Only four battalions of this division were engaged. The infantry showed his normal intrepidity and the enemy was repulsed.

On the 7th, the Viceroy, being informed that the enemy had crossed the Elbe at Dessau, sent the 5th Corps and part of the 11th to support the 2nd Corps commanded by the Duke of Belluno. He proceeded to Stassfurt, where his headquarters was on the 9th, and he brought together his army on the Saale, the left at Elbe, the right against the mountains of the Hartz and the reserve at Magdeburg.

The artillery of General Vandamme's division was arriving at Bremen and at Minden.

The head of a corps composed of two divisions, which is to take a position at Wesel under the orders of General Lemarois, is starting to arrive there.

On the 10th, General Souham had sent a regiment to Erfurt, where we still have no information regarding the enemy's light troops.

The Duke of Ragusa was taking position on the height of Eisenach. The French army of the Main appeared to be in movement in different directions.

The Prince of Neufchâtel was expected at Mayence.

Part of the Emperor's staff had arrived there, which caused us to presume the Sovereign would arrive soon.

—〜—

Moniteur, 17 April 1813

His Majesty the Emperor passed at Metz this morning, 27 hours after his departure from Paris.

Moniteur, 21 April 1813

His Majesty the Emperor arrived at Mayence the 16th of this month, at midnight.

Moniteur, 24 April 1813

Mayence, 18 April, at night

To Her Majesty the Empress-Queen and Regent

His Majesty the Emperor did not come out at all on the 17th; he received the Grand Duke of Bade, the Prince of Hesse-Darmstadt and the Duke of Nassau.

The Count of Saint-Marsan and the Baron of Nicolay were presented to him.

On the 18th, after mass, His Majesty received the authorities of the department.

Afterwards, His Majesty mounted his horse; he traversed Cassel, the new fort of Montebello, the marshes of Monbach, and the fort Meunier.

At five o'clock, the Emperor received the Prince-Primate, Grand Duke of Frankfurt.

The Grand Duke and Grand Duchess of Bade, the Prince Primate, the Princes of Hesse-Darmstadt and the Duke of Nassau had the honour of dining with His Majesty.

Moniteur, 26 April 1813

To Her Majesty the Empress-Queen and Regent

Situation of the French Armies in the North, at 20 April

Danzig, Thorn, Modlin and Zamosé were in the same shape.

Stettin, Custrin, Glogau and Spandau were only slightly blockaded.

Magdeburg was the point of reserve of the Viceroy.

Wittenberg and Torgau were in good shape. The garrison of Wittenberg had repulsed the attack with lively force.

General Vandamme was before Bremen, General Sebastiani was between Celle and the Weser; the Viceroy was in the same position, the left on the Elbe, at the mouth of the Saal, and the right at the Hartz, occupying Bernburg, his reserve at Magdeburg.

The Prince of the Moskova was at Erfurt; the Duke of Ragusa at Gotha, occupying Langensaltza; the Duke of Istria at Eisenach; Count Bertrand at Coburg.

General Souham was at Weimar. The town was occupied by 300 Prussian hussars, who were dispersed during the day of the 19th by a squadron of the 10th Hussars and a Baden squadron under the orders of General Laboissière. We took 60 hussars and four officers of the enemy, among them an aide-de-camp of General Blücher.

Moniteur, 28 April 1813

To Her Majesty the Empress-Queen and Regent

On the 22nd of this month, His Majesty the Emperor passed in review four beautiful regiments of the Old Guard; he showed his satisfaction of the great state of these troops; they arrived at Mayence in post, and took only six days to get there; they were so very little tired that they crossed the Rhine at once.

General Curial arrived at Mayence with the staff of the twelve new regiments of the Young Guard, which are organizing in that town. All the supplies needed to equip these troops arrived at Mayence by accelerated transports.

The Duke of Castiglione has been named military governor of the Grand Duchies of Frankfurt and of Würzburg. The citadel of Würzburg has been armed and supplied with necessary stock.

The rumours that had been made regarding the defeat of General Sebastiani and the death of his aides-de-camp are false and fabricated; on the contrary, hoping to lure the enemy to him, he ordered General Maurin to evacuate Celle; 1,200 Cossacks rushed there immediately. On the 28th, General Maurin precipitately entered Celle pell-mell with the enemy, which was put in a complete rout and lost 50 killed, a great number of wounded and some 100 prisoners.

Meanwhile, General Sebastiani proceeded on Ültzen; he chased from Gross-Ösingen a party of 600 Cossacks, which fell back on Sprakenselh, where the enemy had gathered 1,500 riders. General Sebastiani had them charged and taken out at once; we killed 25 men, wounded many more and took 20 Cossacks; the fugitives were pursued as far as Ültzen.

General Vandamme commands at Bremen; he has under his orders the three divisions of Dufour, Saint-Cyr and Dumonceau.

The effervescence of the spirits is calming down in the 32nd Military Division; the quantity of force they see arriving from all sides, the severe examples that were made of the chiefs of the plots, but mostly the very few people that the enemy showed on that point, have squashed the malevolence.

The Duke of Reggio left Mayence on the 23rd to take command of the 12th Corps of the *Grande Armée*.

On the 24th, the biggest part of the army had crossed the mountains of the Thuringe.

The King of Saxony had judged it necessary to approach Dresden, and proceeded on Prague.

His Majesty the Emperor left Mayence on the 24th, at eight o'clock in the evening.

The Duke of Dalmatia has resumed the functions of Colonel-General of the Guard. His Majesty has dispatched the Duke of Treviso to Wetzlar to organize the Polish corps of General Dombrowski and form this corps into two regiments of infantry, two regiments of cavalry and two battalions of artillery. His Majesty took this corps in his pay since 1 January.

The Prince of Eckmühl joined the 32nd Military Division, to exercise, according to the circumstances, the extraordinary powers delegated by the decree of the Senate of 3 April.

Moniteur, 3 May 1813

Her Majesty the Empress-Queen and Regent has received news regarding the situation of the army to 25 April.

The fortress of Thorn has capitulated, the garrison is to return into Bavaria; it was composed of 600 French and 2,700 Bavarians; of this number of 3,300 men, 1,200 were in the hospitals. No preparations as yet announced the commencement of the siege of Danzig; the garrison was in excellent condition, and master of the ground around it. Modlin and Zamosé were not seriously threatened. At Stettin a brisk engagement had taken place: the enemy having endeavoured to introduce itself between Stettin and Dan has been driven into the marshes, and 1,500

Prussians had been killed or taken. A letter received from Glogau informed us that this place as of 12 April was in the best of state. Nothing new had occurred at Custrin. Spandau was besieged: a powder magazine had blown up there and the enemy, believing it could take advantage of this to give an assault, had been repulsed after having lost 1,000 men killed or wounded. We took no prisoners because we were separated from them by marshes.

The Russians threw some shells into Wittenberg, and burned a part of the town. They attempted an attack by main force, which did not succeed. They lost in it from 500 to 600 men.

The following appears to be the position of the Russian army: a corps of partisans, commanded by a man called Dörnberg who, in 1809, was Captain of the King of Westphalia's Guards, and who betrayed him, was at Hamburg, and made excursions between the Elbe and the Weser. General Sebastiani had set out to cut him off from the Elbe.

The two Prussian corps of Generals Lestocq and Blücher appeared to occupy, the 1st, the right bank of the Lower Saale, the 2nd the right bank of the Upper Saale.

The Russian Generals Winzingerode and Wittgenstein occupied Leipzig.

General Barclay de Tolly was on the Vistula, observing Danzig, General Sacken was before the Austrian corps in the direction of Kraków, on the Pilica.

The Emperor Alexander with the Russian Guard, and General Kutusov, having some 20,000 men, appeared to be on the Oder; they announced that they would be at Dresden on the 12th, afterwards on 20 April; neither of these announcements has been realized. The enemy appeared to want to maintain itself on the Saale. The Saxons were in Torgau.

Here is the position of the French army:

The Viceroy had his headquarters at Mansfeld, the left bearing on the mouth of Saale, occupying Calbe and Bernburg, where the Duke of Belluno is. General Lauriston, with the 5th Corps, occupied Asleben, Sondersleben and Gerbstet. The 31st Division was on Eisleben; the 35th and 36th were in the rear, as a reserve. The Prince of the Moskova had his corps in advance of Weimar. The Duke of Ragusa was at Gotha; the 4th Corps, commanded by General Bertrand, was at Saalfeld; the 12th Corps, under the orders of the Duke of Reggio, arriving at Coburg.

The Guard is at Erfurt, where the Emperor arrived at eleven o'clock in the evening of the 25th. On the 26th His Majesty reviewed the Guard, and inspected the fortifications of the town and citadel. He designated some places for establishing hospitals able to contain 6,000 sick or wounded, having ordered that Erfurt should be the last line of evacuation.

On the 27th the Emperor reviewed the division Bonet, which is part of the 6th Corps under the command of the Duke of Ragusa.

All the army appeared in motion; already all the parties that the enemy had on the left bank of the Saale have fallen back. Three thousand cavalry had marched on Nordhausen, to penetrate into the Harz, and another party advanced on Heiligenstadt, to menace Cassel: all these precipitately retreated, leaving sick, wounded, and stragglers, who have been made prisoners. From the heights of Ebersdorf, to the mouth of the Saale, there are no longer any enemies on the left bank. The junction of the armies of the Elbe and the Main must take place on the 27th, between Naumburg and Merseburg.

Moniteur, 4 May 1813

Her Majesty the Empress-Queen and Regent, has received the following intelligence of the situation of the army to 28 April 1813:

The headquarters of the Emperor were on the 28th at Naumburg: the Prince of the Moskova had crossed the Saale; General Souham had overthrown an advanced guard of 2,000 men who wished to dispute the crossing of the river. The whole corps of the Prince of the Moskova was in order of battle beyond Naumburg.

General Bertrand occupied Jena, and had his corps ranged on the famous battlefield of Jena.

The Duke of Reggio was arriving at Saalfeld with the 12th Corps.

The Viceroy debouched by Halle and Merseburg.

General Sebastiani had marched on the 24th on Velzen; he had overthrown a corps of 4,000 adventurers commanded by the Russian General Czernichev; he had dispersed his infantry, he had taken part of his baggage and artillery, and pursued him, sword in his back, on Lüneburg.

Moniteur, 5 May 1813

Her Majesty the Empress-Queen and Regent, has received the following news relative to the situation of the army to 30 April 1813:

On the 29th His Majesty maintained his headquarters at Naumburg.

The Prince of the Moskova had marched on Weissenfels. His advance guard, commanded by General Souham, arrived near that town at two o'clock in the afternoon, and found himself in presence of the Russian General Lanskoï, commanding a division of 6,000 or 7,000 men, of cavalry and artillery. General Souham had no cavalry, but without waiting for it he marched against the enemy and drove it from its different positions. The enemy unmasked 12 pieces of artillery; General Souham placed a similar number in a battery. The cannonade became very lively and caused ravages in the Russian ranks, which were mounted and uncovered, while our pieces were supported by skirmishers, placed in ravines and the villages. General of Brigade Chemineau distinguished himself. The enemy attempted several charges of cavalry: our infantry received it, formed in squares, and, and by their fire covered the battlefield with Russian corpses and horses. The Prince of the Moskova said that he never had seen, at the same time, more enthusiasm and more sang-froid in the infantry. We entered Weissenfels, but seeing that the enemy wished to keep near the town, the infantry marched to it at the quick charge, with shakos at the end of their muskets, and to the cries of 'Long live the Emperor!' The enemy's division retreated. Our loss in killed and wounded was about 100 men.

On the 27th, Count Lauriston marched on Wetter, where the enemy had a bridge. General Maison erected a battery, which forced the enemy to burn the bridge, and he seized the bridgehead that the enemy had constructed.

On the 28th, Count Lauriston advanced on the Halle, where a Prussian corps occupied a bridgehead, overthrew the enemy and obliged it to evacuate this bridgehead and cut off the bridge. A very brisk cannonade from one bank to the other took place. Our loss was 67 men, that of the enemy was much more considerable.

The Viceroy had ordered Marshal Duke of Tarentum to march on Merseburg. On the 19th, at four in the afternoon, this Marshal arrived before that town; he found 2,000 Prussians who wished to defend themselves there; these Prussians belonged to Yorck's corps, those even whom the Marshal commanded in chief, and who had abandoned him on the Niemen. The Marshal entered by great force, killed some men and took 200 prisoners, among whom was a major, and took possession of the town and bridge.

Count Bertrand had, on the 29th, his headquarters at Dörnberg, on the Saale, occupying the bridge of Jena with one of his divisions.

The Duke of Ragusa had his headquarters at Kösen, on the Saale; the Duke of Reggio had his headquarters at Saalfeld, on the Saale.

The battle of Weissenfels is remarkable because it is a battle between infantry and cavalry, equal in number, on an open plain and the advantage remained with our infantry. Young battalions were seen behaving with as much sang-froid and impetuosity as the oldest troops.

So for the opening of this campaign, the enemy is driven from all that it occupied on the left bank of the Saale; we are masters of all the debouches of this river; the junction between the armies of the Elbe and the Main has been effected, and the important towns of Naumburg, Weissenfels and Merseburg have been taken possession of by vigorous force.

Weimar

30 April 1813
His Majesty the Emperor and King passed here on the 28th at two in the afternoon. The Duke of Weimar and Prince Bernard had gone to meet him as far as the boundaries of the territory. His Majesty went to the palace and conversed with the Duchess for close to two hours; after that, His Majesty mounted his horse to go to Eckarsberg, which is six leagues from here, where his headquarters were. The Princes who had accompanied His Majesty there had the honour of dining with him that night at his headquarters.

The quantity of troops who pass here is innumerable. Never have we seen more beautiful trains of artillery or convoys of military equipment in better shape

Moniteur, 8 May 1813
Situation of the French Armies in the North to 1 May

The Emperor moved his headquarters to Weissenfels; the Viceroy his to Merseburg; General Maison had entered Halle; the Duke of Ragusa had his headquarters at Naumburg; Count Bertrand was at Stohassen, the Duke of Reggio had his headquarters at Jena.

There was much rain on 30 April; on 1 May the weather was better.

Three bridges had been thrown across the Saale at Weissenfels; campaign works had been started at Naumburg, and three bridges have been thrown over the Saale.

Fifteen grenadiers of the 13th Line, between Jena and Saalfeld, were surrounded by 95 Prussian hussars. The Commandant, who was a colonel, advanced, saying, 'Frenchmen, surrender!' The sergeant killed him. The other grenadiers formed a platoon, killed seven Prussians, and the hussars went off faster than they came.

The different parts of the Old Guard have reunited at Weissenfels; General of Division Roguet commands them.

The Emperor visited all the advanced posts, notwithstanding the bad weather. His Majesty enjoys excellent health.

The first blow with the sabre that was given at the renewing of this campaign at Weimar, took off the ear of Major-General Blücher's son. This blow was given by a sergeant of the 10th Hussars. The inhabitants of Weimar remarked that the first

sabre blow given in the campaign of 1806 at Saalfeld, and which killed Prince
Louis of Prussia, was also given by a sergeant of this same regiment.

Battles of Weissenfels and Lützen

*Her Majesty the Empress-Queen and Regent has received the following new intelligence
of the situation of the armies to 2 May 1813 at nine in the morning:*

On 1 May the Emperor mounted on horseback at nine in the morning, with the
Prince of the Moskova and General Souham. General Souham's division put itself
in motion towards the fine plain that commences on the heights of Weissenfels and
extends to the Elbe. This division was formed in four squares of four battalions
each, each square 500 *toises* from the other and having four pieces of artillery.
Behind the square was placed General Laboissière's brigade of cavalry, under the
orders of Count Valmy, who had just arrived. The Gérard and Marchand divisions
came behind in echelon, and formed in the same manner as Souham's division.
Marshal Duke of Istria was on the right with all the cavalry of the Guard.

At eleven o'clock these dispositions were made, the Prince of the Moskova, in
the presence of a cloud of the enemy's cavalry that covered the plain, put himself
in motion on the defile of Poserna. We seized several villages without giving a
blow. On the heights of the defile the enemy occupied one of the finest positions
that can be seen; it had six cannon and presented three lines of cavalry.

The first square passed the defile at the quick charge, amidst cries of 'Long live
the Emperor!' long continued through the line. We seized the height. The four
squares of Souham's division passed the defile.

Two other divisions of cavalry then came to reinforce the enemy with 20 pieces
of artillery. The cannonade became lively. The enemy everywhere gave ground.
Souham's division marched on Lützen; Gérard's took the direction of the Pegau
road. The Emperor, wishing to reinforce the batteries of this last division, sent 12
pieces of the Guard, under the orders of his aide-de-camp, General Drouot, and
this reinforcement performed admirably. The ranks of the enemy's cavalry were
overthrown by grapeshot.

At the same moment the Viceroy marched quickly from Merseburg, with the
11th Corps, commanded by the Duke of Tarentum, and the 5th, commanded by
General Lauriston. General Lauriston's corps was on the left, on the high road
from Merseburg to Leipzig; that of the Duke of Tarentum, where the Viceroy
was, on the right. The Viceroy hearing the brisk cannonade that took place near
Lützen, made a movement to the right; and the Emperor almost at the same
moment, found himself at the village of Lützen.

Marchand's division, and, in succession, the divisions of Brenier and Ricard,
crossed the defile. But the matter was settled when they entered in line.

Fifteen thousand cavalry were therefore driven from these plains, by nearly the
same number of infantry. It was General Winzingerode who commanded these
three divisions, one of which was General Lanskoï's. The enemy displayed but one
division of infantry. Become more prudent by the battle of Weissenfels, and
astonished at the fine order and sang-froid of our march, the enemy dared not
approach any part of our infantry, and was crushed by our grapeshot. Our loss
amounted to 33 men killed and 55 wounded, one a Battalion Chief. This loss may
be considered extremely trifling in comparison to that of the enemy, which had
three colonels, 30 officers and 400 men killed or wounded, besides a great number
of horses; but by one of those fatalities of which the history of the war is full, the
first cannonball which was fired on this day, cut the wrist of the Duke of Istria,
pierced his chest, and killed him instantly. He had advanced 500 paces on the side

of the skirmishers in order to reconnoitre the plain. This Marshal, whom we justifiably call brave and just, was equally commendable for his military *coup-d'oeil*, his great experience in the arms of the cavalry, as by his civil qualities and attachment to the Emperor. His death on the field of honour is most worthy of envy, it was so rapid that it must have been without pain. There are few losses that could have more deeply affected the Emperor's heart: the army and all of France will partake of the grief His Majesty felt.

The Duke of Istria, since the first Italian campaigns, that is to say, for 16 years, had always, in different ranks, commanded the Emperor's Guard whom he had followed in all his campaigns and battles.

The composure, goodwill, and intrepidity of the young soldiers astonished the veterans and all the officers: it is a proof of the saying, that 'To souls well born, virtue does not wait for the number of years.'

On the night between 1 and 2 May, His Majesty had his headquarters at Lützen; the Viceroy is at Markranstädt; General Lauriston at Liebersdorff, the Prince of the Moskova is at Kaïa; and the Duke of Ragusa is at Poserna. General Bertrand was at Stohassen; the Duke of Reggio marching on Naumburg.

At Danzig, the garrison has obtained great advantages and made so successful a sortie that it took prisoner a corps of 3,000 Russians. The garrison of Wittenberg also appears to have distinguished itself, and, in a sortie, to have caused considerable injury to the enemy.

A letter in ciphers, which has this moment arrived from the garrison of Glogau, is written in these terms:

All goes on well, the Russians have made several attempts on this place; they have always been repulsed with much loss; 3- or 4,000 men blockade us, sometimes less, sometimes more. The trenches were opened for two days; the fire from our batteries forced them to abandon their project.

GENERAL LAPLANE

Glogau, 15 April 1813

Her Majesty the Empress-Queen and Regent has received news from His Majesty the Emperor, from the battlefield two leagues in advance of Lützen, 2 May, at ten o'clock in the evening, at the moment when the Emperor had thrown himself on a bed to get some hours' sleep.

The Emperor informs Her Majesty that he has gained the most complete victory over the Russian and Prussian army, commanded in person by the Emperor Alexander and King of Prussia; that in this battle more than 150,000 cannonballs had been fired, that the troops covered themselves with glory and that not withstanding the immense inferiority of cavalry which the French army had, the good-will and courage inherent in Frenchmen supplied everything.

The enemy was briskly pursued.

No Marshal, no person composing the household of the Emperor, was killed or wounded.

Moniteur, 9 May 1813

Her Majesty the Empress-Queen and Regent has received the following intelligence from the army:

The battles of Weissenfels and Lützen were but the prelude of events of the highest importance. The Emperor Alexander and the King of Prussia, who had arrived at Dresden with all their forces at the latter end of April, learning that the

French army had debouched from the Thuringia, adopted the plan of giving it battle on the plains of Lützen, and put themselves in motion to occupy the position, but they were anticipated by the rapidity of the movements of the French army; they, however, persisted in their projects, and resolved to attack the army to drive it from the positions it had taken.

The position of the French army was on 2 May, at nine in the morning, as follows:

The left of the army leaned on the Elster; it was formed by the Viceroy, having under his orders the 5th and 11th Corps. The centre was commanded by the Prince of the Moskova, in the village of Kaïa. The Emperor, with the Young and Old Guard, was at Lützen.

The Duke of Ragusa was at the defile of Poserna, and formed the right with his three divisions. General Bertrand, commanding the 4th Corps, marched to proceed to this defile. The enemy debouched and crossed the Elster at the bridges of Zwenkau, Pegau and Zeitz. The Emperor, hoping to anticipate it in its movement, and thinking that it could not attack until 3 May, ordered General Lauriston, whose corps formed the extreme of the left, to march on Leipzig in order to disconcert the enemy's project and place the French army for the day of the 3rd in a position quite different from that on which the enemy had calculated to find it, and in which it was, in reality, on the 2nd; and by this means carry confusion and disorder into their columns.

At nine in the morning His Majesty, having heard a cannonade coming from Leipzig, proceeded there at full gallop. The enemy defended the small village of Listenau and the bridges in advance of Leipzig. His Majesty only waited the moment when these last positions should be carried to put in motion all his army in that direction, make it pivot on Leipzig, cross to the right bank of the Elster, and take the enemy from the rear; but, at ten o'clock, the enemy's army debouched towards Kaïa, in several columns extremely deep; the horizon was obscured by them. The enemy presented forces which appeared immense: the Emperor immediately made his dispositions. The Viceroy received orders to march on the left of the Prince of the Moskova; but three hours were necessary to execute this movement. The Prince of the Moskova placed his men under arms, and with his five divisions supported the battle, which, at the end of half an hour, became terrible. His Majesty himself marched at the head of the Guard behind the centre of the army, supporting the right of the Prince of the Moskova. The Duke of Ragusa, with his three divisions, occupied the extreme right. General Bertrand had orders to debouch on the enemy's rear, at the moment in which the line should be most strongly engaged. Fortune was please to crown all these dispositions with the most brilliant success. The enemy, who appeared certain of the success of its enterprise, marched to reach our right and gain the road of Weissenfels. General Compans, General of Battle of the first merit, at the head of the first division of the Duke of Ragusa, stopped him quite short. The marine regiments supported several charges with sang-froid, and covered the battlefield with the élite of the enemy's cavalry. But the great efforts of infantry, cavalry and artillery were directed against the centre. Four of the Prince of the Moskova's five divisions were already engaged. The village of Kaïa was taken and re-taken several times. This village had remained in the enemy's power. The Count of Lobau directed General Ricard to re-take the village: it was re-taken.

The battle embraced a line of two leagues, covered with fire, smoke and clouds of dust. The Prince of the Moskova, General Souham and General Gérard were everywhere facing everything; wounded with several bullets, General Gérard wished to remain on the field of battle. He declared he wished to die commanding and directing his troops, as the moment had arrived for all Frenchmen who possessed any heart to conquer or perish.

However, we began to perceive from afar the dust and first fire of General Bertrand's corps. At the same moment, the Viceroy entered in line on the left, and the Duke of Tarentum was attacking the enemy's reserve and reached the village where the enemy rested his right. At this moment the enemy redoubled its efforts on the centre; the village of Kaïa was again taken, our centre gave way, a few battalions fled, but these valorous youths, at the sight of the Emperor, rallied, exclaiming, 'Long live the Emperor!' His Majesty judged that the critical moment that decides the gaining or losing of battles had arrived: there was not a moment to lose. The Emperor ordered the Duke of Treviso to march with 16 battalions of the Young Guard to the village of Kaïa, overthrow the enemy, retake the village and grab everything he found there. At the same moment His Majesty ordered his aide-de-camp General Drouot, an artillery officer of the greatest distinction, to form a battery of 80 pieces and place it in advance of the Old Guard, which was formed in echelons, as four redoubts to support the centre, all our cavalry ranged in battle behind. Generals Dulauloy, Drouot, and Devaux, set out at full gallop, with their 80 pieces of artillery in the same group. The fire became dreadful. The enemy gave way on all sides. The Duke of Treviso obtained possession of the village of Kaïa, overthrew the enemy, and continued to advance, beating the charge. The enemy's cavalry, infantry and artillery all retreated.

General Bonet, commanding one of the Duke of Ragusa's divisions, received orders to make a movement on Kaïa by his left, to support the success of the centre. He sustained several charges of cavalry in which the enemy suffered great losses.

Nevertheless, General Count Bertrand advanced and entered the line. It was in vain that the enemy's cavalry capered about his squares; his march was not slowed by it. To rejoin him quicker, the Emperor ordered a change of direction by pivoting on Kaïa. All of the right made a change in front, the right wing foremost.

The enemy then fled, and we pursued it for a league and a half. We soon arrived at the heights that had been occupied by the Emperor Alexander, the King of Prussia, and the Brandenburg family during the battle. An officer who was taken prisoner there informed us of this circumstance.

We have taken several thousand prisoners. The number could not be more considerable, considering the inferiority of our cavalry, and the desire that the Emperor had shown of sparing it.

At the commencement of the battle the Emperor said to the troops 'It is a battle like those in Egypt: A good infantry supported by artillery should be sufficient for it.'

General Gouré, chief of the Prince of the Moskova's staff, was killed; a death worthy of so good a soldier! Our loss amounts to 10,000 men killed or wounded; that of the enemy may be estimated at 25,000 to 30,000 men. The Royal Prussian Guards was destroyed. The Emperor of Russia's guards have suffered considerably: the two divisions of ten regiments of Russian cuirassiers have been crushed.

His Majesty cannot deliver enough of a eulogy to the good will, courage and intrepidity of the army. Our young soldiers took no danger into consideration. They have in this great instance shown all the nobility of the French blood.

The chief of staff in his report will mention the fine actions that have shed a lustre on this brilliant day, which, like a clap of thunder, has pulverized the chimerical hopes and all the calculations of the destruction and dismemberment of the Empire. The dark plots hatched by the Cabinet of St James during a whole winter are in an instant undone, like the Gordian knot by the sword of Alexander.

The Prince of Hesse Homburg was killed. The prisoners say that the young Prince Royal of Prussia has been wounded and the Prince of Mecklenburg-Strelitz killed.

The infantry of the Old Guard, only six battalions of which had arrived, by their presence kept up the affair with that sang-froid with which they are characterized. They did not fire a shot. Half the army was not engaged; for the four divisions of General Lauriston's corps have done nothing but occupy Leipzig; the three divisions of the Duke of Reggio were still two day's march from the field of battle; Count Bertrand did not charge but with one of his divisions, and so lightly that it did not lose 50 men; his 2nd and 3rd Divisions did not charge at all. The 2nd Division of the Young Guard, commanded by General Barrois, was still five days' march off; it was the same with half the Old Guard, commanded by General Decouz, who was then only at Erfurt: some battery in reserve, made up of more than 100 muzzles, are still marching from Mayence to Erfurt. The Duke of Belluno's corps was also three day's march from the field of battle. General Sebastiani's corps of cavalry, with the three divisions of the Prince of Eckmühl, was on the side of the Bas-Elbe. The allied army, 150,000 or 200,000 men strong, commanded by the two sovereigns with a great number of the Princes of the House of Prussia at its head, has thus been defeated and put to the rout by less than half of the French army.

The field of battle presented the most affecting spectacle: the young soldiers, on seeing the Emperor, forgot their sufferings and exclaimed, 'Long live the Emperor!' 'It is now 20 years,' said the Emperor, 'that I have commanded the French armies, but I have never yet witnessed so much bravery and devotion!'

Europe would at last be at peace if the sovereigns and ministers who direct their cabinets could have been present on the battlefield. They would give up all hopes of causing the star of France to set, and perceive that those councillors who wish to dismember the French Empire and humiliate the Emperor are preparing the ruin of their sovereign.

Moniteur, 10 May 1813

The Empress-Queen and Regent has received the following new intelligence from the army to 3 May at nine o'clock in the evening:

At daybreak of the 3rd, the Emperor traversed the battlefield. At ten o'clock he put himself in motion to follow the enemy. His headquarters was on the evening of the 3rd at Pegau. The Viceroy had his at Wichstanden, halfway between Pegau and Borna. Count Lauriston, whose corps had taken no part in the battle, set out from Leipzig to march on Zwemkau, where he had arrived. The Duke of Ragusa had crossed the Elster, at the village of Leitzkowitz, and Count Bertrand has crossed it at the village of Gredel. The Prince of the Moskova had stayed in position on the battlefield. The Duke of Reggio was supposed to march on Zeist from Naumburg.

The Emperor of Russia and the King of Prussia had passed through Pegau in the evening of the 2nd, and arrived in the village of Loberstadt at eleven o'clock at night. They reposed there four hours, and set out on the 3rd, at three o'clock in the morning, in the direction of Borna.

The enemy has not recovered from its astonishment at finding itself beaten on so large a plain, by an army so greatly inferior in cavalry. Several colonels and superior officers taken prisoner assure us that at the enemy's headquarters they had not learned of the Emperor's presence with the army until the battle had commenced; they had believed the Emperor to be at Erfurt.

As always happens in similar circumstances, the Prussians accuse the Russians of not having supported them. The Russians accuse the Prussians of not having fought well. The greatest confusion prevails in their retreat. Several of those pretended volunteers that were raised in Prussia have been made prisoner; they cause pity. All declare that they were enrolled by force, or otherwise suffer the penalty of seeing their property and families confiscated.

The country people say that a Prince of Hesse Homburg was killed and that several Russian and Prussian generals have been killed or wounded. The Prince of Mecklenburg-Strelitz is also reported killed; but this intelligence is still only the reports of the country.

The joy of these countries at being delivered from the Cossacks is indescribable. The inhabitants speak with contempt of all the proclamations and attempts that have been made to tempt them to insurrection.

The Russian and Prussian army was composed of the corps of the Prussian Generals Yorck, Blücher and Bülow, and those of the Russian Generals Wittgenstein, Winzingerode, Miloradovitch and Tormasov. The Russian and Prussian Guards were likewise there. The Emperor of Russia, the King of Prussia, the Prince Royal of Prussia and all the Princes of the Royal House of Prussia were in the battle.

The combined Russian and Prussian army is estimated at from 150,000 to 200,000 men. All the Russian cuirassiers were there, and have suffered greatly.

Her Majesty the Empress-Queen and Regent has received the following news of the situation of the armies, to the evening of 4 May:
The Emperor's headquarters were, on the evening of the 4th at Borna.

Those of the Viceroy at Colditz.

Those of General Count Bertrand at Freiberg.

Those of General Count Lauriston at Malbus.

Those of the Prince of the Moskova at Leipzig.

Those of the Duke of Reggio at Zeitz.

The enemy is retiring on Dresden in the greatest disorder and by every road.

All the villages in the road of the army are full of Russian and Prussian wounded.

Major-General the Prince of Neufchâtel has given orders for the interment of the Prince of Mecklenburg-Strelitz, on the morning of the 4th, at Pegau, with all honours due his rank.

In the battle of the 2nd, General Dumoustier, who commands the division of the Young Guards, has sustained the reputation that he had already acquired in the preceding campaigns. He bestows high praise on his division.

General of Division Brenier was wounded. Generals of Brigade Chemineau and Grillot were wounded, and have suffered amputation. By a calculation of the number of cannon-shot fired in the battle, it is found to be less considerable than was at first believed; only 39,500 cannon-shot were fired. At the battle of Moskova upwards of 50,000 were fired.

Moniteur, 11 May 1813
Her Majesty the Empress-Queen and Regent has received the following intelligence of the situation of the armies on the evening of 5 May:

The Emperor's headquarters were at Colditz; the Viceroy's at Hartau; the Duke of Ragusa's behind Colditz; General Lauriston's at Würzen; the Prince of the Moskova's at Leipzig; the Duke of Reggio's at Altenburg; and General Bertrand's at Rochlitz.

The Viceroy arrived before Colditz on the 5th, at nine in the morning. The bridge was cut, and some columns of infantry and cavalry with artillery opposed our crossing. The Viceroy, with his division, marched towards a ford which is on the left, crossed the river, and gained the village of Komichau, where he placed a battery of 20 pieces of artillery; the enemy then evacuated the town of Colditz in the greatest disorder, and in defiling were exposed to the fire of our 20 pieces.

The Viceroy pursued the enemy with vigour; it was the remainder of the Prussian army, about 20,000 or 25,000 men strong, which took its direction partly to Leisnig and partly to Gersdorff.

Having arrived at Gersdorff the Prussian troops passed across a reserve which occupied this position: it was the Russian corps of Miloradovitch, composed of two divisions, amounting to nearly 8,000 men under arms. The Russian regiments, consisting of only two battalions of four companies each, and the companies not consisting of not more than 150 men, but having only 100 men present, which does not amount to more than 700 or 800 men per regiment. These two divisions of Miloradovich had arrived at the moment the battle was ending, and could not take any part in it.

As soon as the 36th Division rejoined the 35th, the Viceroy gave orders to the Duke of Tarentum to form the two divisions in three columns, and drive the enemy from its position. The attack was brisk: our brave fellows precipitated themselves on the Russians, penetrated, and drove them towards Hartau. In this engagement we had 500 to 600 wounded, and took 1,000 prisoner. The enemy lost 2,000 men on this day.

General Bertrand arriving at Rochlitz, took several convoys of sick and wounded, some baggage, and made them prisoners; more than 1,200 carriages with wounded had passed by this route.

The King of Prussia and Emperor Alexander had slept at Rochlitz.

An adjutant NCO of the 17th Provisional Regiment, who had been taken prisoner on the 2nd, made his escape and gave information that the enemy had sustained great losses, and was retiring in the utmost disorder; that during the battle, the Russians and Prussians kept their colours in reserve, which was why we could not take any of them; that they have taken 102 prisoners from us, among whom are four officers; that these prisoners were conducted to the rear under the guard of the detachment which had charge of the colours; that the Prussians treated their prisoners very badly; that two prisoners not being able to walk, through extreme fatigue, they ran them through the body with their swords; that the astonishment of the Russian and Prussians at having found such a numerous army, and so well disciplined and supplied with everything, was extreme; that there existed a misunderstanding between them, and that they mutually accused each other as being the cause of their losses.

General Count Lauriston has begun to march from Würzen, on the high road to Dresden.

The Prince of the Moskova has marched towards the Elbe to raise the blockade of General Thielmann, who commands at Torgau, take his position at that point, and raise the blockade of Wittenberg. It appears that this latter place has made a fine defence, and repulsed several attacks, which have cost the enemy very dearly.

The prisoners state that the Emperor Alexander, finding the battle lost, rode through the Russian line to animate the soldiers, by exclaiming, 'Courage! God is with us!'

They add that the Prussian General Blücher is wounded and that there were four other generals of division or brigade either killed or wounded.

Moniteur, 13 May 1813

Her Majesty the Empress-Queen and Regent has received the following intelligence respecting the situation of the armies, to 6 May in the evening;

The headquarters of the Emperor and King were at Waldheim, those of the Viceroy at Ertzdorff, those of General Lauriston at Oschatz, those of the Prince of the Moskova between Leipzig and Torgau, those of Count Bertrand at Mittweyda and those of the Duke of Reggio at Penig.

The enemy had burned a very fine wooden bridge of one arch at Waldheim, which delayed us for some hours. Its rearguard wished to defend it, but was driven back on Ertzdorff. The position of this last point is very fine. The enemy wished to hold it. The bridge being burnt, the Viceroy ordered the village to be turned by the right and left. The enemy was placed behind ravines. A fusillade and a cannonade took place; quickly we marched right to the enemy, and the position was carried. The enemy left 200 dead on the battlefield.

General Vandamme had, on 1 May, his headquarters in Harburg. Our troops have taken a Russian cutter, armed with 20 cannon. The enemy re-crossed the Elbe with so much precipitation that he left on the left bank a number of boats proper for crossing the river in, and much baggage. The movements of the *Grande Armée* had already caused a great consternation at Hamburg; the Hamburg traitors could see the day of vengeance was fast approaching.

General Dumonceau was at Lüneburg.

At the battle of the 2nd, ordnance officers Berenger and Pretel were wounded, but only slightly.

The following is the relation that the enemy has given of the battle. We must expect that they will sing a *Te Deum* at Saint Petersburg, as they did for the battle of Moskova.

Account of the Battle fought on 2 May, on the road from Weissenfels to Leipzig, by an officer of Blücher's corps. (Translated from the German.)

The enemy was turning its back to Leipzig; and we had behind us Naumburg and Weissenfels. The Elster and the Luppe were at a certain distance from the wings of the two armies. Before our right wing we had a village occupied by the enemy. The battle began by the attack of this village, which was carried by the right wing of Blücher's corps. Soon after, the left wing of that corps found itself before another village, before which the enemy brought several batteries; we opposed it with nearly as much artillery, which we covered by our reserve of cavalry, because the infantry had not advanced so far. The other corps came up by degrees, and the battle commenced on the entire length of the line, and extended past the last village on the left; I do not exactly know to what distance. For some hours we occupied the village on our right; but the enemy presented itself there in considerable force, surrounded and took it. It did not keep it above half an hour. We again attacked and took it. We even penetrated beyond it, and took two other villages, by which means we came on the enemy's flanks. From this moment the battle became very obstinate at this point. Almost all the infantry of Blücher's corps, and part of that of the other corps, came up by degrees. We were then very near each other. Victory appeared to incline sometimes to the one side and sometimes to the other. However, we did not lose an inch of the ground we occupied on the enemy's flank. It was now between six and seven in the evening, and at this moment I was wounded in the leg, and forced to leave the battlefield. I am ignorant of what was happening on the left wing, but I perceived that we had likewise gained some ground on that side. The battle is consequently won. I do not as yet know the result. The enemy has occupied Leipzig in its rear. Towards evening reinforcements had arrived from the great army, and Miloradovich's corps was in march.

At this moment I learn the battle is over, and that we are masters, not only of the first battlefield, but likewise of the ground that we have taken from the enemy. Nevertheless, the occupation of Leipzig by the enemy obliges us to make a lateral movement.

Letter from the Emperor to the Duchess of Istria.

From Our Imperial Camp at Colditz, 6 May 1813
My cousin, your husband has died in the field of honour. Your loss, and that of your children, is certainly great but mine is still greater. The Duke of Istria died the noblest of deaths, and without suffering. He has left a reputation without blemish, the fairest inheritance he could bequeath to his children. They have acquired my protection, and they will also inherit the affection that I bore to their father. Find in all these considerations motives of consolation to alleviate your sorrow, and never doubt of my sentiments of regard towards you. This letter having no other end than to assure you of it, I pray god to have you, my dear Cousin, in his holy and worthy keeping.

NAPOLEON

Moniteur, 15 May 1813

Her Majesty the Empress-Queen and Regent has received the following information of the situation of the armies up to the morning of 9 May 1813.
On the 7th, the Emperor's headquarters were at Nossen.

Between Nossen and Wilsdruff, the Viceroy reconnoitred the enemy posted behind a torrent and in a fine situation. He drove the enemy from its post, killed about 1,000 men and made 500 prisoners.

A Cossack who was taken, was bearer of the annexed order (A) for burning the baggage of the Russian rearguard. In effect, 800 Russian wagons were burned; a quantity of baggage and 20 pieces of artillery were taken by us on the roads; several columns of Cossacks were cut off; we pursue them.

The Viceroy entered Dresden at noon on the 8th. Independent of the great bridge which the enemy had restored, they had thrown three bridges over the Elbe. The Viceroy having caused some troops to march towards those bridges, the enemy immediately set fire to them. The three bridgeheads that covered them were carried.

On the same day, the 8th, at nine o'clock in the morning, Count Lauriston arrived at Meissen. There he found three redoubts with blockhouses constructed by the Prussians; they had burned the bridge.

All of the Elbe is free from the enemy.

His Majesty the Emperor arrived at Dresden on the 8th at one o'clock in the afternoon. The Emperor, in making a circuit of the city, immediately went to the building site at the gate of Pirna, and from there to the village of Priesnitz, where His Majesty ordered a bridge to be thrown over the river. At seven o'clock in the evening

His Majesty returned from his reconnaissance to the palace, where he is lodged.

The Old Guard made its entrance into Dresden at eight o'clock in the evening.

On the 9th, at three in the morning, the Emperor caused a battery to be placed on one of the bastions that towers over the right flank, by which the enemy was driven from a position that it occupied on that side.

The Prince of the Moskova is marching on Torgau.

You will find here the relation that the enemy has given of the battle of Lützen (B), which is nothing but a series of falsehoods. We are advised here, that orders had been given to sing a *Te Deum*; but that the people of the country who were charged to have it performed declared it to be ridiculous, and that what might be suitable in Russia would be very absurd in Germany.

The Emperor of Russia left Dresden yesterday morning.

The famous Stein is an object of contempt to an honest people. He wished to cause the mob to revolt against the landowners. We cannot recover from our surprise to see such Sovereigns as the King of Prussia, and more especially the Emperor Alexander, on whom nature has bestowed so many fine qualities, give the sanction of their names to actions which are as criminal as they are atrocious.

Independent of the cannon and baggage taken in the pursuit of the enemy, we likewise took 5,000 prisoners in the battle, and took 10 pieces of artillery. The enemy did not take a single cannon from us, but it took 111 prisoner.

General-in-Chief Kutusov died at Bautzen of a nervous fever, about a fortnight ago. He has been replaced as command-in-chief by General Wittgenstein, who made his debut by the loss of the battle of Lützen.

A: Copy of the Letter of which a Cossack, who was made prisoner, was the bearer.

If the enemy should force you to fall back, you will take the steps prescribed to you in General Winzingerode's orders. I authorize you to destroy all the baggage that might impede your route and cannot be carried off, by burning the wagons and taking the horses with you. Those who are able to escape must run, without relaxation, as far as the Elbe.

[RUSSIAN GENERAL] LANSKOÏ
24th — Chemnitz

I shall set off this day for Freiberg.

B: Official intelligence from the combined armies, from the battlefield

11 April [3 May] 1813

The Emperor Napoleon had left Mayence on 12 [24] April. Having arrived at his army, everything announced that he meant immediately to act on the offensive. In consequence the combined Russian and Prussian armies were united between Leipzig and Altenburg, a central position, and very advantageous in all possible cases. Meanwhile the General-in-Chief, Count Wittgenstein, had soon convinced himself by good and spirited reconnaissance, that the enemy, after having concentrated itself, was debouching with all of his force by Merseburg and Weissenfels, while at the same time, it sent a considerable corps on Leipzig, which appeared to be the principal goal of its operations. Count Wittgenstein immediately decided on taking advantage of the moment when it would be out of the power of this detached corps to co-operate with the main body of the French army, and to attack this immediately with his whole force. For this purpose it was necessary to conceal his movements; and during the night between the 19th and 20th [1st to 2nd], he drew to himself the corps under the orders of the General of Cavalry Tormasov. By this junction he found himself enabled to throw himself *en masse* on the enemy, at a place where the latter might suppose it had only to deal with a detachment, whose aim was to give it disturbance on his flanks. The action commenced. Generals Blücher and Yorck entered into it with an ardour and energy that was quickly shared by the troops. The operation took place between the Elster and Luppe.

The village of Gross-Görschen was the key and centre of the French position. The battle commenced by the attack on this village. The enemy understood all the importance of this point, and wished to maintain itself in it. It was carried by the right wing of the corps under General Blücher's order. At the same time his left wing pushed in front, and soon charged on the village of Klein-Görschen. From this time on the corps came successively into action, which soon became general.

The village of Gross-Görschen was disputed with unexampled obstinacy. It was six times taken and re-taken by the bayonet; but the valour of the Russians and Prussians obtained the superiority, and this village, as well as those of Klein-Görschen and Rham, remained in the hands of the combined armies. The enemy's centre was broken and it was driven off the field of battle. It nevertheless brought forward fresh columns, which having come from Leipzig, we expected to support the left flank of the enemy. Some corps drawn from the reserve, and placed under the orders of Lieutenant General Kanownitzin, were opposed to them. Here, towards evening, a combat commenced, which was likewise exceedingly obstinate, but the enemy was also completely repulsed at this point. Everything was disposed for renewing the attack at sunrise, and orders had been sent to General Miloradovitch, who, with his whole corps, was posted at Zeitz, to join the main army and to be there at daybreak. The presence of an entire fresh corps, with 100 pieces of artillery, left no doubt as to the issue of the day. But towards morning the enemy appeared to be moving towards Leipzig, always falling towards its rearguard. This mode of refusing the challenge made for engaging gave reason for believing that it would endeavour to manoeuvre, either to move towards the Elbe, or on the communications of the combined armies. Under this supposition, it became necessary to oppose manoeuvre against manoeuvre, and by occupying a commanding front between Colditz and Rochlitz, we immediately outmanoeuvred every tentative move of this kind without for such purpose withdrawing too far from the starting points for making an offensive attack.

On this memorable day the Prussian army fought in a manner to fix the admiration of its allies. The King's guards covered themselves with glory. Russians and Prussians rivalled each other in valour and zeal, under the eyes of the two sovereigns, who did not for a moment quit the field of battle. The enemy has lost 16 cannon, and we have taken 1,400 prisoners. Not a single trophy has been conquered from the allied army. Its loss in killed and wounded may amount to 8,000 men; that of the French army is estimated at 12,000 to 15,000. Among the wounded are General of Cavalry Blücher, and Lieutenant Generals Kanownitzin and Scharnhorst. Their wounds are not dangerous.

The enemy, having but few cavalry, endeavoured to get and keep possession of the villages, the ground of which was intersected; consequently the day of 20 April [2 May] has been a continual combat between the infantry. An uninterrupted shower of balls, bullets, grapeshot and shells was kept up on the part of the French, during an action of ten hours.

Moniteur, 16 May 1813

Her Majesty the Empress-Queen and Regent has received the following intelligence respecting the situation of the army, 10 May, at night:

On the 9th, Colonel Lasalle, director of the bridge equipage, began to set up rafts for the bridge, which we cast at the village of Priesnitz. We also set up a ferry-boat at the same time. Three hundred voltigeurs were crossed over to the right bank, under the protection of 20 cannon placed on a height.

At ten in the morning the enemy advanced to drive back these skirmishers into the river: it thought that a battery of 12 pieces would be sufficient to silence our guns; the cannonade began, and the guns of the enemy were shot to pieces; three battalions whom it had pushed forwards were destroyed by our grapeshot: the Emperor hastened to the spot. General Dulauloy took a station with General Devaux, and 18 pieces of light artillery on the left of the village of Priesnitz, a position which covers on the flank all the plain on the right bank; General Drouot advanced on the right with 16 pieces of artillery. The enemy brought forward 30 cannon. We had established a battery of 80.

In the meantime a hollow was traced on the right bank of the river, in the form of a bridgehead, in which our skirmishers sheltered themselves. After having had from 12 to 15 pieces of their cannon shot to pieces, and from 15-to 1,800 men killed or wounded, the enemy understood the folly of its enterprise, and at three in the afternoon marched off.

We worked all night at the bridge, but the Elbe rose, some of our anchors drifted unmoored, and the bridge will not be finished until tonight.

Today, the 10th, the Emperor has marched the Charpentier division into the new town, by the bridge of Dresden. Tonight, the bridge being finished, all the army is crossing over to the right bank of the river. The enemy appears to be retreating to the Oder.

The Prince of the Moskova is at Wittenberg; General Lauriston at Torgau; General Reynier has resumed the command of the 7th Corps, composed of the Saxon contingent, and the division Durutte.

The 4th, 6th, 11th and 12th Corps will cross by the bridge of Dresden at daybreak tomorrow. The Young and Old Guard are around Dresden. The second division of the Guard, commanded by General Barrois, arrived today at Altenburg.

The King of Saxony, who has directed his course towards Prague in order to be near his capital, will arrive in Dresden in the course of tomorrow. The Emperor has sent an escort of 500 of his Guard with his aide General Flahaut to receive and accompany him.

Two thousand of the enemy's cavalry have been cut off from the Elbe, as well as a great quantity of baggage, patrols of light troops, and some Cossacks. They appear to have taken refuge in Bohemia.

Moniteur, 18 May 1813

Her Majesty the Empress-Queen and Regent has received the following accounts with regard to the situation of the Armies, on the evening of 11 May:

The Viceroy had advanced with the 11th Corps to Bischofswerder; General Bertrand, with the 4th Corps, to Königsbruck; the Duke of Ragusa, with the 6th Corps, to Reichenbach; the Duke of Reggio, to Dresden; the Young and Old Guard, to Dresden.

The Prince of the Moskova entered Torgau on the morning of the 11th, and took a position on the right bank, one day's march from that fortress. General Lauriston arrived the same day at Torgau with his corps, at three in the afternoon.

The Duke of Belluno, with the 2nd Corps, has started his march on Wittenberg, along with General Sebastiani's cavalry corps.

The cavalry corps commanded by General Latour-Maubourg crossed the bridge of Dresden at three in the afternoon on the 11th.

The King of Saxony slept at Sedlitz. All the Saxon cavalry must rejoin on the 13th at Dresden. General Reynier has resumed the command of the 7th Corps at Torgau: that corps is composed of two Saxon divisions, consisting of 12,000 men.

His Majesty spent the entire day on the bridge to see his troops defile.

Colonel of Engineers Bernard, aide-de-camp of the Emperor, has exerted great activity in repairing the bridge of Dresden.

General Rogniat, Commander-in-Chief of the Engineers of the Army, has traced out the works that are to cover the new town, and to serve as a bridgehead.

We will find attached the account of the battle of the 2nd that appeared in the Berlin gazette.

We have intercepted a courier from Count Stackelberg, ex-ambassador from Russia at Vienna, to Count Nesselrode, Secretary of State, accompanying the Russian Emperor at Dresden. We have also intercepted a number of dispatch riders from Berlin and Prague.

Her Majesty the Empress-Queen and Regent has received the following account with regard to the situation of army on the evening of 12 May 1813:
On the 12th, at ten o'clock in the morning, the Imperial Guard took up arms and was drawn up in battle formation on the road from Pirna to Gross Garten. The Emperor reviewed them. The King of Saxony, who slept the night before at Sedlitz, arrived at midday. The two Sovereigns alighted from horseback, embraced each other, and then entered Dresden at the head of the Guard, amidst the acclamation of an immense population. It formed a very fine sight.

At three o'clock the Emperor reviewed the division of cavalry of General Fresia, consisting 3,000 horses from Italy. His Majesty was extremely satisfied with this cavalry, the good condition of which is owing to the care and activity of Fontanelli, the Minister of War for the Kingdom of Italy, who spared nothing to put it in a good state.

The Emperor has given orders to the Viceroy to go to Milan, in order to fulfil a special mission. His Majesty has been extremely satisfied with the conduct of this Prince during the whole campaign: that conduct has acquired for the Viceroy a new title to the confidence of the Emperor.

Proclamation of the Emperor to the Army
From our Imperial Camp at Lützen, 3 May 1813
Soldiers! I am satisfied with you. You have fulfilled my expectations! You have supplied everything by your good will, and by your valour. You have, on the memorable 2 May, defeated and routed the Russian and Prussian army, commanded by the Emperor Alexander and the King of Prussia. You have added new lustre to the glory of my Eagles; you have displayed all that the French blood is capable of. The battle of Lützen will be placed above those of Austerlitz, Jena, Friedland and the Moskova! In the last campaign, the enemy found no refuge against our arms but by following the ferocious way of its barbarous ancestors. Armies of Tartars burned down his fields, his cities, sacred Moscow itself! Today

they arrived in our regions, preceded by all the bad subjects and deserters of Germany, France, and Italy, for the purpose of preaching revolt, anarchy, civil war and murder. They became the apostles of every crime. They wished to light up a moral conflagration between the Vistula and the Rhine, in order, according to the usage of the despotic governments, to place deserts between us and them. The madmen! They little knew the attachment of the Germans to their sovereigns, their wisdom, their orderly disposition, and their good sense. They little knew the power and bravery of the French!

In a single day you have counteracted all those parricidal plots. We will drive back these Tartars into their frightful regions, which they ought never to have left. Let them remain in their frozen deserts, the abode of slavery, of barbarism, and of corruption, where man is debased to an equality with the brute. You have deserved well of civilized Europe. Soldiers! Italy, France, and Germany return you thanks!

NAPOLEON

Moniteur, 20 May 1813

Her Majesty the Empress-Queen and Regent has received the following information respecting the situation of the armies on the morning of 13 May:

The fortress of Spandau has capitulated; this event astonishes all military men. His Majesty has ordered that General Bruny, the Commandant of Artillery, and Armand, the Engineer of the place, as well as the Ministers of the Council of Defence, who would not have protested, to be arrested and tried before a Marshal's commission, presided by the Prince Vice-Constable.

His Majesty has likewise ordered that the capitulation of Thorn should be the subject of inquiry.

If the garrison of Spandau has surrendered without a siege, a strong fortress surrounded by marshes, and subscribed to a capitulation that must be the subject of an inquiry and a judgment, the conduct observed by the garrison of Wittenberg has been very different. General La Poype has conducted himself perfectly well, and supported the honour of our arms in the defence of that important point, which is besides but an indifferent fortress, having but one enclosure half destroyed, and which could only owe its resistance to the courage of its defenders.

Baron Montaran, an equerry to the Emperor, followed by a man from the stables, on 6 May lost his way two days' journey from Dresden; he fell into the hands of a patrol of light cavalry consisting of 30 men, and was taken by the enemy.

A new courier sent from Vienna by Mr Stackelberg to Mr Nesselrode at Dresden, has just been intercepted. What is remarkable is that the dispatches are dated the 8th, in the evening, and notwithstanding that fact, they contain congratulations from Stackelberg to the Emperor Alexander, on the brilliant victory he has gained, and on the retreat of the French beyond the Saale.

The Grand Duchess Catherine received at Töplitz a letter from her brother, the Emperor Alexander, which informs her of this great victory of the 2nd. The Grand Duchess, with reason, allowed all the persons taking the waters of Töplitz to read this letter. However, the following day she learned that the Emperor Alexander had returned to Dresden, and that she herself must proceed to Prague. All this has appeared extremely ridiculous in Bohemia. We saw the name of a sovereign compromised, without any reason that politics could justify. All this can only be explained as a Russian custom, resulting from the necessity there is in Russia of imposing on an ignorant populace, and of the facility with which they can be made to believe anything. They should have adopted a different conduct in such a civilized country as Germany.

Her Majesty the Empress-Queen and Regent has received the following intelligence relative to the situation of the army on the morning of 14 May:
The army of the Elbe has been dissolved, and the two armies of the Elbe and the Maine now form only one.

The Duke of Belluno was, on the evening of the 13th, near Wittenberg.

The Prince of the Moskova had left Torgau, to proceed to Lukau.

Count Lauriston was marching from Torgau on Donbrilugk.

Count Bertrand was at Königsbruck.

The Duke of Tarentum, with the 11th Corps, was encamped between Bischofswerder and Bautzen; he on the 11th and 12th briskly pursued the enemy. General Miloradovitch, with a rearguard, consisting of 20,000 men, and 40 pieces of artillery, endeavoured on the 12th to retain the positions of Fischbach, Capellemberg, and Bischofswerder, which brought on three successive battles, in which our troops behaved with the utmost intrepidity. The division of Charpentier distinguished itself in the attack on the right; the enemy was turned in its positions, and dislodged at all points; one of its columns was cut off. We have taken 500 prisoners, and it had upwards of 1,500 men killed or wounded. The artillery of the 11th Corps fired 2,000 cannon-shot in this engagement.

The remains of the Prussian army under the command of the King of Prussia, who passed at Meissen, took the road to Bautzen by Königsbruck to join the Russian army.

Yesterday at noon the Duke of Reggio's corps crossed the bridge of Dresden.

The Emperor has reviewed the corps of cavalry and the fine cuirassiers under General Latour-Maubourg.

It is said that the Russians have advised the Prussians to burn Potsdam and Berlin, and to lay all Prussia waste. They began by setting the example themselves; out of sheer wantonness they burnt the little town of Bischofswerder.

The King of Saxony dined with the Emperor on the 13th.

The second division of the Young Guard, commanded by General Barrois, is expected to arrive tomorrow the 15th at Dresden.

Moniteur, *22 May 1813*

Her Majesty the Empress Queen and Regent has received the following information of the situation of the armies, 16 May 1813, in the evening:
On the 15th, His Majesty the Emperor and His Majesty the King of Saxony reviewed four regiments of Saxon cavalry (one of hussars, one of lancers and two of cuirassiers), which form part of General Latour-Maubourg's corps. Their Majesties afterwards visited the field of battle and the bridgehead of Priesnitz.

The Duke of Tarentum had put himself in motion on the 15th, at five in the morning, to march opposite Bautzen.

He reconnoitred at the debouch from the woods the enemy's rearguard; a few charges of cavalry were attempted against our infantry, but without success. The enemy, however, wishing to maintain itself in this position, a fusillade was exchanged, and it was driven from the post.

We had 250 men killed or wounded in this rearguard affair. The enemy's loss is estimated at from 700 to 800 men, of whom 200 are prisoners.

The second division of the Young Guard, commanded by General Barrois, arrived at Dresden yesterday.

All the army has crossed the Elbe.

Independently of the great bridge of Dresden, two bridges of boats have been established, the one above, the other below the town.

The Berlin Gazette of the 8th contained the regulation for the *Landsturm*. Folly cannot be carried further; but it may be foreseen that the inhabitants of Prussia have too much good sense, and are too much attached to the real principles of propriety, to imitate barbarians, who hold nothing sacred.

At the battle of Lützen, a regiment composed of the élite of the Prussian nobility, and who were called Prussian Cossacks, were almost entirely destroyed; not even 15 men belonging to it remain, which has covered all their families with mourning.

These Cossacks really mimicked Cossacks of the Don: tender, delicate, young men had lances in their hands which they could scarcely support, and were dressed like real Cossacks.

What would Frederick, whose works are full of scorn for these awful troops, say, if he saw his great nephew at this day seek models of uniform and appearance from them?

The Cossacks are ill-clothed, they are mounted on small horses, almost without saddles and harness, because they are irregular militia, which the inhabitants of the Don furnish and which is established at their expense. To go there to seek a model for the Prussian nobility is to show to what point the spirit of folly and inconsequence which directs the affairs of that kingdom is carried.

—

Moniteur, 24 May 1813

Her Majesty the Empress-Queen and Regent has received the following accounts of the situation of the armies on 18 May 1813:

The Emperor was still at Dresden. On the 15th the Duke of Treviso had left it with General Latour-Maubourg's corps of cavalry, and General Dumoustier's infantry division of the Young Guard.

On the 16th the division of the Young Guard, commanded by General Barrois, also left Dresden.

The Duke of Reggio, the Duke of Tarentum, the Duke of Ragusa and Count Bertrand were in line opposite of Bautzen.

The Prince of the Moskova and General Lauriston had arrived at Hoyerswerda.

The Duke of Belluno, General Sebastiani and General Reynier were marching on Berlin. What was foreseen has happened: at the approach of danger the Prussians ridiculed the regulations respecting the Landsturm; a proclamation announced to the inhabitants of Berlin that they were covered by Bülow's corps, but at all events, should the French arrive, they were not to take up arms, but receive them according to the principles of war. There is no German who is inclined to burn his habitation, or to assassinate any one. This circumstance constitutes the eulogy of the German nation. When desperadoes without honour and without principles preach disorder and assassination, the character of this good people repel them with indignation. The Schlegels, the Kotzbues and other agitators equally criminal would transform the upright German into poisoners and assassins; but posterity will remark that they have not been able to seduce a single individual, a single authority, beyond the line of duty and probity.

Count Bubna arrived on the 16th at Dresden. He was the bearer of a letter from the Austrian Emperor to the Emperor Napoleon. He set off on the 17th on his return for Vienna.

The Emperor Napoleon has proposed the meeting of a congress at Prague for a general peace. On the side of France there would arrive at this congress the plenipotentiaries of France, those of the United States of America, of Denmark, the King of Spain and all the allied princes; and on the opposite side those of England, Russia, Prussia, the Spanish insurgents and the other allies of that belligerent mass. In this congress would be established the basis of a long peace. But it is doubtful whether England is inclined to submit her egotistical and unjust principles to the censorship and opinion of the universe; for there is no power, however inconsiderable, that does not preliminarily claim the privileges attached to its sovereignty, and which are consecrated by the articles of the Treaty of Utrecht, respecting maritime navigation.

If England, from that feeling of egotism on which her policy is founded, refuses to co-operate in this grand work of the peace of the world because she wishes to exclude the universe from that element which constitutes three-fourths of the globe, the Emperor, nevertheless, proposes a meeting at Prague of the plenipotentiaries of all the belligerent powers to settle the peace of the Continent. His Majesty even offers to stipulate at the moment when the congress shall be formed, an armistice between the different armies, in order to put a stop to the effusion of human blood.

These principles are conformable with the views of Austria. It now remains to be seen what the courts of England, Russia, and Prussia will do.

The distance of the United States of America ought not to form a reason for excluding them. The congress might still be opened, and deputies of the United States would have time to arrive before the conclusion of the discussions, in order to stipulate for their rights and their interests.

Moniteur, 30 May 1813

Her Majesty the Empress-Queen and Regent has received the following intelligence respecting the events which have passed to the army during the days of the 19th, 20th, 21st, and 22nd, and of the position of the army on the 23rd.

The Emperor Alexander and the King of Prussia attributed the loss of the battle of Lützen to the fault their generals had committed in the direction of the combined forces, and particularly to the difficulties attached to an offensive movement of from 150,000 to 180,000 men. They resolved on taking the position of Bautzen and Hochkirch, already celebrated in the history of the Seven Years War, to unite all their reinforcements, which they expected from the Vistula and other points in their rear; to add to that position everything for which art could furnish the means, and there run the chance of a fresh battle, of which all the probabilities appeared to be in their favour.

The Duke of Tarentum, commanding the 11th Corps, had left Bischofswerder on the 15th. That evening he found himself within cannon-shot of Bautzen, where he found all the enemy army. He took a position.

From this moment the French army marched on the camp at Bautzen.

The Emperor left Dresden on the 18th; he slept at Hartau, and on the 19th, at ten in the morning, arrived before Bautzen. He employed all the day in reconnoitring the enemy's positions. We learned that the Russian corps of Barclay de Tolly, Langeron, and Sass, and Kleist's Prussian corps, had rejoined the combined army, and that its force might be estimated at from 150,000 to 160,000 men.

On the 19th, in the evening, the enemy's position was as follows: its left was supported by mountains, covered with woods, and perpendicular to the course of the Sprée, nearly a league from Bautzen. Bautzen contained the enemy's centre. This town had been entrenched and covered by redoubts. The right of the enemy leaned on fortified rising points, which defended the debouches from the Sprée; on the side of the village of Nimschütz, this very strong position was but a first position.

We distinctly perceived, at 3,000 *toises* distance in the rear, the ground newly dug up, and works which marked their second position. The left was still supported by the same mountains at 2,000 *toises* in the rear of those of the first position, and considerably in advance of the village of Hochkirch. The centre leaned on three entrenched villages, where so many works had been erected, that they might have been considered as strong places. A marshy and difficult ground covered three-quarters of the centre. Lastly, their right leaned in rear of the first position, on villages and a rising round, likewise entrenched.

The enemy's front, either in the first or second position, extended a league and a half.

After this reconnaissance, it was easy to conceive how, notwithstanding a lost battle, like that of Lützen, and eight days retreating, the enemy could still have hopes in the changes of fortune. According to the expression of a Russian officer, who was asked what they intended to do, 'We wish neither to advance nor retire.' 'You are masters of the first point,' replied a French Officer, 'and the event, in a few days, will prove whether you are masters of the other!' The headquarters of the two sovereigns were in the village of Natchen.

On the 19th the position of the French army was as follows:

On the right was the Duke of Reggio leaning on the mountains to the left of the Sprée, and separated from the left of the enemy by the valley. The Duke of Tarentum was before Bautzen straddling the road of Dresden. The Duke of Ragusa was on the left of Bautzen, opposite the village of Niemenschütz. General Bertrand was on the left of the Duke of Ragusa, leaning on a windmill and a wood, and appearing to intend to move out from Jaselitz on the enemy's right.

The Prince of the Moskova, General Lauriston, and General Reynier, were at Hoyerswerda, on the road to Berlin out of the line, and in the rear of our left.

The enemy having learned that a considerable corps was arriving by the road of Hoyerswerda, suspected that it was the Emperor's intention to turn the position by the right, to alter the field of battle, and to cause all these entrenchments to fall, which had been erected with so much pain, and the object of such hopes. Not being yet informed of General Lauriston's arrival, it did not suppose that this column could consist of more than 18,000 or 20,000 men. On the 19th, it therefore detached against them, at four o'clock in the morning, General Yorck with 12,000 Prussians and General Barclay de Tolly with 18,000 Russians. The Russians posted themselves at the village of Klix, and the Prussians at the village of Weissig.

Count Bertrand, in the meantime, had sent General Pery [*sic*, Peyri], with the Italian division, to Königswartha, to keep up our communication with the detached corps. Having arrived there at noon, General Pery made bad dispositions. He did not cause the neighbouring forest to be properly reconnoitred. He placed his posts badly, and at four o'clock he was assailed by a hurrah! which threw a few battalions into disorder. He lost 600 men, among whom was General Balathier of the Italian brigade, wounded, two cannon and three caissons; but the division having taken to their arms, kept themselves to the wood, and faced against the enemy.

Count Valmy, having arrived with the cavalry, put himself at the head of the Italian division, and retook the village of Königswartha. At this very moment, the corps under Count Lauriston, which marched at the head of the Prince of the Moskova, to turn the enemy's position, departed from Hoyerswerda, arrived on Weissig. The battle commenced, and the corps of General Yorck would have been destroyed had it not been for the circumstances of our troops having to pass a defile by which means they could come up only in succession.

After a battle of three hours, the village of Weissig was carried, and Yorck's corps overthrown and driven to the other bank of the Sprée.

The battle of Weissig was, in itself, an important event. A detailed report will shortly make known the particulars concerning it.

On the 19th, Count Lauriston therefore remained in the position of Weissig: the Prince of the Moskova at Mankersdorf, and Count Reynier at the distance of a league in the rear. The right of the enemy's position was evidently outflanked. On the 20th, at eight o'clock in the morning, the Emperor went to the heights in the rear of Bautzen. He gave orders to the Duke of Reggio to cross the Sprée and attack the mountains which supported the enemy's left; to the Duke of Tarentum, to throw a bridge over trestles, over the Sprée, between Bautzen and the mountains, to the Duke of Ragusa, to throw another bridge across the Sprée, in the turn which that river takes to the left, at half a league from Bautzen; to the Duke of Dalmatia, to whom His Majesty had given the command in chief of the centre, to cross the Sprée and disturb the enemy's right; and finally, to the Prince of the Moskova, under whose orders were the third corps, General Lauriston and General Reynier, to push forward on Klix, to cross the Sprée, and turn the enemy's right, and to carry his headquarters from Würschen to Weissenburg.

At noon the cannonade commenced. The Duke of Tarentum had no occasion to throw his bridge across the river, as he found a stone bridge before him, over which he forced his passage. The Duke of Ragusa threw his bridge across, and all of his corps crossed over to the other bank of the Sprée. After six hours of brisk cannonade, and several charges by the enemy without success, General Compans occupied Bautzen; General Bonet occupied the village of Nudkaya, and by a running charge took a plain which rendered himself master of all the centre of the enemy's position. The Duke of Reggio got possession of the heights, and at seven o'clock in the evening, the enemy was driven back on its second position. General Bertrand crossed one of the arms of the Sprée, but the enemy kept the heights that supported its right, and by this means maintained itself between the Prince of the Moskova's corps and our army.

At eight o'clock in the evening the Emperor entered Bautzen and was received by the inhabitants, and the constituted authorities, with sentiments due from allies who were happy in finding themselves delivered from Stein, from Kotzebue, and the Cossacks. This day, which were it isolated might be called the battle of Bautzen, was merely the prelude to the battle of Würschen.

However, the enemy began to comprehend the possibility of being forced in its position. Its hopes were no longer the same; and it must from this moment have had the presage of its defeat. Already all its dispositions were changed. The fate of the battle was no longer to be decided behind its entrenchments. Its immense works and 300 redoubts became useless. The right of its position, which was opposed to the four corps, became its centre, and it was obliged to offer its right, which formed a good part of its army, to oppose the Prince of the Moskova in a place which it had not studied and which it believed beyond his positions.

On the 21st, at five in the morning, the Emperor marched towards the heights, three-quarters of a league in advance of Bautzen.

The Duke of Reggio sustained a lively fire of musketry towards the height, which was defended by the enemy's left. The Russians, who felt the importance of this position, had placed a strong part of their army there, in order that their left should not be turned. The Emperor ordered the Dukes of Reggio and Tarentum to keep up this combat, to prevent the enemy's left from disengaging itself, and to hide from it the real attack, the result of which could not be felt before noon or one o'clock.

At eleven o'clock, the Duke of Ragusa advanced 1,000 *toises* ahead of his position, and engaged in a dreadful cannonade before all the enemy's redoubts and entrenchments.

The Guard and the reserve of the army infantry and cavalry concealed by rising round, had easy debouches to advance by the left or right, according to what the vicissitudes of the day might require. The enemy was thus held in uncertainty respecting the real point of attack.

During this time the Prince of the Moskova overthrew the enemy at the village of Klix, crossed the Sprée, and led, fighting what he had before him, to the village of Preilitz. At ten o'clock he carried the village, but the enemy's reserve having advanced to cover the headquarters, the Prince of the Moskova was driven back, and lost the village of Preilitz. The Duke of Dalmatia began to debouch an hour after noon. The enemy, comprehending all the danger with which it was threatened by the direction the battle had taken, knew that the only means of advantageously supporting the battle against the Prince of the Moskova was to prevent us from debouching. He endeavoured to oppose the Duke of Dalmatia's attack. The moment for deciding the battle had then arrived. The Emperor, by a movement to the left, in 20 minutes marched with the Guard, General Latour Maubourg's four divisions and a great quantity of artillery on the right flank of the enemy's position, which had become the centre of the Russian army.

Morand's division and the Württembergers' division carried the rising ground that the enemy had made his fulcrum.

General Devaux established a battery, the fire of which he directed on the masses that attempted to retake the position. Generals Dulauloy and Drouot, with 60 reserve artillery, advanced. Lastly, the Duke of Treviso, with the divisions Dumoustier and Barrois of the Young Guard, took the road to the Inn of Klein-Baschwitz, cutting off the road from Würschen to Bautzen.

The enemy was obliged to uncover its right to fend off this new attack. The Prince of the Moskova took advantage of it by advancing in front; he took the village of Prelsig, and having overwhelmed the enemy's army, marched on Würschen. It was at three o'clock in the afternoon, and while the army was in the greatest incertitude of success, that a heavy firing was heard along a line of three leagues. The Emperor announced that the battle was won.

The enemy, finding that its right was turned, began to retreat, and this retreat soon became a flight.

At seven o'clock in the evening, the Prince of the Moskova and General Lauriston arrived at Würschen. The Duke of Ragusa, having been ordered to make movement reverse to that which the Guard had made, occupied all the entrenched villages and all the redoubts, which the enemy was obliged to evacuate, advanced in the direction of Hochkirch, and thus took all of the enemy's left in flank, which then fell into an unavoidable rout. The Duke of Tarentum, on his side, briskly pushed the left wing, and did it considerable harm.

The Emperor slept on the road in the midst of his Guard, at the Inn of Klein-Baschwitz. Then the enemy being forced into all its positions, left the battlefield in our power, covered with its dead and wounded, and several thousands of prisoners.

On the 22nd, at four o'clock in the morning, the French army put itself in motion. The enemy had fled all night, by all the roads, and in every direction. We did not find its first posts until past Weissenburg; it did not offer to make any resistance, until it had gained the heights in the rear of Ruckenback. The enemy had not yet seen our cavalry.

General Lefebvre-Desnouettes, at the head of 1,500 horse of the Polish lancers, and the Red Lancers of the Guard, charged and overthrew the enemy's cavalry in the plain of Reichenbach. The enemy, believing that these were alone, caused a division of their cavalry to advance and several divisions were successively engaged. General Latour-Maubourg, with his 14,000 horses, and the French and Saxon cuirassiers, arrived to their assistance and several charges of cavalry took place. The enemy, quite astonished to find 15,000 to 16,000 cavalry before it, while it believed us to be unsupplied with any, retired in disorder. The Red Lancers of the Guard are for a great part composed of the volunteers of Paris and its environs. General Lefebvre-Desnouettes, General Colbert and their colonel bestow the greatest praise on them.

In this affair of cavalry, General Bruyères of the light cavalry, an officer of the highest distinction, had his leg carried off by a cannonball.

General Reynier, with the Saxon corps, gained the heights behind Reichenbach, and pursued the enemy as far as the village of Hotterndorf. Night overtook us a league from Görlitz. Since the day had been extremely long, and we found ourselves now at the distance of eight leagues from the battlefield, and the troops having undergone so much fatigue, the French army would have slept at Görlitz, but the enemy had placed a corps of its rearguard on the heights in front of this town, and it would have required half an hour more daylight to turn it by the left. The Emperor ordered the army to take a position.

In the battle of the 20th and 21st the Württemberg General Franquemont and General Lorencez were wounded. Our loss on these days may be estimated at 11- or 12,000 men, killed or wounded. At seven o'clock in the evening of the day of the 22nd, Grand Marshal of the Palace the Duke of Friuli, being on a small eminence, along with the Duke Treviso and General Kirgener, all three with their feet on the ground, and at a sufficient distance from the fire, one of the last balls fired by the enemy struck down close to the Duke of Treviso, tore the lower part of the Grand Marshal, and killed General Kirgener on the spot. The Duke of Friuli immediately felt that he was mortally wounded, and expired twelve hours after.

As soon as the posts were placed, and the army had taken its bivouacs, the Emperor went to see the Duke of Friuli. He found him perfectly master of himself and showing the greatest composure. The Duke offered his hand to the Emperor, who pressed it to his lips. 'My whole life,' said he to him 'has been consecrated to your service, nor do I regret its loss, but for the use it still might have been to you!' 'Duroc,' said the Emperor, 'there is another life! It is there that you will wait for me, and where we will meet again one day!' 'Yes, Sire! But that will be in 30 years, when you will have triumphed over your enemies and realized all the hopes of our country. I have lived an honest man. I have nothing to reproach myself with. I leave a daughter behind me; Your Majesty will fulfil the place of a father to her.'

The Emperor, grasping the right hand of the Grand Marshal, remained for a quarter of an hour, with his head reclined on his right hand, in deep silence. The Grand Marshal was the first who broke this silence 'Ah, Sire,' cried he, 'go away, this sight gives you pain!' The Emperor, supporting himself on the Duke of Dalmatia and the Master of the Horse, left the Duke of Friuli without being able to say more than these words: 'Farewell, then, my friend!' His Majesty returned to his tent, and would not receive any person all of that night.

On the 23rd, at nine o'clock in the morning, General Reynier entered Görlitz. Bridges were thrown over the Neisse, and the army crossed that river.

On the 23rd, in the evening, the Duke of Belluno was near Boitzenburg. Count Lauriston had his headquarters at Hochkirch, Count Reynier before Trotskendorf, on the road of Lauban; and Count Bertrand in the rear of the same village; the Duke of Tarentum at Schönberg, and the Emperor was at Görlitz.

An emissary sent by the enemy brought several letters, from which it is believed that he wished to negotiate for an armistice.

The enemy's army has retired by the road of Banalau and Lauban, into Silesia. All Saxony is delivered from her enemies, and by tomorrow, the 24th, the French army will be in Silesia.

The enemy has burned a great quantity of its baggage, blown up a number of parks and distributed through the villages a great many wounded. Those whom it was able to take away in carriages did not have their wounds dressed. The inhabitants state their numbers at upwards of 18,000, and more than 10,000 remain in our power.

The town of Görlitz, which contains 8,000 to 10,000 inhabitants, has received the French as their liberators.

The city of Dresden and the Saxon ministry have shown the greatest activity in providing for the army, which has never had a greater abundance of anything.

Although great quantities of ammunition have been consumed, the workmen of Torgau and Dresden, and the convoys that arrive through the attention of General Sorbier, keep our artillery well provided.

We have received intelligence from Glogau, Custrin and Stettin. All these places are in good condition.

This recital of the battle of Würschen can only be considered as a sketch. The Major-General will collect the reports, which will point out such officers, soldiers and corps who have distinguished themselves.

In the minor combat of the 22nd, at Reichenbach, we ascertained that our young cavalry is superior to that of the enemy in equal numbers.

We could not take any flags, as the enemy always carries them off the field of battle. We have only taken 19 cannon, the enemy having blown up its parks and caissons; and besides, the Emperor keeps his cavalry in reserve; and until it is of sufficient numbers, he wishes to spare it.

Moniteur, 2 June 1813

Her Majesty the Empress-Queen has received the following intelligence, respecting the situation of the Armies, on the evening of the 25th:

The Prince of the Moskova, having under his orders Generals Lauriston and Reynier's corps, forced the crossing of the Neisse on 24 May; and on the morning of the 25th, that of the Queiss, and had arrived at Bunzlau. General Lauriston had his headquarters halfway between Bunzlau and Hanau.

The Emperor's headquarters were, on the evening of the 25th, at Bunzlau.

The Duke of Belluno's headquarters was at Wehrau, on the Queiss.

General Bertrand, on the 24th, entered Lauban and on the 25th pursued the enemy.

The Duke of Tarentum, after having crossed the Queiss, had a combat with the enemy's rearguard. The enemy, encumbered with wagons loaded with sick and baggage, wished to make a stand. The Duke of Tarentum had his three divisions engaged. The battle was quick. The enemy suffered much. The Duke of Tarentum had his headquarters at Sligkight on the 25th in the evening.

The Duke of Ragusa was at Ottendorf.

The Duke of Reggio had left Bautzen, marching on Berlin by the Luckau road.

Our advanced posts were but one march from Glogau.

It was at Bunzlau that the Russian General Kutusov died, six weeks ago. Our armies have not found in this country any enthusiasm. The *Landwehr* and *Landsturm* only exist in the journals, at least in this country; and the inhabitants are very far from adhering to the advice of the Russians, of burning their houses and desolating their country.

General Durosnel has remained in the position of Governor of Dresden. He commands all the troops and French garrisons in Saxony.

Several French corps are marching on Berlin, where it appears they are retiring, and have for some days expected to see the army arrive.

Moniteur, 4 June 1813

The Empress-Queen and Regent has received the following intelligence respecting the situation of the armies on the 27th in the evening:

On the 26th, General Count Lauriston's headquarters were in Hanau. A battalion of General Maison was unexpectedly charged at five in the evening by 3,000 cavalry, and obliged to fall back on a village. It lost two cannon and three caissons that were under its guard. The division took to arms. The enemy endeavoured to charge the 153rd Regiment, but it was driven from the battlefield, which it left covered with his dead. Among the killed was the colonel and about a dozen officers of the Prussian *gardes du corps*, the decorations of whom we brought back.

On the 27th the Emperor's headquarters were at Liegnitz, where the Young and Old Guard were, and the corps of Generals Lauriston and Reynier. The Prince of the Moskova's corps was at Hanau; that of the Duke of Belluno manoeuvred on Glogau. The Duke of Tarentum was at Goldberg. The Duke of Ragusa and Count Bertrand were on the road from Goldberg to Liegnitz.

It appears that the enemy's army has taken the road to Jauer and Schweidnitz.

A good number of wounded have been collected. The villages are full of the enemy's wounded.

Liegnitz is a very pretty town of 10,000 inhabitants. The authorities had left it by express orders; this has caused much discontent among the inhabitants and peasantry of the Circle. Count Daru has in consequence been charged to form new magistracies.

All the people who belonged to the Court, and all the nobility who evacuated Berlin, retired to Breslau; now they are evacuating Breslau, and a part is retiring into Bohemia.

The intercepted letters speak of nothing but the consternation of the enemy, and of the enormous losses he experienced at the battle of Würschen.

Her Majesty the Empress-Queen and Regent has received the following intelligence from the army dated 29 May 1813, in the morning:

The Duke of Belluno was marching on Glogau. General Sebastiani met an enemy's convoy near Sprottau, charged it, took 22 pieces of artillery, 80 caissons and 500 prisoners.

The Duke of Ragusa arrived on the evening of the 28th, at Jauer, driving the enemy's rearguard, whose position he had turned, on that point. He took 300 prisoners. The Duke of Tarentum and Count Bertrand had arrived on the heights above that town.

On the 28th, at daybreak, the Prince of the Moskova, with Count Lauriston and General Reynier's corps, had marched on Neumark: thus our advanced guard is within seven leagues of Breslau.

On the 29th, at ten in the morning, Count Schouvalov, aide-de-camp of the Emperor of Russia, and General Kleist, a Prussian General of Division, presented themselves at the advanced posts. The Duke of Vicenza went to negotiate with them. It is believed that this interview is relative to the negotiation of an armistice.

We have accounts from our fortresses, all of which are in the best situation.

The works that defended the field of battle of Würzen are very considerable; therefore the enemy had the greatest confidence in them. An idea of them may be formed when it is known that they were the labour of 10,000 workmen during three months, for the Russians have been labouring on this position, which they considered unattackable, since the month of February.

It appears that General Wittgenstein has given up the command of the combined army: it is General Barclay de Tolly who commands it.

The army is here in the finest country possible. Silesia is a continuous garden, in which the army finds the greatest abundance of everything.

Moniteur, *8 June 1813*

Her Majesty the Empress-Queen and Regent has received the following intelligence from the armies dated 30 May 1813:

A convoy of artillery composed of 50 carriages, which had left from Augsburg, has deviated from the route of the army, and went from Augsburg towards Bayreuth; the enemy partisans attacked this convoy between Zwickau and Chemnitz, which caused the loss of 200 men and 300 horses taken; 7 to 8 pieces of artillery and several carriages which were destroyed; the cannon have been re-taken. His Majesty has ordered an inquiry to find out who decided to change the route of the army. Whether it was a general or a commissioner of war who made this decision, he must be punished according to the rigour of the military laws; the route of the army had been ordered to be from Augsburg by Würzburg and Fulde.

General Poinsot, arriving from Brunswick with a marching regiment of cavalry, 400 men strong, was attacked by 700 to 800 men of the enemy's cavalry near Halle; he has been taken prisoner along with about 100 men; 200 men returned to Leipzig.

The Duke of Padua has arrived at Leipzig, where he assembled his cavalry to sweep the whole left bank of the Elbe.

Her Majesty the Empress-Queen and regent has received the following intelligence from the armies dated 31 May 1813:

The Duke of Vicenza, Count Schouvalov and General Kleist had an 18-hour conference at the convent of Watelstadt, near Liegnitz. They went their separate ways yesterday, 30 May, at five in the afternoon. The result of this conference is still not known. It is said they agree on the principles of an armistice, but they do not seem to agree on the limits that are to form the line of demarcation.

On the 31st, at six in the evening, the conferences renewed near Streigau.

The Emperor's headquarters was at Neumarkt; that of the Prince of the Moskova, having under his command Generals Lauriston and Reynier, was at Lissa. The Duke of Tarentum and Count Bertrand were between Jauer and Streigau. The Duke of Ragusa was between Moys and Neumarkt. The Duke of Belluno was at Steinau on the Oder. Glogau was no longer blockaded. The garrison was successful in all its sorties. This fortress still has enough rations for seven months.

On the 28th, the Duke of Reggio, who had taken position at Hoyerswerda, was attacked by General Bülow's corps, 15,000 to 18,000 men strong. The combat was engaged; the enemy was repulsed on all points and pursued as far as two leagues.

On 22 May, Lieutenant General Vandamme seized Wilhelmsburg, by Hamburg.

On the 24th, the headquarters of the Prince of Eckmühl was at Harburg. Several bombs had fallen on Hamburg and the Russian troops appeared to be evacuating that town, negotiations had been opened for its surrender; the Danish troops made common cause with the French troops.

There was to be, on the 25th, a conference with the Danish generals to set the plan of operations. Count Kaas, Minister of the Interior for the King of Denmark, and charged with a mission in the service of the Emperor, had left to go to the headquarters.

Report to His Most Serene Highness the Prince of Neufchâtel, Major-General of the Army

Hoyerswerda, 27 May 1813

My Lord,

I arrived at Hoyerswerda about six o'clock in the evening with my 13th Division. All the pieces of intelligence from the peasants assured me that the enemy was in town, and I marched cautiously. My advance guard, seeing no scouts, entered the town during a heavy rain from a thunderstorm. The first group of light horse, under the orders of one of my officers, had already gone through different streets without meeting anyone, and then, upon arriving on the square, the Bavarian squadron of light horse, which was following, saw and fell upon two squadrons of Cossacks that were busy loading bread.

Several of those who were on horses were able to escape, but the rest of them were sobered or taken. I have from this affair seven officers, one of whom is a major, one captain, five lieutenants and sublieutenants, and three Prussian officers (not one of them escaped), 61 Cossacks and more than 90 horses.

I am, etc.

MARSHAL DUKE OF REGGIO

Report to His Most Serene Highness the Prince of Neufchâtel, Major-General of the Army

My Lord,

The enemy came to attack me this morning in the position of Hoyerswerda, where I am, and where I am held up, awaiting the division of General Gruyer.

The enemy arrived from Stenftenberg by the two banks of the Schwarz Elster. Its first attack took place at eight o'clock, by Bergen and Newiese, where its cavalry repulsed my advance posts; and at almost the same time, I was attacked on my left, close to Narditz, from where the enemy deployed 30 cannon.

I still did not know on what side the principle attacks would take place, and I was obliged to split up my men between these two points.

The 14th Division formed in squares in the plain of Narditz under a very lively fire of artillery, to which mine responded with advantage.

The enemy, seeing the uselessness of his efforts on that side, took its forces on the right bank; columns of infantry, cavalry and some cannon debouched from there.

Then my artillery, placed in a position of advantage, put the enemy's columns to rout, and at a charge, General Pacthod repulsed this Prussian corps much beyond Bergen, and caused it a lot of mischief. Since that moment, its retreat was made in haste on all points, and I remained master of the terrain, where the enemy left many dead. I cannot praise enough General Pacthod's conduct, as well as that of General Pourailly who, with his brigade, took two villages with the bayonet and in the most forward manner.

We continue to follow the enemy at five o'clock at night.

I am, etc.,

MARSHAL DUKE OF REGGIO

Copy of the letter of General of Division Count Vandamme to Marshal Prince of Eckmühl

Harburg, 13 May 1813, eleven o'clock in the morning

The day before yesterday, we were badly established on the Island of Wilhelmsburg. At nightfall, we were restricted to protecting ourselves militarily.

Yesterday, the 12th, at eight in the morning, the enemy started by disembarking 1,000 to 1,200 men opposite Hamburg. A lively fusillade was engaged with the brigade of light infantry under the command of General Gengoult. I went to survey the affair and saw that this enemy column, expecting to be supported, was attempting to push us off the island.

The enemy, hastening its attack, at first had gained some advantage, and advanced in force with the artillery it has disembarked. I immediately ordered the three battalions of infantry to turn *en masse*; they were supported by the rest of the Dufour division. I ordered a charge, and in one quarter of an hour everything was thrown in the most complete rout. The enemy abandoned all its artillery, its caissons, its munitions, and re-embarked in the biggest order, leaving some prisoners and a large number of dead, among whom were found many Danes. Generals Dufour and Gengoult conducted themselves perfectly in this affair.

I decided to have the brigade of Reuss cross in the island; I planned to have it occupy Altwerden, Kattwick and Rosneuhof. I no sooner had the troops disembarked that I learned that the enemy was attempting to land on the point of Reiherstiegerland, from where he wanted to advance to the point of my crossing. A fusillade was engaged, and seeing that he had been unable to surprise us, the enemy precipitately fell back, losing a few dead, wounded or prisoners.

I established the 152nd in reserve and in observation at the castle of Wilhelmsburg, so that we can proceed everywhere.

Anticipating a new attack, I sent the 37th, which was on the dike, marching. A serious fusillade was engaged. I did not hesitate ordering the 37th to withdraw slowly, while defending the dike, and to let the enemy advance so that we could cut off his retreat or pursue him vigorously.

I at once ordered two battalions of the right of the Dufour division to proceed directly to the bridge where the enemy had crossed, while I had Prince Reuss start a hasty march on the enemy with the two battalions that were at Wilhelmsburg. At first, a fusillade was engaged; and because we can only move over very elevated dikes, I ordered the troops to cease firing, and sent them charging everywhere. The enemy was constrained into retreat and was pursued for one hour, bayonets at its back. Never was there a more complete confusion. All that had thrown themselves in the small boats were drowned or killed. Four hundred and thirty men, unable to embark, lay down their arms.

I cannot praise enough the valour of our troops. I do not remember ever having found more ardour in our old troops. Several officers of all ranks have distinguished themselves. I will have the honour to address their case to Your Excellency, so that she may forward it to the Emperor.

I have the honour etc.,

COUNT VANDAMME

Moniteur, 10 June 1813

Her Majesty the Empress-Queen and Regent has received the following intelligence respecting the situation of the armies on 2 June 1813:

The headquarters of the Emperor were still at Neumarkt and those of the Prince of the Moskova at Lissa. The Duke of Tarentum and Count Bertrand were between Jauer and Striegau; the Duke of Ragusa at the village of Eisendorf; the 3rd Corps at the village of Titersdorf; the Duke of Belluno between Glogau and Liegnitz.

Count Bubna had arrived at Liegnitz, and had conferences with the Duke of Bassano.

General Lauriston entered Breslau at six o'clock in the morning of 1 June. A Prussian division of 6,000 to 7000 men, which covered that town by defending the passage of the Lobe, was beaten at the village of Neukirchen.

The Burgomaster and four Deputies from the town of Breslau were presented to the Emperor at Neumarkt on 1 June at two o'clock in the afternoon. His Majesty told them that they might assure the inhabitants he pardoned everything they might have done to second the spirit of anarchy which Stein and the Scharnhorst wished to excite.

The town is perfectly tranquil and all the inhabitants remain in it. Breslau offers very great resources.

The Duke of Vicenza and the Russian and Prussian plenipotentiaries, Count Schouvalov and General Kleist, exchanged their full powers and neutralized the village of Peicherwitz. Forty infantrymen and 20 cavalrymen furnished by the French army, and the same number of men furnished by the Allied army, respectively occupy the two entrances of the village. On the morning of the 2nd, the plenipotentiaries had a conference to determine the line, which, during the armistice, should determine the position of the two armies. In the meantime, orders have been given from both headquarters that no hostilities should take place. Thus, since 1 June at two in the afternoon, there have been no hostilities committed on either side.

Moniteur, 11 June 1813

Her Majesty the Empress-Queen has received the following intelligence respecting the situation of the armies on 3 June 1813:

The suspension of arms still continues. The respective plenipotentiaries continue their negotiations for the Armistice.

General Lauriston has seized on the Oder more than 60 vessels laden with meal, wine and warlike ammunition which had been destined for the army that besieged Glogau; all these provisions have been forwarded to that fortress.

Our advanced posts are halfway to Breig.

General Hogendorp has been named Governor of Breslau. The greatest order reigns in that town. The inhabitants appear very much discontented, and even indignant, at the dispositions made relative to the *Landsturm*; they attribute these dispositions to General Scharnhorst, who passed for an anarchistic Jacobin. He was wounded at the battle of Lützen.

The Prussian princesses, who hastily withdrew from Berlin to take refuge at Breslau, have left the latter town to seek shelter still farther away.

The Duke of Bassano has gone to Dresden, where he will receive Count Kaas, Minister from Denmark.

The Empress-Queen and Regent has received the following intelligence of the situation of the army on the evening of 4 June 1813:
The armistice was signed on the 4th, at two in the afternoon. The articles are attached.

His Majesty the Emperor set out at daybreak on the 5th to proceed to Liegnitz. It is thought that while the Armistice lasts, His Majesty will spend part of his time at Glogau, and the greater part at Dresden, in order to be nearer his states.

Glogau is provisioned for a year.

Armistice

Today, 4 June [23 May], the plenipotentiaries named by the belligerent powers are the Duke of Vicenza, Grand Ecuyer of France, General of Division, Senator, Great Eagle of the Legion of Honour, Great Cross of the Orders of St Andrew of Russia, of St Leopold of Austria, St Hubert of Bavaria, of the Green Crown of Saxony, of the Fidelity of St Joseph, appointed Minister Plenipotentiary by His Majesty the Emperor of the French, King of Italy, Protector of the Confederation of the Rhine, Mediator of the Swiss Confederation, etc., furnished with full powers by his Highness the Prince of Neufchâtel, Vice-Constable, Major-General of the Army *and* Count Schouvalov, Lieutenant-General and Aide-de-Camp to the Emperor of all the Russias, Grand Cross of the Order of Vladimir of the Second Class, Grand Cross of the Order of St Anne, Knight of the Order of St George, Fourth Class, Commander of the Order of St John of Jerusalem, and Grand Cross of the Red Eagle of Prussia; and Lieutenant-General Kleist, in the service of His Majesty the King of Prussia, Grand Cross of the Red Eagle of Prussia, of St Vladimir of the Second Class, and of St Anne of Russia, Knight of the Order of Merit of the Iron Cross of Prussia and of the Legion of Honour, furnished with full powers by his Excellency the General of Infantry, Barclay de Tolly, General-in-Chief of the Combined Armies.

After having each exchanged their full powers at Gebersdorff on 1 June [20 May], and signed a suspension of arms for 36 hours at the village of Plaswitz, neutralized for that purpose between the advanced posts of the respective armies, in order to continue the negotiations for an Armistice proper and to suspend hostilities between all the belligerent troops, no matter where they are, [they] have agreed on the articles following:

Article I Hostilities shall cease on all points upon notification of the present Armistice.

Article II The Armistice shall last to 8 [20] July inclusive. Hostilities shall not commence without giving six days' notice.

Article III Hostilities shall not consequently re-commence until six days after the denunciation of the Armistice at the respective headquarters.

Article IV The line of demarcation between the belligerent armies is fixed as follows:

In Silesia, the line of demarcation of the combined armies, setting out from the frontiers of Bohemia, shall pass through Dittersback, Pfaffendorff, Landshut; follow the Bobr to Rudolstadt; pass from there through Bolkenhayn, Striegau, follow the Striegauerwasser to Cauth, and join the Oder by passing through Bettlern, Oltaschin, and Althofen.

The combined army shall be at liberty to occupy the towns of Landshut, Rudolstadt, Belkenhayn, Streigau and Cauth, as well as their suburbs.

The line of the French army, also setting out from the frontier which touches Bohemia, shall pass through Sieffershauf, Alt-Ramnitz, follow the course of the small river which falls into the Bobr, not far from Bertelsdoff; afterwards from the Bobr to Lahn. From there to Neukick on the Katzbach, by the most direct line, from whence it will follow the course of that river to the Oder.

The towns of Parschwitx, Liegnitz, Goldberg, and Lahn, no matter on what side of the river they are situated, may, as well as their suburbs, be occupied by the French troops.

All the territory between the line of demarcation of the French and combined armies shall be neutral, and cannot be occupied by any troops, not even by the Landsturm. This disposition consequently applies to the town of Breslau.

From the mouth of the Katzbach, the line of demarcation shall follow the course of the Oder to the frontiers of Saxony, extending along the frontiers of Saxony and Prussia, and join the Elbe starting from the Oder, not far from Mülhrose, and following the frontiers of Prussia, so that all Saxony, the country of Dessau and the small surrounding states of the Princes of the Confederation of the Rhine shall belong to the French army, and all Prussia shall belong to the combined army.

The Prussian enclaves in Saxony shall be considered neutral and shall not be occupied by any troops.

The Elbe, to its mouth, fixes and terminates the line of demarcation between the belligerent armies, with the exception of the points hereafter mentioned:

The French army shall remain in possession of the isles; and everything that it will occupy in the 32nd Military Division on 27 May [8 June], at midnight.

If Hamburg is only besieged, that town shall be treated like other besieged towns. All the articles of the present Armistice, which are relative to them, are applicable to it.

The line of the advanced posts of the belligerent armies at the turn of 27 May [June 8] at midnight shall form for the 32nd Military Division, that of the demarcation of the Armistice, with the military alterations which the respective commandants shall judge necessary. These alterations shall be made in concert with an officer of the staff of each army, on the principle of perfect reciprocity.

Article V The fortresses of Danzig, Modlin, Zamosé, Stettin, and Custrin, shall be restocked every five days, according to the force of their garrisons, through the care of the Commanders of the blockading troops.

A commissioner appointed by the Commandant of each place shall be with one of the besieging troops, to see that the stipulated provisions are exactly supplied.

Article VI During the time of the armistice, every fortress shall have beyond its walls an extent of a French league. This ground shall be neutral. Magdeburg will, consequently, have its frontier a league on the right bank of the Elbe.

Article VII A French officer shall be sent into each of the besieged places to inform the Commandant of the conclusion of the Armistice, and of its re-stocking. A Russian or Prussian officer shall accompany him during the journey, either going or coming back.

Article VIII Commissioners named on both sides in each place shall fix the price of the provisions furnished. This account, settled at the end of each month by the Commissioners charged with maintaining the Armistice, shall be paid at the headquarters by the Paymaster-General of the army.

Article IX Officers of the staff shall be appointed on either side, to regulate, in concert, the general line of demarcation, respecting points that shall not be determined by running water, and on which there could be some difficulty.

Article X All the movements of the troops shall be so regulated that each army shall occupy its new line on 12 June [31 May].

All the corps, or parts of the combined army which may be beyond the Elbe, or in Saxony, shall return into Prussia.

Article XI Officers of the French and Combined Armies shall be dispatched conjointly to cause hostilities to cease on all point, and make the Armistice known.

The respective Commanders-in-Chief shall furnish them with the necessary powers.

Article XII On both sides two Commissioners, general officers, shall be appointed to watch over the execution of the stipulations of the present Armistice. They shall remain in the line of neutrality at Neumarkt to decide on such disputes as may occur.

These Commissioners shall proceed there within 24 hours in order to expedite officers and orders that must be sent in consequence of the present Armistice. Done and completed the present act in 12 articles, etc.

CAULAINCOURT, DUKE OF VICENCE
COUNT SCHOUVALOV
KLEIST

Viewed and ratified by order of the Emperor and King, 4 June 1813

THE PRINCE VICE-CONSTABLE OF FRANCE,
MAJOR-GENERAL OF THE GRANDE ARMÉE, ALEXANDER

Moniteur, 13 June 1813

Her Majesty the Empress-Queen and Regent has received the following intelligence respecting the situation of the armies on 6 June 1813:

The Emperor's headquarters were on the 6th at Liegnitz.

The Prince of the Moskova was still at Breslau.

The Commissioners appointed by the Emperor of Russia for the execution of the Armistice are Count Schouvalov, Lieutenant General, aide-de-camp-general to the Emperor, and Mr Kutusov, Major-General, aide-de-camp-general to the Emperor. Those named on the part of France are General of Division Count Dumoustier, commanding a division of the Guard, and General of Brigade Flahault, aide-de-camp to the Emperor. These Commissioners are at Neumarkt.

The Duke of Treviso, with the Young Guard, takes his headquarters at Glogau. The Old Guard is returning to Dresden, where it is supposed the Emperor is going to establish his headquarters.

The different army corps started marching to form camps in the different positions of Goldberg, Löwenberg, Bunzlau, Liegnitz, Sproteau, Sagan, etc.

The Polish corps of Prince Poniatowski, which crosses Bohemia, is expected at Zittau on 10 June.

Moniteur, 14 June 1813

Her Majesty the Empress-Queen and Regent has received the following intelligence of the situation of the armies on 7 June 1813:

His Majesty's headquarters were at Bunzlau. All the army corps were in march to their cantonments. The Oder was covered with boats which descended from Breslau to Glogau laden with artillery, tools, meal and articles of every description taken from the enemy.

Hamburg was retaken on the 30th, by main force. The Prince of Eckmühl especially praises the conduct of General Vandamme. Hamburg had been lost during the last campaign by the pusillanimity of General Saint-Cyr; it was to the vigour displayed by General Vandamme, on his arrival in the 32nd Military Division, that the preservation of Bremen was owing, and the present retaking of Hamburg. Several hundred prisoners were taken. Two or 300 pieces of artillery were found in the town, 80 of which were on the ramparts. Works had been constructed to place the town in a state of defence.

Denmark marches with us: the Prince of Echmühl intended to march on Lubeck. Thus the 32nd Military Division and all the territory of the Empire are delivered from the enemy.

Orders have been given to fortify Hamburg; it is surrounded by a bastioned rampart, having a large moat full of water, and can in part be covered by inundations. The works are so constructed that communication with Hamburg can be maintained by the islands at all times.

The Emperor has ordered another fortress to be constructed on the Elbe, at the mouth of the Havel. Königstein, Torgau, Wittenberg, Magdeburg, the fortress of the Havel and Hamburg will complete the defence of the line of the Elbe.

The Dukes of Cambridge and Brunswick, Princes of the House of England, arrived in time at Hamburg to give more relief to the success of the French. Their journey was reduced to this: they arrived, and they fled.

The last battalions of the Prince of Eckmühl's five divisions, which are composed of 72 battalions at their full complement, have set out from Wesel.

Since the commencement of the campaign, the French army has delivered

Saxony, conquered half of Silesia, re-occupied the 32nd Military Division and confounded the hopes of our enemies.

Moniteur, 16 June 1813

Her Majesty the Empress Queen and Regent has received the following intelligence of the situation of the Armies on 10 June 1813:

His Majesty arrived at four o'clock in the morning of the 10th at Dresden. The Horse Guard arrived there at noon. The Foot Guard was expected the following day, the 11th.

The Emperor arrived there at the moment when he was least expected; he thus rendered useless the preparations made for his reception.

At noon the King of Saxony came to see the Emperor, who lodges in the suburbs, in the fine house of Marcolini, where there is a grand suite of apartments on the ground floor, and a handsome park; the King's Palace, which the Emperor formerly inhabited, had no garden.

At seven in the evening, the Emperor received Mr Kaas, Minister of the Interior and of Justice of the King of Denmark.

A Danish brigade of the auxiliary division, placed under the Prince of Eckmühl's orders, on 2 June, had taken possession of Lubeck.

The Prince of the Moskova, on the 10th, was at Breslau; the Duke of Treviso, at Glogau; the Duke of Belluno, at Crossen; the Duke of Reggio, on the frontiers of Saxony and Prussia, near Berlin. The armistice has been published everywhere. The troops were making preparations to place their barracks, and encamp in their respective positions, from Glogau and Liegnitz, to the frontiers of Bohemia and at Görlitz.

Moniteur, 20 June 1813

Her Majesty the Empress-Queen and Regent received the following intelligence regarding the situation of the armies at 14 June, at night.

All the troops have arrived in their cantonments. We raise some barracks and form the camps.

The Emperor has a parade every day at 10 o'clock.

A few enemy partisans are still on the rears. Some of them make war for their own account, in the manner of Schill, and refuse to acknowledge the armistice. Several columns are in movement to destroy them.

Her Majesty the Empress-Queen and Regent received the following intelligence from the army, under the date of 13 June.

Baron Kaas, Minister of the Interior of Denmark, and dispatched with letters from the King, has been presented to the Emperor.

After the affairs of Copenhagen, a treaty of alliance was concluded between France and Denmark: by this treaty, the Emperor guaranteed the integrity of Denmark.

During the year 1811, the Swedish court let it be known in Paris that it wished to unite Norway to Sweden and asked the assistance of France. The response was that notwithstanding any desire that France might have to do something agreeable for Sweden, a treaty of alliance had been concluded with Denmark, and, guaranteeing the integrity of that power, His Majesty could never give his consent for the dismemberment of his ally's territory.

From that moment, Sweden moved away from France and entered into negotiations with her enemies.

Since then, a war became imminent between France and Russia. The Swedish court proposed to join the common cause with France, but renewed its proposition relative to Norway. In vain, Sweden tried to show that from the ports of Norway it would be easy to enter Scotland; it is in vain that they maintaincd all the guarantees that the old alliance of Sweden could give to France in regard to the conduct that would be shown towards England. The conduct of the cabinet of the Tuileries remained the same: our hands were tied by the treaty with Denmark.

From that moment, Sweden kept no measures; she made a contract of alliance with England and Russia; and the first stipulation of this treaty was the common engagement to constrain Denmark to cede Norway to Sweden.

The battle of Smolensk and of the Moskova followed the activity of Sweden; she received a few subsidies, made a few preparations, but did not start any hostilities. The events of the winter of 1813 arrived; the French troops evacuated Hamburg. The situation of Denmark became perilous: at war with England, threatened by Sweden and Russia, France appeared to be powerless to support it. The King of Denmark, with the loyalty that characterizes him, appealed to the Emperor in order to get out of that situation. The Emperor, who wishes that his political situation never becomes a burden for his allies, replied that Denmark was free to deal with England to save the integrity of its territory, and that his esteem and friendship for the King would not suffer on account of the new connections that circumstances obliged Denmark to contract. The King expressed his gratitude of this proceeding.

Four crews of very good sailors had been furnished by Denmark and manned four vessels of our fleet of the Escaut. The King of Denmark, meanwhile, had expressed the desire that these sailors be sent back to him; the Emperor sent them back with the most scrupulous punctuality, and expressing to the officers and sailors his satisfaction of their good services.

Meanwhile, events continued.

The allies thought that Burke's dream had been realized. In their minds, the French Empire was already erased from the globe, and that idea had to have culminated to a strange point, because they offered to Denmark, as indemnity for Norway, our departments of the 32nd Military Division, and even all of Holland, in order to reshape in the north a maritime power which would link up with Russia.

The King of Denmark, far from letting himself be surprised by these lures, said to them, 'So, you wish to give me some colonies in Europe, and all that to the detriment of France?'

In view of the impossibility of leading the King of Denmark into such an insane idea, Prince Dolgorouki was sent to Copenhagen to ask Denmark to join the common cause with the allies; and in doing so, the allies would guarantee the integrity of Denmark and also Norway.

The urgency of the circumstances, the imminent dangers that Denmark was facing, distancing itself from the French armies, its own salvation at stake, all these caused Denmark's politics to bend. The King consented, in return for the guarantee of the integrity of his States, to cover Hamburg, and to keep this town safe from the French armies for the duration of the war. He understood how disagreeable this would be to the Emperor; he made all the modifications to it that he could possibly make, and did not sign it until faced with the urgency of those around him, who reminded him of the necessity of saving his States; but he was far from thinking that it was a trap that had just been laid on him. They wanted to put him at war with France, and after causing him to lose, in this way, his natural support in that circumstance, they wanted to break their word and oblige him to subscribe to all the shameful conditions that they would want to impose upon him.

Mr Bernstorf proceeded to London; he believed he would be received with great attention and have only to renew the treaty to which Prince Dolgorouki had consented; but to his astonishment, the Prince-Regent refused to receive the letter from the King, and Lord Castlereagh made him aware that there could be no treaty between Denmark and England if, prior to this, Norway had not been ceded to Sweden. A few days later, Count Bernstorf received an order to return to Denmark.

During that same time, the same speech was given to Count Moltke, dispatched from Denmark to meet with the Emperor Alexander. Prince Dolgorouki was disavowed as having acted beyond his powers, and at the same time the Danes gave notice to the French army, and a few hostilities were taking place!!!

It would be in vain to open the annals of nations to find in them a more immoral politic. It is at the moment when Denmark finds itself engaged in a state of war with France that the treaty to which it believes to be conforming is disavowed both in London and Russia, and that taking advantage of the embarrassment in which this power is placed, a treaty is proposed, as an ultimatum, that engages it to recognize the relinquishment of Norway!

In these difficult circumstances, the King showed the greatest confidence in the Emperor; he declared the treaty nullified. He called his troops back from Hamburg. He ordered his army to march with the French army, and declared that he still considered himself an ally of France and that he relied on the magnanimity of the Emperor.

The President of Kaas was sent to the French headquarters with letters from the King.

At the same time, the King sent to Norway the hereditary Prince of Denmark, a young prince of greatest expectation, and particularly loved by the Norwegians. He left disguised as a sailor in a small fishing boat and arrived in Norway on 22 May.

On 30 May, the French troops entered Hamburg, and a Danish division, who marched with our troops, entered Lubeck.

Baron Kaas, who was at Altona, had to endure another treacherous act equal to the first.

The ally envoys came to his quarters and advised him that the surrender of Norway was renounced, and that under the condition that Denmark would join the common cause with the allies, it would no longer be in question; they implored him to delay his departure. The response of Mr Kass was simple, 'I have my orders, I must execute them.' He then was told that the French armies were defeated; that did not shake him either, and he continued on his way.

However, on 31 May, an English fleet appeared in the harbour of Copenhagen; one of the war vessels anchored in front of the town and Mr Thornton presented himself. He made it known that the allies were about to start hostilities, if in 48 hours Denmark did not subscribe to a treaty, the principal condition of which was to cede Norway to Sweden, giving at once the province of Drontheim as a deposit in trust, and to furnish 25,000 men to march with the allies against France, and conquer the indemnities which would be the portion for Denmark. It was also declared that the proposals made to Mr Kass at Altona were disavowed and should not be considered anything more than military negotiations.

The King rejected this injurious summons with indignation.

Meanwhile, the Royal Prince had arrived in Norway and had published the following proclamation:

Norwegians!

Your King knows and appreciates your unshakeable loyalty to him and the dynasty of the Kings of Norway and Denmark, who, for centuries, reigned over your fathers and you. His paternal desire is to bind tighter the indissoluble band of fraternal affection and of the union that binds the people of the two kingdoms. The heart of Frederic VI is still with us; but his attention on all the branches of the administration of the state deprives him of being surrounded by his Norwegian people. That is why he has sent me to you, as governor, to execute his wishes as if he were present; his orders will by my laws. My efforts will be to gain your confidence. Your esteem and your affection will be my recompense. Perhaps more difficult hardships threaten us… but having trust in Providence, I will meet them without fear; and with your help, loyal Norwegians, I will vanquish all obstacles. I know that I can count on your loyalty to the King; that you wish to conserve the ancient independence of Norway, and that motto which unites us is: For God, the King and the Fatherland!

CHRISTIAN-FREDERIC, PRINCE OF DENMARK AND OF NORWAY,
GOVERNOR OF THE KINGDOM OF NORWAY AND GENERAL-IN-CHIEF

The confidence that the King of Denmark has had in the Emperor is found to be entirely justified, and all the bonds between the two people have been re-established and tightened.

The French army is at Hamburg: a Danish division follows its movement, to support it. The English gain from their politics only shame and confusion; the good wishes of all the great people accompany the hereditary Prince of Denmark to Norway. What makes Norway's position dangerous is the lack of provisions; but Norway will remain Danish; the integrity of Denmark is guaranteed by France.

The bombardment of Copenhagen while an English minister was still with the King, the conflagration of this capital and of the fleet without a declaration of war, without prior hostility, appeared to become the most odious scene in modern history; but the tortuous politics which causes the English to demand the relinquishment of a province, happy for many years under the sceptre of the House of Holstein, and the series of intrigues into which they enter to arrive at this odious result, will be considered as more immoral and more outrageous yet than the fires of Copenhagen. We will recognize in this the kind of politics of which the Houses of Timor and of Sicily were victims, and which stripped them of their states. The English have been accustomed in India never to be stopped by any idea of justice. They follow this politic in Europe.

It appears that in the negotiations that the allies had with England, the powers of the greatest enemy of France were raised against her, by the exaggeration of the pretensions of the English government. The very foundations of the peace of Luneville were declared by the English to be inadmissible as being too favourable to France. Insane people! They are wrong about the latitude, and mistake the French for *Indous*.

Moniteur, *27 June 1813*

Her Majesty the Empress-Queen, and Regent, has received the following intelligence from the army, dated 21 June 1813:

The 8th Corps, commanded by Prince Poniatowski, which traversed Bohemia, has arrived at Zittau, in Lusach.

This corps consisted of 18,000 men, of whom 6,000 are cavalry. All the requisite orders have been given to complete their clothing and furnish them with everything of which they may stand in need.

On the 20th His Majesty went to Pirna and Königstein.

President Kaas, sent by the King of Denmark, has received his audience of leave, and set out from Dresden.

The Prussian free corps, raised in the same manner as those of Schill, has continued since the armistice to levy contributions and arrest isolated men. They were told of the armistice on the 8th, but they declared they would make war on their own account; and as they have continued the same conduct, several columns have been sent against them. Captain Lützow, who commanded one of those bands, has been killed; 400 of his men were killed or taken, and the remainder dispersed. It is not believed that 100 of these brigands succeeded in re-crossing the Elbe. Another band, commanded by a Captain Colomb, is completely surrounded, and it is to be hoped that in a few days the left bank of the Elbe will be entirely purged of the presence of those bands, who are guilty of all kinds of excesses towards the unfortunate inhabitants.

The officer sent to Custrin has returned. The garrison of that fortress consists of about 5,000 men, and has only 150 sick. The fortress is in the best state, and provisioned for six months in wheat, rice, vegetables, fresh meat and all the necessary objects.

The garrison has always been master of the place to the distance of 1,000 *toises*. During these four months, the commandant did not cease to labour in augmenting the means of his artillery, and the fortifications of the fortress.

All the army is encamped; this repose is of the utmost advantage of our troops. The regular distribution of rice greatly contributes to maintain the health of the soldiers.

Situation of the French Army

Paris, 29 June 1813, Moniteur 30 June 1813
Her Majesty, the Empress-Queen and Regent, has received the following news from the army, dated Dresden, 24 June 1813:

Captain Planat, an officer of the staff charged with carrying intelligence of the armistice, has arrived at Danzig. He had much difficulty in getting into the place, because General Rapp, the Governor, fatigued by the great number of parliamentarians which the enemy sent every day, had declared that he would receive no more of them. The officer, therefore, had considerable difficulty in making himself known. It would be difficult to describe the joy that his presence caused that fine and numerous garrison, which is far from having the appearance of a besieged fortress; it is master of all the neighbourhood. The rations that are to be furnished it during the armistice have been fixed at 20,000 each day, which has with justice caused complaints on the part of the Governor.

Several times that garrison, during the five months' blockade, threw shells into the enemy's headquarters, and, as one may say, besieged him.

General Rapp has formed a good battalion of the Foot Guard, which is composed of fatigued or frozen men who took refuge in the fortress.

The fortress has sufficient rations for a year; military men estimate that it could resist open trenches for three months, even supposing that the enemy had a besieging train of 200 pieces of artillery, and without calculating the delay which the sorties from the garrison could occasion to the operations of the siege. But up to that hour, the enemy had in no manner shown an intention of attempting so difficult an enterprise.

—

Moniteur, 3 July 1813

Her Majesty the Empress-Queen and Regent, has received the following intelligence respecting the situation of the army on 25 June 1813:

On the 24th the Emperor dined with the King of Saxony. In the evening, the French comedians gave one of Moliere's pieces in the court theatre, at which their Majesties were present.

The King of Westphalia has arrived at Dresden to see the Emperor.

On the 25th the Emperor visited the different debouches of the forests of Dresden, and travelled about 20 leagues. His Majesty set out about five in the afternoon, and returned at ten in the evening.

Two bridges have been thrown over the Elbe, opposite to the fortress of Königstein. The rock of Silienstein, which is on the right bank within half cannon-shot of Königstein, has been occupied and fortified. Magazines and other military establishments have been prepared in that interesting position. A camp of 60,000 men, thus leaning on the fortress of Königstein and able to manoeuvre on both banks, would be unattackable by any force whatever.

The King of Bavaria has established a camp of 25,000 men around Nymphenburg, near Munich.

The Emperor has given the command of the Bavarian corps of observation to the Duke of Castiglione. This army has assembled at Würzburg. It is composed of six divisions of infantry and two of cavalry.

The Viceroy is assembling, between the Piave and the Adige, the army of Italy, composed of three corps. General Grenier commands one of them.

The new corps that has just been formed at Magdeburg, under the command of General Vandamme, already consists of 40 battalions and 80 pieces of artillery.

The Prince of Eckmühl is at Hamburg. His corps has been reinforced by troops coming from France and Holland, so that on that point there are more troops than there ever were. The Danish division that has joined the corps of the Prince of Eckmühl consists of 15,000 men.

The 2nd Corps, which the Duke of Belluno commands, had but one division during the campaign that has just finished; this corps has been completed, and the Duke of Belluno now commands three divisions.

Circumstances were so urgent at the commencement of this campaign, that battalions of the same regiment were disseminated into different corps. All has been regulated, and each regiment has reunited its battalions. Every day a great number of marching battalions arrive, crossing the Elbe at Magdeburg, at Wittenberg, Torgau and Dresden. His Majesty daily reviews those that arrive at Dresden.

The military supplies of the army are now either in caissons of the old model, or in caissons of the new model (called no. 2), or in carriages *á la Comtoise*, in which provisions are conveyed for all of the army for a month. His Majesty has discovered that the carriages *á la Comtoise*, as well as the caissons of the ancient model, have inconveniences, and has ordered that the supplies, as the equipment may henceforth require replacing, shall be carried in the model no. 2 of the caissons, drawn by four horses and which easily carry 20 quintals.

The army is provided with portable mills, weighing 16 pounds, and each capable of making five quintals of meal daily. Three of these mills have been distributed to each battalion.

360

They are working with the greatest activity in augmenting the fortifications of Glogau.

They are also working to augment the fortifications of Wittenberg. His Majesty wishes to make that town a regular fortress, and as the plan is defective he has ordered it to be covered by three crowns, by nearly following the method which Senator Count Chasseloup-Laubat has put in practice at Alexandria.

Torgau is in good condition.

They are also working with great activity in fortifying Hamburg. General of Engineers Haxo has proceeded there to trace out the citadel and establish in the islands works to connect Hamburg with Haarburgh. The engineers of bridges and causeways are constructing two flying bridges there, on the same system as those at Antwerp, one for the flowing, the other for the ebb tide.

A new fortress on the Elbe has been traced out by General Haxo on the Virden side, at the mouth of the Havel.

The forts of Cuxhaven were in a condition to support a siege, but were abandoned without reason, and that which the enemy had razed is being rebuilt. They are actively working on them; they will no longer be simple enclosed batteries, but a fort, which, like the Imperial fort at the Escaut, will protect the arsenal for construction, and the basin, the establishment of which has been projected on the Elbe, since the engineer Beaupré, who employed two years in sounding that river, discovered it had the same properties as the Escaut, and that the largest squadrons [of boats] could be constructed on it, and collected in its roads [tributaries].

The 3rd Division of the Young Guard, which General Laborde, an officer of consummate merit, commands, is encamped in the woods in advance of Dresden, on the right bank of the Elbe.

The 4th Division of the Young Guard, which General Friant commands, debouches by Würzburg. Some regiments of that division have already passed that town and are marching towards Dresden.

The cavalry of the Guard already has more than 9,000 horses. The artillery consists already of more than 200 pieces of artillery. The infantry forms five divisions, four of which are of the Young and one of the Old Guard.

The 7th Corps, which General Reynier commands, composed of Durutte's division, which is a French division, and two Saxon divisions, is receiving its complement. This corps is encamped in advance of Görlitz. All the Saxon light cavalry has joined it, and is also going to be completed.

The King of Saxony also has completed his two fine regiments of cuirassiers to their full complement.

His Majesty has been extremely satisfied with the kings and grand dukes of the Confederation. The King of Württemberg has particularly distinguished himself. He has made, in proportion, efforts equal to those of France, and his army, infantry, cavalry and artillery have been carried to their full complement. Prince Émile of Hesse-Darmstadt, who commands the contingent of Hesse-Darmstadt, constantly distinguished himself in the last campaign, and in the present, by great sang-froid and much intrepidity. He is a young prince of promise, whom the Emperor greatly esteems. The Princes of Saxony alone are in the rear with their contingent.

Not only is the citadel of Erfurt in good condition and well provisioned, but the fortifications of the town have been re-established; they are covered by advanced walls, and henceforth Erfurt will be a strong fortress of the first importance.

The congress has not yet assembled; we, however, expect that it will in a few days. If a month has been lost, the fault is not with France.

England, who has no money, has not been able to furnish any to the coalesced powers; but she has just imagined a new expedient. A treaty has been concluded between England, Prussia and Russia, by means of which a new paper for several hundred millions will be created guaranteed by the three powers. It is on this resource they depend for meeting the expenses of the war.

In the separate articles England guarantees a third of this paper, so that in reality it is a new debt added to the English debt. It remains to be known in what country this paper will be issued. When this luminous idea was conceived, it was probably conceived that this emission would take place at the expense of the Confederation of the Rhine, and even of France, notably in Holland, Belgium and the departments of the Rhine. Nevertheless, the Treaty regarding this matter has not been ratified since the Armistice. Russia pays the expenses of her army with paper, which the inhabitants of Prussia are obliged to receive; Prussia herself pays her debt with paper; England likewise has her paper. It appears that each of these isolated papers has no longer sufficient credit, as those powers have come to the resolution of creating a common one. It remains for the merchants and bankers to inform us, if we have to multiply the credit of the new paper by the credit of the three powers, or rather if this credit is to be the quotient of it.

Sweden alone appears to have received money from England to amount to 5,000 to 600,000 pounds sterling.

The garrison of Modlin is in good state: the fortifications have been augmented. We have deciphered, at headquarters, the two reports from the Governors of Modlin and Zamosé. The garrisons of those two fortresses remained masters of the country a league round them, the troops who blockaded them being only badly armed and equipped militia.

The Emperor has taken Prince Poniatowski's army into his pay and given it a new organization. Workshops are established to provide it with what is needed. In less than 20 days it will be fresh equipped and in good condition.

However brilliant this situation may be, and although His Majesty really has more power than ever, he only desires peace with more ardour.

The administration has purchased a great quantity of rice, in order that during the excessive heat this product should constitute a quarter of the soldier's ration.

<hr/>

Moniteur, 6 July 1813

Her Majesty the Empress-Queen and Regent has received the following intelligence from the Army:

Count Metternich, Minister of State and of Conferences to His Majesty the Emperor of Austria, has arrived at Dresden, and already had several conferences with the Duke of Bassano.

Russia has just obtained from the King of Prussia that Russian paper should have a forced circulation in the Prussian States; and as the Prussian paper is already at a discount of 70 per cent, this ordinance does not appear calculated to raise the credit of Prussia.

The city of Berlin is tormented in every possible manner, and every day those vexations are felt to their disadvantage. This capital already compares its situation to that of several towns in France in 1793.

His Majesty the Emperor, on the 28th, made an excursion of eight or ten hours length in the environs of Dresden.

We have received accounts from Zamosé and Modlin. These fortresses are in the best condition, whether considered in respect to munitions of war or fortifications.

Moniteur, 8 July 1813

The politics of the English towards Denmark was one of the most striking historical monuments to the treachery and the immorality of their government; and their conduct towards the Bourbons of Sicily is no less an example of the same treachery.

The King and Queen of Sicily lost their kingdom as a result of their hatred of France and their absolute devotion to the English politic.

During the expedition of Malta and Egypt, the Kingdom of Naples and that of Sicily were like English possessions, in comparison to France.

In 1805, at the time peace had just been concluded in Vienna, King Ferdinand made a treaty with the English and welcomed them at Naples, which caused him a declaration of war from France and gave rise to the conquest of Naples. Since that time, this court, having taken refuge in Sicily, has not been any less devoted to England.

As a reward for 20 years of attachment and submission, the King and Queen were arrested; the queen was put on a ship, taken away from Sicily, and taken to Constantinople, where she was given permission to set foot on land. The King, divested, degraded, locked up in a castle, saw his most intimate friends arrested and taken into dungeons. In short, the conduct of the English in Sicily was exactly the same as the conduct they showed the Nabobs of India.

Indeed, we in France are not paid to deplore the misfortune and the catastrophe of the House of Sicily; however, so much ingratitude and treachery on the part of England towards princes who lost themselves for her, and who for 20 years gave her so much proof of their attachment and devotion, nauseates us with indignation!

It is said that the Queen, arrived at Constantinople, obtained from the great lord permission to land and reach Hungary by land, a laborious journey in a country where the roads are not passable for any kind of carriage and which presents all sorts of difficulties for the traveller.

Moniteur, 18 July 1813

Magdeburg, 12 July 1813

The Emperor arrived here today at seven in the morning. His Majesty immediately mounted his horse and visited the fortifications that make Magdeburg one of the strongest fortresses of Europe.

His Majesty had left from Dresden on the 10th at three in the morning. He had eaten lunch at Torgau, visited the fortifications of that fortress and saw there the brigade of Saxon troops commanded by General Lestocq. At six in the evening he arrived at Wittenberg and visited its fortifications.

On the 11th at five in the morning, His Majesty passed in review three divisions (the 5th, 6th and 6th *bis*) arriving from France; he made appointments to fill vacant posts and gave compensation to several officers and soldiers.

Leaving from Wittenberg at three in the afternoon, the Emperor arrived at six at Dessau, where His Majesty reviewed the division of General Philippon.

His Majesty left Dessau at two in the morning and arrived at Magdeburg as early as five in the morning, where the three divisions of the corps of General Count Vandamme are encamped.

Moniteur, 22 July 1813

Dresden, 15 July 1813,

The Emperor left Magdeburg on the 13th, after reviewing the divisions of the corps of General Vandamme, and went to Leipzig.

On the 14th at five in the morning, His Majesty reviewed the 3rd Corps of cavalry under the command of the Duke of Padua.

In the afternoon, His Majesty reviewed on the square of Leipzig the remainder of the Duke of Padua's troops he had not been able to see that morning. He then went by carriage, at five in the evening, to Dresden, where he arrived at one in the morning.

Her Imperial Majesty the Empress-Queen and Regent has received the following intelligence from the army:

The Duke of Vicenza, Grand Equerry, and Count Narbonne, Ambassador from France to Vienna, has been appointed by the Emperor his Ministers Plenipotentiary at Prague.

Count Narbonne set out on the 9th.

It is supposed the Duke of Vicenza will set out on the 18th.

The private Councillor d'Anstett, plenipotentiary from the Emperor of Russia, arrived at Prague on 12 July.

A Convention has been signed at Neumarkt for the prolongation of the Armistice to the middle of August.

Letter from the Emperor to the Duke of Massa, Grand-Judge Minister of Justice

From Our Imperial Camp at Dresden, 14 August 1813

The Duke of Massa, our Grand-Judge Minister of Justice,

We learned with the greatest sadness the scandalous scene that just took place at Brussels at the assize of the Imperial Court. Our good town of Antwerp, after losing millions by the public and acknowledged plundering by agents of the octroi, has lost the suit and has been condemned to pay the costs. The jury, in this instance, has not followed the principles of the law, and several jurors, betraying their oath, applied themselves publicly to the most shameful corruption. In this circumstance, although it is our principle and our will that our tribunals should administer justice in the greatest independence, yet, as they do this in our name and at the discharge of our conscience, we cannot ignore and tolerate such a scandal, nor can we permit that corruption should triumph and walk with heads held high in our good towns of Brussels and Antwerp.

Our intention is that upon reception of this letter, you should order our imperial procurator at the court of Brussels to assemble the judges who presided over the session of assizes, to draw up a report in the form of an inquest as to what they know and what they think pertaining to the scandalous declaration by the jury in the above mentioned affair. Our intention is that you advise our imperial procurator at the court of Brussels that the judgment rendered by the court in consequence of the jury's declaration be regarded as suspended; that in consequence the accused must be brought to justice, and re-apply sequestration of their estates. Finally, our intention is that according to paragraph 4 of Article 55 of Title 5 of the Constitutions of the Empire, you should present yourself, in a private council with the Regent, our beloved spouse whom we authorize to preside over, a project of Senatus-Consultum to annul the judgment of the court of assizes of Brussels, and send this affair to the court of appeals who will designate an imperial court in the front of which the process will be started all over again, and judged in the chambers and without a jury. Our wish is that if corruption is adept at eluding the effect of the law, the corruptors will know that the laws, in their wisdom, have seen to everything. Our intention is also that you should give instructions to our imperial procurator, who will be authorized by an article of the Senatus-Consultum, to pursue those jurors accused by the public of having yielded to corruption in this affair. We hope that our good city of Antwerp will be consoled by this just sovereign decision, and that it will see the solicitude we give to our people, even in the middle of our camps and of the circumstances of the war.

Now, we pray God to keep you in his holy safekeeping.

NAPOLEON

Moniteur, *6 September 1813*

Her Majesty, the Empress-Queen, and Regent, has received the following intelligence from the army, dated 20 August 1813:

The enemies denounced the armistice on the 11th at noon, and stated that hostilities would commence on the 17th after midnight.

At the same time a note from Austrian Foreign Minister Count Metternich addressed to Count Narbonne informed him that Austria had declared war against France.

On the morning of the 17th, the dispositions of the two armies were as follows:

The 4th, 12th and 7th Corps, under the orders of the Duke of Reggio, were at Dahme.

The Prince of Eckmühl with his corps, to which the Danes were joined, encamped before Hamburg, his headquarters being at Bergedorf.

The 3rd Corps was at Liegnitz, under the orders of the Prince of the Moskova.

The 5th Corps was at Goldberg, under the orders of General Lauriston.

The 11th Corps was at Löwenberg, under the orders of the Duke of Tarentum.

The 6th Corps, commanded by the Duke of Ragusa, was at Bunzlau.

The 8th Corps, under the orders of Prince Poniatowski, was at Zittau.

Marshal Saint-Cyr was with the 14th Corps, the left leaning on the Elbe, at the camp at Königstein and on both sides of the great road from Prague to Dresden, pushing the corps of observation to the debouches of Marienburg.

The 1st Corps had arrived at Dresden, and the 2nd at Zittau.

Dresden, Torgau, Wittenberg, Magdeburg and Hamburg each had their garrison, and were armed and provisioned.

The enemy's army was, as far as could be ascertained, in the following position:

Eighty thousand Russians and Prussians had entered Bohemia on the morning of the 10th, and on the 21st were to arrive on the Elbe. That army was commanded by the Emperor Alexander and the King of Prussia, the Russian generals Barclay de Tolly, Wittgenstein and Miloradovich, and the Prussian general Kleist. The Russian and Prussian Guards formed a part of it, which, joined to Prince Schwarzenberg's army, formed the Great Army and a force of 200,000 men. This army was to act on the left bank of the Elbe by crossing that river in Bohemia.

The Silesian army, commanded by the Prussian Generals Blücher and Yorck, and the Russian Generals Sacken and Langeron, appeared to collect on Breslau; it was 100,000 men strong.

Several Prussian and Swedish corps and the insurrectional troops covered Berlin, and were opposite Hamburg and the Duke of Reggio. The force of the army that covered Berlin was estimated at 110,000 men.

All the enemy's operations were made under the idea that the Emperor would re-cross to the left bank of the Elbe.

The Imperial Guard left Dresden, moved on the 15th to Bautzen, and on the 18th to Görlitz.

On the 19th the Emperor went to Zittau, and instantly ordered Prince Poniatowski's troops to march, forced the debouches of Bohemia, crossed the great chain of mountains which separate Bohemia from Lusace, and entered Gobel, while General Lefebvre-Desnouettes, with a division of infantry and cavalry of the Guard, obtained possession of Rumburk, cleared the pass of the mountains at Georgenthal, and the Polish General Reminski took Friedland and Reichenberg.

This operation was intended to disturb the allies at Prague and acquire certain information respecting their designs. There we learned what our spies had already informed us, that the élite of the Russian and Prussian army were traversing Bohemia, and uniting on the left bank of the Elbe.

Our light troops pushed to within 16 leagues of Prague.

The Emperor was at Zittau, on his return from Bohemia on the 20th, at one o'clock in the morning. He left the Duke of Belluno with the second Corps at Zittau, to strengthen the corps of Prince Poniatowski. He placed General Vandamme, with the first Corps at Rumburk, to support General Lefebvre-Desnouettes; these two generals occupying the pass in force, caused redoubts to be thrown up on the height that dominates the pass. The Emperor took the road by Laubau to Silesia, where he arrived on the 20th before seven o'clock in the evening.

The enemy army of Silesia had violated the armistice and passed through the neutral territory as early as the 12th. They had on the 15th insulted all our advanced posts, and carried off some observation posts.

On the 16th, a Russian corps placed itself between the Bobr and the post of Spiller, occupied by 200 men of the division of Charpentier. These brave men, who were reposing themselves on the faith of treaties, flew to arms, passed through the enemy's centre , and dispersed them. They were commanded by Chief of Division Guillermie.

On the 18th, the Duke of Tarentum gave orders to General Zucchi to take the small town of Lahn; he marched there with an Italian Brigade; he bravely executed his orders and caused the enemy a loss of 500 men. General Zucchi is an officer of distinguished merit. The Italian troops attacked the Russians, who were superior in number, with the bayonet.

On the 19th, the enemy encamped at Zobten. A corps of 12,000 Russians crossed the Bobr and attacked the post of Siebenicken, which was defended by three light companies. General Lauriston caused a part of his corps to take to arms, left Löwenberg, marched to the enemy, and drove it into the Bobr. The brigade of General Lafitte, of the division of Rochambeau, distinguished itself.

Meanwhile the Emperor arrived on the 20th at Laubau, and at daybreak on the 21st, he was at Löwenberg, and ordered bridges to be thrown across the Bobr. General Lauriston's corps crossed the river at noon. General Maison, with his accustomed valour, beat down everything that endeavoured to oppose his passage, carried all the positions, and sent the enemy retreating as far as Goldberg. The 5th and 11th Corps supported him. On the left, the Prince of the Moskova caused General Sacken to be attacked by the 3rd Corps, in front of Bunzlau, overthrew them, put them to rout and took some prisoners.

The enemy put itself in retreat.

An engagement took place before Goldberg on 23 August. General Lauriston was there at the head of the 5th and 11th Corps. He had before him the Russians, who covered the position of the Flensburg, and the Prussians, who extended to the right on the road to Liegnitz. At the moment when General Gérard debouched to the left on Nieder–au, a column of 25,000 Prussians appeared on this point. He caused them to be attacked in the middle of the barracks of the old camp; they were beaten on all fronts; the Prussians attempted many charges of cavalry which were repulsed everywhere; they were driven from their positions and left near 5,000 dead on the field of battle, besides some prisoners, etc. To the right, the Flensburg was taken and retaken several times; at length the 135th Regiment threw itself on the enemy and entirely overthrew him. The enemy has lost on this point 1,000 dead and 4,000 wounded.

The allied army retired in disorder, and in great haste towards Jauer.

The enemy being thus defeated in Silesia, the Emperor took with him the Prince of the Moskova, left the command of the army in Silesia to the Duke of Tarentum, and arrived on the 25th at Stolpen. The Old and Young Guards, infantry, cavalry and artillery completed these 40 leagues in four days.

Her Majesty, the Empress-Queen and Regent has received the following intelligence from the army, dated 28 August 1813:
On the 26th, at eight o'clock in the morning, the Emperor entered Dresden. The great Russian, Prussian and Austrian army, commanded by the sovereigns, was before it; it crowned all the hills that surround Dresden, at the distance of a short league on the left bank. Marshal Saint-Cyr, with the 14th Corps and the garrison of Dresden, occupied the entrenched camp and lined the fortifications that surrounded the suburbs with sharpshooters. All was tranquil at noon, but to the skilful eye this calm was the precursor of a storm, and attack appeared imminent.

At four in the afternoon, at a signal of the firing of three cannon, six of the enemy's columns, each preceded by 50 pieces of artillery, formed, and a few moments later descended into the plain; they marched towards the redoubts. In less than a quarter of an hour the cannonade became terrible. The fire of a redoubt being silenced, the assailants turned it, and made efforts at the foot of the fortifications of the suburbs, where a good number met death.

It was near five o'clock: a part of the reserves of the 14th Corps was engaged. Some shells fell in the town; the moment appeared pressing. The Emperor ordered the King of Naples to march with General Latour-Maubourg's cavalry on the enemy's right flank, and the Duke of Treviso to march against the left flank. The four divisions of the Young Guard, commanded by Generals Dumoustier, Barrois, Decouz and Roguet then debouched, two by the gate of Pirna and two by the gate of Plauen. The Prince of the Moskova debouched at the head of Barrois' division. These divisions overthrew everything before them; the fire immediately moved to a distance from the centre to the circumference, and was soon driven back on the hills. The field of battle remained covered with dead, cannon and debris. General Dumoutier is wounded, as are likewise Generals Boyeldieu, Tindal and Combelle. The officer of artillery Béranger is mortally wounded; he was a young man of great hopes. General Gros of the Guard was the first to throw himself into the ditch of a redoubt where the enemy's sappers were already at work cutting down the palisades he received a bayonet wound.

The night became dark and the fire ceased, the enemy having failed in its attack, and left upwards of 2,000 prisoners on the battlefield, which was covered with dead and wounded.

On the 27th the weather was dreadful, and the rain fell in torrents. The soldiers had passed the night in mud and water. At nine in the morning we could plainly perceive the enemy lengthening its left and covering the heights, which were separated from its centre by the valley of Plauen.

The King of Naples departed with the corps of the Duke of Belluno and the division of cuirassiers, and debouched on the road of Freiberg to attack this left wing. He performed it with the greatest success. The six divisions that composed this wing were broken and scattered. Half, with their colours and cannon, were taken prisoner, and among the number are several generals.

In the centre a brisk cannonade fixed the enemy's attention, and some columns showed themselves ready to attack him on his left.

The Duke of Treviso, with General Nansouty, manoeuvred in the plain, with his left to the river and his right to the heights.

Marshal Saint-Cyr's corps joined our left with the centre, which was formed of the Duke of Ragusa's corps.

About two o'clock in the afternoon the enemy decided to retreat; it had lost its great communication with Bohemia on its left and right wings.

The result of this day is 25,000 to 30,000 prisoners, 40 flags and 60 pieces of artillery.

We may reckon that the enemy has lost 60,000 men. Our loss in killed, wounded and captured amounts to 4,000 men.

The cavalry has covered itself with glory. The État-Major of the cavalry will publish the details and mention those who have distinguished themselves.

The Young Guards have merited the praises of the entire army. The Old Guard had two battalions engaged; its other battalions were kept in reserve in the village. The two battalions that were engaged beat down everything before them.

The city of Dresden ran great risks of danger.

The conduct of the inhabitants has been such as we should expect from an allied people. The King of Saxony and his family remained at Dresden, and have shown the example of confidence.

Her Majesty the Empress-Queen and Regent has received the following intelligence from the Army, dated 30 August 1813:
On the 28th, 29th and 30th, we followed up our success. Generals Castex, Doumerc and Audenarde, and General Latour-Maubourg's corps, have taken 1,000 caissons, or wagons, of ammunition and collected many prisoners. The villages are full of the enemy's wounded; we already reckon 10,000 of them.

The enemy, according to the report of prisoners, had eight generals killed or wounded.

The Duke of Ragusa has had several actions of advanced posts, which attest the intrepidity of his troops.

General Vandamme, commanding the 1st Corps, on the 25th debouched by Königstein, and on the 26th took possession of the camp at Pirna, of the town and of Höndorf. He intercepted the great communications from Prague to Dresden. The Duke of Württemberg, with 15,000 Russians, was charged with observing this debouche. On the 28th General Vandamme attacked and defeated him, took 2,000 prisoners, six cannon, and drove him into Bohemia. The Prince of Reuss, General of Brigade, an officer of merit, was killed.

On the 29th General Vandamme took a position on the heights of Bohemia and established himself there. He caused the country to be scoured by different parties of light troops, to obtain intelligence of the enemy, annoy it and seize its magazines.

The Prince of Eckmühl was, on the 24th, at Schwerin. He had had no affair of consequence. The Danes had distinguished themselves in several small affairs.

The opening of the campaign has been most brilliant, and allows us to form great hopes. The quality of our infantry is much superior to that of the enemy.

Moniteur, 8 September 1813

Her Majesty the Empress-Queen and Regent, has received the following intelligence from the army, dated 1 September 1813.

On 28 August, the King of Naples and Duke of Belluno slept at Freiberg; the 29th at Lichtenberg; the 30th at Zittau; the 31st at Sayda.

The Duke of Ragusa, with the 6th Corps, slept at Dippoldiswalde on the 28th, where the enemy has abandoned 1,200 wounded, on the 29th at Falkenhain, the 30th at Altenburg and the 31st at Zinnwald.

The 14th Corps, under the orders of Marshal Saint-Cyr, was at Maxen on the 28th, at Reinhards-Grimma on the 29th, at Dittersdorf on the 30th, at Liebenau on the 31st.

The 1st Corps under General Vandamme was at Hollendorf on the 28th, and at Peterswalde on the 29th, occupying the mountains.

The Duke of Treviso was in position at Pirna on the 28th and 29th.

General Pajol, commanding the cavalry of the 14th Corps, has taken some prisoners.

The enemy retired to the position of Dippoldiswalde and Altenburg. Its left followed the Plauen road, and fell back by Tharandt on Dippoldiswalde, not being able to retreat by the Freiberg road. Its right could neither retire by the causeway of Pirna, nor that of Dohna, and therefore retired to Maxen, and from there to Dippoldiswalde. All that there were of partisans or detached on Meissen were cut off. The Russian, Prussian and Austrian baggage got entangled on the causeway of Freiberg; several thousand carriages were taken there.

Arriving at Altenburg, where the road from Töplitz to Dippoldiswalde became impractical, the enemy took the resolution of abandoning more than 1,000 carriages of ammunition and baggage. This great army re-entered Bohemia, after having lost part of its artillery and baggage.

On the 29th General Vandamme crossed, with eight or ten battalions, the pass of the grand chain and marched on Culm; he there met the enemy, 8,000 or 10,000 strong; the enemy engaged him; not finding himself sufficiently strong, he had all his army corps descend; he would have soon overthrown the enemy. Instead of returning and again placing himself on the heights, he remained and took a position at Culm, without guarding the mountain; this mountain commanded the only causeway; it is high. It was only on the 30th in the evening that Marshal Saint-Cyr and the Duke of Ragusa arrived at the debouche from Töplitz. General Vandamme thought only of closing the road against the enemy, and taking all. To a fleeing army, a bridge of gold must be made, or oppose a barrier of steel. He was not strong enough to form this barrier of steel.

However, the enemy perceiving that this army corps of 18,000 remained alone in Bohemia, separated by high mountains, and that all the others were at the foot of the mountains on the other side saw that it was lost unless it defeated it. He conceived the hope of successfully attacking it, its position being bad. The Russian guards were at the head of the army, which was retreating; to them were joined two fresh Austrian divisions. The remainder of the enemy's army joined them as it debouched, followed by the 2nd, 6th and 14th Corps. These troops reached the 1st Corps. General Vandamme showed a good countenance, repulsed all the attacks, penetrated all that presented itself, and covered the field of battle with dead. Disorder increased in the enemy's army, and it was seen with admiration what a small number of brave men can do against a multitude whose morale is weakened.

At two in the afternoon, the Prussian column of General Kleist, cut off in his retreat, debouched by Peterswalde, to endeavour to penetrate into Bohemia; it met no enemy, and arrived on the top of the mountains without resistance. From there it saw the affair that was going on. The effect of this column on the rear of the army decided the business.

General Vandamme immediately marched against this column, which he repulsed: he was obliged to weaken his line at this delicate moment. Fortune turned: he nevertheless succeeded in overthrowing the column of General Kleist, who was killed; the Prussian soldiers threw away their arms, and precipitated themselves into the fosses and woods. In this fight, General Vandamme disappeared. It is supposed he was killed.

Generals Corbineau, Dumonceau and Philippon determined to profit from the moment, and to withdraw, part by the main road, and part by the cross road, with their divisions, and abandoning all the material, which consisted of 30 pieces of artillery and 300 wagons of all kinds, but keeping all the horses. In the situation in which the affairs were, they could not have acted better. The killed, wounded and prisoners may carry our loss in this affair to 6,000 men. It is thought that the enemy's loss cannot be less than from 4,000 to 5,000 men.

The 1st Corps rallied, half a league from the field of battle, to the 14th Corps. The state of the losses sustained in this catastrophe is thought to be due to a badly calculated ardour of war.

General Vandamme merits regrets: he had a rare intrepidity. He died on the field of honour, a death worthy of the envy of every brave man.

—◦—

Her Majesty the Empress-Queen has received the following intelligence from the army, dated 2 September 1813:

On 21 August the Russian, Prussian and Austrian army, commanded by the Emperor Alexander and the King of Prussia, had entered Saxony, and on the 22nd marched against Dresden with from 180- to 200,000 men, and immense matériel, and full of hope, not only of driving us from the right bank of the Elbe, but even of marching on the Rhine, and nourishing the war between the Elbe and the Rhine. In five days it has seen its hopes confounded; 30,000 prisoners, 10,000 wounded fallen into our power, which makes the number amount to 40,000; 20,000 killed or wounded, and as many sick due to the effects of fatigue and the lack of provisions, (it has been five or six days without bread) have weakened it by nearly 80,000 men.

It does not count today to 100,000 men under arms, it has lost more than 100 pieces of artillery, entire parks, 1,500 ammunition and artillery wagons, which were blown up or fell into our hands; more than 3,000 baggage wagons, which it has burnt or that we have taken. There were 40 flags or standards. Among the prisoners there are 4,000 Russians. The ardour of the French army, and the courage of the infantry, fixed everyone's attention.

The first cannon fired from the batteries of the Imperial Guard on 27 August mortally wounded General Moreau, who had returned from America to enter the Russian service.

Moniteur, *16 September 1813*

Her Majesty the Empress-Queen and Regent has received the following intelligence from the army, dated 6 September 1813, in the evening:

On 2 September the Emperor reviewed the 1st Corps in Dresden, and conferred the command of it on Count Lobau.

This corps is composed of the three divisions of Dumonceau, Philippon and Teste. This corps has lost less than was at first supposed, many men having returned.

General Vandamme was not killed; he was taken prisoner. The Engineer General Haxo, who had been sent on a mission to General Vandamme, was with him at that moment, and was also taken prisoner. The élite of the Russian guard were killed in this affair.

On the 3rd, the Emperor slept at the castle of Harta, on the Silesian road, and on the 4th, at the village of Hochkirch (on the other side of Bautzen). Since His Majesty's departure from Löwenberg, important events had taken place in Silesia.

The Duke of Tarentum, to whom the Emperor had left the command of the army of Silesia, made good dispositions for pursuing the Allies and driving them from Jauer: the enemy was driven from all its positions; its columns were in full retreat. On the 26th the Duke of Tarentum had taken all his measures to turn it; but in the night between the 26th and 27th, the Bobr and all the streams which flow into it overflowed; in less than seven to eight hours, the roads were covered with from three to four feet of water, and all the bridges carried away. Our columns found themselves separated. The one that was to have turned the enemy was not able to arrive. The allies quickly perceived this change of circumstances.

The Duke of Tarentum employed the 28th and 29th to reassemble his columns separated by the inundation. They succeeded in regaining Bunzlau, where the only bridge was that had not been carried away by the waters of the Bobr. But a brigade of General Puthod's division was not able to arrive there. In place of endeavouring to throw himself on the sides of the mountains, the general wished to return to Löwenberg. There, finding himself surrounded by enemies, and the river behind him, after having defended himself with all his means, he was obliged to give way to numbers. All those in the two regiments who could swim saved themselves; we estimate from 700 to 800: the remainder was taken.

The enemy has taken from us, in these different affairs, from 3,000 to 4,000 prisoners, two eagles of two regiments and the cannon of the brigade.

After these circumstances, which had fatigued the army, it successively re-crossed the Bobr, the Queiss and the Neisse. The Emperor found it on the 4th on the heights of Hochkirch. He had it, the same evening, re-attack the enemy, drive it from the heights of Wohlenberg, and pursue it during the whole day of the 5th, with the sword at its back to Görlitz. General Sebastiani executed several charges of cavalry at Reichenbach and took some prisoners.

The enemy hastily re-crossed the Neisse and the Queiss, and our troops took a position on the heights of Görlitz, beyond the Neisse.

On the 6th, at seven in the evening, the Emperor returned to Dresden.

The Council of War of the 3rd Army Corps has condemned to the pain of death General of Brigade Jomini, chief of the staff of that corps, who, from the headquarters of Liebnitz, deserted to the enemy at the moment of the rupture of the armistice.

Moniteur, 20 September 1813

Her Majesty the Empress Queen and Regent has received the following intelligence from the army, dated 7 September:

The Duke of Reggio, with the 12th, 7th and 4th Corps, marched on Berlin on 23 August. He attacked the village of Trebbin, defended by the enemy's army, and forced it. He continued his movement.

On 24 August, the 7th Corps not having succeeded in the battle of Grossbeeren, the Duke of Reggio marched on Wittenberg.

On 3 September, the Prince of the Moskova took the command of the army and marched on Interburg. On the 5th he attacked and defeated General Tauenzien; but on the 6th he was attacked on his march by the enemy army commanded by General Bülow. Some cavalry charges on his rear threw disorder among his parks. He was obliged to retire on Torgau. He lost 8,000 men killed, wounded or prisoners, and 12 pieces of artillery. The enemy's loss must also have been very great.

Report from the Prince of the Moskova

Torgau, 7 September 1813

Sire,

The 12th army Corps attacked the enemy on the 5th, and drove it with great vigour beyond Seyda; we took three flags, several cannon and some hundreds of Prussian prisoners; the battlefield was covered with the enemy's dead.

The following day, the 6th, the 4th Corps debouched at eight in the morning by Neuendorf and Interbock: the enemy held the heights in the rear of Dennewitz. The 7th Corps marched on Rohrbach and the 12th on Obna; I thus refused my left, and was in a condition to support the 4th Corps, which, in lieu of attacking, was to turn Interbock by its right, to mask the movement which I wished to make on Dahme, and on which I had determined with certainty that all of the enemy's army was debouching in great haste on Dennewitz. The enemy's advanced guard was overthrown by General Morand's division, which performed prodigies of valour. General Lorge's division of light cavalry improperly engaged, and brought back in disorder, caused some confusion, which the good countenance of the infantry soon corrected.

The enemy being rapidly reinforced, all of the 4th Corps found itself engaged. The 7th, which had been expected, at last arrived, and I ordered General Reynier to briskly charge the enemy's right while General Morand should renew his attack. This general charge had much success; the enemy had just lost much ground. Durutte's division conducted itself well; 60 pieces of artillery fired grapeshot on the enemy's troops, who were in disorder in the hollow ground between Golsdorf and Welmersdorf; in short, the 12th Corps, which entered briskly into action, drove the enemy's right on his centre, separated from his left by the 4th Corps. At this moment the battle was won; but two divisions of the 7th Corps, the two divisions of Lestocq and Sahrer, failed, and that entire corps suddenly falling back, carrying part of the 12th with it, changed the state of things.

The enemy succeeded in throwing its masses between the 4th and 12th Corps, which still fought with the greatest fury. I imperceptibly brought the 4th from the right of the 12th.

The artillery, from the position placed on heights between the Ohna and Dennewitz, filled the interval; and I then ordered a retreat. The 4th Corps affected it in good order on Dahme, and the 7th and 12th marched on Schweidnitz.

This morning the enemy, in number from 3,000 to 4,000 infantry, with cannon and 120 horses coming from Luckau, briskly attacked Dahme. The 23rd Regiment of Line marched against it, and forced it to precipitately retire. The bridge of Hersberg on the Elbe has been burnt. We have preserved two others, one above, and one below that town. Tomorrow, the 4th Corps, with a division of light cavalry, will proceed from Hersberg to Torgau. The 7th and 12th Corps, and the two other divisions of cavalry, will occupy positions on Torgau.

The loss suffered yesterday is about 8,000 men and 12 pieces of artillery: that of the enemy must have been as considerable, the artillery of the different corps having consumed a great part of their ammunition. We had many prisoners in our power, but they disappeared during the night march.

I am with the most profound respect, Sire,

Your Majesty's very obedient and very humble servant and faithful subject.

THE PRINCE OF THE MOSKOVA.

———

Her Majesty the Empress and Queen has received the following intelligence from the army, of 11 September 1813:

The enemy's great army, beaten at Dresden, took refuge in Bohemia. Informed that the Emperor had gone to Silesia, the allies assembled a corps of 80,000 men composed of Russians, Prussians and Austrians, and on the 5th marched on Hottendorf, the 6th on Gieshubel and the 7th on Pirna.

At noon on the 8th, the Emperor proceeded to Dohna, ordered Marshal Saint-Cyr to attack the enemy's advanced guard, which was driven by General Bonet from the heights of Dohna. That night, the French were on the camp of Pirna.

On the 9th, the French army marched on Borna and Fürstenwalde. The Emperor's headquarters were at Liebstadt.

On the 10th, Marshal Saint-Cyr marched from the village of Fürstenwalde on the Geyersberg, which dominates the Bohemian plain. General Bonnet, with the 43rd Division, descended into the plain near Töplitz. There they saw the enemy's army, which endeavoured to rally after having called back all its detachments from Saxony. If the debouche of the Geyersberg had been practicable for artillery, that army would have been attacked in flank during its march; but all the efforts made to get the cannon down were ineffectual.

General Ornano debouched on the heights of Peterswalde, while General Dumonceau arrived there by Hollendorf.

We have taken some hundreds of prisoners, of which several are officers. The enemy has constantly avoided battle and precipitately retired in all directions.

On the 11th the Emperor returned to Dresden.

———

Moniteur, 24 September 1813

Her Majesty the Empress-Queen and Regent has received the following intelligence from the army, dated 13 September:

The Emperor's headquarters were at Dresden.

The Duke of Tarentum, with the 5th, 11th and 3rd Corps, was placed on the left bank of the Sprée. Prince Poniatowski, with the 8th Corps, was at Stolpen. All these forces were thus concentrated on the right bank of the Elbe, within a day's march of Dresden.

Count Lobau, with the 1st Corps, was at Nollendorf, in advance of Peterswalde; the Duke of Treviso at Pirna, Marshal Saint-Cyr on the heights of Borna, occupying the debouches of Fürstenwalde and the Geyersberg. The Duke of Belluno was at Altenburg.

The Prince of the Moskova was at Torgau, with the 4th 7th and 12th Corps.

The Duke of Ragusa and the King of Naples, with General Latour-Maubourg's cavalry, were marching on Grossenhain.

The Prince of Echmühl was at Ratzeburg.

The enemy's army of Silesia was on the right of the Sprée. That of Bohemia was: the Russians and Prussians, in the plain of Töplitz, and an Austrian corps at Marienburg. The enemy's army of Berlin was at Junterbork.

The French General Margaron, with a corps of observation, occupied Leipzig.

The château of Sonnenstein, above Pirna, had been occupied, fortified and armed.

His Majesty had given the command of Torgau to Count Narbonne. The four regiments of Guards of Honour were attached; the first to the Mounted Chasseurs of the Guard; the second to the Dragoons; the third to the Horse Grenadiers; and the fourth to the 1st Regiment of Lancers. Those regiments of the Guard furnished them with instructors, and whenever they marched to battle were joined to old soldiers, by whom they will be guided, and whose staff they will reinforce. A squadron of each regiment of Guards of Honour was always at the service of the Emperor, with a squadron furnished by each regiment of the Guard, which carried to eight the number of squadrons of service.

Her Majesty the Empress-Queen and Regent has received the following intelligence from the army, dated 17 September:
On the 14th the enemy debouched from Töplitz on Nollendorf, to turn Dumonceau's division, which was on the height. This division retired in good order on Gushabel, where Count Lobau collected his corps. The enemy, having wished to attack the camp at Gushabel, was repulsed and lost many men.

On the 15th the Emperor left Dresden and marched to the camp at Pirna. He directed General Mouton-Duvernet, commanding the 42nd Division, by the villages of Langenhenersdorf and Bera, thus turning the enemy's right. At the same time Count Lobau attacked it in front; the enemy was driven, sword in its back, all the remainder of the day.

On the 16th, he still occupied the heights beyond Peterswalde. At noon we began to pursue him and he was dislodged from his position. General Ornano made some fine charges with his division of the cavalry of the Guard and Prince Poniatowski's brigade of Polish light horse. The enemy was followed and driven in the greatest disorder into Bohemia. It made its retreat with so much activity that we were only able to take a few prisoners from it, among whom was General Blücher, commander of the advanced guard, and son of the Prussian General-in-Chief Blücher.

Our loss was trifling.

On the 16th, the Emperor slept at Peterswalde and on the 17th His Majesty returned to Pirna.

Thielmann, a general who deserted from the Saxon service with a corps of partisans and deserters, has marched on Saal. An Austrian colonel has also, as a partisan, marched on Colditz. Generals Margaron, Lefevre-Desnouettes and Piré have gone with columns of infantry and cavalry in pursuit of those parties, hoping to settle the score.

Moniteur, 27 September 1813

Her Majesty the Empress-Queen and Regent has received the following intelligence from the army, dated 19 September 1813:

On the 17th, at two o'clock in the afternoon, the Emperor mounted on horseback, and in lieu of going to Pirna proceeded to the advanced posts. Having perceived the enemy had prepared a great quantity of battlements to defend the descent from the mountain, His Majesty ordered an attack by General Duvernet, who, with the 42nd Division, seized the village of Abessau and drove the enemy into the plain of Töplitz. He was charged with manoeuvring in such a manner as to reconnoitre thoroughly the enemy's position and oblige him to unmask his forces. This general perfectly succeeded in executing his instructions. He engaged in a brisk cannonade beyond cannon-shot, which did little injury; but an Austrian battery of 24 pieces, having left its position to approach Duvernet's division, General Ornano ordered it to be charged by the red lancers of the guard; they took these 24 pieces and sabred all the artillerymen, but were only able to bring back the horses, two cannon and a limber.

On the 18th, Count Lobau remained in the same position, occupying the village of Abessau and all the debouches of the plain. At four o'clock in the afternoon the enemy sent a division to surprise the height above the village of Keinitz. This division was repulsed sword in its back, and fired at with grapeshot for an hour.

On the 18th, at nine in the evening, His Majesty arrived at Pirna, and on the 19th Count Lobau again resumed his positions before Hollendorf and the camp of Giesherbel.

The rain fell in torrents.

The Prince of Neufchâtel is a little indisposed by an excess of fever.

His Majesty is very well.

Moniteur, 2 October 1813

Her Majesty the Empress-Queen and Regent has received the following intelligence from the army, dated 26 September 1813:

The Emperor passed the days of the 19th and 20th at Pirna. His Majesty ordered a bridge to be thrown across there, and a bridgehead to be established on the right bank.

On the 21st the Emperor came to sleep at Dresden, and on the 22nd went to Hartau. He immediately ordered the 11th Corps, commanded by the Duke of Tarentum; the 5th Corps, commanded by General Lauriston; and the 3rd Corps commanded by General Souham to debouch beyond the forest of Bischofswerder.

The enemy's army of Silesia, which had marched, the right commanded by Sacken, on Camenz, the left commanded by Langeron, on Neustadt to the debouches of Bohemia; and the centre, commanded by Yorck, on Bischofswerder, instantly retreated on all sides. General Gérard, commanding our advanced guard, briskly pushed it and took some prisoners. The enemy was led fighting to the Sprée. General Lauriston entered Neustadt.

The enemy thus refusing battle, the Emperor returned on the 24th to Dresden, and ordered the Duke of Tarentum to take a position on the heights of Weissig.

The 8th Corps, commanded by Prince Poniatowski, has re-crossed on the left bank.

Count Lobau, with the 1st Corps, still occupies Gieshubel.

Marshal Saint-Cyr occupies Pirna, and the position of Borna.

The Duke of Belluno occupies the position of Freiberg.

The Duke of Ragusa with the 6th Corps, and General Latour-Maubourg's cavalry, was beyond Grossenhain: he had repulsed the enemy on the right bank, beyond Torgau, to facilitate the passage of a convoy of 20,000 quintals of meal, which was going up the Elbe in boats and which has arrived at Dresden.

The Duke of Padua is at Leipzig; the Prince of the Moskova is between Wittenberg and Torgau.

General Count Lefebvre-Desnouettes, with 4,000 cavalry, was in pursuit of the traitor Thielmann. This Thielmann is a Saxon, and loaded with favours by the King. As a return for so many benefits, he has shown himself the most irreconcilable enemy to his King and to his country. At the head of 3,000 skirmishers, partly Prussians, partly Cossacks and Austrians, he has plundered the King's stud farms, everywhere levied contributions for his own profit and treated his countrymen with all the hatred of a man tormented by crime. This deserter, decorated with the uniform of a Russian Lieutenant-General, marched to Naumburg, where there neither was Commandant nor garrison, but where he surprised 300 or 400 sick.

However, General Lefebvre-Desnouettes met him on the 19th at Freiberg, took from him the 300 or 400 sick, whom that wretch had torn from their beds to make a trophy of them, took some hundreds of prisoners, took some baggage and re-took some carriages which he had seized. Thielmann then took refuge on Zeitz, where Colonel Munsdorf, an Austrian partisan, joined him. General Lefebvre-Desnouettes attacked them at Altenburg on the 24th, threw them back into Bohemia, and killed many men, among others a Prince of Hohenzollern and a Colonel.

Thielmann's march had caused some delays in the communications from Erfurt and Leipzig.

The enemy's army of Berlin appears to be making preparations for building a bridge at Dessau.

The Prince of Neufchâtel is unwell of a bilious fever; he has for several days kept his bed.

His Majesty was never better.

Moniteur, 6 October 1813

Her Majesty the Empress-Queen and Regent has received the following intelligence of the situation of the armies on 29 September 1813:

The Emperor has given the command of one of the corps of the Young Guard to the Duke of Reggio.

The Duke of Castiglione has marched with his corps to take a position on the debouches of the Saale.

Prince Poniatowski has marched with his corps on Peneg.

On the 26th, General Count Bertrand attacked the enemy's army corps of Berlin, which covered the bridge at Wartenburg, forced it, took some prisoners and drove it fighting to the bridgehead. The enemy has evacuated the left bank and destroyed its bridge. General Bertrand immediately destroyed the bridgehead.

The Prince of the Moskova marched on Oranienbaum and the 7th Corps on

Dessau. A Swedish division that was at Dessau hastened to re-cross on the right bank. The enemy was likewise obliged to destroy its bridge, and the bridgehead has been razed.

The enemy has thrown some shells into Wittenberg from the right bank.

During the day of the 8th, the Emperor reviewed the 2nd Corps of cavalry on the heights of Weissig.

The month of September has been very bad and very wet, contrary to what is usual in this country. One hopes that the month of October will be better.

The Prince of Neufchâtel's bilious fever has ceased; the Prince is convalescent.

Moniteur, 30 October 1813

Her Majesty the Empress-Queen and Regent has received the following intelligence of the situation of the armies on 4 October 1813:

General Count Lefebvre-Desnouettes was attacked on 28 September, at seven o'clock in the morning, at Altenburg, by 10,000 cavalry and 3,000 infantry. He retreated before such superior forces; he made some fine charges and did the enemy much injury. It lost 300 of its infantry; it has arrived on the Saale. The enemy was commanded by the Hetman Platov and General Thielmann. Prince Poniatowski marched on the 2nd on Altenburg, by Nossen, Waldheim and Colditz; he overthrew the enemy, took more than 400 prisoners and drove him into Bohemia.

On the 27th, the Prince of the Moskova took possession of Dessau, which a Swedish division occupied, and drove that division back on the bridgehead. On the following day the Swedes arrived to retake the town. General Guilleminot allowed them to advance until within grapeshot range, then unmasked his batteries and repulsed them with considerable loss.

On 3 October the enemy's army of Silesia marched by Königsbruck and Elsterwerda on the Elster, threw over a bridge at the bend that the Elbe forms at Wartenburg, and crossed that river. General Bertrand was placed on an isthmus, in a fine position, surrounded by banks and marshes. Between nine o'clock in the morning and five in the evening, the enemy made seven attacks and was always repulsed. It left 6,000 dead on the battlefield; our loss was 500 killed or wounded. This great difference was owing to the good position which Morand and Fontanelli's division occupied. In the evening General Bertrand, seeing new forces debouche, thought proper to retreat and took a position on the Mulde with the Prince of the Moskova.

On the 4th, the Prince of the Moskova was on the left banks of the Mulde, at Delitsch. The Duke of Ragusa and General Latour-Maubourg's corps of cavalry were at Eulenburg. The 3rd Corps was at Torgau.

Two hundred and fifty partisans, commanded by a Russian major-general, had marched on Mulhausen, and learning that Cassel was without troops they attempted a surprise on the gates of Cassel. They were repulsed; but the following day the Westphalian troops disbanded, and the partisans entered Cassel. They pillaged everything that fell into their hands, and a few days after left it. The King of Westphalia has retired on the Rhine.

31 October 1813

Her Majesty the Empress-Queen and Regent has received the following intelligence respecting the situation of the armies on 15 October 1813:

On the 7th, the Emperor left Dresden; on the 8th he slept at Würzen, the 9th at

Eulenburg, and on the 10th at Düben.

The enemy's army of Silesia, which had marched on Würzen, immediately retreated and re-crossed to the left bank of the Mulde: it had some engagements in which we took some prisoners and took several hundreds of baggage wagons.

General Reynier had marched on Wittenberg, and having crossed the Elbe, marched on Rosslau, turned the bridge of Dessau, seized it, afterwards marched on Aachen and took possession of the bridge. General Bertrand marched on the bridges of Wartenburg, and seized them. The Prince of the Moskova marched on the town of Dessau; he met a Russian division: General Delmas overthrew it and took 3,000 men and 6 cannon.

Several Cabinet couriers, among others *Sieur* Kraft, were taken with dispatches of high importance.

After having thus obtained possession of all the enemy's bridges, the Emperor's intention was to cross the Elbe, to manoeuvre on the right bank from Hamburg to Dresden; to threaten Potsdam and Berlin, and to take Magdeburg for the centre of operations, which, for this purpose, had been supplied with warlike munitions and provisions: but on the 13th, the Emperor learned at Düben that the Bavarian army had joined the Austrian army and threatened the Lower Rhine. This inconceivable defection made the defection of other Princes be foreseen, and induced the Emperor to come to the resolution of returning towards the Rhine – a painful change, as everything had been prepared to operate on Magdeburg; but it would have been requisite to have remained separated and without communication with France for a month. This would not have been inconvenient at the moment when the Emperor fixed his plans, but the case was no longer the same, when Austria was about to have two new disposable armies: the Bavarian army, and the army opposed to Bavaria. The Emperor, therefore, changed his plans with these unforeseen circumstances, and removed his headquarters to Leipzig.

Meanwhile, the King of Naples, who remained in observation at Freiberg, had received orders on the 7th to make a change of front, and march on Gernig and Frohburg, operating on Würzen and Wittenberg. An Austrian Division, which occupied Augustusburg, rendered this movement difficult; the King received orders to attack it; he defeated it, took several battalions, and afterwards effected his movement to the right. Meanwhile, the right of the enemy's army of Bohemia, composed of Wittgenstein's Russian corps, had marched on Altenburg, on intelligence of the King of Naples's change of front. It marched on Freiberg, and afterwards by the left on Borna, placing itself between the King of Naples and Leipzig. The King did not hesitate respecting the manoeuvre he ought to make; he faced about and marched on the enemy, overthrew it, took 9 cannon, 1,000 prisoners, and drove him beyond the Elster, after having made him experience a loss of from 4,000 to 5,000 men.

On the 15th the position of the army was as follows:

The Emperor's headquarters were at Reidnitz, half a league from Leipzig.

The 4th Corps, commanded by General Bertrand, was at the village of Lindenau.

The 6th Corps was at Libenthal.

The King of Naples, with the 2nd, 8th and 5th Corps, had his right at Dölitz, and his left at Liebertwolkwitz.

The 3rd and 7th Corps were in march from Eulenburg to flank the 6th Corps.

The great Austrian army of Bohemia had Giulay's corps opposite Lindenau, a corps at Zwickau, and the remainder of the army, with the left leaning on Grobern and the right on Naumdorf. The bridges of Würzen and Eulenburg, on the Mulde, the position of Wachau, on the Partha, were occupied by our troops. Everything indicated a great battle.

The result of our different movements in these six days has been 5,000 prisoners, several pieces of artillery and doing much injury to the enemy. Prince Poniatowski has, in these circumstances, covered himself with glory.

Report of General of Division Count Milhaud
Leipzig, 12 October 1813, Moniteur, 6 November 1813
To his Most Serene Highness, Prince of Neuchâtel, Vice-Constable, Major-General

My Prince,

I have the honour of reporting to Your Highness that I arrived at Leipzig today with 26 squadrons composing the 5th Corps *bis* of cavalry. His Excellency Marshal Duke of Castiglione will doubtless have related the military events of our march. We had arrived at Naumburg on the 9th; my light cavalry occupied Wethau, and two regiments of dragoons, the 19th and the 22nd, occupied Flemingen. The enemy attacked Flemingen with 1,000 horses and 4 cannon. Colonel Merhet of the 19th repulsed this attack and lost only 4 horses killed by the artillery. General Subervie was attacked at Wethau by 2,000 horses and 2,000 infantrymen; he avoided the surprise and made his retreat on Naumburg without losing one man.

After the fine retreat of the light cavalry, the enemy occupied the defile of Wethau on the road of Naumburg at Weissenfels.

The next day, the 10th, His Excellency the Duke of Castiglione continued his march on Leipzig and made his dispositions to attack the enemy and chase it from the defile of Wethau. Three battalions of light infantry under the command of General Aymard were enough to seize the position, and our young infantrymen, in spite of the fusillade and the cannonade of the enemy, made themselves masters of the bridge of Wethau and all the small woods which surround this difficult position. The light cavalry passed the defile quickly, supported by echelons by the dragoons; it charged on the plateau which leads to Stölgen and Pletsch, the rearguard of the enemy cavalry, turned the infantry which was forced to throw itself back into the ravines, killed one hundred men of cavalry and infantry, and protected the rush of the light infantry; the efforts of these two arms caused 300 infantrymen to lay down their arms, and we took 20 horses from the enemy.

Ahead of this plateau there is a small defile in the middle of the woods, and in the front a vast plain that leads to the village of Pletsch and the small town of Zeitz.

The light artillery of my cavalry had already done a lot of harm to the enemy. I had the woods defile pass very quickly, and I ordered all the cavalry to debouch in a tight column, in order to hide its force from the enemy, which had a force at least twice superior; but I wished to engage it in a charge, to let it learn the valour of our old soldiers of cavalry.

The enemy took out at a gallop its pieces of artillery and immediately marched against us with the regiment of the old dragoons of La Tour and the Chevauxleger 'Kaiser'. The 6th Dragoons of our Emperor rushed at the head of the column against those two regiments; the mêlée became serious; I deployed on the right and left the squadrons and the brigade of General Montélégier, and the two enemy regiments surrendered the ground to us, leaving many dead Austrians there.

The enemy advanced eight squadrons of the dragoons of Hohenzollern and two squadrons of Black Prussian hussars to support the dragoons that used to be of La Tour, today Saint-Vincent. The French 2nd Dragoons took these new regiments in flank and overthrew them totally, at the moment when one squadron of the 13th, surrounded by 800 horses, was forming a circle, and struck with death all that was around: that squadron was under the command of Squadron Chief Ligniville.

At the same time, the light cavalry under the command of General Subervie, having just driven down an equal number of Prussian hussars and one squadron of Uhlans, was being outflanked by twice the number. But Colonel Mermet who, in the absence of the General of Brigade, was in command of the 18th, 19th, 22nd and 24th Dragoons, received the order to deploy his column; the 18th and 19th overthrew ten squadrons. The light cavalry and our dragoons crushed the enemy everywhere, who left 600 dead on the battlefield, 100 riders and several officers prisoner, and 120 horses. We have to regret the loss of the captain of the élite company of the 11th Dragoons, 14th Chasseurs and 4th Dragoons. Generals Montélégier and Subervie have distinguished themselves. All the officers and soldiers, during four successive charges on a ground of one quarter of a league, fought to the cries of 'Long live the Emperor!'

The regiments of dragoons of Saint-Vincent, of Hohenzollern and the Chevauxleger 'Kaiser' were destroyed in this fine affair. We have 18 dead, 120 chasseurs, dragoons or hussars wounded; but 100 will return into the ranks in about seven to eight days.

The enemy corps were under the command of General Thielmann, the Princes Lichtenstein and Biron Courlande: the enemy had 4,000 horses and we only had 2,600. The old dragoons of La Tour and the Chevauxleger Kaiser were from the élite Austrian cavalry.

In my report to the Duke of Castiglione, I mentioned the name of several brave men; but all are worthy of the favours of His Majesty, by their intrepidity and devotion.

I am, etc.

GENERAL OF DIVISION COUNT MILHAUD

Excerpt of a letter from the Emperor to the Empress
Frankfort, 1 November 1813
Madam and very dear spouse,

I am sending you 20 flags taken by my arms at the battles of Wachau, of Leipzig and of Hanau; it is an homage that I like to pay to you. I desire that you should see in this a token of my great satisfaction of your conduct during the regency with which I have entrusted you.

NAPOLEON

Her Majesty, the Empress-Queen, and Regent, has received the following intelligence respecting the situation of the armies on the evening of 16 October 1813:
On the 15th, Prince Schwarzenberg, commanding the enemy's army, announced in the orders of the day, that the following day, the 16th, there would be a general and decisive battle. Accordingly, on the 16th, at nine in the morning, the great allied army marched on us; it constantly operated to extend itself on its right. At first three large columns were seen marching, one along the river Elster, against the village of Dölitz, the second against the village of Wachau and the third against that of Liebertwolkwitz. These three columns were preceded by 200 pieces of artillery.

380

The Emperor immediately made his dispositions.

At ten o'clock the cannonade was most violent, and at eleven the two armies were engaged in the villages of Dölitz, Wachau and Liebertwolkwitz. These villages were attacked six or seven times; the enemy was constantly repulsed, and covered the approaches with its dead. Count Lauriston, with the 5th Corps, defended the village on the left (Liebertwolkwitz); Prince Poniatowski, with his brave Poles, defended the village on the right (Dölitz); and the Duke of Belluno defended Wachau.

At noon the sixth attack of the enemy had been repulsed; we were masters of the three villages and had taken 2,000 prisoner.

Nearly at the same moment, the Duke of Tarentum debouched by Holzhausen, marching on an enemy's redoubt, which General Charpentier carried at the quick charge, seizing the artillery and taking some prisoners.

The moment appeared decisive.

The Emperor ordered the Duke of Reggio to march on Wachau with two divisions of the Young Guard. He equally directed the Duke of Treviso to march against Liebertwolkwitz with two other divisions of the Young Guard, and take possession of an extensive wood that is on the left of the village. At the same time he caused to be advanced on the centre a battery of one 150 cannon, which General Drouot directed.

All of those dispositions had the success that was expected from them. The enemy's artillery withdrew a distance. The enemy retired, and the entire battlefield remained in our possession.

It was three o'clock in the afternoon; all the enemy's troops had been engaged. It has recourse to its reserve. Count Merveldt, who commanded in chief the Austrian reserve with six divisions, supported all the troops in all the attacks, and the Russian Imperial Guard, which formed the reserve of the Russian army, supported the centre.

The cavalry of the Russian Guard, and the Austrian cuirassiers, threw their left on our right; they seized Dölitz, and engaged in prancing about the Duke of Belluno's squares.

The King of Naples marched with Latour Maubourg's cuirassiers, and charged the enemy's cavalry by the left of Wachau; at the same time the Polish cavalry and dragoons of the Guard, commanded by General Letort, charged by the right. The enemy's cavalry was defeated: two entire regiments remained on the field of battle. General Letort took 300 Austrians and Russians prisoners. General Latour-Maubourg took some hundreds of men of the Russian Guard.

The Emperor immediately ordered Curial's division of the Guard to advance to support Prince Poniatowski. General Curial marched on the village of Dölitz, attacked it with the bayonet, carried it without firing a shot and took 1,200 prisoner, among whom was the General-in-Chief Merveldt.

Affairs being thus re-established on our right, the enemy retreated and the battlefield was no longer disputed with us.

The reserve artillery of the Guard, which General Drouot commanded, was with the skirmishers: the enemy's cavalry came and charged them. The artillerymen formed their pieces, which they had the precaution to load with grapeshot, in a square and fired with so much agility that in an instant the enemy was repulsed. On these developments the French cavalry advanced to support these batteries.

General Maison, commanding a division of the 5th Corps, an officer of the greatest distinction, was wounded. General Latour-Maubourg, commanding the cavalry, had his thigh carried off by a ball. Our loss on this day has been 2,500 men killed and wounded. It will not be exaggerating to estimate that of the enemy at 25,000 men.

One cannot over-eulogize the conduct of General Lauriston and Prince Poniatowski during this day. To give the latter a proof of his satisfaction, the Emperor on the battlefield appointed him a Marshal of France, and granted a great number of decorations to the regiments of his corps.

General Bertrand was at the same time attacked in the village of Lindenau by Generals Giulay, Thielmann and Lichtenstein. We deployed from different parts about 50 pieces of artillery. The combat lasted six hours, without the enemy being able to gain an inch of ground. At five in the evening, General Bertrand decided the victory by making a charge with his reserve, and not only rendered vain the enemy's designs, who rushed to seize the bridges of Lindenau and the suburbs of Leipzig, but even constrained him to evacuate the battlefield.

On the right of the Partha, a league from Leipzig and nearly four leagues from the field of battle where the Emperor was, the Duke of Ragusa was engaged. By one of those fatal circumstances which often have an influence over the most important affairs, the 3rd Corps, which was to support the Duke of Ragusa, hearing nothing on that side at ten in the morning, and, on the contrary, hearing a terrible cannonade on the side where the Emperor was, thought proper to march there, and thus lost the day in marches. The Duke of Ragusa, abandoned to his own forces, defended Leipzig and maintained his position during the day, but he suffered losses that were not compensated by those he inflicted on the enemy, however great they were. Some battalions of marine artillerymen conducted themselves feebly. Generals Compans and Frédéricks were wounded. In the evening, the Duke of Ragusa, himself slightly wounded, was obliged to contract his position on the Partha. In this movement He was obliged to abandon several dismounted cannon and several wagons.

Her Majesty the Empress-Queen and Regent has received the following intelligence respecting the situation of the armies on 24 October 1813:
The battle of Wachau disconcerted all the enemy's projects; but its army was so numerous that it still had resources. The enemy hastily called in, during the night, the corps that it had left on its line of operations and the divisions that remained on the Saale; and it pressed the march of General Bennigsen, who was coming up with 40,000 men.

After the movement in retreat that it made on the evening of the 16th and during the night, the enemy occupied a fine position two leagues in the rear. It was requisite to employ the 17th in reconnoitring and fully determining the point of attack. That day it was also necessary to allow the parks of reserve to arrive, and replace the 80,000 cannonballs that had been expended in the battle. The enemy had therefore time to re-assemble its troops that it had scattered when it delivered itself up to his chimerical projects, and to receive the reinforcements that it expected.

Having received information of the arrival of these reinforcements, and knowing that the position of the enemy was very strong, the Emperor resolved to draw it to another ground. The 18th, at two o'clock in the morning, he approached two leagues closer to Leipzig, and placed his army with the right at Connewitz, his centre at Probstheyda and the left at Stötteritz, placing himself at the mill of Ta.

On his part, the Prince of the Moskova had placed his troops opposite the army of Silesia, on the Partha; the 6th Corps at Schönfeld; and the 3rd and 7th along the Partha at Neutzsch and at Teckla. The Duke of Padua, with General Dombrowski, guarded the position and the suburbs of Leipzig, on the road to Halle.

At three o'clock in the morning the Emperor was at the village of Lindenau and ordered General Bertrand to march on Lützen and Weissenfels, to sweep the plain and secure the debouches of the Saale, and the line of communication with Erfurt. The light troops of the enemy dispersed, and at noon General Bertrand was master of Weissenfels and the bridge on the Saale.

Having thus secured his communications, the Emperor waited the approach of the enemy with firmness.

At nine o'clock the scouts announced that the enemy was marching on the whole line. At ten o'clock the cannonade commenced.

Prince Poniatowski and General Lefol defended the bridge of Connewitz. The King of Naples, with the 2nd Corps, was at Probstheyda, and the Duke of Tarentum at Holzhausen.

All the efforts of the enemy during the day against Connewitz and Probstheyda failed. The Duke of Tarentum was outflanked at Holzhausen. The Emperor ordered him to take a position at the village of Stötteritz. The cannonade was dreadful. The Duke of Castiglione, who defended a wood in the centre, maintained himself there all of the day.

The Old Guard was drawn up in reserve, on a rising ground, in four massive columns directed towards the four principal points of attack.

The Duke of Reggio was sent to support Prince Poniatowski, and the Duke of Treviso to guard the debouches of the city of Leipzig.

The success of the battle was at the village of Probstheyda. The enemy attacked it four times in considerable force, and four times it was repulsed with great loss.

At five o'clock in the evening, the Emperor caused the artillery of the reserve to advance, and drove back the fire of the enemy, which withdrew to the distance of a league from the battlefield.

In the meantime, the army of Silesia attacked the suburb of Halle. All its attacks, repeated a number of times during the day, failed. It attempted, with the greater part of its force, to cross the Partha at Schönfeld and Saint Teckla. Three times it succeeded in gaining a footing on the left bank, and three times the Prince of the Moskova repulsed and overthrew it at the point of the bayonet.

At three o'clock in the afternoon the victory was ours, as well on this side against the army of Silesia, as on the side of the Emperor against the great army. But at this instant the Saxon army, infantry, cavalry and artillery, and the Württemberg cavalry, passed altogether to the enemy. Of the Saxon army there remained only General Zeschau, the commander-in-chief, and 500 men. This treason not only caused a vacancy in our lines, but also delivered up to the enemy the important debouche confided to the Saxon army, who carried their infamy so far as instantly to turn their 40 pieces of artillery against the division of Durutte. A moment of disorder succeeded; the enemy crossed the Partha, and marched on Reudnitz, which it occupied: it was now, therefore, only half a league from Leipzig.

The Emperor sent his Horse Guard, commanded by General Nansouty, with 20 pieces of artillery, to take in flank the troops that were advancing along the Partha to attack Leipzig. He proceeded in person with a division of the Guard to the village of Reudnitz. The promptitude of these movements restored order. The village was retaken, and the enemy driven to a great distance.

The battlefield remained entirely in our power, and the French army remained victorious in the fields of Leipzig as they had in those of Wachau.

At nightfall, the fire of our canon had, at all points, repulsed that of the enemy to the distance of a league from the field of battle.

Generals of Division Vial and Rochambeau died gloriously. Our loss on this day may be estimated at 4,000 men killed or wounded; that of the enemy must have been considerable in the extreme. It took no prisoners from us, and we took from it 500 men.

At six in the evening, the Emperor ordered his dispositions for the following day; but at seven o'clock, Generals Sorbier and Dulauloy, commanding the artillery of the army and of the Guard, came to his bivouac to inform him of the expenditure of the day: 95,000 cannonballs had been fired. They informed him that the ammunition in reserve was exhausted, and that there remained only 16,000 cannonballs; that this would scarcely suffice for a cannonade of two hours, after which no ammunition would remain for ulterior events; that the army had in five days fired upwards of 220,000 cannonballs, and that a further supply could only be furnished at Magdeburg or Erfurt.

This state of things rendered necessary a prompt movement on one of our two largest depots. The Emperor decided for that of Erfurt, for the same reason that induced him to come to Leipzig, to enable him to appreciate the influence of the defection of Bavaria.

The Emperor immediately gave orders that the baggage, the parks and the artillery should pass the defiles of Lindenau; he gave similar orders with respect to the cavalry, and to different corps of the army and then repaired to the Prussian hotel, in the suburbs of Leipzig, where he arrived at nine o'clock in the evening.

This circumstance obliged the French army to renounce the fruits of the two victories in which they had, with so much glory, beaten troops greatly superior in numbers, and the armies of the whole Continent.

But his movement was not without difficulty. From Leipzig to Lindenau there is a defile of two leagues, with from five to six bridges on the road. It was proposed to place 6,000 men and 60 cannon in Leipzig, which is a walled town; to occupy that town as a head of defile and burn its vast suburbs in order to prevent the enemy from effecting a lodgment therein, and to allow full scope to bring our artillery on the ramparts into play.

However odious the treason of the Saxon army was, the Emperor could not resolve to destroy one of the finest cities in Germany, to deliver it up to the disorders of every kind inseparable from such a defence; and that, too, under the eyes of the King, who had been pleased to accompany the Emperor from Dresden, and who was so poignantly afflicted by the conduct of his army. The Emperor chose rather to expose himself to the loss of a few hundred wagons than to adopt this barbarous measure.

At daybreak, all the parks, the baggage, all of the artillery, the cavalry, the Guard and two-thirds of the army, had already passed the defile.

The Duke of Tarentum and Prince Poniatowski were charged to hold the suburbs, and to defend them long enough to allow everyone to debouch, and then themselves to execute the passage of the defile towards eleven o'clock.

At six o'clock in the morning the Magistrates of Leipzig sent a deputation to the Prince of Schwarzenberg, to beg that he would not make the city the scene of an action that would occasion its ruin.

At nine o'clock the Emperor mounted his horse, entered Leipzig, and paid a visit to the King. He left this prince at full liberty to do as he pleased, and not to leave his dominions, leaving them to be exposed to that seditious spirit which had been fomented amongst the soldiers. A Saxon battalion had been formed at Dresden, and joined the Young Guard. The Emperor caused it to be drawn up at Leipzig, in front of the King's palace, to serve him as a guard, and protect him from the first movement of the enemy.

Half an hour after, the Emperor repaired to Lindenau, there to await the evacuation of Leipzig, and to see the last troops cross the bridges before putting himself in march.

Meanwhile the enemy was speedily apprised that the greater part of the army had evacuated Leipzig, and that there remained there only a strong rearguard. It briskly attacked the Duke of Tarentum and Prince Poniatowski; it was repeatedly repulsed, and in the act of defending the suburbs, our rearguard effected its retreat. But the Saxons that had remained in the city fired on our troops from the ramparts, which obliged them to accelerate their retreat, and occasioned some disorder.

The Emperor had ordered the engineers to form charges under the great bridge which is between Leipzig and Lindenau, in order to blow it up at the last moment, and thus to retard the march of the enemy and give time for our baggage to file off. General Dulauloy had entrusted this operation to Colonel Montfort. This Colonel, instead of remaining on the spot to direct it and to give the signal, ordered a corporal and four sappers to blow up the bridge the instant the enemy should appear. The corporal, an ignorant fellow, and but ill comprehending the nature of the duty with which he was charged, on hearing the first shots discharged from the ramparts of the city, set fire to the charges and blew up the bridge. A part of the army was still on the other side with a park of 80 pieces of artillery and some hundreds of wagons.

The advance of this part of the army, which was approaching the bridge, seeing it blow up, conceived it was in the power of the enemy. A cry of dismay spread from rank to rank 'The enemy are close on our rear, and the bridges are destroyed!' The unfortunate soldiers dispersed and endeavoured to effect their escape as well as they could. The Duke of Tarentum swam across the river; Count Lauriston, less fortunate, was drowned[1]; Prince Poniatowski, mounted on a high-spirited horse, darted into the water, and appeared no more. The Emperor was not informed of this disaster until it was too late to remedy it. In fact no remedy would have been possible. Colonel Montfort and the corporal of sappers have been handed over to a court-martial.

It is impossible as yet to ascertain the losses occasioned by this unfortunate event, but they are estimated at 12,000 men and several hundred wagons. The disorder that it has occasioned in the army has changed the state of affairs. The French army, though victorious, is arriving at Erfurt as a defeated army would have arrived there. It is impossible to describe the regret that the army feels for Prince Poniatowski, Count Lauriston, and all the brave men who perished in consequence of this fatal event. We have no accounts of General Reynier; it is not known whether he is taken or killed. The profound grief of the Emperor may be easily conceived, who sees, from inattention to his wide dispositions, the results of so many fatigues and labours completely vanishing.

---

1   Lauriston was actually taken prisoner and lived until 1828.

On the 19th the Emperor slept at Markranstädt; the Duke of Reggio remained at Lindenau.

On the 20th the Emperor crossed the Saale at Weissenfels.

On the 21st the army crossed the Unstrut at Freiberg; General Bertrand took a position on the heights of Kösen.

On the 22nd the Emperor slept at the village of Ollendorf.

On the 23rd he arrived at Erfurt.

The enemy, which had been struck with consternation by the battles of the 16th and 18th, has, by the disaster of the 19th, resumed the courage and ascendance of victory. The French army, after such brilliant successes, has lost its victorious attitude.

We have found at Erfurt provisions, ammunition, clothing, all that the army stood in need of.

The staff will publish the reports of the different chiefs of the army as to the officers who distinguished themselves in the great battles of Wachau and of Leipzig.

~~

Moniteur, 5 November 1813

Her Majesty the Empress-Queen and Regent has received the following accounts respecting the situation of the army 31 October 1813.

The two regiments of the King of Saxony's cuirassiers, forming part of the 1st Corps of cavalry, had remained with the French army. After the Emperor left Leipzig, he made the Duke of Vicenza write them the accompanying letter, and sent them back to Leipzig to serve as guard to the King.

When we were certain of the defection of Bavaria, a Bavarian battalion was still with the army; His Majesty caused the accompanying letter to be written by the Major-General to the commandant of that battalion.

The Emperor left Erfurt on the 25th.

Our army tranquilly operated its movement on the Main. Arriving on the 29th at Gelnhausen, we saw an enemy's corps of from 5,000 to 6,000 men, cavalry, infantry and artillery, which we knew by prisoners to be the advanced guard of the Austrian and Bavarian army. This advanced guard was repulsed and obliged to retreat. We quickly re-established the bridge the enemy had destroyed. We soon learned from prisoners that the Austrian and Bavarian army, announced from 60,000 to 70,000 men strong, coming from Braunau, had arrived at Hanau, supposedly to prevent the passage of the French army.

On the 29th, in the evening, the skirmishers of the enemy's advanced guard were driven beyond the village of Langensebolde, and at seven in the evening the Emperor and his headquarters were in that village at the Castle of Isselburg.

The following day, the 30th, at nine in the morning, the Emperor mounted on horseback. The Duke of Tarentum advanced with 5,000 skirmishers under the orders of General Charpentier. General Sebastiani's cavalry, the division of the Guard commanded by General Friant, and the cavalry of the Old Guard followed; the remainder of the army was one march in the rear.

The enemy had placed six battalions in the village of Ruchingen, in order to cut off all the roads that could lead towards the Rhine. Some discharges of grapeshot and a charge of cavalry made these battalions precipitately recoil.

Arriving on the skirt of the wood within two leagues of Hanau, the skirmishers did not delay long in engaging. The enemy was driven to that point in the wood where the old and the new roads join. Not being able to oppose anything to the

386

superiority of our infantry, it endeavoured to profit by its great numbers; it extended the fire on its right. A brigade of 2,000 skirmishers of the 2nd Corps, commanded by General Dubreton, was engaged to check the enemy, and General Sebastiani caused several successful charges to be executed on the enemy's skirmishers in the open parts of the wood. Our 5,000 skirmishers thus checked all the enemy's army, by gaining time until three in the afternoon.

The artillery having arrived, the Emperor ordered General Curial to march at the quick charge on the enemy with two battalions of chasseurs of the Old Guard and drive it beyond the debouch; General Drouot to immediately debouch with 50 cannon; General Nansouty, with all the corps of General Sebastiani and the cavalry of the Old Guard to vigorously charge the enemy in the plain.

All those dispositions were executed.

General Curial overthrew several enemy battalions. At the aspect of the Old Guard alone, the Austrians and Bavarians were terrified. Fifteen pieces of artillery, and successively to the number of 50, were placed in battery with the activity and intrepid sang-froid that distinguishes General Drouot. General Nansouty marched on the right of these batteries, and caused 10,000 of the enemy's cavalry to be charged by General Levesque, Major of the Old Guard, by the division of cuirassiers Saint-Germain, and successively by the grenadiers and dragoons of the cavalry of the Guard. All these charges had the happiest result. The enemy's cavalry were overthrown and sabred; several squares of infantry were penetrated; the Austrian Jordis regiment and the Prince of Schwarzenberg's Uhlans have been entirely destroyed. The enemy precipitately abandoned the Frankfort road, which it had closed, and all the ground that its left occupied. It put itself in retreat, and was soon after in complete rout.

It was five o'clock. The enemy made an effort on its right to disengage its left, and give the latter time to reform. General Friant sent two battalions of the Old Guard to a farmhouse situated on the old Hanau road. The enemy was soon driven from its advantageous post, and its right was obliged to fall back, and put itself in retreat; it re-crossed, in disorder, the small river of the Kinzig, before six in the evening.

Victory was complete.

The enemy, which pretended to shut up all the country, was obliged to evacuate the road of Frankfort and of Hanau. We have taken 6,000 prisoners, and taken several flags and several pieces of artillery. The enemy had six generals killed or wounded. Its loss has been about 10,000 men, in killed, wounded, or prisoners. Ours is but from 400 to 500 killed or wounded. We had only engaged 5,000 skirmishers, four battalions of the Old Guard and about 80 squadrons of cavalry and 120 pieces of artillery.

At daybreak on the 30th, the enemy retired in the direction of Aschaffenburg. The Emperor continued his movement, and at three in the afternoon His Majesty was at Frankfort.

The flags taken in this battle, as well as those that were taken in the battles of Wachau and Leipzig, have been sent off for Paris.

The cuirassiers, the mounted grenadiers, the dragoons, made brilliant charges. Two squadrons of the Guards of Honour of the 3rd Regiment, commanded by Major Saluces, particularly distinguished themselves, and give reason for presuming what may be expected from this corps next spring, when they will be perfectly organized and disciplined.

General of Artillery of the Army Noury, and General Devaux, Major of Artillery of the Guard, were distinguished. General Letort, Major of Dragoons of the Guard, although wounded in the battle of Wachau, would charge at the head of his regiment, and had his horse killed.

On the 31st, in the evening, the main headquarters were at Frankfort.

The Duke of Treviso, with two divisions of the Young Guard, and the first corps of cavalry, was at Gelnhausen. The Duke of Reggio arrived at Frankfort.

Count Bertrand and the Duke of Ragusa were at Hanau.

General Sebastiani was on the Nidda.

Letter from the Duke of Vicenza to the Captain Commanding the two regiments of Saxon Cuirassiers, employed in the corps of cavalry of Count Latour-Maubourg.

Markranstädt, 19 October 1813

I hasten to inform you, Commandant, that the Emperor authorizes the two regiments of Saxon Cuirassiers of the Guard, and of Zeschwitz, which were serving in his armies, to proceed to Leipzig, His Majesty thinking that it will be agreeable to your good King to have these troops of his Guard near his person, under existing circumstances.

General Latour-Maubourg, who is informed of this disposition, will afford you all the necessary facilities, that the return of these troops may suffer no difficulty. I have the honour to be, etc.

CAULAINCOURT, DUKE OF VICENZA

Letter from the Major-General to the Lieutenant-Colonel commanding the Bavarian troops

Erfurt, 24 October 1813

The King, your Master, forgetting what the Emperor has done for him, has declared war against France. Under such circumstances the Bavarian troops that are with the army should be disarmed and made prisoners of war, but that would be contrary to the confidence that the troops under his orders should have in him. In consequence, Sir, His Majesty's intention is that you should collect your battalion. You shall have magazines given you, four day's provisions, and you shall set out from hence to proceed by Coburg on Bamberg where you will take your orders from the Minister of His Majesty the King of Bavaria. It would likewise be equally contrary to the sentiments of honour and loyalty that you should bear arms against France. In consequence it is the Emperor's wish that you and your officers should give your word of honour that neither you nor your soldiers shall serve against France for one year.

THE PRINCE VICE-CONSTABLE MAJOR-GENERAL, ALEXANDER

Moniteur, 8 November 1813

Her Majesty the Empress-Queen and Regent has received the following accounts of the situation of the army on 3 November 1813.

On 30 October, at the moment when the battle of Hanau was fought, General Lefebvre-Desnouettes, at the head of his division of cavalry and of the 5th Corps of cavalry commanded by General Milhaud, flanked all the right of the army near Brucköbel and Nieder-Issengheim. He found himself in the presence of the corps of Russian and allied cavalry of from 6,000 to 7,000 men: the combat commenced; several charges, all to our advantage, took place and that enemy's corps formed by the junction of two or three partisans was broken, and briskly pursued. We took from it 150 mounted prisoners. Our loss consisted of about 60 men wounded.

The day following the battle of Hanau the enemy was in full retreat; the Emperor did not wish to pursue it, the army being fatigued, and His Majesty, far from attaching any importance to it, could only have seen with regret, the destruction of 4,000 or 5,000 Bavarians which would have been the result of that pursuit. His Majesty, therefore, contented himself with causing the enemy's rearguard to be slightly pursued, and left General Bertrand on the right bank of the Kinzig River.

About three o'clock in the afternoon, the enemy, knowing that that army had fled, retraced its steps, hoping to obtain some advantage over General Bertrand's corps. The Morand and Guilleminot divisions allowed it to make his preparations for the crossing of the Kinzig, and when it had crossed the river, marched on it with fixed bayonets and drove it into the river, where the greater part of its people were drowned. The enemy lost 3,000 men in this affair.

The Bavarian General Wrede, Commander-in-Chief of that army, has been mortally wounded, and we noticed that all the relations which he had in the army perished in the battle of Hanau; among others his son-in-law, the Prince of Oettingen.[2]

A Bavarian-Austrian division entered Frankfort at noon on the 30th, but on the approach of the scouts of the French army it retired on the left bank of the Main, after having destroyed the bridge.

On 2 November the French rearguard evacuated Frankfort and marched on the Nidda.

The same day, at five o'clock in the morning, the Emperor entered Mayence.

It is supposed among the people that General Wrede has been the author and principal agent of the defection of Bavaria. That General had been loaded with favours by the Emperor.

Moniteur, *10 November 1813*

Her Majesty the Empress-Queen and Regent has received the following accounts of the situation of the Army on 7 November:

The Duke of Tarentum was at Cologne, where he is organizing an army for the defence of the Lower Rhine.

The Duke of Ragusa was at Mayence.

The Duke of Belluno was at Strasburg.

The Duke of Valmy had gone to take the command of all the reserve at Metz.

Count Bertrand, with the 4th Corps composed of four divisions of infantry and a division of cavalry, and about 40,000 strong, occupied the right bank before Cassel. His headquarters were at Hocheim. For four days they have been working up an entrenched camp, on the heights a league in advance of Cassel. Several works have been traced out and considerably advanced.

All the remainder of the army have crossed the Rhine.

His Majesty, on the 7th, signed the re-organization of the army, and appointments to all vacant places.

The advanced guard under General Bertrand has not yet seen any of the enemy's infantry, but only some troops of light cavalry.

All the fortresses on the Rhine are being armed and provisioned with the greatest activity.

---

2 Wrede actually survived his wounds, fought additional battles against Napoleon, attended the Congress of Vienna and lived until 1838.

The national guards recently levied are proceeding from all sides to the fortress, to form the garrisons of them, and leave the army disposable.

General Dulauloy has re-organized the 207 pieces of artillery belonging to the Guard. General Sorbier was occupied in re-organizing 100 foot and horse batteries, and in repairing the loss of horses that the artillery of the army has suffered.

It is believed that His Majesty will not delay proceeding to Paris.

Imperial Notification

Paris, 10 November 1813

The Emperor arrived at Saint Cloud on the 9th at five o'clock in the afternoon.

His Majesty had left Mentz the 8th, at one o'clock in the morning.

CAMPAIGN IN FRANCE
1814

The allies did not stop at the borders of France. By now, only the complete defeat and removal of Napoleon would satisfy them. One by one Napoleon's allies had deserted him. Even his brother-in-law, Prince Joachim Murat, King of Naples, negotiated an understanding with Austria in an effort to preserve his throne. Napoleon could have used his superb cavalry talent, but it was denied him.

The end was clearly near; even Napoleon had authorized negotiations to proceed without any preconditions. Yet, as long as Napoleon was commanding his troops they had success. But he could not be everywhere at once, and the allies advanced on Paris, defeating his marshals as they went. As the Bulletins point out, the allies were content to ignore the fortresses in their rear, feeling that if they could take Paris, Napoleon would be finished. When Napoleon realized this, he also began to race for Paris, but he arrived half a day too late.

All was not completely lost, however, until Marshal Marmont, the Duke of Ragusa, defected, causing the loss to Napoleon of the 11,000 men of his 6th Corps. This treachery, along with the political treachery of Talleyrand, was too much to overcome, and Napoleon abdicated.

Imperial Decrees
Paris, Tuileries Palace, 26 December 1813, Moniteur, *28 December 1813*
Napoleon, Emperor of the French, etc.

We have decreed and decree the following:

Article 1 There will be some Senators or Councillors of State sent in the military divisions, in the capacity of our extraordinary commissioners.
They will be accompanied by masters of petitions or by auditors.

Article 2 Our extraordinary commissioners are charged with accelerating:
1st The conscription levies;
2nd The clothing, the equipment and the arming of the troops;
3rd The completion of supplying the fortresses;
4th The gathering of the horses required for the service of the army;
5th The levying and organization of the National Guard, in accordance with our decrees.
The said commissioners will be able to extend the dispositions of the said decrees to the towns and fortresses that are not yet included in them.

Article 3 Those of the said commissioners who will be sent into countries threatened by the enemy will order massive levies and all other measures necessary to the defence of the territory and governed by the duty to oppose any progress of the enemy.
Furthermore, they will be given special instructions, according to the particular situation of the departments where their mission will take them.

Article 4 Our commissioners have the authority to order all high police measures that may be required by circumstances and to maintain public order.

Article 5 They are in the same way authorized to form military commissions and to try, before them or before special courts, all persons known to favour the enemy, of having secret dealings with it or to threaten public tranquility.

Article 6 They will be able to make proclamations and to pass decrees. The said decrees will be obligatory for all citizens. The judicial, civil and military authorities will be obliged to conform to them and to execute them.

Article 7 Our commissioners will stay in communication with our ministers regarding the subjects relating to each ministry.

Article 8 They will enjoy, in their respective quality, the honours that are given to them according to our regulations.

Article 9 Our ministers are charged with the execution of the present decree, which will be inserted in the Bulletin of the Laws.

NAPOLEON

By the Emperor, THE MINISTER SECRETARY OF STATE, THE DUKE OF BASSANO

Moniteur, Friday 21, Saturday 22, Sunday 23, Tuesday 25 and Thursday 26 January 1814
Army of the North

The defection of eight battalions of the 3rd and 4th Foreign Regiments, and of two battalions composed of Dutch who made up the major portion of General Molitor's division, having left Holland without defence, and the towns of Amsterdam and of La Haye being in a state of insurrection, General Molitor immediately sent a garrison in Naarden, and General Rampon shut himself up with 4,000 men in Gorcum. Some troops were at once sent into Bois-le-Duc: Bergen op Zoom received a garrison of 5,000 men. The events happening with rapidity, terror took hold among those who, at Antwerp, directed the military dispositions. The evacuation of the important fortresses of Willemstad and of Brede was ordered. The enemy took advantage of such a mistake and at once took both these fortresses, and Willemstad became for him the point of support for his disembarkment. General Graham took advantage of this, and landed a column of English troops of 4,000 to 5,000 men. During the evacuation of Willemstad, we lost our head to such a point that we left there the powder, the artillery and a flotilla, the equipment of which was almost ready and was almost sufficient to defend the place. An investigation into this affair has been ordered. The Minister of War immediately ordered General Roguet to march on Brede and attempt to re-take this fortress before the enemy could supply it and establish himself solidly there.

On 22 December, General Roguet proceeded to the town of Brede, overthrew its advance posts, surrounded it and threw some shells in it; he had the hope of taking it, when learned than an English corps, having landed at Tholen, was advancing between him and Antwerp; he deemed it appropriate to get nearer this place, and took position at Hoogstraten.

General Maison was named commander of the 1st Corps of the army of Antwerp: he hastened to complete the stocking of Bergen op Zoom for nine months. The forts of Batz, Lillo and Liekenseek were provided with arms and provisions; Flessingue and Teerveer received rations for a year; and then the fortresses of the left bank of the Escaut, such as Ysendik, Hultz and the forts of the island of Cadzand, were furnished with complete armament and provisions. General Maison attended to the need to increase his corps with all the battalions that were almost completed in the fortresses of Flanders.

On 14 January, General Bülow debouched from Brede with a corps of 10,000 to 12,000 men, and proceeded to Hoogstraten. General Roguet had his left at

Wustvesel, his centre at Hoogstraten. The Aymard brigade, which formed his right, occupied Turnhout: it received the order to advance on Lier, and this kept it from taking part in the affair. An enemy column debouched by Meer, while another column of 12 battalions was marching on Wortel. General Roguet had placed a battalion of the 12th Tirailleurs [skirmishers] in the cemetery of Minderhout: this battalion repulsed all the enemy's attacks and covered itself with glory. The road of Meer was defended with equal success; the enemy was repeating his attacks on all the points of the line; he was repulsed everywhere with enormous losses, and without being able to deploy before Hoogstraten.

General Roguet having learned that night that an enemy column coming from Rosendäl, and made up of 4,000 English under the orders of Graham, was moving toward Antwerp, and ignoring the strength of the different enemy corps that were attacking him, judged it necessary to get closer to Antwerp, to better appreciate their deployment and to concentrate his defence; he proceeded on Winigeem, where he placed his right; his left joined the corps that had come from Antwerp, which occupied Merxen and Deurne. The day of the 12th was spent moving and making dispositions in order to receive the enemy well, who, after the enormous losses he had suffered on the 11th, was only proceeding tentatively.

On the 13th, at eight o'clock in the morning, the Bülow corps debouched by the roads of Braashet and Turnhout, while a column of light infantry arriving by Schoten was trying to separate General Roguet from the village of Deurne, defended by a brigade of the Young Guard. At the same moment, the Graham corps was attacking Merxen, which was occupied by four battalions of the 1st Corps and a naval works battalion. The cannonade was immediately engaged on all the line, and the enemy advanced in force on Winigeem: our artillery crushed him; the enemy was making great efforts and even sacrificed some soldiers in order to force the village.

General Roguet proceeded to the front with five battalions and completely repulsed the fight of the enemy. The death of General of Brigade Avy had caused some disorder on our left: a battalion of the 4th Light Infantry distinguished themselves by their good countenance and re-established order. The village of Merxen was occupied for a moment by the enemy. Our troops regrouped at Dame, and soon the enemy was repulsed everywhere; Bülow's corps quickly fell back on Turnhout, and Graham's corps by the road of Bergen op Zoom.

On the 12th, General Maison, deceived by false information, believing that the enemy was advancing on Diest and Louvain by the Campine, had taken with him the Aymard brigade of the corps of General Roguet, had joined it to the Barrois division that was in reserve at Liers, and with the cavalry had proceeded in the direction he presumed the enemy was taking. As soon as he recognized that the information he had received was false, he became certain that the victory was already determined and that the enemy was in full retreat. Without this circumstance, which momentarily deprived us of a part of our forces, it would have been possible, in briskly pursuing the enemy, to throw him back beyond the Waal and to raise the siege of Gorcum.

The troops of the enemy that are in the north are busy blockading Veselie, Naarden, Gorcum, Deventer and the Helden.

As soon as the brave Admiral Verhuel learned that the enemy had entered Holland, he pulled back to the Helder, sent troops to occupy the forts of Lasalle, Morland and other fortified points that cover the Helden and the Moerdijk. He was approached with all the measures possible to engage him to betray his duty. 'I have enough rations for ten months,' he said; 'I took an oath of loyalty to the Emperor of the French.'

The fine system of defence that protected the Helder was due to the great work of the Colonel of Engineers, Paris. If several millions had been spent, we gained the invaluable advantage of holding there the key to the Zuider Zee. It is because the Republic of Holland did not take that precaution that they lost two squadrons since 1793. The garrison of the Helder has made several sorties and has repulsed the enemy as far as Alkmaar. The Gorcum garrison has also, during the course of several sorties, caused the enemy many losses.

Army of the Duke of Tarentum

The Duke of Tarentum, who was charged with the defence of the Rhine as far as Nijmegen, repulsed all of the enemy's attacks. General Sebastiani, who was in charge of Cologne, has taken 5,000 to 6,000 prisoners in several circumstances. The Duke of Tarentum had the forts of Grave, Venloo Juliers and Maastricht set in condition of defence.

From the beginning of January, the enemy, having taken the offensive on Brede, under the orders of General Bülow, and on Mayence, under the orders of General Blücher, the Duke of Tarentum concentrated his forces; his headquarters was at Maastricht on the 14th, occupying Liège and Charlemont, and observing the right flank of General Blücher. On the 18th, his headquarters was at Namur.

Crossing of the Rhine by the Army said of Silesia, composed of Prussians and of Russians

On 1 January, the army of Silesia crossed the Rhine on several points. The corps that were part of this army proceeded, namely: the Russian division of General Langeron before Mayence with his advance guard on Trèves, and the divisions of Sacken and Yorck on the Sarre: the Kleist division in reserve. These four divisions, including the cavalry, can be estimated at 50,000 men.

The Duke of Ragusa retired before these corps without suffering any loss. He took position on the Sarre, had supplies brought to Sarrelouis and Bitche, advanced on Metz, and sojourned a few days before this town in order to evacuate all that was not necessary to its defence, and to complete stocking it for a year. He occupied Saint Mihiel and was in the front of Verdun on the 19th of this month, having had no significant encounters. The town of Verdun was well supplied, armed and in good state of defence.

The Sacken division was on Pont-à-Mousson, that of Yorck before Metz, that of Kleist before Thionville, and that of Langeron before Mayence.

The infantry of this army is entirely employed at blockading the fortresses.

The rigour of the season, the bad weather, the many bivouacs, have increased the ravage of the sick among these troops, whose health has already been altered by the fatigue of the campaign. The hospitals are full at the rear of the army, and the roads are covered with dead horses.

The Prefect and the Mayor of Metz, the Sub-Prefect of Thionville, and generally all of the population of the Messin country, have earned the praises of the Emperor.

Entry into Switzerland of the army of Prince Schwarzenberg, composed of Austrians, Russians, Bavarians, Württembergers and Badois

On 20 December, the Duke of Belluno had his headquarters at Strasburg. The 5th Corps of cavalry, with a division of infantry, occupied Colmar. The forts of Landau, Strasburg, Schelestadt, Neuf-Brisach and Huningue had been furnished with their supplies and armaments. Count Roederer, Commissioner Extraordinary, and Baron Belleville, Master of Petitions, had wanted to remain at Strasburg to arouse the National Guard.

The army of Schwarzenberg, evaluated at 100,000 men, including 15,000 Bavarians, 8,000 Württembergers, 4,000 Badeners and the Russian corps of Wittgenstein, entered Switzerland on 21 December. General Bubna, in command of the advance guard, proceeded to Berne, and from there to Geneva, where he arrived on the 28th. This fortress, which has an enclosure fortified with bastions, opened its gates, following the bad conduct of the prefect, the bad dispositions of the inhabitants and the madness prevalent at that moment. The magnificent lords of the small council believed the moment to be favourable for re-establishing their aristocracy, and a proclamation appeared, signed by all of them. But the democratic party became indignant of this usurpation: the Austrian General declared that he could not interfere in these quarrels, and that this was a French town that he occupied following the events of the war. The magnificent lords, after 24 hours had passed, came down from their siege of sovereigns: the French municipality reclaimed it functions and justice continued to be served in the name of the Emperor. As of 16 January, there was only one garrison of 800 Austrians in Geneva. The French advance posts were at a cannon-shot's distance of the town. Baron Finot, Prefect of the Mont Blanc territory, had rapidly organized some free-corps, and the levies in mass, the commandant of which had been taken by General of Division Count Dessaix. The Mont Blanc territory appeared to be sheltered from any assault. Fort Barreau had been supplied with provisions; the assembling of the troops of the line, the National Guard and the corps of volunteers that were forming at Chambéry increased everyday; it was already 8,000 men strong.

The department of Isère has again distinguished itself by the patriotism of which they have given proof at all times. The whole department raised up at the sound of the voice of the Commissioner Extraordinary, Count Saint-Vallier. General Marchand is commander of the National Guard and the levy in mass. On the 16th, we could count at Grenoble 15,000 men under arms: we were organizing there with great activity a park of 60 guns. The forts of Briançon, Fenestrelle and Mont-Dauphin were all supplied with all that was necessary.

The Drôme department, which had not thus far demonstrated the same ardor as the department of Isère, started to put itself in movement. The troops of line of Toulon and Marseille and the National Guard of Provence were marching to reinforce the army of the Dauphiné.

Some advance guard troops of General Bubna, having entered the Ain department, had occupied Bourg, after experiencing some resistance from the inhabitants.

On the 19th, the enemy's advance posts were located within three leagues of Lyon.

Marshal Duke of Castiglione had proceeded to the Dauphiné in order to rally all the troops and march in force on Lyon and Geneva. General Musnier occupied Lyon, and was to act on the right bank of the Saône.

The commissioner extraordinary Count Chaptal, and Count de Bondy, Prefect of the Rhône, did everything that we had the right to expect from them. The inhabitants of Lyon showed great ardour and patriotism. The town being threatened, many families had left, and it was estimated that the value of merchandise transported into the mountains was more than 100 millions.

From Bourg, Count Bubna sent some advance guards of light troops in all directions. Fifteen hussars presented themselves before Mâcon. There were troops and some National Guards there to defend the town; but the mayor of Mâcon and that of Saint Laurent betrayed the public's confidence and let the enemy occupy the bridge on the Saône with 50 men. On the 16th, the enemy's force at Mâcon was 300 cavalrymen. This conduct is an unforgettable task for the inhabitants of that town: it is in sharp contrast with the heroism and devotion of those of Châlons.

As an enemy party had presented itself in front of this latter town, the Châlonais had run to arm themselves; the National Guard of Autun marched to assist them; the inhabitants of the Charolais came down from the mountains; they pulled out four iron cannons from Creusot; the bridges were barricaded; some redoubts were built, and all was placed in a state of defence. As of the 18th, the enemy had been repulsed in all his attacks.

Another division of Prince Schwarzenberg's army had advanced on Besançon. Count Marulaz had taken command of the town. Seconded by Baron de Bry, Prefect of the Doubs, he had totally supplied Besançon in two days, which was armed and in a state of defence. General Marulaz sent out several parties, which surprised and slaughtered some enemy detachments. The Austrian troops that are before Besançon are estimated to be 15,000 to 16,000 men strong, and from where are sending parties in all directions.

One of these parties appeared before Dôle. One hundred and fifty men of cavalry sufficed to occupy that town. Having since then received reinforcements of infantry, they proceeded to Auxonne; but the garrison came out, defeated them and threw them back beyond Dôle.

The inhabitants of the small town of Saint Jean de Losne defended their bridge and took 14 prisoners: one squadron chief of the enemy was killed with a sabre hit, delivered by a retired officer who had placed himself at the head of the National Guard.

Another corps of Prince Schwarzenberg had advanced to Huningue, and after bombarding that place for four days, had converted the siege into a blockade.

As of the 17th, the news from Huningue, Schelestadt and all the fortresses of the Rhine was very satisfying.

Some troops of the same army had advanced before Béfort, and after losing 1,500 men in a brisk attack had also converted the siege into a blockade.

At the date of the 16th, the news from that place was satisfying.

Another of Prince Schwarzenberg's army corps had marched on Épinal, and from there on Nancy.

On the 19th, his advance posts were before Toul. The Duke of Belluno was behind the Meuse at Void, occupying Commercy and joining with the Duke of Ragusa.

On the 12th, the Duke of Treviso was at Langres. He had in his presence the corps of General Giulay, which is also part of the army of Prince Schwarzenberg.

On the 13th and 14th, the Duke of Treviso ordered a march against the enemy's advance guard, 1,800 men strong. Three hundred chasseurs of the Young Guard's infantry, led by people from the country, at one o'clock in the morning advanced into the rear of the enemy, which had just taken up arms, approached it with the bayonet, killed 500 to 600 men and took 150 prisoner.

On the 19th, according to the general dispositions, the Duke of Treviso had taken position at Chaumont, where two new divisions and a park of 70 pieces of artillery had joined him.

Two Württemberger battalions coming from Épinal had compromised themselves, and the Duke of Treviso, after cannonading them for ten minutes, had them approached at the point of the bayonet by 60 grenadiers, volunteers of the Guard. These two battalions were repulsed by cold steel, by 60 men and thrown into the river. We took 80 prisoners.

Some reserve camps are being formed at Meaux, at Soissons, at Châlons, at Troyes and at Arcis-Sur-Aube.

One hundred squadrons of reserve cavalry are gathering at Meaux and at Melun, under the command of Generals of Division Bordesoulle and Pajol.

The National Guards of Normandy, of Poitou and of Brittany are marching to reinforce the camps of Meaux, of Soissons and of Troyes.

A park of 600 pieces of artillery, under the orders of General of Division Ruty, is put together at Châlons.

The moment has come when, from all the points of this vast empire, the French who wish to promptly free the territory of the fatherland, and wish to conserve the national honour inherited from our fathers, must take up arms and march towards the camps, which are the meeting place of the brave and real French.

The enemy announces that he invades France with 200,000 men. He has 20,000 in the Brabant; 50,000 in the army said of Silesia, before Mayence, Sarrelouis, Luxemburg, Thionville and Metz, and 100,000 in the army of Prince Schwarzenberg, who is at Bourg, before Besançon, before Huningue, before Schelestadt, before Béfort and the area of Langres.

Army of Italy

On the 12th, the Viceroy had his headquarters at Verona. He was in communication with Venice, which has a numerous garrison; Palma-Nova and Osoppo are fully supplied for ten months, as are Mantua and Legnago. The army of the Viceroy is of 60,000 men present under arms, not including the garrisons.

The army of reserve of Alexandria is 24,000 men strong. This fortress is completely armed and supplied, as is the citadel of Torino.

The armies of Italy are going to start their movements.

The conscription of 1815 is being raised in Piedmont to reinforce the army of reserve of Alexandria. The inhabitants of the departments beyond the Alps are showing their best spirit.

Frontiers of Spain

Lord Wellington was announcing everywhere that he wanted to force the crossings of the Nive and of the Adour, surround the town of Bayonne and march on Bordeaux; he totally failed in his project: the combats that took place from 9–13 December have been to his disadvantage; he had more than 15,000 men disabled; our loss has not been one quarter of that number. The consternation is in the English army. Lord Wellington limits his pretensions and is working to retrench all of the parts of his line.

On 20 December, a numerous garrison occupied Bayonne; three divisions of the army, under the orders of General Belle, occupied the retrenched camps and were finishing the work; General Clauzel was rapidly advancing, with three other divisions, on the left bank of the Bidousse by Peyrhorade; a large corps covered the banks of the Adour and the Bidousse.

The Duke of Dalmatia took his headquarters at Peyrhorade, to be within range to direct his movements on the right flank of the enemy.

During the last days of December, the position of the English became more and more critical: the lack of food was taking its toll; their convoys, beaten by the storm, ran aground on the coast of the Landes; our detachments were collecting cargo of cattle, salt provisions and clothing; at Bayonne, we even made some distributions of compressed hay that had been sent from England in the cargo.

The position taken by General Clauzel worried Lord Wellington; he feared for the safety of his posts at Saint Jean de Luz, where his headquarters was. He ordered the attack of Saint Jean Pied de Port, but he was repulsed. General Harispe had taken the command of our extreme left, organized the levy of the Basques, and each day he dispersed the enemy foragers.

On 1 January, an English detachment presented itself with cannon on the left bank of the Adour, in front of the island of Broc; he was immediately repulsed and constrained to abandon the banks with much loss.

The Duke of Dalmatia, assured of the good defence of Bayonne and the Adour, placed General Clauzel behind Joyeuse. On 3 January, we chased an English regiment from the old fortress of Clarence. General Paris advanced across from Bouloc, where the enemy had a strong detachment. The days of 4 and 5 January were passed doing manoeuvres in tranquillity; our light cavalry, filled with ardour, took a few prisoners and worried the enemy very much. Lord Wellington had hastened from Saint Jean de Luz; he had left only a few detachments before Bayonne and the Adour; his line formed on Hasparren.

On the 6th, he deployed 20,000 men, and at three in the afternoon he attacked a battalion of the 6th Division, placed before the old fort of Clarence as an advance post. This battalion withdrew in order; the two armies remained in the presence of each other until ten o'clock on the morning of the 7th; the battle appeared imminent; but the English army retreated in different directions, and completely disappeared: Wellington had just become aware that the part of the French army that had stayed in the retrenchments of Bayonne was debouching on his rear, and was going to cut off his retreat on Saint Jean de Luz.

Bayonne is now one of the most formidable boulevards of the Empire.

The misunderstanding between the Spanish and English troops seems to increase each day.

24 January 1814
His Majesty the Emperor and King, having to leave at once to place himself at the head of his armies, conferred, for the duration of his absence, the regency to Her Majesty the Empress-Queen, by patent letters dated yesterday the 23rd.

The same day, Her Majesty the Empress-Queen gave an oath, as Regent, in the hands of the Emperor, and in a council composed of the French Princes, the grand dignitaries, the ministers of the cabinet and the ministers of state.

25 January 1814
This morning at seven, His Majesty the Emperor and King left to go place himself at the head of his armies.

Moniteur, 29 January 1814
The enemy had been here for two days, committing the ugliest vexations: it respected neither age nor sex; the women and the old men were exposed to its violence and its outrages. The wife of *Sieur* Canard, a rich farmer, 50 years old, died of the bad treatment she received: her husband, over 70 years old, is near death. It would be much too painful to enter in this report the list of all the other victims. The arrival of the French troops entering our town yesterday put an end

to our misfortunes. The enemy tried to show some resistance, but was soon routed and suffered considerable loss. The arrival of the Emperor gave way to some very touching scenes. The entire population gathered around him; all the horrors seemed forgotten. He gave us back the security for all that is very dear to us. An old colonel, Mr Bouland, 70 years old, threw himself at his feet, which he covered with tears of joy. He was expressing, all at the same time, the pain felt by a brave soldier who saw the enemy defiling his natal land, and the happiness at seeing them flee before the Imperial Eagles.

We learn that the same enthusiasm that had burst out here has been manifested at Bar upon the arrival of our troops. The enemy had already fled.

Moniteur, 5 February 1814

Her Majesty the Empress-Queen and Regent has received the following news of the situation of the armies as of 3 February 1814:

The Emperor arrived at Vitry on 26 January.

General Blücher, with the army of Silesia, had crossed the Marne and was marching on Troyes. On the 27th, the enemy entered Brienne and continued its march; but it had to lose some time in re-establishing the bridge of Lesmont on the Aube.

On the 27th, the Emperor ordered that Saint Dizier be attacked. The Duke of Belluno presented himself before that town. General Duhesme overthrew the enemy's rearguard, which was still there, and took several hundred prisoner. At eight in the morning the Emperor arrived at Saint Dizier; it is difficult to portray the intoxication and joy of the inhabitants at this moment. The excesses of all kinds committed by the enemy, and especially by the Cossacks, are beyond all description.

On the 28th, the Emperor advanced on Montierender.

On the 29th, at eight in the morning General Grouchy, who commands the cavalry, gave information that General Milhaud, with the 5th Corps of cavalry, was between Maizières and Brienne in presence of the enemy's army, commanded by General Blücher, and which was estimated at 40,000 Russians and Prussians; the Russians are commanded by General Sacken.

At four o'clock the small town of Brienne was attacked. General Lefebvre-Desnouettes, commanding a division of the cavalry of the Guard, and Generals Grouchy and Milhaud executed several fine charges on the right of the road and made themselves masters of the heights of Perthe. The Prince of the Moskova put himself at the head of six battalions in close columns, and advanced on the town by the road of Maizières. General Château, chief of staff of the Duke of Belluno, at the head of two battalions, turned to the right and entered the castle of Brienne through the park.

At this moment the Emperor directed a column on the road to Bar-sur-Aube, which appeared to be the enemy's point of retreat; the attack was vigorous and the resistance obstinate. The enemy did not expect so severe an attack, and had only time to recall its parks from the bridge of Lesmont, where it reckoned on crossing the Aube, in order to march forward. This countermarch had greatly blocked it.

Night did not put an end to the combat. The Decouz division of the Young Guard, and a brigade of the Meunier division, were engaged: the great number of the enemy's forces, and the fine situation of Brienne, afforded it many advantages; but the capture of the castle, which it had neglected to guard in force, occasioned the loss of these advantages.

Towards eight o'clock, the enemy, seeing that it could not maintain its position, set fire to the town, and the flames spread with rapidity, all the houses being of wood.

Profiting from this event, the enemy endeavoured to retake the castle, which the brave Battalion Chief of the 56th defended with intrepidity. He covered with dead all the approaches to the castle, and particularly the staircases on the side of the park. This last defeat decided the enemy's retreat, which was favoured by the conflagration of the town.

On the 30th, at eleven in the morning, General Grouchy and the Duke of Belluno pursued the enemy beyond the village of La Rothière, where they took a position.

The 31st was employed by us in repairing the bridge of Lesmont-sur-Aube, the Emperor wishing to advance on Troyes in order to operate on the columns, which were directing their march on Sens, by Bar-sur-Aube and the route of Auxerre.

The bridge of Lesmont could not be re-established until 1 February, in the morning. A part of our troops instantly filed across it.

At three o'clock in the afternoon, the enemy, having been reinforced by its whole army, marched on La Rothière and Dienville, which we still occupied. Our rearguard kept in good order. General Duhesme distinguished himself in preserving La Rothière, and General Gérard in preserving Dienville. The Austrian corps of General Giulay, which endeavoured to cross from the left bank to the right and to force the bridge, had several of its battalions destroyed. The Duke of Belluno held the whole day at the hamlet of La Gibérie, in spite of the enormous disproportion of his forces to those of the enemy by which he was attacked.

This day, in which our rearguard supported itself in a vast plain against the enemy's whole army, five times its own force, is one of the finest achievements of the French army.

In the midst of the obscurity of the night a battery of artillery of the Guard, following the movements of a column of cavalry that rushed forward to repel a charge of the enemy, mistook its way and was taken. When the cannoneers perceived the ambush into which they had fallen, and saw that they had not time to form themselves in battery, they immediately formed in squadron, attacked the enemy, and saved their horses and harness. They lost 15 men, killed or taken prisoner.

At ten o'clock at night, the Prince of Neufchâtel visited the posts and found the two armies so near each other that he frequently mistook the posts of the enemy for our own. One of his aides-de-camp, finding himself within ten paces of a mounted sentry, was made prisoner. The same accident happened to many Russian officers who were carrying orders and who fell into our posts, thinking that they had reached their own.

There were few prisoners taken on either side. We have taken 250.

On 2 February, at daybreak, all the rearguard of the army was in battle in front of Brienne. It took successively different positions, in order to accomplish the passage of the bridge of Lesmont, and rejoin the rest of the army.

The Duke of Ragusa, who had taken up a position on the bridge of Rosnay, was attacked by an Austrian corps, which had passed behind the woods. He repulsed it, took 300 prisoner and charged the enemy beyond the little river of Voire.

On the 3rd, at noon, the Emperor entered Troyes.

We have lost in the battle of Brienne the brave General Baste. General Lefebvre-Desnouettes has been wounded by a bayonet thrust. General Forestier has been severely wounded. Our loss in these two days may amount to between 2- or 3,000 men, killed or wounded. That of the enemy is at least double.

A division detached from the corps of the enemy's army, which observes Metz, Thionville and Luxemburg, and amounting to 12 battalions, has advanced on Vitry [le François]. The enemy intended to enter that town, which General Montmarie and the inhabitants defended. It was in vain that the enemy threw shells in order to intimidate the inhabitants; it was received by cannon-shot, and driven back a league and a half. The Duke of Tarentum arrived at Châlons, and marched on that division.

On the morning of the 4th, Count de Stadion, Count Razoumofski, Lord Castlereagh and Baron de Humboldt reached Châtillon-sur-Seine, where the Duke of Vicenza had already arrived. The first visits were made on both sides, and on the evening of the same day the first conference of the plenipotentiaries was to take place.

Moniteur, 12 February 1814
Her Majesty the Empress-Queen and Regent has received today the following intelligence regarding the situation of the army.
Yesterday at Champaubert, the Emperor attacked the enemy, consisting of 12 regiments and having 40 cannon.

General-in-chief Ousouwieff has been taken, with all his generals, all his colonels, officers, cannon, caissons and baggage.

We have taken 6,000 prisoner; the remainder were driven into a pond or killed on the battlefield.

The Emperor briskly pursues General Sacken, who is separated from General Blücher.

Our loss has been extremely light; we have not 200 men to regret.

His Majesty King Joseph today, reviewing the grenadiers of the National Guard of Paris, was pleased to communicate this news to them.

Moniteur, 13 February 1814
Mr Alfred de Montesquiou, aide-de-camp to the Prince of Neufchâtel, dispatched by His Majesty the Emperor, has brought to her Majesty the Empress-Queen and Regent the following news:
On 11 February, at daybreak, the Emperor, having left Champaubert after the day of the 10th, pushed a corps towards Châlons to keep in check the enemy's columns that had thrown themselves on this side.

With the rest of his army he took the road to Montmirail.

A league beyond he met the corps of General Blücher, and after an action of two hours all of the enemy's army was overthrown.

Never did our troops display more ardour.

The enemy, everywhere broken, is completely routed: infantry, artillery, ammunition, all is in our power or overthrown.

The results are immense; the Russian army is destroyed.

The Emperor is extremely well, and we have lost no person of rank.

Moniteur, 14 February 1814
Her Majesty the Empress-Queen and Regent has received the following news of the situation of the armies:
On 12 February His Majesty followed up his successes. Blücher endeavoured to

gain Chateau-Thierry. His troops were driven from position to position.

A whole corps, which had remained united and which protected his retreat, was taken.

This rearguard was composed of four Russian battalions, three Prussian battalions and three pieces of artillery. The general who commanded it was also taken.

Our troops entered Chateau-Thierry pell-mell with the enemy, and are pursuing, on the road to Soissons, the wrecks of this army, which is in dreadful confusion.

The results of today, the 12th, are 30 cannon and an innumerable quantity of baggage wagons.

The number of prisoners was already 3,000; more are brought in every minute. We have still two hours' daylight.

Among the prisoners are five or six generals, who are sent to Paris.

It is believed that the General-in-Chief Sacken has been killed.

~—

Moniteur, 16 February 1814

Her Majesty the Empress-Queen and Regent has received the following account of the situation of the armies as of 7 February:

On 3 February, two hours after his arrival at Troyes, His Majesty had the Duke of Treviso depart to Maison Blanches. An Austrian division, commanded by Prince Maurice Lichtenstein, had advanced to this point, which is two leagues from the town; it was vigorously repulsed and driven two leagues beyond.

On the evening of the 4th, the headquarters of the Emperor of Russia were at Lusigny, near Vandövre, two leagues from Troyes, where the Russian Guard and the enemy's army was. The enemy intended to enter Troyes that evening. It marched on the bridge of La Guillotière, where it found a warm resistance. Its first attack was repulsed: some cavalry who were made prisoners told it that the Emperor was at Troyes: then it thought it necessary to take other measures. At the same moment the Duke of Treviso caused an attack to be made on the bridge of Clerey, which was occupied by the division of General Bianchi. The enemy was driven away. General of the Division Briche made a charge with his dragoons, in which he took 160 men and killed 100.

On the 5th, the Emperor was preparing to cross the bridge of La Guillotière and attack the enemy, when His Majesty learned that it had sounded a retreat and fell back one march towards Vandövre.

On the 6th, arrangements were made to menace Bar-sur-Seine. Some attacks took place on that road. We took from the enemy 30 men, one piece of artillery and a caisson.

During this time the army started marching for Nogent, in order to fall on the enemy's columns, which have occupied Châlons and Vitry and which threatened Paris from Ferté-sous-Jouarre and Meaux.

On the 7th, in the morning, the Duke of Tarentum had his headquarters near Chaville, between Épernay and Châlons. The élite divisions of the National Guard arriving at Montereau from Normandy and Brittany put themselves in motion under the command of General Pajol.

The division of the army of Spain, under the command of General Laval, is arriving at Provins; the others follow. These troops are composed of soldiers who took part in the campaigns in Austria and Poland. They are replaced in the army of Spain by the five divisions of reserve.

At noon today, the 7th, the Emperor arrived at Nogent.

All is in motion to manoeuvre.

The inhabitants are exasperated to the highest degree. The enemy everywhere commits the most horrible excesses.

All measures are taken for surrounding it as soon as it withdraws one step.

Millions of arms wait only for the moment to be raised. The sacred land that the enemy has violated will become a land of fire that will devour it.

Battle of Montmirail

11 February 1814

Her Majesty the Empress-Queen and Regent, has received the following news of the situation of the armies to 12 February 1814:

On the 10th the Emperor had his headquarters at Sézanne.

The Duke of Tarentum was at Meaux, having caused the bridges of La Ferté and Tréport to be cut down.

General Sacken and General Yorck were at La Ferté, General Blücher at Vertus and General Alsuffiew at Champaubert. The army of Silesia was only three marches from Paris. This army, under the commander-in-chief General Blücher, was composed of the corps of Sacken and Langeron, forming 60 regiments of Russian infantry, and the élite of the Prussian army.

At daybreak on the 10th, the Emperor advanced to the heights of Saint Prix to cut the army of General Blücher in two. At ten o'clock, the Duke of Ragusa crossed the marshes of Saint Gond and attacked the village of Baye. The 9th Russian Corps, under General Alsuffiew, 12 regiments strong, was deployed and presented a battery of 24 cannon. The Lagrange and Ricard divisions, with the cavalry of the first Corps, turned the enemy's position by his right. At one o'clock in the afternoon we were masters of the village of Baye.

At two o'clock, the Imperial Guard deployed in the fine plains between Baye and Champaubert. The enemy began its retreat. The Emperor ordered General Girardin, with two squadrons of the Guard Service Squadrons, to put himself at the head of the 1st Corps of cavalry and to turn the enemy in order to cut it off from the road to Châlons. The enemy, which perceived this movement, fell into disorder. The Duke of Ragusa carried the village of Champaubert. At the same time, the cuirassiers charged on the right and pressed the Russians against a wood and a lake, between the road to Épernay and that to Châlons. The enemy had but little cavalry. Seeing itself without retreat, its masses became confused; artillery, cavalry, infantry, all fled pell-mell into the wood; 2,000 men were drowned in the lake; 30 pieces of artillery and 200 carriages were taken. The General-in-Chief, the generals, the colonels, more than 100 officers and 400 men were made prisoners.

This corps of two divisions and 12 regiments ought to have consisted of 18,000, but sickness, long marches and battles had reduced it to 8,000; scarcely 1,500 escaped by means of the woods and the darkness. General Blücher remained at his headquarters at Vertus, where he witnessed the disasters of this part of his army without being able to remedy them.

Not a man of the Guard was engaged, except two of the four service squadrons, who behaved valiantly. The cuirassiers of the 1st Corps of cavalry had displayed the rarest intrepidity.

At eight o'clock in the evening, General Nansouty having departed on the causeway, advanced on Montmirail with the division of the cavalry of the Guard of Generals Colbert and Laferrière, and took the town and 600 Cossacks who occupied it.

The 11th, at five in the morning, the division of cavalry of General Guyot also advanced on Montmirail. Several divisions of infantry were delayed by being obliged to wait for their artillery. The roads from Sézanne to Champaubert are awful; our artillery would not have passed them but for the diligence of the cannoneers, and by the assistance furnished by the inhabitants, who brought their horses.

The action at Champaubert, where a part of the Russian army was destroyed, did not cost us more than 200 men killed or wounded.

General of Division Count Lagrange is among the latter, having a slight wound in the head.

At ten in the morning on the 11th, the Emperor arrived half a league in advance of Montmirail. General Nansouty was in his position with the cavalry of the Guard, and kept in check the army of Sacken, which began to show itself. Informed of the disasters of a part of the Russian army, this general had left La Ferté-sous-Jouarre on the 10th, at nine in the evening, and marched all night. General Yorck has also left Chateau-Thierry. At eleven in the morning of the 11th, he began to form, and all foreboded the battle of Montmirail, the issue of which was of such vast importance. The Duke of Ragusa, with his corps and the first Corps of cavalry, had placed his headquarters at Étoges, on the road to Châlons.

The Ricard division and the Old Guard arrived at ten in the morning. The Emperor ordered the Prince of the Moskova to line the village of Marchais with troops, by which it seemed the enemy's intention to debouche. This village was defended by the brave division of General Ricard with rare firmness; it was taken and retaken several times during the course of the day.

At noon the Emperor ordered General Nansouty to advance to the right, cutting off the road to Château-Thierry, and formed the sixteen battalions of the 1st division of the Old Guard, under the command of General Friant, in a single column along the road, the battalion columns being 100 paces from each other.

During this time our batteries of artillery successively arrived. At three o'clock the Duke of Treviso, with the 16 battalions of the 2nd Division of the Old Guard that had left Sézanne in the morning, debouched on Montmirail.

The Emperor would have wished to wait for the arrival of the other divisions, but night was approaching. He ordered General Friant to march with four battalions of the Old Guard, two of the 2nd Regiment of Gendarmerie, and two of the 2nd Regiment of Chasseurs, on the farm of Épine-aux-Bois, which was the key of the position, and to carry it. The Duke of Treviso, with six battalions of the 2nd Division of the Old Guard advanced to the right of General Friant's attack.

The success of the day depended on the position of the farm of Épine-aux-Bois. The enemy understood this. It had placed 40 pieces of artillery there, had lined the hedges with a triple row of skirmishers, and formed behind masses of infantry.

Meantime, to render this attack easier, the Emperor ordered General Nansouty to extend his line to the right, which made the enemy apprehensive of being cut off and forced to uncover a part of its centre to cover its right. At the same time he ordered General Ricard to yield a part of the village of Marchais, which also induced the enemy to uncover its centre to reinforce this attack, on the success of which it supposed the gaining of the battle depended.

As soon as General Friant had begun his movement, and the enemy had weakened its centre to take advantage of its apparent success, which it believed real, General Friant attacked the farm of Haute-Épine with the four battalions of the Old Guard. They came up to the enemy at full charge, and produced on it the effect of the head of Medusa. The Prince of the Moskova marched first and showed them the road to honour. The skirmishers retired in terror on the masses of infantry that were attacked. The artillery could no longer play a role; the firing of small arms became dreadful, and success was in the balance; but at the same moment General Guyot, at the head of the 1st Regiment of Lancers, old dragoons and old grenadiers of the Imperial Guard, filed along the high road in full trot, and with cries of Long Live the Emperor! passed to the right of Haute-Épine. They fell on the rear of the masses of infantry, broke them, threw them into disorder and killed all that were not taken prisoner. The Duke of Treviso, with six battalions of the division of General Michel, seconded there the attack of the Old Guard, reached the wood, carried the village of Fontanelli and took a whole park of the enemy.

The division of the Guards of Honour filed off after the Old Guard on the high road, and having arrived at the height of Épine-aux-Bois, turned to the left to carry what had advanced on the village of Marchais. General Bertrand, Grand Marshal of the Palace, and the Duke of Danzig, at the head of two battalions of the Old Guard, marched on the village, and placed it between two fires. All who were in it were killed or taken.

In less than a quarter of an hour a profound silence succeeded to the noise of the cannon and a dreadful fire of musketry. The enemy no longer sought safety but in flight: generals, officers, soldiers, infantry, cavalry and artillery, all fled pell-mell.

At eight in the evening, the night being obscure, it was necessary to take a position. The Emperor placed his headquarters at the farm of Épine-aux-Bois.

General Michel of the Guard has been wounded by a bullet in the arm. Our loss amounts at most to 1,000 killed or wounded. That of the enemy is at least 8,000 killed or prisoners. We have taken many cannon, and six stands of colours. This memorable day, which confounds the pride and boasting of the enemy, has annihilated the élite of the Russian army. A quarter of our army has not been engaged.

At nine in the morning the next day, the 12th, the Duke of Treviso followed the enemy on the road of Chateau-Thierry. The Emperor, with two divisions of the cavalry of the Guard, and some battalions, went to Vieux-Maisons, and from there took the road which goes straight to Chateau-Thierry. The enemy covered its retreat with eight battalions, which arrived late the preceding evening, and had not been engaged. It supported them with a few squadrons, and three cannon. Having arrived at the small village of Coquerets, it appeared determined to defend the position that is behind the rivulet, and to cover the road to Château-Thierry.

A company of the Old Guard marched on La Petite-Nue and overthrew the enemy's skirmishers, who were pursued to its last position. Six battalions of the Old Guard, at proper distances for deploying, occupied the plain on both sides of the road.

General Nansouty, with the divisions of cavalry of General Laferrière and Defrance, had orders to make a movement to the right, and march between Chateau-Thierry and the enemy's rearguard. This movement was executed with equal skill and intrepidity.

The enemy's cavalry marched from all points on his left to oppose the French cavalry. It was overthrown, and obliged to disappear from the battlefield.

The brave General Letort, with the dragoons of the 2nd Division of the Guard, after having repulsed the enemy's cavalry, charged on the flanks and rears of eight masses of infantry that formed the enemy's rearguard. This division, burning with desire to equal what the light horse, the dragoon and the mounted grenadiers of General Guyot had done the preceding evening, surrounded those masses on all sides and made a horrible carnage among them. The three pieces of artillery and the Russian General Freudenreich, who commanded this rear guard, were taken. All who composed its battalions have been killed or taken prisoner. The number of prisoners taken in this brilliant affair amounts to more than 2,000. Colonel Curley of the 10th Hussars distinguished himself. We then arrived on the heights of Chateau-Thierry, from where we saw the remainder of that army fleeing in the greatest disorder and with all haste gaining its bridges. The great roads were cut off from them; they sought their salvation on the right bank of the Marne. Prince William of Prussia, who had remained at Chateau-Thierry with a reserve of 2,000 men, advanced to the head of the suburbs to protect the flight of this disorganized mass. Two battalions of the Guard arrived at full charge. At the sight of them, the suburbs' left bank was cleared; the enemy burnt its bridges, and unmasked a battery of 12 cannon on the right bank: 500 men of the reserve of Prince William were taken.

On the 12th in the evening, the Emperor had his headquarters in the small castle of Nesles.

At daybreak on the 13th, we were busy repairing the bridges of Château-Thierry.

The enemy not being able to retreat either on the road of Épernay, from which it was cut off, or by that which passes through the town of Soissons, which we occupy, has taken the back road in the direction of Reims. The inhabitants assert that of all the army not 10,000 men have passed through Chateau-Thierry, and they in the greatest disorder. A few days before they had seen it flourishing and full of boasting. General Yorck said that ten howitzers would be sufficient to render him master of Paris. In going, these troops only talked of Paris; on returning, it was peace that they invoked.

One cannot form an idea of the excesses committed by the Cossacks; there are no vexations, cruelties, crimes, which those hordes of barbarians have not committed. The peasantry pursue them, track them in the woods like ferocious beasts, seize them and bring them to wherever there are French troops. Yesterday they led more than 300 of them to Vieux-Maisons. All those who hid themselves in the woods to escape the conquerors fell into their hands, and augment at each moment the number of prisoners.

Her Majesty the Empress-Queen and Regent has received the following news from the army, to the morning of 15 February 1814:
On the 13th, at three in the afternoon, the bridge of Château-Thierry was re-established. The Duke of Treviso crossed the Marne and put himself in pursuit of the enemy, who, in frightful disorder, appeared to have retired on Soissons and Reims by the crossroad of La Fère, in Tardenois.

General Blücher, Commander-in-Chief of all the army of Silesia, had constantly remained at Vertus during the three days that have annihilated his army. He collected 1,200 men of the remains of General Alsuffiew's corps, beaten at Champaubert, which he united to a Russian division of the corps of Langeron, arrived from Mayence and commanded by Lieutenant General Ouroussov. He was too weak to attempt anything, but on the 13th he was joined by a Prussian corps of

General Kleist composed of four brigades. He then put himself at the head of these 20,000 men and marched against the Duke of Ragusa, who still occupied Étoges. In the night of the 13th and 14th, not deeming his forces sufficient to meet the enemy, the Duke of Ragusa put himself in retreat and supported himself on Montmirail, where he was in person on the 14th, at seven in the morning.

The Emperor set out the same day from Château-Thierry at four in the morning, and at eight arrived at Montmirail. He immediately attacked the enemy, who had just taken up a position with the body of his troops at the village of Vauchamps. The Duke of Ragusa attacked this village. General Grouchy, at the head of the cavalry, turned the enemy's right by the villages and the woods and advanced a league beyond the enemy's position. While the village of Vauchamps was vigorously attacked, and vigorously defended, taken and re-taken several times, General Grouchy arrived at the rear of the enemy, surrounded and sabred three squares and backed the rest into the woods. At the same moment the Emperor caused a charge to be made from our right by his four service squadrons, commanded by the Squadron Chief of the Guard, Labiffe. This charge was as brilliant as it was fortunate. A square of 2,000 men was pierced and taken. All the cavalry of the Guard then arrived at a sharp trot, and the enemy was pushed sword in its back. At two o'clock we were at the village of Fromentières; the enemy had lost 6,000 men taken prisoner, 10 flags and 3 cannon.

The Emperor ordered General Grouchy to advance on Champaubert, a league in rear of the enemy. In fact the enemy, continuing its retreat, arrived on that point at night. It was surrounded on all sides, and all would have been taken had the bad state of the roads permitted 12 pieces of light artillery to follow the cavalry of General Grouchy. Nevertheless, though the night was dark, three squares of the enemy's infantry were broken, killed or taken, and the others were briskly pursued as far as Étoges; the cavalry also took three pieces of artillery. The Russian division formed the rearguard of the enemy; it was attacked by the 1st Regiment of the Marine [infantry] of the Duke of Ragusa, charged with the bayonet, broken, and lost 1,000 prisoners, including Lieutenant-General Ouroussov, who commanded it, and several colonels.

The results of this brilliant day are 10,000 prisoners, 10 cannon, 10 flags and a great number of the enemy killed.

Our loss does not exceed 300 or 400 men, killed or wounded, which is owing to the boldness with which our troops attacked the enemy, and the superiority of our cavalry, which convinced the enemy as soon as it saw it to put its artillery in retreat; so that it marched constantly exposed to the fire of 60 pieces of artillery, while, of the 60 cannon which it had, it opposed us with only two or three.

The Prince of Neufchâtel, the Grand Master of the Palace, Count Bertrand, the Duke of Danzig and the Prince of the Moskova were constantly at the head of the troops.

General Grouchy bestows the highest praise on the Saint-Germain and Doumerc divisions of cavalry. The cavalry of the Guard covered itself with glory; nothing could equal its intrepidity. General Lion of the Guard was slightly wounded. The Duke of Ragusa makes particular mention of the 1st Regiment of Marine; the rest of the infantry, both of the Guard and the Line, did not fire a shot.

Thus this army of Silesia, composed of the Russian corps of Sacken and Langeron, the Prussian corps of Yorck and Kleist, and about 80,000 strong, was in four days beaten, dispersed, annihilated, without a general action, and without occasioning any loss proportioned to such great results.

Moniteur, *18 February 1814*

Her Majesty the Empress-Queen and Regent has received the following news from the army, to 17 February 1814 in the morning:

The Emperor, in setting out from Nogent on the 9th to manoeuvre on the enemy's corps which was advancing by La Ferté and Meaux on Paris, left the corps of the Duke of Belluno and of General Gérard before Nogent; the 7th Corps of the Duke of Reggio at Provins in charge of the defence of the bridges of Bray and Montereau, and General Pajol near Montereau and Melun.

The Duke of Belluno, having received information that several divisions of the Austrian army had marched from Troyes during the day on the 10th to advance on Nogent, had his army corps re-cross the Seine, leaving General Bourmont with 1,200 men at Nogent for the defence of the town.

The enemy presented itself on the 11th to enter Nogent. It renewed its attacks all the day, and always in vain; it was briskly repulsed with the loss of 1,500 men killed or wounded. General Bourmont had barricaded the streets, crenellated the houses and taken every measure for a vigorous defence. This general, who is an officer of distinction, was wounded in the knee; Colonel Ravier replaced him. The enemy renewed the attack on the 12th, but still to no purpose. Our young troops covered themselves with glory.

These two days have cost the enemy more than 2,000 men.

The Duke of Belluno, having learned that the enemy had crossed at Bray, judged it proper to cause the bridge of Nogent to be destroyed, and marched on Nangis. The Duke of Reggio ordered the bridges of Montereau and Melun to be blown up, and retired on the river Yères.

On the 16th, the Emperor arrived at the Yères, and marched his headquarters to Guignes.

The evening of the battle of Vauchamps (the 14th), the Duke of Ragusa ordered the attack on the enemy at eight o'clock at Étoges; he took nine pieces of artillery from it, and he has finished the destruction of the Russian division: there were counted on this point alone of the battlefield 1,300 dead.

The successes obtained at the battle of Vauchamps have been much more considerable than was announced.

The exasperation of the inhabitants of this country is at its height. The atrocities committed by the Cossacks surpass all that can be imagined. In their ferocious intoxication they have carried their indecent assaults on women of 60 years and young girls of 12; they have plundered and destroyed the habitations. The peasants, breathing only vengeance, conducted by old retired military men and armed with muskets of the enemy collected on the battlefield, beat the woods and lay hands on all that they meet. They estimate already those that they have taken at more than 2,000; they have killed several hundred of them. The frightened Russians surrender to our columns to find asylum. The same causes will produce the same effects throughout the Empire; and those armies that entered, they said, in our country to carry peace, happiness, the sciences and the arts, shall find in it their annihilation.

Letters from the army, written from Nangis on the 17th, announce that the Emperor, who had attacked the enemy, had in his power at this time 6,000 prisoners, among whom were several generals and a great number of officers, plus 14 pieces of artillery.

His Majesty continues his successes.

Today at noon, 6,000 prisoners, taken yesterday morning in the battle of Nangis, will arrive in Paris, by the gateway of Charenton.

Moniteur, 20 February 1814

The Emperor ordered a march in the morning of the 18th on the bridges of Bray and Montereau.

The Duke of Reggio started towards Provins.

His Majesty having been informed that the corps of General Wrede and of the Württembergers was in position at Montereau, headed there with the corps of the Duke of Belluno and that of General Gérard, the Guard on foot as well as on horse.

General Pajol was marching from Melun to Montereau.

The enemy defended the position.

It was overthrown so quickly that the town and the bridges on the Yonne and the Seine were taken with vigorous force and are in such great shape we are able to cross them to follow the enemy.

At this moment we have about 3,000 Bavarians and Württembergers prisoners, one of which is a general, and five cannon.

Moniteur, 21 February 1814

Her Majesty the Empress-Queen and Regent has received the following news of the situation of the armies to 19 February 1814:

The Duke of Ragusa was marching on Châlons, when he learned that a column of the Russian Imperial Guard composed of two divisions of grenadiers was marching on Montmirail. He faced about, marched on the enemy, took 300 men, repulsed it on Sézanne, from where the movements of the Emperor have compelled this corps to proceed by forced marches towards Troyes.

Count Grouchy, with the division of infantry of General Leval and three divisions of the second Corps of cavalry, was passing la Ferté-sous-Jouarre.

The advanced posts of the Duke of Treviso had entered Soissons.

On the 17th, at daybreak, the Emperor marched from Guignes on Nangis. The battle of Nangis has been one of the most brilliant.

Russian General-in-Chief Wittgenstein was at Nangis with three divisions, which formed his army corps.

General Pahlen commanding the 3rd and 14th Russian Divisions and much cavalry, was at Mormant.

General of Division Gérard, an officer of the highest promise, debouched at the village of Mormant on the enemy. A battalion of the 32nd Regiment of Infantry, always worthy of its past reputation that caused it to be honoured 20 years ago by the Emperor in the battles of Castiglione, entered the village at a charge. The Count of Valmy, at the head of the dragoons of General Trelliard coming from Spain, and who arriving at the army, turned the village by its left. Count Milhaud, with the 5th Corps of cavalry, turned it by its right. Count Drouot advanced with numerous batteries. In an instant all was decided. The squares formed by the Russian divisions were broken. All were taken, generals and officers: 6,000 prisoners, 10,000 muskets, 16 pieces of artillery and 40 caissons fell into our hands. General Wittgenstein was almost captured; he fled in great haste in the direction of Nogent. He had announced to *sieur* Billy, with whom he lodged at Provins, that he would be at Paris on the 18th. On returning, he stopped but a quarter of an hour, and had the frankness to say to his host, 'I have been well beaten; two of my divisions were taken, and in two hours you will see the French.'

Count Valmy marched on Provins with the Duke of Reggio, the Duke of Tarentum on Donnemarie.

The Duke of Belluno marched on Villeneuve-le-Comte. General Wrede, with his two Bavarian divisions, was in position there. General Gérard attacked them and put them to rout. The 8,000 or 10,000 men who composed the Bavarian corps would have been lost if General L'Héritier, who commanded a division of dragoons, had charged as he ought to have done; but this general, who has on so many occasions distinguished himself, allowed this one chance which offered itself to escape him. The Emperor has conveyed his discontent to him. He has transmitted this to a council of inquiry, certain that, as at Hoff in Prussia and at Znaim in Moravia, where he commanded the 10th Regiment of Cuirassiers, he will merit eulogies and repair his fault.

His Majesty has expressed his satisfaction to the Count of Valmy, to General Trelliard and his division, and to General Gérard and his army corps.

The Emperor passed the night between the 17th and 18th at the castle of Nangis.

On the 18th, at daybreak, General Château marched on Montereau. The Duke of Belluno was to arrive there on the evening of the 17th. He halted at Salins: this was a grave mistake. The occupation of the bridges of Montereau would have gained the Emperor a day, and enabled him catch the Austrian army red-handed.

General Château arrived before Montereau at ten a.m. But as early as nine o'clock General Bianchi, commanding the first Austrian corps, had taken a position with two Austrian divisions and the Württemberg division on the heights before Montereau, covering the bridges and the town. General Château attacked him; not being supported by the other divisions of the army corps, he was repulsed. *Sieur* Lecouteulx, who in the morning had been sent on a reconnaissance, having had his horse killed, was taken. He is an intrepid young man.

General Gérard supported the battle during the whole morning. The Emperor proceeded there at full gallop. At two p.m. he ordered the attack on the plateau. General Pajol, who marched by the road of Melun, arrived while these affairs were going on, executed a brilliant charge, overthrew the enemy and drove it into the Seine and the Yonne. The brave 7th Chasseurs debouched on the bridges, which the grapeshot from more than 60 cannon prevented from being blown up, and we at the same time obtained the double advantage of being able to cross the bridges at the quick charge, take 4,000 men, four pairs of flags, six pieces of artillery from the enemy and kill 4,000 or 5,000 men.

The squadrons of service of the Guard debouched in the plain. General Duhesme, an officer of rare intrepidity and long experience, debouched on the road of Sens; the enemy was driven in every direction and our army defiled on the bridges. The Old Guard had only to show itself: the ardour of the troops of General Gérard and General Pajol prevented it from participating in the affair. The inhabitants of Montereau had not remained idle: musket shots, fired from the windows, augmented the enemy's embarrassment. The Austrians and Württembergers threw away their arms. A Württemberg general has been killed, an Austrian general taken, as well as several colonels, among whom is the colonel of the regiment of Colloredo, taken with his chief of staff and his flags.

On the same day, Generals Charpentier and Allix debouched from Melun traversed the forest of Fontainebleau and drove the Cossacks and an Austrian brigade from it. General Allix arrived at Moret.

The Duke of Tarentum arrived before Bray.

The Duke of Reggio pursued the enemy's parties from Provins towards Nogent.

General of Brigade Montbrun, who had been charged with 18,000 men to defend Moret and the forest of Fontainebleau, abandoned them and retired on Essones. Yet the forest of Fontainebleau could be disputed foot by foot. The Major-General suspended General Montbrun and sent him before a council of inquiry.

A loss that has noticeably affected the Emperor is that of General Château. This young officer, who gave the utmost promise, was mortally wounded on the bridge of Montereau, where he was with the skirmishers. If he dies, and the report of the surgeons give little reason for hope, he will at least die accompanied with the regret of all the army; a death worthy of envy, and much preferable to existence, for all military men who cannot preserve it but by surviving his reputation, and by stifling the sentiments with which, in these great circumstances, the defence of the country and the honour of the French name ought to inspire him.

The palace of Fontainebleau has been preserved. The Austrian General Hardegg, who had entered the town, placed sentinels to defend it against the excesses of the Cossacks, who, however, succeeded in pillaging the doors, and carrying away the horsecloths from the stables. The inhabitants do not complain of the Austrians, but of those Tartars, monsters that dishonour the sovereign who employs them, and the armies that protect them. These brigands are covered with gold and jewels. There have been found from eight to ten watches on those whom the soldiers and the peasants have killed; they are true highway thieves.

The Emperor, on his march, met the national guards of Brest and Poitou. He passed them in review. 'Show,' said he to them, 'of what the men of the west are capable; they were at all times the faithful defenders of their country and the firmest support of the monarchy.'

His Majesty passed the night of the 19th at the castle of Survilliers, situated on the heights of Montereau.

The inhabitants complain greatly of the vexations of the Prince Royal of Württemberg.

Thus, the army of Schwarzenberg found itself affected by the defeat of Kleist, this corps having always constituted part of it, by the defeat of Wittgenstein, by that of the Bavarian corps, of the Württemberg division and of General Bianchi's corps.

The Emperor has granted to the three divisions of the Old Guard cavalry 500 decorations of the Legion of Honour. He has also granted a similar number to the Old Guard infantry. He has given 100 to the cavalry of General Treilhard and a like number to the cavalry of General Milhaud.

We have collected a great number of the decorations of St George, St Vladimir and St Anne, taken from the men who cover the different battlefields.

Our loss in the battles of Nangis and Montereau does not exceed 400 men killed or wounded; this, although exceedingly improbable, is nevertheless the exact truth.

The town of Épernay having been informed of the successes of our army, sounded the tocsin, barricaded its streets, refused passage to a column of 2,000 men and took some prisoner. Let this example be imitated everywhere, and it can be presumed that very few men of enemy armies will re-cross the Rhine.

The towns of Guise and Saint Quentin have also shut their gates and declared that they would open them only if a sufficient force of infantry presented itself in front of them. They have not acted like Reims, which had the weakness to open its gates to 150 Cossacks, and which for eight days has complimented and treated them well. Our annals will preserve the recollection of the populations that have failed in what they owed to themselves and to honour. They will exalt on the contrary those who, like Lyons, Châlons-sur-Saône, Tournus, Sens, Saint Jean de Losne, Vitry, Châlons-sur-Marne, have paid their debt to the country and understood the requirements for the great glory to be called French. Franche-Compté, the Vosges and Alsace will not forget the moment of the retrograde movement of the allies. The Duke of Castiglione, who has collected an élite army at Lyons, is marching up to block the enemy's retreat.

Moniteur, 24 February 1814
Her Majesty the Empress-Queen and Regent has received the following intelligence respecting the situation of the army to 21 February:
Baron Marulaz, commandant at Besançon, writes the following:

On 31 January, the enemy made an attack, in the night, close to the town of Bréguille; it put in motion towards the town two batteries of howitzers and cannons and attempted an attack on the fort of Chandonne: it was repulsed everywhere to the cries of 'Long live the Emperor!' It lost more than 1,200 men. Anywhere the enemy presents itself, we are well prepared to meet it.

All the Cossacks, who had spread as far as Orléans, fall back hastily. Everywhere the peasants pursue them, taking and killing a large number of them. At Nogent, these Tartars, who have no human qualities, burned barns, setting fire to them by hand. The inhabitants who had cause to put out the fires were charged by the Cossacks who then re-ignited the fire. In a village of the Yonne, while the Cossacks were busy setting a farm on fire, the alarm bell rang and the people threw 30 Cossacks in the fire.

The Emperor Alexander slept at Bray on the 17th; he had sent his headquarters to Fontainebleau for the next day. The Austrian emperor did not leave Troyes.

The Emperor Napoleon had his headquarters at Nogent, the 20th at night.

All the enemy army is heading for Troyes.

General Gérard arrived at Sens with his corps and the division of cavalry of General Roussel. He has his advance guard at Villeneuve-l'Archevêque. The advance guard of the Duke of Reggio is halfway between Nogent and Troyes, at Chartres and at Mesgrigny. The advance guard of the Duke of Tarentum is at Pavillon.

The Duke of Ragusa is at Sézanne, observing the movements of General Winzingerode, who, after leaving Soissons, marched by Reims towards Châlons to join the debris of General Blücher. The Duke of Ragusa would hit his left flank if he began an action again.

Soissons is a place sheltered from an action. General Winzingerode, in charge of 4,000 to 5,000 men of light troops, ordered the town to surrender. General Rusca responded as was appropriate. Winzingerode put his 12 pieces of artillery in battery: unfortunately, the first shot killed General Rusca. The only garrison in the place was made up of 1,000 national guards; they became terror-stricken and the enemy entered Soissons, where it committed all sorts of unimaginable horrors. The generals who were there and who were to take command after the death of General Rusca will be arraigned for an inquest, because this town was not to be taken.

The Duke of Treviso re-occupied Soissons on the 19th and reorganized its defence.

General Vincent writes from Château-Thierry that 250 mounted enemy scouts having returned to Fère in Tardenois, Mr d'Arbaud-Missun marched against them with 60 horses of the 3rd Regiment of the Guards of Honour he had gathered; and with the help of the national guards of the villages he defeated these scouts, killed several of them and chased away the rest.

General Milhaud met the enemy at Saint Martin le Bosnay, on the old road from Nogent to Troyes. The enemy had about 800 horses. He had the enemy attacked by 300 men who overthrew it, took 160 prisoner, killed 20 men and took 100 horses. He pursued the enemy and pursues it still, sword at its back.

The Duke of Castiglione leaves from Lyon with a considerable army corps composed of élite troops, to march towards the Franche-Comté and Switzerland.

The congress at Châtillon continues, but the enemy does all it can to impede its progress. The Cossacks constantly stop the couriers and send them through so many detours that even though we are only at 30 leagues in a straight line from Châtillon, the couriers arrive after four or five days of running. It is the first time we see the rights of people so violated. In the less civilized nations, the couriers of the ambassadors are respected and no obstacles created to impede the communications between the negotiators and their government.

The people of Paris could expect the greatest misfortune, if, the enemy at their door, they had surrendered their town without defence. The plunder, devastation and conflagration would have put an end to the destiny of this beautiful capital.

It is extremely cold. This has been favourable to our enemies as they were able to evacuate their artillery and baggage in all directions. If not for that, more than half of their carriages would have been in our hands.

Moniteur, 27 *February* 1814

Her Majesty the Empress-Queen and Regent has received the following accounts of the situation of the armies to 24 February 1814:

The Emperor returned on the 22nd, at two o'clock in the afternoon, to the little town of Méry-sur-Seine.

General Boyer attacked at Méry the remains of the corps of Generals Blücher, Sacken and Yorck, which had crossed the Aube in order to rejoin the army of Prince Schwarzenberg at Troyes. General Boyer attacked the enemy at the charge step, overthrew it and made himself master of the town. The enemy, in its rage, set fire to the town with so much rapidity that it was impossible to pass through the flames in order to pursue it. We have taken 100 prisoner.

From the 22nd to the 23rd, the Emperor had his headquarters at the little town of Chartres.

On the 23rd, Prince Wenzel-Lichtenstein arrived at the headquarters. This new parliamentary was sent by Prince Schwarzenberg to propose an armistice.

General Milhaud, commanding the cavalry of the 5th Corps, has made prisoners of 200 cavalry between Pavillon and Troyes.

General Gérard having set out from Sens and marching by Villeneuve-l'Archevêque, Villemont and Saint Liebsut, came up to the rearguard of Prince Maurice of Lichtenstein and took from him six cannon and 600 mounted men, who were surrounded by General Roussel's brave division of cavalry.

On the 23rd our troops surrounded Troyes on all sides. A Russian aide-de-camp came to the advanced posts to demand time to evacuate the city; otherwise it would be burnt. This consideration arrested the movements of the Emperor.

The city was evacuated in the night, and we entered it this morning.

It is impossible to give an idea of the vexations to which the inhabitants have been a prey during the 17 days of its occupation by the enemy. It would be equally difficult to describe the enthusiasm and exaltation of feeling that they displayed on the arrival of the Emperor. A mother who sees her infants snatched from death, slaves who behold their fetters broken after the cruellest captivity, do not experience a joy more lively than that which the inhabitants of Troyes manifested. Their conduct has been honourable and worthy of praise. The theatre was open every evening, but neither man nor woman, even of the lowest classcs, chose to appear there.

The *Sieur* Gau, an old emigrant, and the *Sieur* Viderange, an old *garde-du-corps*, declared themselves in favour of the enemy, and wore the cross of St Louis. They have been brought before a commission of provost marshal, and condemned to death. The former has undergone his sentence, and the latter has been condemned *in absentia*.

All the population requested to march. 'You were right,' the inhabitants exclaimed while surrounding the Emperor, 'to tell us to rise in mass. Death is preferable to the vexations, the bad treatment, the cruelties which we have experienced for these 17 days.'

In all the villages the inhabitants are in arms; everywhere they grab the enemies whom they met. The isolated men, the prisoners, voluntarily present themselves to the gendarmes, whom they no longer regard as jailors but as protectors.

General Vincent writes from Château-Thierry on the 22nd, that the enemy having wished to exact requisitions from the communes of Bazzi, Passy and Vincelle, the national guards assembled and repelled the enemy, after taking from it and wounding several men. The same general writes on the same date that a part of Russian and Prussian cavalry having approached Château-Thierry, he ordered them attacked by a detachment of the 3rd Regiment of the Guards of Honour, commanded by Squadron Chief D'Andlaw, and supported by the national guards of Chateau-Thierry and of the communes of Bienne and Crezensi. The enemy was chased and put to route; 12 Cossacks and 14 horses were taken. The national guards were in quest of the remainder of this troop, which took refuge in the woods. His Majesty has granted three decorations of the Legion of Honour to the detachment of the 3rd Regiment of Guards of Honour, and an equal number to the national guards.

Count Valmy marched today, the 24th, on Bar-sur-Seine. Arrived at Saint Paar, he found the rearguard of General Giulay, charged it, put it to rout and took 1,200 prisoner. It is probable that Count Valmy will be this evening at Bar-sur-Seine.

General Gérard set out from the bridge of La Guillotière, supported by the Duke of Reggio; he has advanced on Lusigny and crossed the Barse. General Duhesme has taken a position at Montieramey, near Vandoeuvre.

Count Flahaut, aide-de-camp of the Emperor Napoleon; Count Ducea, aide-de-camp of the Emperor of Austria; Count Schouvalov, aide-de-camp of the Emperor of Russia; and General Rauch, chief of the military engineering corps of the King of Prussia, have assembled at Lusigny, in order to draft the conditions of a suspension of arms.

Thus in the day of the 24th, the capital of Champagne has been delivered, and we have taken about 2,000 prisoner, of whom a considerable number are officers. We also found in the hospitals of the city 1,000 wounded officers and soldiers, abandoned by the enemy.

Moniteur, 1 March 1814

Her Majesty the Empress-Queen and Regent has received the following account respecting the situation of the armies to 27 February 1814:

On the 26th the headquarters were at Troyes.

The Duke of Reggio was at Bar-sur-Aube with General Gérard and the 2nd Corps of cavalry, commanded by Count Valmy.

The Duke of Tarentum had his headquarters at Mussy-l'Évêque, and his advanced posts at Châtillon: he was marching on the Aube and on Clairvaux.

The Duke of Castiglione, who has under his command an army of 40,000 men, the greatest part composed of élite troops, was in motion.

General Marchand was at Chambéry, General Dessaix under the walls of Geneva and General Musnier had entered Macon.

Bourg and Nantua were also in our power. The Austrian General Bubna, who had threatened Lyons, was retreating on all sides. As early as the 20th his loss was already estimated at 1,500 men, of whom 600 are prisoners.

The Prince of the Moskova is at Arcis-sur-Aube; the Duke of Belluno at Plancy; the Duke of Padua at Nogent. Troops are marching in the rear of the remains of the corps of Blücher, Sacken, Yorck and Kleist, who had received reinforcements from Soissons and were manoeuvring on the corps of the Duke of Ragusa, who was at La Ferté-Gaucher. General Duhesme took Bar-sur-Aube at the point of the bayonet, and took some prisoners, among whom are several Bavarian officers.

Moniteur, 7 March 1814

Her Majesty the Empress-Queen and Regent has received the following intelligence of the situation of the armies on 5 March 1814:

His Majesty the Emperor and King had, on the 5th, his headquarters at Berry-au-Bac, on the Aisne.

The enemy army of Blücher, Sacken, Yorck, Winzingerode, and of Bülow was in retreat: without the treason of the commandant of the village of Soissons, who handed over his gates, this army was lost.

General Corbineau has entered Reims at four in the morning on the 5th.

We have fought the enemy in the actions of Lisy-sur-Ourcq and of May.

The results of these diverse affairs are 4,000 prisoners, 600 baggage wagons, many pieces of artillery and the deliverance of the city of Reims.

Moniteur, 10 March 1814

Craonne, 7 March 1814

Today there was a battle here that was very glorious for the French Armies.

His Majesty the Emperor and King fought the corps of enemy generals Winzingerode, Woronzov and Langeron, reunited with the remnants of the corps of General Sacken.

We already have 2,000 prisoners and many pieces of artillery.

Our army is in pursuit of the enemy on the road to Laon.

Moniteur, 12 March 1814

Her Majesty the Empress-Queen and Regent has received the following intelligence of the situation of the armies to 9 March 1814:

The army of General Blücher, composed of the remains of the corps of Generals Sacken, Kleist and Yorck, retired after the battles of Montmirail and Vauchamps,

415

by Reims on Châlons. It there received the two last divisions of the corps of General Langeron, which had remained before Mayence. The loss had been such that it was obliged to reduce its cadres in half, though several convoys of recruits from its reserved had arrived.

The army, called the Army of the North, composed of four Russian divisions under the orders of Generals Winzingerode, Woronzov and Stroganov, and one Prussian division under the orders of General Bülow, replaced the army of Silesia at Châlons and at Reims.

The latter crossed the Aube at Arcis, while Prince Schwarzenberg lined the right of the Seine, and, in consequence of the action of Nangis and Montereau, evacuated all the country between the Seine and the Yonne.

On 22 February General Blücher appeared before Méry. He had already crossed the bridge when General of Division Boyer marched against him with the bayonet, overthrew him and drove him to the other side of the river; but the enemy set fire to the bridge and the little town of Méry, and the conflagration was so violent that for 48 hours it was impossible to cross.

On the 24th the Duke of Reggio proceeded against Vandövre and the Duke of Tarentum on Bar-sur-Seine.

It appears that the army of Silesia had marched on the left of the Aube to join the Austrian army and fight a general battle; but the enemy having renounced this project, General Blücher re-crossed the Aube and directed his course on Sézanne.

The Duke of Ragusa watched this corps, checked its march, and retreated before it without any loss. He arrived on the 25th at Ferté-Gaucher, and at La Ferté-sous-Jouarre on the 26th effected his junction with the Duke of Treviso, who observed the right of the Marne and the corps of the army called the army of the North, which were at Châlons and Reims.

On the 27th General Sacken moved on Meaux and appeared before the bridge placed at the further end of Meaux, on the road to Nangis, which had been cut. He was received with grapeshot. Some of his stragglers advanced to the bridge of Lagny.

However, the Emperor left Troyes on the 27th, slept the same night at the village of Herbisse, on the 28th at the castle of Esternay, and on 1 March at Jouarre.

The army of Silesia was thus extremely exposed. It had no other part to take but to cross the Marne. It threw bridges over it and moved on the Ourcq.

General Kleist crossed the Ourcq and proceeded on Meaux by Varede. The Duke of Treviso met up with him on the 28th, in position at the village of Gué-à-Trême, on the left bank of the Térouenne. He attacked him straight on. General Christiani, commanding a division of the Old Guard, covered himself with glory. The enemy was closely pursued for several leagues. We took several hundred men, and a great number remained on the battlefield.

At the same time the enemy had crossed the Ourcq at Lisy. The Duke of Ragusa threw it back on the other side.

The retreat of the army of Blücher was strong. All filed off on Ferté-Milon and Soissons.

The Emperor left from La Ferté-sous-Jouarre on the 3rd, his advance guard arrived the same day at Rocourt.

The Dukes of Ragusa and Treviso pushed the enemy's rearguard; they attacked it quickly on the 3rd at Neuilly-Saint-Front.

The Emperor arrived early on the 4th at Frismes. Prisoners were taken, along with many baggage wagons.

The city of Soissons was armed with twenty cannon and was in a good condition to defend itself. The Dukes of Ragusa and Treviso proceeded on that city to cross the Aisne, while the Emperor marched on Mezy. The enemy's army was in the most dangerous position; but the general commanding at Soissons, by an unaccountable cowardice, abandoned the place at four in the afternoon of the 3rd by a capitulation, calling itself honourable because the enemy permitted him to leave the city with his troops and artillery, and retired with his garrison and artillery to Villers-Cotterêts. At the moment the enemy's army thought itself lost, it was informed that the bridge of Soissons was in its power and had not been destroyed. The general who commanded in the city, and the members of the Council of Defence, are ordered before a commission of enquiry. They appear so much the more culpable, because during all of the 2nd and 3rd we had heard from the city the cannonading of our army which was approaching Soissons, and that a battalion of the Vistula, which was in the place and which left it with tears in their eyes, had given the greatest proofs of intrepidity.

General Corbineau, aide-de-camp of the Emperor, and General of Cavalry, Laferrière, had proceeded on Reims, which they entered at four in the morning of the 5th, by turning an enemy's corps of four battalions which covered the town, and the troops of which were made prisoners. Everything in Reims was taken.

On the 5th, the Emperor slept at Berry-au-Bac. General Nansouty forced a crossing by the bridge of Berry, routed a division of cavalry that covered it, obtained possession of its two pieces of cannon, and took 300 cavalry, among whom was Colonel Prince Gagarine, who commanded a brigade.

The enemy's army was divided into two parts. The eight Russian divisions of Sacken and of Winzingerode had taken a position on the heights of Craonne, and the corps of Prussia on the heights of Laon.

On the 6th the Emperor came to sleep at Corbani. The heights of Craonne were attacked and carried by two battalions of the Guard. The orderly officer Caraman, a young officer of hope, turned to the right at the head of a battalion. The Prince of the Moskova marched on the farm of Urtubie. The enemy retired and took position on a height, which was reconnoitred at daybreak on the 7th. This gave rise to the battle of Craonne.

The position was very good, the enemy having its right and left supported on two ravines, and a third ravine in its front. He defended the only passage, 100 *toises* broad, which joined its position to the plateau of Craonne.

The Duke of Belluno marched with two divisions of the Young Guard to the abbey of Vaucler, to which the enemy had set fire. He drove the enemy from it, and passed the defile that the enemy defended with 60 pieces of artillery. General Drouot overcame it with several batteries. At the same moment the Prince of the Moskova crossed the ravine from the left and debouched on the enemy's right. The cannonade was very heavy for an hour. General Grouchy debouched with his cavalry. General Nansouty with two cavalry divisions crossed the ravine on the right of the enemy. The defile being passed, and the enemy forced in its position, it was pursued four leagues and cannonaded by 80 pieces of artillery with grapeshot, which caused it to sustain a great loss. The plateau by which it was retreating having also ravines on the right and left, the cavalry could not get to attack it.

The Emperor moved his headquarters to Bray.

On the next day, the 8th, we pursued the enemy beyond the defile of Urcel, and on the same day entered Soissons, where it had left bridge equipment.

The battle of Craonne is extremely glorious to our arms. The enemy lost six generals and estimates their loss at from 5,000 to 6,000 men. Ours has been 1,800 killed or wounded.

The Duke of Belluno was wounded by a bullet. General Grouchy, and also General Laferrière, a cavalry officer of great distinction, were also wounded in marching at the head of their troops.

General Belliard has taken the command of the cavalry.

The result of all these operations is a loss to the enemy of from 10,000 to 12,000 men, and 30 pieces of artillery.

The intention of the Emperor is to manoeuvre with the army on the Aisne.

Moniteur, 14 march 1814

The Empress-Queen and Regent has received the following news of the situation of the armies to 12 March 1814:

The day after the battle of Craonne (the 8th) the enemy was pursued by the Prince of the Moskova to the village of Étouvelles.

General Voronzov, with 7,000 or 8,000 men, guarded this position, which was very difficult to approach because the road that leads to it runs for a league between two impassable marshes.

Baron Gourgaud, first ordinance officer of His Majesty and an officer of distinguished merit, set off at eleven that night from Chavignon, with two battalions of the Old Guard, turned the position, and proceeded by Challevois on Chivi. He reached the enemy, whom he attacked with the bayonet at one in the morning. The Russians were awakened with the cries of 'Long live the Emperor!' and pursued to Laon. The Prince of the Moskova debouched by the defile.

At daybreak on the 9th, we reconnoitred the enemy, which had joined the Prussians corps. The position he occupied was such as to be deemed un-attackable. We took a position.

The Duke of Ragusa, who had slept on the 8th at Corbeni, appeared at two in the afternoon at Veslud, overthrew the enemy's advanced guard, attacked the village of Athis, which he carried, and was successful during the whole day. At half-past six he took up a position. At seven the enemy made a dash of cavalry, one league in the rear, where the Duke of Ragusa had a park of reserve. The Duke of Ragusa proceeded there quickly, but the enemy had time to carry off 15 pieces of artillery. A great part of the personnel got away.

On the same day General Charpentier, with his division of the Young Guard, carried the village of Clacy. On the next day the enemy attacked this village seven times, and were seven times repulsed. General Charpentier took 400 prisoner. The enemy left the avenues covered with his dead. The Emperor's headquarters were on the 9th and 10th at Chavignon.

His Majesty, judging that it was impossible to attack the heights of Laon, fixed his headquarters on the 11th at Soissons. The Duke of Ragusa occupied Berry-au-Bac on the same day.

General Corbineau praises the good disposition of the inhabitants of Reims.

On the 7th, at eleven in the morning, General Saint-Priest, commanding a Russian division, appeared before the town of Reims and summoned it to surrender. General Corbineau replied with cannon. General Defrance then arrived with his division of Guards of Honour. He made a fine charge, and drove off the enemy. General Saint-Priest set fire to two great manufactories and to 50 houses that were on the outside of the town; a conduct worthy of a turncoat. In all times turncoats have been the most cruel enemies of their country.

Soissons has suffered much; the inhabitants have conducted themselves in the most honourable manner. There are no praises too great for the regiment of the Vistula, which formed the garrison; there are no praises that the regiment of the Vistula deems too great for the inhabitants. His Majesty has granted this brave corps 30 decorations of the Legion of Honour.

The plan of the enemy's campaign appears to have been a kind of general mad dash on Paris. Neglecting all the forts of Flanders, and only observing Berg-op-Zoom and Antwerp with troops inferior by half in number to the garrisons of those towns, the enemy penetrated on Avesnes. Neglecting the fortresses of the Ardennes, Mézières, Rocroi, Philippeville, Givet, Charlemont, Montmédy, Maastricht, Vanloo and Juliers, it passed by impracticable roads to arrive on Avesnes and Rethel. These places communicate together, are not observed, and their garrisons alarm the rear of the enemy considerably. At the same time that General Saint-Priest burned Reims, his brother was arrested by the inhabitants and sent off prisoner to Charlemont. Neglecting all the forts of the Meuse, the enemy had advanced by Bar and Saint Dizier. The garrison of Verdun has come to Saint Mihiel. Near Bar, a Russian General, who remained a few moments with 15 men after the departure of his troops, was killed with his escort by the peasants in revenge for the atrocities he had ordered. Metz pushes its sorties as far as Nancy, Strasburg and the other places of Alsace, being observed but by small parties, there is free ingress and egress, and provisions arrive in abundance. The troops of the garrison of Mayence go as far as Spire. The departments having hastened to complete the cadres of battalions that are in all those places, where they are armed, equipped, and exercised, we may say that there are several armies in the rear of the enemy. His position cannot but become more dangerous daily. We see by the reports that have been intercepted that the regiment of Cossacks, whose force was 230 men, have lost upwards of 120, without having been in action, but only by the hostilities of the peasants.

The Duke of Castiglione manoeuvres on the Rhone, in the department of the Ain, and in Franche-Comté. Generals Dessaix and Marchand have driven the enemy from Savoy. Fifteen thousand men are crossing the Alps to reinforce the Duke of Castiglione.

The Viceroy has obtained great successes at Borghetto, and has driven the enemy on the Adige.

General Grenier, who set out from Placentia on 2 March, beat the enemy at Parma, and chased it beyond the Taro.

The French troops that occupied Rome, Civita-Vecchia and Tuscany, are entering Piedmont to cross the Alps.

The exasperation of the population increases daily in proportion to the atrocities which are committed by these hordes, more barbarous still than their climate, who would dishonour the human race, and whose military existence has for its object pillage and crime, instead of honour and renown.

The conferences of Lusigny for the suspension of arms have failed. We could not agree on the line of demarcation. We were in accord on the points of occupation to the north and east, but the enemy wished not only to extend its line on the Saône and the Rhone but also to enclose Savoy in it. We replied to this unjust pretension by proposing to adopt on this line the status quo, and to leave the Duke of Castiglione and Count Bubna to settle it on the line of their advanced posts. This was rejected. It was then necessary to renounce the idea of an armistice for 15 days, which was attended with more inconveniences than advantages. The Emperor, besides, did not believe he had the right to place numerous populations under the iron yoke from which they had been delivered. He would not consent to abandon our communications with Italy, which the enemy had so often and so vainly attempted to intercept, while our troops were not yet reunited.

The weather has been constantly very cold; the bivouacs are very harsh during this season; but we have also felt the suffering on all sides. It appears even that sickness creates great havoc in the enemy's army, while ours has but few sick.

Moniteur, 16 March 1814
Her Majesty the Empress-Queen and Regent has received the following intelligence of the situation of the armies to 14 March 1814:
General Saint-Priest, Commander-in-Chief of the 8th Russian Corps, had been for several days in position at Châlons-sur-Marne, having an advanced guard at Sillery. This corps, composed of three divisions, which ought to have formed 18 regiments and 36 battalions, had actually only 8 regiments or 16 battalions totalling about 5,000 or 6,000 men.

General Jagow, commanding the last column of the Prussian reserve and having under his orders 4 regiments of the Landwehr of Prussian Pomerania and the Marches, forming 16 battalions, or 7,000 men, who had been employed in the sieges of Torgau and Wittenberg, joined the corps of General Saint-Priest, whose forces in the end were about 15,000 or 16,000 men, cavalry and artillery included.

General Saint-Priest resolved to surprise Reims, in which General Corbineau was stationed at the head of the National Guard and three battalions of the *levée en masse*, with 100 cavalry and eight pieces of artillery. General Corbinau had placed General Defrance's division of cavalry at Châlons-sur-Vesle two leagues from the town.

On the 12th, at five in the morning, General Saint-Priest presented himself at the different gates. He made his principal attack on the gate of Laon, which the superiority of his numbers enabled him to force. General Corbineau operated his retreat with three battalions of the *levée en mass* and his 100 cavalry, and fell back on Châlons-sur-Vesle. The National Guard and the inhabitants behaved very well in these circumstances.

On the 13th, at four o'clock in the evening, the Emperor was on the heights of Moulin-à-Vent, a league from Reims. The Duke of Ragusa formed the advanced guard. General of Division Merlin attacked, surrounded and took several battalions of Prussian militia. General Sebastiani, commanding two divisions of cavalry, advanced on the town. One hundred pieces of artillery were engaged on the one side and on the other. The enemy crowned the heights in front of Reims. While the attack was under way, the bridges of Saint Brice were repaired, in order to turn the town. General Defrance made a superb charge with the Guards of Honour, who covered themselves with glory, particularly General Count Segur, commanding the 3rd Regiment. They charged between the town and the enemy, which they drove into the suburbs and from which they took 1,000 cavalry and its artillery.

Meanwhile, General Count Krasinski having cut off the road from Reims to Berry-au-Bac, the enemy abandoned the town, fleeing in disorder on all sides. The results of this day, which did not cost us 100 men, are 22 cannon, 5,000 prisoners, 100 artillery and baggage wagons.

The same battery of light artillery that killed General Moreau before Dresden mortally wounded General Saint-Priest, who had come at the head of the Tartars of the desert to ravage our beautiful country.

The Emperor entered Reims at one in the morning, amidst the acclamations of the inhabitants of that great city, and has established his headquarters there. The enemy is retreating, partly on Châlons, partly on Rethel and partly on Laon. It is pursued in all these directions.

The 10th Regiment of Hussars, as well as the 3rd Regiment of the Guards of Honour, particularly distinguished itself.

General Count Ségur has been severely wounded, but his life is not in danger.

Moniteur, 22 March 1814

Her Majesty the Empress-Queen and Regent has received the following intelligence of the situation of the armies to 20 March 1814:

General Wittgenstein, with his army corps, was at Villenoxe. He had thrown up bridges at Pont, where he had crossed the Seine, and he marched on Provins.

The Duke of Tarentum had united his troops at that town. On the 16th, the enemy manoeuvred to march on his left. The Duke of Reggio engaged his artillery, and the whole day passed in cannonade. The movement of the enemy appeared to be on Provins and Nangis.

On the other side, Prince Schwarzenberg, the Emperor Alexander and the King of Prussia were at Arcis-sur-Aube.

The corps of the Prince Royal of Württemberg had moved on Villers–aux–Corneilles.

General Platov, with his 3,000 barbarians, had thrown himself on Fère-Champenoise and Sézanne.

The Emperor of Austria had just arrived from Chaumont to Troyes.

The Prince of the Moskova entered Châlons-sur-Marne on the 16th.

The Emperor slept on the 17th at Épernay; on the 18th at Fère-Champenoise; and on the 19th at Plancy.

General Sebastiani, at the head of his cavalry, caught up with General Platov at Fère-Champenoise, overthrew him, and pursued him to the Aube, taking some prisoners from him.

On the 19th, in the afternoon, the Emperor crossed the Aube at Plancy. At five in the afternoon he crossed the Seine at a ford, and turned Méry, which was occupied.

At seven o'clock at night, General Letort, with the Chasseurs of the Guard, arrived at the village of Chartres, cutting off the road from Nogent to Troyes, but the enemy was already in retreat. Yet General Letort was able to reach his park of pontoons, which had served for the bridge at Pont-sur-Seine, took them all, and 100 baggage wagons; he took some prisoners.

On the 17th, General Wrede withdrew rapidly on Arcis-sur-Aube. In the night of the 17th, the Emperor of Russia retired on Troyes. On the 18th, the Allied Sovereigns evacuated Troyes and proceeded in all haste on Bar-sur-Aube.

His Majesty the Emperor arrived at Arcis-sur-Aube on the 20th, in the morning.

Moniteur, 28 March 1814

Boulevent, 25 March 1814

The headquarters of the Emperor is here. The French army occupies Chaumont, Brienne; it is in communication with Troyes and its patrols are as far as Langres. On all sides prisoners are restored.

His Majesty's health is very good.

Moniteur, 29 March 1814

The 26th of this month, His Majesty the Emperor has battled General Winzingerode at Saint Dizier; he has 2,000 prisoners, he has taken the cannons and many baggage wagons. This corps has been pursued very far.

Bulletin of 31 March 1814

Her Majesty the Empress-Queen and Regent has received this news regarding the situation of the armies to 29 March:

General of Division Béré entered Chaumont on the 25th, and has cut the enemy's line of operation; he has intercepted many military couriers, and taken from the enemy baggage, many pieces of artillery, the stores of clothing and a great part of the hospitals. He was perfectly seconded by the inhabitants of the area, who are everywhere in arms and exhibiting the greatest ardour. Baron de Wissemberg, Austrian minister to England, returned from London with Count Pulsy, his secretary of legation; the Swedish Lieutenant General Sessile de Brand, Swedish Minister to the Emperor of Russia, with a Swedish Major; the Prussian councillor of war, Peguilhen; Messrs Tolstoï and Marcof, and two other Russian ordinance officers, are in active mission to different headquarters of the allies and were halted by the general citizen activities and were taken to the headquarters. The capture of these people, and of their papers, which were all taken, is a matter of great importance.

The park of the Russian army and all its equipment was at Bar-sur-Aube. At the first news of the movements of the army, they evacuated toward Bedfort; thus we deprived the enemy of its artillery munitions, of its transports of rations reserve material and many other objects that it needed badly.

The enemy army having decided to take its operation between the Aube and the Marne, had left Russian General Winzingerode at Saint Dizier with 8,000 cavalrymen and two divisions of infantry to maintain their line of operations and facilitate the arrival of artillery, munitions and rations the enemy greatly needs.

The division of dragoons of General Milhaud, and the cavalry of the Guard, commanded by General Sebastiani, forded the Valcoeur on 22 March, have marched on that cavalry, and, after beautiful charges, they were routed. Three thousand Russian cavalrymen, including many of the Imperial Guard, are dead or taken. The 18 pieces of artillery of the enemy were taken as well as their baggage. The enemy left the woods and prairies covered with their dead. All the corps of cavalry were distinguished to the envy of many. The Duke of Reggio has pursued the enemy as far as Bar-sur-Ornain [Bar-le-Duc], where he entered the 27th. On the 29th, the headquarters of the Emperor was at Troyes. Two convoys of prisoners, of which the number must be more than 6,000 men, follow the army.

In all the villages, the inhabitants take to arms; exasperated by the violence, the crimes and the ravages of the enemy, they make it a fierce war, which is for the enemy the greatest danger.

The following was posted at Rennes on 5 April 1814

The bulletin composed at Troyes could not appear in the Paris Journals, the enemy's army having marched on that city.

1 April 1814

The Emperor, who had moved his headquarters to Troyes on the 29th, headed out in forced marches by Sens toward his capital. On the 31st, His Majesty was at

Fontainebleau; there he was apprised that the enemy, arriving 24 hours before the French army, occupied Paris, after having encountered a strong resistance in which it suffered great loss.

The corps of the Dukes of Treviso and Ragusa, and that of General Compans, which had joined for the defence of the capital, were united between Essones and Paris, where His Majesty had taken a position with the whole army who arrived from Troyes.

The occupation of the capital by the enemy is a misfortune that deeply afflicts the heart of His Majesty, but there is no need for alarm. The presence of the Emperor and his army at the gates of Paris will prevent the enemy from committing its usual excesses in so populous a city, which it will not retain without rendering its position very dangerous.

Proclamation annexed to the Bulletin

The Emperor is well and watches out for the safety of everyone.

Her Majesty the Empress and the King of Rome are in a safe place.

The King-brothers of the Emperor, the grand dignitaries, the ministers, the Senate and State Council have gone on the banks of the Loire, where the centre of the government is temporarily established.

Thus the action of the government will not be paralysed; the good citizens, the real French people, may be afflicted by the occupation of the capital but they need not be alarmed; they can count on the activity and the genius of the Emperor for our deliverance! But they should know that under these great circumstances the national honour and our interests as well, command us more than ever to rally around our sovereign! Let us support his efforts, and let us not regret any sacrifice needed to put an end to this terrible struggle against enemies who, not content enough to fight our armies, come still to strike each citizen in what is dearest to him, and ravage this beautiful country whose glory and prosperity have been, at all times, the object of their jealous hatred.

In spite of the success obtained by the allied army and for which it will not be elated much longer, the war theater is still far from us; but if a few skirmishers, lured by the hope of pillage, dared to scatter in our fields, they will find you armed to defend your wives, your children and your properties.

Proclamation of the Empress-Queen and Regent

Blois, 3 April 1814

French people,

The events of the war have placed the capital under foreign power.

The Emperor hastened to defend it and is at the head of his armies that have been so often victorious.

They are in the presence of the enemy, at the walls of Paris. It is from the residence that I have chosen, and from the ministers of the Emperor, that will emanate the only orders that you will recognize.

Any city under the enemy's power ceases to be free; any directive coming from there is a foreigner's speech and that which suits the propagation of the enemy's hostile views.

You will be loyal to your oaths, you will listen to the voice of a princess who gives hereafter to understand your faith, whose glory it is to be French and to be associated with the destiny of the Sovereign whom you have chosen freely.

My son was less convinced of your hearts during our more prosperous times.

His rights and his person are under your safekeeping.

MARIE LOUISE

Speech of Napoleon to his Guard when he learned the allied forces had entered Paris

Officers, NCOs, and soldiers of the Old Guard! The enemy has stolen three marches from us and has entered Paris. I made an offer of peace to the Emperor Alexander, a peace purchased at the cost of great sacrifices: France with her old boundaries, renouncing her conquests and giving up all that we had gained since the Revolution. Not only did he refuse, he did more than that; from suggestions made to him by treacherous men, whose lives I have spared, whom I gratified with favours, he authorizes them to wear the white cockade and soon he will want to substitute it for our national cockade... in a few days, I will go and attack him in Paris. I rely on you... Am I right? (At this moment we hear numerous cries of: 'Long live the Emperor!', 'Yes, to Paris, to Paris')... We will prove to them that the French nation knows how to be mistress at home; that if she has been so often mistress in another's house, she will always be mistress on her own soil, and furthermore she is quite capable of defending her cockade, her independence and the wholeness of her territory. Go and communicate these sentiments to your soldiers.

Order of the Day

Fontainebleau, 4 April 1814

The Emperor thanks the army for the affection it shows him, and especially because it recognizes that France is in him, and not in the people of the capital. A soldier follows the success as well as the misfortune of his general, his honour and his religion. The Duke of Ragusa did not inspire these sentiments among his companions in arms; he fell into the hands of the allies. The Emperor cannot approve of the conditions under which he took this measure; he cannot accept life, or liberty, from the mercy of a subject. The members of the Senate allowed themselves to dispose of the French government; they have forgotten that they owe to the Emperor the power they are now abusing; that it is the Emperor who saved many of them from the thunder of the Revolution, pulled from obscurity and protected others against the nation's hatred. The Senate relies on the articles of the constitution to topple it. They are not ashamed of the reproaches they make to the Emperor, taking no notice that, like the first corps of the state, they took part in all events. They went so far as to dare accuse the Emperor of having changed some documents in the publication; the entire world knows that he did not need such ruse: a sign was an order for the Senate, always daring more than we desired from it. The Emperor has always been accessible to his ministers' sage remonstrances, and he expected of them, in this circumstance, the most undefined justification for the measures he had taken. If great enthusiasm became tangled in the public speeches, then the Emperor has been deceived; but those who spoke this way must assume responsibility for the disastrous consequences of their flatteries. The Senate is not ashamed to speak of the libels published against foreign governments; the Senators forget, having drafted them themselves.

So long as good fortune remained loyal to their sovereign, these men too remained loyal, and there were no complaints heard in regard to the misuse of power. If the Emperor had scorned men, as some have reproached him, then the world would today recognize that he has had reasons that motivated his scorn. He

424

possessed his dignity from God and from the nation; only they could deprive him of it: he has always considered it to be a burden, and when he accepted it, it was in the conviction that he alone was capable of bearing it with dignity. His happiness seemed to be his destination: today, as good fortune has turned against him, only the wishes of the nation could persuade him to remain on the throne. If he must consider himself the only obstacle to peace, he makes this last sacrifice for France: consequently, he has sent the Prince of the Moskova and the Dukes of Vicence and of Tarentum to Paris to start the negotiations. The army can be certain that his happiness will never be in contradiction with the happiness of France.

Act of Abdication of the Emperor Napoleon
At the Palace of Fontainebleau, 11 April 1814
The allied powers having proclaimed that the Emperor Napoleon was the only obstacle to re-establishing the peace in Europe, the Emperor Napoleon, loyal to his oath, declares that he renounces, for him and his heirs, the thrones of France and Italy, and that there is no personal sacrifice, even that of life itself, that he would not make in the interest of France.

Last Speech of Napoleon to his Guard
Generals, officers, non-commissioned officers and soldiers of my Old Guard, I bid you farewell. For the last 20 years, I have been happy with you. I have always found you on the road of glory.

The allied powers armed all of Europe against me; a part of the army has betrayed its duties, and France herself has wanted other destinies.

With you and the braves who remained loyal to me, I could have maintained the civil war for three years; but France would have been unhappy, which would be contrary to the goal I had proposed myself.

Be loyal to the new king chosen by France; do not abandon our dear fatherland, much too long unhappy! Love her always, love her well, this dear fatherland.

Do not feel sorry for my fate; I will always be happy, as long as I know that you are happy.

I could have died; nothing could have been easier; but I will always follow the road of honour. I still have to write what we have done.

I cannot embrace all of you; but I will embrace your General... Come, General...(he pressed General Petit in his arms). Someone bring me my eagle...(he kisses it). Dear eagle! May these kisses resound in the heart of all the braves!... Adieu, my children!... My wishes accompany your always; preserve memory of me.

Conclusion
These Bulletins end with Napoleon's abdication and his farewell speech to his Old Guard, delivered in the courtyard of Fontainebleau. His saga was not over. He was exiled to Elba, returned for the One Hundred Days, was defeated at Waterloo, and finally exiled to Saint Helena. He died there in 1821 after working hard to successfully create a legend that has survived to this day. Thus ended the life of one of history's most fascinating people. There are many ways to measure and judge those who have so greatly influenced history; there are many windows into the minds of great men and women. For Napoleon, few windows offer a better view than the Bulletins of the *Grande Armée*.

SELECT GUIDE TO PEOPLE AND TITLES

The Bulletins sometimes refer to marshals and others by their titles (e.g., the Duke of Danzig) rather than by their names. The following list should be helpful in determining which titles go with which individuals. Note that Prince Poniatowski was made a Marshal shortly before he was killed, and had no additional title beyond his Polish title of Prince.

Abrantès, Duke of — General Jean Andoche Junot
Auerstädt, Duke of — Marshal Louis Nicolas Davout
Bassano, Duke of — Hughes–Bernard Maret
Belluno, Duke of — Marshal Claude-Victor Perrin (also known as Victor)

Bénévent, Prince of — Charles Maurice de Talleyrand
Castiglione, Duke of — Marshal Charles Augereau
[Cleves and] Berg, Grand Duke of — Marshal Joachim Murat
Dalmatia, Duke of — Marshal Nicolas Jean de Dieu Soult
Danzig, Duke of — Marshal François Joseph Lefebvre
Eckmühl, Prince of — Marshal Louis Nicolas Davout
Elchingen, Duke of — Marshal Michel Ney
Friuli, Duke of — Géraud-Christophe-Michel Duroc
Holland, King of — General Louis Bonaparte, brother to Napoleon

Horse, Master of the — General Armand de Caulaincourt
Istria, Duke of — Marshal Jean Baptiste Bessières
Montebello, Duke of — Marshal Jean Lannes
Moskova, Prince of the — Marshal Michel Ney
Naples, King of — Marshal Joachim Murat
Neufchâtel, Prince of — Marshal Louis Alexandre Berthier
Otranto, Duke of — Joseph Fouché
Palace, Grand Marshal of the — Géraud-Christophe-Michel Duroc
Ponte Corvo, Prince of — Marshal Jean Baptiste Bernadotte
Prince Poniatowski — Marshal Josef Anton Poniatowski
Ragusa, Duke of — Marshal Auguste-Frédéric Louis Viesse de Marmont

Reggio, Duke of — Marshal Nicolas-Charles Oudinot
Rivoli, Duke of — Marshal André Masséna
Rovigo, Duke of — General Jean René Savary
Spain, King of — Joseph Bonaparte, Napoleon's oldest brother
Tarentum (Tarente), Duke of — Marshal Etienne Jacques, Joseph Alexandre Macdonald

Treviso, Duke of — Marshal Edouard Mortier
Valmy, Duke of — Marshal François Christophe de Kellermann
Vicenza, Duke of — General Armand de Caulaincourt
Viceroy (of Italy) — His Serene Highness, Eugene Beauharnais, Napoleon's stepson

Westphalia, King of — Jérôme Bonaparte, Napoleon's youngest brother

A PARTIAL LIST OF OTHER IMPORTANT PEOPLE MENTIONED IN THE BULLETINS

Alexander I, Tsar of all the Russias   Son of Tsar Paul I, Alexander at first was friendly to Napoleon, but joined the Third Coalition against Napoleon, only to be defeated at Austerlitz. After meeting with Napoleon on a raft after the battle of Tilsit in 1807, he again became enamoured with Napoleon and joined him in his quest against England. The Continental System and the Polish question eventually led to a break between the two. After Napoleon's retreat from Russia, Alexander moved with his armies to the gates of Paris. Here he befriended Josephine and tempered the punitive efforts of his allies towards France.

Bagration, General Peter   A Russian commander from Georgia, he fought at numerous battles including Austerlitz, Eylau and Friedland. He commanded the Russian army of the west, but feuded with Barclay de Tolly. He was given command of the left wing at Borodino, was wounded, and died two weeks later.

Barclay de Tolly, Field Marshal Prince Mikhail   A man of Scottish descent who joined the Russian army, he commanded Russian troops and served as Minister of War. In 1812 he commanded one of the wings of the Russian army, but his personal difficulties with General Bagration led to a loss at Smolensk and the giving of overall command to Kutusov. He later commanded the Russian forces in France in 1814.

Bennigsen, General Levin, Count   A German serving the Russian army, Bennigsen was Russian commander at Eylau in 1807 and commanded the Russian centre at Borodino in 1812. The Tsar made him Count after Leipzig in 1813.

Blücher, Field Marshal Gebhard Leberecht von   An excellent general with an unusual hatred for France, Blücher fought Napoleon in the campaign of 1806 and was defeated. In 1813, he led the Prussian forces in successful actions against the French. In 1814 he was repeatedly defeated by Napoleon, but the allies took Paris anyway. In his 70s and with poor health, he expected to retire, but the Waterloo campaign brought him back into action. Defeated and nearly captured at Ligny, he withdrew in good order and his late appearance on the French flank at Waterloo is probably the main reason for Napoleon's defeat in that battle.

Ferdinand, Archduke d'Este   Austrian commander in 1805 who left Ülm before Napoleon surrounded it.

Ferdinand, Prince Louis   Prussian commander and leader of the war faction in the Prussian court, he died at the battle of Saalfeld in 1806.

Francis I, Emperor of Austria   Repeatedly defeated by General Bonaparte in Italy and Napoleon I in the rest of Europe, Francis was pleased to have Napoleon marry his daughter, Marie Louise, in 1810 after marriage negotiations with the Russians failed. This blood alliance lasted all of three years, and after the armistice of 1813, Francis joined the Sixth Coalition and helped defeat Napoleon.

Frederick Augustus I   Frederick first served as Elector and then, as a reward for his loyalty to Napoleon, King of Saxony in 1806. His lands included the Grand Duchy of Warsaw, which put him at odds with Russia, and his loyalty to Napoleon eventually cost him much of his territory.

Frederick William III, King of Prussia   Though he was briefly part of the Third Coalition in 1805, he played little role and it was his refusal to help the Russians and Austrians at Austerlitz that sealed their fate. His wife, Queen Louise, who hated the French (and who is mentioned extensively in the Bulletins) urged him to make war on Napoleon in 1806 as part of the Fourth Coalition. His forces were destroyed at Jena and Auerstädt. He was an unwilling ally of Napoleon's in 1812, but was quick to turn on him in 1813. The Prussians played a major role in Napoleon's ultimate defeat, especially at the battle of Waterloo in June, 1815.

Kleist, Field Marshal Friedrich Baron   Prussian commander who fought throughout the period and led Prussian forces at Leipzig in 1813 and in the campaign of France in 1814.

Kutusov, Field Marshal Mikhail, Prince   Defeated and wounded at Austerlitz in 1805, Kutusov later became the commander of Russian forces in 1812. His age, health and the Tsar's lack of support cost him his command in 1813, and he died during that campaign.

Mack, General Karl Freiherr   Austrian general who commanded the Austrian army at Ülm in 1805. He surrendered to Napoleon, giving the French a great victory without much difficulty. For this he was sentenced to death by his government, but after spending some time in prison he was eventually released.

Metternich, Clemens Lothar Wensceslas, Count / Prince   After serving as ambassador to France, Metternich became Minister of Foreign Affairs for Austria. For years he promoted good relations with the French, and was instrumental in arranging Napoleon's marriage to Marie Louise, but after 1812 he believed that Austria's interests lay elsewhere. In 1813 he arranged for Austria to join the Sixth Coalition. After Napoleon's fall, Metternich became perhaps the dominant political figure in Europe, a role he played until the Revolutions of 1848.

Schwarzenberg, Field Marshal Karl Philip, Prince   Commander of Austrian forces, he escaped Ülm in 1805, commanded troops under Napoleon in 1812, was defeated at Dresden by Napoleon in 1813, but defeated Napoleon at Leipzig that same year.

Suvorov, Field Marshal Alexander Count   Russian commander, very popular with his troops, had great success against the French in Italy in 1799, but died in 1800.

Wrede, Field Marshal Carl Phillipp, Prince of   A Bavarian general who fought on the side of the French until after the battle of Leipzig, when he changed sides and participated in the invasion of France.

Württemberg   A German territory that was governed by Frederick I as Elector in 1803, and after 1806, as King.

GLOSSARY

Army corps: a self-contained military unit that contained artillery, cavalry, infantry and all necessary support staff and personnel.

Biscaïen: long-barrelled musket and its rather large bullet.

Caisson: ammunition wagon.

Carabinier: a member of the élite company of light infantry or, if mounted, a type of heavy cavalry.

Chasseurs: light infantry or cavalry.

Cuirassiers: heavy cavalry wearing breast-plates (cuirasses) and helmets, usually with large plumes. These were the 'shock troops' of the *Grande Armée.*

Debouch (verb): to march from a narrow place out into the open; to appear on the battlefield.

Debouch (noun): an opening through which troops may march onto the field. Sometimes used to mean the field where troops form.

Defile (verb): to march past, usually in columns or lines.

Defile (noun): a narrow passage, including dikes, bridges and the like, or a narrow valley between mountains.

Department: an administrative district of France, of which there were 83.

Dragoons: regular cavalry of line.

Eagle: an Imperial Eagle given to certain units to carry atop a standard; it was considered a disgrace to lose your unit's Eagle.

État-major: staff of the army

Fusilier: a member of an ordinary (non-élite) company of line infantry.

Grenadier: the best of the infantrymen, so named because originally they carried grenades.

Guard, or Imperial Guard: Napoleon's élite fighting force, usually held in reserve until the last possible moment. The Guard was expanded in 1806, and after 1809 the newer recruits served in units called the Young Guard and veteran soldiers in older regiments were called the Old Guard.

Hussars: élite light cavalry with a reputation for a fast life on and off the field.

Infantry of Line: the regular infantry, not a member of any special units, such as the Imperial Guard.

Landwehr: militia raised in Austria or Germany.

League: a unit of distance equivalent to 3 miles or 4.8 kilometres.

Limber: a two-wheeled cart used with artillery.

Parole: a word of honour given by a captured officer not to fight until exchanged or until the end of hostilities. Enlisted men were not given this opportunity and were instead imprisoned.

Petard: explosive cartridge

Sapper: an engineer trained to construct trenches or tunnels, or to undermine or destroy enemy fortifications or emplacements.

Sieur: legal or honorary title, perhaps somewhere between Sire and Mister.

Toise: a French unit of measure equal to 6.395 feet, or 1.949 metres.

Uhlan: Russian, Prussian or Polish lancers.

Verst: a Russian measure of distance equivalent to 3500 feet, 0.6629 miles or 1.067 kilometres.

Voltigeurs: élite light infantrymen in line regiments, and skirmishers in light infantry regiments. Some Young Guard regiments were made up entirely of voltigeurs.

INDEX OF NAMES